Analysing English Sentence Structure

Andrew Radford has acquired an unrivalled reputation over the past forty years for writing syntax textbooks in which difficult concepts are clearly explained without excessive use of technical jargon. *Analysing English Sentence Structure* continues in this tradition, offering a well-structured intermediate course in English syntax and contemporary syntactic theory. Chapters are split into core modules, each focusing on a specific topic, and the reader is supported throughout with learning aids such as summaries, lists of key hypotheses and principles, extensive references, exercises with handy hints, and a glossary of terminology. Both teachers and instructors will benefit from the book's free online resources, which comprise an open-access *Students' Answerbook*, and a password-protected *Teachers' Answerbook*, each containing comprehensive answers to exercises, with detailed tree diagrams. The book and accompanying resources are designed to serve both as a coursebook for use in class, and as a self-study resource for use at home.

Andrew Radford is Emeritus Professor at the University of Essex. He has written a number of popular textbooks, including *Transformational Grammar* (1988) and *Minimalist Syntax* (2004), and research monographs on *Colloquial English* (2018) and *Relative Clauses* (2019).

Analysing English Sentence Structure

An Intermediate Course in Syntax

Andrew Radford

University of Essex

CAMBRIDGE
UNIVERSITY PRESS

CAMBRIDGE
UNIVERSITY PRESS

Shaftesbury Road, Cambridge CB2 8EA, United Kingdom

One Liberty Plaza, 20th Floor, New York, NY 10006, USA

477 Williamstown Road, Port Melbourne, VIC 3207, Australia

314–321, 3rd Floor, Plot 3, Splendor Forum, Jasola District Centre,
New Delhi – 110025, India

103 Penang Road, #05–06/07, Visioncrest Commercial, Singapore 238467

Cambridge University Press is part of Cambridge University Press & Assessment,
a department of the University of Cambridge.

We share the University's mission to contribute to society through the pursuit of
education, learning and research at the highest international levels of excellence.

www.cambridge.org
Information on this title: www.cambridge.org/highereducation/isbn/9781009322966
DOI: 10.1017/9781009322980

First published 2024

A catalogue record for this publication is available from the British Library.

*A Cataloging-in-Publication data record for this book is available from the Library of
Congress*

ISBN 978-1-009-32296-6 Hardback
ISBN 978-1-009-32293-5 Paperback

This book is dedicated to a very special person – my dear wife Khadija. Thank you for the unstinting love, friendship, happiness and laughter you have brought me over the past four decades, for sharing your ever-welcoming family with me, and for broadening my cultural horizons to include couscous and (through your two amazing sons, Karim and Mourad) Olympique Marseille: *Allez l'OM!*

Contents

Preface

Aims

This book is a response to the question: 'What kind of course materials can we use for an intermediate course intended as a follow-up to an introduction to English syntax?' Some teachers use handbooks, and others use sets of original research articles, but both of these can be too demanding for many students, and do not contain essential teaching materials such as exercises with helpful hints and model answers, or a glossary of terminology. This book aims to fill this gap in the market, and to serve as an intermediate coursebook in syntactic analysis and English syntax, designed as a follow-up to introductory syntax books. It aims to give readers:

- a thorough grounding in syntactic analysis and argumentation, and in how the syntactic component of a grammar works
- an appreciation of how data can be used to evaluate the strengths and weaknesses of competing accounts of syntactic phenomena
- familiarity with a wide range of phenomena in English syntax, and how they can be analysed using concepts and constructs discussed in the book
- an understanding of Minimalist and Cartographic approaches to syntax, and how they handle specific phenomena
- hands-on experience of analysing specific phenomena through the extensive exercise material in the 'Workbook' module of each chapter
- detailed feedback on exercise answers for students and teachers in the (free) online Answerbooks (one for students, another for teachers)

It is a dual-purpose book, designed to function both:

- as a coursebook, providing extensive materials for lectures, seminars, workshops, classes, and assignments; and
- as a self-study aid for students working from home

Level of the book

The book is designed as a follow-up course for students who have already taken an introductory course in syntax (such as Radford 2016 or Radford 2020) and presupposes familiarity with:

- approaches to grammar; the goals of linguistic theory; the nature of categories and features; words, phrases, clauses and sentences; universals; variation
- syntactic structure: X-bar syntax: heads, complements, specifiers and adjuncts; the classic CP+TP+VP model of clause structure; tests for constituent structure
- null constituents: null subjects; null T and C heads; null D and P heads
- Head Movement operations; Auxiliary Inversion; Auxiliary Raising; Verb Raising
- Movement to spec-CP; Wh-Movement in interrogatives, exclamatives and relatives; Topicalisation; Focusing; Constraints on movement

For readers who may need reminding about some of these topics, Chapter 1 provides a *Background* summarising the key ideas that are taken as assumed knowledge in the rest of the book.

Key features

Key features of the book include the following:

- It is written in an accessible style and adopts a hands-on approach in which students get to do syntax for themselves, with extensive practice exercise material in the Workbook modules of the book, and model answers and detailed solutions provided in the accompanying free online Answerbooks for students and teachers
- It makes extensive use of authentic materials from a wide variety of written and spoken sources, and covers a range of unusual structures which tend to be neglected in most textbooks, thereby offering an interesting perspective on microvariation
- It takes an in-depth look at a range of topics not touched on in any detail in earlier books of mine, with two chapters devoted to the syntax of the clause periphery, another to the syntax of the subperiphery, and another to the syntax of abbreviated registers of English (as found e.g. in recipe books, social media, newspaper headlines, etc.)
- It has a modular structure, with each chapter including a number of core modules, each tackling a distinct topic and having its own set of

dedicated exercise materials (with answers in the Answerbooks): for example, Exercise 2.1 is linked to Module 2.1, Exercise 2.2 to Module 2.2, Exercise 2.3 to Module 2.3, and so on. This modular structure makes it easier to regulate the pace of learning (e.g. for teachers/learners to decide whether to cover one, two, or more modules per week), and to skip specific modules or chapters if so desired (e.g. modules on non-standard structures, or the chapter on Agreement, etc.)

- All modules within chapters are subdivided into sections, so breaking up the material into shorter (and more readable) units
- The book begins with a Background chapter reminding students of key ideas that they will have covered in an earlier introductory course, some of which they may – Heaven forbid! – have forgotten
- The core chapters in the book contain extensive materials designed to help students, including an overview and summary of the main points and key constructs in each chapter, and a set of bibliographical notes that form a useful starting point for a literature review for research projects on a wide range of topics
- Each chapter also includes a 'Workbook' component containing extensive exercise material (one exercise for each core module in the chapter), and helpful hints for students on how to tackle exercises, plus a list of key constructs for students to utilise in tackling exercise examples
- Some Workbook exercise examples have an [M] after them, and this means that a model answer is provided in the *Students' Answerbook* (see below). Other exercise examples have an [S] after them, indicating that they are for self-study (so that after reading the relevant module, helpful hints and model answer associated with the exercise, students can analyse the self-study examples on their own, and then compare their answers with those provided in the *Students' Answerbook*). The remaining exercise examples are intended for teachers to use as the basis for hands-on problem-solving work in workshops, seminars, classes, or assignments: answers to all of these non-self-study examples are given in the *Teachers' Answerbook* (along with model answers, and answers to self-study exercises).
- There is a detailed Glossary of technical terms and abbreviations at the end of this book

Free online resources

This book is published in conjunction with the following free online Answerbooks which provide comprehensive written answers to exercise examples, with detailed argumentation and evaluation of alternative analyses along with discussion of the theoretical implications of particular analyses:

- A *Students' Answerbook* providing a model answer for every exercise, together with a set of comprehensive written answers to all the self-study material in the Workbook modules of each chapter
- A *Teachers' Answerbook* providing comprehensive written answers to every single exercise example in the Workbook modules

The *Students' Answerbook* is available for readers to download for free at www.cambridge.org/analysingenglish. The *Teachers' Answerbook* can be downloaded for free by teachers, and can be accessed from a password-protected website at www.cambridge.org/analysingenglish.

Acknowledgements

I am grateful to the following for providing the help set out below:

- Five anonymous reviewers at Cambridge University Press for extensive comments, suggestions, and criticisms of an earlier draft of the book
- Helen Barton (Commissioning Editor) and her team at Cambridge University Press for helping steer me through the protracted publication process ever since I submitted a first draft of the manuscript in October 2021
- Gordon Lee (copy-editor) and Preethika Ramalingam (typesetter) for invaluable help in preparing the manuscripts and proofs for publication
- Mike Jones and Andrew Weir for comments on a draft of Chapter 7
- Giuliano Armenante and Ingo Reich, for sharing their ideas with me on tense drop in Module 7.4
- The following for kindly providing me with example sentences: Alison Henry for the Belfast English examples (2, 3) in Chapter 2; Johannes Gisli Jónsson for the Icelandic example (40) in Chapter 2; Andrew Spencer for the Russian example (16) in Chapter 3.

And a footnote from the Rolling Stones

In 1965, when I was an undergraduate at Trinity College Cambridge, the Rolling Stones released their hit single *The Last Time.* The chorus line goes like this:

> Well this could be the last time
> This could be the last time
> Maybe the last time
> I don't know, oh no, oh no

I've been publishing syntax books with Cambridge University Press since my *Italian Syntax* book way back in 1977. I've just celebrated my 77th birthday (in Morocco, with my wife's family) and there may simply not be enough time left for me to publish another (since writing another book and the accompanying answerbooks would take three years, and the publication process would take at least another year). So, this could indeed be my last ever book. If so, let me just say: it's been challenging for me writing them, and I hope it has been equally challenging for you reading them!

1 | Background

1.0 Overview

Since this is an intermediate book intended as a follow-up to an introduction to syntax, it presupposes that (before tackling it) readers will already have taken an introductory course in syntax (let's call it *Syntax 101*), and acquired a grounding in the basics of syntax. But just in case *Syntax 101* wasn't quite as memorable as you had hoped, I thought it might be useful to start with a chapter which serves as a reminder of key ideas that will no doubt have been covered in *Syntax 101* (and which are taken as assumed background knowledge in Chapters 2–7). To signpost key terms in this Background chapter, I print them in **bold**.

1.1 Basic concepts

This module provides a brief introduction to approaches to syntax, to the nature of data in syntax, and to the role played by categories and features in syntactic description.

1.1.1 Prescriptive and descriptive grammar

Linguists analysing the syntax of a particular language attempt to devise a grammar of the language that describes the range of structures found in the language. However, in order to attain a deeper understanding of the nature of natural (i.e. human) language, they seek to investigate the extent to which the grammar of any given language reflects universal properties (i.e. properties shared by the grammars of all languages), and the extent to which there is variation between different languages. Consequently, the ultimate goal of the study of grammar is to develop a theory of **Universal Grammar/UG** which identifies universal properties shared by all languages on the one hand, and parameters of variation between different languages (or language varieties) on the other.

The goal of a linguist describing the syntax of a specific language (e.g. English, the focus of this book) is to seek to understand the ways in which words are combined together to form phrases, clauses and sentences.

However, a fundamental methodological question that needs to be resolved at the outset concerns what kind of approach to adopt in studying grammar. One traditional view sees the role of grammar as being essentially **prescriptive** (i.e. prescribing norms for grammatical correctness, linguistic purity and literary excellence). However, a more modern view sees the role of grammar as being inherently **descriptive** (i.e. describing the way people speak or write their native language). We can illustrate the differences between these two approaches in relation to the following TV dialogue between the fictional Oxford detective Morse and his assistant Lewis, as they are examining a dead body (where italics mark items of grammatical interest):

(1)   MORSE: I think he was murdered, Lewis
        LEWIS: *Who by*, sir?
        MORSE: *By whom*, Lewis, *by whom*. Didn't they teach grammar at that comprehensive school of yours?

Morse was educated at a grammar school – that is, an elitist school which sought to give pupils a 'proper education' and taught them grammar, so that they could learn to speak and write 'properly' (i.e. in a prestigious form of standard English). Lewis, by contrast, was educated at a comprehensive school – that is, a more socially inclusive type of school which admitted pupils from a much broader social spectrum and didn't force-feed them with grammar. The linguistic skirmish between Lewis and Morse in (1) revolves round the grammar of an italicised phrase which comprises the preposition *by* and the pronoun *who(m)*. The differences between what the two men say relates to (i) the form of the pronoun (*who* or *whom?*), and (ii) the position of the pronoun (before or after the preposition *by?*). Lewis uses the pronoun form *who*, and positions the pronoun <u>before</u> the preposition when he asks *Who by?* Morse corrects Lewis and instead uses the pronoun form *whom* and positions the pronoun <u>after</u> the preposition when he says *By whom?* But why does Morse correct Lewis? The answer is that Morse was taught traditional prescriptive grammatical rules at his grammar school, including two which can be outlined informally as follows:

(2)   (i) The form *who* is used as the subject of a finite verb, and *whom* as the object of a verb or preposition
        (ii) Never end a phrase, clause or sentence with a preposition

When Lewis asks *Who by?* he violates both prescriptive rules. This is because the pronoun *who(m)* is the object of the preposition *by* and rule (2i) stipulates that *whom* must therefore be used, and rule (2ii) specifies that the preposition should not be positioned at the end of a phrase. The corrected form *By whom?* produced by Morse obeys both rules, in that *whom* is used in conformity with rule (2i), and *by* is positioned in front of its object *whom*, thereby avoiding violation of (2ii).

The more general question raised by our discussion here is the following. When studying syntax, should we adopt a descriptive approach and <u>describe</u> what ordinary people like Lewis actually say, or should we adopt a prescriptive approach and <u>prescribe</u> what people like Morse think they ought to say? There are several reasons for rejecting the prescriptive approach. For one thing, it is elitist and socially divisive in that a privileged elite attempts to lay down grammatical norms and impose them on everyone else in society. Secondly, the grammatical norms which prescriptivists seek to impose are often derived from structures found in 'dead' languages like Latin, which is somehow regarded as a model of grammatical precision and linguistic purity: and so, because Latin made a distinction between subject and object forms of pronouns, English must do so as well; and because Latin (generally) positioned prepositions before their objects, English must do so as well. Such an approach fails to recognise typological diversity in languages – that is, that there are many different types of structure found in the world's 8,000 or so known languages. Thirdly, the prescriptive approach fails to recognise sociolinguistic variation – that is, that different types of structure are found in different styles and varieties of English (e.g. *By whom?* is used in formal styles of English, and *Who by?* or *By who* in non-formal styles). Fourthly, the prescriptive approach also fails to recognise that languages are constantly evolving, and that structures used centuries ago may no longer be in use today (e.g. *whom* is an archaic form which has largely dropped out of use and is no longer part of the grammar of teenagers today). And fifthly, prescriptive rules are very often oversimplistic, in the sense that they paint an oversimplified picture of what is in fact a more complex linguistic reality (as our discussion of *by who/m* and *who by* illustrates). For reasons such as these, the approach taken to grammar in work over the past sixty years or so has been descriptive.

What this means is that in attempting to devise a grammar of (for example) English, contemporary linguists aim to describe the range of grammatical structures found in present-day English. But how do we determine what is or isn't grammatical in present-day English? What kinds of data can we use? This is the question addressed in the next section.

1.1.2 Syntactic data

One way of collecting syntactic data is to study **usage** (i.e. the range of structures used by people when they speak or write). Contemporary linguists who adopt this kind of approach rely on data from a **corpus** (e.g. a computerised database such as the British National Corpus) containing authentic examples of spoken or written English. Such corpora offer the advantage that they contain millions of sentences, and the sentences have usually been codified/tagged by a team of researchers, so simplifying the task of searching for examples of a particular construction. Some linguists treat the web as a form of corpus, and use a search engine to find examples from the internet of the kind of structures they are interested in.

However, although usage data (from corpora or the web) provide a useful source of information about what people say or write, there are some downsides associated with a usage-based approach. For one thing, a corpus may contain relatively few examples of low-frequency structures. Secondly, it is generally not possible to ask the speakers who produced the sentences in the corpus questions (e.g. 'How would you negate this sentence?'). Thirdly, a corpus may contain examples of production errors (slips of the tongue, or pen, or keyboard) which would probably be judged as unacceptable even by the people who produced them. And (in the case of internet examples), it is sometimes unclear whether someone producing a given sentence (who may use an identity-concealing pseudonym like *CutiePie* or *MasterBlaster* as their name) is a native speaker of English or not (i.e. someone who has acquired and used English as a first language in an English-speaking environment from birth or early childhood, and who speaks the language fluently), and if so what variety/dialect of English they speak.

A very different approach to grammaticality is to rely on **introspective judgements** by native speakers (i.e. their 'gut feelings' or 'intuitions' about whether a particular sentence is or isn't grammatical in their native language). For example, any native speaker of English would readily accept *I don't like syntax* as a grammatical sentence of English, but not **I no like syntax* (where the asterisk marks ungrammaticality). Consequently, an approach widely used by linguists over the past seven decades (particularly by Noam Chomsky and his followers) has been to devise grammars on the basis of native-speaker intuitions about grammaticality. Where linguists are describing aspects of their own native language, they often rely primarily on their own introspective grammaticality judgements.

However, although extensively used, this approach of relying on introspective judgements about the grammaticality of sentences has been criticised by some as being unscientific (hence yielding potentially unreliable results). One problem is that people are sometimes (whether consciously or subconsciously) influenced by prescriptive rules inculcated at school, and hence may give a prescriptive judgement about the grammaticality of a particular sentence which reflects the 'proper English' they were taught to use at school, rather than a descriptive judgement about the 'real English' which they actually use when talking to their friends.

A second problem which arises from asking native speakers whether such-and-such a sentence is grammatical or ungrammatical in their variety of English arises in relation to so-called **marginal sentences** – that is, sentences of doubtful grammaticality, such as the following:

(3)   a. He ought to apologise, *oughtn't he?*
        b. He ought to apologise, *shouldn't he?*

Such sentences are referred to as tag questions (with the italicised part of the sentence following the comma being the tag). Normally in tag questions, the auxiliary in the tag is a (contracted negative) copy of that used in main clause (i.e. the part of the sentence preceding the comma). However, use of the *oughtn't* tag in (3a) results in a relatively degraded sentence for speakers like me, simply because the contracted negative form *oughn't* is obsolete in my variety of English. Instead, I'd prefer to use *should* in the tag (which can freely have the contracted negative form *shouldn't*), as in (3b): but since this results in a structure with mismatching auxiliaries (*ought* in the main clause, *shouldn't* in the tag), it still feels ungainly. Thus the problem posed by asking people to make a judgement on whether a given sentence is grammatical or ungrammatical is that such a binary judgement is problematic for marginal sentences like (3a, 3b) which are neither clearly grammatical nor clearly ungrammatical. More generally, marginal sentences pose a problem for the use of introspective judgements about sentence acceptability for a number of reasons. Firstly, different individuals may disagree in their judgements of particular sentences (and may have different tolerance thresholds): this means that relying on the intuitions of one person alone could give misleading results. Secondly, the same individual may sometimes give conflicting judgements about the same sentence on different occasions. Thirdly, it can sometimes be very difficult to judge the grammaticality of a sentence in isolation (without an appropriate context). Fourthly, grammaticality is sometimes a matter of degree rather than an absolute property (e.g. a given sentence may be more acceptable than some sentences but less acceptable than others). Fifthly, native speakers who are not linguists very often have no clear idea what it means for a sentence to be 'grammatical' or not (since grammaticality is a technical term which non-linguists may have little conception of): rather, all that non-experts can do is say how acceptable they find a sentence, and this may depend on a range of factors which have little to do with grammaticality, including how frequent a given structure is, whether it contains taboo language or concepts, and so on. And sixthly, linguists who rely on their own grammaticality judgements tend to give different judgements from non-linguists, and are vulnerable to the accusation that (however unwittingly) they may tailor their grammaticality judgements to fit their analysis (e.g. they may judge a given sentence to be grammatical because their analysis predicts that it should be).

Because of the potential unreliability of informal intuitions, some linguists prefer to adopt an **experimental approach** to eliciting native-speaker judgements, particularly when dealing with marginal structures whose grammaticality status is not clearcut. One type of experiment involves asking a group of native speakers to judge the grammaticality of a large set of test sentences which are flashed up on a computer screen one at a time, with subjects being asked to rate the acceptability of each sentence on a seven-point scale on which 7 means 'completely acceptable' and 1 means 'completely unacceptable'. Using this scale, a marginal sentence might be rated as 4, for example.

However, it should be acknowledged that there are a number of drawbacks to experimental studies. For one thing, they require considerable time and money to set up: it can take months to design an experiment, collect the data, and process the results; and a design flaw (or problematic results) may require the whole experiment to be re-designed and subsequently re-run. Moreover, it is in the nature of experiments that (in order to meet stringent methodological requirements on experimental design) they can only be used to collect data relating to a specific (and narrow) set of phenomena. Furthermore, experiments can sometimes produce results which are skewed by the design of the experiment. In addition, how acceptable (or otherwise) people perceive a sentence to be may depend on a whole range of extraneous factors other than its grammaticality: these extraneous factors include, for example, how interesting it is, how long it is, how plausible it is, how frequent the relevant type of structure is, how easy it is to imagine a context where it could be used, and whether or not the sentence expresses ideas which offend cultural or religious sensibilities or contains taboo words. Furthermore, the results which experiments yield can be far from straightforward to interpret: for example, they sometimes produce results which represent acceptability in terms of many different shades of grey, rather than as a black-and-white issue. Moreover, in order to achieve statistical significance in results, it may be necessary to discard outliers (i.e. atypical results).

The approach that I will adopt in this book is a hybrid one, combining my own introspective judgements with usage data I have collected from live unscripted radio and TV broadcasts, supplemented with internet-sourced examples. I should add two caveats to this. The first is that I tend to accept a wider range of structures than many other people do: for example, one reviewer noted that he found some of the examples of complex structures in Chapter 4 unacceptable in his English. And the second is that my corpus data reveal many types of structure which are widely considered to be ungrammatical in standard English. For example, below are a few types of non-standard structures reported in earlier books of mine:

(4) a. *What a mine of useless information* **that** I am (Sir Terry Wogan, BBC Radio 2; Radford 1988: 501)

b. That's the guy **who** I think*'s sister* is the lead singer in a new band (Radio presenter, Top Shop, Oxford Street, London; Radford 1988: 526)

c. *What* is thought **has** happened to him? (Reporter, BBC Radio 5; Radford 2004a: 429)

d. *To which* of these groups do you consider that you belong **to**? (Form issued by the Council in the town where I live; Radford 2009a: 233)

e. This is a team [*which* Fabio Capello has seen **them** play] (Gabriel Marcotti, BBC Radio 5; Radford 2019: 90)

These sentences are unusual from the perspective of standard English in several respects. For instance, the use of *that* in (4a) is odd because *that* is neither used in main clauses nor in wh-clauses in standard varieties. In (4b), the affix *'s* is separated from its potential host *who*, resulting in (non-standard) affix stranding (whereas standard English requires 'That's the guy *whose sister* I think is the lead singer in a new band'). In (4c), the pronoun *what* has undergone a Passivisation operation which moves it from being the subject of *has* to a position at the front of the main clause, in spite of the widespread claim that subjects can't be extracted out of finite clauses in standard English. In (4d), we find (non-standard) preposition doubling, resulting in one copy of the preposition *to* being placed at the beginning of the sentence, and another at the end. In (4e), we find use of the resumptive pronoun *them* to reprise the relative pronoun *which*, so giving rise to a (nonstandard) resumptive relative structure.

Sentences like those in (4) raise important questions about whether such sentences are grammatical in English. One perspective is that they are un-grammatical, and are perhaps the result of accidental processing errors. On this view, we might conjecture that people who produce preposition doubling structures like (4d) forget that they already fronted the preposition *to* along with *which*, and so spell out the preposition again at the end of the sentence – and indeed, a processing account of this kind is outlined in Radford et al. (2012). Still, it is much less obvious what kind of processing errors could give rise to the other types of sentences in (4). Moreover, some of the structures in (4) are relatively frequent (in that I have collected hundreds of examples of them): for example, one linguist told me (after finishing a PhD on relative clauses!) that his initial reaction to resumptive relatives was to treat them as ungrammatical, but that after reading my

(2019) book on relative clauses in everyday English, he began to notice just how frequent they are in everyday conversation. Of course, it might be that some of the structures in (4) originated as processing errors, and then became grammaticalised (i.e. treated as part of the grammar) in some varieties.

An alternative perspective (which I defend in a book-length study in Radford 2018) is to suppose that what we are dealing with in sentences like (4) is microvariation between different varieties of English: for example, there are varieties of English (including mine) which allow use of *that* in exclamatives in main and subordinate clauses alike; there are varieties (including mine) which allow resumptive relatives; there are varieties (including mine) which allow subjects to be extracted out of certain finite clauses; there are varieties (not including mine) which allow affix-stranding in possessive structures, and so on. In this book, I will adopt the microvariation approach, and accordingly some of the sentences discussed in the core of the book (or set as exercises in the Workbook modules) involve analysing interesting non-standard structures in English.

1.1.3   Categories and features

As noted at the beginning of §1.1.1, the goal of a linguist describing the syntax of a given language is to seek to understand the ways in which words are combined together to form larger structures (phrases, clauses and sentences). Properties of individual words determine the range of structures they can appear in, and these properties for centuries have been described by grouping words into **categories** on the basis of grammatical properties they share in common. Traditional categories include nouns like *dog* (denoting an object), verbs like *sing* (denoting an action), adjectives like *happy* (denoting a state), adverbs like *cleverly* (denoting the manner in which something is done), and prepositions like *under* (denoting a location): these are generally termed **lexical categories** because most lexical items (= dictionary items = words) belong to categories like these. Lexical categories typically have a very large membership: for example, there are dozens of prepositions in English, and thousands of nouns. Words belonging to lexical categories are traditionally called **content words** because they have descriptive content (e.g. *dog* is a noun, and it's easy enough to draw a picture of a dog).

Work since the 1950s, however, has placed increasing emphasis on so-called **functional categories** – that is, categories whose members are words with a grammatical function, serving to mark properties such as definiteness, tense, mood, aspect, clause type etc. These include determiners like *the/this/that/these/those*, quantifiers like *all/both/each/several/many*, auxiliaries/auxiliary verbs such as *will/would/can/could/may/might*, and complementisers (i.e. clause-introducing particles) like the italicised words at the beginning of the bracketed clause below:

(5)   I didn't know [*that/if/whether* she would be there]

Functional categories tend to have a very small membership: for example, there are only around a dozen auxiliaries in English. It has become standard practice to abbreviate the names of categories using capital letters, and employ (for example) N for noun, V for verb, P for preposition, A for adjective, ADVP for adverb, D for determiner, Q for quantifier, AUX for auxiliary, and C for complementiser.

The categorial status of a word determines its **distribution** – that is, what range of positions it can occupy in sentences. For example, consider what kind of single word can occur in the gap (–) position in a sentence like the following:

(6)   He – go home early

The answer is: an auxiliary like *will/would/can/could/may/might/must/did*, but not, for example, a determiner like *the*, or a complementiser like *if*, or an adjective like *happy* (and so on).

However, categories alone aren't sufficient to describe the grammatical properties of words. This is because many words have different forms, depending on the types of structure in which they occur. By way of illustration, consider the words *this* and *that*. These both belong to the category D/determiner, and yet they have different forms in different uses – as can be illustrated by the examples below (where a prefixed asterisk indicates ungrammaticality):

(7)   a. Do you like *this/that/*these/*those* dress?
         b. Do you like *these/those/*this/*that* dresses?

In (7a), we can fill the italicised position with *this/that* but not *these/those*, whereas conversely in (7b) we can fill the italicised position with *these/those* but not *this/that*. Why should this be? The answer does not lie in the categorial status of the words (both are determiners), but rather in a finer-grained property which is generally described in terms of the grammatical **features** carried by words. More specifically, the forms *this/that* are singular forms which are used to modify a singular noun like *dress*, whereas *these/those* are plural forms used to modify a plural noun like *dresses*. One way of handling this is to suppose that nouns and determiners inflect for **number**, and carry the feature [singular-number] in sentences like (7a), and the feature [plural-number] in sentences like (7b). Determiners and the nouns they modify agree in number (i.e. they have the same number value – for example, a plural determiner modifies a plural noun), and this type of agreement between a noun and a determiner modifying it is traditionally termed **concord**. Features are enclosed in square brackets, and are often abbreviated to save space: they typically comprise an attribute/property and a value – as in [Sg-Num] 'singular number', where [Num] is the attribute and [Sg] the value.

Another class of words whose subcategorial properties can be described in terms of features are pronouns like *I/we/you/he/she/it/they*. Although these are traditionally categorised as personal pronouns, they differ from each other in a number of respects. For example, *I* is a singular pronoun and *we* a plural pronoun, and this difference can be captured by positing that *I* carries the number feature [Sg-Num], and *we* [Pl-Num]. Likewise, *he* is a masculine pronoun, *she* a feminine one, and *it* a neuter/inanimate pronoun; these differences can be captured by treating them as carrying **gender** features, with *he* being [Masc-Gen], *she* [Fem-Gen] and *it* [Inan-Gen]. A further difference between the various types of pronoun relates to their **person** properties: the pronouns *I/we* are first person pronouns denoting the speaker/s, *you* is a second person pronoun denoting the addressee/s (i.e. the person or persons being spoken to), and *he/she/it/they* are third person pronouns denoting one or more entities that are neither speaking nor being addressed. These differences can be captured by supposing that *I/we* carry the person feature [1-Pers], *you* [2-Pers], and *he/she/it/they* [3-Pers].

An additional property of pronouns which can be captured in terms of features is that they inflect for **case**, as can be illustrated in terms of the italicised items below:

(8)   *He* says that *his* house has bankrupted *him*

The pronoun HE is traditionally said to have three distinct case forms: the nominative form *he*, the accusative form *him* and the genitive form *his*. These differences can be captured by supposing that *he* carries the feature [Nom-Case], *him* [Acc-Case], and *his* [Gen-Case]. It can also be argued that nouns too carry case – for example, a noun like JOHN has the common nominative/accusative form *John*, and the genitive form *John's*: see **case** in the Glossary at the end of the book for a table of the different case forms of nouns and pronouns in English.

Another class of words which have a complex range of different forms that can be captured in terms of features are verbs. These are traditionally divided into two distinct types – namely **lexical verbs** and **auxiliary verbs**. Lexical verbs are verbs which have inherent descriptive content (e.g. *pour* describes an action, *die* an event, and *think* a cognitive state), whereas auxiliary verbs have no descriptive content but rather mark grammatical properties such as tense, mood and aspect. Auxiliaries also differ from lexical verbs in their syntactic properties. For example, an auxiliary like *will* can undergo Inversion (and move to a position in front of its bold-printed subject) in a question like (9a) below, but a lexical verb like *want* cannot (as we see from the ungrammaticality of 9b) and instead requires the support of the auxiliary *do* (as in 9c):

(9)   a. *Will* **he** visit Paris?
       b. **Wants* **he** to visit Paris?
       c. *Does* **he** want to visit Paris?

For obvious reasons, this phenomenon is referred to as **Do–support**.

Some auxiliaries are used to mark **aspect** (i.e. whether an action is in progress or completed) – as illustrated by the contrast between the auxiliaries italicised below:

(10)   a. He *is* writing a novel
       b. He *has* written a novel

In (10a), the novel-writing activity is still in progress, whereas in (10b) it is completed. A traditional way of describing this difference is to suppose that the auxiliary BE in (10a) marks **progressive aspect**, whereas the auxiliary HAVE in (10b) marks **perfect aspect** (i.e. marks the perfection/completion of the relevant act). This difference can be captured in terms of an aspectual feature if we posit that (in the relevant uses) BE carries the feature [Prog-Asp] and HAVE [Perf-Asp].

Features can also be used as a way of characterising the properties of verb forms which are marked for **mood**. In this respect, consider the italicised verb forms below:

(11)   a. I *am* surprised that he *was* arrested
       b. The judge ordered that he *be* released
       c. '*Be* quiet!', he said

The italicised verb BE in these examples is traditionally said to be indicative in mood in declarative (i.e. statement-making) clauses like those in (11a), subjunctive in mood in (11b) where it denotes a hypothetical event, and imperative in mood in a sentence like (11c) where it conveys an order. In much the same way, the complementiser *that* can be treated as signalling that the clause it introduces is indicative in mood in (11a), but subjunctive in mood in (11b): the two complementisers differ in that (for many speakers) indicative *that* can be omitted, but subjunctive *that* cannot. These mood differences can be characterised in terms of features such as [Ind-Mood], [Subj-Mood] and [Imp-Mood].

Indicative verb forms have the property that they inflect for **tense** and **agreement** – as can be illustrated by the italicised forms below:

(12)   a. He *is*, and always *was*, passionate about politics
       b. I *am*, you *are*, and he *is* passionate about politics

In (12a), *is* marks present tense and *was* past tense, and this difference can be characterised in terms of features such as [Pres-Tns] and [Past-Tns]. In (12b), *am* is used with a first person singular subject like *I*, *are* with a second person subject like *you* (or with a plural subject like *we/they*), and *is* with a third person singular subject like *he*. In traditional terms, an indicative verb is said to agree in person and number with its subject: on one implementation of this view, the features [1-Pers, Sg-Num] of the first person singular pronoun *I* are copied onto the verb BE, so that BE carries the same features in this use and hence is spelled out in its first person singular present tense form *am* in a sentence like *I am hungry*.

Verb forms that are marked for tense/mood are traditionally termed **finite**, whereas those not so marked are termed **nonfinite**. In this connection, consider the contrast between the italicised clauses below:

(13)   a. Mary was glad *that he* **apologised**
       b. Mary demanded *that he* **apologise**
       c. I can't imagine *him* **apologising**
       d. It would be sensible *for him to* **apologise**
       e. It's important to know *when to* **apologise**

The italicised clauses in (13a, 13b) are finite, since they contain a bold-printed verb marked for tense/mood: in (13a) the verb *apologised* is finite by virtue of marking past tense and indicative mood; and in (13b), the verb *apologise* is finite by virtue of marking subjunctive mood. A clause containing a verb in the indicative mood (like that italicised in (13a) can be used to denote a real (or **realis**, to use the relevant grammatical term) event or state occurring at a specific point in time; by contrast, a subjunctive clause (like that italicised in 13b) denotes a hypothetical or unreal (= **irrealis**) event or state which has not yet occurred and which may never occur. By contrast, the bold-printed verbs italicised in (13c–13e) are nonfinite, in that they are not marked for tense or mood. For example, the verb *apologising* in (13c) is nonfinite because it is a tenseless and moodless **gerund** form. Likewise, the verb *apologise* in (13d, 13e) is a tenseless and moodless **infinitive** form (as we see from the fact that it follows the infinitive particle *to*).

A second property which differentiates finite from nonfinite verbs is that finite verbs permit a nominative subject (like *I*, *we*, *he*, *she* or *they*), whereas nonfinite verbs permit either an accusative subject (like *me*, *us*, *him*, or *them*) or a silent (i.e. unpronounced) subject. On the basis of the form of their subjects, we can therefore categorise the verbs *apologised/apologise* in (13a, 13b) as finite, since they have a nominative subject (*he*). By contrast, the italicised clauses in (13c, 13d) are nonfinite, since they have an accusative subject (*him*). Similarly, the italicised clause in (13e) is also nonfinite, because it has a silent subject – that is, an 'understood' but 'unpronounced' subject which is a silent counterpart of the overt subject pronoun *you* in 'It's important to know when *you* have to apologise'.

To summarise: our discussion in Module 1.1 has served to illustrate the different types of data that linguists use in syntactic analysis, and has shown how categories and features play an important role in syntactic description.

You should now be able to tackle Exercise 1.1.

1.2 Generating syntactic structures

Syntax explores the ways in which words can be combined together to **generate** (= form) larger structures (phrases, clauses and sentences). In the conception of the organisation/architecture of a grammar assumed in much work inspired by Noam Chomsky, grammars contain three **components**. One of these is a **syntactic component** that generates/forms syntactic structures. These syntactic structures are in turn inputted into two other components. One is the **PF/phonological component**, and this serves to map/ convert syntactic structures into PF representations (i.e. representations of their **phonetic form**, telling us how they are pronounced). The second component which syntactic structures are inputted into is the **LF/semantic component** and this maps/converts syntactic structures into LF representations (representations of their logical form – i.e. of linguistic aspects of their meaning). Thus, the three components of a grammar are interconnected in the manner shown in schematic form below:

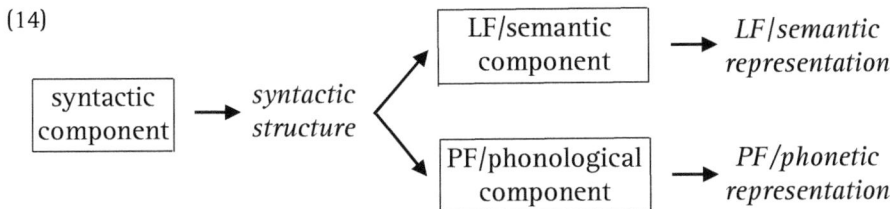

(14)

| | | | LF/semantic component | → | *LF/semantic representation* |

syntactic component → *syntactic structure*

| | | | PF/phonological component | → | *PF/phonetic representation* |

On this view, for each sentence, the syntactic component generates a syntactic structure which feeds into the LF component where it is assigned an LF representation, and also feeds into the PF component where it is assigned a PF representation. In this module, we'll start by looking at key syntactic operations used to build syntactic structures.

1.2.1 Merge

A core operation which the syntactic component uses to generate syntactic structures is **merge**, which combines pairs of categories together to form a larger unit. To illustrate this, consider the italicised sentence produced by speaker B in the dialogue below:

(15)   SPEAKER A: What did the manager say about the customer?
         SPEAKER B: *That he had complained about something*

Let's first reflect on the category that each of the italicised words in (15B) belongs to. *That* is a C/**complementiser**, in that it is a clause-introducing word that tells us that the clause it introduces is indicative in mood and declarative in force/type, so that the clause expresses a statement. *Had* is an auxiliary marking past tense, and so let's take it to belong to the category of T (= auxiliary inflected for tense). *Complained* is a V/verb; and *about* is a P/preposition.

More problematic is the status of *he* and *something*. These are tradition-ally termed pronouns, and since *pro-* is a prefix meaning 'in place of', this might suggest that pronouns are used in place of nouns. However, senten-ces such as the following suggest that this is not the case:

(16)   a. He had complained about *something*
         b. He had complained about *some trivial matter*
         c. He had complained about *some mistake with his bill*
         d. He had complained about *some meal he had eaten*

Thus, in place of the pronoun *something* in (16a) we can have a quantifier phrase/QP like *some trivial matter* in (16b), *some mistake with his bill* in (16c), or *some meal he had eaten* in (16d). Sentences like (16) suggest that *something* has the same distribution (i.e. can occupy the same range of positions) as a QP/quantifier phrase, and thus *something* functions as a pronominal QP (i.e. a pronoun which occupies a position that could alter-natively be occupied by a QP like *some trivial matter*).

Similar considerations hold in the case of *he* (traditionally called a per-sonal pronoun, as noted in §1.1.3). Sentences like (17) below illustrate the types of expression which *he* can stand in place of:

(17)   a. *He* had complained about something
         b. *The guy* had complained about something
         c. *The owner of the car* had complained about something
         d. *The man who was in room 13* had complained about something

In place of the pronoun *he* in (17a) we can have a determiner phrase/DP like *the guy* in (17b), *the owner of the car* in (17c), or *the man who was in room 13* in (17d). This suggests that *he* has the same distribution as a DP/ determiner phrase (like *the guy* etc.), and thus functions as a pronominal DP (i.e. a pronoun which occupies a position that could alternatively be occupied by a DP like *the guy*).

Given these background assumptions, let's return to the structure of the italicised sentence produced by speaker B in (15) above. On the assumption that merge is an operation which combines one **constituent** (i.e. syntactic unit) with another to form a larger constituent, we can suppose that speaker B's sentence is formed as follows.

The P/preposition *about* merges with the pronominal QP *something* to form the PP/prepositional phrase *about something,* with the structure below:

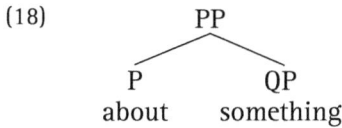

(18)
```
        PP
       /  \
      P    QP
   about  something
```

The V/verb *complained* then merges with the PP in (18) to form the VP/verb phrase *complained about something,* with the structure below:

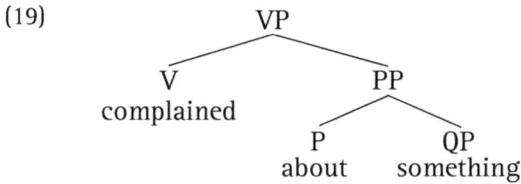

(19)
```
              VP
            /    \
         V         PP
    complained    /  \
                 P    QP
               about  something
```

Next, the T auxiliary (i.e. past tense auxiliary) *had* merges with the VP in (19) to form the larger constituent *had complained about something.* But what is the categorial status of this larger constituent? A plausible assumption would be that it is a TP/tense phrase. But full phrases like VP, PP etc. can serve as sentence fragments (i.e. self-contained utterances used e.g. as short replies to questions) – as illustrated by the replies produced by speaker B below:

(20)   SPEAKER A: What did the customer do?
        SPEAKER B: *Complain about the bill* (VP)

(21)   SPEAKER A: What did the customer complain about?
        SPEAKER B: *About the bill* (PP)

By contrast, the phrase *had complained about something* can't be used as a sentence fragment – as we see from the ungrammaticality of speaker B's reply in (22) below:

(22)   SPEAKER A: What had the customer done to upset the manager?
        SPEAKER B: **Had complained about something*

On the other hand, the fuller reply given by speaker B in (23) below is fully grammatical:

(23)   SPEAKER A: What had the customer done to upset the manager?
        SPEAKER B: *He had complained about something*

Why should it be that the shorter reply *Had complained about something* can't be used as a sentence fragment in (22B), but the longer reply *He had complained about something* in (23B) can?

The answer given to this question within work dating back to the mid-1970s (following pioneering work by Jackendoff 1974, 1977a) is the following. Let's suppose that merging a T/tensed auxiliary with a VP/verb phrase forms an intermediate constituent which is larger than a word but smaller than a complete phrase: let's call this a T′ (T-bar) constituent. Let's further assume that merging this intermediate T-bar constituent *had complained about something* with its subject (here, the pronominal DP *he*) forms a full phrase, namely the TP/tense phrase *he had complained about something*, with the structure shown below:

(24)

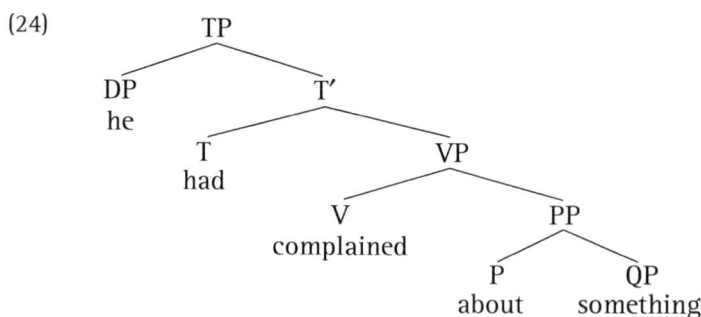

Merging the C/complementiser *that* with the TP/tense phrase in (24) above will in turn form the CP/complementiser phrase in (25) below:

(25)

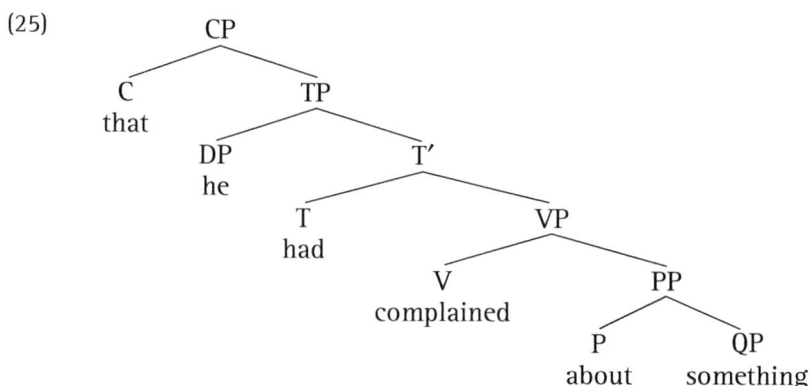

If we suppose that only full phrases can function as sentence fragments, the analysis in (25) can account for the CP *that he had complained about something* being able to be used as a sentence fragment in (15B), the VP *complain about the bill* in (20), the PP *about the bill* in (21), and the TP *he had complained about something* in (23) – but not the T-bar *had complained about something* in (22), because this is an incomplete phrase (lacking the subject that it requires).

1.2.2 X-bar syntax

The tree diagram in (25) represents a classic analysis of clause structure (widely adopted in work since the 1980s) which sees clauses as CP+TP+VP structures. Example (25) illustrates a number of key properties of syntactic structures assumed in this approach to syntax. Firstly, syntactic structures are **binary-branching** in nature: that is to say, each mother has two daughters, in the sense that each non-terminal constituent (i.e. each constituent which is not at the foot/bottom of the tree) branches down into two other constituents immediately beneath it: for example, in (25), CP branches down into C and TP; TP into DP and T-bar; T-bar into T and VP; VP into V and PP; and PP into P and QP.

A second assumption embodied in (25) is that every phrase has a matching **head**: for example, PP *about something* is headed by P *about*; VP *complained about something* is headed by V *complained*; TP *he had complained about something* is headed by T-*had*; and CP *that he had complained about something* is headed by C-*that*. An alternative (but equivalent) terminology is to say that every phrase is a **projection** of its head, in the sense that the properties of a phrase are determined by the nature of its head (e.g. *complained about something* is a verb phrase precisely because its head is the verb *complained*). In these terms, PP is a projection of P, VP a projection of V, TP a projection of T, and CP a projection of C. By extension, a constituent like TP/CP etc. is sometimes referred to as tense projection/complementiser projection (as an alternative to the equivalent term tense phrase/complementiser phrase).

A third assumption made in (25) is that there are three different types of projection: a **minimal projection** (i.e. a head or word-level category X); an **intermediate projection** (X′/X-bar) which is larger than a head but smaller than a complete phrase; and a **maximal projection** (XP) which represents a full phrase. Since what is novel in this approach (compared to earlier models of syntax) is the postulation of intermediate X-bar projections, this model has become known as **X-bar Syntax**.

A fourth assumption in (25) is that syntactic structures are built up by a series of merge operations. For example, by merging P *about* with its QP complement *something* we form the PP *about something*; by merging V *complained* with its PP complement *about something* we form the VP *complained about something*; and by merging C *that* with its TP complement *he had complained about something* we form the CP *that he had complained about something*. However, the picture becomes more complicated when we consider what the T/tense auxiliary *had* is merged with, because this is merged with two different constituents. To introduce some new terminology, T-*had* **first-merges** with its VP complement *complained about something* to form T-bar *had complained about something*, and then

T-*had* **second-merges** with the pronominal DP *he* to form the TP *he had complained about something.* In structures in which a head merges with two separate constituents, the constituent which the head first-merges with is called its **complement**, and the constituent which the head second-merges with is called its **specifier**: thus, the VP *complained about something* is the complement of T-*had* in (25), and the DP *he* is the specifier of T-*had* (or, equivalently, VP occupies comp-TP/the complement position in TP, and DP occupies spec-TP/the specifier position in TP). Complements differ from specifiers in that complements follow the head that they are (first-) merged with, whereas specifiers precede the head that they are (second-) merged with.

The structure in (25) also illustrates a fifth property of syntactic structures – namely that each merge operation involves merging a minimal projection with a maximal projection (i.e. merging a head H with an XP). So, for example, the set of merge operations which give rise to (25) are the following: P merges with QP; V merges with PP; T first-merges with VP and second-merges with DP; and C merges with TP.

A sixth property of syntactic structures illustrated by (25) is that there are different types of maximal projection/XP. Some (like TP in 25), are SPECIFIER+HEAD+COMPLEMENT structures; others (like CP, VP and PP in 25) are HEAD+COMPLEMENT structures; and yet others (like QP and DP in 25) have no complement or specifier and contain just a head (recall that *he* is analysed as a DP and not just as a D because it occupies a position which could alternatively be occupied by a DP like *the guy*, but not by a D like *the*).

A tacit assumption made in our discussion above is that the **derivation** of structures (i.e. the set of operations used to form them) proceeds in a **bottom-up** fashion, with lower constituents in a tree like (25) being formed before higher ones. Thus, the initial merge operation that applies in (25) is that P-*about* merges with QP *something* to form PP *about something*; next, V-*complained* merges with this PP to form VP *complained about something*; then T-*had* first-merges with this VP to form T-bar *had complained about something*, and T-*had* subsequently second-merges with DP *he* to form TP *he had complained about something*; finally, C-*that* merges with this TP to form CP *that he had complained about something.* In each case, smaller constituents are formed before larger ones.

1.2.3   Adjunction

Although our discussion so far has assumed that syntactic structures are built up by merge operations, traditional work dating back to the 1960s posits that there is a second type of structure-building operation by which structures can be formed – namely **adjunction**. Two types of adjunction are assumed in such work. One involves a **head adjunction** operation by which

which one head adjoins to another to form a complex head. To illustrate this, compare the following sentences:

(26) a. He will run up the stairs
  b. *Up the stairs* he will run
  c. He will pick up the bag
  d. **Up the bag* he will pick

At first sight, the verb phrases *run up the stairs* and *pick up the bag* might look as if they have the same kind of structure, and comprise a V (*run/pick*) which is merged with a PP complement headed by P-*up* (= *up the stairs/ up the bag*) to form a VP (= *run up the stairs/pick up the bag*). And yet, the *run*-VP and the *pick*-VP behave very differently in certain respects.

For one thing, *up the stairs* can be fronted/preposed in a sentence like (26a) in order to highlight it as in (26b), but *up the bag* in (26c) cannot be fronted for highlighting purposes – as we see from the ungrammaticality of (26d). What this suggests is that *up the stairs* is a prepositional phrase in (26a) since it can be preposed for emphasis in (26b): hence we can say that *run* is a prepositional verb here (i.e. a verb with a PP complement). Conversely, the fact that fronting *up the bag* in (26c) results in the ungrammatical sentence (26d) suggests that it is not a PP. Rather, *pick up* seems to be a complex verb comprising the verb *pick* and the prepositional particle *up*, and thus can be termed a particle verb. One way of capturing these differences is to suppose that *up* is the head of a separate PP in the VP *run up the stairs* but is adjoined to the verb *pick* in the VP *pick up the bag* so that the two verb phrases have the respective structures shown below:

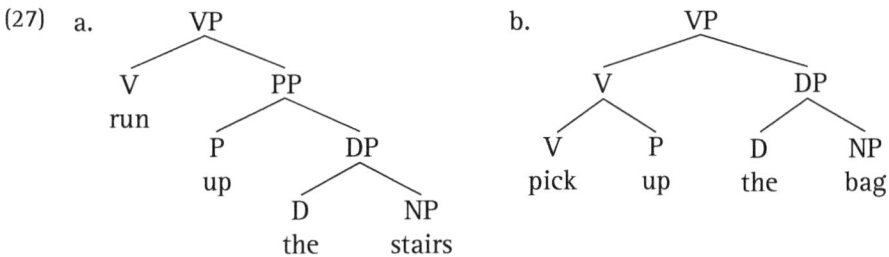

(27) a.
```
            VP
           /  \
          V    PP
         run  /  \
             P    DP
             up  /  \
                D    NP
               the  stairs
```

b.
```
            VP
           /  \
          V    DP
         / \   / \
        V   P  D   NP
      pick  up the  bag
```

What the analyses in (27) claim is that *up* is a preposition which projects into the prepositional phrase *up the stairs* in (27a), but *up* is a particle adjoined to the verb *pick* in (27b) to form the complex verb *pick up*. This correctly predicts that the string *up the stairs* can be fronted in (26a/26b) because it is a PP, but not in the verb+particle structure in (26c/26d) because the string *up the bag* is not a constituent there. It also predicts that *pick up* (being a V, albeit one with a complex internal structure) can be coordinated with another V (like *carry* in 'John will **pick up** and *carry* the bag').

A second type of adjunction operation assumed in earlier work is **phrasal adjunction** – that is, an operation by which a phrase/XP is adjoined to a constituent larger than a head. To illustrate this, consider the role played by the italicised prepositional phrases in the clause bracketed below:

(28)   I feel [that *in all likelihood* the president *before long* may face a backlash]

Here, the PP *before long* modifies the T-bar *may face a backlash*, and the PP *in all likelihood* modifies the TP *the president before long may face a backlash*. If modifiers are adjuncts, this means that the PP *before long* (as used here) adjoins to the T-bar *may face a backlash* to form the even larger T-bar *before long may face a backlash*; and that the PP *in all likelihood* adjoins to the TP *the president before long may face a backlash* to form the even larger TP *in all likelihood the president before long may face a backlash*. Given these assumptions, the *that*-clause bracketed in (28) above will have the structure in (29) below:

(29)   I feel

On this view, phrasal adjunction involves adjoining a maximal projection to a projection larger than a head (i.e. to an intermediate or maximal projection). Thus, the PP *before long* (a maximal projection) adjoins to the T-bar *may face a backlash* (an intermediate projection) to form an even larger T-bar; and the PP *in all likelihood* (a maximal projection) adjoins to the TP *the president before long may face a backlash* (a maximal projection) to form an even larger TP. Introducing some technical terminology, we can say that the PP *before long* in (29) is a **T-bar adjunct**, whereas the PP *in all likelihood* is a **TP adjunct**.

An interesting property of adjunction is that adjuncts can typically be positioned to the left or right of constituents they adjoin to. This can be illustrated by the following set of examples (where 30a, 30b, and 30c are alternative replies that could be given by speaker B to the question that speaker A asks):

(30)   SPEAKER A: What has the crash done to the car door?

SPEAKER B: (a)   Dented it

(b)   *Slightly* dented it

(c)   Dented it *slightly*

In (30a), the complement of the T auxiliary *has* is the italicised verb phrase/ VP *dented it*. In (30b), this VP is enlarged by adjoining *slightly* to the left of it, forming the larger VP *slightly dented it*. And in (30c), *slightly* is instead adjoined to the right of the VP *dented it*, forming the larger VP *dented it slightly*. We can take *slightly* to be an ADVP/adverbial phrase here (and not an ADV/adverb) because it can be substituted by a phrase like *ever so slightly* which is clearly an ADVP. Given the assumption that *slightly* in (30) is an ADVP which adjoins to VP to form a larger VP, (30b/30c) will have the respective structures shown in (31a/31b) below:

(31)   a.   b.

In both structures, *slightly* is a **VP adjunct** – that is, a constituent that adjoins to a VP to form an even larger VP.

Adjunction differs from merge in three main respects. One is that whereas merge gives rise to a fixed ordering of constituents (e.g. a head first-merges with a complement that follows it, and second-merges with a specifier that precedes it), phrasal adjuncts can typically either precede or follow the constituent they adjoin to (so that the two PPs in 29 above can alternatively be positioned to the right of the constituents they adjoin to). The second is that whereas merge gives rise to a constituent different in kind from the head involved in the operation (e.g. first-merging T with its complement forms a T-bar; and second-merging T with its specifier forms a TP), adjunction gives rise to a larger constituent of the same kind (e.g. adjoining *slightly* to a VP forms another VP). The third is that adjunction is a potentially **recursive** operation, in the sense that (for example) you can go on adding more and more adjuncts to a given VP (forming successively larger and larger VPs), whereas by contrast, a head can only have (i.e. second-merge with) a single specifier.

The recursive nature of adjunction can be illustrated by what speaker B says in the dialogue below:

(32)   SPEAKER A: What has Sherlock Holmes decided to do with the sample?

SPEAKER B: **Examine** it *carefully, under a microscope, in the lab, tomorrow*

Here, the bold-printed VP *examine it* has three italicised XPs adjoined to it. The ADVP *carefully* adjoins to the VP *examine it* to form the larger VP *examine it carefully*; then the PP *under a microscope* adjoins to the resulting VP to form the even larger VP *examine it carefully, under a microscope*; next, the PP *in the lab* adjoins to this VP to form the even larger VP *examine it carefully, under a microscope, in the lab*; and finally, the ADVP *tomorrow* adjoins to the structure thereby formed to derive the structure shown below (simplified by not showing the internal structure of the two PPs, for lack of space):

(33)

```
                                              VP
                                   ┌──────────┴──────────┐
                                  VP                    ADVP
                         ┌─────────┴─────────┐         tomorrow
                        VP                   PP
                ┌────────┴────────┐        in the lab
               VP                PP
         ┌──────┴──────┐   under a microscope
        VP           ADVP
    ┌────┴────┐     carefully
    V        DP
 examine     it
```

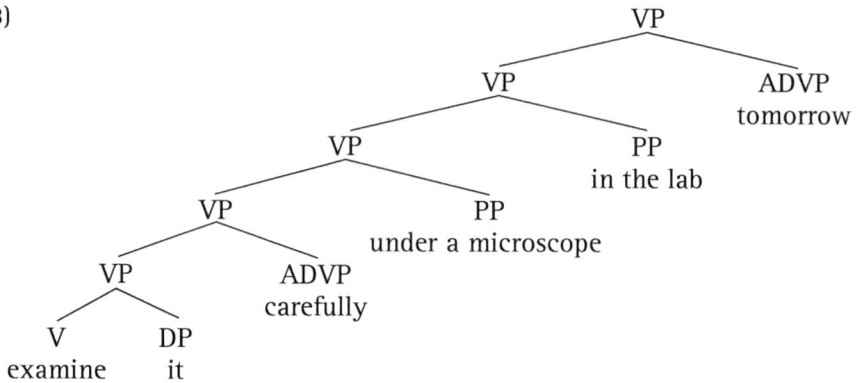

A further property of phrasal adjuncts is that they can be recursively stacked on top of the constituent they modify in any order. Thus, a prediction made by the analysis in (33) is that the adjuncts can be freely ordered with respect to each other. And, as the sentences below show, this is indeed the case:

(34)   a. He has decided to examine it *carefully, under a microscope, in the lab, tomorrow*
        b. He has decided to examine it *carefully, in the lab, tomorrow, under a microscope*
        c. He has decided to examine it *tomorrow, carefully, under a microscope, in the lab*
        d. He has decided to examine it *under a microscope, carefully, in the lab, tomorrow*

The free ordering of the italicised constituents following the VP *examine it* makes it plausible to suppose that they can all function as VP adjuncts.

To summarise: in Module 1.2 we have seen how syntactic structures can be formed by successive merge and adjunction operations which build up structures (one layer at a time) in a bottom-up fashion.

You should now be able to tackle Exercise 1.2.

1.3   Invisible structure and structural relations

In this module we will see that part of the structure of sentences can some-times be invisible/inaudible, because sentence structures can contain **null constituents** (also referred to as **empty categories**) – that is, constituents which have morphological, syntactic and semantic properties, but have no overt/audible phonetic form. We will then go on to look at a structural relation (**c-command**) which plays a key role in governing how syntactic operations apply.

1.3.1   Null constituents

A key assumption underlying much contemporary work in syntax is that lan-guages make widespread use of null constituents. One way such constituents can arise is through **ellipsis** (i.e. omission of redundant material) – as in the sentence below (where ~~strikethrough~~ marks material undergoing ellipsis):

(35)   a. I know I should *see the dentist*, but I just don't want to ~~see the dentist~~
      b. There are two *cans of paint* on the shelf, and three ~~cans of paint~~ on the floor
      c. If he is *fond of her* (and I'm sure he is ~~fond of her~~), he should tell her

The sentence in (35a) contains two occurrences of the VP/verb phrase *see the dentist*. To avoid repetition, the second occurrence of this VP can undergo ellipsis and thereby be omitted, as indicated by strikethrough. Likewise, the second occurrence of the noun phrase/NP *cans of paint* can undergo ellipsis in (35b), as can the second occurrence of the adjectival phrase/ AP *fond of her* in (35c). I shall assume here that constituents undergoing ellipsis are present in the syntax, but are given a silent spellout (and so are unpronounced/silent) in the phonology. A general assumption in relevant research is that ellipsis is subject to a **Recoverability Condition** specifying that constituents can only undergo ellipsis if their contents are recoverable (i.e. if we can recover what has been omitted). The recoverability require-ment is satisfied in (35) because the omitted VP/NP/AP is mentioned earlier in the sentence (the earlier occurrences being italicised).

In addition to null constituents which arise from ellipsis, there are other constituents which are inherently null (and hence have no phonetic form). In this respect, consider the expressions highlighted in the sentence below:

(36)   He bought **roses** and *several orchids*

Here, *several orchids* is a QP/quantifier phrase which has been coordi-nated (i.e. joined together by *and*) with the expression *roses*. On the tra-ditional assumption that only likes (i.e. constituents that are alike/of the same type) can be coordinated, it follows that *roses* must have the same status as the QP *several orchids* and hence *roses* must also be a QP. But if so, what is the head quantifier of this QP? The answer given in much contemporary research is that the relevant QP is headed by a null quantifier with a meaning paraphrasable as 'an unspecified quantity of'. On this view, *roses* in (36) will be a QP with the structure below (where ø denotes an inherently null item):

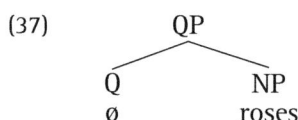

(37)

```
        QP
       /  \
      Q    NP
      ø    roses
```

On the assumption that merge involves a head combining with an XP/maximal projection, it follows that *roses* will be an NP/noun phrase, and not just an N. This predicts that in place of *roses* we can have a larger NP like *bunches of roses*. The assumption that indefinite nominal arguments are QPs headed by an overt or null quantifier is known as the **QP Hypothesis**.

Now consider the sentence below:

(38)   I saw **John** and *the waiter* arguing

Here, *the waiter* is a DP/determiner phrase (denoting a definite/specific individual) which has been coordinated with *John*. Assuming that only likes can be coordinated, it follows that *John* must have the same DP status as *the waiter* and hence must likewise be a DP; and since the DP containing *John* has no overt determiner, it must be headed by a null determiner and have the structure below:

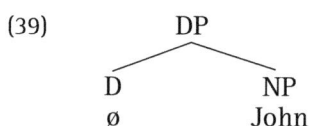

(39)

```
        DP
       /  \
      D    NP
      ø    John
```

Since DPs mark definiteness/specificity, the DP in (39) will have a meaning paraphrasable as 'the specific individual John'. The assumption that all definite expressions are DPs is known as the **DP Hypothesis**. Of course, it follows from the DP Hypothesis that a definite pronoun like *he* will also be a DP – as is the case in (25) above.

A further type of constituent which can be argued to contain a null head is nominals (i.e. expressions containing or comprising a noun) like those italicised below which are said in traditional grammar to have an adverbial function:

(40)   a. I'll see you *Sunday*

b. I'll do it *my own way*

c. I'm staying *home* today

An interesting property of the italicised nominals in (40) is that they can be substituted by PPs like those highlighted below in which the italicised nominal is the complement of a (bold-printed) preposition:

(41)   a. I'll see you **on** *Sunday*
        b. I'll do it **in** *my own way*
        c. I'm staying **at** *home* today

It is therefore plausible to take adverbial nominals like those italicised in (40) to be PPs headed by a null counterpart of the preposition *on/in/at*.

Some evidence for analysing adverbial nominals as the complement of silent prepositions comes from examples such as the following:

(42)   a. Do you want to go *home* or **to the supermarket?**
        b. I'm going to be busy *tomorrow* and **at the weekend**
        c. Shall we stay *a week*, or **for a couple of weeks?**

The fact that in each case the italicised adverbial nominal is coordinated with a bold-printed PP headed by an overt preposition (*to/at/for*) suggests that adverbial nominals are PPs headed by a null preposition (given the assumption that only like constituents can be coordinated).

The null P analysis of adverbial nominals can be extended to adverbial pronominals like *here/there/where/then/when/why*. These are traditionally analysed as adverbs, but can be taken to be pronouns functioning as the object of a null preposition, with *here* meaning 'at/to/in this place', *there* meaning 'at/to/in that place', *then* meaning 'at that time', *where* meaning 'at/to/in what place', *when* meaning 'at what time', and *why* meaning 'for what reason'. Some support for a PP analysis of such adverbs comes from the observation that the relevant preposition can sometimes be spelled out overtly, as shown by the bold-printed prepositions below:

(43)   a. *Where* is he going **to?**
        b. *Where* is he staying **at?**
        c. I've had a change of heart in the last week and I'll tell you **for** *why*
           (www.trollishdelver.com)

Such considerations suggest the hypothesis that adverbial (pro)nominals are PPs headed by a null preposition: let's call this the **PP Hypothesis**. Given this, adverbs like *there* (as in *He went there*) or *where* (as in *Where did he go?*) will be PPs with the respective structures shown below:

(44)   a.   PP   b.   PP
              ┌─────────┴─────────┐   ┌─────────┴─────────┐
              P   DP   P   QP
              ø   there   ø   where

In (44a), *there* will be a pronominal DP meaning 'that place', whereas in (44b) *where* will be a pronominal QP meaning 'what place' (if we treat *what* as an interrogative quantifier); and the null preposition in both sentences (*He went there/Where did he go?*) can be taken to be a null counterpart of *to*.

A further type of null constituent can be found in the following sentence:

(45)   She said [**she was feeling tired**] and [*that she was going to bed*]

Here, *that she was going to bed* is a CP/complementiser phrase headed by a C/complementiser *that* which serves to mark the clause it introduces as declarative (i.e. as a statement). But on the assumption that only likes can be coordinated, it follows that the first bracketed clause (*she was feeling tired*) must also be a CP; and given that it contains no overt complementiser, it must be headed by a null complementiser, and thus have the structure below:

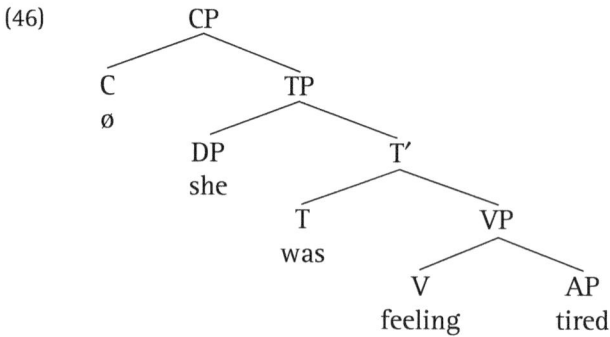

(46)

```
                CP
          _____|_____
         C             TP
         ø         _____|_____
                  DP          T'
                  she      ___|___
                          T        VP
                         was    ___|___
                               V        AP
                            feeling    tired
```

Since this is an indicative clause, we can suppose that the null complementiser in (46) serves to mark the clause as indicative in mood, and declarative in force (i.e. having the force of a statement).

An interesting property of CP+TP+VP structures like (46) above is that each separate type of projection/layer of structure serves a different function. Thus, the VP layer identifies the type of action or event involved; the TP layer marks tense, and hence situates the action/event in time; and the CP layer marks clause type (i.e. whether the clause is declarative, interrogative, exclamative or imperative in force). From this perspective, it could be argued that it is a matter of conceptual necessity for complete/non-defective clauses to contain all three types of projection. This means that main clauses too (even though they are not introduced by overt complementisers like *that/if/whether*) must be CP+TP+VP structures, and hence a sentence like *It is raining* must have the CP+TP+VP structure below:

(47)

```
            CP
          /    \
        C        TP
        ∅      /    \
           DP        T'
           it      /    \
                  T        VP
                  is     raining
```

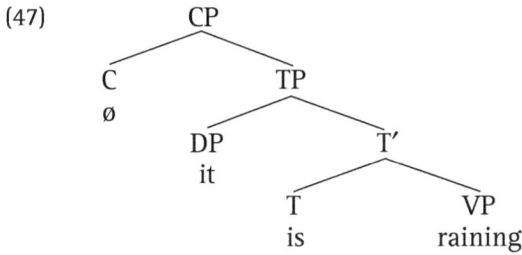

The VP *raining* identifies the event taking place, the TP headed by *is* indicates the (present) time of the event, and the CP layer serves to mark the sentence as declarative in force, hence as making a statement. (Note that *raining* is a VP rather than just a V in 47 because a head can only merge with a maximal projection/XP, hence the T head *is* can only merge with a VP, not with a V. Moreover, *raining* can be substituted by a larger expression which is clearly a VP, like *raining cats and dogs*.)

The assumption that clauses always contain a TP headed by a T which marks (present or past) tense proves potentially problematic for a clause like that produced by speaker B below:

(48)   SPEAKER A: What are you trying to establish?
        SPEAKER B: *Whether they lied to me*

The italicised clause produced by speaker B contains a CP layer headed by the interrogative complementiser *whether*, and a VP layer headed by the verb *lie*, but doesn't (at first sight) seem to contain any TP layer headed by a present or past tense T auxiliary. However, on the assumption that subjects occupy the specifier position in TP (e.g. *it* is in spec-TP in 47 above, and *she* is in spec-TP in 46), it follows that the subject *they* in (48B) must also occupy the specifier position in a TP. But if so, what is the head of the relevant TP?

An answer given in work dating back in spirit to Chomsky (1955, 1957) is that tensed clauses which contain no present or past tense auxiliary are TPs whose head T constituent contains a (present or past) tense affix/*Af*. On this view, the clause produced by speaker B in (48) above has the syntactic structure shown below, where *Af* denotes a past tense affix:

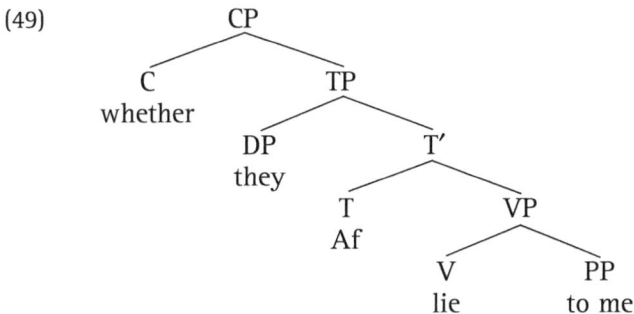

(49)

```
              CP
           /      \
         C          TP
      whether     /    \
               DP        T'
               they    /    \
                      T        VP
                      Af     /    \
                           V        PP
                          lie      to me
```

(The structure is simplified by not showing the internal structure of the PP *to me*, because this is not relevant to our discussion here.) At the end of the syntactic derivation (i.e. when all syntactic operations have finished applying), the resulting structure is sent to the LF/semantic component (to be assigned a logical form representing linguistic aspects of its meaning), and to the PF/phonological component (to be assigned a phonetic form determining how it is pronounced). In the PF component, the past tense affix in T is lowered onto the head V of VP by an operation traditionally termed **Affix Hopping** – as shown by the arrow below:

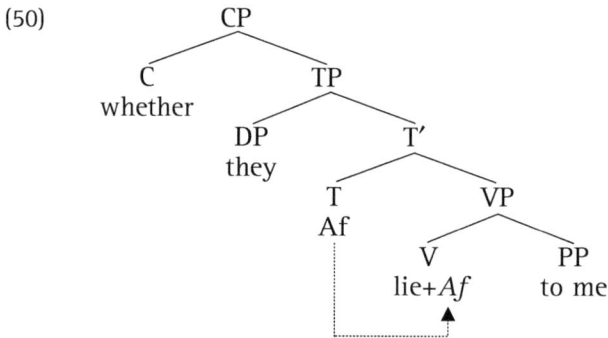

(50)

```
                    CP
            ┌────────┴────────┐
            C                 TP
         whether      ┌────────┴────────┐
                      DP                T'
                     they        ┌──────┴──────┐
                                 T             VP
                                 Af      ┌──────┴──────┐
                                 ┊       V             PP
                                 ┊     lie+Af        to me
                                 ┊       ▲
                                 └───────┘
```

Spellout rules in the phonology specify that a past tense affix is spelled out on a regular verb in the default form *+d* (where the default form is the form used with verbs that don't form their past tense in some other way). As a result, the verb is ultimately spelled out as *lie+d* (written as *lied*). The head T position of TP (once it has been vacated by the affix) is silent/empty/null.

1.3.2   Case-marking and c-command

Thus far, we have concentrated on the structure of finite clauses (i.e. clauses which contain an auxiliary or non-auxiliary verb marked for mood/tense). But what about nonfinite clauses (i.e. clauses not containing any AUX/V marked for mood/tense)? As a case in point, consider the structure of the clause produced by speaker B below:

(51)   SPEAKER A: What was his suggestion?

        SPEAKER B: *For us to meet up*

What speaker B says in (51) can be accommodated within the CP+TP+VP model of clause structure if we treat *for* as an infinitival complementiser, and *to* as an infinitival T/tense particle (here with future time reference), as shown below (simplified by not showing the internal structure of the VP *meet up*):

(52)

```
              CP
           /      \
          C        TP
         for      /   \
               DP       T'
               us      /   \
                      T      VP
                      to   meet up
```

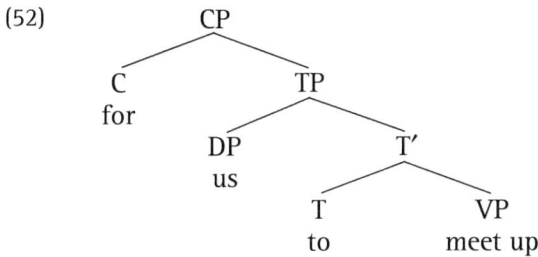

Here, the complementiser *for* serves not only to mark clause type (in that it tells us that the clause it introduces denotes an irrealis event – that is, a hypothetical one which hasn't yet taken place and may never do so), but also to determine the case of the clause subject, in the sense that *for* requires the subject to have accusative case (hence the use of the accusative subject *us* rather than its nominative counterpart *we*). This suggests that complementisers case-mark the subject of their clause. But how exactly does case assignment work?

An assumption made in work in syntax since the 1960s is that the structural relation **c-command** (an abbreviation of constituent-command) plays a key role in syntactic operations – including case-marking. This assumption can be embodied in the principle below (very loosely based on Chomsky 1986a):

(53)   **Structure Dependence Principle**
         Syntactic operations and conditions are structure dependent in the
         sense that they are sensitive to hierarchical structure, and canonically
         involve a c-command relation between a given constituent and
         another constituent that it c-commands. For example:
   (i)   movement involves a head attracting (i.e. triggering movement of)
          another constituent that it c-commands
   (ii)   case-marking involves a head assigning case to a constituent that it
          c-commands
   (iii) anaphora involves an anaphor (like *himself*) being bound by (i.e.
          taking its reference from) a constituent that c-commands it
   (iv)   polarity items are subject to a condition that they be c-commanded
          by an appropriate licenser (e.g. *any* is licensed by being
          c-commanded by *not* in 'I did **not** ask for *any* help')

We can define the relation c-command as follows:

(54)   **C-command**
         One constituent X c-commands another Y if the two are independent
         (i.e. if neither contains the other), and if the mother of X contains Y

In the light of (53) and (54), consider the role that c-command plays in case-marking in a structure like (52) above. On the assumption that the complementiser *for* is an accusative case assigner (i.e. in traditional terms, *for* is transitive), it follows that the subject DP *us* in (52) is assigned accusative case by the complementiser *for*, because C *for* c-commands DP *us* (in that the mother of C *for* is CP, and CP contains DP *us* as one of its constituents).

The c-command analysis of case-marking can be extended to finite clauses like the CP whose structure is shown below (where ø denotes a null C):

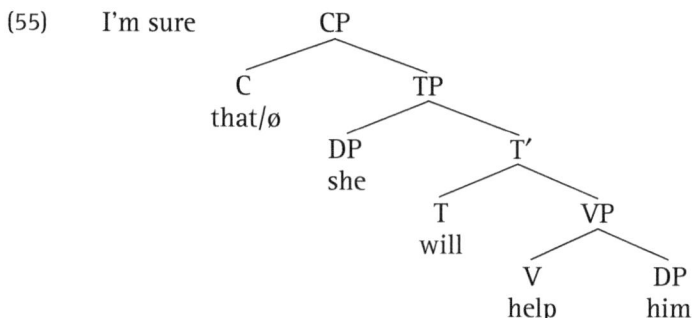

(55)   I'm sure

```
                        CP
                    ╱       ╲
              C               TP
            that/ø        ╱       ╲
                       DP           T′
                       she       ╱     ╲
                              T           VP
                            will      ╱     ╲
                                    V          DP
                                  help        him
```

If we follow Chomsky (2001) in supposing that finite complementisers are nominative case assigners, it follows that the subject DP *she* will be assigned nominative case by the finite complementiser *that/ø* which c-commands it in (55); and likewise, *they/she* will be assigned nominative case by the finite complementisers *whether/ø* in (50/46) above.

Still, an issue which arises with the c-command account of case-marking outlined here is the following. In a structure like (55) above, the finite complementiser *that* c-commands two different pronominal DPs – namely *she* on the one hand and *him* on the other. This raises the question of why *that* doesn't (wrongly) assign nominative case to *him* as well as (rightly) assigning nominative case to *she* (leading to the ungrammatical outcome *I'm sure that she will help he*). The answer given in work dating back to the 1980s is to suppose that UG/Universal Grammar contains a set of principles which regulate how grammatical operations apply. One of these (given the fuller name the Relativised Minimality Condition by Rizzi 1990) can be characterised informally as follows (where *above* means 'c-commanding' and *below* means 'c-commanded by'):

(56)   Minimality Condition
        A constituent can only enter into a syntactic relation with the minimal
        (= closest) constituent of the relevant type above or below it

One implication of (56) is that the complementiser *that/ø* can only case-mark the closest pro/nominal that it c-commands in (55) – namely *she*. Conversely, a second implication is that the pronoun *him* can only be case-marked by the closest case assigner that c-commands *him* – namely by the transitive (i.e. accusative case-assigning) verb *help*. Consequently, the effect of the Minimality Condition (56) on case assignment in (55) is to ensure that the complementiser *that/ø* assigns nominative case to *she*, and that the transitive verb *help* assigns accusative case to *him*.

We can broaden our discussion of clause structure and case marking by turning to consider the type of infinitive clause bold-printed below:

(57)   He is arranging **to see a cardiologist** and *for you to see an optician*

The italicised infinitival clause *for you to see an optician* is a CP introduced by the infinitival complementiser *for*. But given the assumption that only likes can be coordinated, the bold-printed clause *to see a cardiologist* must also be a CP. However, if this is so, why does it appear to contain no complementiser, and no subject? The answer given in research which dates back in spirit to work in the 1960s is that clauses like that bold-printed in (57) contain a null infinitival complementiser, and a null pronominal DP subject (denoted as PRO), so that the bold-printed clause has the structure below (where I take the indefinite article *a* to be an ART/article constituent which projects into an ARTP/article phrase):

(58)

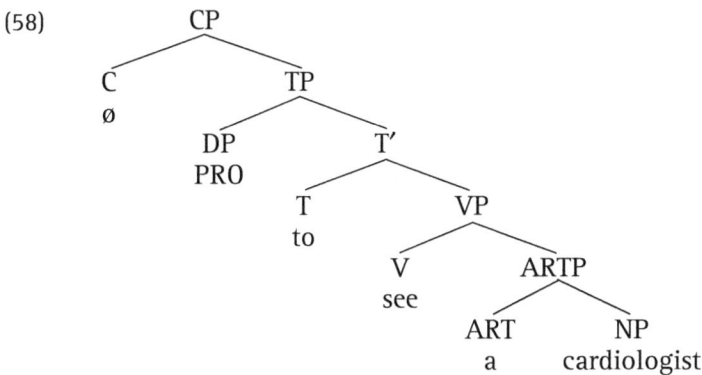

In such structures, PRO is said to be assigned **null case** by the null infinitival complementiser which c-commands it. Since case determines how a pronoun is spelled out (e.g. a third person masculine singular pronoun is spelled out as *he* if nominative, *him* if accusative, and *his* if genitive), it is plausible to suppose that PRO (since it has a null spellout) carries null case.

To summarise: in Module 1.3, I have argued that syntactic structures contain null constituents which have morphological, syntactic and semantic properties of their own (so that, for example, the PRO subject in 58 will carry null case, and be third person masculine singular by virtue of referring back to *he*). I also argued that the syntactic relation c-command plays a key role in regulating how syntactic operations and conditions apply.

You should now be able to tackle Exercise 1.3.

1.4   Movement operations

In addition to the merge and adjunction operations discussed in Module 1.2, the derivation/formation of syntactic structures can also involve **movement** operations. In this section, I outline three different types of movement operation, termed **A–bar Movement, A–Movement** and **Head Movement**.

1.4.1   A–bar Movement

One type of movement operation can be illustrated in terms of the exclamative sentences below (sourced by me from live, unscripted radio and TV broadcasts, and from the internet; capitals in 59b mark emphatic stress):

(59)   a.   *What a career* **that** she's had! (Laura Robson, BBC Radio 5)
b.   *What a race* **that** HE ran as well! (Steve Cram, BBC2 TV)
c.   *What a mine of useless information* **that** I am! (Terry Wogan, BBC Radio 2)
d.   *How cool* **that** she is! (forums.soompi.com)
e.   *How often* **that** I give it my all to finish a task or job! (friendspeaceteams.org)

To understand what's going on here, let's take a closer look at (59a), supposing that *what* is an exclamative quantifier and that *what a career* is a QP/quantifier phrase (comprising Q-*what* and the ARTP/article projection *a career*). This QP functions as the (direct object) complement of the verb *had*, and thus originates in the same position as the phrase *such a good career* in 'She's had *such a good career*'. This being so, the derivation of (59a) will proceed as follows.

The V/verb *had* merges with the QP *what a career* to form the VP *had what a career*. The T/present tense auxiliary *has* first-merges with this VP to form the T-bar *has had what a career*, and second-merges with the pronominal DP *she* to form the TP *she has had what a career*. The C/complementiser *that* then merges with this TP to form the C-bar *that she has had what a career*, with the structure shown below (simplified by not showing the internal structure of QP):

(60)

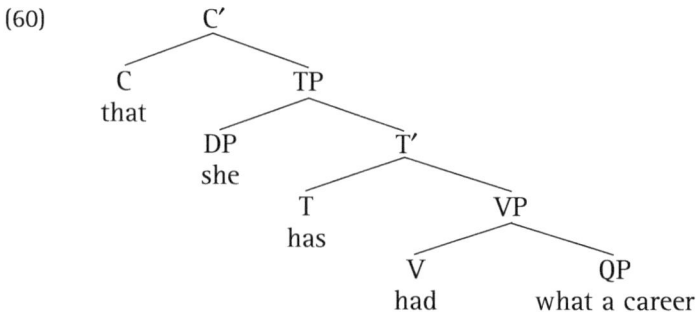

In an exclamative structure like (60), C attracts an exclamative wh-XP to move to the edge of the projection headed by C to become its specifier. If we suppose that (in conformity with the Structure Dependence Principle 53 above) movement involves a head attracting some other constituent which it c-commands, it follows that C-*that* can only attract an exclamative wh-XP that it c-commands (thereby underlining that the relation c-command plays a central role in syntactic operations). Furthermore, given the Minimality Condition (56), it follows that C-*that* must attract the closest exclamative wh-XP that it c-commands. The *QP what a career* is the only exclamative wh-XP c-commanded by C-*that* in (60), and consequently C-*that* attracts this QP to become its specifier, so resulting in the movement arrowed below:

(61)

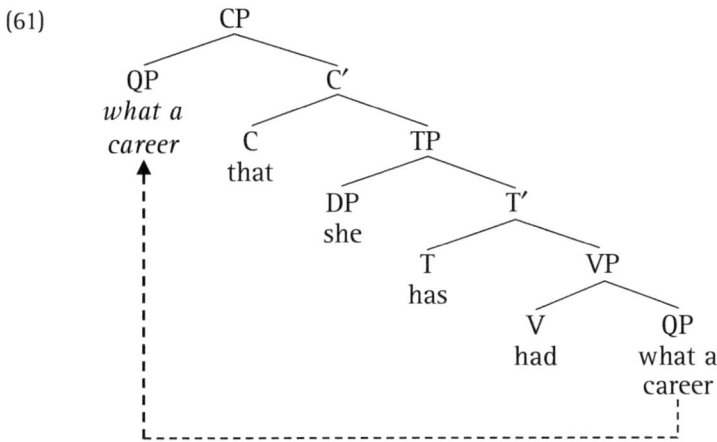

The arrowed movement of a wh-XP (i.e. a maximal projection comprising or containing a word beginning with *wh*-) is traditionally termed **Wh-Movement**: in this case, the wh-QP *what a career* moves from comp-VP (i.e. complement position within VP) into spec-CP (i.e. specifier position within CP).

Under the **Copy Theory of Movement** developed by Chomsky (1993), movement is a composite operation which creates a copy of the constituent to be moved, and then merges this newly created copy in a new position at the top of the tree. On this view, Wh-Movement in (60) involves creating a copy of the QP *what a career* and second-merging it as the specifier of *that*. This generates a syntactic structure like (61) above containing two copies of the QP *what a career*: the original one in comp-VP, and a second (italicised) copy in spec-CP. The syntactic structure in (61) is then handed over to the PF/phonological component, and this contains spellout rules that specify which copies of moved constituents are pronounced/overt, and which are silent/null. In default of any other spellout rule applying (i.e. if no other spellout rule applies), the following rule will apply:

(62)   Default Spellout Rule/DSR
        For a constituent whose spellout is not determined in some other way,
        the highest copy of the constituent is overtly pronounced, and any lower
        copies are silent

This means that the higher copy of the QP *what a career* in (61) will be
spelled out overtly, but the lower copy will be silent, resulting in (63) below
(where strikethrough marks a silent copy):

(63)   What a career that she has had ~~what a career~~!

    A point of detail to note, however, is that most speakers of standard
varieties of English don't like the use of *that* in exclamatives, and prefer to
use a null complementiser ø instead – so that in place of (63) above they
use (64) below:

(64)   What a career ø she has had ~~what a career~~!

I made use of a (non-standard) structure containing the overt complementiser *that* in (61/63) above in order to underline the point that the QP
what a career moves to a position in which it becomes the specifier of a
complementiser (i.e. it moves to spec-CP).
    Wh-Movement of a wh-XP to spec-CP is also found in other types of
clause, including interrogative clauses like that bracketed in (65a) below,
and relative clauses like that bracketed in (65b):

(65)   a. I wonder [*which film* she was watching –]
        b. That's the film [*which* she was watching –]

On the assumption that Wh-Movement involves movement of a wh-XP
from a position below C to spec-CP, the bracketed clauses in (65) above
will have the respective structures shown in (66a/66b) below (simplified
by not showing the internal structure of the DP *which film*, for space
reasons)

(66)

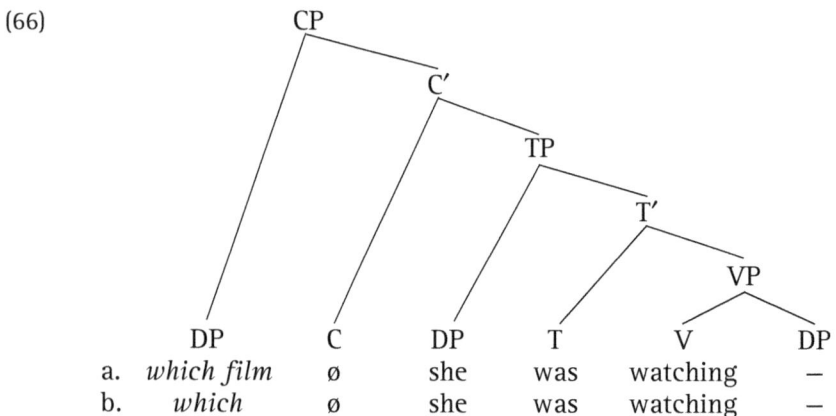

	DP	C	DP	T	V	DP
a.	*which film*	ø	she	was	watching	–
b.	*which*	ø	she	was	watching	–

In both cases, the italicised wh-DP *which (film)* originates in the gap position (−) and from there moves to become the specifier of the null complementiser ø which is the head C of CP. Under the Copy Theory of Movement, the gap position in comp-VP will contain a silent copy of the moved wh-DP *which film/which.*

Although our discussion thus far has been concerned with Wh-Movement, in reality Wh-Movement is simply one instance of a wider class of movement operations which move a maximal projection/phrase/XP to spec-CP. Other operations of this type include the **Focusing** operation by which the italicised nominals move to spec-CP (to become the specifier of a null complementiser) in sentences such as those in (67B) below in order to mark them as focused (i.e. conveying new information), and the **Topicalisation** operation by which the italicised nominal moves to spec-CP (again becoming the specifier of a null complementiser) in a sentence such as the second one in (68) below, in order to mark it as a topic conveying familiar/old information;

(67)   SPEAKER A: What are the subjects you enjoy most and least?

        SPEAKER B: *Syntax* I enjoy most. *Phonetics* I enjoy least

(68)   He had witnessed acts of horrific violence, mutilation and torture. *Such brutality,* he prayed that he would never again encounter as long as he lived

A more generic term for operations which move a constituent into spec-CP is **A-bar Movement** (so that Wh-Movement, Focusing and Topicalisation are specific instances of A-bar Movement). It is important to note here that the suffix *-bar* has a very different meaning from that found in category labels like T-bar (where it denotes an intermediate constituent larger than T but smaller than TP). By contrast, in the term A-bar Movement, the -bar suffix marks negation, so that A-bar Movement denotes 'movement to a non-A position' (i.e. to a position which is not an A-position). This of course raises the question of what the difference is between an A-position and an A-bar position. This can be illustrated in relation to a clause such as that produced by speaker B in the dialogue below:

(69)   SPEAKER A: What don't you understand?

        SPEAKER B: [$_{CP}$ Why [$_{TP}$ you are blaming yourself]]

An **A-position** is one which can only be occupied by an **argument** (e.g. the subject or complement of a verb) but not by an adjunct, which can control agreement, and from which an anaphor (like *yourself*) can be bound; by contrast, an **A-bar position** is one which is not restricted to arguments (so can contain either an adjunct or an argument), but cannot control agreement, and cannot bind (i.e. serve as the antecedent of) an anaphor.

Given these criteria, the spec-TP position occupied by *you* in (69B) is an A-position because the pronoun *you* that it contains is an argument (of the verb *blaming*), it controls the agreement properties of the auxiliary *are*, and it serves as the antecedent of the anaphor *yourself*. By contrast, the spec-CP position occupied by *why* in (69B) is an A-bar position because *why* is an adjunct, does not control agreement with *are*, and cannot bind an anaphor.

1.4.2 A-Movement

Alongside A-bar Movement, we find a second type of XP movement operation which is termed **A-Movement**, since it involves movement into an A-position (like spec-TP). In this connection, consider the position of the QP/quantifier phrase *several suspects* in the three sentences below:

(70)   a. They detained *several suspects*
      b. There were detained *several suspects*
      c. *Several suspects* were detained

(70a) is an active sentence, (70b) is an expletive passive sentence (i.e. one with the expletive pronoun *there* as its subject), and (70c) is a non-expletive passive sentence. In the active sentence (70a) and the expletive passive (70b), the QP *several suspects* occupies comp-VP (i.e. the complement position within VP). But in the non-expletive passive (70c), the QP *several suspects* occupies spec-TP, in that it serves as the specifier of the past tense auxiliary *were*. But how does the QP get from the comp-VP position that it occupies in (70a, 70b) to the spec-TP position that it occupies in (70c)? The answer given in work dating back in spirit to Chomsky (1955, 1957) is that the QP *several suspects* originates in comp-VP and from there moves to spec-TP via an operation traditionally referred to as **Passivisation**. Let's look more closely at passives like (70b, 70c).

The V/verb *detained* merges with the QP *several suspects* to form the VP *detained several suspects*. The past tense T auxiliary *were* first-merges with this VP to form the T-bar *were detained several suspects*, which has the structure below:

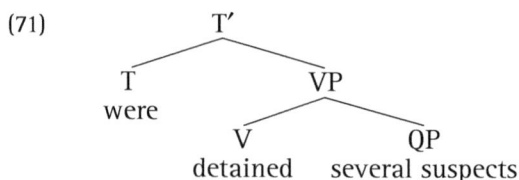

(71)

$$T'$$

T — VP

were

V — QP

detained   several suspects

T constituents carry a feature (traditionally called an **EPP feature**) requiring them to second-merge with an appropriate nominal or pronominal specifier/subject. One way of satisfying this EPP requirement is by merging the expletive pronominal DP *there* in spec-TP. Merging the resulting TP with a null declarative complementiser forms the expletive passive structure below:

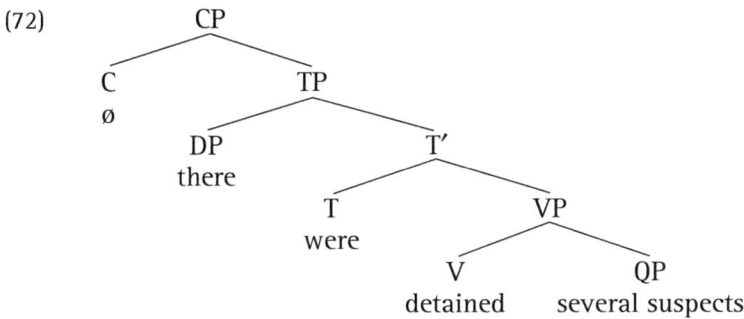

(72)

```
                    CP
           ┌─────────┴─────────┐
           C                   TP
           Ø          ┌─────────┴─────────┐
                      DP                  T′
                     there        ┌────────┴────────┐
                                  T                 VP
                                were        ┌────────┴────────┐
                                            V               QP
                                        detained      several suspects
```

The reason why the feature requiring T to have a specifier/subject is termed an EPP feature is that in earlier work its function was seen as being to satisfy an Extended Projection Principle (= EPP) requiring T to project not only into T-bar, but also to have an extended projection into a TP formed by second-merging T with a nominal or pronominal subject.

However, an alternative way of satisfying the EPP feature on T is for T to attract a nominal or pronominal DP/QP to become its subject. In consequence of the Structure Dependence Principle (53) and the Minimality Condition (56), T will attract the closest QP/DP that it c-commands; and in the case of the structure in (71) above, this is the QP *several suspects*. Accordingly, this QP moves from comp-VP to spec-TP, in the manner shown by the arrow below:

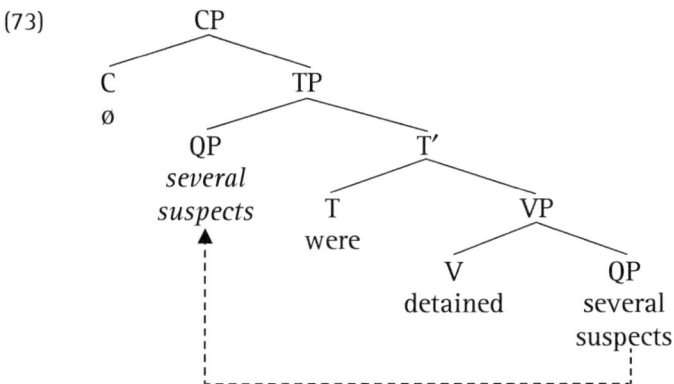

(73)

```
                    CP
           ┌─────────┴─────────┐
           C                   TP
           Ø          ┌─────────┴─────────┐
                      QP                  T′
                    several       ┌────────┴────────┐
                   suspects       T                 VP
                      ▲         were        ┌────────┴────────┐
                      ┊                     V               QP
                      ┊                 detained          several
                      ┊                                   suspects
                      └┄┄┄┄┄┄┄┄┄┄┄┄┄┄┄┄┄┄┄┄┄┄┄┄┄┄┄┄┄┄┄┘
```

This movement is traditionally termed Passivisation, but (as we will see in more detail in Chapter 2) it is a particular subtype of a more general movement operation known as **A-Movement**, because it involves movement into an A-position (spec-TP). Under the Copy Theory of Movement, Passivisation results in a structure containing two copies of the QP *several suspects* (a lower one in comp-VP, and a higher one in spec-TP), but in accordance with the Default Spellout Rule (62), only the higher copy is overtly spelled out in the phonology.

1.4.3   Head Movement

A more general conclusion to be drawn from our discussion so far in this module is that there are two distinct types of XP movement operation found in the grammars of natural languages: A-bar Movement of an XP from a position below C to spec-CP; and A-Movement of an XP from a position below T to spec-TP. However, it is not only XP constituents (i.e. maximal projections/phrases) which can undergo movement, as the bold-printed auxiliaries below illustrate:

(74)   a. *What colour* **have** you chosen?
         b. *No leniency* **will** the judge show

The italicised phrases *what colour/no leniency* are QPs headed by the interrogative/negative quantifiers *what/no*. These QPs originate as the complement of the verb *chosen/show*, as we see from the corresponding in situ sentences (i.e. sentences in which no movement takes place) below:

(75)   a. You **have** chosen *what colour?*
         b. The judge **will** show *no leniency*

In each of the two sentences in (75), the interrogative/negative QP originates in comp-VP (as the complement of the verb *chosen/show*) and from there moves to spec-CP in sentences like (74). But in both (74a) and (74b), movement of the italicised QP to spec-CP triggers concomitant Inversion of the bold-printed auxiliary *have/will* – in the sense that the auxiliary moves from a position following the subject *you/the judge* in (75) to a position preceding the subject in (74). But what kind of movement operation does Auxiliary Inversion involve?

   Since the bold-printed auxiliaries in (75) occupy the canonical (post-subject) T position for finite auxiliaries, and since (via Inversion) they end up in the same (pre-subject) C position in (74) as is occupied by the complementiser *that* in (61) above, it is plausible to suppose that Auxiliary Inversion involves T-to-C movement (i.e. movement of an auxiliary from the T position following the subject to the C position preceding the subject). On one classic implementation of this idea, the derivation of (74a) proceeds as follows. The V *chosen* merges with the QP *what colour* to form the VP *chosen what colour*. The (present tense) T auxiliary *have* first-merges with this VP to form the T-bar *have chosen what colour*, and second-merges with the pronominal DP *you* to form the

TP *you have chosen what colour*. The resulting TP is then merged with a null complementiser (C-ø) to form the C-bar *ø you have chosen what colour*. The null complementiser/C attracts the interrogative QP *what colour* to become its specifier, and concomitantly attracts the T auxiliary *have* to adjoin to the null C, so resulting in the two movement operations arrowed below:

(76)

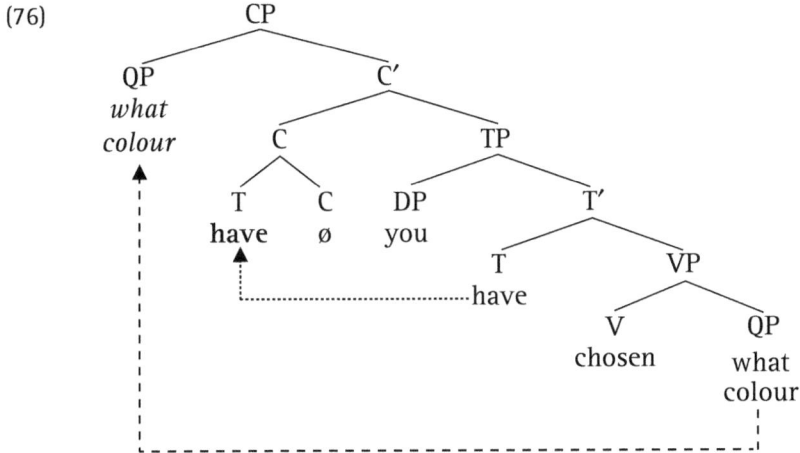

On this view, movement of the interrogative QP *what colour* to spec-CP triggers concomitant movement of the auxiliary *have* from T to adjoin to a null complementiser in C. In each case, only the highest/italicised copy of the moved QP in spec-CP (and the highest/bold-printed copy of the auxiliary in C) is spelled out overtly in the phonology, in conformity with the Default Spellout Rule (62). Note that, in conformity with the Structure Dependence Principle (53i) and the Minimality Condition (56), C-ø in (76) attracts the closest auxiliary that it c-commands (namely the T auxiliary *have*) to adjoin to C-ø.

The assumption that Auxiliary Inversion in sentences like (74) is triggered when C has an interrogative or negative specifier raises the question of what triggers Inversion of the bold-printed auxiliary in a yes–no question like:

(77)   **Have** you chosen the colour?

A traditional answer given in research dating back decades is that in yes–no questions, C has a null yes–no question **operator** as its specifier, and it is this operator which (by virtue of being interrogative) triggers Auxiliary Inversion in main clause questions. It is called a yes–no question operator because it has the semantic function of operating on a proposition to convert it into a yes–no question which questions the truth value of the proposition (e.g. 77 asks whether it is true that you have chosen the colour). If we denote this abstract/silent yes–no question operator as Op_{YNQ} (and take it to be an ADVP like *why/how/when/where*), the yes–no question in (77) will have the derivation below:

(78)

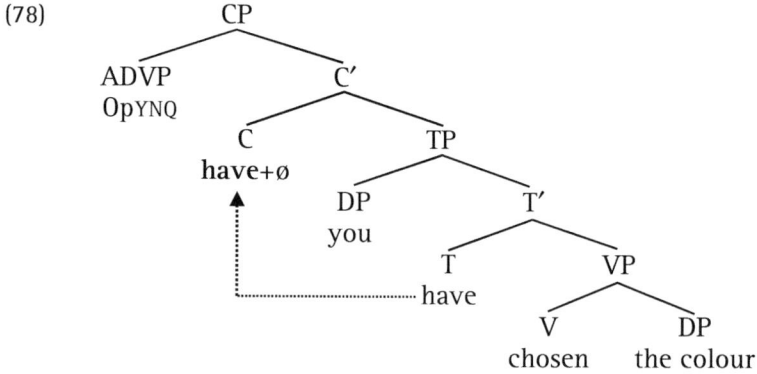

On the assumption that a C with an interrogative or negative specifier triggers Auxiliary Inversion, the T auxiliary *have* in (78) will undergo Inversion and thereby adjoin to the null complementiser in C (as shown in simplified form above), because the complementiser has an interrogative operator as its specifier. Given the Default Spellout Rule (62), only the higher copy of the auxiliary *have* (in C) will be overtly spelled out in the phonology.

An interesting question arising from the yes–no question operator analysis is what function the operator serves. A plausible answer is that having an interrogative operator on the edge of CP (i.e. inside CP but outside TP) provides a way of signalling what type a given clause is (e.g. whether it is interrogative, or exclamative, etc. in force). Reasoning along these lines, let's suppose that in the semantic component of the grammar, clauses are typed (i.e. interpreted as being of a specific type) in accordance with the Clause Typing Conditions in (79) below:

(79)   **Clause Typing Conditions**
    (i) A clause is interpreted as being of a given type (interrogative or exclamative etc.) if it has a peripheral clause-typing specifier of the relevant type
    (ii) An indicative clause is interpreted as declarative in type by default if it contains no peripheral clause-typing specifier

Note that a *peripheral* constituent is one positioned on the edge of the clause periphery; and we can give a more concrete idea of what the clause periphery comprises if we represent the structure in (78) in terms of the highly simplified labelled brackets below:

(80)   [CP Op_YNQ [C **have+ø**] [TP you [T ~~have~~] chosen the colour]]

The periphery of a clause/CP comprises that part of the structure positioned above TP (i.e. the part boxed in 80): consequently, the bold-printed constituents positioned on the edge of CP (i.e. inside CP but outside TP) are in the clause periphery in (80). Given the clause-typing conditions in (79), it follows from (79i) that the presence of the interrogative yes–no question operator in spec-CP in (78/80) will type the relevant clause as having the force of a yes–no question. And in essentially the same way, the presence of the exclamative QP *what a career* in spec-CP in (61) above will type (61) as an exclamative clause. Likewise, the presence of the interrogative phrase *which film* in spec-CP in (66a) will type the relevant clause as a wh-question. By contrast, the absence of any clause-typing constituent in the clause periphery (= on the edge of CP) in structures like (72) and (73) above will ensure that the relevant clauses are typed as declarative in force by default (via 79ii), assuming that the null C marks indicative mood.

Returning now to the main theme of this module: movement operations typically move a constituent (either a maximal projection XP or a head X) to the edge of a functional projection. So, for example, A-bar Movement moves an XP from a position below C into spec-CP; A-Movement moves an XP from a position below T into spec-TP; and Head Movement (in the case of Auxiliary Inversion) moves a head from T into C. Still, if movement operations move an X or XP to the edge of CP or TP, we'd expect to find a further type of Head Movement operation by which a head moves from V to T. And indeed it has long been argued that English does indeed have just such a V-to-T Movement operation by which the verb BE (when used as a **copula** – i.e. a verb which links a subject to a non-verbal predicate) can raise from the head V position of VP into the head T position of TP. This can be illustrated by sentences such as the following:

(81)   a.   He may not *be* at home
            b.   He *is* not at home

In (81a) the copular verb BE occupies the head V position of VP, and hence follows *not* (which is taken in much recent work to be the specifier of a NEGP/negative phrase constituent positioned between TP and VP). In (81b), the verb BE (in the guise of *is*) ends up in front of *not*, so can be taken to have moved from V into T. Let's take a closer look at what is involved in this type of movement.

Consider first (81a), which we can take to have the following structure:

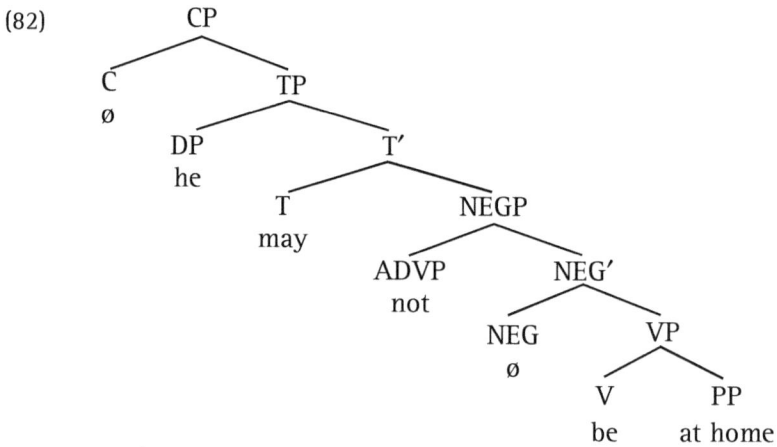

(82)

```
                    CP
          C                  TP
          ø          DP              T'
                     he      T              NEGP
                             may     ADVP          NEG'
                                     not     NEG         VP
                                             ø       V       PP
                                                     be    at home
```

In (81a/82) *be* occupies the head V position of VP, and hence follows the NEGP containing the negative adverb *not*. But things are different in three respects in (81b): firstly, there is no auxiliary like *may* in T; secondly, in place of *be* we find the finite form *is*; and thirdly, *is* precedes *not* (whereas in 81a/82, *be* follows *not*). How can we account for these differences?

A plausible answer is to suppose that BE has auxiliary-like properties which enable it to raise from the V position which it occupies in (82) above to adjoin to a present tense affix in T – in the manner shown by the arrow in (83) below:

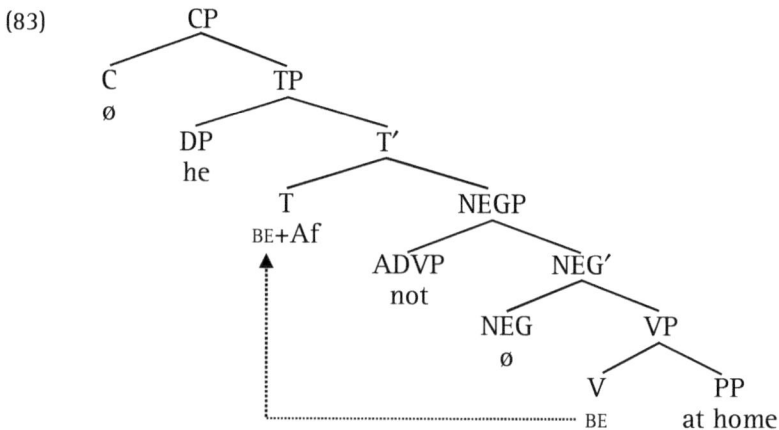

(83)

```
                    CP
          C                  TP
          ø          DP              T'
                     he      T              NEGP
                           BE+Af     ADVP          NEG'
                             ↑       not     NEG         VP
                             :               ø       V       PP
                             :.......................... BE    at home
```

Since the affix in T is present tense (and third person singular by agreement with *he*), the resulting complex T head BE+*Af* will be spelled out in the phonology as the irregular third person singular present tense form *is* (and the overall sentence as 81b *He is not at home*). On the assumption that only an affix that needs to attach to a verbal stem can attract the verb BE to adjoin to it (and that T contains such an affix but NEG does not), movement from V to T will satisfy the Minimality Condition (56) (which requires a constituent to move to the closest appropriate position above it), since the verb BE moves to adjoin to the closest head above it that contains the kind of affix that attaches to a verb – namely T. It will also satisfy the Structure Dependence Principle (53i), since (prior to movement) T-*Af* c-commands the V-BE constituent that it attracts to adjoin to it.

Once BE has raised to T, the BE+*Af* head thereby formed can undergo Auxiliary Inversion in questions and thereby move to C, as in a yes–no question such as *Is he at home?* with the (simplified) superficial structure shown below:

(84)

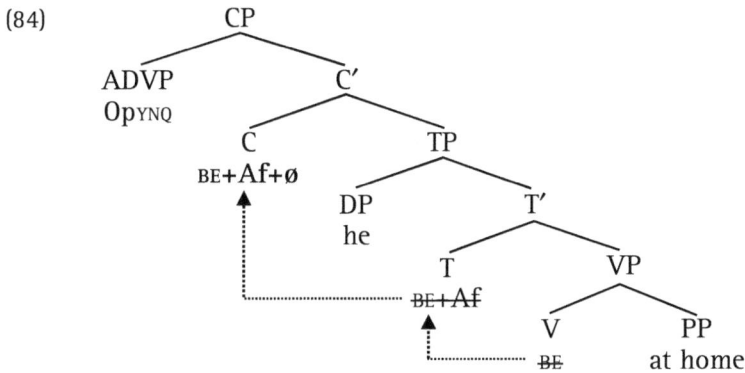

The verb BE first moves from V to T (adjoining to a null present tense affix in T), and then the resulting BE+*Af* structure (ultimately spelled out as *is*) moves from T to C (adjoining to a null complementiser in C). The V and T positions are empty after movement (and so end up as gaps), but under the Copy Theory of Movement, these gaps represent null copies of moved items.

In earlier varieties of English (e.g. in Shakespearean English), lexical/ main verbs could also raise from V to T, so resulting in auxiliariless finite clauses like those in (85) below, where the (bold-printed) main verb is positioned in front of *not*: cf.

(85)　　a.　I **care** *not* for her (Thurio, *Two Gentlemen of Verona*, V.iv)

　　　　b.　He **heard** *not* that (Julia, *Two Gentlemen of Verona*, IV.ii)

　　　　c.　My master **seeks** *not* me (Speed, *Two Gentlemen of Verona*, I.i)

　　　　d.　I **know** *not* where to hide my head (Trinculo, *The Tempest*, II.ii)

In such sentences, the bold-printed verb raises from V (across the intervening NEGP containing *not*) to adjoin to a present or past tense affix in T. However, in present-day English, only a handful of verbs can now undergo movement to T – namely items which have little (if any) lexical semantic content and thus are auxiliary-like, such as BE and (in some varieties) some uses of HAVE.

To summarise: I have argued in Module 1.4 that there are three main types of syntactic movement operation: (i) A-bar Movement of an XP from a position below C into spec-CP; (ii) A-Movement of an XP from a position below T into spec-TP; and (iii) Head Movement from a lower head position to adjoin to a higher one (e.g. from T to adjoin to null C, or from V to adjoin to an affix in T).

You should now be able to tackle Exercise 1.4.

1.5   Blocking mechanisms

Ever since the 1960s, linguists have argued that grammars need to contain mechanisms which block illicit syntactic operations (termed **constraints**), and also mechanisms which block illicit superficial syntactic structures (termed **filters**). In this module, we'll look at how these two different mechanisms can be used to block illicit operations and structures.

1.5.1   Constraints

Pioneering work by Chomsky (1964a) and Ross (1967) argued that principles of UG/Universal Grammar impose constraints (i.e. restrictions) on the types of syntactic operation which are permissible. Using a picturesque metaphor, Ross (1967) argued that certain types of syntactic structure are **islands** in the sense that any constituent inside an island is marooned there and can't be got off the island by any movement operation. He proposed a family of constraints on movement which can be characterised informally as follows:

(86)   **Island Constraints**
No movement operation can extract any constituent out of an island such as the following:
(i)   a subject
(ii)   an adjunct
(iii)   a clause contained inside an NP (forming a complex NP)
(iv)   a coordinate structure

These island constraints have the effect of blocking movement from the gap to the italicised position in sentences such as the following:

(87)   a.   *The motorway*, everyone knows that [the closure of −] will cause chaos
      b.   *The FBI*, the CIA were working on the case [independently of −]
      c.   *This course*, there are [students [who hate −]]
      d.   *The princess*, the police are guarding [the prince and −]

The reason is the following. In (87a), the italicised topic is extracted out of a bracketed subject, in violation of the Subject Island Constraint (86i).

In (87b), the italicised topic is extracted out of a bracketed ADVP which is an adjunct to the VP *working on the case*, in violation of the Adjunct Island Constraint (86ii). In (87c), the italicised topic is extracted out of a relative clause *who hate* which is contained inside the NP *students who hate*, in violation of the Complex NP Constraint (86iii). And in (87d), the italicised topic is extracted out of a bracketed coordinate structure, in violation of the Coordinate Structure Constraint (86iv).

In the decades since Ross's original work, considerable research has been undertaken into constraints. One strand of this research has sought to conflate several of Ross's Constraints into a single, more general constraint. A constraint along these lines (proposed by Cattell 1976, Cinque 1978, and Huang 1982) can be characterised informally as follows:

(88)   **Constraint on Extraction Domains/CED**
        Only complements allow material to be extracted out of them, not
        specifiers or adjuncts

Since subjects are specifiers, the ungrammaticality of (87a) can be attributed to a CED violation because the DP *the motorway* is extracted out of a DP (*the closure of the motorway*) which is the specifier of the T auxiliary *will*. And since (87b) involves extraction out of an adjunct, it too gives rise to a CED violation. Similarly, CED is violated in (87c), because *this course* is extracted out of a bracketed *who*-clause inside a bracketed NP containing *students*, and in (87d), because *the princess* is extracted out of a bracketed coordinate structure.

Much other work on constraints has focused on locality conditions which impose restrictions on how far constituents can move in any single movement operation. The Minimality Condition (outlined in 56 above) is one of these, requiring a moved constituent to move to the closest appropriate landing site above it. Another locality constraint (dating back to work by Chomsky 1998) can be characterised informally as follows (where *impenetrable* means 'inaccessible', and – to be strictly accurate – *below* means 'c-commanded by', and *above* means 'c-commanding'):

(89)   **Impenetrability Condition**
        Anything below the head C of a CP is impenetrable to anything above
        the CP

The condition/constraint in (89) has the effect of barring syntactic operations from applying across the edge of a CP (i.e. across the head C of a CP and any specifier that it has). The effect of the constraint can be illustrated below:

(90)   *They consider [$_{CP}$ that [$_{TP}$ *each other* should apologise]]

In this sentence, *each other* is a reciprocal anaphor, and like all anaphors it needs to be bound by (i.e. linked to) a local/nearby antecedent which c-commands it. However, while *they* c-commands *each other* in (90), the resulting sentence is ill-formed. Why should this be? A plausible answer is that the Impenetrability Condition (89) prevents *they* from binding *each other* across the edge of the intervening (bracketed) CP containing *that*. And since there is no other possible binder/antecedent for *each other*, the resulting sentence (90) is ungrammatical.

Locality constraints like the Minimality and Impenetrability Conditions have important implications for how long-distance (i.e. cross-clausal) movement works – as can be illustrated in relation to:

(91)   What do you think [that he wants]?

Here, the interrogative wh-QP *what* originates as the complement of the verb *wants*, and subsequently (via Wh-Movement/A-bar Movement) moves out of the bracketed *wants*-clause to the front of the *think*-clause. But how does this long-distance movement (out of one clause into the other) take place? At first sight, it might seem plausible to suppose that movement takes place in a single step, in the manner shown in highly simplified form below:

(92) $[_{CP2}$ *What* $[_{C2}$ do] you think $[_{CP1}$ $[_{C1}$ that] he wants ~~what~~]]

That is, the wh-QP *what* moves directly from being the complement of the verb *want* to becoming the specifier of the inverted auxiliary *do* in the main clause; and in accordance with the Default Spellout Rule (62), only the higher copy of *what* (in spec-CP$_2$) is spelled out overtly.

However, the single-step movement arrowed in (92) violates locality constraints on movement. For one thing, since Wh-Movement involves movement of a wh-XP to become the specifier of a CP above it, the Minimality Condition (56) requires a wh-moved XP to become the specifier of the closest CP above it – and in the case of (92), the closest CP above/to the left of the position in which *what* originates (as the complement of *want*) is CP$_1$, and not CP$_2$. Secondly, the single-step movement in (92) also violates the Impenetrability Condition (89) – which bars movement across the edge of an intervening CP – by moving *what* across the complementiser *that* on the edge of CP$_1$. In short, the single-step movement in (92) violates two separate locality conditions (Minimality and Impenetrability), and hence is untenable. And yet, the resulting sentence (*What do you think that he wants?*) is fully grammatical. How come?

The answer is that although the single-step movement arrowed in (92) is ruled out by locality constraints, there is an alternative way of deriving the sentence which satisfies locality requirements. This is to suppose that the wh-QP *what* moves in two successive steps, moving first to become the specifier of the lower clause (CP$_1$), and then to become the specifier of the higher clause (CP$_2$) – as shown by the two numbered arrows below:

(93)   [$_{CP2}$ *What* [$_{C2}$ do] you think [$_{CP1}$ ~~what~~ [$_{C1}$ that] he wants ~~what~~]]

                          (2)   (1)

The wh-QP *what* originates in comp-VP (as the complement of the verb *want*), and first of all moves into spec-CP$_1$: since CP$_1$ is the closest CP above the comp-VP position in which *what* originates, this movement does not violate the Minimality Condition (56). Nor does movement (1) in (93) violate the Impenetrability Condition (89), since it involves movement to a position <u>inside</u> CP$_1$ (not to a position <u>outside</u>/<u>above</u> CP$_1$). Subsequent movement of *what* from spec-CP$_1$ to spec-CP$_2$ does not violate the Minimality Condition either, since in moving to spec-CP$_2$ *what* moves to the closest spec-CP position above spec-CP$_1$. Nor does movement (2) induce an impenetrability violation, since *what* moves from a position <u>above</u> (not <u>below</u>) C$_1$ to a position above CP$_1$. In short, locality (minimality and impenetrability) constraints permit long-distance movement to take place only in a **successive-cyclic** fashion (i.e. in a succession of small steps, with the relevant constituent moving first to the front of the lowest clause, then to the front of the next lowest clause, and so on).

A different kind of constraint on movement is posited by Wexler & Culicover (1980: 119), and can be outlined informally as follows:

(94)   **Freezing Principle**
         The constituents of a moved phrase are frozen internally within (and so cannot be extracted out of) the moved phrase

How the principle works can be illustrated by the examples below:

(95)   a. *Which hotel* do you think he is staying **in**?
         b. **In** *which hotel* do you think he is staying?
         c. **Which hotel* do you think **in** he is staying?

In these sentences the wh-phrase *which hotel* originates as the complement of the preposition *in*. In (95a), *which hotel* undergoes Wh-Movement on its own, stranding the preposition *in* at the end of the sentence. In (95b), the preposition *in* is dragged (or, to use a technical term, **pied-piped**) along with *which hotel*, so that the whole PP *in which hotel* undergoes Wh-Movement. Given the arguments presented in our discussion of (91–93) above that long/cross-clausal Wh-Movement is successive-cyclic, the PP *in* *which hotel* will move first to the edge of the CP in the embedded clause before moving to the edge of the CP in the main clause in (95b). But this assumption raises the question of what would prevent us from moving the PP *in which hotel* to the front of the embedded clause CP_1, and then moving the wh-phrase *which hotel* on its own to the front of the main clause CP_2, leaving the preposition *in* stranded in the bold-printed position below, at the beginning of the embedded clause CP_1:

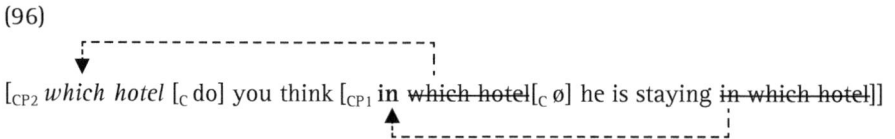

(96)

$[_{CP2}$ *which hotel* $[_C$ do$]$ you think $[_{CP1}$ **in** ~~which hotel~~$[_C$ ø$]$ he is staying ~~in which hotel~~$]]$

Why does the derivation in (96) crash and lead to the ungrammatical outcome in (95c)? The answer is that the movement shown by the upper arrow violates the Freezing Principle (94), because *which hotel* has been extracted out of a larger phrase (= the PP *in which hotel*) which has itself undergone movement, in that the PP *in which hotel* undergoes the Wh-Movement operation indicated by the lower arrow.

Yet another kind of constraint on movement operations can be illustrated by the following contrast:

(97)   a. Nobody can have *no secrets*
         b. **No secrets* can **nobody** have

Let's suppose that the expressions *nobody* and *no secrets* are both negative QPs/quantifier phrases. Let's also suppose that (97b) involves the negative QP *no secrets* moving from its initial position as the complement of *have* to the specifier position in the CP at the beginning of the sentence (and that this triggers concomitant Auxiliary Inversion) – as shown by the arrow below:

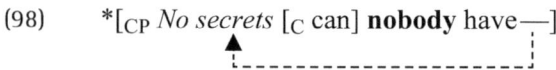

(98)   *$[_{CP}$ *No secrets* $[_C$ can$]$ **nobody** have —$]$

So why is the resulting sentence (97b) ungrammatical? The answer lies in a constraint formulated by Abels (2012: 247) in the following terms:

(99)   **Intervention Condition**
         Likes cannot cross likes (*likes* = 'constituents which are alike')

The problem posed by the arrowed movement in (98) is that it involves one negative QP (*no secrets*) crossing another negative QP (*nobody*), in violation of the Intervention Condition (99). We will encounter a number of other constraints on movement operations in later chapters of the book.

1.5.2 Filters

In work dating back to the 1960s, it has been argued that (in addition to imposing constraints on syntactic operations), natural language grammars also impose constraints on the types of superficial syntactic structure that they allow. These constraints on superficial structures have been termed **filters**, because they have the effect of filtering out structures at the end of a syntactic derivation that do not meet the relevant requirements.

By way of illustration, consider the clauses bracketed below (from sentences I recorded from live, unscripted radio/TV broadcasts):

(100)   a. It shows [*what a fantastic squad* **that** they have] (Gordon Strachan, ITV)

            b. You just wonder [*how long* **that** America can hang on] (Gary Lineker, BBC1 TV)

            c. I'm aware of the speed [*with which* **that** they work] (Tim Vickery, BBC Radio 5)

In each case, the bracketed clause is a CP whose edge comprises a wh-XP (exclamative in the case of *what a fantastic squad* in 100a, interrogative in the case of *how long* in 100b, and relative in the case of *with which* in 100c) immediately followed by the complementiser *that* – as shown in the structures below (simplified by not showing the internal structure of TP):

(101)

	wh-XP	C	TP
a. It just shows	*what a fantastic squad*	**that**	they have
b. You just wonder	*how long*	**that**	America can hang on
c. I'm aware of the speed	*with which*	**that**	they work

However, while I have recorded hundreds of similar *wh+that* structures from radio, TV and the internet, it is nonetheless true that speakers of standard varieties of English typically don't like such structures, and regard them as ungrammatical. Why?

A traditional answer (dating back to work by Chomsky & Lasnik 1977) is that standard varieties of English impose a requirement on superficial syntactic structures that can be outlined informally as follows:

(102)   **Doubly Filled COMP Filter/DFCF**

        At the end of a syntactic derivation, any superficial structure in which the edge of a projection headed by an overt complementiser is doubly filled (i.e. contains some other overt constituent) is filtered out as ungrammatical

(Note that the edge of a projection XP comprises its head X and any other constituent/s of XP above/c-commanding X; most commonly, the edge of XP will comprise the head X and any specifier that it has.) Speakers with DFCF in their grammar find *wh+that* structures like (100/101) ungrammatical, because the edge of the relevant CP is doubly filled (by virtue of comprising an overt complementiser *that* with an overt wh-XP as its specifier). Such speakers avoid violating DFCF by using a structure in which the relevant CP contains a null C-*ø* in place of C-*that*, resulting in the structures bracketed below:

(103)   a. It shows [$_{CP}$ *what a fantastic squad* [$_C$ *ø*] they have]
        b. You just wonder [$_{CP}$ *how long* [$_C$ *ø*] America can hang on]
        c. I'm aware of the speed [$_{CP}$ *with which* [$_C$ *ø*] they work]

Since the clauses bracketed in (103) do not contain an overt complementiser, they do not give rise to any DFCF violation. By contrast, speakers (like me) of varieties of English which do not have DFCF in their grammar accept both *wh+that* CPs like those in (100/101), and *wh+ø* CPs like those in (103). Thus, varieties of English can differ with respect to whether specific filters (like DFCF) operate in their grammar.

A second type of filter which operates in standard varieties of English (again proposed by Chomsky & Lasnik 1977: 451) can be characterised informally as follows:

(104)   **COMP-Trace Filter/CTF**
        Any structure at the end of a syntactic derivation in which an overt COMP/complementiser is immediately adjacent to and c-commands a trace (i.e. a gap/null copy left behind by a moved constituent) is filtered out as ill-formed

Types of structure which CTF allows/disallows can be illustrated below:

(105)   a. *Who* do you think that he should help – ?
        b. **Who* do you think that – should help him?

In (105a), the fronted wh-QP *who* originates as the complement of the verb *help*, and from there moves first to spec-CP in its own clause, and then to spec-CP in the main clause – as shown in simplified schematic form below:

(106)   Who do you think

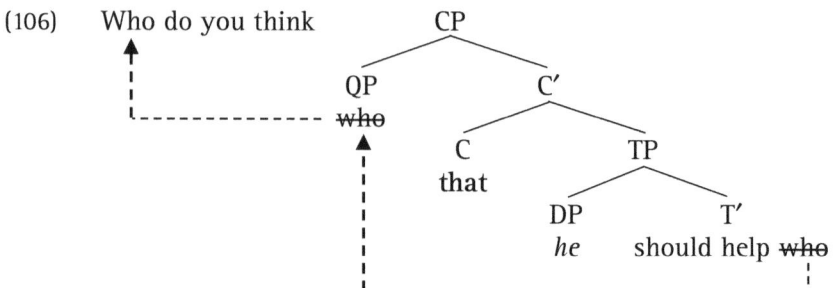

The two-step Wh-Movement operation arrowed above is forced by the Minimality Condition (56) and the Impenetrability Condition (89). It results in a superficial syntactic structure (106) which does not violate the COMP-Trace Filter (104), because the italicised constituent immediately following (and c-commanded by) the bold-printed complementiser *that* is the overt pronoun *he*, not a trace/null copy of a moved constituent. Since the resulting structure (106) does not violate CTF, the corresponding sentence (105a) is grammatical.

But now compare what happens in (105b). Here, Wh-Movement results in the pronoun *who* undergoing the (two-step) Wh-Movement operation arrowed below:

(107)   *Who* do you think

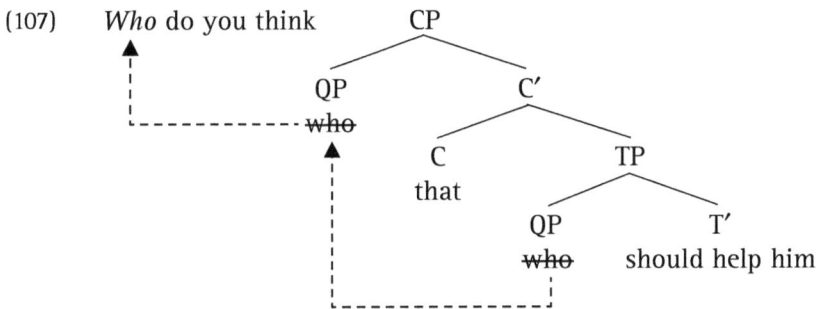

More specifically, *who* first moves from spec-TP to spec-CP in the complement clause (i.e. the *should*-clause), and then moves to spec-CP in the main clause. But this results in a structure (107) in which the overt complementiser *that* immediately precedes and c-commands a trace/null copy of the moved pronoun *who*. This results in a violation of the COMP-Trace Filter (104) which causes the resulting structure to be filtered out as ungrammatical. The corresponding sentence (105b) is therefore ungrammatical, by virtue of violating CTF.

While CTF violations lead to ungrammaticality in standard varieties of English, it should be noted that there are non-standard varieties which do not have CTF in their grammar, and thus allow structures such as those in (108) below, where an italicised constituent has been extracted out of a position (marked by the gap) and leaves behind a trace/null copy which immediately follows and is c-commanded by a bold-printed complementiser:

(108)   a. *Michael Owen*, I'm sure **that** – will be touted round many clubs (Stan Collymore, talkSPORT Radio)

   b. *Who* did you feel **that** – ran the dressing room? (Michael Vaughan, BBC Radio 5)

   c. *What* are we hoping [**that** – can come from this]? (Jonny Gould, talkSPORT Radio)

       d. I probably played under 25 managers, *which* I'm not sure **whether** −
         is a good thing (Danny Mills, BBC Radio 5)
       e. *Chamak* it looks as **if** − will be joining West Ham (Jason Cundy,
         talkSPORT Radio)

This suggests that the restrictions on the class of admissible syntactic structures imposed by filters may be variety-specific. It is also interesting to note that both of the filters discussed here (the Doubly Filled COMP Filter in 102, and the COMP-Trace Filter in 104) relate to properties of overt complementisers.

To summarise: Module 1.5 has shown how constraints limit the ways in which syntactic operations can apply, and how filters limit the kinds of superficial syntactic structure which they can give rise to.

You should now be able to tackle Exercise 1.5.

1.6   Summary

This chapter has set out to provide an outline of key concepts and constructs underlying the classic CP+TP+VP model of clause structure developed in the 1980s.

In Module 1.1, I compared descriptive and prescriptive approaches to syntax (§1.1.1), noting that contemporary work in Linguistics takes a purely descriptive stance. I went on (§1.1.2) to discuss the relative merits of three different types of data used in syntactic analysis: corpus data, introspective grammaticality judgements, and experimental data. I then turned (§1.1.3) to outline the key role played by categories and features in syntactic analysis.

In Module 1.2, we looked at the nature of syntactic structures, and the operations which generate/build them. We began by looking at the operation merge (§1.2.1), by which a head combines with a maximal projection to form a larger constituent. We saw that in more complex structures, a head X first-merges with a following complement to form an intermediate X-bar projection, and then second-merges with a specifier to form a maximal projection XP. So, for example, in a sentence like *He is helping her*, the verb *helping* merges with the pronoun/pronominal DP *her* to form the VP *helping her*. The (present tense) T auxiliary *is* first-merges with this VP to form the T-bar *is helping her*, and then T-*is* second-merges with the pronoun/pronominal DP *he* to form the TP *He is helping her*. As this example illustrates, syntactic structures are formed in a bottom-up fashion, in the sense that lower parts of the structure are formed before higher parts. This particular model of syntax is known as X-bar syntax (§1.2.2). In addition to merge, syntactic structures can also be generated by a separate type of operation termed adjunction (§1.2.3). There are two types of adjunction. One type (called head adjunction) involves adjoining one head to another to form a complex head: for example, by adjoining the prepositional particle *up* to the verb *pick* we form the complex verb *pick up*. A second type of adjunction (termed phrasal adjunction) involves adjoining a phrase (more precisely, a maximal projection/XP) to a constituent larger than a head (i.e. to an intermediate projection/X-bar or to a maximal projection/XP) to form an even larger constituent of the same type. For example, if we take the verb phrase/VP *examine it* and adjoin the prepositional phrase/PP *under a microscope* to the right of this VP, we form the larger VP italicised in 'He will *examine it under a microscope*'. We briefly looked at a number of differences between adjunction and merge.

In Module 1.3, we saw that parts of the structure of a sentence can be invisible, because syntactic structures can contain null constituents. One way this can come about is through ellipsis (a process whereby a constituent present in the syntax is silent/unpronounced in the phonology): for example, in order to avoid unnecessary repetition, we can omit the <bracketed> occurrence of the noun phrase *cans of beer* in a sentence like 'I had four cans of beer, and you had three <cans of beer>' (§1.3.1). Some types of head can be inherently null: for example, in a sentence like 'People don't trust Boris', *people* can be argued to be a QP/quantifier phrase headed by an inherently null quantifier Q-ø with a meaning paraphrasable as 'an unspecified number of'; likewise, *Boris* can be argued to be a DP headed by an inherently null definite determiner (so that *Boris* has a meaning roughly paraphrasable as 'the specific individual Boris'). And the overall sentence can be argued to be a CP headed by an inherently null complementiser which serves the function of marking the clause as indicative in mood and declarative in force (i.e. as having the force of a statement).

I went on to argue that hierarchical structure (and the relation c-command in particular) plays a central role in syntactic operations and conditions (§1.3.2), and we saw that this can be captured in terms of the following principle:

(53)   **Structure Dependence Principle**
        Syntactic operations and conditions are structure dependent in the
        sense that they are sensitive to hierarchical structure, and canonically
        involve a c-command relation between a given constituent and another
        constituent that it c-commands. For example:
        (i)   movement involves a head attracting (i.e. triggering movement of)
               another constituent that it c-commands
        (ii)   case-marking involves a head assigning case to a constituent that it
               c-commands

(iii) anaphora involves an anaphor (like *himself*) being bound by (i.e. taking its reference from) a constituent that c-commands it

(iv) polarity items are subject to a condition that they be c-commanded by an appropriate licenser (e.g. *any* is licensed by being c-commanded by *not* in 'I did **not** ask for *any* help')

The relation c-command was defined as follows:

(54) **C-command**

One constituent X c-commands another Y if the two are independent (i.e. neither contains the other), and if the mother of X contains Y

I also argued that other principles of Universal Grammar determine how syntactic operations apply, and that these include the following condition (where *above* means 'c-commanding', and *below* means 'c-commanded by'):

(56) **Minimality Condition**

A constituent can only enter into a syntactic relation with the minimal (= closest) constituent of the relevant type above or below it

We can illustrate the role played by (53, 54, 56) by looking at how case-marking applies in relation to a sentence such as *I am keen for them to help him*. Each of the pronouns will be assigned case by the closest case-assigning head which c-commands it. Consequently, *him* will be assigned accusative case by the transitive verb *help*; *them* will be assigned accusative case by the transitive complementiser *for*; and *I* will be assigned nominative case by the invisible null complementiser above it (given the assumption made here that finite clauses are CPs headed by an overt or null complementiser).

In Module 1.4, we examined three different types of movement operation. We began by looking at **A-bar Movement** (§1.4.1) and saw that this involves C attracting an XP below it (e.g. one that is wh-marked, or topicalised or focused) to become its specifier (and thereby move to spec-CP). In consequence of the Structure Dependence Principle (53) and the Minimality Condition (56), C will attract the closest XP of the relevant type to become its specifier. I noted that under the Copy Theory of Movement developed by Chomsky (1993), movement is a composite operation which creates a copy of the constituent to be moved, and then merges this newly created copy in a new position at the top of the tree. Spellout rules in the phonology determine which copies of a moved constituent are spelled out overtly and which are given a silent/null spellout (and so are unpronounced). In default of any other spellout rule applying (i.e. if no other spellout rule applies), the following spellout rule will apply:

(62)   Default Spellout Rule/DSR

   For a constituent whose spellout is not determined in some other way,
   the highest copy of the constituent is overtly pronounced, and any lower
   copies are silent

We went on to look at a second type of XP-movement operation known
as **A-Movement**, whereby (in conformity with the Structure Dependence
Principle and the Minimality Condition) T attracts the closest DP/QP that
it c-commands to become its specifier (§1.4.2). Thus, in a passive sentence
such as *Several demonstrators were arrested*, the QP *several demonstrators* originates in comp-VP as the complement of the verb *arrested*, and is
attracted by the T auxiliary *were* to move to spec-TP, so deriving *Several
demonstrators were arrested* – (where the position marked by the gap contains a null copy of the passivised QP *several demonstrators*).

   We also looked at a third type of movement operation termed **Head Movement** (§1.4.3), whereby a head attracts another head that it c-commands
to adjoin to it. One particular instance of Head Movement is Auxiliary
Inversion – an operation by which a null complementiser (C-ø) that has an
interrogative or negative XP as its specifier attracts a T auxiliary to adjoin
to C-ø. Thus, in a sentence such as *What decision have you come to?* the
QP *what decision* originates as the complement of the preposition *to*, and
the auxiliary *have* originates in the head T position of TP (as in the in situ
structure *You have come to what decision?*). A null complementiser above
TP attracts (a copy of) the QP *what decision* to move to spec-CP by A-bar
Movement, and concomitantly attracts (a copy of) the auxiliary *have* to
undergo Inversion and thereby adjoin to C-ø via Head Movement, as shown
in simplified form below (where the upper/dotted arrow marks Head Movement, and the lower/dashed arrow marks A-bar Movement):

(109)   [$_{CP}$ *what decision* [$_C$ **have**+ø] [$_{TP}$ you [$_T$ ~~have~~] come to ~~what decision~~]]

Lower copies of the two moved constituents receive a null spellout in the
phonology (marked by strikethrough in 109) via the Default Spellout Rule (62).

   An interesting question posed by the claim that a null C triggers Inversion (i.e. attracts a T constituent below C to adjoin to C) when C has an
interrogative or negative specifier is how to deal with yes–no questions like
Have you come to a decision? An answer dating back in spirit to work in the
1960s is that in such cases, C has a null yes–no question operator (Op_{YNQ})
as its specifier, and that (by virtue of having an interrogative specifier), C
triggers Auxiliary Inversion (i.e. attracts a present/past tense auxiliary in
T to adjoin to it) in essentially the same way as in a wh-question. On this

view, the periphery of a yes–no question like *Have you come to a decision?* will be a CP with the structure shown in highly simplified form below:

(110)   [$_{CP}$ Op$_{YNQ}$ [$_C$ **have**+ø] you come to a decision]

However, a question raised by this analysis is what semantic function is served by the yes–no question operator on the edge of CP. The answer given here is that the yes–no question operator serves to type the relevant clause as being a yes–no question, in accordance with the Clause Typing Conditions below:

(79)   Clause Typing Conditions
    (i) A clause is interpreted as being of a given type (interrogative or exclamative etc.) if it has a peripheral clause-typing specifier of the relevant type
    (ii) An indicative clause is interpreted as declarative in type by default if it contains no peripheral clause-typing specifier

It would then follow that the presence of the interrogative yes–no question operator in spec-CP in (110) will type the relevant clause as having the force of a yes–no question. Likewise, the presence of an interrogative wh-XP in spec-CP in a structure like (109) will type the relevant clause as a wh-question; and the presence of an exclamative wh-XP in spec-CP in a sentence like *What a great time we had!* will type the sentence as exclamative in force.

In Module 1.5, I noted that work dating back to the 1960s has posited that grammars contain mechanisms which block illicit syntactic operations and structures. One such mechanism are constraints which govern how syntactic operations can (and can't) apply. An early constraint of this kind (deriving from work by Cattell 1976, Cinque 1978, and Huang 1982) is the following:

(88)   Constraint on Extraction Domains/CED
    Only complements allow material to be extracted out of them, not specifiers or adjuncts

Another (dating back to work by Wexler & Culicover 1980: 119) is the following:

(94)   Freezing Principle
    The constituents of a moved phrase are frozen internally within (and so cannot be extracted out of) the moved phrase

In addition, numerous locality constraints have been proposed which limit how far a constituent can move in any single movement operation

(§1.5.1). These include the Minimality Condition in (56) above, and the Impenetrability Condition in (89) below:

(89) **Impenetrability Condition**
      Anything below the head C of a CP is impenetrable to anything above the CP

The Minimality Condition requires a moved constituent to move to the closest position of the appropriate kind above it, while the Impenetrability Condition bars movement across the edge of an intervening CP (i.e. across a complementiser and any specifier that it has). In consequence of such constraints, Wh-Movement in a sentence like *Where do you think that he has gone?* moves *where* from its initial position as the complement of *gone* in two successive steps: *where* moves first to spec-CP in the *that*-clause, and then from there into spec-CP in the *do*-clause.

A different kind of constraint on movement operations is the following:

(99) **Intervention Condition**
      Likes cannot cross likes (*likes* = 'constituents which are alike'):

In a sentence like *Nobody would do nothing if they saw someone drowning*, this prevents the negative QP *nothing* from being moved across the negative QP *nobody* to form *Nothing would nobody do if they saw someone drowning*.

In addition to imposing restrictions on syntactic operations, grammars also impose restrictions on the class of syntactic structures they produce: such restrictions are termed **filters** (since they filter out illicit structures as ungrammatical). Two such filters (discussed in §1.5.2) are the following:

(102) **Doubly Filled COMP Filter/DFCF**
       At the end of a syntactic derivation, any superficial structure in which the edge of a projection headed by an overt complementiser is doubly filled (i.e. contains some other overt constituent) is filtered out as ungrammatical

(104) **COMP-Trace Filter/CTF**
       Any structure at the end of a syntactic derivation in which an overt COMP/complementiser is immediately adjacent to and c-commands a trace (i.e. a gap/null copy left behind by a moved constituent) is filtered out as ill-formed

DFCF filters out for example, 'I'm not sure [$_{CP}$ *how amenable* that [$_{TP}$ he will be]]', because the edge of the bracketed CP is doubly filled, in that it contains an overt complementiser (*that*) with an overt specifier (*how amenable*). CTF filters out for example, '*What* do you think [$_{CP}$ that [$_{TP}$ — has made him change his mind]]?' because the overt complementiser *that* immediately precedes and c-commands a gap which represents a trace/ null copy of the moved wh-QP *what*. As noted in the text discussion, both DFCF and CTF concern properties of complementisers, and both seem to be variety-specific (in the sense that they hold in standard English, but not in some other varieties).

1.7   Bibliographical notes

For examples of the **prescriptive** approach to grammar discussed in Module 1.1, see Heffer (2011), and Gwynne (2013). On the **who/whom** distinction, see Sobin (1997) and Lasnik & Sobin (2000). For discussion of the relative merits and reliability of different methods of collecting **linguistic data**, see Schütze (1996), Cowart (1997), Hoffmann (2011: ch.2), Weskott & Fanselow (2011), and Schütze & Sprouse (2014). On the drawbacks of collecting linguistic data from a **corpus** (or from the web), see Schütze (2009). For a defence of the use of **introspective judgement data** rather than other sources of data, see Newmeyer (2003, 2005, 2006a, 2006b) on **usage-based data**, and Sprouse (2011), Sprouse, Schütze & Almeida (2013), and Sprouse & Almeida (2011a, 2011b, 2012, 2013) on **experimental data**. For evidence that the **grammaticality judgements of linguists** about sentences may differ from those of non-linguists, see Dąbrowska (2010). On **grammatical categories** in English see Quirk et al. (1985), Biber et al. (1999), Huddleston & Pullum (2002), and Radford (2016: 60–110). On **determiners**, see Giusti (1997), Adger (2003), Spinillo (2004), and Isac (2006). On **pronouns** see Cardinaletti & Starke (1999), Wiltschko (1998, 2001), Freidin & Vergnaud (2001), and Déchaine & Wiltschko (2002). On treating **personal pronouns as DPs**, see Postal (1966), Abney (1987), Longobardi (1994), and Lyons (1999). On **grammatical features** and their relation to grammatical categories, see Chomsky (1965, 1970), Radford (1997a, 1997b, 2004a, 2016) and Ramat (2014); on **gender** features in English, see Namai (2000).

   The claim made in Module 1.2 that phrases are formed by a **merge** operation which combines heads with complements and specifiers dates back to the model of X-bar Syntax developed in Jackendoff (1974, 1977a, 1977b): for a textbook introduction, see Radford (1981, 1988). The idea that syntactic structures are **headed** dates back in spirit to Bloomfield (1935), though it should be noted that Bloomfield assumed that some structures are headless. The idea that all syntactic structure is **binary-branching** was put forward and defended in Kayne (1981, 1984): for a review of evidence for and against binary-branching structures, see Stradmann (2013). The idea that clauses contain a **TP projection** headed by a T constituent containing an auxiliary or affix in finite clauses and the particle *to* in infinitive clauses dates back in spirit to Chomsky (1981, 1986b); the idea that (non-defective) clauses also contain a **CP projection** is due to Fassi-Fehri (1980), Chomsky (1981, 1986b) and Stowell (1981). In earlier work (e.g. Chomsky 1957, 1965) nominal expressions like *the nose* or *several people* were taken to have the status of **NP/Noun Phrase**; however, in much work since the mid-1960s they have been analysed as having the status of **DP/determiner phrase** or **QP/quantifier phrase** constituents (see e.g. Fukui 1986, Fukui & Speas 1986, Hellan 1986, Abney 1987, Löbel 1989, and Olsen 1989 – though it should be noted that the DP analysis is not without problems: see for example Bruening 2009, and Bruening et al. 2015). An alternative to the **bottom-up model** of syntax developed by Chomsky and outlined in the main text is the **top-down model** presented in Phillips (1996, 2003), Richards (1999), Shan & Barker (2006), and Bruening (2014): but see Chomsky (2007) for arguments that the bottom-up/top-down dichotomy may be a false one.

For a textbook account of (head and phrasal) **adjunction** operations, see Radford (2020: 108–151). The type of adjunction operation dealt with here was termed 'Chomsky-adjunction' by Ross (1967: 259, fn. 12) on the grounds that it was 'first noted by Chomsky', and this term was widely used in earlier work. The treatment of **verb+particle structures** as complex verbs involving a particle adjoined to a verb dates back to Chomsky (1955) and Fraser (1965), and was widely adopted in much subsequent work (e.g. Radford 1988, Johnson 1991, Neeleman 1994, Haegeman & Guéron 1999, Dehé 2002, etc.): for a critical review of a range of analyses of verb+particle structures, see Capelle (2005), Elenbaas (2009), and Larsen (2014). The analysis of **TP adjuncts** presented here dates back in spirit to earlier work by Ross (1967: 289), Baltin (1978: 156, and 1982: 16–22), Lasnik & Saito (1992: 81) and Haegeman & Guéron (1999: 102). The analysis of PPs and ADVPs which modify VPs as **VP adjuncts** dates back to Emonds (1970: 187), who argues that the italicised PP in 'John told us the game was cancelled *at the airport*' is an adjunct to the VP *told us the game was cancelled*.

For a more detailed textbook account of various types of **null constituent** discussed in Module 1.3, see Radford (2016: 172–244), or Radford (2020: 152–208). The idea that certain types of null constituent can arise via **ellipsis** dates back to Hankamer (1971), Hankamer & Sag (1976), Sag (1980), Kuno (1981), Pesetsky (1982a), Hardt (1993), McCawley (1993), Lobeck (1995), Schwarz (1999, 2000), Merchant (1999, 2001, 2002, 2003, 2004a, 2008a, 2008b, 2013a, 2013b), Johnson (2001) etc. The idea that bare nominals (i.e. noun expressions not modified by an overt determiner or quantifier) can contain a **null determiner/null quantifier** has a long history, dating back to a suggestion made by Chomsky (1965: 108) which was taken up and extended in later work by Abney (1987), Bernstein (1993, 2001), and Longobardi (1994, 1996, 2001). On the nature of quantified expressions see Löbel (1989), Giusti (1991a), and Shlonsky (1991). On determiners and determiner phrases, see Abney (1987), Bernstein (1993), Giusti (1997), Alexiadou & Wilder (1998), Lyons (1999), Zamparelli (2000), Grohmann & Haegeman (2002), and Ticio (2003, 2005). The idea that apparently complementiserless clauses contain a **null complementiser** dates back in spirit several decades (see e.g. Stockwell et al. 1973: 599): for discussion of factors governing the use of null or overt complementisers in finite clauses, see Hawkins (2001), and Nomura (2006). The idea that certain infinitive clauses are introduced by null complementiser dates back to Bresnan (1970); on treating infinitive complements of verbs like *want* as CPs headed by a null counterpart of *for*, see Sawada (1995) and Nomura (2006). The **Affix Hopping** account of verb morphology dates back in spirit to Chomsky (1955, 1957), and is revised in Lasnik (1981). The **c-command** relation dates back to Klima (1964): a defence of its primitive nature can be found in Frank & Vijay-Shanker (2001). However, it should be noted that Bruening (2014) argues for alternative accounts of many phenomena traditionally handled in terms of c-command. On the idea that finite complementisers assign **nominative case**, see Chomsky (2001). The idea that PRO subjects in English carry **null case** derives from Chomsky & Lasnik (1993), Chomsky (1995), and Martin (1996, 2001). On the claim that null case is assigned to a PRO subject by C, see Rizzi (1997: 304) and Collins (2005: 104). On the (Relativised) **Minimality Condition**, see Rizzi (1990, 2003), Chomsky (1995), Friedmann et al. (2009), and Takano (2013).

For a more detailed textbook account of the **A-bar Movement** operation discussed in Module 1.4, see Radford (2016: 317–477), or Radford (2020: 265–331). The idea that A-bar Movement involves C attracting a (specific kind of) XP to second-merge with C and thereby move to spec-CP derives from Chomsky (1981, 1986b, 1998, 2008). The **Copy Theory of Movement** derives from Chomsky (1995); on why (generally) only the highest copy of a moved constituent is overtly spelled out, see Nunes (1995, 1999, 2001, 2004). On the **A-Movement** operation by which T attracts a DP/QP to move from a position below T to spec-TP (e.g. in passives), see the detailed discussion in Chapter 2 of this book. On the nature of the **EPP feature** of T which requires T to have a specifier/subject, see Chomsky (1982, 1995, 1998), Rothstein (1983), Alexiadou & Anagnostopoulou (1998), Déprez (2000), Grohmann et al. (2000), Holmberg (2000), Kiss (2001), Bošković (2002), Roberts & Roussou (2002), Rosengren (2002), Haeberli (2003), Miyagawa (2005, 2006a, 2010), van Craenenbroeck & den Dikken (2006), Landau (2007), and Lin (2011).

For a textbook account of **Head Movement**, see Radford (2016: 245–316), or Radford (2020: 209–64). The idea that **Auxiliary Inversion** involves a null C attracting a finite auxiliary to adjoin to it dates back to Chomsky (1981); on earlier analyses, see Radford (2018: 11–17). The view that **yes–no questions** contain a null yes–no question operator is put forward in Katz & Postal (1964), Bresnan (1970), Larson (1985), Grimshaw (1993), Roberts (1993a), den Dikken (2006), and Haegeman (2012). On the notion of **clause typing**, see Cheng (1997); the idea that indicative clauses are interpreted as declarative by default is suggested by Roberts & Roussou (2002). The analysis of BE-**Raising** whereby finite forms of the copula BE involve BE raising from V to adjoin to a tense affix in T dates back in spirit to Klima (1964); see Nomura (2006: 303–14) for discussion of HAVE/BE-Raising in subjunctive clauses.

The idea outlined in Module 1.5 that syntactic operations are regulated by putatively universal principles/conditions/constraints dates back to pioneering work by Chomsky (1964a) and Ross (1967). The **Impenetrability Condition** (preventing operations applying across the edge of a CP) is a simplified version of the Phase Impenetrability Condition of Chomsky (1998); its historical roots lie in the Subjacency Condition of Chomsky (1973) (amended by Rizzi 1982), the Barrierhood Condition of Chomsky (1986b), and the Relativised Minimality Condition of Rizzi (1990). On the **Intervention Condition** (barring likes from crossing likes), see Starke (2001), Rizzi (2004a), Endo (2007a), Friedmann et al. (2009), Haegeman (2012), and Abels (2012).

The idea that grammars contain **filters** which rule out illicit superficial structures at the end of a syntactic derivation dates back to pioneering work by Perlmutter (1968, 1971). On the **Doubly Filled COMP Filter**, see Chomsky & Lasnik (1977), Seppänen & Trotta (2000), Koopman (2000), Koopman & Szabolsci (2000), Zwicky (2002), Collins (2007), Baltin (2010), Collins & Radford (2015), and Radford (2018). On the **COMP-Trace Filter**, see Perlmutter (1968, 1971), Chomsky & Lasnik (1977), Pesetsky (1982b), Sobin (1987, 2002, 2009), Browning (1996), Szczegielniak (1999), Roussou (2000), Pesetsky & Torrego (2001, 2004), Ackema & Neeleman (2003), Kandybowicz (2006), Lohndal (2009), Ackema (2010), Ha (2010), Llinàs-Grau & Fernández Sánchez (2013), Sato & Dobashi (2013), Erlewine (2014, 2017a), Bošković (2016), Pesetsky (2016), Sobin (2016), and Douglas (2017).

The approach adopted in this book can be described as **representational** (in that more emphasis is placed on getting the precise details of syntactic structures right), rather than **algorithmic** (in the sense that less attention is devoted to the mechanical details and formal properties of operations like Merge, Agree, and Adjoin that apply in the course of derivations): see Müller (2015) on this distinction. For an alternative (more formal and algorithmic) approach, see especially Collins & Stabler (2016), and additionally Chomsky (1995, 2013, 2014, 2015), Citko (2005), Di Sciullo & Isac (2008),

Hornstein & Nunes (2008), Hornstein (2009), Fukui (2011), Larson (2014), Merchant (2014, 2019), Epstein et al. (2015), Collins (2017), Müller (2017), and Zyman (2022).

1.8   Workbook

In the exercises below, an [M] after an example sentence indicates that a model answer is provided in the free-to-download *Students' Answerbook* (and in the *Teachers' Answerbook* as well). You will find it helpful to look at this model answer before attempting to tackle other examples in the exercise. Some other exercise examples have an [S] after them, indicating that they are for self-study: this means that after reading the relevant module (and those preceding it), and looking at the helpful hints and model answer associated with the exercise, students should be able to analyse these self-study examples on their own, and then compare their answers with those provided in the *Students' Answerbook*. The remaining exercise examples (i.e. those not marked with [M] or [S] after them) are intended for teachers to use as the basis for hands-on problem-solving work in seminars, classes, or assignments: answers to all of these non-self-study examples are provided in the *Teachers' Answerbook*. Note that Exercise 1.1 tests you on Module 1.1, Exercise 1.2 on Module 1.2, and so on; and that each exercise in a given chapter presupposes familiarity with material covered in earlier chapters and in earlier modules of the same chapter.

EXERCISE 1.1

This exercise is designed to be attempted after reading Module 1.1.

Comment on the potential problems posed by relying on usage data to determine grammaticality in relation to the following example sentences (recorded by me from live, unscripted radio/TV broadcasts). Say what (if anything) is odd about them, and what potential problems they highlight with usage data:

1   We look at Arsenal and we see what the squad they have (Steve Claridge, BBC Radio 5) [M]
2   They have not withstood up to the pressure (Graeme Souness, Sky Sports TV)
3   The speed that which they go at these days leaves no margin for error (Darren Gough, talkSPORT Radio) [S]
4   As Gary Neville was saying at the start of our coverage, that it has usually been easy for Manchester United at White Hart Lane (Martin Tyler, Sky Sports TV)

5   One of the first things you're taught as a batsman is to don't leave your
    ground while the ball is live (Dominic Cork, talkSPORT Radio) [S]
6   First of all, let's me bring you an update on this dreadful fire we heard about
    (Rachel Burden, BBC Radio 5) [S]
7   What would've England asked from you? (Dominic Cork, talkSPORT Radio) [S]
8   You do feel sorry for him as the rain run downs the back of his neck (Adrian
    Chiles, ITV)
9   We entirely agree that there needs to be changes (Angela Knight, BBC Radio 5)
10 This is someone who now finds themself in line for considerable
    compensation (Reporter, BBC Radio 5)

In addition, comment on the issue arising from using experimental methods to determine grammaticality in relation to the experiment outlined
below. As noted in Module 1.1, in everyday English we find structures
like *Who by?* where the preposition *by* and its object *who* are 'inverted'.
These are said to be instances of *Swiping* (an acronym for 'Sluicing With
Inverted Prepositions In North Germanic', where *Sluicing* is a type of ellipsis, involving deleting redundant material like that marked by strikethrough
in a sentence such as *He is coming back, but I'm not sure when he is coming
back*). Numerous published studies have claimed that Swiping is only grammatical in wh-questions (like the *when*-question in the preceding sentence),
not in other types of clause. In order to verify whether this is indeed the
case, I asked Philip Hofmeister (and he kindly agreed) to include Swiping
sentences like those in 11 below in an online experiment he ran to test the
acceptability of a wide range of different types of sentence structure. Each
of the sentences in 11 below contains a bracketed elliptical clause in which
the italicised object of a bold-printed preposition is positioned in front of
the preposition:

11   a. I wonder where she bought that awful tie, and [*who* **for**] [M]
        b. Whenever we argue and [*whatever* **about**], we always make up
            afterwards
        c. I'm amazed at how much he bought on eBay and [*how little* **for**]!
        d. I'm going away, but [*not long* **for**]
        e. The fewer presents we send and [*the fewer people* **to**], the happier
            Scrooge will be
        f. So hard has he trained and [*so long* **for**] that he is sure to win the race

The italicised object of the preposition is interrogative in 11a, unconditional
(in the terminology of Rawlins 2008) in 11b, exclamative in 11c, negative in 11d, comparative in 11e, and consecutive in 11f. Sixty-four native
speakers of American English were asked to rate the acceptability of a set
of sentences including those in 11 using a seven-point numerical scale on

which 7 denotes 'extremely natural' and 1 denotes 'extremely unnatural'. The mean scores for each sentence were as follows: 5.13 for the interrogative 11a; 4.95 for the unconditional 11b; 4.50 for the exclamative 11c; 4.27 for the negative 11d; 3.92 for the comparative 11e; and 2.69 for the consecutive 11f. (The above results are reported in Radford & Iwasaki 2015; note that this is an abridged version of an exercise in Radford 2020.)

Helpful hints

In relation to the sentences in 1–10, bear in mind the possibility that some of them may involve accidental production errors, perhaps resulting from a memory lapse of some kind (e.g. forgetting how you started your sentence). This sometimes results in the formation of what are termed 'blends', that is, structures in which parts of two different (but related) structures are blended/combined together. Bear in mind, too, that some structures which strike you as odd may be used in other varieties of English, even if not in your own. In relation to the acceptability scores reported for each of the sentences in 11, discuss the issue they pose for the assumption in much work in traditional syntax that sentences are either grammatical or ungrammatical (in that a sentence marked by a prefixed star/asterisk is ungrammatical, and one not so marked is grammatical).

EXERCISE 1.2

This exercise is designed to be attempted after reading Module 1.2 and the module preceding it.

Discuss the derivation of the sentences produced by speaker B below:

1   SPEAKER A: What did he say about your offer?
    SPEAKER B: That he will carefully consider it [M]

2   SPEAKER A: What did he ask you?
    SPEAKER B: If she really did enjoy the meal

3   SPEAKER A: What do the police say?
    SPEAKER B: That in all probability someone is lying [S]

4   SPEAKER A: What did John say?
    SPEAKER B: That he may reluctantly give up the job soon [S]

5   SPEAKER A: What did you ask the engineers?
    SPEAKER B: Whether they had previously run into this problem

6   SPEAKER A: What was the advice you gave to Boris?
    SPEAKER B: For him immediately to apologise unreservedly

Helpful hints

Discuss the set of merge and adjunction operations used to form the relevant sentences, and say how merge and adjunction differ from each other. Comment on any additional points of interest arising in relation to your analysis – for example, why in 1 the personal pronouns *he/it* are DPs, and why *carefully* is an ADVP. In 3, treat *in all probability* as a PP, but don't concern yourself with its internal structure. In 4 and 5, be mindful of the distinction between particle verbs (i.e. verbs like *pick up* in which a prepositional particle is an adjunct to the verb *pick*), and prepositional verbs (i.e. verbs like *run* which have a prepositional phrase as their complement in a sentence like 'He ran *up the hill*'): note that prepositional verbs allow the P to be fronted along with its complement (as in '*Up which hill* did he run?'), and also allow *straight* to intervene between V and P (as in 'He will *run* **straight** *up* the hill'), but particle verbs don't exhibit either of these properties.

EXERCISE 1.3

This exercise is designed to be attempted after reading Module 1.3 and the modules preceding it.

Discuss the derivation of the sentences below, paying particular attention to the syntax of the null constituents in 1–3, and to the case-marking of (overt or null) personal pronouns in 4–6:

1   John will now undergo tests [M]
2   Students are going home this weekend [S]
3   Boris thinks politicians should show leadership
4   She intended to examine them thoroughly [S]
5   He must be keen for us to vote for him
6   I would like you to be nice to them

Helpful hints

Bear in mind the following assumptions made in the book. (Non-defective) clauses are CPs headed by an overt or null C/complementiser; in relation to 6, note that *like* in this kind of use is traditionally classed as a *for*-deletion verb (i.e. a verb which selects a CP complement headed by a null counterpart of the complementiser *for*). Finite TPs are headed either by a finite auxiliary in T, or by an affix in T which lowers onto the closest verb below it in the phonology by Affix Hopping; infinitival TPs are headed by the infinitive particle *to*. Definite nominal arguments are DPs headed by an overt or null determiner, and indefinite nominal arguments can be QPs headed by a null quantifier (with a meaning paraphrasable as 'an unspecified quantity of'). Adverbial (pro)nominals are PPs headed by a null preposition; since prepositional phrases can often contain the modifiers *straight/right* (as in '**straight** *to the point*' or '**right** *on time*') one test of PP status is to see whether a given constituent can be modified by *straight* or *right*. (Pro)nominal constituents are assigned case by the closest case-assigning head above/c-commanding them, with transitive heads assigning accusative case, finite complementisers assigning nominative case, and a null infinitival complementiser assigning null case (to a PRO subject).

EXERCISE 1.4

This exercise is designed to be attempted after reading Module 1.4 and the modules preceding it.

Discuss the merge, movement and adjunction operations involved in the derivation of the following sentences:

1   What chaos there was! [M]
2   No concessions will they make
3   Where can he now go? [S]
4   How was the parcel wrapped?
5   Were there any complaints? [S]
6   Could anyone imagine what a struggle it was?

Helpful hints
Bear in mind the following assumptions made in the book. Expletive *there* sentences involve a pronominal DP *there* in spec-TP, with a QP associate that originates in comp-VP (as the complement of an appropriate verb). A-bar Movement (e.g. Wh-Movement) involves movement of an XP from a position below C into spec-CP; A-Movement (e.g. Passivisation) involves movement of an XP from a position below T into spec-TP; Head Movement involves movement of a lower head to adjoin to a higher one (e.g. an auxiliary moving from T to C, or verb like BE from V to T). A null C with an interrogative or negative specifier triggers concomitant Auxiliary Inversion/T-to-C movement); yes–no questions contain a null interrogative operator in spec-CP. Movement involves copying, and (in consequence of the Default Spellout Condition), only the highest copies of moved constituents are (generally) overtly spelled out in the phonology.

In consequence of Clause Typing Conditions, clauses are interpreted as being interrogative/exclamative etc. in force if they contain a clause-typing specifier of the relevant kind in their periphery (i.e. in spec-CP); indicative clauses with no clause-typing specifier in their periphery are interpreted as declarative in type by default.

In 6, take the phrase *what a struggle* to be an exclamative QP, headed by the quantifier *what*. Its internal structure need not concern you: but one possibility is that the phrase *what a struggle* is derived by merging the ART/article *a* with the NP *struggle* to form the ARTP/article phrase *a struggle*, and then merging the exclamative quantifier *what* with this ARTP to form the QP *what a struggle*.

EXERCISE 1.5

This exercise is designed to be attempted after reading Module 1.5 and the modules preceding it.

Discuss the derivation of the sentences below, and the role played by constraints and/or filters in accounting for their ungrammaticality:

1   *Who did he ask if was fired? [M]
2   *What document were which parts of redacted? [S]
3   *Few things would I say never should you try [S]
4   *Who did you wonder where had gone to?
5   *The weekend, she asked who he was with at
6   *The accident, they know which car that the driver of caused

Helpful hints
Consider the role played by constraints in blocking illicit syntactic operations, especially the following (N.B. in 8 and 9, *below* = c-commanded by; *above* = c-commanding):

7   **Constraint on Extraction Domains/CED**
    Only complements allow material to be extracted out of them, not specifiers or adjuncts
8   **Minimality Condition**
    A constituent can only enter into a syntactic relation with the minimal (= closest) constituent of the relevant type above or below it
9   **Impenetrability Condition**
    Anything below the head C of a CP is impenetrable to anything above the CP
10 **Intervention Condition**
    Likes cannot cross likes (*likes* = 'constituents which are alike')

Consider also the possible role of filters in blocking illicit superficial syntactic structures, especially the following:

11 **Doubly Filled COMP Filter/DFCF**
    At the end of a syntactic derivation, any superficial structure in which the edge of a projection headed by an overt complementiser is doubly filled (i.e. contains some other overt constituent) is filtered out as ungrammatical

12 **COMP-Trace Filter/CTF**
    Any structure at the end of a syntactic derivation in which an overt COMP/complementiser is immediately adjacent to and c-commands a trace (i.e. a gap/null copy left behind by a moved constituent) is filtered out as ill-formed

Assume that all yes–no question clauses (including those introduced by the complementiser *if/whether*) have a null yes–no question operator (Op_{YNQ}) in spec-CP. Take the word *of* to be a K/case particle which merges with a nominal or pronominal complement to form a KP/case phrase (rather than treating *of* as a preposition – though this assumption does not affect the analysis in any material way). For the purposes of this exercise, treat *which?* as an interrogative Q/quantifier (like *what?*) – though a case could be made for treating *which?* as an interrogative D/determiner because it is definite/specific in sense, in that for example, *which book* means 'which book out of a specific set'. In relation to 5, consider the possibility that there is an Anti-Iteration Filter which bars iteration of likes: that is, it bars superficial structures containing likes (e.g. words of the same form or type) which are immediately adjacent to each other.

2 | A-Movement

2.0 Overview

In this chapter, we take a closer look at the syntax of subjects. Subjects generally occupy the specifier position within TP and remain there (unless the subject undergoes A-bar Movement and so moves to spec-CP). However, here I will argue that subjects originate internally within the verb phrase as arguments of verbs, and are subsequently raised into the specifier position within TP, with the relevant movement operation being triggered by an EPP feature carried by T. Since spec-TP is an A-position (i.e. an agreement-related position occupied by an argument which can bind an anaphor), the operation by which subjects move into spec-TP is known as **A-Movement**.

2.1 VP-Internal Subject Hypothesis

This module outlines evidence for positing that subjects originate internally within VPs (a claim known as the VP-Internal Subject Hypothesis), and from there subsequently raise to their superficial position in spec-TP

2.1.1 Subjects in Belfast and Standard English

Let's begin our discussion of the syntax of subjects by looking at some interesting data from Belfast English. Alongside Standard English structures like (1a, 1b), Belfast English also has structures like (2a, 2b):

(1) a. *Some students* should get distinctions
     b. *Lots of students* have missed the classes

(2) a. There should *some students* get distinctions
     b. There have *lots of students* missed the classes

Sentences like (2a, 2b) are called expletive structures because they contain the expletive pronominal DP *there*. (The fact that *there* is not a locative DP meaning 'that place' in this kind of use is shown by the impossibility of replacing it by locative *here* or questioning it by the interrogative locative *where?* or focusing it by assigning it contrastive stress.) For the time being, let's concentrate on the derivation of Belfast English sentences like (2a, 2b) before turning to consider the derivation of Standard English sentences like (1a, 1b).

One question to ask about the sentences in (2a, 2b) is where the expletive pronoun *there* is positioned. Since *there* immediately precedes the tensed auxiliary *should/have*, a reasonable conjecture is that *there* is the subject/ specifier of *should/have* and hence occupies spec-TP. If so, we'd expect to find that the auxiliary can move in front of the expletive subject (via Auxiliary Inversion, i.e. T-to-C Movement) in questions – and this is indeed the case, as the Belfast English sentences in (3) below illustrate:

(3)   a. **Should** *there* <u>some students</u> get distinctions?
         b. **Have** *there* <u>lots of students</u> missed the classes?

But where are the underlined quantified expressions *some students/lots of students* positioned in (3)? Since they precede the verbs *get/missed* and since subjects precede verbs, it seems reasonable to conclude that the expressions *some students/lots of students* function as the subjects of the verbs *get/missed* and (since subjects are typically specifiers) occupy spec-VP (i.e. specifier position within VP). If these assumptions are correct, (2a) will have the structure (4) below (simplified by not showing the internal structure of the expressions *some students/distinctions*: we can take both of these to be QP/Quantifier Phrase constituents, headed by the overt quantifier *some* in one case and by a null quantifier $[_Q$ ø] in the other):

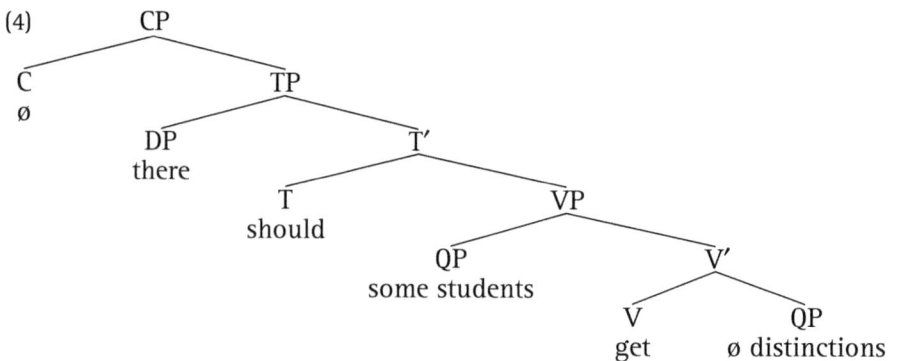

(4)

```
            CP
          /    \
         C      TP
         ø     /  \
            DP      T'
           there   /  \
                  T      VP
               should   /  \
                      QP      V'
                some students / \
                            V     QP
                           get   ø distinctions
```

The analysis in (4) claims that the sentence contains two subjects/specifiers: the pronominal DP *there* is the specifier (and subject) of *should*, and the QP *some students* is the specifier (and subject) of *get*. The two subjects serve two different functions: the expression *some students* has the semantic function of denoting the recipients of the distinctions, and so could be said to be the semantic subject of the sentence; by contrast, the pronoun *there* satisfies the syntactic requirement of the EPP feature on T (requiring T to have a specifier which is a noun or pronoun expression), and so could be said to be the syntactic subject of the sentence.

Given the assumptions in (4), sentence (2a) will be derived as follows. The verb *get* first-merges with the QP *ø distinctions* to form the V-bar (intermediate verb expression) *get ø distinctions*, and *get* then second-merges with the QP *some students* (itself formed by merging the quantifier *some* with the NP *students*), so deriving the VP *some students get ø distinctions*. The past-tense auxiliary T-*should* first-merges with this VP forming the T-bar *should some students get ø distinctions*. Let's suppose that every T constituent has an EPP feature requiring it to second-merge with a noun or pronoun expression that serves as its specifier (and subject). In sentences like (2a, 2b) in Belfast English, the EPP requirement for T to have a specifier can be satisfied by second-merging T-*should* with expletive *there* to form the TP *There should some students get ø distinctions*. The resulting TP is then merged with a null indicative complementiser, forming the CP in (4) above. In the semantic component, this CP is interpreted as declarative in type by default, in accordance with the Clause Typing Condition (5ii) below (introduced in §1.4.3):

(5)   **Clause Typing Conditions**
   (i)   A clause is interpreted as being of a given type (interrogative or exclamative etc.) if it contains a peripheral clause-typing specifier of the relevant type
   (ii) An indicative clause is interpreted as declarative in type by default if it contains no peripheral clause-typing specifier

Our discussion of subjects in Belfast English here invites questions about the derivation of the corresponding Standard English sentence (1a) *Some students should get distinctions*. Let's suppose that the derivation of (1a) starts out in the same way as that of (2a). So, once again, the verb *get* first-merges with the QP *ø distinctions* to form the V-bar *get ø distinctions*, and then *get* second-merges with the QP *some students* to derive the VP *some students get ø distinctions*. This VP is in turn first-merged with the past-tense auxiliary T-*should*, forming the T-bar *should some students get ø distinctions*. As before, let's assume that T-*should* has an EPP feature requiring it to project a structural subject/specifier. But let's also suppose that the requirement for T-*should* to have a specifier of its own cannot be satisfied by merging expletive *there* in spec-TP because in standard varieties of English *there* can generally only occur in structures containing an intransitive existential verb like *be, become, exist, occur, arise, remain* etc. Instead, the EPP requirement for T to have a subject is satisfied by moving the subject *some students* from its original position in spec-VP, and merging it in a new position in spec-TP – as shown by the arrow in (6) below:

(6)

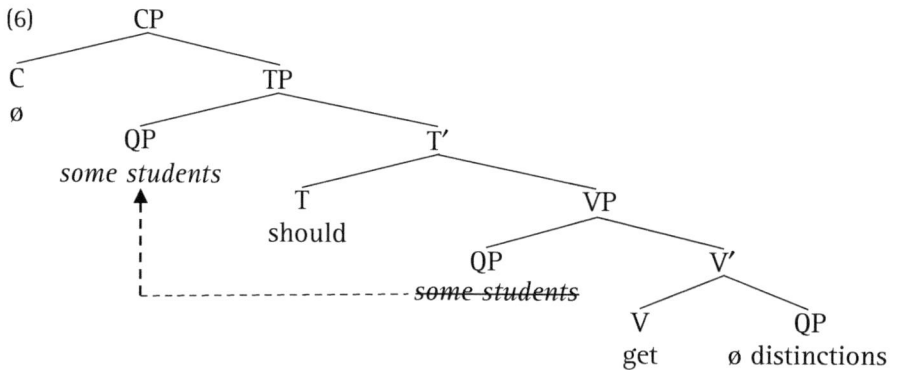

Since spec-TP is an A-position, the kind of movement operation illustrated by the arrow in (6) is termed A-Movement. This is in contrast to the kind of operation which moves a focused, topicalised or wh-marked constituent to spec-CP, which (since spec-CP is an A-bar position) is known generically as A-bar Movement.

Given that other movement operations (e.g. Head Movement and A-bar Movement) are composite operations involving copying, we would expect the same to be true of A-Movement. This would mean that when the QP *some students* moves to its italicised position in spec-TP in (6) above, it leaves behind a copy of itself in spec-VP. Only the higher copy of the QP (= the one in spec-TP) is spelled out overtly, in consequence of the Default Spellout Rule, which was given the following formulation in §1.4.1:

(7)   **Default Spellout Rule/DSR**
       For a constituent whose spellout is not determined in some other way,
       the highest copy of the constituent is overtly pronounced, and any lower
       copies are silent

One piece of evidence in support of a copying analysis of A-Movement comes from scope properties in relation to sentences such as (8a) below, which will have the syntactic structure shown in simplified form in (8b) if *everyone* originates as the specifier of the verb *finished* and is then raised up (by A-Movement) to become the specifier of the present tense auxiliary *has* (as shown by the arrow in 8b):

(8)   a. Everyone hasn't finished it yet
       b. [CP [C ø] [TP *Everyone* [T has] [NEGP [NEG n't] [VP ~~everyone~~ [V finished] it yet]]]]

For some speakers, sentences like (8a) are ambiguous between (i) a reading on which the quantifier expression *everyone* has scope over the negative particle *n't* so that the sentence means much the same as 'Everyone is in the position of not having finished it yet', and (ii) another reading on which *everyone* falls within the scope of the negative particle (so that the sentence means much the same as 'Not everyone is yet in the position of having finished it'). We can account for this scope ambiguity in a principled fashion if we suppose that A-Movement involves copying, that scope is defined in terms of c-command (so that a scope-bearing constituent has scope over a scope-sensitive constituent which it c-commands), and that the scope of a universally quantified expression like *everyone* in negative structures like (8b) can be determined either in relation to the initial position of *everyone* or in relation to its final position. In (8b) *everyone* is initially merged in a position (marked by ~~strikethrough~~) in which it is c-commanded by (and so falls within the scope of) *n't*; but via A-Movement it ends up in an (italicised) position in which it c-commands (and so has scope over) *n't*. The scope ambiguity in (8a) therefore reflects the different positions occupied by the initial and final copies of *everyone* in structure in (8b).

2.1.2   Further evidence for VP-internal subjects

The claim made in §2.1.1 that (non-expletive) subjects like *some students/ lots of students* in sentences like (1) originate internally within the VP containing the relevant verb (and from there move into spec-TP in sentences like 1 above) is known in the relevant literature as the VP-Internal Subject Hypothesis (= VPISH), and this has been almost universally adopted in research since the mid-1980s. Let's take a look at some of the evidence in support of VPISH.

One piece of evidence comes from the syntax of quantifiers in sentences such as following:

(9)   a. **All** *the students* have done the assignment
        b. *The students* have **all** done the assignment

In both sentences, the universal quantifier *all* is construed as modifying the DP *the students*. So how does *all* come to end up in two different positions in (9a) and (9b)? A plausible answer is that the QP *all the students* originates in spec-VP as the subject of *done the assignment*, and either the whole QP can undergo A-Movement to spec-TP as shown in simplified form in (10a) below, or alternatively the DP *the students* can undergo A-Movement on its own, leaving the quantifier *all* behind in the spec-VP position that it occupies in (10b):

(10)a.

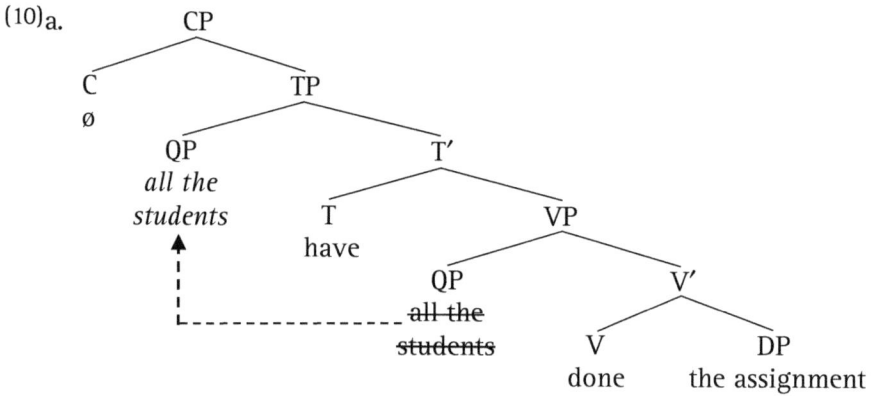

b.

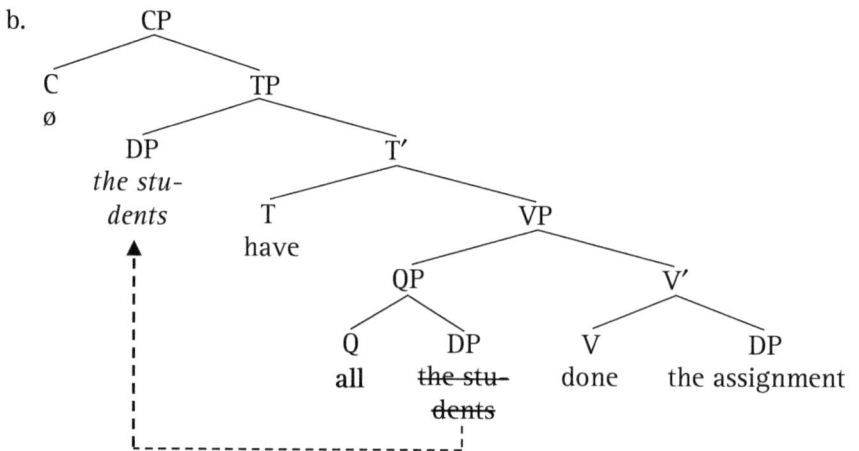

In a structure like (10b), *all* is said to be stranded, in the sense that it is detached from (and occupies a lower position than) the higher italicised DP *the students* that it modifies. The fact that the quantifier is stranded in spec-VP in (10b) provides us with evidence that the QP *all the students* originates in spec-VP.

An additional piece of evidence that subjects originate internally within VP comes from the syntax of idioms. We can define idioms as expressions (like those italicised below) which have an idiosyncratic meaning that is not a purely compositional function of the meaning of their individual parts:

(11)   a. Let's have a couple of drinks to *break the ice*
         b. Be careful not to *upset the applecart*
         c. The president must *bite the bullet*

There seems to be a constraint that only a string of words which forms a unitary constituent (i.e. a non-discontinuous constituent) can be an idiom. So, while we find idioms like those in (11) which are of the form *verb+-complement* (but where the subject isn't part of the idiom), we don't find idioms of the form *subject+verb* where the verb has a complement which isn't part of the idiom: this is because in *subject+verb+complement* structures, the verb and its complement form a unitary constituent (a V-bar), whereas the subject and the verb do not – and only unitary constituents can be idioms.

In the light of the constraint that an idiom is a unitary constituent with an idiosyncratic interpretation, consider idioms such as the following:

(12)   a.   All hell broke loose (= 'There was pandemonium')
         b.   The shit hit the fan ('The situation became chaotic')
         c.   The cat got his tongue (= 'He was speechless')

In (12), not only is the choice of verb and complement fixed, but so too is the choice of subject. In such idioms, we can't replace the subject, verb or complement by near synonyms – as we see from the fact that sentences like (13) below are ungrammatical (on the intended idiomatic interpretation):

(13)   a.   *The whole inferno escaped
         b.   *Camel dung was sucked into the air conditioning
         c.   *A furry feline bit his lingual articulator

However, what is puzzling about idioms like (12) is that one or more (italicised) auxiliaries can freely be positioned between the subject and verb, as we see from the examples below:

(14)   a.   All hell *had* broken loose
         b.   All hell *could* break loose
         c.   All hell *would have* broken loose
         d.   All hell *might have been* breaking loose

How can we reconcile our earlier claim that only a string of words which form a unitary constituent can constitute an idiom with the fact that *all hell ... break loose* is a discontinuous string in (14), since the subject *all hell* and the expression *break loose* are separated by the intervening auxiliaries *had/could/would have/might have been*? To phrase the question another way: how can we account for the fact that although the choice of subject, verb and complement is fixed, the choice of auxiliary is not?

The VP-Internal Subject Hypothesis provides us with a principled answer, if we suppose that subjects originate internally within VP, and that clausal idioms like those in (12) are VP idioms which require a fixed choice of head, complement and specifier in the VP containing them. For instance, in the case of (12a), the relevant VP idiom requires the specific word *break* as its head verb, the specific adjective *loose* as its complement, and the specific quantifier phrase *all hell* as its subject/specifier. We can then account for the fact that *all hell* surfaces in front of the auxiliary *had* in (14a) by positing that the QP *all hell* originates in spec-VP as the subject of *break loose*, and is then raised (via A-Movement) into spec-TP to become the subject of *had broken loose*. Given these assumptions, sentence (14a) *All hell had broken loose* will be derived as follows.

The (perfect participle) verb *broken* merges with the AP/adjectival projection *loose* to form the idiomatic V-bar *broken loose*. This is then merged with its QP subject *all hell* to form the idiomatic VP *all hell broken loose*. The resulting VP is merged with the (past tense) auxiliary T-*had* to form the T-bar *had all hell broken loose*. Since finite auxiliaries carry an EPP feature requiring them to have a nominal constituent like QP or DP as their subject/specifier, the QP *all hell* moves from being the specifier of *break* to becoming the specifier of *had* – as shown by the arrow below:

(15)

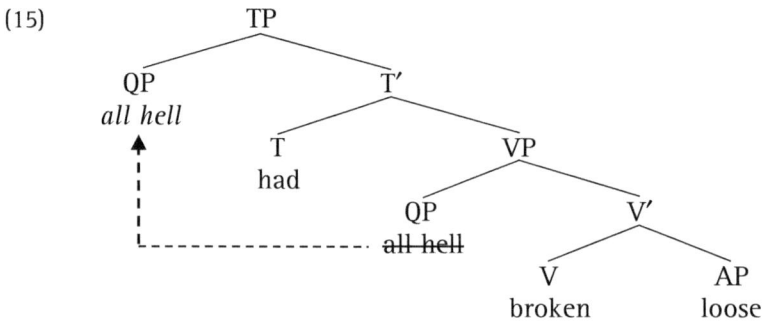

We can then say that (in the relevant idiom) *all hell* must be the sister of *broken loose*, and that this condition will be met only if *all hell* originates in spec-VP as the specifier (and sister) of the V-bar *broken loose*. We can account for how the subject *all hell* comes to be separated from its predicate *broken loose* by positing that subjects originate internally within VP and from there raise to spec-TP (via A-Movement) across an intervening T constituent like *had*, so that the subject and predicate thereby come to be separated from each other – movement of the subject to spec-TP being driven by an EPP feature carried by the T auxiliary *had* requiring *had* to have a nominal or pronominal subject. Subsequently, the TP in (15) is merged with a null indicative complementiser, so deriving the structure associated with (14a) *All hell had broken loose*: the resulting CP is interpreted as declarative by default in accordance with the Clause Typing Condition (5ii).

To summarise: in Module 2.1 we have seen that data from expletive structures in Belfast English, quantifier scope, floating quantifiers and idioms provide evidence in support of the VP-Internal Subject Hypothesis/VPISH, whereby subjects originate internally within the verb phrase/VP, and from there move into spec-TP via an operation known as A-Movement. In the next module, we will see that considerations relating to argument structure provide further support for VPISH.

You should now be able to tackle Exercise 2.1.

2.2 Argument structure and theta roles

The assumption that subjects originate internally within VP ties up in interesting ways with a traditional idea from predicate logic maintaining that propositions (which can be thought of as representing the substantive semantic content of clauses) comprise a predicate and a set of arguments. In this module, we'll explore key ideas embodied in this work.

2.2.1 Predicates and arguments

Simplifying somewhat, we can say that a predicate is an expression denoting an activity or event, and an argument is an expression denoting a participant in the relevant activity or event. For example, in sentences such as those in (16) below, the italicised verbs are predicates and the bracketed expressions represent their arguments:

(16)   a. [The guests] have *arrived*
       b. [The police] have *arrested* [the suspect]

In other words, the arguments of a verb are typically its subject and complement. A verb like *arrive* when used with a single [bracketed] argument in a structure like (16a) is said to be a one-place predicate; and a verb like *arrest* when used with two [bracketed] arguments in a structure like (16b) is said to be a two-place predicate. It has been widely assumed in work spanning more than half a century that complements of verbs are contained within a projection of the verb – for example, *the suspect* in (16b) is the direct object complement of *arrested* and is contained within the verb phrase headed by the verb *arrested* (serving as the complement of the verb). Under the VP-Internal Subject Hypothesis, we can go further than this and hypothesise that all the arguments of a predicate (not just its complement, but also its subject) originate within a projection of the predicate. Such an assumption allows us to maintain that there is a uniform mapping/relationship between syntactic structure and semantic argument structure – more specifically, between the position in which arguments are initially merged in a syntactic structure and their semantic function.

   To see what this means in practice, consider the derivation of (16b) *The police have arrested the suspect*. The verb *arrested* first-merges with its direct object complement *the suspect* (a DP formed by merging the determiner *the* with the NP *suspect*) to form the V-bar *arrested the suspect*; the verb *arrested* then second-merges with the subject DP *the police* (formed by merging the determiner *the* with the NP *police*) to form the VP shown in (17) below (simplified by not showing the internal structure of the two DPs):

(17)

```
              VP
        ┌──────┴──────┐
       DP             V′
    the police    ┌───┴───┐
                  V       DP
               arrested  the suspect
```

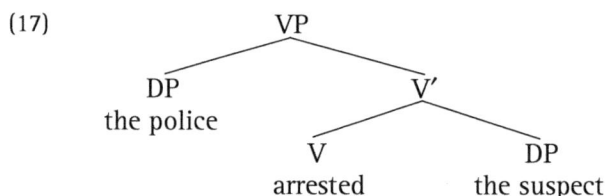

In a structure such as (17), the complement *the suspect* is said to be the internal argument of the verb *arrested* (in the sense that it is the argument contained within the immediate V-bar projection of the verb, and hence is a sister of the verb), whereas the subject *the police* is the external argument of the verb *arrested* (in that it occupies a position external to the V-bar constituent which is the immediate projection of the verb *arrested*, and is an aunt of the verb). The VP in (17) is then merged with the present tense auxiliary T-*have*, forming the T-bar *have the police arrested the suspect*. T-*have* has an EPP feature requiring it to second-merge with a subject of its own, and this EPP feature allows *have* to attract the DP *the police* to move from being the subject of *arrested* to becoming the subject of T-*have*, so forming *The police have ~~the police~~ arrested the suspect*. Merging the resulting TP with a null complementiser (marking the sentence as indicative in mood) in turn derives the structure shown in simplified form in (18) below, with the arrow showing the A-Movement operation involved:

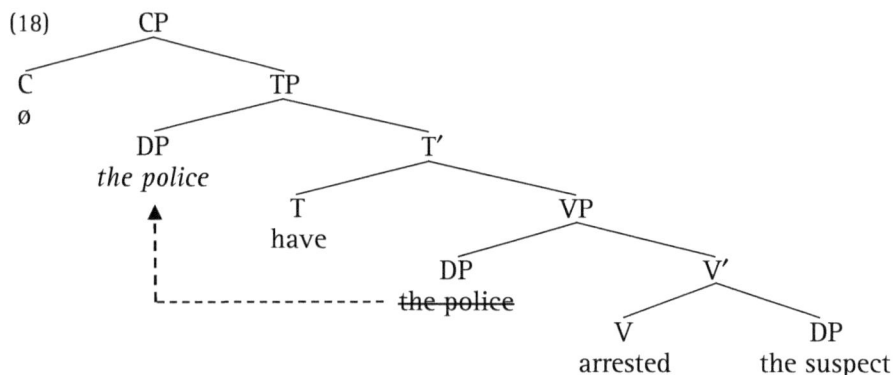

(18)

```
          CP
      ┌────┴────┐
      C         TP
      Ø     ┌────┴──────┐
           DP           T′
       the police   ┌────┴──────┐
                    T           VP
                  have     ┌─────┴─────┐
                          DP           V′
                       the police  ┌───┴───┐
                                   V       DP
                                arrested  the suspect
```

Under the analysis in (18), the argument structure of the verb *arrest* is directly reflected in the internal structure of the VP which it heads, since *the suspect* is the internal (direct object) argument of *arrested* and *the police* was initially merged as its external (subject) argument – and indeed a silent copy of *the police* is left behind in spec-VP, marking the spec-VP position as associated with *the police*. The overall CP is interpreted as declarative in force in accordance with (5ii).

However, there is an important sense in which it is not enough simply to say that in a sentence such as (16b) *The police have arrested the suspect* the verb *arrest* is a predicate which has two arguments – the internal argument *the suspect* and the external argument *the police*. After all, such a description fails to account for these two arguments playing very different semantic roles in relation to the act of *arrest* – that is, it fails to account for *the police* being the individuals who perform the act (and hence get to handcuff suspects and bundle them into the back of a police vehicle), and *the suspect* being the person who suffers the consequences of the act (e.g. being handcuffed and bundled into the back of a police vehicle). Hence, any adequate account of argument structure should provide a description of the semantic role which each argument plays. In the next section, we'll look at how this can be done.

2.2.2 Theta roles

In research spanning more than half a century, linguists have attempted to devise a universal typology of the semantic roles played by arguments in relation to their predicates. In (19) below are listed a number of terms used to describe some of these roles (the convention being that terms denoting semantic roles are CAPITALISED), and for each role an informal gloss is given, together with an illustrative example sentence (in which the italicised expression has the semantic role specified):

(19)   **List of roles played by arguments with respect to their predicates**

Role	Gloss	Example
THEME	Entity undergoing the effect of some action	*Mary* fell over
AGENT	Entity instigating some action	*Debbie* killed Harry
EXPERIENCER	Entity experiencing some psychological state	*I* like syntax
LOCATIVE	Location in which something is situated or takes place	He hid it *there*
GOAL	Entity representing the destination of some other entity	John went *home*
SOURCE	Entity from which something moves	He returned *from Paris*
INSTRUMENT	Means by which something comes about	He hit it *with a hammer*

We can illustrate how the terminology in (19) can be used to describe the semantic roles played by arguments in terms of the following examples:

(20)   a. [The FBI]   arrested   [Larry Luckless]
            [AGENT]   [THEME]
        b. [The suspect]   received   [a caution]
            [GOAL]   [THEME]

c. [The audience] enjoyed [the play]

[EXPERIENCER]   [THEME]

d. [The president] went [to Boston]

[THEME]   [GOAL]

e. [They] stayed [in a hotel]

[THEME]   [LOCATIVE]

f. [The noise] came [from the car]

[THEME]   [SOURCE]

Given that – as we see from these examples – the THEME role is a central one, it has become customary to refer to the relevant semantic roles as thematic roles; and since the Greek letter θ (= *theta*) corresponds to *th* in English and the word *thematic* begins with *th*, it has also become standard practice to use the synonymous expression theta role or θ-role (with theta pronounced [θiːtə] by some and [θeiːtə] by others). Using this terminology, we can say (for example) that in (20a) *the FBI* is the AGENT argument of the predicate *arrested*, and that *Larry Luckless* is the THEME argument of *arrested*.

Thematic relations (like AGENT and THEME) have been argued to play a central role in the description of a range of linguistic phenomena. For example, it has been claimed that the distribution of certain types of adverb is thematically determined. For instance, Gruber (1976) maintains that adverbs like *deliberately* can only be associated with AGENT arguments:

(21)   a. *John* (= AGENT) **deliberately** rolled the ball down the hill

b. *The ball (= THEME) **deliberately** rolled down the hill

Likewise, Fillmore (1970) argues that the adverb *personally* (in the use illustrated below) can only be associated with an (italicised) EXPERIENCER argument:

(22)   a. **Personally,** *I* (= EXPERIENCER) don't like roses

b. **Personally,** your proposal doesn't interest *me* (= EXPERIENCER)

c. ***Personally,** *I* (= AGENT) hit you

d. ***Personally,** you hit *me* (= THEME)

And in much the same vein, Anderson (1977: 267–71) argues that only verbs with AGENT subjects have *by*-phrase nominal counterparts:

(23)   a. *The mayor* (= AGENT) protested

b. the protest *by the mayor*

(24)   a. *The mayor* (= THEME) died

b. *the death *by the mayor*

Many other aspects of sentences have also been argued to be subject to thematic constraints. For example, selection restrictions (i.e. restrictions which hold between a predicate and its choice of arguments) are a function of the semantic properties of the predicate on the one hand, and the thematic role of its arguments on the other. This can be illustrated by comparing the following sentences:

(25) a. John rolled *the ball* down the hill
      b. *The ball* rolled down the hill

Although *the ball* has a different constituent structure status in these two sentences (= complement of the verb *rolled* in 25a, but the subject of *rolled* in 25b), it has the same thematic function of THEME (i.e. entity which undergoes the rolling motion) in both cases. Accordingly, *the ball* is subject to the same selection restrictions in the two uses – as illustrated below (where *!* marks semantic/pragmatic anomaly):

(26) a. John rolled *the ball/the rock/!the theory/!sincerity* down the hill
      b. *The ball/the rock/!the theory/!sincerity* rolled down the hill

Such data suggest that selection restrictions correlate with thematic structure rather than syntactic structure.

In a similar vein, Fillmore (1970) argues that constraints on coordinate structures like (27c) below suggest that only constituents with the same thematic function can readily be coordinated:

(27) a. *John* (= AGENT) broke the window
      b. *A hammer* (= INSTRUMENT) broke the window
      c. *!John* (= AGENT) and *a hammer* (= INSTRUMENT) broke the window

And Jackendoff (1972) argues that a number of constraints on passive structures can be accounted for in thematic terms. For example, he argues (1972: 44) that the ill-formedness of passive sentences like:

(28) a. *Five dollars are cost by this book
      b. *Two hundred pounds are weighed by Bill

is attributable to violation of the following constraint (formulated in thematic terms):

(29) **Passive Thematic Hierarchy Condition**
      The passive *by*-phrase must be higher on the Thematic Hierarchy than the superficial subject

The hierarchy referred to in (29) is the following:

(30) **Thematic Hierarchy**
      AGENT > LOCATIVE/SOURCE/GOAL > THEME

Jackendoff maintains that the *by*-phrase in both examples in (28) is a THEME argument of the relevant verb, whereas the superficial subject is a LOCATIVE argument. Since THEME is lower on the hierarchy (30) than LOCATIVE, sentences like (28) violate the condition (29) and so are ungrammatical.

2.2.3 Theta-marking

Having seen that theta roles play a key role in accounting for a variety of aspects of the use of sentences, let's reflect more generally on how theta-marking (i.e. assignment of theta roles) works, and what constraints it is subject to. In order to determine this, let's take another look at the sentences in (20) above, repeated as (31) below:

(31)   a. [The FBI]   arrested   [Larry Luckless]
            [AGENT]   [THEME]
        b. [The suspect]   received   [a caution]
            [GOAL]   [THEME]
        c. [The audience]   enjoyed   [the play]
            [EXPERIENCER]   [THEME]
        d. [The president]   went   [to Boston]
            [THEME]   [GOAL]
        e. [They]   stayed   [in a hotel]
            [THEME]   [LOCATIVE]
        f. [The noise]   came   [from the car]
            [THEME]   [SOURCE]

If we look closely at the examples in (31), we see a fairly obvious pattern emerging. Each of the bracketed argument expressions in (31) carries one and only one θ-role, and no two arguments of any predicate carry the same θ-role: for example, in (31a), the FBI is assigned the AGENT role, and Larry Luckless the THEME role. Chomsky (1981) suggested that these thematic properties of arguments are the consequence of a principle of Universal Grammar outlined below:

(32)   **Theta Criterion/θ-criterion**
        Each argument bears one and only one θ-role, and each θ-role is
        assigned to one and only one argument (Chomsky 1981: 36)

A principle along the lines of (32) has been assumed (in some form or other) in much subsequent work.

However, a question which arises from (32) is how θ-roles are assigned to arguments. In V-bar constituents of the form *verb+complement,* the thematic role of the complement is determined by the semantic properties of the verb. As examples like (31a–31c) above illustrate, the θ-role associated with complements is often that of THEME (though this is not always the case – e.g. the complement *me* of the verb *bother* in *Personally, it doesn't bother me* has the thematic role of EXPERIENCER).

But how are subjects assigned theta roles? Marantz (1984: 23ff.) and Chomsky (1986a: 59–60) argue that although verbs directly assign theta roles to their internal arguments (i.e. complements), it is not the verb but rather the whole verb+complement (i.e. V-bar) constituent which determines the theta role assigned to its external argument. The evidence they adduce in support of this conclusion comes from sentences such as:

(33)   a. John threw a ball
        b. John threw a fit

(34)   a. John broke the window
        b. John broke his arm

Although the subject of the verb *threw* in both (33a) and (33b), *John* plays a different thematic role in the two sentences – that of AGENT in the case of *threw a ball*, but that of EXPERIENCER in *threw a fit*. Likewise, although the subject of the verb *broke* in both (34a) and (34b), *John* plays the role of AGENT in (34a) but that of EXPERIENCER on the most natural (accidental arm-breaking) interpretation of (34b). From examples such as these, Marantz and Chomsky conclude that the thematic role of the subject is not determined by the verb alone, but rather is compositionally determined by the whole verb+complement structure – that is, by V-bar. On this view, a verb assigns a θ-role directly to its internal argument, but only indirectly (as a compositional function of the semantic properties of the overall V-bar) to its external argument. To use the relevant technical terminology, we can say that predicates directly θ-mark their complements, but indirectly θ-mark their subjects/specifiers.

A related observation is that auxiliaries seem to play no part in determining the assignment of theta roles to subjects, as can be illustrated in relation to:

(35)   a. John *will* throw a ball/a fit
        b. John *was* throwing the ball/a fit
        c. John *had been* throwing the ball/a fit
        d. John *might have been* throwing the ball/a fit

Here, the thematic role of the subject *John* is determined purely by the choice of V-bar constituent (i.e. whether it is *throw the ball* or *throw a fit*), and is not affected in any way by the presence of the italicised auxiliaries. Clearly, any theory of θ-marking should offer us a principled answer to questions such as the following: How are θ-roles assigned? Why do some constituents (e.g. verbs) play a key role in θ-marking, while others (e.g. auxiliaries) do not?

We can provide a principled answer to these questions if we suppose that theta roles are assigned to arguments in accordance with the hypothesis below:

(36)   **Predicate-Internal Theta-Marking Hypothesis**
         An argument is theta-marked internally within a projection of a
         predicate, either directly by being merged with the predicate, or indirectly
         by being merged with an intermediate projection of the predicate

In the light of (36), consider our earlier sentence (16b) *The police have arrested the suspect.* Here, the DP complement *the suspect* will be assigned the θ-role of THEME argument of *arrested* when the verb *arrested* merges with this DP to form the V-bar *arrested the suspect.* In a similar fashion, the subject DP *the police* will be assigned the θ-role of AGENT when the V-bar *arrested the suspect* is merged with the subject DP to form the VP *the police arrested the suspect.* The resulting VP is then merged with the auxiliary *have* to form the T-bar *have the police arrested the suspect.* Because T has an EPP feature, T-*have* attracts the subject DP *the police* to raise to spec-TP, deriving *The police have ~~the police~~ arrested the suspect.* However, the subject *the police* does not receive a theta role from the auxiliary *have*, since auxiliaries are not predicates (unlike main verbs) and hence do not theta-mark their subjects. The resulting TP is ultimately merged with a null complementiser to form the CP shown in (18) above, which is the structure associated with (16b) *The police have arrested the suspect.* Since both arguments of *arrested* (the complement DP *the suspect* and the subject DP *the police*) are assigned a single theta role, and each has a different theta role (*the police* being an AGENT, and *the suspect* a THEME), the Theta Criterion (32) is satisfied.

To summarise: our discussion in Module 2.2 suggests that the semantic role played by arguments with respect to their associated predicates can be described in terms of a set of theta roles, and that thematic considerations lend further support to the VP-Internal Subject Hypothesis. By positing that subjects originate internally within VP, we can arrive at a unitary and principled account of θ-marking in terms of the operation merge, in that an argument is θ-marked when merged with a predicate or with an intermediate projection of a predicate.

You should now be able to tackle Exercise 2.2.

2.3   Unaccusative structures

The overall conclusion to be drawn from our discussion hitherto is that subjects originate internally within VP, as theta-marked arguments of the verb. In all the structures we have looked at so far, the verb phrase has contained both a complement and a specifier (the specifier being the subject of the verb). However, in this module we look at a special class of VPs which contain a verb and a complement but no specifier, and where it is the complement of the verb which subsequently moves to spec-TP.

2.3.1 Unaccusative predicates

One class of verb phrases which have a complement but no specifier are those headed by a special subclass of intransitive verbs which have the property that they can be used both in expletive structures such as (37a, 38a, 39a) below, and in non-expletive structures like those in (37b, 38b, 39b):

(37)   a.   There <u>have</u> **arisen** *several complications*
       b.   *Several complications* have **arisen**

(38)   a.   There <u>could</u> have **occurred** *a diplomatic incident*
       b.   *A diplomatic incident* could have **occurred**

(39)   a.   There <u>does</u> still **remain** *some hope of finding survivors*
       b.   *Some hope of finding survivors* does still **remain**

I shall argue here that the italicised arguments originate as the complements of the bold-printed verbs in both types of structure: they remain in situ as the complement of the verb in the expletive (a) structures, but raise to become the subject of the underlined T auxiliary *have/could/does* in the non-expletive (b) structures. However, the bold-printed verbs in (37–39) differ from transitive verbs taking a nominal expression as their complement in that they don't assign accusative case to their complement, but rather nominative case. Although the nominative-accusative case contrast is invisible on noun expressions in English, it is visible in languages like Icelandic with a richer case system. And in Icelandic, the (italicised) complement of an unaccusative verb receives *nominative* (= NOM) case even in expletive structures where it remains in situ and follows the verb – as the following example illustrates:

(40)   Það   hafa   **komið**   *nokkrir*$_{NOM}$ *gestir*$_{NOM}$
       There   have   come   some   guests

And it may be that the nominative case borne by unaccusative arguments can be illustrated from English by use of *I* in archaic structures such as:

(41)   There but for the grace of God go *I*

Because they don't assign accusative case to their complements, verbs like those bold-printed in (37–39) are known as unaccusative predicates.

     Given that the complements of unaccusative predicates are not assigned accusative case, it would be only natural to question whether they actually are complements (rather than e.g. subjects which end up positioned after the unaccusative verb rather than in front of it). In fact, there is strong syntactic evidence in support of analysing them as complements. Part of the evidence comes from their behaviour in relation to a constraint on movement operations (dating back to work by Cattell 1976, Cinque 1978, and Huang 1982) which was given the following characterisation in §1.5.1:

(42)   **Constraint on Extraction Domains/CED**
        Only complements allow material to be extracted out of them, not specifiers or adjuncts

We can illustrate how CED works in terms of the following contrasts:

(43)   a.   He was taking [pictures of *who*]?
        b.   *Who* was he taking [pictures of ~~who~~]?

(44)   a.   [Part of *what*] has broken?
        b.   *What* has [part of ~~what~~] broken?

(45)   a.   He was angry [because she did *what*]?
        b.   *What* was he angry [because she did ~~what~~]?

(43a, 44a, 45a) are questions in which the wh-pronoun *who/what* remains in situ, while (43b, 44b, 45b) are their Wh-Movement counterparts. In (43b), *who* is extracted out of a bracketed nominal expression which is the complement of the verb *taking*, and yields a grammatical outcome because there is no violation of CED (extraction out of complements being permitted by CED). By contrast, in (44b) *what* is extracted out of a bracketed expression which is the subject (and hence specifier) of the auxiliary *has*, and since CED blocks extraction out of specifiers, the resulting sentence is ungrammatical. Likewise, in (45b) *what* is extracted out of a bracketed adjunct clause, and since CED blocks extraction out of adjuncts, the sentence is ungrammatical.

In the light of CED, consider a sentence such as:

(46)   *How many survivors* does there remain [some hope of finding −]?

Here, the wh-phrase *how many survivors* has been extracted (via Wh-Movement) out of the bracketed expression *some hope of finding how many survivors*, moving from the gap position marked by − to the italicised position. Given that the Condition on Extraction Domains tells us that only complements allow material to be extracted out of them, it follows that the bracketed expression in (46) must be the complement of the unaccusative verb *remain*. By extension, we can assume that the italicised expressions in (37–39) likewise originate as the complements of the bold-printed unaccusative verbs.

A further argument supporting the claim that unaccusative subjects are initially merged as complements comes from observations about quantifier stranding in the West Ulster variety of English. McCloskey (2000) notes that West Ulster English allows wh-questions such as those below which have the interpretation 'What are all the things that you got for Christmas?':

(47)   a. **What** *all* did you get for Christmas?
        b. **What** did you get *all* for Christmas?

He argues that when the universal quantifier *all* is used to modify a wh-word like *what*, Wh-Movement can either move the whole expression *what all* to the front of the sentence (as in 47a) above, or can move the word *what* on its own, thereby stranding the quantifier in situ (as in 47b). In the light of his observation, consider the following sentence:

(48)   **What** happened *all* at the party last night?

The fact that the quantifier *all* is stranded in a position following the unaccusative verb *happened* suggests that the wh-expression *what all* originates in postverbal position as the complement of the verb *happened*. More generally, sentences like (48) provide empirical evidence in support of positing that unaccusative subjects are initially merged as complements.

2.3.2   Unaccusatives compared with other predicates

Although unaccusative verbs allow their arguments to be positioned after them in expletive structures like (37a, 38a, 39a) above, there are other types of predicate which do not – as we see from the ungrammaticality of sentences such as (49) below:

(49)   a. *When the Snail Rail train arrived five hours late, there complained *many passengers*
        b. *In the dentist's surgery, there groaned *a toothless patient*
        c. *Every time General Wynott Nukem goes past, there salutes *a guard at the gate*

Intransitive verbs like *complain/groan/salute* are known as unergative verbs: they differ from unaccusative verbs in that the subject of an unergative verb has the thematic role of an AGENT argument, whereas the subject of an unaccusative verb has the thematic role of a THEME argument.

In addition to those already noted, there are a number of other important syntactic differences between unaccusative verbs and other types of verb (e.g. unergative verbs or transitive verbs). For example, Henry (1995) observes that in one dialect of Belfast English (which she calls dialect A) unaccusative verbs like those bold-printed below can have (italicised) post-verbal subjects in imperative structures like:

(50)   a. **Leave** *you* now!
        b. **Arrive** *you* before 6 o'clock!
        c. Be **going** *you* out of the door when he arrives!

By contrast, other (e.g. unergative or transitive) verbs don't allow post-verbal imperative subjects, so that imperatives such as those below are ungrammatical in the relevant dialect:

(51)   a. *__Read__ *you* that book!
        b. *__Eat__ *you* up!
        c. *Always **laugh** *you* at his jokes!

Additional evidence for positing that unaccusative verbs are syntactically distinct from other verbs comes from auxiliary selection facts in relation to earlier stages of English when there were two perfect aspect auxiliaries (HAVE and BE), each taking a complement headed by a specific kind of verb. Unaccusative verbs differed from transitive or unergative verbs in being used with the perfect auxiliary BE, as the sentences below (taken from various plays by Shakespeare) illustrate:

(52)   a. Mistress Page *is* **come** with me (Mrs Ford, *Merry Wives of Windsor*, V.v)
        b. How chance thou *art* **returned** so soon? (Antipholus, *Comedy of Errors*, I.ii)
        c. I *am* **arriv'd** for fruitful Lombardy (Lucentio, *Taming of the Shrew*, I.i)
        d. You shall hear I *am* **run** away (Countess, *All's Well That Ends Well*, III.ii)
        e. She *is* **fallen** into a pit of ink (Leonato, *Much Ado About Nothing*, IV.i)
        f. Did he not say my brother *was* **fled**? (Don Pedro, *Much Ado About Nothing*, V.i)
        g. And now *is* he **become** a man (Margaret, *Much Ado About Nothing*, III.iv)
        h. Why *are* you **grown** so rude? (Hermia, *Midsummer Night's Dream*, III.ii)

We find a similar contrast with the counterparts of perfect HAVE/BE in a number of other languages – for example, Italian and French (Burzio 1986), Sardinian (Jones 1994), German and Dutch (Haegeman 1994), and Danish (Spencer 1991).

A further difference between unaccusative predicates and others relates to the adjectival use of their perfect participle forms. As the examples below indicate, (italicised) perfect participle forms of unaccusative verbs can be used adjectivally (to modify a noun), for example, in sentences such as:

(53) a. The train *arrived* at platform 4 is the delayed 8.28 for London Euston
     b. The vice squad arrested a businessman recently *returned* from Thailand
     c. Several facts recently *come* to light point to his guilt
     d. Brigadier Bungle is something of a *fallen* hero

By contrast, perfect participle forms of (active) transitive verbs (like those in 54a, 54b below) or unergative verbs (like those in 54c, 54d) cannot be used in the same way, as we see from the ungrammaticality of examples like the following:

(54) a. *The man *committed* suicide was a neighbour of mine
     b. *The thief *stolen* the jewels was never captured
     c. *The man *overdosed* was Joe Doe
     d. *The *yawned* student eventually fell asleep in class

In this respect, unaccusative verbs resemble passive participles, which can also be used adjectivally (cf. *a changed man, a battered wife, a woman arrested for shoplifting*, etc.).

Further support for the subjects of unaccusative predicates originating as complements comes from thematic considerations. In this respect, consider alternations such as the following:

(55) a. A torpedo sank the ship
     b. The ship sank

In (55a) the subject *a torpedo* is an INSTRUMENT argument of *sank* (representing the means used to destroy the ship), and the complement *the ship* is a THEME argument (representing the entity undergoing the effects of sinking). In (55b), *the ship* is again a THEME argument, but this time it is the subject of *sank*, rather than its complement. Baker (1988) argued at length that there is a uniform mapping between thematic and syntactic structure, and he captured this in terms of a principle of Universal Grammar/UG which can be outlined informally as follows:

(56) **Uniform Theta Assignment Hypothesis/UTAH**
     Constituents which fulfil the same thematic role with respect to a given predicate occupy the same initial position in the syntax.

So, since *the ship* is a THEME argument of *sank* in both sentences in (55), and since it is the complement of *sank* in (55a), it is plausible to suppose (on the basis of UTAH) that it originates as the complement of *sank* in (55b) also, and from there moves into spec-TP via A-Movement, in the manner shown by the arrow below:

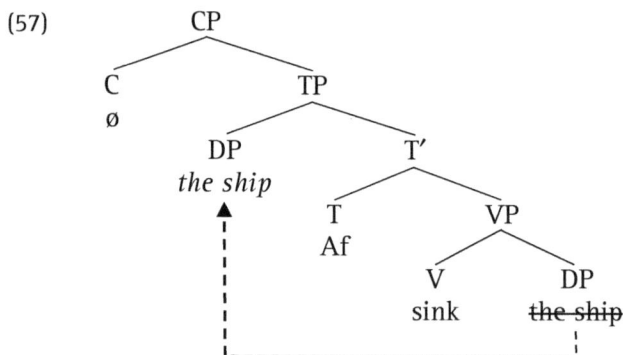

(57)

```
                    CP
                  /    \
                C        TP
                ø       /   \
                     DP        T'
                  the ship    /   \
                    ▲        T       VP
                    ┊        Af     /   \
                    ┊             V       DP
                    ┊            sink   the ship
                    ┊                      ┊
                    ┊_____┊
```

In the PF component, the higher (italicised) copy of the DP *the ship* will receive an overt spellout and the lower copy a silent spellout (marked by strikethrough), in accordance with the following spellout rule (repeated from 7 above):

(58)   **Default Spellout Rule/DSR**
        For a constituent whose spellout is not determined in some other way,
        the highest copy of the constituent is pronounced at PF, and any lower
        copies are silent

In addition, the past tense affix in T will lower onto the verb *sink* in (57) via Affix Hopping, so that this is spelled out at PF as the past tense form *sank*.

Verbs which (when used intransitively) are unaccusative predicates include motion predicates such as *arrive/come/fall/go/leave/return/rise* etc. and existential predicates (i.e. verbs indicating the existence or coming into being of a state of affairs, or a change of state, or the cessation of a state) like *appear/arise/be/become/begin/change/die/exist/happen/occur/remain/start/ stay/stop/turn*. An unaccusative verb like *fall* typically allows inanimate as well as animate subjects (cf. *My wife fell off a stool/The temperature fell sharply*), whereas an unergative predicate like *complain* typically allows only an animate subject (cf. *My wife complained/!The temperature complained*).

2.3.3   The syntax of unaccusative subjects

As we have seen in §2.3.2, there is empirical evidence that unaccusative subjects behave differently from subjects of other (e.g. unergative or transitive) verbs. Why should this be? The answer given by the VP Internal Subject Hypothesis is that the subjects of unaccusative verbs do not originate as the subjects of their associated verbs at all, but rather as their complements, and that unaccusative structures with postverbal arguments involve leaving the relevant argument in situ in VP-complement position – for example, in unaccusative expletive structures such as (37–39) above, and in Belfast English unaccusative imperatives such as (50). This being so, a sentence such as (37a) *There have arisen several complications* will have the following derivation (slightly simplified). The QP *several complications* is merged as the complement of the unaccusative verb *arisen*, forming the VP *arisen several complications*. This VP is merged with the auxiliary T-*have*, thereby forming the T-bar below:

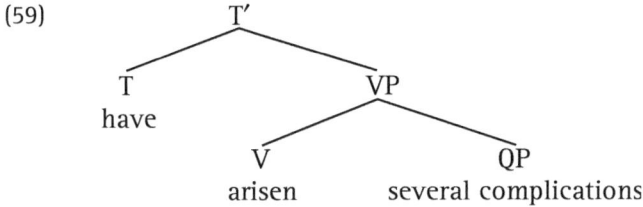

(59)

```
              T′
         ┌────┴────────┐
         T             VP
       have      ┌──────┴──────┐
                 V             QP
              arisen    several complications
```

The finite T auxiliary *have* carries an EPP feature (not shown in 59) which requires it to have a pro/nominal constituent as its specifier. One way of satisfying this requirement is by second-merging T-*have* with the expletive pronominal DP *there* in spec-TP, and the resulting TP *there have arisen several complications* is then merged with a null complementiser (marking indicative mood) to form the CP shown in (60):

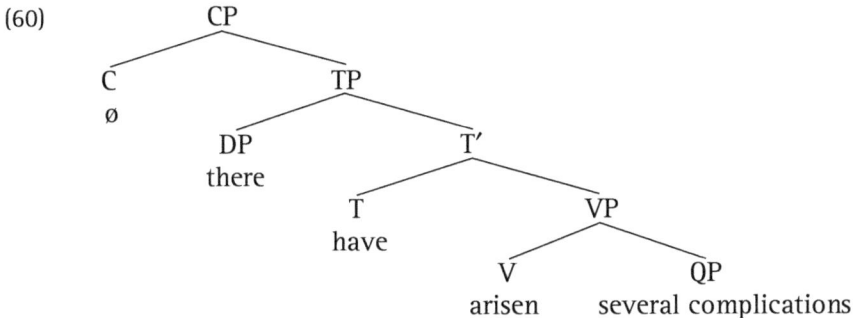

(60)

```
                    CP
          ┌─────────┴────────┐
          C                  TP
          ∅         ┌────────┴────────┐
                    DP               T′
                  there        ┌──────┴──────┐
                               T             VP
                             have     ┌──────┴──────┐
                                      V             QP
                                   arisen    several complications
```

The CP in (60) is spelled out at PF as (37a) *There have arisen several complications*, and is interpreted as declarative in force in conformity with the Default Clause Typing Condition (5ii).

However, an alternative way for the T constituent in (59) to satisfy the EPP requirement for it to have a pro/nominal specifier is not to use an expletive, but instead allow T to attract a pro/nominal to move to spec-TP. Let's suppose that (in such a case) T attracts the closest pro/nominal which it c-commands, in consequence of a principle (termed the Relativised Minimality Condition in Rizzi 1990, 2003) which was given the following characterisation in §1.3.2:

(61)   **Minimality Condition/MC**
        A constituent can only enter into a syntactic relation with the minimal
        (= closest) constituent of the relevant type above/below it

(where *above/below* mean 'c-commanding/c-commanded by'). Since the closest nominal below T in (59) is the QP *several complications* (not the NP *complications*), T attracts this QP to move to spec-TP in the manner shown in (62):

(62)

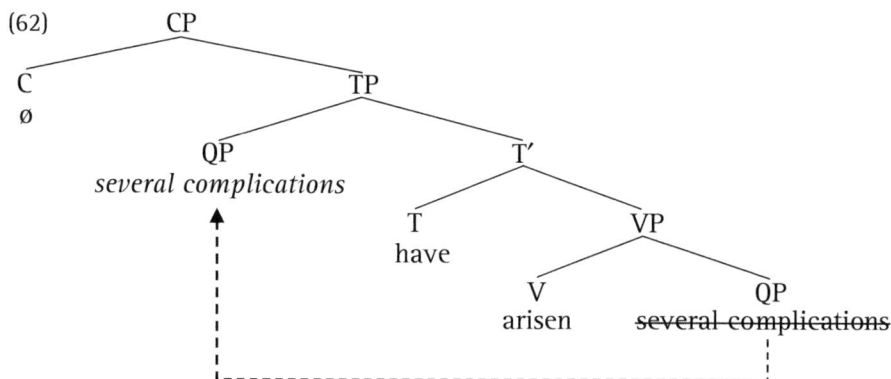

The type of movement involved is the familiar A-Movement operation which moves an argument from an A-position lower down in a sentence to an A-position higher up in the sentence: in the case of (62), the arrowed A-Movement operation moves the QP *several complications* from comp-VP (i.e. complement position within VP) into spec-TP (i.e. specifier position within TP). In the PF component, the higher (italicised) copy of the moved QP receives an overt spellout, and the lower copy (marked by strikethrough) a null spellout, in accordance with the Default Spellout Rule (58) above. Consequently, the structure in (62) is spelled out at PF as (37b) *Several complications have arisen.*

The derivation in (62) illustrates a characteristic property of A-Movement. Since comp-VP is a thematic A-position/θ-position (i.e. an A-position which is assigned a theta role by the relevant predicate/verb) but spec-TP is a θ-bar position (i.e. an A-position to which no theta role is assigned), we can see that an A-Movement structure like (61) involves movement from a thematic A-position within VP into a non-thematic A-position in spec-TP. This results in the formation of an A-chain (i.e. a movement chain created by A-Movement) which satisfies the Theta Criterion (32) by virtue of the relevant A-chain being assigned only one theta role: more specifically, the null copy of the QP *several complications* at the foot of the A-chain in (62) is assigned the θ-role of THEME complement of *arisen*, but the overt copy of the same QP at the head of the movement chain is in a θ-bar position in spec-TP where it receives no additional θ-role (but instead inherits the θ-role of its lower copy). This suggests that the Theta Criterion (32) can be taken to be a condition on A-chains, requiring each A-chain to carry one and only one theta role.

The A-Movement analysis of unaccusative subjects in (62) above allows us to provide an interesting account of sentence pairs like that below:

(63) a. All hope of finding survivors has gone
      b. All hope has gone of finding survivors

Since GO is an unaccusative verb, the QP *all hope of finding survivors* will originate as the complement of *gone*. Merging *gone* with this QP will derive the VP *gone all hope of finding survivors*. The resulting VP is merged with the T auxiliary *has* to form the T-bar *has gone all hope of finding survivors*. The QP *all hope of finding survivors* is attracted by the EPP feature on T-*has* to raise to the bold-printed spec-TP position, leaving a copy behind in the italicised position in which it originated – as shown in (64):

(64)

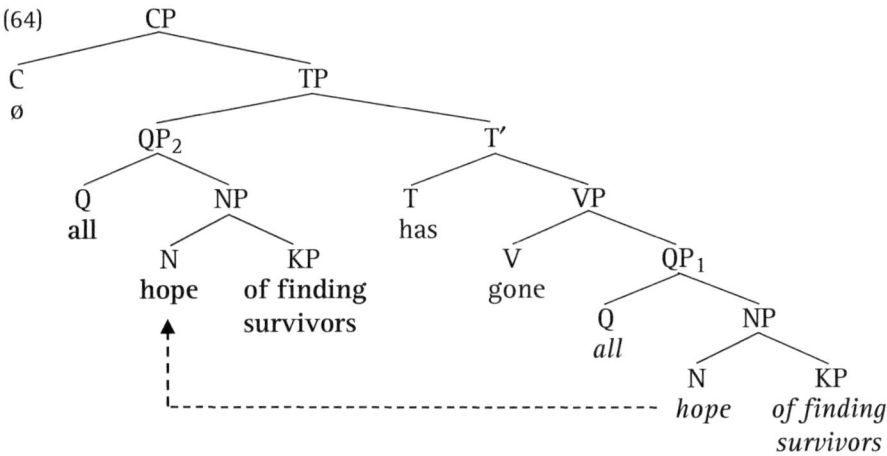

In the case of (63a), the higher copy of the moved QP *all hope of finding survivors* is spelled out in the bold-printed spec-TP position which it moves to, and the lower copy (QP₁) in the italicised VP-complement position is given a null spellout (in accordance with the Default Spellout Rule 58) – as shown in simplified form in (65):

(65)

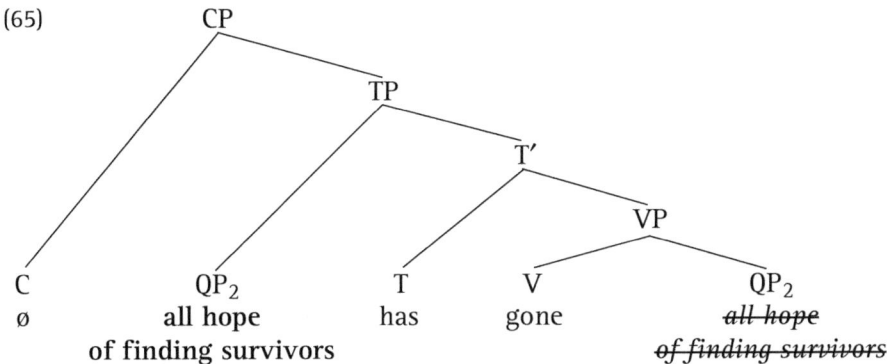

By contrast, in the case of (63b), the quantifier *all* and the noun *hope* are spelled out in the bold-printed position that they move to in (64), but the KP *of finding survivors* is spelled out in the VP-complement position in which it originates – as shown in (66):

(66)

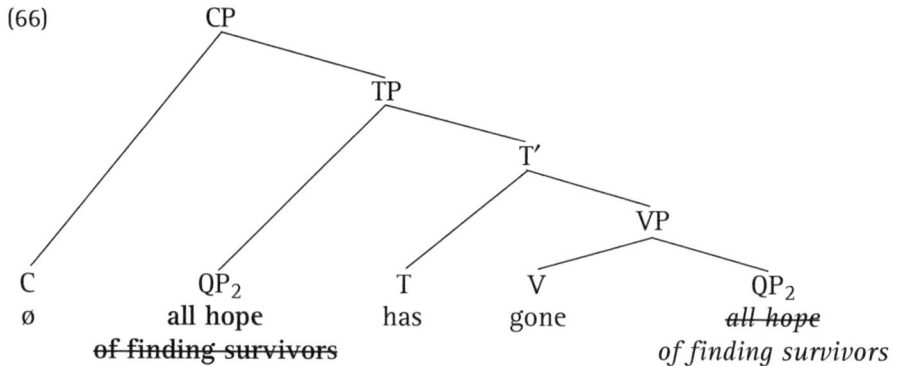

The exceptional spellout pattern in (66) is the result of the application of a special Low Spellout Rule which is given the following informal characterisation in Radford (2020: 277):

(67)   **Low Spellout Rule/LSR**
A KP/PP/CP which is the lowest/rightmost constituent of a larger phrase that undergoes movement can be spelled out on a lower copy of the moved phrase

(67) allows the KP/case phrase *of finding survivors* to be spelled out on the lower (italicised) copy of the moved QP, while the remainder of the QP is spelled out on the higher (bold-printed) copy, giving rise to discontinuous/split spellout. This split spellout pattern provides evidence in support of taking A-Movement (like other movement operations) to be a composite operation involving copying and deletion. An interesting observation about sentences like (63) is that they allow the archaic use of BE as a perfect auxiliary (as in *All hope is now gone of finding survivors*), so underlining their unaccusative status.

   To summarise: in Module 2.3 we have looked at the syntax of unaccusative predicates like *arise/remain/occur* etc. We saw that the thematic argument of an unaccusative verb originates as its complement but differs from the complement of a transitive verb in that (in a finite clause) it receives nominative rather than accusative case. We examined a number of further differences between unaccusative predicates and other types of predicate (e.g. in relation to the position of subjects in Belfast English imperatives, and auxiliary selection in earlier varieties of English). We also looked at how split spellout patterns can arise in unaccusative clauses like *All hope has now gone of finding survivors*.

   You should now be able to tackle Exercise 2.3.

2.4 Passive structures

In this module, we turn to examine the syntax of passive structures. We will see that passives are similar in certain respects to unaccusative structures. We begin by looking at simple passive structures (i.e. those which involve Passivisation applying internally within a single clause).

2.4.1 Simple passives

Traditional grammarians maintain that the bold-printed verbs in sentences such as (68a, 69a, 70a) below are in the active voice, whereas the italicised verbs in the corresponding sentences in (68b, 69b, 70b) are in the passive voice (so that the italicised verbs have the status of passive participles):

(68) a. Hundreds of passers-by **saw** the attack
b. The attack was *seen* by hundreds of passers-by

(69) a. Lex Luthor **stole** the kryptonite
b. The kryptonite was *stolen* by Lex Luthor

(70) a. They **took** everything
b. Everything was *taken*

There are four main properties which differentiate passive sentences from their active counterparts. One is that passive (though not active) sentences generally require the auxiliary BE (as in 70b 'Everything *was* taken'). Another is that the main verb in passive sentences is in the passive participle form (cf. *seen/stolen/taken*), which is often the same as the perfect participle form (cf. *He has stolen it*). A third is that passive sentences may contain a *by*-phrase in which the complement of *by* plays the same thematic role as the subject in the corresponding active sentence: for example, *hundreds of passers-by* in the active structure (68a) serves as the subject of *saw the attack*, whereas in the passive structure (68b) it serves as the complement of the preposition *by* (though in both cases it has the thematic role of EXPERIENCER argument of *see*). The fourth difference is that the expression which serves as the complement of an active verb surfaces as the subject in the corresponding passive structure: for example, *the attack* is the complement of *saw* in the active structure (68a), but is the subject of *was* in the passive structure (68b). Since this chapter is concerned with A-Movement (and hence the syntax of subjects), we focus on the syntax of the superficial subjects of passive sentences, setting aside the derivation of *by*-phrases.

Passive predicates resemble unaccusatives in that alongside structures like those in (71a–73a) below containing (bold-printed) preverbal subjects, they also allow expletive structures like (71b–73b) in which the relevant argument can occupy the italicised postverbal position (providing it is an indefinite expression):

(71)   a. **No evidence of any corruption** was found
        b. There was found *no evidence of any corruption*

(72)   a. **Several cases of syntactophobia** have been reported
        b. There have been reported *several cases of syntactophobia*

(73)   a. **A significant change of policy** has been announced
        b. There has been announced *a significant change of policy*

How can we account for the dual position of the highlighted constituents in such structures?

The answer given within the framework utilised here is that a passive subject is initially merged as the thematic complement of the main verb (i.e. it originates as the complement of the main verb as in 71b, 72b, 73b) and so receives the θ-role which the relevant verb assigns to its complement. It then moves from comp-VP (i.e. complement position within VP) into spec-TP in passive sentences such as (71a, 72a, 73a), via a specific type of A-Movement operation traditionally termed Passivisation.

On this view, the derivation of sentences like (71) will proceed as follows. The quantifier *any* merges with the NP *corruption* to form the QP *any corruption*. The resulting QP is then merged with the case particle/K *of* to form the KP/case phrase *of any corruption*. This KP in turn is merged with the noun *evidence* to form the NP *evidence of any corruption*. The resulting NP is merged with the negative quantifier *no* to form the QP *no evidence of any corruption*. This QP is merged as the complement of the passive verb *found* (and thereby assigned the thematic role of THEME argument of *found*) to form the VP *found no evidence of any corruption*. The VP thereby formed is merged with the T auxiliary *was* forming the T-bar *was found no evidence of any corruption*. The auxiliary T-*was* carries an EPP feature requiring it to have a specifier. This requirement can be satisfied by merging the expletive pronominal DP *there* in spec-TP, deriving the TP *There was found no evidence of any corruption*. Merging this TP with a null complementiser marking indicative mood will derive the structure shown in simplified form in (74) below:

(74)

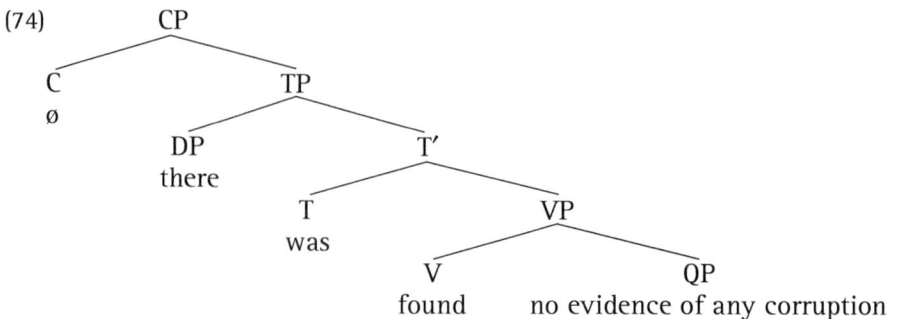

However, an alternative way of satisfying the EPP feature of T-*was* is not to merge *there* in spec-TP, but rather to passivise the QP *no evidence of any corruption* – that is, move it from being the thematic complement of *found* to becoming the specifier/subject of T-*was*. Merging the resulting TP with a null complementiser derives the CP shown in simplified form in (75) below (with the dotted arrow showing the A-Movement operation involved in Passivisation):

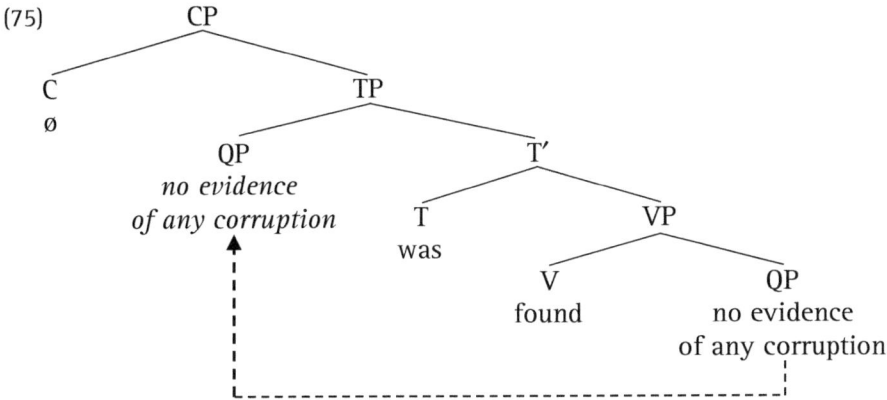

(75)

```
                        CP
              ┌──────────┴──────────┐
              C                     TP
              ø           ┌──────────┴──────────┐
                         QP                     T′
                    no evidence         ┌────────┴────────┐
                   of any corruption    T                 VP
                         ▲             was        ┌────────┴────────┐
                         ┊                        V                 QP
                         ┊                      found          no evidence
                         ┊                                    of any corruption
                         ┊                                             ┊
                         └─────────────────────────────────────────────┘
```

The arrowed Passivisation operation by which QP moves from being the complement of the verb *found* to becoming the specifier of T-*was* is a particular instance of the more general A-Movement operation which serves to create structural subjects (i.e. to move some constituent from a position below T into spec-TP in order to satisfy the EPP feature of T).

Note that an assumption implicit in the analyses in (74) and (75) is that verb phrases headed by intransitive passive participles remain subjectless throughout the derivation, because the T auxiliary *was* is the head which requires a structural subject by virtue of its EPP feature, not the verb *found* (suggesting that it is functional heads like T and C which trigger movement, not lexical heads like V). Note also that the A-Movement operation in (75) satisfies the Theta Criterion (32) because the QP *no evidence of any corruption* is assigned a θ-role (as THEME argument of the verb *found*) in its original position in comp-VP, but is not assigned a second theta role when it moves to spec-TP, because spec-TP is a θ-bar position. The resulting A-chain thus carries one and only one θ-role, and hence satisfies the Theta Criterion.

In the case of (71a) *No evidence of any corruption was found*, the whole of the QP *no evidence of any corruption* is spelled out in the italicised spec-TP position in (75) at the head (i.e. on the highest link) of the movement chain, and all the material in the comp-VP position at the foot (i.e. on the lowest link) of the movement chain is silent, in accordance with the Default Spellout Rule/DSR (58) above. However, an alternative possibility is for the Low Spellout Rule/LSR (67) to apply. LSR would allow the KP *of any corruption* to be spelled out on the lower link of the chain (as shown in italics in 76), and the remainder of the moved QP would then be spelled out on the higher link of the chain by DSR (as shown in bold print), so resulting in the following split spellout pattern:

(76)

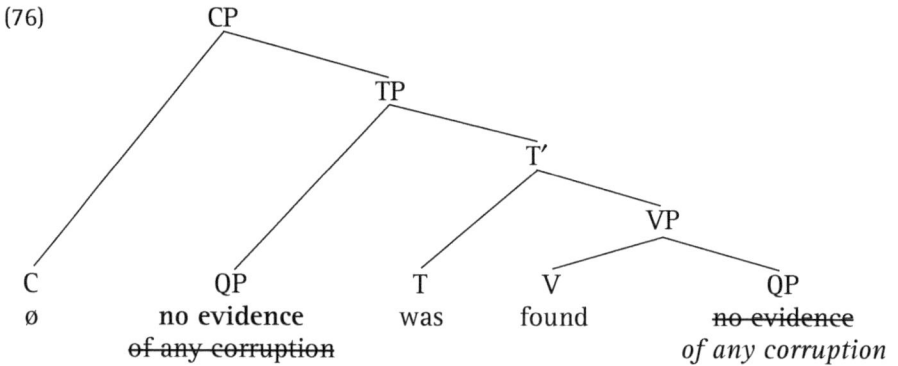

And (76) is the structure associated with the sentence *No evidence was found of any corruption*. Note that the postverbal position of the KP *of any corruption* in (76) provides us with evidence that the subject of a passive predicate originates in comp-VP.

Split spellout passive structures like (76) provide evidence that passive subjects originate as complements. Further evidence comes from the distribution of idiomatic nominals like those italicised in (77)–(79):

(77) a. They **paid** *little heed* to what he said
       b. *Little heed* was **paid** to what he said

(78) a. They **paid** *due homage* to General Ghouly
       b. *Due homage* was **paid** to General Ghouly

(79) a. The FBI **kept** *close tabs* on the CIA
       b. *Close tabs* were **kept** on the CIA by the FBI

In expressions such as *pay heed/homage to* and *keep tabs on*, the verb *pay/keep* and the noun expression containing *heed/homage/tabs* together form an idiom. Given the arguments in §2.1.2 that idioms are unitary constituents, it is apparent that the bold-printed verb and the italicised noun expression must form a unitary constituent when they are first introduced into the derivation. This will clearly be the case if we suppose that the noun expression originates as the complement of the associated verb (as in 77a, 78a, 79a), and becomes the subject of the passive auxiliary *was/were* in (77b, 78b, 79b) via Passivisation/A-Movement.

Additional evidence that passive subjects are initially merged as complements comes from quantifier stranding in West Ulster English structures such as the following (from McCloskey 2000: 72):

(80)   **What** was said *all* at the meeting?

Recall from our earlier discussion of sentences like (47, 48) that McCloskey argues that stranded quantifiers modifying wh-expressions are left behind via movement of the wh-expression without the quantifier. This being so, sentences such as (80) provide evidence that *what all* originates as the complement of the passive participle *said* (with *what* subsequently being passivised on its own, stranding *all*) – and more generally, that passive subjects are initially merged as thematic complements.

A claim which is implicit in the hypothesis that passive subjects originate as thematic complements is that the subjects of passive verbs and the complements of active verbs have the same thematic function. Evidence that this is indeed the case comes from the observation that the two are subject to the same selection restrictions on the choice of expression which can occupy the relevant position, as we see from sentences such as the following (where ?/?!/! mark increasing degrees of anomaly):

(81)   a. *The students/?the camels/?!The flowers/!The ideas* were arrested

        b. They arrested *the students/?the camels/?!the flowers/!the ideas*

We can account for this if we suppose that selection restrictions on the choice of admissible arguments for a given predicate depend jointly on the semantic properties of the predicate and the thematic role of the argument: it will then follow that two expressions which fulfil the same thematic role in respect of a given predicate will be subject to the same restrictions on argument choice. Since passive subjects like those italicised in (81a) originate as complements, they will have the same θ-role (and so be subject to the same pragmatic restrictions on argument choice) as active complements like those italicised in (81b).

We can arrive at the same conclusion (that passive subjects originate as thematic complements) on theoretical grounds. Earlier, we hypothesised that thematic structure is mapped into syntactic structure in a uniform fashion, in consequence of the Uniform Theta Assignment Hypothesis/ UTAH, outlined in (56) above. Consequently, it follows from UTAH that if passive subjects have the same theta role as active complements, they must originate in the same comp-VP position as active complements.

2.4.2   Cross-clausal passives

Thus far, the instances of Passivisation which we have looked at have been clause-internal in the sense that they have involved movement from comp-VP to spec-TP within the same clause. However, Passivisation is also able to apply across certain types of clause boundary – for example, across the infinitive clause boundary bracketed in (82):

(82)   a. There are alleged [to have been **stolen** *several portraits of the queen*]

        b. *Several portraits of the queen* are alleged [to have been **stolen**]

It seems clear that the italicised QP *several portraits of the queen* is the thematic complement of the bold-printed verb *stolen* in the bracketed infinitive clause. In (82a) this QP remains in situ as the complement of the bold-printed verb; but in (82b) it moves to become the structural subject of the auxiliary *are*. Let's look rather more closely at the derivation of these two sentences.

(82a) has the following derivation (slightly simplified). The noun *portraits* merges with the KP/case phrase *of the queen* to form the NP *portraits of the queen*. The quantifier *several* merges with this NP to form the QP *several portraits of the queen*. The verb *stolen* merges with (and assigns the thematic role of THEME argument to) its QP complement *several portraits of the queen*, thereby forming the VP *stolen several portraits of the queen*. The resulting VP is then merged with the passive VOICE auxiliary *been* to form the VOICEP *been stolen several portraits of the queen*. This VOICEP is in turn merged with the perfect aspect auxiliary/PERF *have* to form the PERFP *have been stolen several portraits of the queen*. The PERFP thereby formed is merged with the infinitival tense particle T-*to*, forming the T-bar *to have been stolen several portraits of the queen*. Infinitival *to* (like all T constituents) has an EPP feature which requires it to have a noun or pronoun expression as its subject/specifier. One way of satisfying this requirement is for expletive *there* to be merged in spec-TP, forming the TP shown in (83) below:

(83)

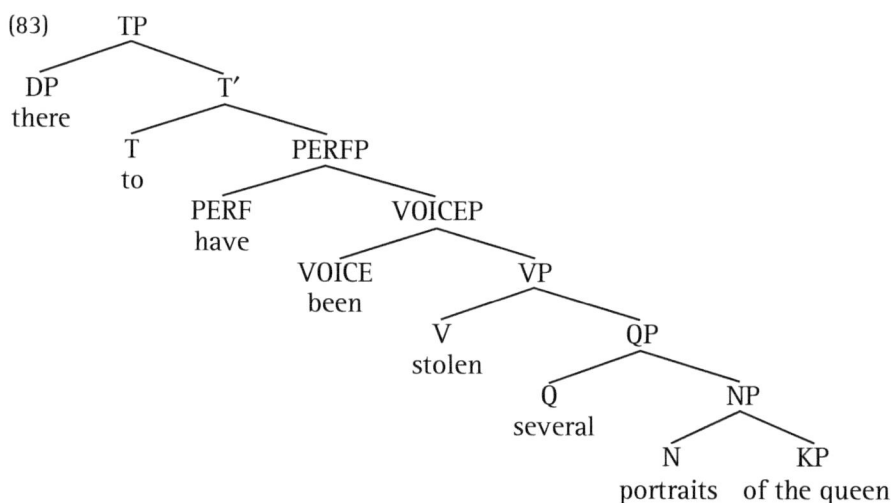

The resulting TP is merged as the complement of the (passive participle) verb *alleged* to form the VP *alleged there to have been stolen several portraits of the queen*. This VP is then merged with the present-tense auxiliary T-*are* to form the T-bar *are alleged there to have been stolen several*

portraits of the queen. T-*are* has an EPP feature which can attract expletive *there* to become its subject (via Passivisation/A-Movement), so forming the TP *there are alleged* ~~there~~ *to have been stolen several portraits of the queen.* This TP is then merged with a null C (marking indicative mood), so deriving the following structure (simplified by not showing the internal structure of VOICEP, which is as shown in 83 above):

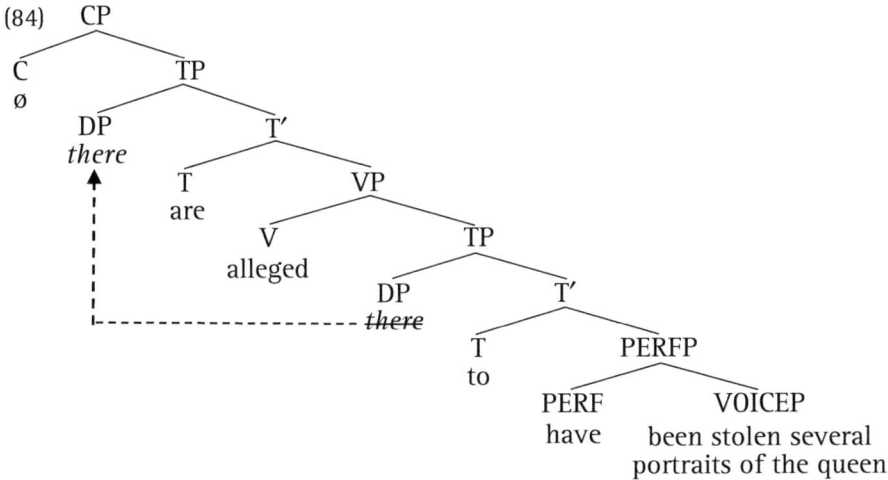

(84)

CP
C (ø)
TP
DP *there*
T′
T *are*
VP
V *alleged*
TP
DP ~~*there*~~
T′
T *to*
PERFP
PERF *have*
VOICEP *been stolen several portraits of the queen*

The overall CP is interpreted as declarative in type by the Default Clause Typing Condition (5ii), and is spelled out at PF as (82a) *There are alleged to have been stolen several portraits of the queen.*

Now consider the derivation of (82b) *Several portraits of the queen are alleged to have been stolen.* Assume that the derivation proceeds as for (82a) until we reach the stage where we have formed the T-bar *to have been stolen several portraits of the queen.* But this time, suppose that the requirements of the EPP feature on T-*to* are satisfied by moving the QP *several portraits of the queen* to spec-TP to become the subject of T-*to*, so forming the TP *several portraits of the queen to have been stolen.* The resulting TP is merged with the passive verb *alleged* to form the VP *alleged several portraits of the queen to have been stolen.* This VP is then merged with the present-tense T auxiliary *are* to form the T-bar *are alleged several portraits of the queen to have been stolen.* Since the T auxiliary *are* has an EPP feature, it can attract the closest noun or pronoun expression (= the QP headed by *several*) to become its subject/specifier, so forming the TP *several portraits of the queen are alleged to have been stolen.* The resulting TP is then merged with a null C (marking indicative mood), forming the CP below (simplified by abbreviating lower copies of the QP *several portraits of the queen* to *spotq*, in order to save space):

(85)

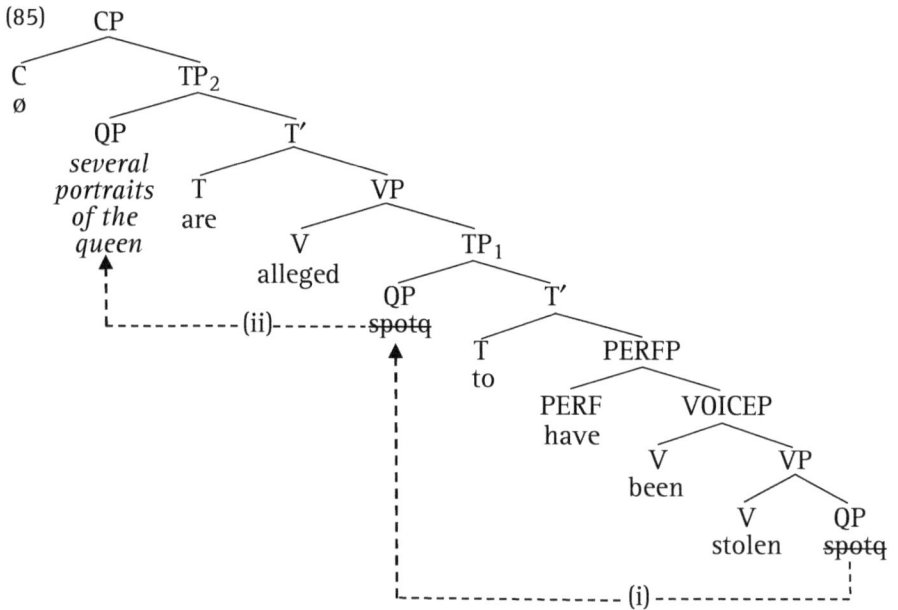

Our discussion illustrates that (in consequence of the EPP feature on each T), cross-clausal Passivisation takes place in a successive-cyclic fashion (i.e. in a succession of short steps), moving the passivised constituent one TP at a time. More specifically, cross-clausal Passivisation involves multiple applications of the familiar A-Movement operation: consequently, each of the two numbered movements arrowed in (85) is a particular instance of A-Movement.

In the previous section (§2.4.1), Passivisation was treated as an operation by which the complement of a VP is raised to become the subject/specifier of a TP above it: this holds true of the lower Passivisation operation numbered (i) in (85) above, where the passivised QP *several portraits of the queen* moves from being the complement of the verb *stolen* to becoming the specifier of TP$_1$. However, it is not true of the higher Passivisation operation numbered (ii), since this involves the QP *several portraits of the queen* moving from spec-TP$_1$ to spec-TP$_2$. This shows that Passivisation is an instance of a more general A-Movement operation which moves a constituent from a lower (complement or specifier) A-position into a higher one.

And indeed independent evidence that subjects/specifiers can be passivised comes from sentences such as:

(86)   a. *All hell* was said to have **broken loose**
        b. *The shit* is expected to **hit the fan**

In (86a, 86b) the italicised passivised nominal is an idiomatic expression which originates as the subject of the bold-printed expression – demonstrating that Passivisation can target subjects as well as complements. The derivation of (86b) proceeds as follows. The verb *hit* merges with the DP *the fan* to form the V-bar *hit the fan*. This V-bar in turn merges with the DP *the shit* to form the (idiomatic) VP *the shit hit the fan*. The resulting VP is merged with the infinitival T constituent *to*, forming the T-bar *to the shit hit the fan*. In conformity with the Minimality Condition (61), the EPP feature on T-*to* attracts the closest (pro)nominal constituent (= DP *the shit*) to become its subject, so forming the TP *the shit to ~~the shit~~ hit the fan*. The resulting TP is merged as the complement of the passive verb *expected*, forming the VP *expected the shit to ~~the shit~~ hit the fan*. This VP is then merged as the complement of the present-tense T auxiliary *is*, forming the T-bar *is expected the shit to ~~the shit~~ hit the fan*. In conformity with the Minimality Condition (61), the EPP feature on the T auxiliary *is* attracts the closest nominal (= *the shit*) to become the subject of T-*is*, so forming the TP *The shit is expected ~~the shit~~ to ~~the shit~~ hit the fan*. Merging this TP with a null indicative complementiser derives (87) below, with the structure being interpreted as declarative in force via the Default Clause Typing Condition (5ii) above:

(87)

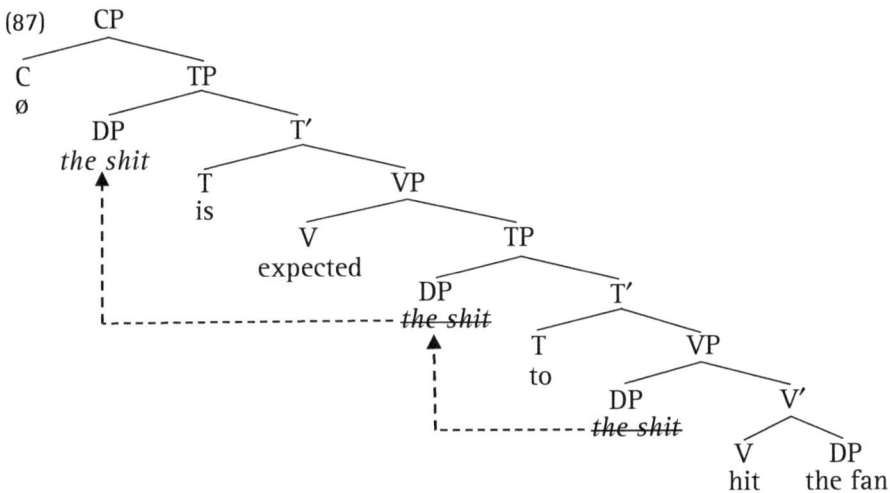

Although a structure like (87) – and likewise the structure in (85) above – is traditionally said to involve long(-distance) Passivisation (because it moves a constituent out of a lower clause into a higher one), in actual fact it involves two separate local A-Movement operations by which the idiomatic nominal *the shit* moves first to become the specifier of the lower TP (thereby becoming the subject of infinitival *to*) and then to become the specifier of the higher TP (thereby becoming the subject of *is*).

2.4.3　Constraints on Passivisation

The analyses of Passivisation in (84, 85, 87) satisfy a number of familiar constraints/conditions. One is the Minimality Condition in (61) above, repeated as (88) below (where *above/below* mean 'c-commanding/c-commanded by'):

(88)   **Minimality Condition**
A constituent can only enter into a syntactic relation with the minimal
(= closest) constituent of the relevant type above/below it

It follows from this condition that, just as an XP undergoing A-bar
Movement is attracted by the closest C head above it, so too an XP undergoing A-Movement is attracted by the closest T head above it. So, for
example, A-Movement in (87) above conforms to the Minimality Condition,
in that the passivised DP *the shit* is first attracted to become the specifier
of the closest T constituent c-commanding it (= the embedded clause T
constituent containing infinitival *to*), and then attracted to become the specifier of the next closest T constituent c-commanding it (= the main clause
T constituent containing *is*).

A key assumption made in (84–87) is that the *to*-infinitive complement
of the verb *alleged/expected* is a TP and not a CP. This is in line with the
traditional assumption that *allege/expect* are ECM/Exceptional Case Marking verbs when used with an infinitival complement, and that the infinitive complement clause is a defective clause (lacking the CP layer found in
complete clauses) and hence a TP (for reasons outlined in Radford 2020:
192–94). We have independent evidence in support of this claim from contrasts such as the following (where − denotes the gap left behind by Passivisation of *you*):

(89)   a. They didn't intend [$_{TP}$ *you* to get hurt]
         b. *You* weren't intended [$_{TP}$ − to get hurt]

(90)   a. They didn't intend [$_{CP}$ for *you* to get hurt]
         b. **You* weren't intended [$_{CP}$ for − to get hurt]

These examples show that an italicised constituent contained within a TP
complement like that bracketed in (89) can passivise, but not one contained
within a CP complement like that bracketed in (90). Passivisation of a constituent inside a CP is prevented by a constraint (deriving from Chomsky
1998) which was given the following informal characterisation in §1.5.1
(where *below* can be characterised more precisely as 'c-commanded by' and
above as 'c-commanding):

(91)   **Impenetrability Condition**
Anything below the head C of a CP is impenetrable to anything above
the CP

(In simpler terms, this condition prevents syntactic operations from applying across the edge of an intervening CP.) Since *you* in (90b) occupies the
gap position below the complementiser *for* prior to moving to become the
subject of the main clause, it is impenetrable to the T auxiliary *weren't*

(and so cannot be attracted by T-*weren't* to become its subject) because T-*weren't* c-commands the complementiser *for*; or, in simpler terms, the intervening complementiser *for* forms an impenetrability barrier to the relevant movement. Conversely, however, the fact that *the shit* can passivise in (87) suggests that the *to*-infinitive complement of *expected* must be a TP, and not a CP.

The assumption that the A-Movement operation involved in Passivisation obeys the Impenetrability Condition offers potential insight into why Passivisation is possible out of a nonfinite clause like that bracketed in (92a) below, but not out of a finite clause like that bracketed in (92b):

(92) a. *The prisoners* were said [− to have been tortured −]
      b. **The prisoners* were said [that/ø − were tortured −]

In both cases, the DP *the prisoners* originates as the complement of *tortured*, then (via one application of A-Movement) becomes the subject of the bracketed complement clause, and subsequently (via another application of A-Movement) moves into the italicised position as the subject of the main clause auxiliary *were*. If we suppose that – as in (84, 85, 87) above – the infinitive complement in (92a) is a TP, nothing prevents movement out of the bracketed TP. But now suppose that 'all finite clauses are CPs' (Radford 2020: 180). This means that the bracketed complement clause in (92b) will be a CP (irrespective of whether introduced by an overt or null complementiser), and that Passivisation in (92b) will involve the two A-Movement operations arrowed (i) and (ii) below:

(93)

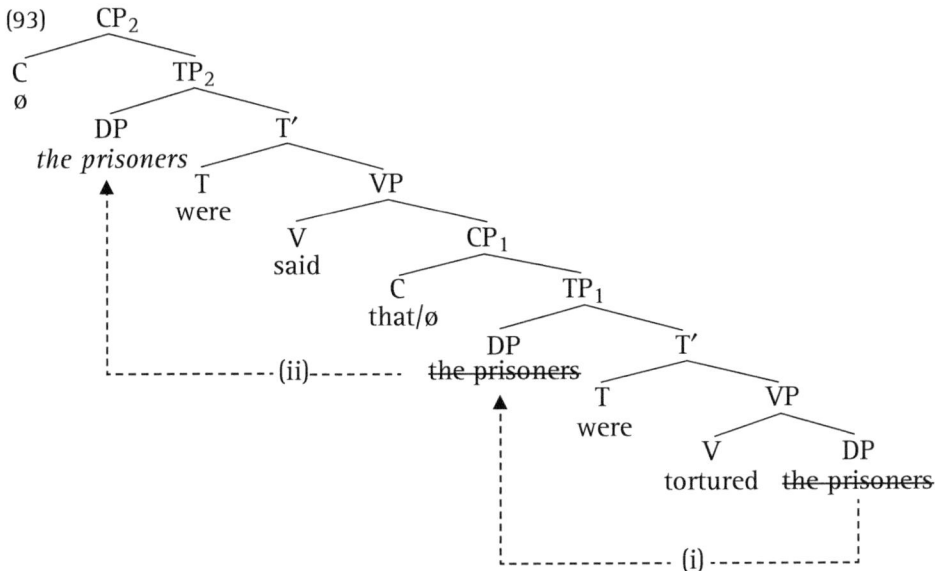

However, there are problems which arise with the derivation in (93).

One is that the Impenetrability Condition (91) will block movement (ii) from spec-TP$_1$ to spec-TP$_2$, since this involves illicit movement across the edge of a CP (i.e. across the overt/null complementiser which is the head C of CP$_1$). Moreover, if *that* is used, (93) will also violate a filter (proposed by Chomsky & Lasnik 1977: 451) which was characterised as follows in §1.5.2:

(94)   **COMP-Trace Filter/CTF**
        Any structure at the end of a syntactic derivation in which an overt
        COMP/complementiser is immediately adjacent to and c-commands a
        trace (i.e. a gap/null copy left behind by a moved constituent) is filtered
        out as ill-formed

The violation of CTF arises in (93) if *that* is used because *that* c-commands and immediately precedes a null copy/trace of the moved subject *the prisoners*.

To summarise: in Module 2.4, we began by looking at the structure of simple passive clauses, and I argued that a passive subject originates as the thematic complement of a subjectless passive participle, and is raised into spec-TP (via A-Movement) in order to satisfy the EPP feature of T. We also saw that Passivisation can be a cross-clausal/long-distance operation involving movement of an argument contained within an infinitival TP which is the complement of a passive participle. I observed that (in consequence of every T carrying an EPP feature requiring it to have a subject), the passivised nominal moves in a successive-cyclic fashion, first into the closest spec-TP position above it, then into the next closest spec-TP position above it (and so on). I went on to argue that Passivisation obeys traditional constraints on syntactic operations (including the Minimality and Impenetrability Conditions), and the COMP-Trace Filter.

You should now be able to tackle Exercise 2.4.

2.5   Raising and Control structures

In this module, we turn to examine the syntax of seemingly subjectless infinitive clauses. We will see that these are of two types. On the one hand, in a sentence like *Jim does seem to support them*, the superficial subject *Jim* originates as the specifier/thematic subject of the VP headed by the verb *support*, and from there moves to become the specifier of the TP headed by infinitival *to*; subsequently, it raises to become the specifier of the higher TP headed by the auxiliary *does*, leaving behind a trace/null copy of the raised subject *Jim* in the infinitival clause (and for this reason infinitives of this kind are called Raising structures). By contrast, in a sentence such as 'Jim does want to support them' the infinitive complement has a null

PRO subject which originates as the specifier/thematic subject of *support them* and from there moves to become the specifier of infinitival *to*; this PRO subject is controlled by (i.e. refers back to) the main clause subject *Jim*, and for this reason infinitives like this are referred to as Control structures. Thus, the two types of infinitive differ in respect of whether the null subject of the infinitive clause is a trace (i.e. a copy of a raised subject), or PRO. In this module, we look at differences between Raising and Control Structures, starting with a look at the former.

2.5.1   Raising structures

The Raising operation by which an argument expression is moved out of one clause to become the subject of another clause can be illustrated by the (b) examples in (95–98) below:

(95)   a. There does **seem** [to remain *some hope of peace*]
         b. *Some hope of peace* does **seem** [to remain]

(96)   a. There does **appear** [to have been made *remarkably little progress*]
         b. *Remarkably little progress* does **appear** [to have been made]

(97)   a. It would **seem** [that *Senator Slyme* has been lying to Congress]
         b. *Senator Slyme* would **seem** [to have been lying to Congress]

(98)   a. It would **appear** [that *they* have underestimated her]
         b. *They* would appear [to have underestimated her]

In (95), the italicised expression *some hope of peace* is the thematic complement of the unaccusative predicate *remain*; it remains in situ in the expletive structure (95a), but raises to become the subject of the *seem*-clause in (95b). In (96), the italicised expression *remarkably little progress* is the thematic complement of the passive verb *made*; it remains in situ in the expletive structure (96a) but raises to become the subject of the *appear*-clause in (96b). In (97), the italicised expression *Senator Slyme* is the thematic subject of the verb *lying*: if the complement clause is a finite clause as in (97a), it surfaces as the subject of the complement clause; but if the complement clause is infinitival as in (97b), it surfaces as the subject of the *seem* clause. Likewise, in (98) the italicised pronoun *they* is the thematic subject of the verb *underestimate*: if the complement clause is finite as in (98a), it surfaces as the subject of the complement clause; if the complement clause is infinitival as in (98b), it surfaces as the subject of the *appear* clause.

Examples like (95–98) suggest that verbs like *seem* and *appear* resemble passive verbs in that they allow an expression which is a theta-marked argument of a predicate in a lower clause to raise to become the subject of the (head T of TP in the) *seem-/appear*-clause. Given this assumption, sentence

(95b) will have the following simplified derivation. The unaccusative verb *remain* merges with the QP *some hope of peace* to form the VP *remain some hope of ø peace*. This VP is then merged with the infinitival tense particle *to*, forming the T-bar *to remain some hope of peace*. Infinitival *to* (like all T constituents) has an EPP feature requiring it to have a noun or pronoun expression as its subject. One way of satisfying this requirement is by merging the expletive pronoun *there* in spec-TP, so deriving the TP *there to remain some hope of peace*. The resulting infinitival TP is then merged with the verb *seem* to form the VP *seem there to remain some hope of peace*. This VP in turn is merged with the present-tense auxiliary *does* to form the T-bar *does seem there to remain some hope of ø peace*. Like all T constituents, T-*does* has an EPP feature which enables it to attract the closest noun or pronoun expression (= the expletive pronoun *there*) to become its subject, so forming the TP *There does seem ~~there~~ to remain some hope of peace*. This TP is then merged with a null indicative complementiser, so deriving the structure shown in simplified form below:

(99)

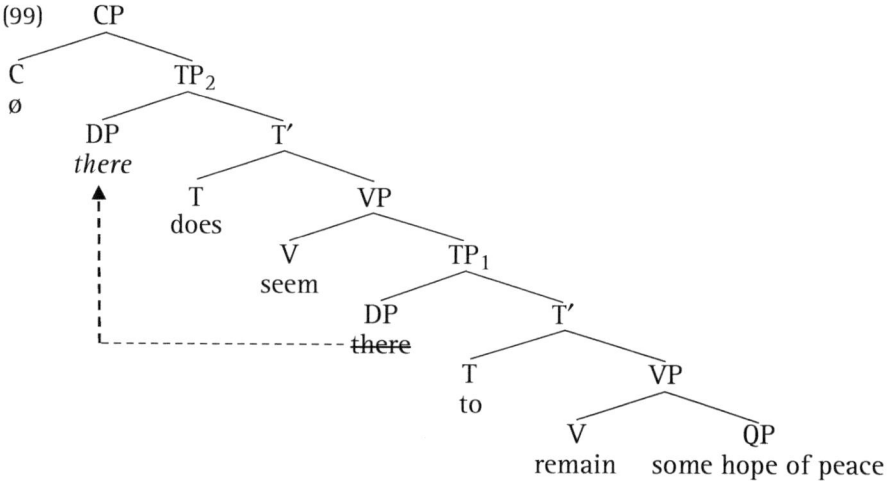

In accordance with the Default Spellout Rule (58), only the higher copy of *there* is spelled out overtly, and the overall structure in (99) is spelled out as (95a) *There does seem to remain some hope of peace*. The sentence is interpreted as declarative in force via the default Clause Typing Condition (5ii).

Now consider the derivation of (95b) *Some hope of peace does seem to remain*. Assume that this proceeds as for (95a) until we have formed the T-bar *to remain some hope of peace*. Since infinitival *to* (like all T constituents in English) has an EPP feature, it can (in conformity with the Minimality Condition 61) attract the closest nominal (= *some hope of peace*) to become its subject, so forming the TP *some hope of peace to remain ~~some hope of peace~~*. The resulting TP is then merged with the verb *seem* to form the VP *seem some hope of peace to remain ~~some hope of ø peace~~*. This VP is in turn merged with the present-tense T auxiliary *does* to form the T-bar *does seem some hope of peace to remain* ~~some hope of peace~~. Like all T-constituents, the T auxiliary *does* has an EPP feature which allows it to attract the closest nominal (= *some hope of peace*) to become its subject, so forming the TP *some hope of peace does seem* ~~some hope of peace~~ *to remain* ~~some hope of peace~~. Merging this TP with a null indicative complementiser forms the following structure (with arrows indicating A-Movement operations which take place in the course of the derivation):

(100)

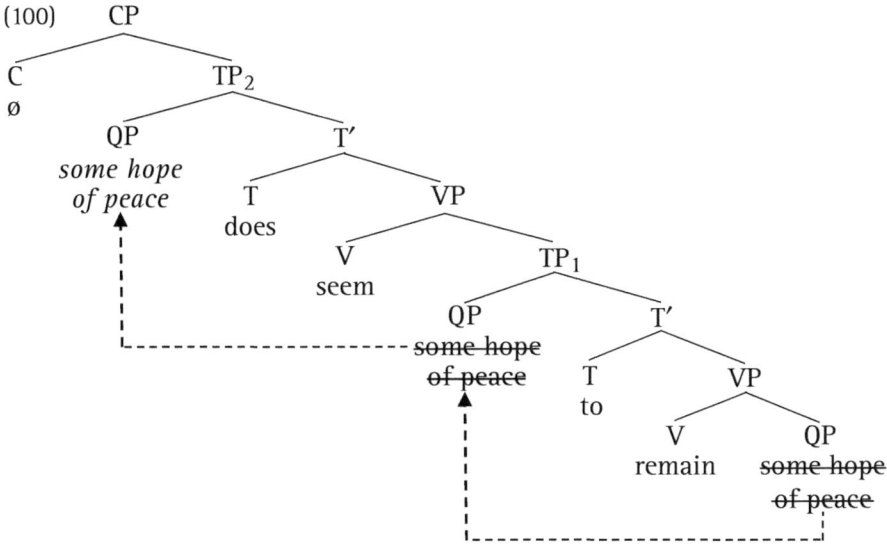

The movement operation denoted by the upper arrow by which the QP *some hope of peace* moves from being the subject of a lower TP to becoming the subject of a higher TP in (100) is traditionally known as (Subject) Raising, because it raises a noun or pronoun expression from being the subject of a lower clause to becoming the subject of a higher clause; but in reality it is yet another instance of the more general A-Movement operation by which T attracts the closest nominal which it c-commands to become its specifier (and thereby move to spec-TP). Words like *seem/appear* (when used with an infinitival complement) have the property that the subject of the *seem/ appear*-clause is created by being raised out of a complement clause, and so (for this reason) they are known as Raising predicates. The parallels between Raising in structures like (100) and long-distance Passivisation in structures like (87) are self-evident.

Although all constituents of the QP *some hope of peace* are spelled out on the highest link in the movement chain in (100) above (in accordance with the Default Spellout Rule in 58), an alternative possibility allowed for by the Low Spellout Rule (67) is that the KP/case phrase *of peace* is spelled out on the lowest link in the movement chain, and the remaining constituents of the QP (bold-printed below) on the highest link, so giving rise to the split spellout pattern below:

(101)   **Some hope** does seem to remain *of peace*

The fact that the KP *of peace* is positioned after the verb *remain* in (101) provides additional evidence that the QP *some hope of peace* originates as the complement of *remain*.

Note in addition that the assumption that the nominal *some hope of peace* moves from its underlying position as the complement of the verb *remain* into its superficial position as the subject of *does* in two successive steps (moving one TP at a time) means that A-Movement in (100) obeys the Minimality Condition (61), which requires a constituent undergoing A-Movement to become the specifier of the closest T constituent above it each time it moves. The derivation in (100) also obeys the Theta Criterion (32), since the QP *some hope of peace* originates in a θ-position in comp-VP (as the THEME argument of the verb *remain*) and from there moves to a θ-bar position as specifier of T-*to*, before going on to move to a further θ-bar position as specifier of T-*does*. Since the resulting A-chain is assigned only one theta role, it obeys the Theta Criterion.

2.5.2   Control structures

It might at first sight seem tempting to conclude from our discussion of cross-clausal Passivisation structures like (87) and Raising structures like (100) that all clauses containing a structure of the form *verb+to+infinitive* have a derivation in which some expression is raised out of the infinitive complement to become the subject of the main clause. However, any such conclusion would be undermined by the traditional claim that some verbs which take *to+infinitive* complements are Control predicates whose complement contains a PRO subject which is controlled by (i.e. takes its reference from) an antecedent in the matrix/higher clause. In this connection, consider the difference between the two types of infinitive structure below:

(102)   a. He does *seem* [to scare them]
         b. He does *want* [to scare them]

As they are used in (102), the verb *seem* is a Raising predicate, but the verb *want* is a Control predicate. We will see that this reflects the fact that the verbs *seem* and *want* differ in respect of their argument structure. We can illustrate this by sketching the derivation of the two sentences.

In the Raising structure (102a), the verb *scare* merges with (and assigns the EXPERIENCER θ-role to) its internal argument/thematic complement *them*. The resulting V-bar *scare them* then merges with (and assigns the AGENT θ-role to) its external argument/thematic subject *he*. The resulting

VP *he scare them* is subsequently merged with the infinitival tense particle *to*, so forming the T-bar *to he scare them*. Like all T constituents, T-*to* has an EPP feature which enables it to attract the closest noun or pronoun expression to become its subject, so forming the TP *he to ~~he~~ scare them*. This TP in turn merges with the Raising verb *seem* to form the VP *seem he to ~~he~~ scare them*. The resulting VP is then merged with the T auxiliary *does*. The EPP feature carried by T-*does* enables it to attract *he* to become its subject, so forming the TP *he does seem ~~he~~ to ~~he~~ scare them*. This TP is merged with a null indicative C, so deriving the structure shown in simplified form in (103) below (where the personal pronouns *he/them* are analysed as pronominal DPs):

(103)

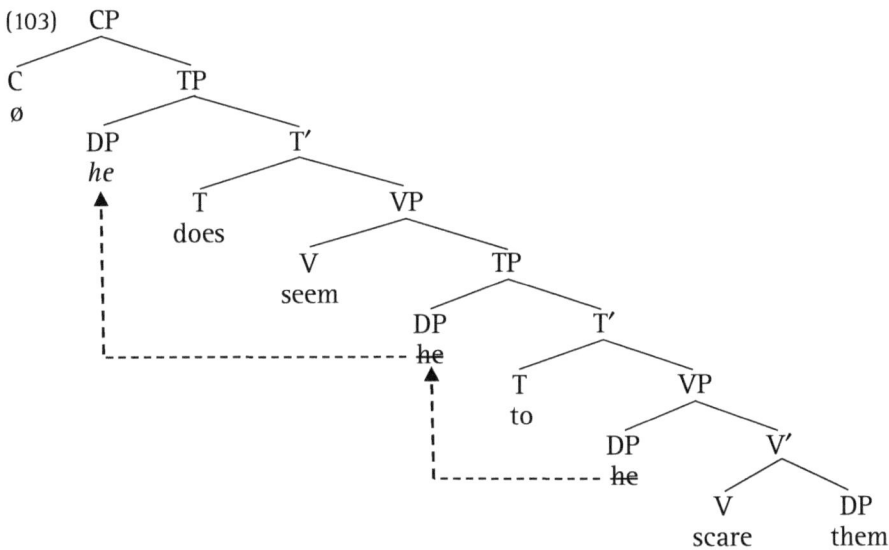

The successive-cyclic (one-TP-at-a-time) application of A-Movement in (103) satisfies the Minimality Condition (61), which requires an A-moved constituent to become the specifier of the closest T above it each time it moves: accordingly, *he* first becomes the specifier of the embedded clause T constituent *to* before moving on to become the specifier of the main clause T constituent *does*.

A key assumption made in the Raising analysis in (103) is that the verb *seem* (as used there) is a one-place predicate whose only argument is its infinitival TP complement, to which it assigns an appropriate θ-role – that of THEME argument of *seem*. This means that the VP headed by *seem* has no thematic subject: note, in particular, that the verb *seem* does not θ-mark the pronoun *he*, since *he* is θ-marked by *scare*, and the Theta Criterion (32) rules out the possibility of any argument being θ-marked by more than one predicate. Nor does the VP headed by *seem* have a structural subject at any stage of derivation, since *he* raises to become first the subject of the lower

TP headed by infinitival *to*, and then to become the subject of the higher TP headed by the present-tense T auxiliary *does* (with the movement in both cases being driven by an EPP feature on T). This underlines the point that syntactic movement operations typically move a constituent to the edge (i.e. head or specifier position) of a functional projection like TP or CP.

The property of having a THEME complement but no thematic subject means that Raising predicates like *seem* have essentially the same thematic properties as unaccusative verbs like *come* discussed in Module 2.3. Not surprisingly, therefore, many intransitive verbs like those below allow a dual use as (i) an unaccusative verb with an italicised nominal complement as in each (a) example in (104–107) below, and (ii) a Raising verb with an underlined infinitival TP complement as in the corresponding (b) example:

(104)   a. There appeared *a grotesque face* at the window
        b. His attitude appears <u>to have changed</u>

(105)   a. There has never before happened *anything quite so momentous*
        b. It happened <u>to be raining at the time</u>

(106)   a. There remain *doubts about his competence*
        b. That remains <u>to be seen</u>

(107)   a. There began *a long period of negotiation*
        b. The situation began <u>to get worse</u>

In such sentences, a Raising verb is a one-place predicate with a TP as its complement, whereas an unaccusative verb is a one-place predicate with a noun or pronoun expression as its complement.

Having looked at the Raising infinitive structure (102a), let's now turn to consider the derivation of the Control infinitive structure (102b) *He does want to scare them*. As before, the verb *scare* merges with (and assigns the EXPERIENCER θ-role to) its internal argument/thematic complement *them*. The resulting V-bar *scare them* then merges with (and assigns the AGENT θ-role to) its external argument. Given the traditional assumption that Control infinitives have a particular kind of null pronominal subject known as 'big PRO' (because PRO is written in upper case letters), the thematic subject of *scare them* will be PRO, and this will be merged in spec-VP (in accordance with the VP-Internal Subject Hypothesis), and thereby be assigned the θ-role of AGENT argument of *scare*. The resulting VP *PRO scare them* then merges with the infinitival tense particle T-*to*, forming the T-bar *to PRO scare them*. The EPP feature of infinitival *to* enables it to attract PRO to become its subject, so forming the TP *PRO to ~~PRO~~ scare them*. Given the assumption that Control infinitives are CPs (for reasons set out in Radford 2020: 207–10), this TP will in turn merge with a null infinitival complementiser to form the CP *ø PRO to ~~PRO~~ scare them*. The CP thereby formed serves as the internal argument (and thematic complement) of the verb *want*, so is merged with *want* and thereby assigned the θ-role of THEME argument of *want*. The resulting V-bar *want ø PRO to ~~PRO~~ scare them* then merges with its external argument (and thematic subject) *he*, assigning *he* the thematic role of EXPERIENCER argument of *want*. The resulting VP *he want ø PRO to ~~PRO~~ scare them* is then merged with the T auxiliary *does*, forming the T-bar *does he want ø PRO to ~~PRO~~ scare them*. The EPP feature carried by T-*does* enables it to attract the closest noun or pronoun expression which it c-commands (= *he*) to become its subject, so forming the TP *he does ~~he~~ want ø PRO to ~~PRO~~ scare them*. Merging the resulting TP with a null indicative complementiser to form a CP which is interpreted as declarative in force by default forms the structure shown in simplified form in (108) below (with arrows marking A-Movement operations):

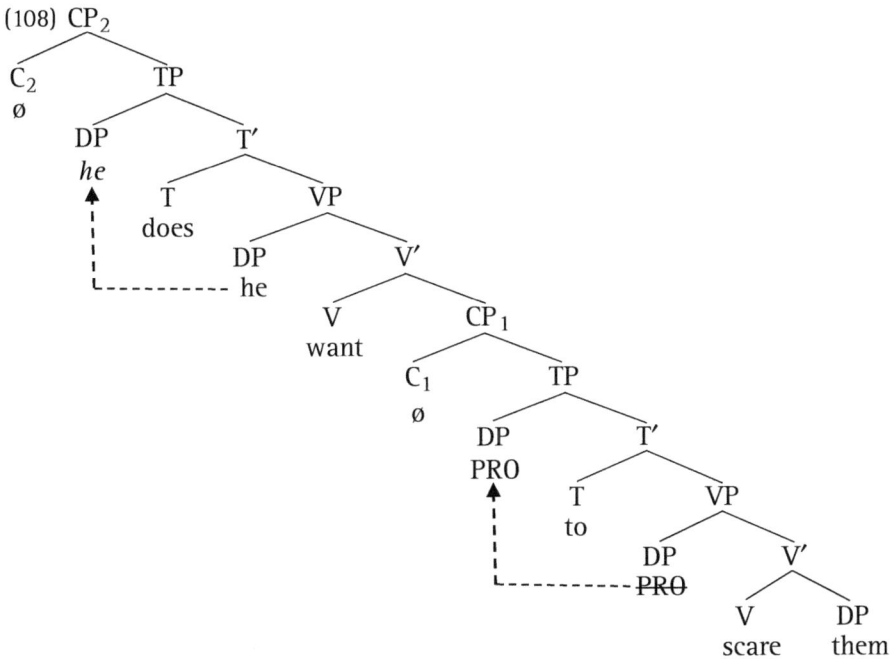

(108) CP_2

[Tree diagram:
CP_2 branches to C_2 (ø) and TP.
TP branches to DP (*he*, with upward arrow) and T'.
T' branches to T (*does*) and VP.
VP branches to DP (*he*, connected by dashed arrow from *he*) and V'.
V' branches to V (*want*) and CP_1.
CP_1 branches to C_1 (ø) and TP.
TP branches to DP (PRO, with upward arrow) and T'.
T' branches to T (*to*) and VP.
VP branches to DP (~~PRO~~, connected by dashed arrow) and V'.
V' branches to V (*scare*) and DP (*them*).]

The resulting structure satisfies the Theta Criterion (32) (which requires each argument to be assigned a single θ-role, and each θ-role to be assigned to a single argument), in that *he* is the EXPERIENCER argument of *want*, the bracketed CP is the THEME complement of *want*, PRO is the AGENT argument of *scare*, and *them* the EXPERIENCER argument of *scare*. The main clause subject *he* is assigned nominative case by the finite complementiser in C_2, and the complement clause subject PRO is assigned null case by the null infinitival complementiser in C_1.

The analysis of Control predicates presented here assumes that the PRO subject of a Control infinitive like that bracketed in (102b) *He does want to scare them* is initially merged in spec-VP. The requirement for PRO to be generated in spec-VP follows from the VP-Internal Subject Hypothesis and the Predicate-Internal Theta-Marking Hypothesis which posit that arguments are generated and theta-marked internally to a projection of their predicate, so that PRO (by virtue of being the AGENT argument of *scare*) is generated as the specifier of the VP headed by *scare*. However, given that all T constituents in English have an EPP feature, the EPP feature on infinitival *to* will attract PRO to move out of the VP in which it originates into the specifier position of the TP headed by infinitival *to*. Since movement of an empty category like PRO out of the VP into spec-TP is by nature invisible, an obvious question which arises is whether there is any empirical evidence that PRO moves to spec-TP rather than remaining in situ within VP. The answer, as we shall see, is 'Yes'.

One piece of evidence suggesting that PRO does indeed move to spec-TP in Control infinitives comes from the syntax of constituents like those italicised in (109) below which have the property that they are construed as modifying a bold-printed antecedent which is not immediately adjacent to them:

(109)   a. **They** were *both* priding themselves on their achievements
         b. I don't *myself* think that Hubert Hedge-Hogge should manage the hedgefund
         c. **He** was *personally* held responsible

In (109a), *both* is a floating quantifier (and *each/all* can be used in a similar fashion); in (109b), *myself* is a floating emphatic reflexive; and in (109c), *personally* is an argument-oriented adverb (construed as modifying an argument, in this case *he*). In each sentence in (109), the italicised expression is construed as modifying the bold-printed subject of the clause. Contrasts such as those in (110) and (111) suggest that a floating modifier must be c-commanded by its bold-printed antecedent:

(110)   a. **Two republican senators** were *themselves* thought to have been implicated
         b. *There were *themselves* thought to have been implicated **two republican senators**

(111)   a. **Two republican senators** are *both* thought to have been implicated
         b. *There are *both* thought to have been implicated **two republican senators**

In the light of the requirement for a floating modifier to be c-commanded by its antecedent, consider the syntax of the bracketed clauses in the following sentences:

(112)   a. [To *both* be betrayed by their friends] would be disastrous for Romeo and Juliet
   b. [To *themselves* be indicted] would be unfair on the company directors
   c. It was upsetting [to *personally* have been accused of corruption]

In each of these examples, the bracketed clause is a Control clause containing a PRO argument. In each case, PRO is the thematic complement of a passive participle (viz. *betrayed/indicted/accused*). Hence, if Control *to* had no EPP feature and PRO remained in situ in comp-VP, the TP in the bracketed infinitive complement in (112b) would have the skeletal structure (113a) below (if we take *be* to be a passive VOICE auxiliary heading a VOICEP projection); but if (as claimed here) Control *to* has an EPP feature, this will trigger movement of PRO to become the structural subject of *to*, resulting in the structure (113b):

(113)   a. $[_{CP} [_C \text{ø}] [_{TP} [_T \text{ to}] [_{VOICEP} \text{ themselves } [_{VOICE} \text{ be}] [_{VP} [_V \text{ indicted}] \text{ PRO}]]]]$
   b. $[_{CP} [_C \text{ø}] [_{TP} \text{ PRO } [_T \text{ to}] [_{VOICEP} \text{ themselves } [_{VOICE} \text{ be}] [_{VP} [_V \text{ indicted}] \text{ ~~PRO~~}]]]]$

Given the requirement for a floating emphatic reflexive to be c-commanded by its antecedent, and given that PRO is the intended antecedent of *themselves* in (113), it is clear that (113a) cannot be the right structure, since PRO does not c-command *themselves* in (113a). By contrast, movement of PRO to spec-TP in (113b) means that PRO will indeed c-command *themselves*, so correctly predicting that (112b) is grammatical. Thus, sentences such as (112) provide empirical evidence that PRO moves to spec-TP in Control clauses, and thereby becomes the subject of infinitival *to*. This in turn is consistent with the more general claim that all T-constituents in English have an EPP feature requiring them to have a subject/specifier.

2.5.3   Differences between Raising and Control

An important syntactic difference between Raising and Control structures concerns the status of the infinitival complement of the two types of verb. In this connection, compare the derivation of the Raising structure in (103) above with that of the Control structure in (108). Whereas the infinitive complement of the Raising verb *seem* in (103) is a TP, by contrast the infinitive complement of the Control verb *want* in (108) is a CP. Theoretical considerations lend support to this conclusion. Since the subject of a Raising verb is raised out of its infinitive complement, the infinitive complement of a Raising verb cannot be a CP, because the Impenetrability

Condition (91) prevents A-Movement from applying across a CP boundary. Conversely, if (as claimed in §2.3.2) PRO is assigned null case by a c-commanding null complementiser, it follows that the infinitive complement of the Control verb *want* in (108) must be a CP headed by a null complementiser.

Having compared the syntax of Control predicates with that of Raising predicates, let's look briefly at the question of how we can determine whether a given predicate which selects an infinitival *to* complement is a Control predicate or a Raising predicate. There are a number of differences between them which are a direct reflection of the different thematic properties of these two types of predicate. For example, Raising predicates like *seem* can have expletive *it/there* subjects, whereas Control predicates like *want* cannot: cf.

(114)   a. *It* seems/*wants to be assumed that he lied to Congress
         b. *There* seem/*want to remain several unanswered questions

(The expletive nature of *it* in 114a is shown by the fact that it cannot be substituted by a referential pronoun like *this/that*, or questioned by *what?* Likewise, the expletive nature of *there* in 114b is shown by the fact that it cannot be substituted by a referential locative pronoun like *here*, or questioned by *where?*) This is because Control predicates like *want* are two-place predicates which project a thematic subject (an EXPERIENCER in the case of *want*, so that the subject of *want* must be an expression denoting a sentient entity capable of experiencing desires), and non-referential expressions like expletive *it/there* clearly do not denote sentient entities and so cannot serve as the thematic subject of a verb like *want*. By contrast, Raising predicates like *seem* do not theta-mark their subject, and hence impose no restrictions on the choice of structural subject in their clause, so allowing a (non-thematic) expletive subject.

Similarly, Raising predicates like *seem* (but not Control predicates like *want*) allow idiomatic subjects such as those italicised below:

(115)   a. *All hell* seems/*wants to break loose whenever they meet
         b. *The fur* seems/*wants to fly whenever they meet
         c. *The cat* seems/*wants to get his tongue whenever they meet

The ungrammaticality of sentences like **All hell wants to break loose* can be attributed to the fact that *want* is a Control predicate, and hence (in order to derive such a structure) it would be necessary to assume that *all hell* originates as the subject of *want*, and that *break loose* has a separate PRO subject of its own: but this would violate the requirement that (in its idiomatic use) *all hell* can only occur as the subject of *break loose*, and conversely *break loose* (in its idiomatic use) only allows *all hell* as its subject.

By contrast, *All hell seems to break loose* is grammatical because *seem* is a Raising predicate, and so *all hell* will originate as the subject of *break loose* and then be raised up to become the subject of (the present tense affix in T in) the *seem* clause.

A further property which differentiates the two types of predicate is that Raising predicates like *seem* allow long Passivisation with preservation of synonymy, so that (116a) below is synonymous with (116b):

(116)　a.　John seems to have helped Mary
　　　　b.　=Mary seems to have been helped by John

By contrast, Control predicates like *want* do not preserve synonymy in long passives, as we see from the fact that (117a) below is not synonymous with (117b):

(117)　a.　John wants to help Mary
　　　　b.　≠Mary wants to be helped by John

Moreover, there are selection restrictions on the choice of subject which Control predicates like *want* allow (in that the subject generally has to be an animate being, not an inanimate entity) – as we see from (118) below (where ! marks anomaly):

(118)　*My cat/!My gesture* wants to be appreciated

By contrast, Raising predicates like *seem* freely allow animate or inanimate subjects:

(119)　*My cat/My gesture* seems to have been appreciated

The different properties of the two types of predicate stem from the fact that Control predicates like *want* θ-mark their subjects, whereas Raising predicates like *seem* do not: so, since *want* selects an EXPERIENCER subject as its external argument (and a prototypical EXPERIENCER is an animate being), *want* allows an animate subject like *my cat*, but not an inanimate subject like *my gesture*. By contrast, since Raising predicates like *seem* do not θ-mark their subjects, they impose no restrictions on their choice of subject.

An important point to note is that although our discussion of Raising and Control predicates has revolved around verbs, a parallel distinction is found in adjectives. For example, in sentences such as (120), the adjective *likely* is a Raising predicate and *keen* a Control predicate:

(120)　a.　*John* is **likely** to win the race
　　　　b.　*John* is **keen** to win the race

We can see this from the fact that *likely* allows expletive and idiomatic subjects, but *keen* does not: cf.

(121)   a.   *There* is **likely/*keen** to be a strike
          b.   *All hell* is **likely/*keen** to break loose

Moreover, Raising structures like (120a) typically allow an impersonal finite clause paraphrase in which the *likely*-clause has an (italicised) non-thematic expletive subject:

(122)   a.   *It* is **likely** that John will win the race
          b.   *There* is every **likelihood** that John will win the race

By contrast, Control structures like (120b) typically allow a personal finite clause paraphrase in which the main and complement clauses have (coreferential) personal/thematic subjects (like those italicised below):

(123)   *John* is keen that *he* should win the race

The fact that adjectives can have the same range of complements as verbs is one reason why I have talked about different types of <u>predicate</u> (drawing a distinction between Raising and Control predicates) rather than different types of verb.

A final point to note is the following. Although a distinction has been drawn here between Raising and Control predicates, some predicates have a range of different uses, and are able to function as Raising predicates in one use, but as Control predicates in another. This can be illustrated by the sentences below:

(124)   a.   *John* **promised** to do his duty
          b.   *There* is **promising** to be a spectacular end to the season

The verb *promise* in (124a) shows the hallmarks of a Control predicate, as we see below:

(125)   a.   **It* promised that *John* would do his duty
          b.   *John* promised that *he* would do his duty
          c.   John *solemnly* promised to do his duty
          d.   What John promised was *to do his duty*

Thus, *promise* requires an animate subject like *John* in (124a) and does not allow an expletive subject like *it* in (125a). Moreover, (124a) has a personal (*John ... he*) paraphrase in (125b), its subject can be modified by a thematic adverb like *solemnly* (i.e. one which can modify a thematic subject) in (125c), and its complement can appear in focus position in a pseudo-cleft like (125d).

By contrast, *promise* in (124b) behaves like a Raising predicate in allowing an expletive pronoun like *there* as its subject in (126a) below, in not allowing the use of a thematic adverb like *solemnly* in (126b), and in not allowing its complement to be focused in a pseudo-cleft sentence like (126c):

(126)   a. *There is promising that there will be a spectacular end to the season
        b. *There is solemnly promising to be a spectacular end to the season
        c. *What there is promising is to be a spectacular end to the season

So, while there are clear differences between Raising and Control predicates (as we have seen), we need to bear in mind that some predicates exhibit dual behaviour (functioning as Raising predicates in one type of use, and as Control predicates in another).
        You should now be able to tackle Exercise 2.5.

2.6   Mixed structures

Modules 2.3–2.5 in this chapter have provided an introduction to four different types of structure: unaccusative, passive, raising and control structures. Although our discussion of these structures above dealt with each separately, it is important to note that any given sentence can involve two or more of them, thereby giving rise to mixed structures. In this module, I'll briefly illustrate this by looking at just two (of the many) different types of mixed structure.

2.6.1   A mixed Passive, Control and Raising sentence
An example which illustrates how different types of structure can be combined within a single sentence is the following:

(127)   He seems to be keen to be promoted

As we saw in §2.5.3, the verb seem behaves like a Raising predicate in not theta-marking its subject, and hence allows an unrestricted choice of subjects (including an expletive subject in 128a below and an idiomatic subject in 128b), and also allows cross-clausal Passivisation in (128c):

(128)   a. There seems to be no easy answer
        b. All hell seems to have broken loose
        c. The plan seems [to have been changed –]

By contrast, the adjective keen functions as a Control predicate, in that it assigns the theta role of EXPERIENCER to its subject, and hence keen does not allow non-thematic (e.g. expletive or idiomatic) subjects as in (129a, 129b) below, nor does it allow long/cross-clausal Passivisation in sentences like (129c):

(129)   a. *There is keen to be peace
        b. *All hell is keen to break loose
        c. *The plan is keen [to be changed –]

As a Control predicate, *keen* selects/takes a CP complement with a PRO subject; but because *to be promoted* is a passive clause, PRO originates as the complement of the passive participle *promoted*, and from there moves to become the specifier/subject of infinitival *to* in *to be promoted*; the controller of PRO (i.e. the constituent which PRO refers back to) is the pronoun *he*.

Evidence that *keen* takes a CP complement comes from the observation that when it has a *to*-infinitive complement like that italicised below, its infinitive complement can be coordinated with a (bold-printed) infinitival CP headed by the infinitival complementiser *for*:

(130)   He is keen *to go to Rome*, and **for me to go with him**

Moreover, *to be promoted* in our example sentence (127) is paraphrasable as a CP headed by C-*for*, or as a CP headed by C-*that* – as below:

(131)   a.   He seems to be keen [$_{CP}$ [$_C$ *for*] *himself to be promoted*]
          b.   He seems to be keen [$_{CP}$ [$_C$ *that*] *he should be promoted*]

Given these (and other) assumptions, our example sentence (127) will be derived as follows.

The PRO subject of the infinitive *to be promoted* will originate as the THEME complement of the passive participle *promoted* and be attracted by the EPP feature on the infinitive particle *to* in T to move to spec-TP where it is assigned null case by the null infinitival complementiser heading CP, thereby deriving the structure in (132) below (where the arrow marks the Passivisation operation which PRO undergoes, and the position out of which PRO moves is shown as a gap):

(132)

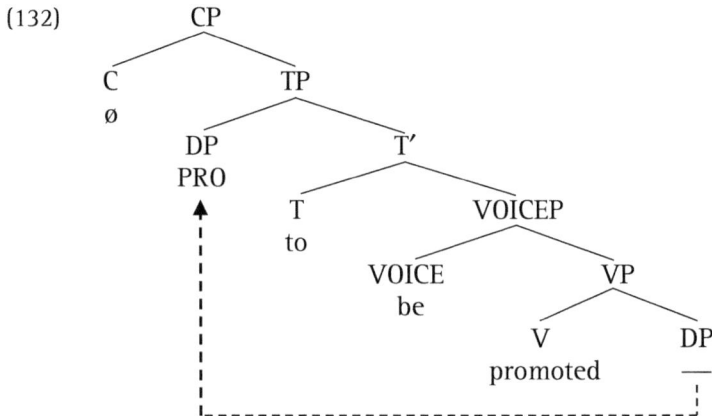

The resulting CP is then merged as the complement of the A/adjective *keen*, forming the AP *keen ø PRO to be promoted –*. The verb *be* is first-merged with this AP, and second-merged with the pronoun/pronominal DP *he*, forming the VP *he be keen ø PRO to be promoted –* (where *he* has the thematic role of the EXPERIENCER argument of *be keen*). The resulting VP is merged with the infinitive particle T-*to*, and the EPP feature on T-*to* attracts *he* to move (via the A-Movement operation arrowed below) to become its specifier, so deriving the following structure (simplified by not showing the internal structure of CP, which is given in 132 above):

(133)

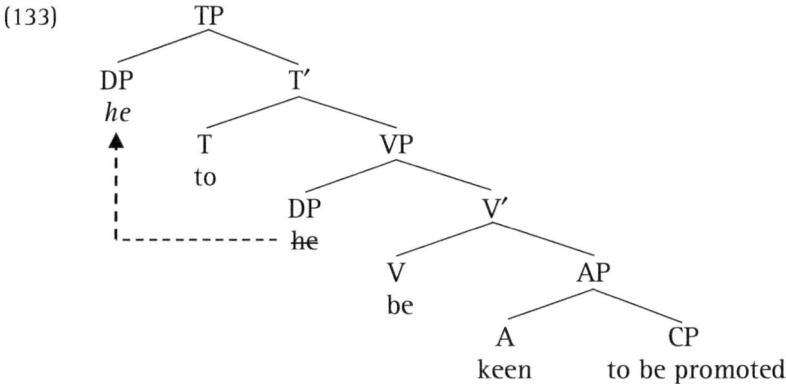

The resulting TP is then merged with the verb *seem*, forming a VP which can be represented in simplified form as *seem he to be keen to be promoted*. This VP is then merged with a T head containing a present tense affix (T-*Af*), and this affix carries an EPP feature which attracts the pronoun *he* to undergo the Raising operation arrowed in (134) below, and thereby move to spec-TP. Merging the TP thereby formed with a null complementiser forms the CP below (simplified by not showing the internal structure of the VP *be keen to be promoted*):

(134)

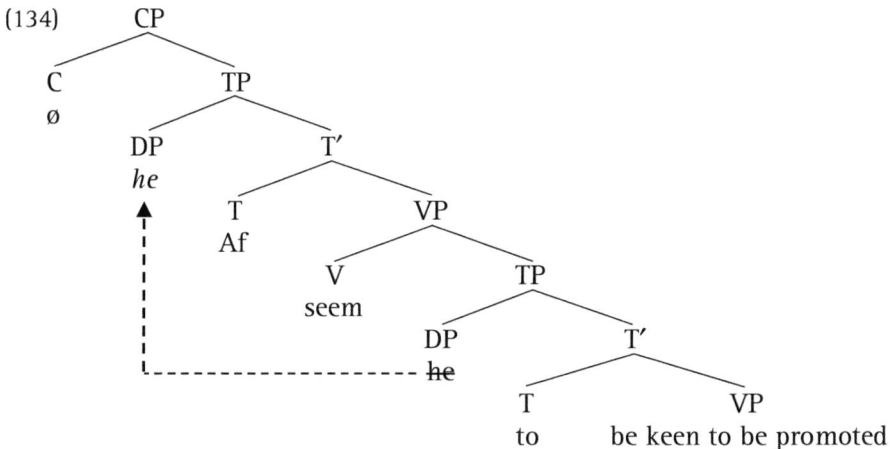

The pronoun *he* is assigned nominative case by the null finite complementiser immediately above it. The present tense affix in the main clause lowers from T onto the verb *seem* by Affix Hopping in the PF component, with the result that the verb is spelled out as *seems*. The derivation satisfies the Theta Criterion, since each argument carries a single theta role: PRO is the THEME argument of *promoted*, and *he* the EXPERIENCER argument of *be keen*. Both PRO and *he* originate internally within VP, in accordance with the VP-Internal Subject Hypothesis. None of the movements arrowed in (132–134) violates the Impenetrability Condition, since none involves movement across the edge of an intervening CP. But for present purposes, what is more important is that our example sentence (127) *He seems to be keen to be promoted* has a mixed structure which involves Passivisation, Control and Raising.

2.6.2   A mixed Unaccusative and Raising sentence

Another type of mixed structure can be found in the sentence below:

(135)   Several details have started to emerge of the proposals

In this sentence, the KP/case phrase *of the proposals* originates as the complement of the noun *details*. We can see this from the observation that the relevant KP can be positioned immediately after the noun *details* (as expected if it is the complement of *details*) in a sentence like:

(136)   Several details <u>of the proposals</u> have started to emerge

Consequently, it is plausible to take *several details of the proposals* to be a QP. This QP originates as the complement of the unaccusative verb *emerge*, as we see from the observation that it can follow *emerge* in an expletive sentence such as:

(137)   There have started to emerge *several details of the proposals*

But if the QP *several details of the proposals* originates as the complement of the verb *emerge*, how does it come to end up as the subject of the *started* clause?

A relevant point to note in this regard is that *start* can function as a Raising predicate in not theta-marking its subject, and hence allowing an unrestricted choice of subjects (including an expletive subject as in 138a below, and an idiomatic subject as in 138b), and also allowing cross-clausal Passivisation (as in 138c):

(138)   a. *There* are starting to be problems
         b. *All hell* is starting to break loose
         c. *A plan* is starting [to be developed –]

These considerations (and others) suggest that the QP *several details of the proposals* originates in comp-VP as the complement of the unaccusative verb *emerge* in (135), and then raises up (in a successive-cyclic fashion) first to become the specifier of infinitival *to*, and then to become the specifier of

T-*have* (in each case, attracted by an EPP feature on T-*to*/T-*have*), so resulting in the A-Movement operations shown by the arrows below:

(139)

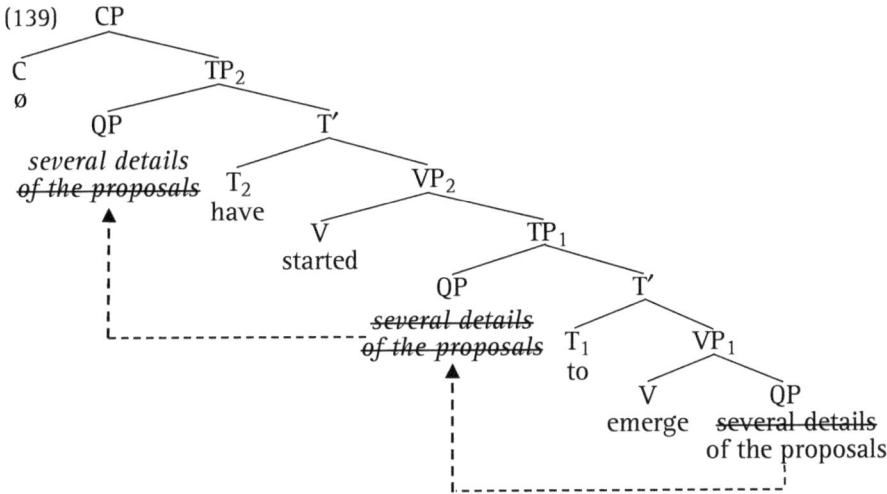

When the structure in (139) is handed over to the PF component, spellout rules determine what is overtly spelled out, and what is silent. One possibility is that (via the Low Spellout Rule 67) the lowest copy of the KP *of the proposals* and the highest copy of the string *several details* are spelled out overtly, so giving rise to the discontinuous spellout pattern that we find in (135) '*Several details* have started to emerge of the proposals'. However, for the purposes of this module, the more important point to underline is that (135/139) is a mixed *Raising+unaccusative* structure, serving to underline the key point made in this module that sentences can be built up out of a number of different types of structure.

You should now be able to tackle Exercise 2.6.

2.7   Summary

This chapter has been concerned with the syntax of subjects. In Module 2.1, I argued that Belfast English sentences such as *There should some students get distinctions* provide us with evidence that subjects originate internally within VP, and I noted that this claim is known as the VP-Internal Subject Hypothesis/VPISH. I also argued that standard English sentences such as *Some students should get distinctions* involve movement of *some students* from the specifier position within VP to the specifier position within TP, and we saw that the relevant movement operation is known as A-Movement. I went on to argue that idiomatic structures like *All hell will break loose* provide empirical support for the VPISH.

In Module 2.2, I noted that the VP-Internal Subject Hypothesis allows us to posit a uniform mapping (i.e. relationship) between thematic argument structure and syntactic structure, if we suppose that all arguments of a predicate originate (and are theta-marked) internally within a projection of the predicate.

In Module 2.3, we looked at the syntax of unaccusative predicates like *arise/remain/occur* etc. and we saw that the subject of an unaccusative verb originates as its complement but differs from the complement of a transitive verb in that (in a finite clause) it receives nominative rather than accusative case. We examined a number of further differences between unaccusative predicates and other types of predicate (e.g. in relation to the position of subjects in Belfast English imperatives, and auxiliary selection in earlier varieties of English).

In Module 2.4, we began by looking at the structure of simple passive clauses, and I argued that a passive subject originates as the thematic complement of a subjectless passive participle, and is raised into spec-TP (via A-Movement) in order to satisfy the EPP feature of T. We also saw that Passivisation can be a long-distance operation involving cross-clausal movement of an argument contained within an infinitival TP which is the complement of a passive participle. I observed that (in consequence of every T carrying an EPP feature requiring it to have a subject), the passivised nominal moves in a successive-cyclic fashion, first into the closest spec-TP position above it, then into the next closest spec-TP position above it (and so on), in conformity with the Minimality Condition.

In Module 2.5, I argued that predicates like *seem/appear* function as Raising predicates in the sense that their subjects originate internally within their infinitive complement, and from there are raised into the spec-TP position within the *seem/appear*-clause: hence, in a sentence such as *All hell would appear to have broken loose*, the idiomatic expression *all hell* originates as the subject of *broken loose* and from there is raised up (one TP at a time) first to become the specifier/subject of the lower TP headed by infinitival *to*, and then to become the specifier/subject of the higher TP headed by the auxiliary *would*. I contrasted Raising predicates with Control predicates, noting that they differ in that Control predicates theta-mark their subjects (and hence require an animate subject) and have a CP complement, whereas Raising predicates do not theta-mark their subjects (and hence freely allow inanimate, expletive and idiomatic subjects) and have a TP complement. We also saw that (unlike Control predicates), Raising predicates allow long/cross-clausal Passivisation.

In Module 2.6, I argued that complex sentences can contain a mixture of different types of (e.g. unaccusative, passive, raising and/or control) predicates, so giving rise to what I termed 'mixed structures'.

Key constructs which our discussion in this chapter made use of include the following (where *below* = 'c-commanded by', and *above* = 'c-commanding'):

(32)   Theta Criterion/θ-criterion
       Each argument bears one and only one θ-role, and each θ-role is
       assigned to one and only one argument (Chomsky 1981: 36)

(36)   Predicate-Internal Theta-Marking Hypothesis
       An argument is theta-marked internally within a projection of a
       predicate, either directly by being merged with the predicate, or
       indirectly by being merged with an intermediate projection of the
       predicate

(56)   Uniform Theta Assignment Hypothesis/UTAH
       Constituents which fulfil the same thematic role with respect to a given
       predicate occupy the same initial position in the syntax

(61)   Minimality Condition/MC
       A constituent can only enter into a syntactic relation with the minimal
       (= closest) constituent of the relevant type above/below it

(91)   Impenetrability Condition
       Anything below the head C of a CP is impenetrable to anything above
       the CP

(94)   COMP-Trace Filter/CTF
       Any structure at the end of a syntactic derivation in which an overt
       COMP/complementiser is immediately adjacent to and c-commands a
       trace (i.e. a gap/null copy left behind by a moved constituent) is filtered
       out as ill-formed

2.8   Bibliographical notes

Evidence adduced in support of the **VP-Internal Subject Hypothesis** outlined in Module 2.1 can be found in a variety of works dating back to the mid-1980s, including Kitagawa (1986, 1994), Speas (1986), Sportiche (1986, 1988), Contreras (1987), Zagona (1987), Kuroda (1988), Rosen (1990), Ernst (1991), Koopman & Sportiche (1991), Woolford (1991), Burton & Grimshaw (1992), McNally (1992), Guilfoyle et al. (1992), Huang (1993), and McCloskey (1997). On **in-situ subjects** (i.e. structures in which subjects remain in situ internally within VP), see Haider (2005) and Wurmbrandt (2006) for German; Alexiadou & Anagnastopoulou (2001) for Greek; Tateishi (1995) for Japanese; Öztürk (2005) for Turkish; and Berger (2015) for Spanish.

For discussion of **quantifier scope** in A-Movement structures, see Lebeaux (1995), Hornstein (1995), Romero (1997), Sauerland (1998), Lasnik (1998, 1999), Fox (2000), Boeckx (2000, 2001) and Fox & Nissenbaum (2004). In relation to the **EPP feature**, it should be noted that some linguists have attempted to eliminate EPP as a factor in driving movement of a subject out of VP into spec-TP (e.g. Grohmann et al. 2000, Epstein et al. 2005, Bošković 2007, Castillo et al. 2009, Cable 2012, and Chomsky 2015). On **expletive** *there* structures in Belfast English, see Borsley (2010); and on the semantics of expletive *there*, see Moro (1997, 2006), and Kayne (2016, 2019). The ideas on **theta roles** discussed in Module 2.2 date back to pioneering work by Gruber (1965, 1976), Fillmore (1968, 1970), and Jackendoff (1972). On the **Theta Criterion**, see Chomsky (1981, 1986a, 1995, 2021), and Collins (2021); for a critical perspective, see Heim & Kratzer (1998), Bruening (2013), Legate (2014), and Alexiadou et. al. (2015). The discussion of **unaccusative predicates** in Module 2.3 and the idea that unaccusative subjects originate as the complements of their associated verbs dates back to work by Burzio (1986) on Italian, and Contreras (1986) on Spanish.

On the **Constraint on Extraction Domains/CED**, see Nunes & Uriagereka (2000), Sabel (2002), Rackowski & Richards (2005), Chomsky (2005, 2008), Stepanov (2007), Müller (2010), Jurka (2010), Jurka et al. (2011), Sheehan (2013a, 2013b), and Sprouse et al. (2013). On potential problems with CED, see Starke (2001: 40, fn.10), Stepanov (2001, 2007), Truswell (2007, 2009, 2011), Chomsky (2008), Chaves (2012, 2013), Haegeman et al. (2014), and Muñoz Pérez et al. (2021).

For a range of views on the nature of the **COMP-Trace Filter**, see Perlmutter (1968, 1971), Chomsky & Lasnik (1977), Pesetsky (1982b, 2016), Bayer (1984a), Sobin (1987, 2002, 2009, 2016), Browning (1996), Szczegielniak (1999), Roussou (2000), Pesetsky & Torrego (2001, 2004), Ackema & Neeleman (2003), Kandybowicz (2006), Lohndal (2009), Ackema (2010), Ha (2010), Bošković (2011a), Llinàs-Grau & Fernández Sánchez (2013), Sato & Dobashi (2013), Erlewine (2014, 2017a), Bošković (2016), Brillman & Hirsch (2016), Douglas (2017), and Pesetsky (2021).

The use of (the counterpart of) BE rather than HAVE as a perfect aspect (or past tense) auxiliary with **unaccusative verbs** is found in a number of languages – for example, Italian and French (Burzio 1986), Sardinian (Jones 1994), German and Dutch (Haegeman 1994), and Danish (Spencer 1991): see Sorace (2000) for further discussion of auxilary selection. On unaccusative structures like *The stockmarket dropped 250 points today*, see Nakajima (2006).

On the syntax of **passives** (and the use of *by*-phrases) in structures like those discussed in Module 2.4, see Jaeggli (1986), Roberts (1987), Baker et al. (1989), Åfarli (1989), Mahajan (1994), Goodall (1997), Embick (1998), Bowers (2002), Collins (2005, 2018, 2021), Meltzer-Asscher (2012), Alexiadou &

Schäfer (2013), Bruening (2013), Legate (2014), Alexiadou et al. (2015, 2018), and Angelopoulos et al. (2020). On the syntax of *get*-passives like *John got arrested*, see Haegeman (1985), Fox & Grodzinsky (1998), Authier & Reed (2009), Brownlow (2011), and Reed (2011). The **Uniform Theta Assignment Hypothesis** was devised by Baker (1988: 46; 1997: 74), but it is rejected (inter alia) by proponents of the Movement Theory of Control (see below). For evidence that **long/cross-clausal A-Movement** applies in a successive-cyclic fashion, see Bošković (2002), Lasnik (2006), and Boeckx (2007).

For more detail on the properties of Raising predicates discussed in Module 2.5 and on the differences between **Control and Raising predicates**, see Davies & Dubinsky (2004). For evidence that Control infinitives are CPs, see Rizzi (1982), van Riemsdijk (1985), Kayne (1989, 1991), Wilder (1989), Branigan (1992) and Sabel (1996). Note that some verbs (e.g. *begin, continue, fail*, and *start*) are ambiguous between being Raising or Control verbs (in the sense that they can be used as either): see Perlmutter (1970), and (on the learnability problem which this poses for children) Becker (2006).

Finally, it should be noted that this chapter presents the classical theory of Control assumed by Chomsky in his own work. An alternative **Movement Theory of Control** has been developed by Bowers (1973), O'Neil (1995), Hornstein (1999, 2001, 2003), Boeckx (2000, 2007), Manzini & Roussou (2000), Boeckx & Hornstein (2003, 2004, 2006a, 2006b), and Grohmann (2003): the key assumption of the movement analysis is that in a sentence such as *Jim will try to open it*, the nominal *Jim* originates as the subject of the embedded clause verb *open* and then raises up to become the subject of (and acquire an additional theta role from) the main clause verb *try*. For a critique of the movement analysis, see Landau (2006). For a very different account of Control which posits that PRO does not exist and that Control clauses are subjectless, see Jackendoff & Culicover (2003), and Culicover & Jackendoff (2001, 2005, 2006).

2.9   Workbook

In the exercises below, an [M] after an example sentence indicates that a model answer is provided in the free-to-download *Students' Answerbook* (and in the *Teachers' Answerbook* as well). You will find it helpful to look at this model answer before attempting to tackle other examples in the exercise. Some other exercise examples have an [S] after them, indicating that they are for self-study: this means that after reading the relevant module (and those preceding it), and looking at the helpful hints and model answer associated with the exercise, students should be able to analyse these self-study examples on their own, and then compare their answers with those

provided in the *Students' Answerbook*. The remaining exercise examples
(i.e. those not marked with [M] or [S] after them) are intended for teachers
to use as the basis for hands-on problem-solving work in seminars, classes,
or assignments: answers to all of these non-self-study examples are provided in the *Teachers' Answerbook*. Note that Exercise 2.1 tests you on
Module 2.1, Exercise 2.2 on Module 2.2, and so on; and that each exercise
in a given chapter presupposes familiarity with material covered in earlier
chapters and in earlier modules of the same chapter. Unparenthesised numbers like 4 refer to material in the exercises, whereas parenthesised numbers
like (22) refer to examples and conditions in the main text of the book.

EXERCISE 2.1

*This exercise is designed to be attempted after reading Module 2.1 and the
chapter preceding it.*

In §2.1.2, it was suggested that evidence from floating quantifiers (i.e.
quantifiers which 'float' in a position below – and are separate from – the
subject which they are construed as modifying) provides an argument
in support of the VP-Internal Subject Hypothesis, if subjects originate
internally within VP and from there move to spec-TP by A-Movement.
Bearing in mind the helpful hints below and the two alternative analyses
sketched in the model answer in the Answerbook, discuss whether this
claim is compatible with the syntax of the universal quantifiers *all/both* in
sentences such as the following:

1a Both the detectives have examined the body [M]
1b The detectives have both examined the body [M]
2a Both the boys were proud of her
2b The boys were both proud of her
3a Both the boys must have been playing golf [S]
3b The boys must have been both playing golf [S]
3c The boys must have both been playing golf [S]
3d The boys must both have been playing golf [S]
4a All the men were arrested
4b The men were all arrested
4c *The men were arrested all

Helpful hints
Consider the possibility that floating quantifiers occupy positions which
the phrases they head originate in (or transit through) on the way to
spec-TP. Compare the two different accounts of floating quantifiers
given in the model answer (in the *Answerbook*), and see how (or indeed

whether) either analysis can account for each of the example sentences. For the purposes of this exercise, assume that *have* in 1a and 1b is a finite auxiliary directly generated in T (setting aside the possibility that it may originate as the head of a PERFP/perfect aspect phrase projection, and from there move to T). In 2a and 2b, bear in mind the traditional view that the copula BE (when finite) originates in the head V position of VP and (by virtue of being auxiliary-like) from there moves to the head T position of TP in finite clauses (adjoining to a null tense affix in T). In 3a–3d, assume that *been* occupies the head PROG position of a PROGP/ progressive aspect phrase, that *have* occupies the head PERF position of a PERFP/perfect aspect phrase, and that *must* occupies the head T position of TP (ignoring the possibility that *must* may originate as the head of a lower MP/modal projection and from there move to T). In relation to 4a– 4c, assume that the passivised subject *the prisoners* originates in comp-VP (as the complement of the verb *arrested*) and from there moves to spec-TP, via A-Movement/Passivisation. Bear in mind that the Minimality Condition means that A-Movement is successive-cyclic, and consider the possibility of the subject moving first to the closest non-thematic specifier position above it (e.g. as the specifier of the closest auxiliary), then to the next closest ... and so on. Bear in mind the spellout rules discussed in the model answer in the *Answerbook*, and take into account the following conditions on extraction/movement:

5   **Constraint on Extraction Domains/CED** (= 42)
       Extraction is only possible out of a complement, not out of a specifier or adjunct

6   **Freezing Principle** (from §1.5.1)
       The constituents of a moved phrase are frozen internally within (and so cannot be extracted out of) the moved phrase

EXERCISE 2.2

This exercise is designed to be attempted after reading Module 2.2 and the module and chapter preceding it.

Discuss the role that thematic structure can play in accounting for similarities/differences between the two or three sentences in each numbered set below:

1a   John handed Mary the phone [M]
1b   John handed the phone to Mary [M]
2a   John smashed the window with a brick [S]

2b   A brick smashed the window [S]

2c   The window smashed [S]

3a   John got an invitation from Mary [S]

3b   Mary got John an invitation [S]

4a   The police deliberately killed the prisoner

4b   *The prisoner deliberately died

5a   Personally, syntax bores me

5b   *Personally, my wife beats me

6a   The bombing of the airport by the terrorists was tragic [S]

6b   The disappearance of/* by the terrorists was mysterious [S]

7a   Mary brought John a lot of happiness last summer

7b   Last summer brought John a lot of happiness

7c   !Mary and last summer brought John a lot of happiness

In addition, discuss any problems posed for the claim that thematic relations play a key role in accounting for the syntax of adverbial/prepositional constituents and coordination by sentences such as the following (where ! denotes semantic/pragmatic anomaly):

8a   Personally, I have never sent a Christmas card to Boris

8b   Personally, I have never been sent a Christmas card by Boris

8c   Personally, I have never been sent to Boris

9a   Gradual economic decline by Britain has led to worsening unemployment [S]

9b   Any further fall by stocks and shares could undermine the economy [S]

10a !John and a tin of paint fell off the ladder

10b !I hit John and the ground with my stick

10c !I saw John and a daffodil in the park

Helpful hints

Do not attempt to draw tree diagrams representing the structure of the relevant phrases and sentences. Instead, identify the thematic roles played by key constituents, and say what part theta roles play in accounting for (i) how constituents occupying different positions can nonetheless have essentially the same semantic function, (ii) the distribution of adverbs and prepositional phrases, and (iii) the types of constituent that can be coordinated.

EXERCISE 2.3

This exercise is designed to be attempted after reading Module 2.3 and the modules and chapter preceding it.

Discuss the derivation of the sentences below: those in 6 and 7 are taken from Shakespeare's play *Measure for Measure*; and those in 8 and 9 were produced by the children whose names and ages in years; months are shown in parentheses (the relevant child data being from Pierce 1992).

1   On the wall, a portrait of Karl Marx had *hung* [M]
2   At which window did a ghostly figure *appear*? [S]
3   An opportunity for us to go to Rome has *arisen* [S]
4   Allegations of police corruption have *emerged*
5   Several of the prisoners have *escaped*
6   Now are they *come* (Duke, *Measure for Measure*, IV.ii) [S]
7   Is the duke *gone*? (Duke, *Measure for Measure*, V.i)
8   *Fall* the cradle (Peter 2;2 = 'The cradle fell')
9   *Come* Cromer? (Adam 2;3 = 'Has Mr Cromer come?')

Helpful hints

Consider whether the italicised verbs in the above sentences are unaccusative predicates, and if so what evidence there is for such an assumption. For the purposes of this exercise, take the PPs *on the wall/at which window* in 1/2 and the ADVP *now* in 6 to be generated in spec-CP (ignoring the possibility that they may originate in some lower position below C and from there move to spec-CP). Treat *a/an*-phrases as having the status of ARTP/article projections, and *of*-phrases as having the status of KP/case projections, but do not concern yourself with the internal structure of these ARTP/KP constituents. In relation to 6 and 7, assume that Shakespearean English is a verb-second/V2 language in which a null C with a specifier in a root/main clause attracts an (auxiliary or non-auxiliary) verb in T to adjoin to C. In 7, assume that yes–no questions contain an ADVP comprising a null yes–no operator/Op_{YNQ} in spec-CP. Compare two different accounts of child utterances like those in 8 and 9. On one (structural deficit) view, two-year-old children's sentence structures are smaller than their adult counterparts in that they can lack functional projections like CP and TP found in adult sentences, and are simply VPs; on an alternative (continuity) view, two-year-old's sentences have the same CP+TP+VP structure as their adult counterparts, but the children may have not yet mastered the morphophonology and syntax of functional heads (e.g. how tense/agreement morphology on T is spelled out, and how/when T and C trigger movement).

In devising your answers, you might want to bear in mind the following:

10   **Low Spellout Rule** (= 67)
      A KP/PP/CP which is the lowest/rightmost constituent of a larger phrase
      that undergoes movement can be spelled out on a lower copy of the
      moved phrase

11   Default Spellout Rule/DSR (= 7)

For a constituent whose spellout is not determined in some other way, the highest copy of the constituent is overtly pronounced, and any lower copies are silent

12   Clause Typing Conditions (= 5)

(i) A clause is interpreted as being of a given type (interrogative or exclamative etc.) if it contains a peripheral clause-typing specifier of the relevant type

(ii) An indicative clause is interpreted as declarative in type by default if it contains no peripheral clause-typing specifier

EXERCISE 2.4

This exercise is designed to be attempted after reading Module 2.4 and the modules and chapter preceding it.

Discuss the derivation of the passive sentences below, accounting for why they are (un)grammatical:

1   They are said to have made allegations of corporate corruption [M]
2   *They are said that have made allegations of corporate corruption [M]
3   Allegations of corporate corruption were said to have been made [S]
4   Allegations were said to have been made of corporate corruption [S]
5   There were said to have been made allegations of corporate corruption
6   *There were said allegations of corporate corruption to have been made
7   *Allegations of corporate corruption were said that had been made
8   Allegations of corporate corruption are expected (*for) to be made

Helpful hints

For the purposes of this exercise, make the simplifying assumption that finite auxiliaries occupy the head T position of TP, but that nonfinite auxiliaries are the heads of auxiliary projections below T (e.g. *have* is the head PERF constituent of a PERFP/perfect aspect phrase, and *been* in passive uses is the head VOICE constituent of a passive VOICEP/voice projection). Assume that definite nominal or pronominal arguments are DPs, and that indefinite nominal arguments are QPs headed by an overt or null Q. Bear in mind the role of the Impenetrability Condition in 9 below in blocking movement across the edge of an intervening CP, and also bear in mind the role of the

COMP-Trace Filter in 10 in filtering out certain types of superficial syntactic structure as illicit:

9   **Impenetrability Condition** (= 91)
     Anything below the head C of a CP is impenetrable to anything above the CP (where *below* = c-commanded by, and *above* = c-commanding)

10   **COMP-Trace Filter/CTF** (= 94)
     Any structure at the end of a syntactic derivation in which an overt COMP/complementiser is immediately adjacent to and c-commands a trace (i.e. a gap/null copy left behind by a moved constituent) is filtered out as ill-formed

Consider also the possibility that some of the sentences may involve split/discontinuous spellout, and in this connection, bear in mind the following two PF spellout rules:

11   **Low Spellout Rule/LSR** (= 67)
     A KP/PP/CP which is the lowest/rightmost constituent of a larger phrase that undergoes movement can be spelled out on a lower copy of the moved phrase

12   **Default Spellout Rule/DSR** (= 7)
     For a constituent whose spellout is not determined in some other way, the highest copy of the constituent is overtly pronounced, and any lower copies are silent

Finally, note that nothing in the account of Passivisation given in the book accounts for the ungrammaticality of sentences like 6. See if you can suggest possible factors that might account for the ungrammaticality of such sentences.

EXERCISE 2.5

This exercise is designed to be attempted after reading Module 2.5 and the modules and chapter preceding it.

Discuss the derivation of each of the sentences below, saying whether the italicised verb in each sentence functions as a Raising or Control predicate (or is potentially ambiguous between the two), and adducing evidence in support of your analysis.

1   Employers *tend* to exploit employees [M]
2   He has *decided* to do it [M]

3 He's *beginning* to irritate me [M]

4 We *came* to appreciate the classes (in the sense of 'We ended up appreciating the classes') [S]

5 They will *have* to do something

6 They have *failed* to score enough goals [S]

7 He *tried* to sabotage the car [S]

8 He *refused* to sign the petition

9 They *attempted* to pervert the course of justice

10 I *happened* to be passing the house

11 He is *going* to help me

12 He is *bound* to win the election

13 He *needs* to have a shave

14 We are *hoping* to get a visa [S]

15 He is *threatening* to sue the CIA [S]

Helpful hints

Bear in mind that because Raising predicates don't theta-mark their subjects, they allow an unrestricted choice of subjects (including inanimate, expletive, and idiomatic subjects); by contrast, because Control predicates theta-mark their subjects, they impose selection restrictions on their choice of subject (typically allowing animate subjects, but not expletive, idiomatic or inanimate subjects). For similar reasons, Raising predicates (if they allow a finite clause paraphrase) typically allow a finite clause paraphrase with an impersonal/expletive main-clause subject, whereas Control predicates (if they allow a finite clause paraphrase) typically allow a finite clause paraphrase with a personal/thematic main-clause subject. Bear in mind that Raising predicates select an infinitival TP complement, whereas Control predicates select an infinitival CP complement: so (like other CPs), the complement of a Control predicate can generally appear in focus position in a pseudo-cleft (but the complement of a Raising predicate cannot). Another difference is that Raising predicates allow long/cross-clausal Passivisation across their TP complement, but Control predicates do not (because they have a CP complement, and the Impenetrability Condition blocks A-Movement across the edge of an intervening CP). A complication to bear in mind is that some predicates allow a dual use, and can function either as Raising or Control predicates. Consider whether your derivation satisfies requirements imposed by the conditions below (where *above* means 'c-commanding', and *below* means 'c-commanded by'):

16   Theta Criterion/θ-criterion (= 32)
      Each argument bears one and only one θ-role, and each θ-role is assigned to one and only one argument

17   Minimality Condition/MC (= 61)
        A constituent can only enter into a syntactic relation with the minimal
        (= closest) constituent of the relevant type above/below it

18   Impenetrability Condition (= 91)
        Anything below the head C of a CP is impenetrable to anything above
        the CP

For the purposes of the exercise, assume that the infinitive complement of
each of the italicised predicates has the thematic role of being the THEME
argument of the relevant italicised predicate; and assume, too, that only
T constituents (containing a finite auxiliary, a tense affix or the infinitive particle *to*) carry an EPP feature. In addition (again for the purposes
of this exercise) make the simplifying assumption that finite auxiliaries
are directly generated in T, rather than originating as the head of a lower
auxiliary projection and from there raising to adjoin to a tense affix in T.
In 6, take *enough goals* to be a QP/quantifier phrase, and in 13–14, take *a
shave/a visa* to be ARTP/article phrase constituents.

EXERCISE 2.6

*This exercise is designed to be attempted after reading Module 2.6 and the
modules and chapter preceding it.*

Discuss the derivation of each of the examples in 1–5 below, presenting
evidence in support of your analysis:

1 The negotiations do seem likely to prove difficult [M]
2 No traces would appear to have been found of any dinosaurs
3 He is thought to be intending to sell it [S]
4 No soldier expects to die
5 Evidence of impropriety is starting to emerge

In addition, discuss the derivation of sentences 6–10 below (recorded by
me from live, unscripted radio broadcasts), saying what is unusual/non-
standard about them:

6 Six venues are planned to be used (Journalist, BBC Radio 5)
7 Next of kin are still trying to be identified (Reporter, BBC News TV) [S]
8 Some of these are thought will have medicinal values (dailymail.co.uk) [S]
9 These works are hoped will start during February 2013 (nwpcp.org.uk)
10 They are deemed that they are too expensive (Spokeswoman for the National
   Health Service, BBC Radio 5; both instances of *they* refer to drugs for treating
   cancer)

Helpful hints

Note that the examples in this exercise are mixed structures involving a combination of clauses containing Raising/Control/passive/unaccusative predicates: you might find it useful to bear in mind the helpful hints given for Exercises 2D and 2E. Bear in mind too the following additional hints in relation to the sentences in 6–10:

- Some speakers may allow an item which normally selects a CP complement to select a TP complement
- Some speakers may allow some Control predicates to be used without a thematic subject as Raising predicates
- Conditions like the Impenetrability Condition and the COMP-Trace Filter mean that A-Movement is not possible across an intervening CP (though is possible across an intervening TP)
- Structures in which constraints on movement prevent a gap inside some island from having an antecedent outside the island can be repaired if an overt copy is used in place of a gap/null copy

In relation to 2, bear in mind the possibility of split spellout arising from applying the Low Spellout Rule in 11 below, rather than the Default Spellout Rule in 12:

11   **Low Spellout Rule/LSR (= 67)**
       A KP/PP/CP which is the lowest/rightmost constituent of a larger phrase that undergoes movement can be spelled out on a lower copy of the moved phrase

12   **Default Spellout Rule/DSR (= 7)**
       For a constituent whose spellout is not determined in some other way, the highest copy of the constituent is overtly pronounced, and any lower copies are silent

Where relevant, bear in mind the following filter:

13   **COMP-Trace Filter (= 94)**
       Any structure at the end of a syntactic derivation in which an overt COMP/complementiser is immediately adjacent to and c-commands a trace (i.e. a gap/null copy left behind by a moved constituent) is filtered out as ill-formed

In 6, take *six venues* to be a NUMP/numeral projection, but don't concern yourself with its internal structure. In 7, take *still* to be an ADVP which adjoins to the VP headed by *trying* to form an even larger VP; and treat *next of kin* as a QP headed by a null quantifier *ø* meaning 'an unspecified number of' (but don't try to analyse the internal structure of this QP). In 8, take *some of these* and *medicinal values* to be QPs (in the latter case, headed by a null quantifier ø meaning 'an unspecified number of'), but don't concern yourself with their internal structure. In 9 take *during February 2013* to be a PP which is an adjunct to the VP headed by *start*, but do not concern yourself with the internal structure of this PP. In 10 take *too expensive* to be an AP/adjectival phrase, but don't concern yourself with its internal structure; and in addition, take *are* (in *are too expensive*) to be a copular verb which originates as the head V of VP, and from there moves to adjoin to a present tense affix in the head T position of TP.

3 Agreement

3.0 Overview

In this chapter, we take a look at the syntax of agreement. I begin by arguing that agreement involves a relation between a probe and a goal (though it should be noted that the term 'goal' in this chapter is used in an entirely different way from the term GOAL – written in capital letters – which was used to denote the thematic role played by a particular kind of argument in relation to its predicate in the Chapter 2). I then go on to explore how agreement works in a range of structures, and the role which agreement plays in A-Movement on the one hand and Case-marking on the other.

3.1 Agreement, A-Movement and Case-marking

This module begins by considering the nature of Agreement, and goes on to explore its relation to A-Movement and Case-marking.

3.1.1 Agreement and A-Movement

In traditional grammars, finite auxiliaries are said to agree with their subjects in person and number. Since (in the classic CP+TP+VP model outlined in Chapter 1) finite auxiliaries occupy the head T position of TP and their subjects are in spec-TP, in earlier work agreement was taken to involve a specifier-head relationship between T and its specifier – as illustrated below:

(1) a. *Numerous complications* **have** arisen
     b. *The responsibility of taking decisions* **has** lain on senators
     c. *His rivals* **have** amassed a much smaller fortune than Senator Swindle
     d. *Inflation* **has** gone up, and *standards of living* **have** come down
     e. *The negotiations* **have** been so protracted that progress is slow

In each of the above examples, the bold-printed T auxiliary HAVE agrees with its italicised superficial subject, making it seem plausible to suppose that agreement involves a spec(ifier)-head relation between an auxiliary in T and its specifier in spec-TP.

However, a spec–head account of agreement proves problematic in that it fails to account for agreement between the auxiliary and its subject in cases where the subject is postverbal (perhaps remaining in situ inside VP) – as is the case with agreement between the bold-printed auxiliary HAVE and its italicised postverbal subject in structures like those below:

(2)   a. There **have** arisen *numerous complications*
       b. On senators **has** lain *the responsibility of taking decisions*
       c. Senator Swindle has acquired a larger fortune than **have** *his rivals*
       d. Up **has** gone *inflation*, and down **have** come *standards of living*
       e. So protracted **have** been *the negotiations* that progress is slow

Since the agreeing subject is postverbal in (2a–2e) above, it is clear that any account of agreement as involving a relation between T and its specifier would be potentially problematic in such cases.

So let's explore an alternative account which makes use of the VP-Internal Subject Hypothesis, and let's suppose that agreement involves a relation between a T constituent (e.g. a finite auxiliary) and a VP-internal constituent which it c-commands. To see how this works, consider the derivation of the sentence produced by speaker B below:

(3)   SPEAKER A: What happened to the protestors?
       SPEAKER B: *They were arrested*

In particular, let's look at the features carried by the pronoun *they* on the one hand, and the auxiliary *were* on the other, and how these are central to agreement and movement. In (3B), we can suppose that a third person plural pronoun is required in order to refer back to the third person plural constituent *the protestors*, and that a past tense auxiliary is required because the event described took place in the past. So (as it were) the person/number features of *they* and the past tense feature of *were* are determined in advance, before the items enter the derivation. By contrast the case feature assigned to *they* and the person/number features assigned to *were* are determined in the course of the derivation: for example, if the subject had been the third person singular pronoun *one*, the auxiliary would have been third person singular via agreement with *one* (as in 'One **was** arrested'); and if THEY had been used as the object of a transitive verb, it would have been spelled out in the accusative form *them* (as in 'The police *arrested* **them**').

Generalising at this point, let's suppose that noun and pronoun expressions like THEY enter the syntax with their person and number features intrinsically valued, but their case feature unvalued. (The notation THEY is used here to provide a case-independent characterisation of the word which is variously spelled out as *they/them/their* depending on the case assigned to it in the syntax.) Using a transparent feature notation, let's say that THEY enters the derivation carrying the features [3-Pers, Pl-Num, u-Case], where 3 = third, Pers = person, Pl = plural, Num = number, and u = unvalued. Similarly, let's suppose that finite T constituents enter the derivation with their tense feature already valued, but their person and number features as yet unvalued (because they will be valued in the course of the derivation via agreement with an appropriate constituent). This means that the auxiliary BE (as used in 3B) enters the derivation with the features [Past-Tns, u-Pers, u-Num], where Tns = tense. Let's also make the traditional assumption that T constituents carry an EPP feature. And finally, since (3B) is a passive sentence, let's take the pronoun THEY to originate as the thematic complement of the passive participle *arrested*. Given these assumptions, the derivation will proceed as follows.

The verb *arrested* merges with its complement THEY to form the VP *arrested THEY*. This VP is then merged with the passive auxiliary BE, forming the T-bar shown in simplified form in (4) below (where the auxiliary and pronoun are shown in their dictionary citation forms BE/THEY in order to indicate that their morphological spellout can't yet be determined):

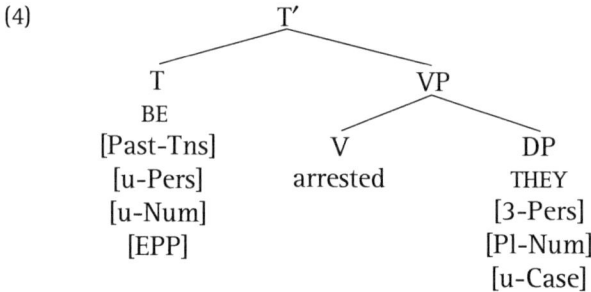

(4)

```
                    T′
        ┌───────────────────────┐
        T                       VP
        BE              ┌──────────────┐
     [Past-Tns]         V              DP
      [u-Pers]        arrested        THEY
      [u-Num]                        [3-Pers]
       [EPP]                         [Pl-Num]
                                     [u-Case]
```

The tense auxiliary T-BE needs to agree with an appropriate nominal within the structure containing it. Given the Structure Dependence Principle of §1.3.2 (requiring syntactic operations to be sensitive to hierarchical relations – and to the relation c-command in particular), let's suppose that T agrees with a nominal which it c-commands. Accordingly, once the structure in (4) is formed, T-BE searches for a nominal which it c-commands to agree with in person and number.

Introducing some new technical terminology at this point, let us say that by virtue of being the highest head in the overall structure (4) at this point in the derivation, BE serves as a <u>probe</u> which searches for a c-commanded (pro)nominal <u>goal</u> which can value its unvalued person and number features (where a probe is a head/X and a goal is a maximal projection/XP). It is conventional to refer to person and number features together as φ-features (where φ is the Greek letter *phi*, pronounced as [fai] in English): using this terminology, we can say that the probe T-BE searches for a goal which can value its φ-features.

In addition, let's also assume that operations like Agreement, A-Movement and Case-marking can only apply if both the probe and the goal are active, and that the following conditions determine this:

(5)   **Activity Conditions**
- (i) A head can only be an active probe for Agreement or A-Movement or Case-marking if it carries some unvalued φ-feature/s, and becomes inactive once its φ-feature/s have been valued (**Probe Condition**)
- (ii) An XP can only be an active goal for Agreement, A-Movement, or Case-marking if it has an unvalued case feature, and becomes inactive once its case feature is valued (**Goal Condition**)
- (iii) If a constituent is part of a movement chain at a given point in a derivation, only the highest copy in the chain can be active for operations like Agreement, A-Movement or Case-marking (**Highest Copy Condition**)

Furthermore, let's suppose that agreement and case-marking are subject to the conditions in (6) below:

(6)   **Feature Valuation Conditions**
- (i) When an active probe like T c-commands an active XP goal, each unvalued φ-feature on the probe will be valued by the goal – that is, assigned a value which is a copy of the corresponding feature value on the goal (**Agreement**)
- (ii) Only a φ-complete XP (i.e. one with person and number) can serve as a goal valuing unvalued features on a probe, and conversely only a φ-complete probe (i.e. one with person and number) can value unvalued features on a goal (**Completeness Condition**)
- (iii) Each feature on a constituent must be valued (i.e. assigned a single, appropriate value) in order for the constituent to be legible at the PF/LF interfaces; if not, the derivation will crash (**Legibility Condition**)

(A structure is legible at the PF interface if it can be assigned an appropriate phonetic/PF representation, and legible at the LF interface if it can be assigned an appropriate semantic/LF representation.) Finally, let's also suppose that the EPP feature on T works in conjunction with person agreement, in accordance with the following condition:

(7)   **EPP Condition**
An EPP feature on a probe T attracts the closest XP goal that T agrees with in person to undergo A-Movement to spec-TP, and the EPP feature is stripped from T (and removed from the derivation) once the movement has taken place

The reason for supposing that the EPP feature on T attracts an XP that it agrees with in <u>person</u> is in order to ensure that T attracts a (pro)nominal goal (and not e.g. an ADVP or PP goal) to move to spec-TP. Of course, it follows from the Goal Condition (5ii) that the XP goal can only be attracted by the EPP feature on T if the goal is active (by virtue of carrying an unvalued case feature). The reason for positing that the EPP feature is stripped from T (and thereby removed from the derivation entirely) once it has done its work is that the EPP feature is illegible in the PF and LF components (since EPP has no phonetic spellout and no semantic interpretation), and hence will cause the derivation to crash if it is not removed.

The reason that I use the term <u>stripped</u> (meaning 'removed from the derivation entirely') in (7) rather than <u>deleted</u>, is that deletion is classically taken to involve giving a null phonological spellout in the PF component to a constituent which nonetheless remains in the syntax and is assigned a semantic interpretation in the LF/semantic component. To illustrate how deletion works, consider the NP Deletion operation which deletes the bracketed NP in (8) below:

(8)   He drank three cans of beer, and I drank four [$_{NP}$ ~~cans of beer~~]

In this structure, the second (bracketed) occurrence of the NP *cans of beer* can be deleted for economy reasons (to avoid redundant repetition of the NP *cans of beer*). What this means is that the bracketed NP is present in the syntax, and is inputted into both the LF component (where it is assigned a meaning paraphrasable as 'cans of beer') and the PF component (where it is given a silent spellout). However, when (7) specifies that the EPP feature is stripped from T (once it has done its work), this means that it is eliminated from the derivation entirely, and thus is no longer present in the syntax, and hence plays no further role in the syntax and is not inputted into the LF or PF components.

A further point to note is that the EPP feature on T is different in kind from other features. For example, a feature like [Past-Tns] comprises an attribute (= the property tense) and a value (= past). By contrast, the EPP feature on T is an instruction specifying 'Attract an XP goal that I agree with in person to become my specifier'. It is arguably because it does not have the canonical attribute-value format of other features that an EPP feature is illegible at the PF and LF interfaces, so has to be removed from the derivation once it has triggered movement. Another reason for assuming that EPP is removed once it has moved some constituent to spec-TP is to prevent it triggering a second movement which would result in T (illicitly) ending up with two specifiers. One way of accounting for EPP not having the attribute-value structure of other features would be to suppose that the person feature on T has the property of attracting a goal carrying a person feature: this could be marked (e.g.) by eliminating the EPP feature altogether, and instead asterisking the person feature on T in (4), so that T-BE has the features [Past-Tns, u-Pers*, u-Num], with the asterisk interpreted as an instruction to 'attract an XP that can value my person feature to become my specifier'. However, I will retain the traditional EPP notation here (because it will be familiar to many readers), and take it to operate as specified in (7) above.

We can take the conditions in (5–7) to be principles of UG/Universal Grammar, in keeping with the goal of linguistic theory being to establish general principles governing how linguistic operations apply. In the light of these conditions, let's return to consider what happens once we have formed the structure in (4) above. At this point, the T auxiliary BE serves as a probe by virtue of being the highest head in the structure; T-BE is rendered active for Agreement and A-Movement by its unvalued (person/number) φ-features. T-BE searches for the closest active goal which it c-commands that can value its φ-features, locating THEY (which is active by virtue of its unvalued case feature). Let's see how these two operations apply.

Consider first Agreement. Since THEY is φ-complete (i.e. it carries both person and number), it can value the unvalued φ-features on the T-probe BE, in conformity with the Completeness Condition (6ii). Via the Agreement operation (6i), the values of the (third) person and (plural) number features on the goal THEY are copied onto the probe BE, so that BE is thereby given the feature values shown in italics below:

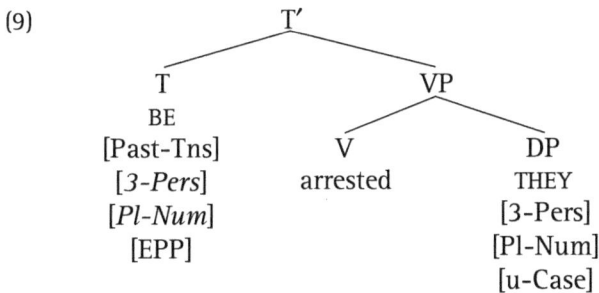

(9)

```
                          T′
              _____/ _____
             /                         \
            T                          VP
           BE                      ___/  \___
        [Past-Tns]               /          \
         [3-Pers]               V            DP
         [Pl-Num]           arrested        THEY
          [EPP]                           [3-Pers]
                                          [Pl-Num]
                                          [u-Case]
```

In accordance with the EPP Condition in (7), the EPP feature on the probe BE attracts the closest XP goal c-commanded by BE which it agrees with in person – namely THEY (which is active through its unvalued case feature). This means that BE attracts (a copy of) THEY to move to spec-TP in the manner shown by the arrow below (with the EPP feature thereafter being stripped from T and removed from the derivation), resulting in the following structure (simplified by showing the position out of which

THEY moves as a gap, though in reality the gap position is occupied by a null copy of THEY):

(10)

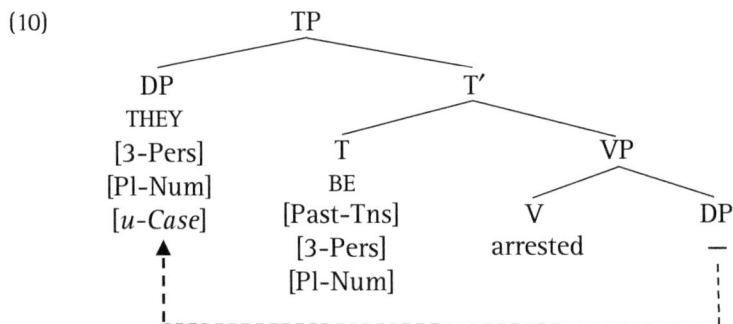

However, there is unfinished business in (10), because the italicised case feature on the subject THEY has not yet been valued – and if it doesn't get valued, the derivation will fall foul of the Legibility Condition (6iii) and crash (because the PF component will be unable to determine whether to spell out THEY as nominative *they*, accusative *them* or genitive *their*). So how does THEY get case-marked here? This is a question addressed in the next section.

3.1.2   Case-marking

Let's suppose that the derivation continues by merging the TP in (10) above with a null finite complementiser which carries an indicative mood feature [Ind-Mood]. On the assumption that a finite (i.e. mood-specified) complementiser with a TP complement assigns nominative case to a c-commanded goal with an unvalued case feature, the unvalued case feature on THEY will be valued as nominative by the finite complementiser. However, since the Completeness Condition (6ii) specifies that only a φ-complete probe can value an unvalued feature on a goal, this means that Case-marking must involve agreement in person and number between the complementiser and the goal that it case-marks. Given this assumption, Case-marking can be given an agreement-based account along the lines outlined informally in (11) below:

(11)   **Case Conditions**

A φ-complete case-assigning probe values an unvalued case feature on an XP goal that it agrees with in respect of one or more φ-features, and assigns the goal a case value that depends on the nature of the probe – namely:

(i)   *nominative* if the probe is a finite C with a TP complement (where a finite C is one that is indicative, subjunctive or imperative in mood)

(ii)   *null* if the probe is an intransitive infinitival C with a TP complement

(iii) *accusative* if the probe is transitive

(I use the term *transitive* to denote a probe which is an accusative case-assigner, and *intransitive* to denote a probe which is not an accusative case-assigner. Note that this is a minor departure from the traditional assumption that an intransitive item is one with no complement: you can use the term *non-transitive* instead if you prefer.) Given these assumptions, the complementiser will enter the derivation carrying an indicative mood feature [Ind-Mood], as well as unvalued person and number φ-features (with unvalued features shown in italics below):

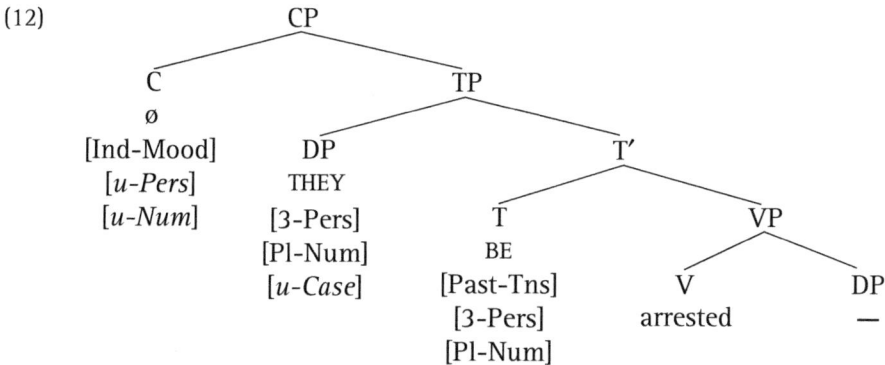

(12)
```
                        CP
              ┌──────────┴──────────┐
              C                     TP
              Ø            ┌─────────┴─────────┐
         [Ind-Mood]        DP                  T'
          [u-Pers]        THEY        ┌─────────┴─────────┐
          [u-Num]        [3-Pers]     T                   VP
                         [Pl-Num]     BE           ┌───────┴───────┐
                         [u-Case]   [Past-Tns]     V               DP
                                    [3-Pers]    arrested           —
                                    [Pl-Num]
```

Agreement between the complementiser probe and the DP goal THEY will result in the φ-features on the complementiser being valued as third person plural via Agreement (6i), and the unvalued case-feature on the goal THEY being valued as nominative via the Nominative Case Condition (11i), so deriving the structure below (where the features on the complementiser and subject which have been valued via Agreement and Case-marking are shown in italics):

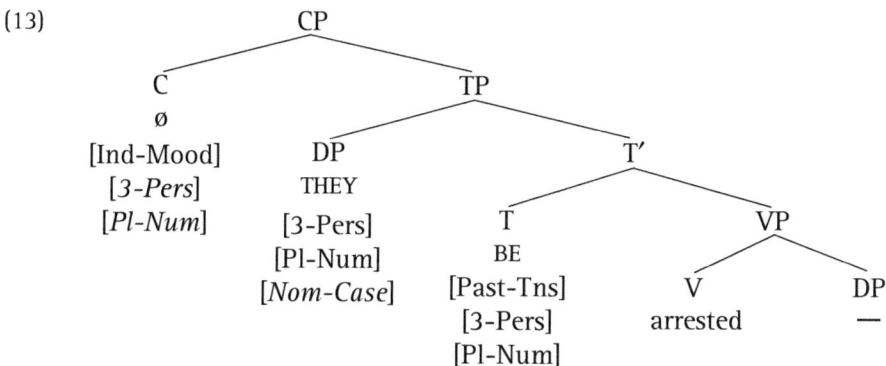

(13)
```
                        CP
              ┌──────────┴──────────┐
              C                     TP
              Ø            ┌─────────┴─────────┐
         [Ind-Mood]        DP                  T'
          [3-Pers]        THEY        ┌─────────┴─────────┐
          [Pl-Num]       [3-Pers]     T                   VP
                         [Pl-Num]     BE           ┌───────┴───────┐
                         [Nom-Case] [Past-Tns]     V               DP
                                    [3-Pers]    arrested           —
                                    [Pl-Num]
```

The resulting structure (13) satisfies the requirement imposed by the Legibility Condition (6iii) for every feature to be valued at the end of a syntactic derivation. The structure (13) is subsequently transferred to the LF and PF components, and PF spellout rules determine that the pronoun THEY is spelled out in its nominative form *they*, and the auxiliary BE in its third person plural past tense form *were*. The overall sentence is spelled out at PF as *They were arrested*. (A point of detail to note is that the T auxiliary BE will also carry an indicative mood feature, perhaps copied from the head C of CP: but I will set aside this detail here, for the sake of presentational simplicity.)

An aspect of the analysis outlined above which might at first sight seem implausible is the postulation of an (abstract/invisible) agreement relation between complementiser and subject. However, there are both theoretical and empirical arguments in support of this assumption. The theoretical argument is that the Completeness Condition (6ii) requires a probe which values a feature on a goal to be φ-complete (i.e. to carry both person and number). The empirical argument is that there are languages in which a finite complementiser agrees overtly in person and number with the subject of its clause, including varieties of Flemish (Haegeman 1992), and of German and Dutch (van Koppen 2017). This phenomenon can be illustrated in terms of the following West Flemish data (from van Koppen 2017):

(14) a. K   peinzen   **da/*dan**   *dienen*   *student*   nen   buot   gekocht   eet

I   think   that$_{3.SG}$/   that   student   a   boat   bought   has

that $_{3.PL}$

'I think that that student has bought a boat'

b. K   peinzen   **dan/*da**   *die*   *studenten*   nen   buot   gekocht   een

I   think   that$_{3.PL}$/   those   students   a   boat   bought   have

that $_{3.SG}$

'I think that those students have bought a boat'

The bold-printed complementiser in these examples (= the West Flemish counterpart of English *that*) agrees in person and number with the italicised subject of the clause it introduces, and thus is third person singular ($_{3.SG}$) by agreement with the third person singular subject *dienen*$_{that}$ *student*$_{student}$ in (14a), and third person plural ($_{3.PL}$) by agreement with the third person plural subject *die*$_{those}$ *studenten*$_{students}$ in (14b). Data such as (14) thus provide cross-linguistic evidence of the existence of complementiser-subject agreement. Given the impoverished nature of English morphology, however, complementiser-subject agreement is abstract in English, in the sense that it has no overt phonetic reflex and so is invisible/inaudible. Still, abstract agreement is an idea that is widely utilised in English: for example, if we make the traditional assumption that indicative verbs/auxiliaries agree with their subjects in person and number, it follows that in the same way as *helps* agrees overtly with its subject *he* in 'He **helps** her', so too *helped* agrees (albeit abstractly/invisibly/inaudibly) with its subject in 'He **helped** her'; and in the same way as the auxiliary *is* agrees overtly with its subject in '*He* **is** helping her', so too the auxiliary *will* agrees abstractly with its subject in '*He* **will** help her'.

The discussion of case-marking above is simplified insofar as the constituent assigned nominative case is a single word (the pronoun/pronominal DP *they*). But what if in place of *they* we had phrases like those italicised in the clauses bracketed below?

(15)   a. Everyone knows [**that** *we foreigners* are exploited]

b. Some people think [**that** *all the foreign workers* are exploited]

c. We feel [**that** *some of us* are exploited]

On the assumptions made here, the DP *we foreigners* in (15a), the QP *all the foreign workers* in (15b), and the QP *some of us* in (15c) are all assigned nominative case by the finite complementiser *that*. But precisely which words in these phrases receive nominative case? Let's look at each example in turn.

If we take *we foreigners* in (15a) to be a DP headed by the first person plural D/determiner *we*, it is clear that the head D of this DP receives nominative case, since it is spelled out in the nominative form *we*. Since *we* is the head D of the DP, and phrases are projections of their heads, it follows from theoretical considerations that the head D of a nominative DP will carry nominative case. But does its complement (*foreigners*) also carry nominative case? This is not straightforward, because nouns don't overtly inflect for nominative/accusative case in present-day English – though nouns did inflect for case in Old English, and still do in many other languages like German and Russian. So, one possible approach would be to suppose that nouns always carry case, but that nominative and accusative case have no visible reflex on nouns in contemporary English.

Now consider the case of the QP *all the foreign workers* in (15b). Since this QP is assigned nominative case (as we see from the possibility of substituting the QP by the nominative pronoun *they*), it follows from theoretical considerations that its head quantifier *all* must carry nominative case (albeit this is invisible). But does the determiner *the* also carry (invisible) nominative case? Since the determiner *we* in (15a) carries nominative case, the most consistent assumption would be that all determiners carry case in English, even though (because of the impoverished nature of English case morphology) this is nearly always invisible. But what of the noun *workers?* Since I argued for treating the noun *foreigners* in (15a) as carrying nominative case, the most consistent assumption would be to suppose that all nouns carry case – and hence that *workers* carries an invisible nominative case feature in (15b). And what of the adjective *foreign?* In a language like Russian (with a richer case morphology than

English), both adjectives and nouns overtly inflect for case – as illustrated by the following example:

(16)   Krasiva*ya* dyevushk*a* vsunula chornu*yu* koshk*u* v pustu*yu* korobk*u*
        Beautiful girl   put   black   cat   in empty   box
        'The beautiful girl put the black cat in the empty box'

The nouns and adjectives in (16) carry (italicised) case endings (-*a* is a nominative suffix, and -*u* an accusative suffix). So (on one view), the broader conclusion that we might draw from our overall discussion here is that crosslinguistic evidence makes it plausible to suppose that nouns and their modifiers (determiners, quantifiers, adjectives) carry case, albeit the relevant case features are no longer directly visible in present-day English.

Now consider the QP *some of us* in (15c). This QP is assigned nominative case (and so can be substituted by *we*), and hence its head quantifier *some* will be nominative. However, it is clearly not the case that all three words in the QP *some of us* are nominative: after all, the pronoun *us* has accusative case, and the case particle *of* (like prepositions) is not the kind of word which inflects for case (even in a language like Russian with a richer case morphology – as we see from the Russian preposition v_{in} being uninflected in 16 above). How can a nominative QP like *some of us* in (15) contain an accusative pronoun? To try and understand what's going on here, consider the structure of the bracketed clause 'that *some of us* are exploited' in (15c), which is as below (simplified by not showing the internal structure of the T-bar *are exploited*, because this is not relevant to our discussion of case here):

(17)

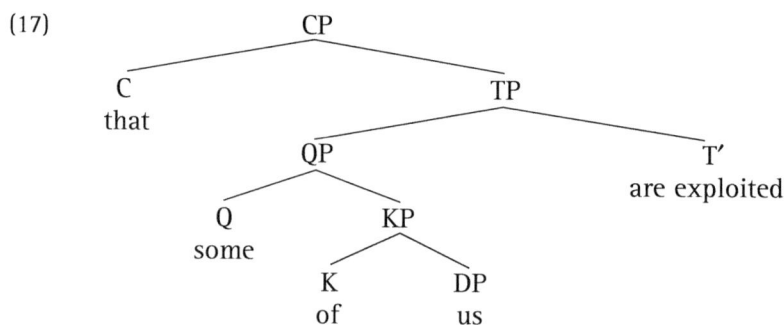

Let's suppose that (in consequence of the Minimality Condition introduced in §1.3.2), constituents are case-marked by the minimal/closest case-assigner above (i.e. c-commanding) them. What this means is that the pronoun/pronominal DP *us* will be assigned accusative case by the transitive case particle *of* in accordance with the case condition (11iii) above, since *of* is the closest case-assigner c-commanding *us*. By contrast, the closest case assigner c-commanding the quantifier *some* in (17) is the complementiser *that*, and since finite complementisers assign nominative case via (11i), this means that *some* will be assigned nominative case. Since case assigners typically don't themselves carry case, this means that both the case particle *of* and the complementiser *that* will be caseless. Thus, in the nominative QP *some of us*, the head quantifier *some* carries (invisible) nominative case, the case particle *of* is caseless, and the pronoun *us* is accusative. So, an important conclusion to draw from our discussion here is that when a complex DP or QP is assigned (say) nominative case, this does not mean that every one of the subconstituents in that DP or QP carries nominative case. In order to simplify our subsequent discussion of case-marking, I shall henceforth simply talk about the case assigned to a given DP or QP, and not be concerned with the case assigned to individual subconstituents of those DPs or QPs which have a complex internal structure.

3.1.3 Valued and unvalued features

Our discussion of how agreement and case-marking work in a sentence such as (3B) *They were arrested* has wider implications. One of these is that items enter the derivation with some of their features already valued and others unvalued: for example, THEY enters the derivation in (4) with its (third) person and (plural) number features valued, but its case feature unvalued. This raises the question of which features are initially valued when they first enter the derivation, which are initially unvalued – and why.

Chomsky (1998, 1999) argued that the difference between valued and unvalued grammatical features correlates with a related distinction between those grammatical features which are <u>interpretable</u> (in the sense that they play a role in semantic interpretation) and those which are <u>uninterpretable</u> (and hence play no role in semantic interpretation). For example, it seems clear that the case feature of a pronoun like THEY is uninterpretable, since a subject pronoun surfaces as nominative, accusative or genitive depending on the type of [bracketed] clause it occurs in, without any effect on meaning – as the examples below illustrate:

(18)   a. It seems [*they* were arrested]
        b. He expected [*them* to be arrested]
        c. He was shocked at [*their* being arrested]

By contrast, the (person/number/gender) φ-features of pronouns are interpretable, since for example, a first person singular pronoun like *I* clearly differs in meaning from a third person plural pronoun like *they*, and a masculine pronoun like *he* differs in meaning from a feminine pronoun like *she*.

Now consider the interpretable and uninterpretable features carried by finite auxiliaries like those italicised below:

(19)   a. She *is* working/She *was* working
        b. He *is* writing the assignment/He *has* written the assignment
        c. He insists that she *is* respected/He insists that she *be* respected
        d. They *are* working/*They *am* working

The tense feature on the present/past tense auxiliary *is/was* in (19a) determines whether the sentence is interpreted as describing a present or past state of affairs, and so tense is clearly an interpretable feature. Likewise, the choice between the progressive aspect auxiliary *is* and the perfect aspect auxiliary *has* in (19b) determines whether the sentence is interpreted as describing an action which is in progress or one which is completed, and so aspect is also an interpretable feature of the auxiliary. In much the same way, the choice between the indicative mood auxiliary *is* and its subjunctive mood counterpart *be* in (19c) determines whether the sentence is interpreted as describing a realis (i.e. existing) state of affairs or an irrealis one (i.e. one which does not exist at present but which may exist in the future), and so mood must also be an interpretable feature of auxiliaries.

By contrast, the person/number φ-features of auxiliaries are uninterpretable, in that they serve purely to mark agreement with a particular (pro)-nominal: consequently, if we replace the third person plural auxiliary *are* by the first person singular form *am* in a sentence like (19d) which has a third person plural subject, we do not change the meaning of the sentence but rather simply make the resulting sentence ungrammatical (**They am* *working*).

We can summarise the picture which emerges from the discussion above in terms of the schema in (20) below:

(20)   **Interpretable and uninterpretable features**

constituent	interpretable features include	uninterpretable features include
T AUXILIARY	tense, aspect and mood	person and number
(PRO)NOMINAL	person, number and gender	case

Each structure generated by the syntactic component of the grammar is subsequently transferred to the PF component of the grammar to be spelled out (i.e. assigned a PF representation which provides a representation of its phonetic form). Since unvalued features are illegible to (i.e. cannot be processed by) the PF and LF components, it follows that every feature which enters the derivation unvalued must be valued in the syntax, or else the derivation will crash (i.e. fail) at the PF interface because the PF component is unable to spell out unvalued features: in the words of Chomsky

(2007: 13) 'If transferred to the interface unvalued, uninterpretable features will cause the derivation to crash' – an idea embodied in the Legibility Condition (6iii). In more concrete terms, this amounts to saying that unless the syntax specifies whether we require (for example) a first person singular or third person plural present tense form of BE, the derivation will crash at the phonetics interface because the PF component cannot determine whether to spell out BE as *am* or *are*.

In addition to being sent to the PF component, each structure generated by the syntactic component of the grammar is simultaneously transferred to the semantic component, where it is assigned an appropriate semantic representation. Clearly, interpretable features play an important role in computing semantic representations. Equally clearly, however, uninterpretable features play no role in this process; and since they are illegible to the semantic component, it is clear that uninterpretable features are not processed in the semantic component. Nonetheless, we need to ensure that uninterpretable features are processed in the PF component (since e.g. PF needs to know whether a third person masculine singular pronoun has been assigned nominative, accusative or genitive case in order to know whether to spell it out as *he*, *him* or *his*). Thus, the overall conclusion to draw from this is: all features (both interpretable and uninterpretable) are processed in the PF/phonological component, but only interpretable features are processed in the LF/semantic component.

However, Chomsky's idea that features entering the derivation valued are interpretable and those entering the derivation unvalued are uninterpretable proves over-simplistic in certain respects. For example, this assumption is problematic for languages which have so-called 'arbitrary gender' – that is, languages in which nouns may carry a gender feature that is unpredictable (e.g. not correlated with their meaning). For example, the word for *sea* in Italian (*mare*) is masculine in gender, but there is no obvious rationale for this, since its counterpart in French (*mer*) is feminine. There are two words for *table* in Italian, one of which is masculine in gender (*tavolo*) and the other feminine (*tavola*). The Italian word *paio* 'pair' is masculine in gender in its singular form, but feminine in its plural form (*paia*). The German word *Mädchen* 'girl' is neuter in gender, in spite of denoting a female human being. Such examples suggest that (rather than assuming that gender is an interpretable feature), it is more appropriate to suppose that gender is an <u>inherent</u> lexical feature of nouns/pronouns (specified in their lexical/dictionary entry), and that inherent features enter the derivation valued. On this view the person/number/gender features of a personal pronoun like HE are <u>inherent</u> features of the pronoun (in the sense that the pronoun carries these features irrespective of the type of structure in which it occurs), whereas its case feature (which determines whether the pronoun is spelled out in the nominative form *he*, the accusative form *him* or the genitive form *his*) is a <u>contextual</u> feature – that is, one determined by the syntactic context (i.e. the type of syntactic structure) in which the word occurs. Contextual features enter the derivation unvalued, and are assigned a value via operations like Agreement and Case-marking in the syntax. (For a theoretical discussion of grammatical features, and views on the relation between valued/unvalued features and interpretable/uninterpretable features, see Pesetsky & Torrego 2007, Willim 2012, and Svenonius 2017.)

To summarise: we have seen in Module 3.1 how (subject-verb) Agreement involves a relation between a finite T-probe and a nominal or pronominal XP goal which it c-commands: the T-probe is made active by unvalued (person/number) φ-features which it carries when it enters the derivation, and its (pro)nominal goal is made active by its unvalued case feature. More generally, the probe and goal enter the derivation carrying a set of valued inherent features, and a set of unvalued contextual features which are valued by operations like Agreement and Case-marking in the course of the derivation. We have also seen that Case-marking is contingent on a person/ number agreement relation between probe and goal, and that A-Movement involves T attracting the closest goal it agrees with in person. At the end of the syntactic derivation, both interpretable and uninterpretable features are processed in the PF component, but only interpretable features are processed in the LF/semantic component.

You should now be able to tackle Exercise 3.1.

3.2   Agreement and case in expletive clauses

So far, all the sentences we have looked at have involved agreement between a (T or C) probe and a thematic nominal or pronominal DP or QP. However, English has two expletive pronouns (*it* and *there*) which differ from other pronouns in that they are non-thematic (in the sense that they cannot occupy a position to which a theta role is assigned) and non-referential (in that they cannot refer back to some other expression, they cannot be substituted by referential pronouns like *this/that*, and they cannot have their reference questioned by interrogative pronouns like *what/where*). In this module, we look at how agreement works in expletive clauses.

3.2.1   Expletive *it* clauses

Typical examples of sentences with an expletive *it* subject are given below:

(21)   a. *It* has transpired that he was cheating
         b. *It* does not matter that the economy is shrinking

    c. *It* can be difficult to cope with long-term illness

    d. *It* was unfortunate that she couldn't attend the meeting

    e. *It* was claimed that Boris knew nothing about Partygate

The pronoun *it* in sentences like these appears to be an expletive, since it cannot be substituted by a referential pronoun like *this* or *that*, and cannot be questioned by *what*. Let's take a closer look at the syntax of expletive *it*, beginning by looking at the features that it carries.

    Since expletive *it* is intrinsically a third person singular pronoun, let us suppose that it enters the derivation carrying the inherent φ-features [3-Pers, Sg-Num]. An interesting question which arises in this regard is whether the person/number features on expletive *it* are interpretable. Some evidence that they may be comes from the observation that expletive *it* can serve as the controller/antecedent for PRO in sentences such as:

(22)   a. *It* can sometimes rain after [PRO snowing] (cf. Chomsky 1981: 324)

       b. *It* can be difficult to overcome depression without [PRO being impossible]

Since the semantic component needs to identify expletive *it* as the antecedent of PRO in such cases, it needs to be able to 'see' the person/number features of *it* in order to determine whether they match the features of PRO. This means that the person/number features of expletive *it* must be visible at the semantics interface, and hence they must be interpretable. Chomsky (1981: 325) suggests that expletive *it* is a quasi-argument (in that it exhibits some but not all of the properties of true arguments). For example, it has the argumental property of being able to occupy an A-position like spec-TP (a position which only arguments can occupy), and being able to serve as the antecedent of PRO.

    Now consider the issue of whether expletive *it* carries a gender feature. It is plausible to suppose that the pronoun *it* carries an interpretable (neuter/inanimate) gender feature when used as a referential pronoun (e.g. in a sentence like *The book has lots of exercises in it*, where *it* refers back to *the book*). However, I shall assume that in its use as an expletive pronoun, *it* is genderless and so carries no interpretable gender feature (which may be why it can't serve as the antecedent of the floating neuter anaphor *itself* in **'It can itself be hard to master syntax'*).

    Finally, consider whether expletive *it* has case. An interesting point to note in this connection is that expletive *it* can undergo Raising/A-Movement in sentences such as:

(23)   *It* does not seem to matter that the economy is shrinking

Given the VP-Internal Subject Hypothesis, expletive *it* will originate as the subject of the verb *matter* and from there raise up to become first the subject of infinitival *to* and then the subject of *does*. However, the Goal Condition (5ii) specifies that a pronoun can only be an active goal for A-Movement if it has an unvalued case feature, so it follows that expletive *it* must enter the derivation with an unvalued case feature. The case feature on expletive *it* will be valued as nominative in a sentence like (24a) below, and accusative in a sentence like (24b):

(24)   a. *It* is irresponsible to behave like that
       b. I consider *it* to be irresponsible to behave like that

In addition, we find expletive *it* used in the genitive form *its* as the subject of a gerund (like *being*) in sentences such as the following:

(25)   a. In the event of *its* being impossible to complete the work of removal and neutralization in time, the party concerned shall mark the spot by placing visible signs there (Agreement on the Cessation of Hostilities in Laos, 1954)
       b. But it was understood that such preparations would now be made as would render it possible to give effect to the blockade measures proposed, in the event of *its* being necessary to take such action (Papers from the Paris Peace Conference, 1919)
       c. In 1856 a Committee of the other House was appointed in consequence of *its* being necessary to renew the Act ... (hansard. parliament.uk)
       d. In 1936 Edward VIII abdicated, and spoke on the radio of *its* being impossible 'to discharge my duties as King ... without the help and support of the woman I love' (thetimes.co.uk)

This suggests that expletive *it* carries a case feature; on the assumptions made here, it will enter the derivation unvalued for case.

   If the reasoning in the paragraphs above is along the right lines, expletive *it* enters the derivation carrying the features [3-Pers, Sg-Num, u-Case]. Given the VP-Internal Subject Hypothesis, we can suppose that (like other subects) expletive *it* originates internally within VP (e.g. as the complement of an unaccusative or passive verb, but as the specifier of other types of verb). To see what all of this means in more concrete terms, let's look at the derivation of the *it*-clause in (21a) *It has transpired that he was cheating.* This proceeds as follows.

   The verb *transpired* merges with its CP complement *that he was cheating* to form the V-bar *transpired that he was cheating*. This V-bar is then merged with the quasi-argument *it* to form the VP *it transpired that he was cheating*. The resulting VP is in turn merged with the T auxiliary HAVE, so forming the T-bar below (where only features on constituents of immediate interest are shown, with uninterpretable features being in italics, and inter-pretable ones in non-italic print):

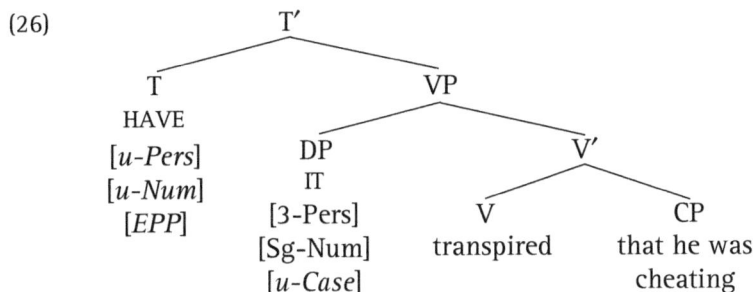

(26)

```
                          T′
              ┌───────────┴───────────┐
              T                       VP
            HAVE             ┌─────────┴─────────┐
          [u-Pers]          DP                   V′
          [u-Num]           IT          ┌────────┴────────┐
           [EPP]          [3-Pers]       V               CP
                          [Sg-Num]    transpired     that he was
                          [u-Case]                     cheating
```

For the reasons given in §3.1.3, I have assumed in (26) that the finite T auxiliary HAVE enters the derivation carrying an interpretable present-tense feature, unvalued (and uninterpretable) person/number φ-features, and an EPP feature which is illegible at the PF and LF interfaces because it has no form or meaning.

The T auxiliary HAVE is a probe which is active for Agreement and A-Movement by virtue of its unvalued person and number features. Accordingly, HAVE searches for a c-commanded goal which can value its person and number features, locating the expletive pronoun IT (which is active for Agreement and A-Movement by virtue of its unvalued case feature). Via Agreement (6i), the goal IT values the unvalued person/number features on the probe HAVE as third person singular. Since the goal IT carries a complete set of (person and number) φ-features, there is no violation of the Completeness Condition (6ii).

In addition, in accordance with the EPP Condition (7) above, the EPP feature on the T auxiliary HAVE in (26) attracts the closest XP that it agrees with in person (namely the pronominal DP IT) to move to spec-TP, and the EPP feature (being illegible at both PF and LF interfaces) is thereafter stripped from T (and thereby removed from the derivation), resulting in the structure below (with the arrow showing A-Movement of IT):

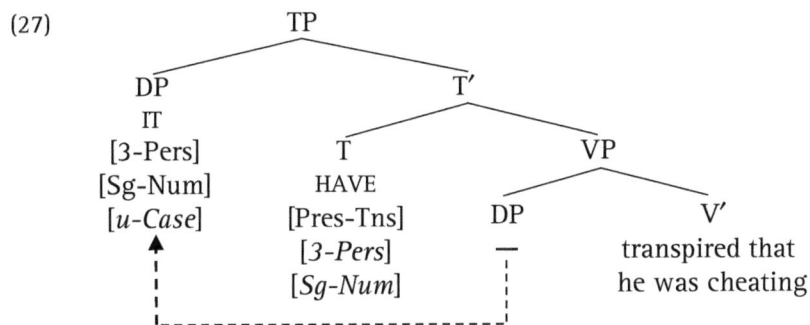

(27)

```
                                TP
                  ┌─────────────┴─────────────┐
                 DP                            T′
                 IT                  ┌─────────┴─────────┐
              [3-Pers]               T                   VP
              [Sg-Num]             HAVE          ┌────────┴────────┐
              [u-Case]          [Pres-Tns]      DP                V′
                 ▲              [3-Pers]         —          transpired that
                 │              [Sg-Num]         │           he was cheating
                 └───────────────────────────────┘
```

This TP is then merged with a null complementiser carrying an interpretable indicative-mood feature, and uninterpretable (and unvalued) person and number φ-features, so forming the CP below (with uninterpretable features italicised):

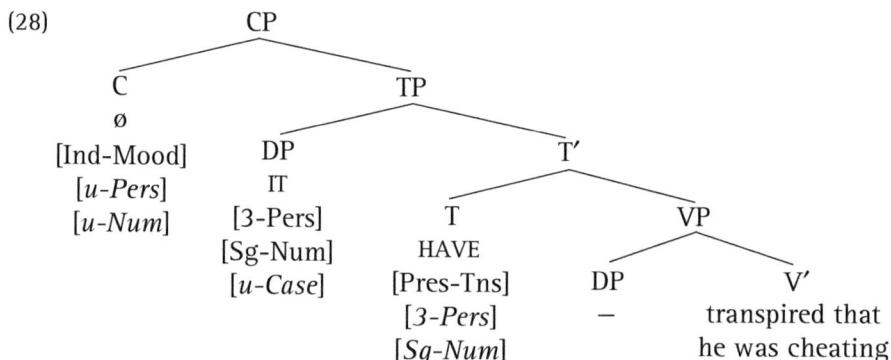

(28)

```
                            CP
              ┌──────────────┴──────────────┐
              C                             TP
              ø                ┌─────────────┴─────────────┐
          [Ind-Mood]          DP                           T′
          [u-Pers]            IT              ┌─────────────┴─────────────┐
          [u-Num]          [3-Pers]           T                          VP
                           [Sg-Num]          HAVE              ┌──────────┴──────────┐
                           [u-Case]        [Pres-Tns]          DP                    V′
                                           [3-Pers]            –          transpired that
                                           [Sg-Num]                       he was cheating
```

The null complementiser in (28) serves as a probe (active by virtue of its unvalued person and number φ-features) and searches for an XP goal which can value these, locating the pronominal DP IT (which is active by virtue of its unvalued case feature, and φ-complete by virtue of its person and number features). Via the Agreement operation (6i), the unvalued φ-features on the null complementiser are valued as third person singular by agreement with IT. At the same time, the complementiser (being finite and φ-complete) values the unvalued case feature on IT as nominative via the Nominative Case Condition (11i). Application of Agreement and Case-marking map (28) above into (29) below:

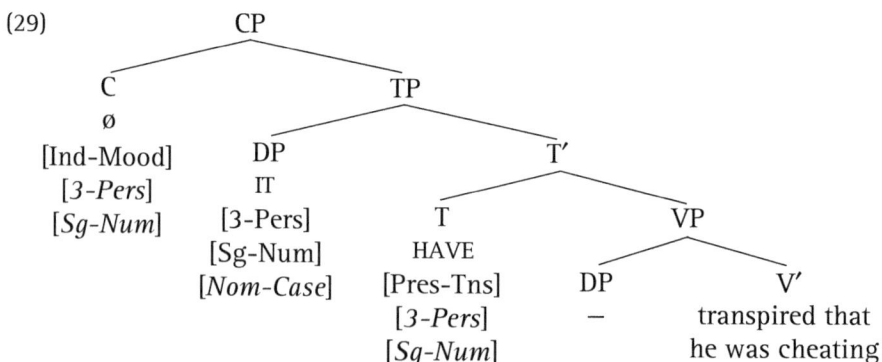

(29)

```
                            CP
              ┌──────────────┴──────────────┐
              C                             TP
              ø                ┌─────────────┴─────────────┐
          [Ind-Mood]          DP                           T′
          [3-Pers]            IT              ┌─────────────┴─────────────┐
          [Sg-Num]          [3-Pers]          T                          VP
                           [Sg-Num]          HAVE              ┌──────────┴──────────┐
                           [Nom-Case]       [Pres-Tns]         DP                    V′
                                           [3-Pers]            –          transpired that
                                           [Sg-Num]                       he was cheating
```

The tree (29) meets the requirement imposed by the Legibility Condition (6iii) for all features to be valued at the end of a syntactic derivation.

The structure (29) then undergoes transfer to the PF and LF components. The PF component processes all the features in (29), and thus spells out HAVE as the third person singular present tense form *has*, and spells out expletive IT in its nominative form *it*. The italicised uninterpretable features are (by their nature) not processed in the semantic component, so that only the non-italic interpretable features are assigned an interpretation at the semantics interface.

I will briefly conclude this section by addressing four issues raised by an anonymous reviewer in relation to the analyses sketched here. One is why expletive *it* should be taken to originate inside VP, rather than being direct-ly merged in spec-TP in order to satisfy the EPP feature on T. One answer lies in Chomsky's treatment of expletive *it* as a quasi-argument: given that (under the VP-internal Subject Hypothesis) arguments originate in a pos-ition where they are first- or second-merged with a predicate, it is plausible to suppose that the same is true of quasi-arguments. A second answer is that, given the account of agreement outlined here under which a finite T constituent agrees with a (pro)nominal that it c-commands, it follows that in a structure like (26) above, expletive *it* must originate in a (VP-internal) position below T-*have* in order for *have* to agree with it.

A second (related) question asked by the reviewer is what theta role ex-pletive *it* is assigned if it originates in an argument position within VP. One possibility is that it has the thematic role of EXPLETIVE argument of the predicate it merges with (though of course, this is merely an ad hoc stipula-tion). Another is to suppose that a predicate like *transpire* has the property that (when used with a CP complement) it assigns the theta role THEME to its complement, but assigns no theta role to its highest argument (i.e. to its subject/specifier); and we will explore another type of structure in which a verb does not theta-mark its subject in §3.4.3.

A third question asked by the reviewer is whether, if expletive *it* lacks gender it won't be φ-complete, and the Completeness Condition (6ii) will prevent expletive *it* from triggering agreement on an auxiliary like *has* in a sentence like (21a) '*It* **has** transpired that he was cheating'. However, note that (6ii) defines a φ-complete constituent as 'one with person and number', and does not mention gender at all: this is because finite verbs/auxiliaries agree with their subjects in person and number only in English, not in gender. So, being φ-complete in a given language means possessing all the features which are involved in agreement in the relevant language: and for English, this means person and number (but not gender). Thus, if (as claimed here) expletive *it* has person and number (but not gender), this will not prevent it from participating in agreement operations.

A fourth question raised by the reviewer is why (under the formulation of the EPP Condition in 7), EPP should be taken to involve T attracting the closest active goal that it agrees with in <u>person</u>. One reason is that this accounts for why T attracts (pro)nominal constituents to become its spe-cifier, since these have person (whereas APs, PPs, ADVPs etc. do not carry person, and so cannot be attracted by T). Another answer is that EPP can attract expletive *there* to move to spec-TP, and this is a defective pronoun which carries only person (not number or gender) – as we will now see in the next section.

3.2.2   Expletive *there* clauses

Typical examples of sentences with expletive *there* subjects are given below:

(30)   a.   *There* have **been** several clashes with the police
       b.   *There* **exists** a passion for comprehension, just as *there* **exists** a passion for music (forbes.com)
       c.   *There* **remain** several unresolved issues
       d.   *There* **persists** a widespread assumption that all Africans are 'indigenous' (*Huffington Post*)
       e.   *There* **endures** a disparity in budget allocation between offline and online worlds (bbh-labs.com)
       f.   Deep in the heart of the Derbyshire dales, *there* **survives** a medieval sport where almost anything goes except murder (matt-blake.co.uk)

In such sentences, expletive *there* is said to be existential in use, since it occurs as the subject of an existential predicate like *be/exist/remain/persist/ endure/survive* (*remain/persist/endure/survive* being existential predicates in that they have a meaning loosely paraphrasable as 'continue to exist'). There are other uses of *there* (e.g. locative and presentational), but I will set these aside here and concentrate on existential uses of expletive *there.*

Consider first the features carried by expletive *there.* An interesting property illustrated below is that expletive *there* can only occur with a third person verb (like *is* in 31a below), not with a first person verb (like *am* in 31b), nor with a second person verb (like *are* in 31c):

(31)   a.   There *is* only me/you taking the Fantasy Syntax course
       b.   *There *am* only I taking the Fantasy Syntax course
       c.   *There *are* only you taking the Fantasy Syntax course

This suggests that expletive *there* is intrinsically third person and so carries an inherent [3-Pers] feature. By contrast, expletive *there* can freely occur both with a singular verb (like *is* in 32a below) and with a plural verb (like *are* in 32b):

(32)   a.   There *is* only one student taking the Fantasy Syntax course
       b.   There *are* only two students taking the Fantasy Syntax course

This suggests that expletive *there* does not have an inherent number feature.

Some support for the claim that expletive *there* is numberless comes from the observation that (unlike expletive *it*: see the examples in 22 above), it cannot serve as the antecedent of PRO, for example, in a sentence like:

(33)   *There* can't be a divorce without [*there*/*PRO being a marriage first]

If PRO requires an antecedent with person and number features, we can account for why expletive *there* cannot serve as the antecedent of PRO by supposing that *there* carries person but not number.

But what about gender? Since expletive *there* never has an antecedent, it is reasonable to conclude that it does not carry a gender feature either. By contrast, expletive *there* seems to enter the derivation with an unvalued case feature which makes it active for undergoing Raising/A-Movement in a structure such as the following (where *there* originates as the subject of *been* and raises up to become the subject of T-*to* and then of T-*do*):

(34)   *There* do seem [~~there~~ to have ~~there~~ been several clashes with the police]

The unvalued case feature on *there* will be valued as nominative in a sentence like (35a) below, and as accusative in a sentence like (35b):

(35)   a. *There* is no good excuse for bad behaviour
        b. I consider *there* to be no good excuse for bad behaviour

And indeed for some speakers, expletive *there* has the genitive form *there's* – as shown by the internet-sourced examples below, where the genitive expletive *there's* is used as the subject of the gerund *being*:

(36)   a. Squidward was ranting about *there's* being no culture in Bikini
            Bottom … (amazing-everything.fandom.com)
        b. People always complain about *there's* being too many swordmen on
            smash, and Sothis also said this (gamefaqs.gamespot.com)
        c. I'd been singing (in my horrible voice) the song about *there's* being
            'no way to stop it', a song not used in the movie (solopassion.com)
        d. *There's* being no other business, the meeting was adjourned by the
            chairman at 18:30 (hksbo.org)
        e. Whites how do you feel about *there's* being a WHITE terrorist
            that has killed lot of people because he's simply a bigoted racist?
            (answers.yahoo.com)
        f. You started off very aggressively in multiple posts in the beginning
            of the thread about *there's* being nothing OP can do (imamother.com)

This suggests that (like expletive *it*), expletive *there* carries case. (People who don't use the genitive form *there's* may well treat *there* as defective in the same way as other pronouns which have no genitive form – e.g. *this/that/what*.)

The considerations outlined above suggest that expletive *there* enters the derivation with an inherently valued [3-Pers] feature, and with an unvalued case feature [u-Case]. In the light of this assumption, let's consider the derivation of our earlier sentence (30a) *There have been several clashes with the police*. This will proceed as follows.

The verb *been* merges with the QP complement *several clashes with the police* to form the V-bar *been several clashes with the police*. This V-bar is then merged with the expletive pronoun *there* to form the VP *there been several clashes with the police*. Given our conclusion in the previous paragraph that expletive *there* enters the derivation with the features [3-Pers, u-Case], the VP headed by the verb *been* will have the following structure (if we set aside the features on *been*):

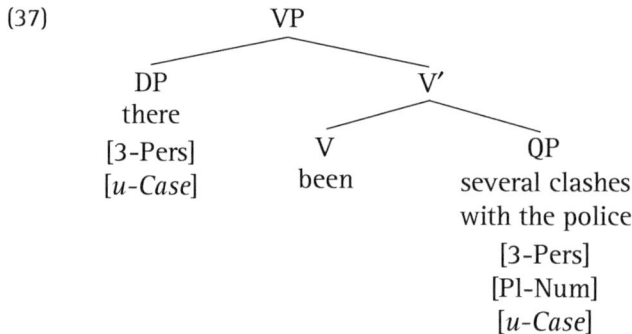

(37)

```
                    VP
         ┌──────────┴──────────┐
        DP                     V′
       there           ┌───────┴───────┐
      [3-Pers]         V               QP
      [u-Case]       been        several clashes
                                 with the police
                                    [3-Pers]
                                   [Pl-Num]
                                   [u-Case]
```

The VP in (37) is merged with the T auxiliary HAVE (which carries an interpretable present-tense feature, along with uninterpretable and unvalued person and number features, and an EPP feature), so deriving (38) below:

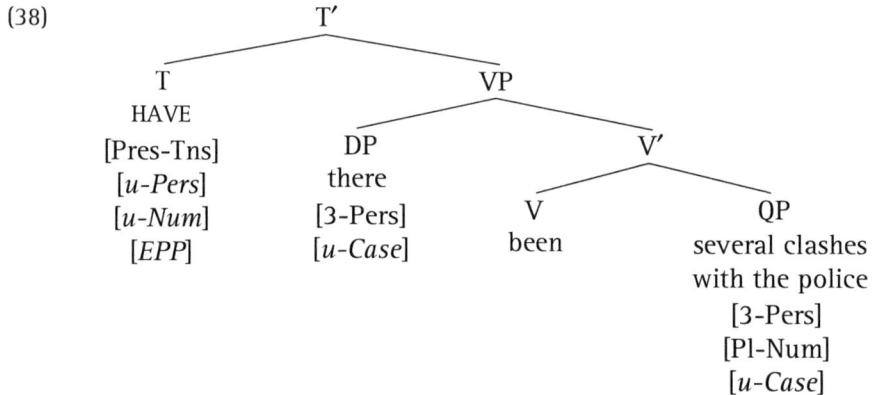

(38)

```
                         T′
         ┌───────────────┴───────────────┐
         T                                VP
       HAVE                    ┌──────────┴──────────┐
      [Pres-Tns]              DP                      V′
      [u-Pers]               there           ┌────────┴────────┐
      [u-Num]               [3-Pers]         V                 QP
      [EPP]                 [u-Case]       been          several clashes
                                                         with the police
                                                            [3-Pers]
                                                           [Pl-Num]
                                                           [u-Case]
```

The T auxiliary HAVE is active as a probe for Agreement and A-Movement at this point (by virtue of its unvalued φ-features) and so HAVE searches for goals which can value its unvalued person and number features. Let us suppose that (in consequence of the Minimality Condition) an agreement probe searches for the minimal (i.e. closest and smallest) set of one or more active goals that can value all its unvalued agreement features. So, a probe first locates the closest goal that it c-commands, and then (if that goal is unable to value all of the probe's unvalued features), the probe then locates the next closest goal ... and so on, until the point where all unvalued features of the probe have been valued (at which point the probe stops searching for further goals).

Accordingly, when T-HAVE probes in (38) above, it locates *there* as the closest goal (with *there* being rendered active by its unvalued case feature). However, *there* (being numberless) cannot value the unvalued number feature on BE; indeed, *there* cannot value the person feature on HAVE either, since *there* is a defective goal (by virtue of lacking number) and it follows from the Completeness Condition (6ii) that only a complete goal (i.e. one carrying both person and number) can value a feature on a probe.

Consequently, T-HAVE continues to probe and locates the QP *several clashes with the police* as a second goal. Thus, T-HAVE locates two active goals: one is *there* (which is active by virtue of its unvalued case feature); the other is the QP *several clashes with the police* (which is likewise active by virtue of its unvalued case feature). When a probe locates more than one active goal, it undergoes simultaneous multiple agreement with all active goals accessible to it. Accordingly, via the Agreement operation (6i), the T-probe HAVE agrees in person with both goals (the third-person constituents *there* and *several clashes with the police*) and the unvalued person feature on HAVE is thereby valued as third person (i.e. HAVE is assigned a value for its person feature which matches that of both goals). However, HAVE also agrees in number with the plural goal *several clashes with the police*, and so the unvalued number feature on HAVE is valued as plural.

In addition, in accordance with the EPP Condition (7), T-HAVE attracts the closest goal that it agrees with in person (namely expletive *there*, active through its unvalued case feature) to move to spec-TP (and the EPP feature on T-HAVE is thereafter stripped/removed from the derivation). Consequently, application of Agreement and A-Movement (arrowed below) derives the following structure:

(39)

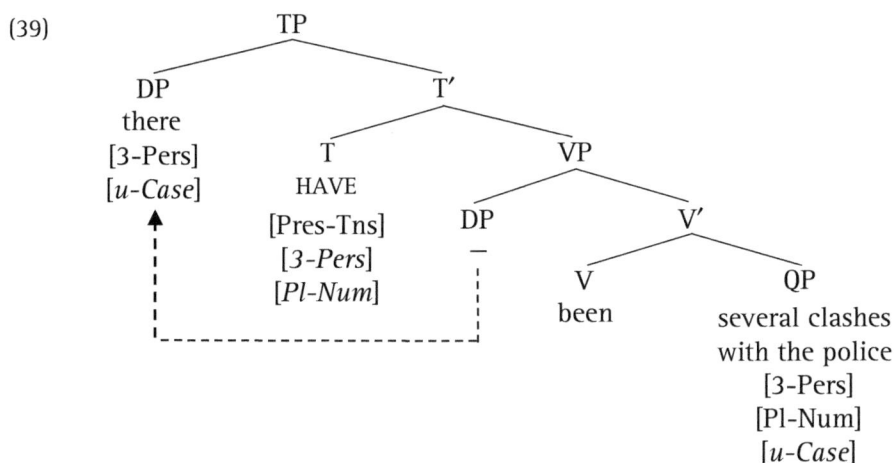

The resulting TP is then merged with a null complementiser which enters the derivation carrying an interpretable indicative-mood feature, and uninterpretable (and unvalued) person and number features, so forming the CP in (40) below:

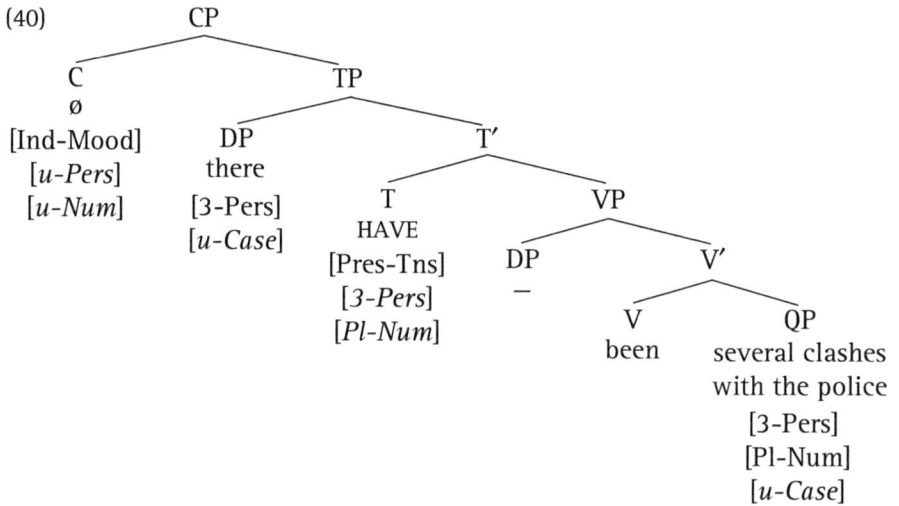

(40)

```
                    CP
            ┌────────┴────────┐
            C                 TP
            ø          ┌──────┴──────┐
        [Ind-Mood]     DP            T′
         [u-Pers]     there    ┌─────┴─────┐
         [u-Num]     [3-Pers]  T           VP
                     [u-Case]  HAVE   ┌─────┴─────┐
                             [Pres-Tns] DP        V′
                              [3-Pers]  −    ┌─────┴─────┐
                              [Pl-Num]       V          QP
                                            been   several clashes
                                                   with the police
                                                     [3-Pers]
                                                     [Pl-Num]
                                                     [u-Case]
```

The indicative complementiser in (40) serves as a probe (active by virtue of its unvalued person and number φ-features) and searches for active goals which can value these φ-features, locating the pronominal DP THERE and the QP *several clashes with the police*. The unvalued φ-features on the null complementiser are valued as third person plural via multiple agreement with THERE and *several clashes with the police*. At the same time, the unvalued case features on DP THERE and QP *several clashes with the police* are both valued as nominative via the Nominative Case Condition (11i). Accordingly, application of Agreement and Case-assignment maps (40) above into the structure in (41) below:

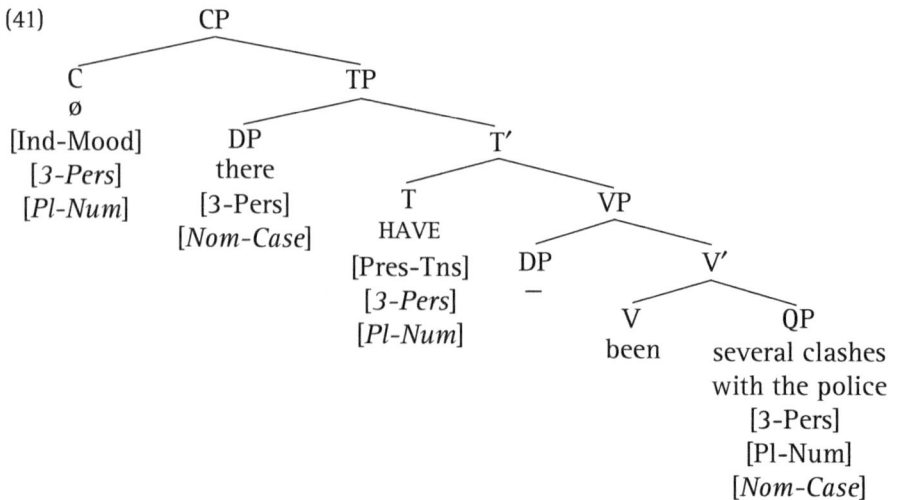

(41)

```
                    CP
            ┌────────┴────────┐
            C                 TP
            ø          ┌──────┴──────┐
        [Ind-Mood]     DP            T′
         [3-Pers]     there    ┌─────┴─────┐
         [Pl-Num]    [3-Pers]  T           VP
                    [Nom-Case] HAVE   ┌─────┴─────┐
                             [Pres-Tns] DP        V′
                              [3-Pers]  −    ┌─────┴─────┐
                              [Pl-Num]       V          QP
                                            been   several clashes
                                                   with the police
                                                     [3-Pers]
                                                     [Pl-Num]
                                                     [Nom-Case]
```

Since all features are valued at the end of the syntactic derivation, the Legibility Condition (6iii) is satisfied.

The structure (41) then undergoes transfer to the PF and LF components. The auxiliary HAVE is spelled out at PF in its third person plural present tense form *have*, and expletive THERE in its nominative form *there* (rather than e.g. in its genitive form *there's*). Likewise, the QP is spelled out in its nominative form *several clashes with the police.* Accordingly, the overall structure in (41) is ultimately spelled out as the PF string (30a) *There have been several clashes with the police.* When the structure (41) is transferred to the semantic component, only the non-italic interpretable features are processed there.

The discussion above highlights a further interesting property of expletive *there* which differentiates it from expletive *it*. This is that expletive *there* must always be associated with another goal (like the QP *several clashes with the police* above) which can value the number feature on T (and on C). This additional goal is referred to as the <u>associate</u> of the expletive (e.g. *several clashes with the police* is the associate of *there* in 41). By contrast, expletive *it* does not require an associate (as we see from sentences like *It is raining*) precisely because it has a full set of person and number features of its own.

Our discussion of agreement in (41) above claims that the null complementiser assigns nominative case to the QP goal *several clashes with the police.* But an important question of detail which this claim raises is which of the words in this QP carries nominative case – an issue discussed earlier in relation to the examples in (15) above. Let's suppose that (as in languages like Latin with a richer system of overt case marking), nouns and the determiners and quantifiers which modify them carry case, and hence all enter the derivation carrying an unvalued case feature. Let's also suppose that (in consequence of the Minimality Condition), a constituent with an unvalued case feature is case-marked by the closest case assigner above (i.e. c-commanding) it. For the words *several* and *clashes*, the closest case-assigner above them in (41) is the null complementiser C-ø at the top of the tree; hence (since C-ø is indicative in mood and thus a nominative case assigner), *several* and *clashes* are assigned nominative case. By contrast, the closest case assigner above *the* and *police* is the transitive preposition *with*; hence *the* and *police* are assigned accusative case by *with*. Thus, in saying that the QP goal *several clashes with the police* is assigned nominative case, what we really mean is that case features on *several* and *clashes* are valued as nominative: the preposition *with* assigns (but does not itself have) case.

Our assumption that T in (41) undergoes multiple agreement with both the expletive goal *there* and the non-expletive goal *several prizes* and that *there* is intrinsically third person carries with it the tacit implication that the associate of the expletive must likewise be a third person expression, since a probe cannot agree with multiple goals which have different person properties (because this will mean that the probe cannot be assigned a person value which matches that carried by each of its goals – that is, there will be feature mismatch). Such an assumption accounts for contrasts like:

(42) a. *Only I* **am** representing the club
      b. **There* **am/is** *only I* representing the club
      c. There **is** *only me* representing the club

In (42a), the only goal for the T-probe BE is the (italicised) first person singular expression *only I*, and consequently BE agrees with this (single) goal and is marked as first person singular. But in (42b), BE has two (italicised) goals which it must agree with – namely the third person expletive *there* and its first person singular associate *only I*. If BE agrees in person and number with the associate *only I*, it will be marked as first person singular and ultimately be spelled out as *am*: but this will mean that *am* does not agree in person with the third person expletive *there*, causing the derivation to crash. Conversely, if BE agrees in person with *there* and in number with the associate *only I*, it will be marked as third person singular and ultimately be spelled out as *is*: but this will mean that *is* does not agree in person with *only I*. Because of the resulting feature mismatch, (42b) is ungrammatical.

What is at first sight puzzling is the pattern of agreement in (42c), where use of the third person form *is* suggests that both of its goals (*there* and *only me*) must be third person. How can this be? The answer would appear to be that *only me* has the property of being able to function as a third person singular expression, as we see from third person singular agreement on the bold-printed verb/auxiliary in (internet-sourced) sentences such as the following:

(43) a. Now *only me* **is** working on it (fsdeveloper.com)
      b. *Only me* **is** capable of breaking a spoon on my second spoonful of sonic ice cream! (Kylie Morton on Twitter)
      c. So at the moment, *only me* **has** access to normally blocked sites (edugeek.net)
      d. *Only me* **knows** why (Title of a song by Harold Walden)
      e. *Only me* **doesn't** have kids (forums.whirlpool.net.au)

How can we account for this? A plausible answer is that *only me* has a more abstract structure akin to that of a QP/quantifier phrase like *nobody but me* (where *but* functions as a preposition like *except*, according to Householder 1987). This would account for third person agreement, because *nobody* requires third person singular agreement (e.g. 'Nobody *is* that stupid'). It would also account for the use of the accusative pronoun *me*, if *me* is the complement of an invisible transitive preposition like *but/except* (i.e. if *only me* can have a structure akin to that of 'nobody *but/except* me').

Support for this analysis of *only*-structures comes from the singular agreement found in sentences such as the following where *only* has a plural pronoun after it:

(44)   a. I thought there **was** *only us* (L. Lowry, *The Giver*, Bantam, New York, 1993)

        b. And then there **was** *only us* (Title of book by K. Buff, Polar Bear Books, 2015)

        c. When there **was** *only us* (Title of song by Aether, on Spotify)

        d. I have no friends, there **is** *only you two* (M. Clark, 2000, *Terrorists*, Google Books)

        e. As you watch, there **is** *only them*, and you are transfixed (iai.tv)

If we analyse *only us/only you two/only them* in (44) as having a more abstract structure paraphrasable as 'nobody except us/you two/them', we can account for singular agreement on the verbs *was* and *is* in structures like these by positing that the head of the structure is a singular pronoun like *nobody*. Of course, as an anonymous reviewer rightly points out, such an analysis raises the question of how 'nobody except' comes to be spelled out as *only*.

3.2.3   Conditions on the use of expletives

An important question to ask in the context of our discussion of expletive *it* in §3.2.1 and expletive *there* in §3.2.2 is what conditions govern the use of expletives. What I shall suggest here is that expletives are subject to the following conditions:

(45)   **Expletive Conditions**

    (i)   <u>External Argument Condition</u>

    An expletive can only be merged as the highest argument of a verb with no external argument

    (ii) <u>Indefiniteness Condition</u>

    Existential *there* can only be merged as the specifier of an existential verb with an indefinite (pro)nominal complement

    (iii) <u>Inactivity Condition</u>

    Expletive *it* can only be merged with a constituent which does not contain an active nominal or pronominal (i.e. one carrying an unvalued case feature)

Let's briefly illustrate how these conditions work.

Consider first the External Argument Condition (45i). If a verb phrase can only have one external argument/specifier (either a thematic argument, or an expletive quasi-argument) and if the italicised external argument of the verb in a transitive structure like (46a) below originates as the specifier of the verb, then it follows that the verb cannot also have an expletive external (quasi-) argument like that bold-printed in (46b):

(46)   a. *A spokeman for the president* has denied allegations of impropriety
        b. ***There** has *a spokesman for the president* denied allegations of impropriety

If an expletive is 'the last argument to be added' in a derivation (Felser & Rupp 2001: 314), it follows that (in a sentence like *There occurred several unfortunate incidents*), the QP *several unfortunate incidents* will be the first argument to be merged with the verb *occur* (as its complement), and expletive *there* the second/last argument (as the specifier of the VP headed by the verb *occur*).

Note that the condition that an expletive is merged as the highest argument of a predicate does not imply that it should always be merged as the specifier of the predicate. This is because, in cases where the expletive is the only argument of a predicate it will initially be merged as the complement of the predicate. A case in point is 'weather *it*' in sentences such as:

(47)   It has been raining/snowing all night long

Here, expletive *it* is the only argument of the unaccusative predicate *rain/snow*, and thus *it* will initially be merged in comp-VP as the complement of the verb *rain/snow*, before raising up to spec-TP to become the subject/specifier of the T auxiliary *has*. Cross-linguistic evidence that *rain/snow* are unaccusative verbs comes from the observation that the Italian counterparts of the verbs *rain/snow* can be used with the Italian counterpart of the perfect auxiliary BE – as is typical of unaccusative verbs:

(48)   È   piovuto/nevicato   tutta   la   notte
        is   rained/snowed   all   the   night
        'It has been raining/snowing all night long'

Since Italian is a null subject language, the Italian counterpart of *it* has a null spellout in (48).

Now consider the Indefiniteness Condition (45ii). This is illustrated by Kayne (2016) in terms of contrasts such as the following:

(49)   a. *Three/many/several/no/some books* were on the table
        b. There were *three/many/several/no/some books* on the table

(50)   a. *The treasure/it* definitely exists, so keep looking
        b. *There definitely exists *the treasure/it*, so keep looking

Kayne (2016: 1) formulates the condition as follows: 'When co-occurring with expletive *there* (or a counterpart of it in other languages), existential verbs only combine with indefinite noun phrases' – hence with indefinite (pro)nominal expressions like those italicised in (49), but not with definites like those italicised in (50).

However, this raises the question of why an expletive should be used at all in sentences like (49b). Use of an expletive in association with an indefinite internal argument may well be motivated by semantic considerations. Thus, indefinites which move to spec-TP are ambiguous between a specific and a non-specific reading, whereas indefinites which remain in situ within VP in expletive structures allow only a non-specific reading – as illustrated by the contrast below:

(51)   a. *A man* is in the room
         b. There is *a man* in the room

So, while *a man* in (51a) can have either a specific or a non-specific interpretation, in (51b) it can only have a non-specific interpretation. This suggests that the use of an expletive pronoun in sentences like (51b) is a device for ensuring that the associated indefinite expression does not receive a specific interpretation.

Finally, consider the Inactivity Condition (45iii). In this respect, consider the following contrast:

(52)   <u>There</u>/*<u>It</u> exists no tangible proof of his involvement

Here, expletive *there* can be used in conjunction with the indefinite QP *no tangible proof of his involvement* (in conformity with the Indefiniteness Condition in 45ii), but expletive *it* cannot be used in place of *there*. How come? The answer is that expletive *it* would be merged as the specifier of the V-bar *exists no tangible proof of his involvement*, but this V-bar contains the QP *no tangible proof of his involvement* which is active (when it enters the derivation) by virtue of its unvalued case feature: hence, the Inactivity Condition blocks the use of *it* here. The condition ensures that expletive *it* is only used in a structure which would otherwise lack a goal active for agreement, with *it* serving to provide an active goal which can value unvalued φ-features on a T-probe.

To summarise: in Module 3.2 we have looked at the syntax of clauses with an expletive subject. I argued that expletive *it* enters the derivation with inherently valued third-person and singular-number features and an unvalued case feature, and that its person/number features value those of the auxiliary HAVE in sentences such as *It has transpired that he was cheating*, while the unvalued case feature on *it* is valued by (abstract/invisible) agreement with the null complementiser introducing the main clause. I suggested that expletive subjects (being quasi-arguments) originate within VP (like other arguments), and from there are attracted by the EPP feature on T to move to spec-TP. I went on to argue that expletive *there* enters the derivation with an inherently valued third person feature and an unvalued case feature, and that the expletive and its associate jointly value the unvalued features on the auxiliary (or affix) in T via multiple agreement. The unvalued case features on expletive *there* and its associate are in turn valued via (abstract) agreement with the complementiser introducing the clause.

You should now be able to tackle Exercise 3.2.

3.3   Agreement, A-Movement and case in infinitives

So far, our discussion of agreement has focused on finite clauses. I have argued that T and C in such clauses enter the derivation carrying valued interpretable features (e.g. indicative-mood in the case of C, present/past-tense in the case of T), and unvalued uninterpretable (person and number) φ-features. The φ-features on T make (an auxiliary or tense-affix in) T active as a probe for Agreement and A-Movement, while the φ-features on C make the complementiser active as a probe for case assignment. However, a question which has not been addressed so far concerns what role (if any) agreement plays in infinitival clauses; and this is the topic tackled in this module.

English has a range of different types of infinitive clause, including those bracketed below:

(53)   a. There do seem [to have been some problems]
        b. We believe [him to be telling the truth]
        c. He is believed [to be telling the truth]

(54)   a. We are anxious [for the agreements to be ratified]
        b. They want [the president to be impeached]
        c. It will be essential [to prepare myself]

For reasons outlined in Radford (2020: §4.4–§4.5), the infinitive clauses bracketed in (53) are TPs, whereas those bracketed in (54) are CPs. More specifically, the bracketed infinitival TP in (53a) is the complement of the Raising verb *seem*, that in (53b) is the complement of the ECM (i.e. exceptional case-marking) verb *believe*, and that in (53c) is the complement of the passive participle *believed*. By contrast, the bracketed CP in (54a) is a *for*-infinitive, that in (54b) is a *for*-deletion infinitive (i.e. a CP headed by a null/deleted counterpart of *for*), and that in (54c) is a Control infinitive headed by a null complementiser. The question which concerns us here is how Agreement, A-Movement and Case-marking work in infinitive clauses. In order to answer this, we'll take a look at each of the sentences in (53, 54) in turn – starting with the Raising structure in (53a).

3.3.1   Raising infinitives

In (53a), the expletive pronominal DP *there* is superficially in spec-TP, but given the VP-Internal Subject Hypothesis, the expletive will originate as the specifier of the VP headed by the verb *been*. It is clear that the auxiliary DO carries agreement properties, since it overtly inflects for agreement (e.g. here it is in the third person plural form *do*, but we require the third person singular form *does* in 'There *does* seem to have been a problem'). By contrast, infinitival *to* doesn't overtly inflect for agreement at all, though there are theoretical reasons for thinking that infinitival *to* must carry a person feature (albeit this is abstract/invisible).

The reason is that infinitival *to* attracts expletive *there* to become its specifier at the intermediate stage of derivation represented by the bold-printed copy of *there* in (55) below, when *there* moves from being the specifier of the bracketed VP to becoming the specifier of the bracketed TP within the infinitive clause:

(55)   *There* do seem [$_{TP}$ ~~**there**~~ to have [$_{VP}$ ~~there~~ been some problems]]

Under the person agreement account of A-Movement outlined in Module 3.1, a T-constituent carrying an EPP feature triggers movement in accordance with the condition in (56) below (repeated from 7 above):

(56)   **EPP Condition**
        An EPP feature on a probe T attracts the closest XP goal that T agrees
        with in person to undergo A-Movement to spec-TP, and the EPP feature
        is stripped from T (and removed from the derivation) once the movement
        has taken place

What this means is that infinitival *to* in (55) must carry an (abstract) person feature in order to be able to attract the goal *there* to become its specifier. Let us suppose that (for economy reasons), person is the only φ-feature carried by infinitival *to* (since there is no theoretical or empirical rationale for positing that infinitival *to* carries number as well: e.g. unlike the T auxiliary *do*, infinitival *to* can't carry third person singular -*s* in 'He *does* seem *to*/**tos* be unwell').

Given the assumptions made above (and others), sentence (53a) *There do seem to have been some problems* will be derived as follows. The verb *been* is first-merged with the QP *some problems* and second-merged with expletive *there*, forming the VP *there been some problems*. The resulting VP is merged with the perfect aspect auxiliary *have* to form the PERFP *have there been some problems*. The resulting PERFP is then merged with T-*to*, forming the T-bar below:

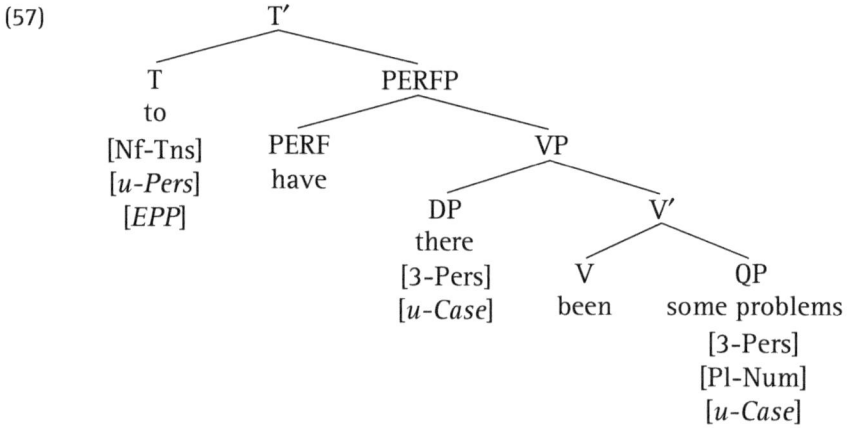

(57)

```
                          T′
            _____
           T                          PERFP
           to               _____
        [Nf-Tns]         PERF                       VP
        [u-Pers]         have               _____
         [EPP]                             DP               V′
                                          there         _____
                                        [3-Pers]       V          QP
                                        [u-Case]     been    some problems
                                                              [3-Pers]
                                                              [Pl-Num]
                                                              [u-Case]
```

Let us suppose that expletive *there* is a pronominal DP which enters the derivation carrying a third person feature and an unvalued case feature. Let's also suppose that infinitival *to* enters the derivation carrying an interpretable feature [Nf-Tns] denoting nonfinite tense, an uninterpretable (and unvalued) person feature, and an EPP feature which is illegible at the PF and LF interfaces, by virtue of having neither form nor meaning. (I note in passing that the idea that infinitives carry an abstract person-agreement feature gains potential cross-linguistic support from the observation that European Portuguese has infinitives which overtly inflect for agreement in both person and number with their subject: see Raposo 1987, Ambar 2007, and Gonçalves et al. 2014.)

In accordance with the Probe Condition (5i), the infinitive particle T-*to* is active as a probe (for Agreement and A-Movement) by virtue of its unvalued person feature, and searches for an active goal which can value this feature. The closest such goal is expletive *there*, which is active by virtue of its unvalued case feature; however, *there* is not φ-complete (since it carries person but not number), and so cannot value the unvalued person feature on T-*to* by itself. Consequently, T-*to* probes deeper into the structure and locates the QP *some problems* as the next closest goal, and this is φ-complete (since it carries both person and number), and active (by virtue of its unvalued case-feature). The two active goals *there* and *some problems* can thus jointly value the unvalued person feature on T-*to* as third person via Agreement (on the assumption that the Completeness Condition 6ii is satisfied as long as one of the agreeing goals is φ-complete).

In addition, the EPP feature on T-*to* attracts the closest goal that it agrees with in person to move to spec-TP: the closest such goal c-commanded by

T-*to* is the expletive pronoun *there*, which is active by virtue of its unvalued case feature. Agreement and A-Movement result in the structure below (with the arrow showing A-Movement, and the position out of which *there* moves being shown as a gap −, and the EPP feature being stripped from T-*to* once it has done its job in triggering A-Movement):

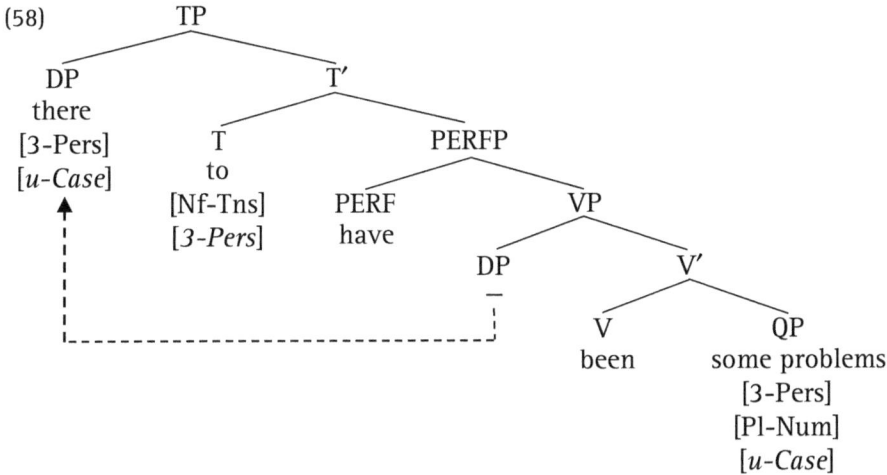

(58)

```
                      TP
         ┌────────────┴────────────┐
        DP                         T′
       there          ┌────────────┴────────────┐
      [3-Pers]         T                       PERFP
      [u-Case]         to          ┌────────────┴────────────┐
         ▲          [Nf-Tns]      PERF                      VP
         ┊          [3-Pers]      have          ┌────────────┴────────────┐
         ┊                                     DP                        V′
         ┊                                      −              ┌──────────┴──────────┐
         └──────────────────────────────────────              V                    QP
                                                             been          some problems
                                                                             [3-Pers]
                                                                             [Pl-Num]
                                                                             [u-Case]
```

The resulting TP is then merged as the complement of the Raising verb *seem*, forming the VP *seem there to have − been some problems*. This VP is in turn merged as the complement of the T auxiliary *do* (which enters the derivation carrying an interpretable present-tense feature, uninterpretable and unvalued person and number features, and an EPP feature which is illegible at both interfaces), forming the T-bar shown below (simplified by showing only features on those constituents which remain active for A-operations at this point, in order to avoid distracting details):

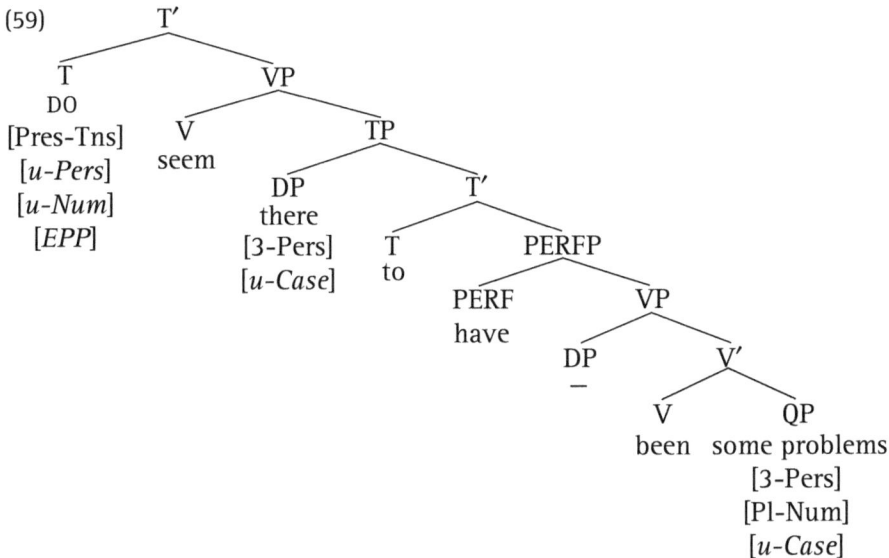

(59)

```
              T′
    ┌─────────┴─────────┐
    T                   VP
   DO         ┌─────────┴─────────┐
 [Pres-Tns]   V                  TP
 [u-Pers]    seem      ┌──────────┴──────────┐
 [u-Num]              DP                     T′
 [EPP]              there         ┌──────────┴──────────┐
                  [3-Pers]        T                   PERFP
                  [u-Case]        to        ┌──────────┴──────────┐
                                          PERF                   VP
                                          have         ┌──────────┴──────────┐
                                                      DP                    V′
                                                       −          ┌──────────┴──────────┐
                                                                  V                    QP
                                                                been          some problems
                                                                                [3-Pers]
                                                                                [Pl-Num]
                                                                                [u-Case]
```

At this point, the T auxiliary DO is active as a probe (for Agreement and A-Movement) by virtue of its unvalued person and number features, and searches for an active goal which can value these. The closest goal c-commanded by DO is expletive *there*, which is active by virtue of its unvalued case feature. However, *there* is a defective goal (since it carries no number feature), and hence the Completeness Condition (6ii) prevents *there* from valuing any of the φ-features on DO on its own. Consequently, DO probes further down into the structure, locating the QP *some problems* as the next closest goal (active by virtue of its unvalued case feature). Since this QP carries both person and number and is therefore φ-complete, multiple agreement can take place at this point between the active probe DO, and its two active goals (*there* and *some problems*). Via agreement, the third person features on *there* and *some problems* jointly value the unvalued person feature on DO as third-person, and the plural number feature on *some problems* values the unvalued number feature on *do* as plural.

The EPP feature on DO then attracts the closest goal it agrees with in person (expletive *there*) to move to spec-TP, and the EPP feature is thereafter stripped from T, and thereby removed entirely from the derivation because it is illegible at the PF and LF interfaces. The resulting TP is merged with a null complementiser, deriving the CP below (with the arrow showing A-Movement):

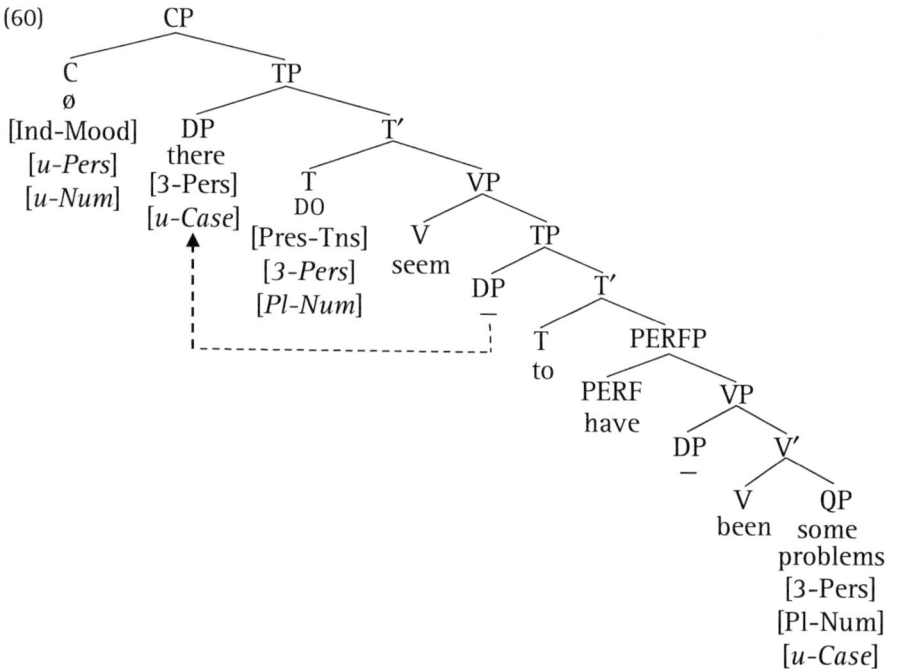

(60)

```
                        CP
          ┌──────────────┴──────────────┐
          C                             TP
          ∅              ┌───────────────┴───────────────┐
    [Ind-Mood]          DP                               T′
      [u-Pers]         there          ┌──────────────────┴──────────────┐
      [u-Num]         [3-Pers]         T                                VP
                      [u-Case]        DO            ┌────────────────────┴───┐
                         ↑        [Pres-Tns]        V                       TP
                         ┊         [3-Pers]       seem         ┌─────────────┴──────┐
                         ┊         [Pl-Num]                    DP                   T′
                         ┊                                      –        ┌──────────┴──────┐
                         ┊                                               T               PERFP
                         └─ ─ ─ ─ ─ ─ ─ ─ ─ ─ ─ ─ ─ ─ ─ ─ ─ ─ ─ to       ┌──────────┴──────┐
                                                                        PERF             VP
                                                                        have      ┌────────┴────┐
                                                                                  DP           V′
                                                                                   –      ┌─────┴─────┐
                                                                                          V          QP
                                                                                        been        some
                                                                                                  problems
                                                                                                  [3-Pers]
                                                                                                  [Pl-Num]
                                                                                                  [u-Case]
```

The null complementiser at the top of the tree is active as a probe (for Agreement and Case-marking) by virtue of its unvalued person and number features, and searches for an XP goal which can value these. The closest goal c-commanded by C-ø is the expletive DP *there*, which is active by virtue of its unvalued case feature. However, *there* is a defective goal (lacking a number feature), and so cannot value any of the φ-features on C-ø. Consequently, the complementiser probes further down into the structure, locating the QP *some problems* as the next closest potential goal (active by virtue of its unvalued case feature). Since this QP carries both person and number and is therefore φ-complete, multiple agreement can take place at this point between the complementiser and its two active goals (*there* and *some problems*). Via multiple agreement, the third person features on *there* and *some problems* jointly value the unvalued person feature on the complementiser as third-person, and the plural number feature on *some problems* values the unvalued number feature on the complementiser as plural. Since the complementiser is finite (in that it carries an indicative mood feature) and φ-complete (in that it carries both person and number), it can value the unvalued case features on the two goals (*there* and *some problems*) as nominative, so resulting in the final derived syntactic structure below:

(61)

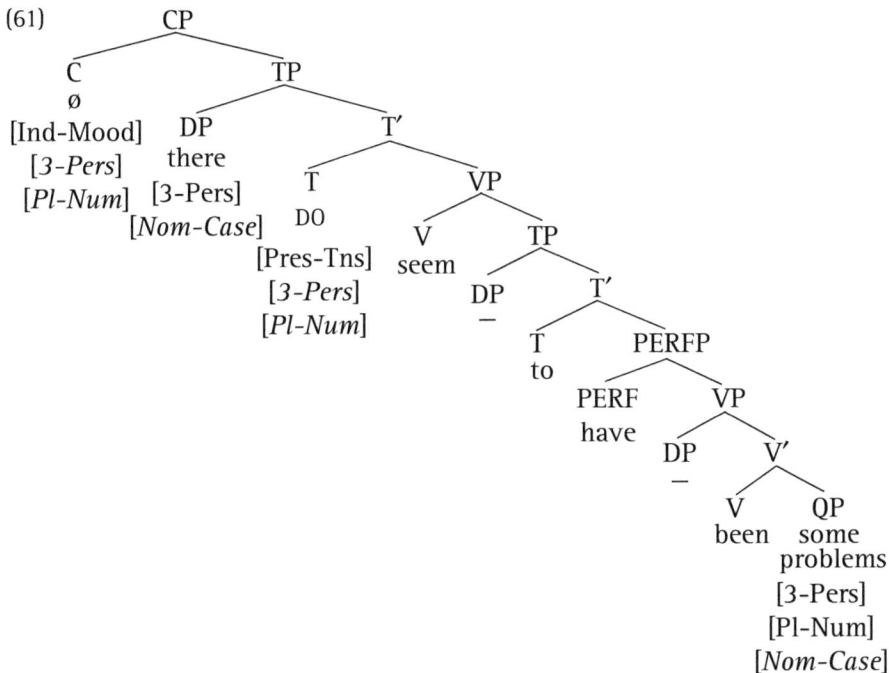

The structure in (61) satisfies the requirement imposed by the Legibility Condition (6iii) for all features to be valued at the end of the syntactic derivation.

When the tree in (61) undergoes transfer to the PF component, the T auxiliary DO is spelled out in its third person plural present tense form *do*, the expletive is spelled out in its nominative form *there*, and the QP *some problems* is likewise spelled out in its nominative form *some problems*. The overall structure is spelled out as the sentence (53a) *There do seem to have been some problems.*

3.3.2   ECM infinitives

Now let's turn to consider the derivation of the ECM infinitive structure (53b) *We believe him to be telling the truth.* The infinitive clause can be argued to be a TP on the grounds that its subject can passivise (as in 53c '*He* is believed to be telling the truth'), and Passivisation is possible across a TP boundary, but not across a CP boundary (because the Impenetrability Condition bars movement across the edge of an intervening CP). Given the VP-Internal Subject Hypothesis, the infinitive subject HE (used as a case-independent designation of the pronoun variously spelled out as *he/him/his*) will originate as the specifier of *telling the truth*, and then (via A-Movement) will be raised to become the specifier of the infinitive particle T-*to*, where it is assigned accusative case by the transitive verb *believe* in the higher clause. Let's take a closer look at the mechanics of this.

The verb *telling* first-merges with the DP *the truth* and second-merges with the pronominal DP HE to form the VP HE *telling the truth*. The resulting VP is merged with the progressive aspect auxiliary/PROG *be* to form the PROGP *be* HE *telling the truth*, and this in turn is merged with the infinitival particle T-*to*, thereby forming the T-bar below (simplified by showing only features on constituents relevant to our discussion of agreement/movement/case-marking here – hence for example, omitting the masculine-gender feature on HE, because this plays no part in person/number agreement):

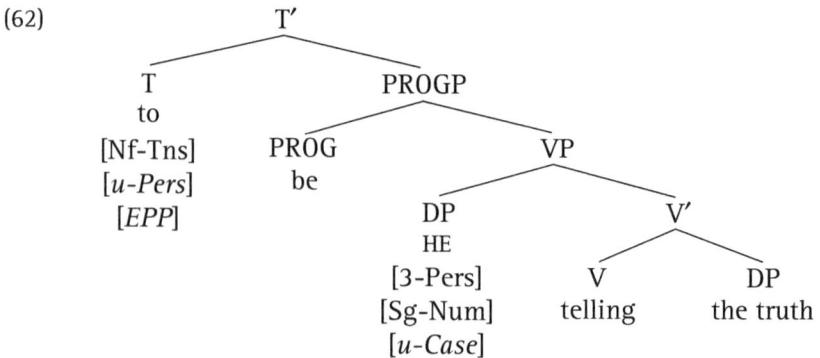

(62)

```
                              T′
              ┌───────────────┴───────────────┐
              T                              PROGP
              to                    ┌──────────┴──────────┐
           [Nf-Tns]               PROG                    VP
           [u-Pers]                be            ┌─────────┴─────────┐
            [EPP]                                DP                  V′
                                                 HE          ┌───────┴───────┐
                                              [3-Pers]       V              DP
                                              [Sg-Num]    telling       the truth
                                              [u-Case]
```

At this point, the infinitive particle T-*to* is active as a probe for Agreement and A-Movement by virtue of its unvalued person feature, and searches for an XP goal which can value this feature. The closest such goal c-commanded by T-*to* is the pronominal DP HE, which is active by virtue of its unvalued case-feature. The pronoun HE is φ-complete (since it carries both person and number), and so can value the unvalued person feature on T-*to* as third person via Agreement (6i). In addition, the EPP feature on T-*to* attracts the closest goal that T-*to* agrees with in person to move to spec-TP: the closest such goal is the third-person pronoun HE, which is active by virtue of its unvalued case feature. After A-Movement takes place, T-*to* is stripped of its EPP feature (because EPP has neither form nor meaning, and so is illegible at the PF and LF interfaces). Agreement and A-Movement thus give rise to the structure below (where the A-Movement operation is arrowed):

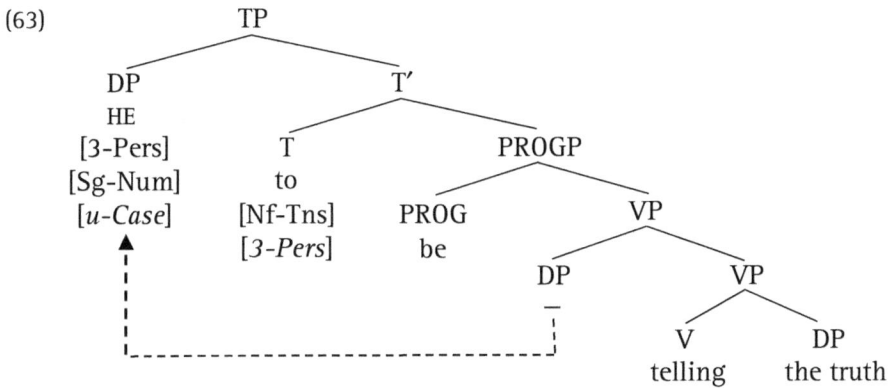

(63)

```
                        TP
           ┌────────────┴────────────┐
          DP                        T′
          HE                 ┌───────┴───────┐
        [3-Pers]            T              PROGP
        [Sg-Num]            to         ┌─────┴─────┐
        [u-Case]         [Nf-Tns]    PROG         VP
           ▲             [3-Pers]     be      ┌────┴────┐
           ┆                                 DP        VP
           ┆                                  ¦     ┌───┴───┐
           ┆                                  ¦     V      DP
           └──────────────────────────────────┘  telling  the truth
```

The resulting VP is then merged with the transitive verb *believe*, which is responsible for assigning accusative case to the pronoun HE. Since Case-marking (under the account in 11 above) is contingent on the case assigner being φ-complete (i.e. carrying person and number) and agreeing with the case assignee in respect of one or more φ-features, this means that the verb *believe* will carry an abstract/invisible set of agreement features. Merging the verb *believe* with the TP in (63) above will form the V-bar shown below (simplified by not showing the internal structure of the VP *telling the truth*):

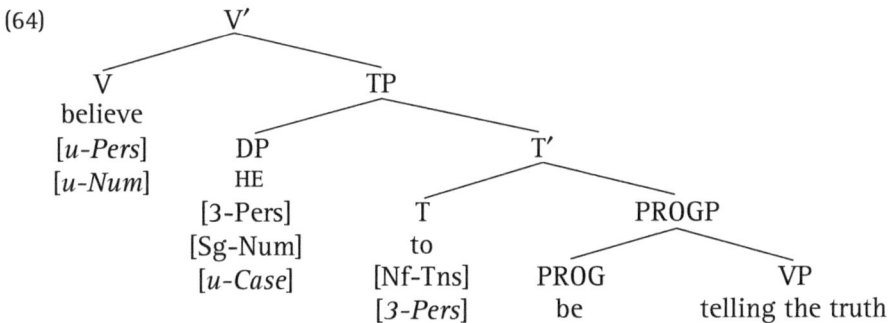

(64)

```
                  V′
        ┌─────────┴─────────┐
        V                  TP
     believe        ┌───────┴───────┐
     [u-Pers]      DP              T′
     [u-Num]       HE        ┌──────┴──────┐
                 [3-Pers]    T           PROGP
                 [Sg-Num]    to       ┌────┴────┐
                 [u-Case]  [Nf-Tns]  PROG      VP
                           [3-Pers]   be   telling the truth
```

The verb *believe* serves as an active probe for Agreement and Case-marking at this point, by virtue of its unvalued person and number features. V-*believe* searches for the closest goal that can value its unvalued φ-features, locating the pronoun HE (which is active by virtue of its unvalued case feature). Being φ-complete, HE can value the unvalued φ-features on V-*believe* as third person singular. Conversely, the φ-complete probe V-*believe* (being transitive) can value the unvalued case feature on HE as accusative, resulting in the structure below:

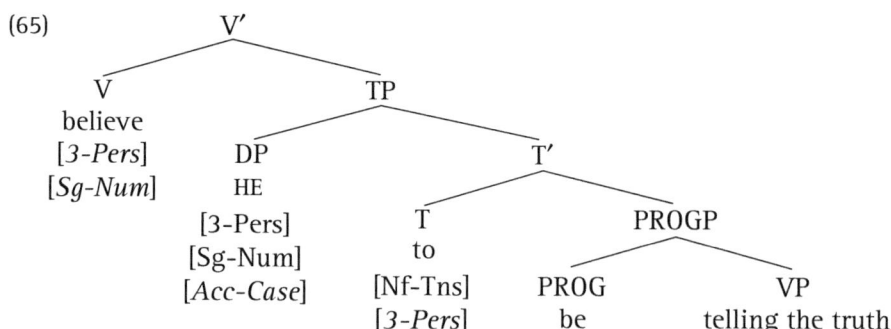

(65)

```
              V'
      ┌───────┴───────┐
      V               TP
   believe      ┌──────┴──────┐
   [3-Pers]    DP             T'
   [Sg-Num]    HE       ┌──────┴──────┐
            [3-Pers]    T           PROGP
            [Sg-Num]    to      ┌─────┴─────┐
            [Acc-Case]  [Nf-Tns] PROG        VP
                        [3-Pers]  be    telling the truth
```

Consequently, the pronoun HE is ultimately spelled out at PF in its accusative form *him*. Since the agreement features on *believe* and *to* are abstract (i.e. invisible), they have no visible reflex on the spellout of these items. The derivation in (65) will then continue until it eventually results in the structure associated with (53b) *We believe him to be telling the truth*, but I will not be concerned with the relevant details here, since my main focus is on agreement and case-marking in the infinitive clause.

An interesting issue raised by the analysis in (65) is how the syntax 'knows' that the verb *believe* is transitive (i.e. is an accusative case assigner). One possibility would be to assume that this is because *believe* has an external argument (its thematic subject *we*, not shown in 65); however, this would clearly not account for why a transitive complementiser like infinitival *for* or a transitive preposition like *about* are also accusative case assigners (since neither has an external argument/thematic subject).

An alternative possibility would be that case assigners carry a feature which specifies the case that they assign. On this view, a transitive verb such as *believe* in a structure like (64) above would carry a feature like [Ass-Acc] 'Assign accusative case to any agreeing goal(s) with an unvalued case feature'. We can suppose that (like EPP features) case-assignment features on probes are stripped (and thereby removed from the derivation entirely) once they have done their work in assigning case to one or more appropriate goals, since they have no form (e.g. a preposition like *about* doesn't inflect for its ability to assign accusative case), and no meaning (e.g. the fact that *about* assigns accusative case to its complement doesn't affect its meaning), and thus they are illegible at the PF and LF interfaces. Indeed, we might similarly treat the EPP feature as being of the form [Attr-Pers] 'Attract the closest XP with person to become my specifier'. I will not speculate on these issues any further here, however (though Exercises 3.3 and 3.4 will give you an opportunity to explore this idea).

A further issue raised by the analysis outlined above concerns the rationale for positing that transitive verbs agree abstractly with constituents they assign accusative case to. The rationale is partly theoretical, in that it follows from the Completeness Condition (6ii) that only a φ-complete probe can value features on a goal. In addition, there is cross-linguistic empirical evidence in support of this assumption, from languages where verbs can agree overtly with constituents to which they assign accusative case – as in the following Hungarian example from Bárány (2015), where OBJ denotes an object agreement suffix:

(66)   Lát-om   a   sajtburger-t
        See-1SG.OBJ   the   cheeseburger-ACC
        'I see the cheeseburger'

Here, the verb *lát*~see~ overtly agrees with the DP *a*~the~ *sajtburger-t*~cheeseburger-ACC~ that it assigns accusative case to, and this lends cross-linguistic plausibility to the idea that accusative case assignment involves agreement (albeit this type of agreement is abstract/invisible in English).

3.3.3   Passive infinitives

Now let's turn to consider the derivation of the passive infinitive structure (53c) *He is believed to be telling the truth*. Let's suppose that this proceeds as for (53b) *We believe him to be telling the truth* until we have formed the infinitival TP *HE to be − telling the truth* in (63) above. At this point, this TP is merged with the passive verb *believed* to form the VP *believed HE to be − telling the truth*. The resulting VP is then merged with the T auxiliary BE, forming the structure below (simplified, inter alia, by showing only features playing a part in Agreement, Case-marking, and A-Movement):

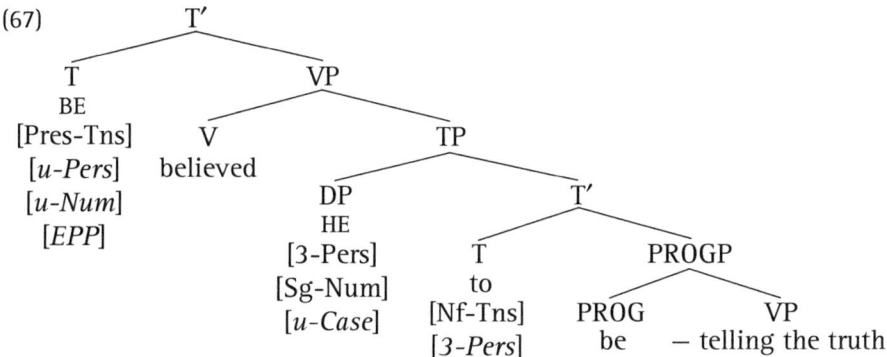

(67)

```
                        T′
         _____
        T                           VP
       BE                _____
  [Pres-Tns]            V                           TP
   [u-Pers]          believed            _____
   [u-Num]                              DP                           T′
    [EPP]                               HE                _____
                                     [3-Pers]            T                 PROGP
                                     [Sg-Num]            to           _____
                                     [u-Case]         [Nf-Tns]       PROG         VP
                                                       [3-Pers]       be    − telling the truth
```

The finite T auxiliary BE (at the top of the tree) enters the derivation carrying an interpretable present-tense feature, uninterpretable (and unvalued) person and number features, and an EPP feature; the verb *believed* is a passive participle here, so is intransitive and therefore does not have the ability to assign accusative case (and consequently, let us suppose, *believed* does not carry agreement features either).

The T auxiliary BE is active as a probe by virtue of its unvalued person and number features, and searches for the closest XP goal that can value these, locating the pronominal DP HE (whose unvalued case feature makes it active). Since HE is φ-complete (through having both person and number), it can value the unvalued person and number features on T-BE as third person singular. At the same time, the EPP feature on T-BE searches for the closest (and only) goal that it agrees with in person (namely the third person pronoun HE, which is active through its unvalued case feature), and attracts HE to move to spec-TP. The resulting TP is merged with a null complementiser carrying an interpretable indicative mood feature and uninterpretable person and number features, forming the CP shown below (where the internal structure of the T-bar *to be telling the truth* is not shown, and arrows mark the two A-Movement operations undergone by the pronoun HE):

(68)

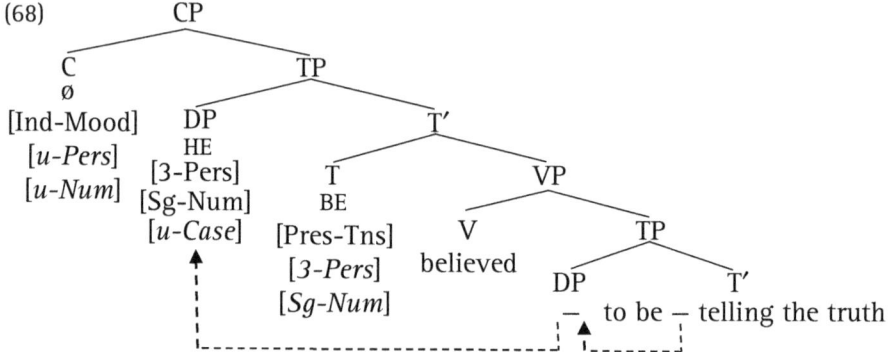

The null complementiser in (68) is active as a probe for Agreement and Case-marking by virtue of its unvalued person and number features, and searches for an active XP goal which can value these. The closest goal c-commanded by the complementiser is the pronominal DP HE, which is active by virtue of its unvalued case feature. Since this DP carries both person and number and is therefore φ-complete, it can value the unvalued person and number features on the complementiser as third person singular. Since the complementiser is finite (in that it carries an indicative-mood feature) and φ-complete (in that it carries both person and number), it can in turn value the unvalued case feature on the pronoun HE as nominative, so resulting in the final derived syntactic structure below:

(69)

```
              CP
      _____|_____
     C               TP
     ø         _____|_____
 [Ind-Mood]   DP            T'
  [3-Pers]    HE       _____|_____
  [Sg-Num]  [3-Pers]  T          VP
            [Sg-Num]  BE      ____|____
          [Nom-Case] [Pres-Tns] V      TP
                      [3-Pers] believed _|_
                      [Sg-Num]         DP    T'
                                    — to be — telling the truth
```

The structure in (69) satisfies the requirement imposed by the Legibility Condition (6iii) for all features to be valued at the end of the syntactic derivation.

When (69) undergoes transfer to the PF component, the T auxiliary BE is spelled out in its third person singular present tense form *is*, and the pronoun HE is spelled out in its nominative form *he*. The overall sentence is spelled out as (53c) *He is believed to be telling the truth.*

3.3.4   Infinitival CPs

Having looked at the case/agreement properties of infinitival TPs, let's now turn to look at those of infinitival CPs, like the italicised complement clause introduced by the complementiser *for* in (54a) above 'We are anxious *for the agreements to be ratified.*' Since the *for*-clause is passive, its superficial subject (the DP *the agreements*) originates as the complement of the passive participle *ratified*, and the derivation proceeds as follows.

The (passive) verb *ratified* merges with the DP *the agreements* to form the VP *ratified the agreements*. This VP is then merged with the passive voice auxiliary *be*, forming the VOICEP *be ratified the agreements*. The resulting VOICEP is in turn merged with the infinitival T-particle *to*, forming the T-bar below:

(70)

```
                T'
        _____|_____
       T              VOICEP
       to         _____|_____
    [Nf-Tns]    VOICE          VP
    [u-Pers]     be       _____|_____
     [EPP]              V            DP
                     ratified   the agreements
                                  [3-Pers]
                                  [Pl-Num]
                                  [u-Case]
```

In accordance with our earlier assumptions, the infinitive particle T-*to* enters the derivation carrying an interpretable nonfinite-tense feature, an uninterpretable (and unvalued) person feature, and an EPP feature.

At this point, T-*to* is active as a probe for Agreement and A-Movement by virtue of its unvalued person feature, and searches for an XP goal which can value this feature. The closest such goal c-commanded by *to* is the DP *the agreements*, which is active by virtue of its unvalued case feature. This DP is φ-complete (since it carries both person and number), and so can value the unvalued person feature on T-*to* as third person via Agreement (6i). In addition, the EPP feature on T-*to* attracts the closest goal that it agrees with in person to move to spec-TP: the closest (and only) such goal is the DP *the agreements*, which is active by virtue of its unvalued case feature. After A-Movement takes place, T-*to* is stripped of its EPP feature, which has neither form nor meaning and so is illegible at the PF and LF interfaces. The resulting TP is merged with the infinitival complementiser *for* to form the CP below, with the arrow showing Passivisation/A-Movement applying to the DP *the agreements*:

(71)

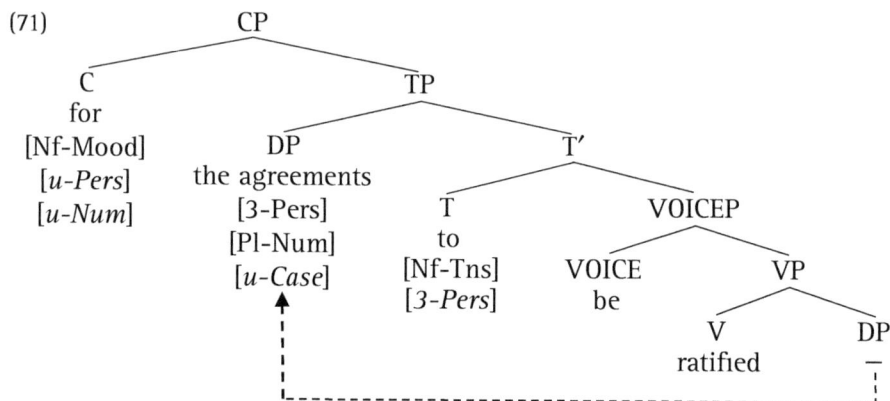

Because it is a case assigner, and case-assigners are φ-complete in consequence of the Completeness Condition (6ii), the complementiser *for* enters the derivation carrying a complete set of uninterpretable (and unvalued) φ-features, together with an interpretable nonfinite-mood feature [Nf-Mood]. The nonfinite-mood feature carried by infinitival complementisers generally has much the same irrealis interpretation as we find in the corresponding subjunctive clause italicised in 'We are anxious *that the agreements be ratified*' – although the two types of clause differ in the case assignment properties of their complementisers (*that* being a nominative case assigner, and *for* an accusative case assigner).

The complementiser *for* in (71) is active as a probe for Agreement and Case-marking by virtue of its unvalued person and number features, and searches for an XP goal which can value these. The closest goal c-commanded by the complementiser is the DP *the agreements*, which is active by virtue of its unvalued case feature. Since this DP carries both person and number and is therefore φ-complete, it can value the unvalued person and number features on the complementiser as third person plural. Since the complementiser *for* is φ-complete (in that it carries both person and number) and transitive (like its prepositional counterpart in 'Don't feel sorry **for** *me*'), it can in turn value the unvalued case feature on the DP *the agreements* as accusative in accordance with the Case Condition (11iii), so resulting in the final derived syntactic structure below:

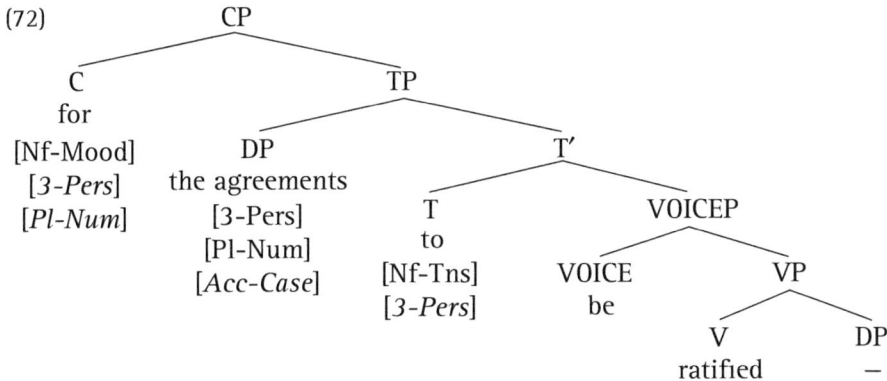

(72)

```
                         CP
          ┌───────────────┴───────────────┐
          C                               TP
         for              ┌───────────────┴───────────────┐
     [Nf-Mood]            DP                              T′
      [3-Pers]      the agreements        ┌───────────────┴───────────────┐
      [Pl-Num]         [3-Pers]           T                             VOICEP
                       [Pl-Num]          to                ┌─────────────┴─────────────┐
                      [Acc-Case]      [Nf-Tns]           VOICE                         VP
                                      [3-Pers]            be              ┌────────────┴────────────┐
                                                                          V                        DP
                                                                       ratified                     –
```

Although the accusative case assigned to the DP *the agreements* is not directly visible, it is indirectly visible in the sense that if we replace the DP by a personal pronoun, we require the accusative form *them* (as in 'We are anxious for *them* to be ratified'). The structure in (72) satisfies the requirement imposed by the Legibility Condition (6iii) for all features to be valued at the end of the syntactic derivation. Because φ-features on complementisers and on nonfinite T constituents are abstract/invisible in English, the φ-features on the complementiser *for* and the infinitive particle *to* have no overt spellout in the PF component. The overall sentence is ultimately spelled out as (54a) 'We are anxious *for the agreements to be ratified.*'

Now consider the derivation of the italicised infinitive clause in (54b) 'They want *the president to be impeached.*' If we make the traditional assumption that this is a *for*-deletion structure (i.e. one in which the italicised complement clause is headed by a null counterpart of the transitive complementiser *for*), it follows that the derivation will be essentially parallel to that outlined in (70–72) above, save for minor lexical differences (i.e. differences in the choice of words). Hence, I will not go into the details here, to avoid unnecessary repetition.

Finally, consider the derivation of a Control infinitive clause like that italicised in (54c) 'It will be essential *to prepare myself.*' The classic analysis of such clauses assumes that infinitival *to* has a PRO subject with null case. In this use, PRO is interpreted as referring to the speaker: this means that PRO (as used here) is a first person singular pronoun (and hence can bind the first person singular anaphor *myself*). Under the VP-Internal Subject Hypothesis, PRO will originate as the specifier of the VP headed by the verb *prepare*. Given this assumption (and others), the complement clause will be derived as follows.

The verb *prepare* first-merges with the reflexive anaphor *myself* and second-merges with PRO to form the VP *PRO prepare myself*. The resulting VP is merged with the infinitive particle T-*to*, forming the T-bar below (where only features on the constituents of direct relevance to our discussion here are shown, and where PRO and *myself* are pronominal DPs):

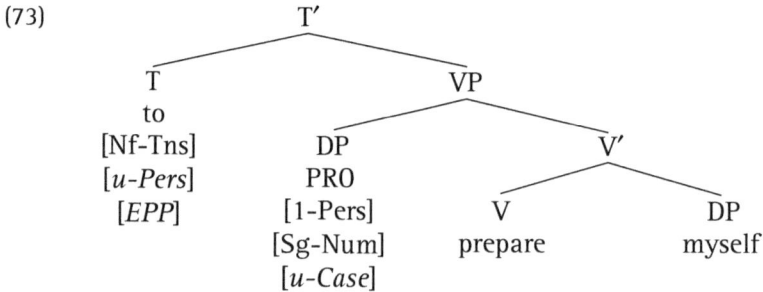

(73)

```
                        T'
          ┌─────────────┴─────────────┐
          T                          VP
          to                ┌─────────┴─────────┐
       [Nf-Tns]            DP                   V'
       [u-Pers]           PRO            ┌──────┴──────┐
        [EPP]           [1-Pers]         V            DP
                        [Sg-Num]      prepare       myself
                        [u-Case]
```

T-*to* enters the derivation carrying an interpretable nonfinite-tense feature, an uninterpretable (and unvalued) person feature, and an EPP feature.

At this point, the infinitive particle T-*to* is active as a probe for Agreement and A-Movement by virtue of its unvalued person feature, and searches for an active XP goal which can value this feature. The closest such goal c-commanded by *to* is PRO, which is active by virtue of its unvalued case-feature. PRO is φ-complete (since it carries both person and number), and so can value the unvalued person feature on T-*to* as first person via Agreement (6i). In addition, the EPP feature on T-*to* attracts the closest goal that it agrees with in person to move to spec-TP: the closest such goal is PRO, which is active by virtue of its unvalued case feature. After A-Movement takes place, T-*to* is stripped of its EPP feature, which has neither form nor meaning, and so is illegible at the PF and LF interfaces. The resulting TP is merged with a null complementiser/C-*ø* carrying a nonfinite mood feature [Nf-Mood] to form the CP below (with the arrow showing A-Movement of PRO):

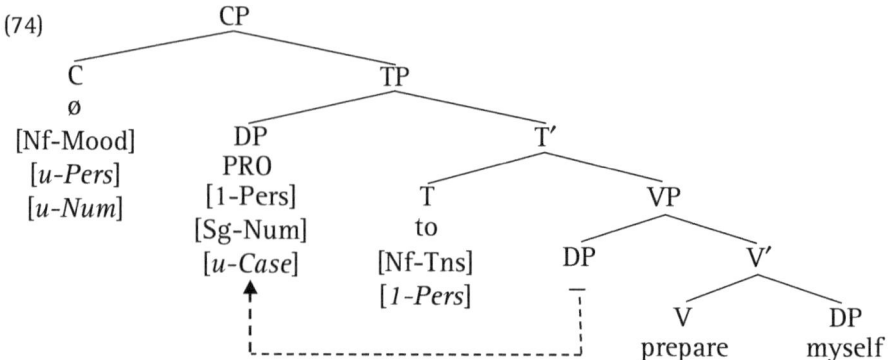

(74)

```
                      CP
          ┌───────────┴───────────┐
          C                       TP
          ø            ┌──────────┴──────────┐
      [Nf-Mood]       DP                     T'
       [u-Pers]      PRO          ┌──────────┴──────────┐
       [u-Num]     [1-Pers]       T                    VP
                   [Sg-Num]       to           ┌────────┴────────┐
                   [u-Case]    [Nf-Tns]       DP                V'
                       ↑        [1-Pers]       ⌐        ┌────────┴────────┐
                       ┊                       ┊        V               DP
                       └───────────────────────┘     prepare         myself
```

Because it is a case assigner, and the Completeness Condition (6ii) requires case-assigners to be φ-complete, the null complementiser enters the derivation carrying a complete set of uninterpretable (and unvalued) person and number φ-features, together with an interpretable nonfinite mood feature.

The null complementiser in (74) is active as a probe for Agreement and Case-marking by virtue of its unvalued person and number features, and searches for an active XP goal which can value these. The closest such goal c-commanded by the complementiser is PRO, which is active by virtue of its unvalued case feature. Since PRO carries both person and number and is therefore φ-complete, it can value the unvalued person and number features on the complementiser as first person singular. Since the complementiser is nonfinite, intransitive and φ-complete (in that it carries both person and number), it can in turn value the unvalued case feature on PRO as null in accordance with the Case Condition (11ii), so resulting in the final derived syntactic structure below:

(75)

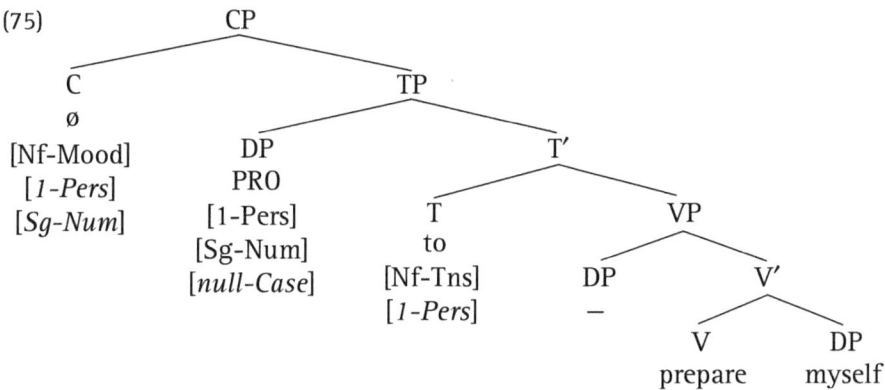

The structure in (75) satisfies the requirement imposed by the Legibility Condition (6iii) for all features to be valued at the end of the syntactic derivation. Since the infinitive subject has been assigned null case, it receives a null spellout as PRO in the PF component.

To summarise: I have argued in Module 3.3 that infinitival *to* (although not overtly inflecting for agreement) enters the derivation carrying an unvalued person feature which (in conjunction with the EPP feature on infinitival *to*) serves to attract the closest XP goal carrying person to undergo A-Movement to spec-TP and thereby become the subject of infinitival *to* (provided that the XP goal is active). If the resulting *to*-infinitive TP is subsequently embedded as the complement of an item which is not a case-assigner (like the Raising verb *seem* in 53a 'There do **seem** *to have been some problems*' or the passive participle *believed* in 53c 'He is **believed** *to be telling the truth*'), the subject will continue to move until it ends up in a position within the domain of a case-assigner. However, if the infinitival TP is embedded as the complement of a case-assigner (e.g. an ECM verb like *believe* in 53b 'We **believe** *him to be telling the truth*', or a complementiser like *for* in 54a 'We are anxious **for** *the agreements to be ratified*'), the subject in spec-TP will be case-marked via agreement with the relevant case assigner, and will thereafter become inactive for further A-operations.

You should now be able to tackle Exercise 3.3.

3.4   Cross-clausal agreement

In the previous module, we saw that A-Movement and Agreement can extend across an infinitive clause boundary. In this module, we will look at an interesting class of non-standard structures in which agreement applies across a finite clause boundary.

3.4.1   Agreement across a finite TP

As we see from (76) below, cross-clausal agreement is possible across a (bracketed) infinitive clause boundary, so allowing agreement between the bold-printed T auxiliary *do* and the italicised QP *some problems*:

(76)   There **do** seem [to have been *some problems*]

By contrast, agreement is not possible across a finite clause boundary like that bracketed in (77) below:

(77)   *There **do** seem [that have been *some problems*]

Why should this be? A plausible answer is that the bracketed infinitive clause in (76) is a TP (as shown in 60 above), whereas the bracketed finite clause in (77) is a CP (headed by the complementiser *that*), and syntactic operations (including movement and agreement) are barred from applying across the edge of an intervening CP by the Impenetrability Condition, which was given the following informal characterisation in §1.5.1 (where above/below mean 'c-commanding/c-commanded by'):

(78)   **Impenetrability Condition/IC**
        Anything below the head C of a CP is impenetrable to anything above the CP

Since the QP *some problems* is positioned below the complementiser *that* in (77) and the T auxiliary *do* is positioned above the bracketed CP headed by *that*, it follows that the Impenetrability Condition blocks cross-clausal agreement here (and it likewise blocks expletive *there* from raising out of the *that*-clause to become the subject of *do*). By contrast, IC does not block cross-clausal agreement in the corresponding infinitive structure (76), because the bracketed infinitive complement clause in (76) is a TP (as in 60 above), not a CP, and the Impenetrability Condition only prevents operations from applying across the edge of a CP. If (as claimed in Radford 2020: 184) 'All finite clauses have the status of CPs', then we should expect that (because of the Impenetrability Condition) syntactic operations like movement and agreement will never apply across the edge of a finite clause.

However, the claim that agreement and movement cannot apply across a finite clause boundary is potentially called into question by Raising of the (italicised) subject out of a finite clause which is the complement of a (bold-printed) Raising predicate such as *likely/seem* in sentences like (79) below, and by Passivisation of the (italicised) subject of a finite clause which is the complement of a (bold-printed) passive participle in sentences like (80):

(79)   a.   *China* is **likely** will field a ground-based laser weapon (WION, on Facebook)
       b.   *An advanced rider* is **likely** will opt for a variety of bearings (ospreyactionsports.co.uk)
       c.   *The additional risk of further borrowing* is **likely** will be reflected in the interest rate offer you are likely to receive (assetsure.com)
       d.   *He* **seems** might be the honey I need now (lyrics to a song by Grace, lyricsontop.com)
       e.   *He* **seems** is very active and shows no sign of illness (labradorforums.co.uk)
       f.   Another thing to like about Kizer is that *he* **seems** has that 'it' factor (slapthesign.com)
       g.   *Juan Mata* **appears** just has to pass a medical (Alan Brazil, talkSPORT Radio)

(80)   a.   *He* was **believed** had lured Olga from her apartment ... (Medicine Hat News, August 7th 1962, p.1)
       b.   *He* is **expected** will become a prominent face in showbiz in the future (teamdantes.com)
       c.   *He* was **considered** was a hero in Turkey ... (quizlet.com)
       d.   *He* was **deemed** was no longer acceptable for naval service ... (navalhistory.org)
       e.   *Approximately 30% of those* were **thought** were students (warwick.ac.uk)
       f.   *He* was **said** was advised 'by his Turkish community' that the 'best way to pass his theory was to arrange a Bluetooth cheat' (dailymail.co.uk)

Such structures (although widely attested in both spoken and written English) tend to be stigmatised as non-standard by prescriptive grammarians (and are characterised as 'bizarre' by one anonymous reviewer) – and indeed, they would be expected to be ungrammatical on our existing assumptions. To see why, consider the derivation of (79a) *China is likely will field a ground-based laser weapon.*

Under the VP-Internal Subject Hypothesis, *China* will originate as the thematic subject of the verb *field*, and the derivation of the sentence will proceed as follows. The verb *field* first-merges with its complement *a ground-based laser weapon* and second-merges with its thematic subject *China* to form the VP *China field a ground-based laser weapon*. The resulting VP is in turn merged with the auxiliary T-*will* to form the T-bar shown in simplified form below (where I have assumed that T-*will* is morphologically a present-tense form carrying unvalued person/number agreement features and an EPP feature, and that *China* is a DP headed by a null determiner, with a meaning paraphrasable as 'the entity China'):

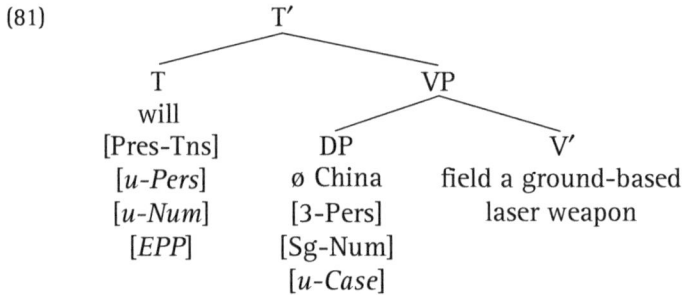

(81)

```
                        T′
          ┌─────────────┴─────────────┐
          T                           VP
         will                 ┌───────┴────────┐
      [Pres-Tns]             DP                V′
       [u-Pers]           ø China      field a ground-based
       [u-Num]            [3-Pers]          laser weapon
        [EPP]             [Sg-Num]
                          [u-Case]
```

The unvalued person/number features on T-*will* make it active as a probe for Agreement and A-Movement, so it searches for an active XP goal that can value these. The closest goal c-commanded by T-*will* is the DP *ø China*, which is active by virtue of its unvalued case feature. Being φ-complete, the DP *ø China* can value the unvalued φ-features on T-*will* as third person singular (although these φ-features have no overt spellout on a modal like *will*). In addition, the EPP feature on T-*will* attracts the closest goal that T-*will* agrees with in person (= the DP *ø China*) to move to become the specifier of *will* (as shown by the arrow below), and the EPP feature is thereafter stripped from T (because EPP is illegible at the PF and LF interfaces), giving rise to the following structure:

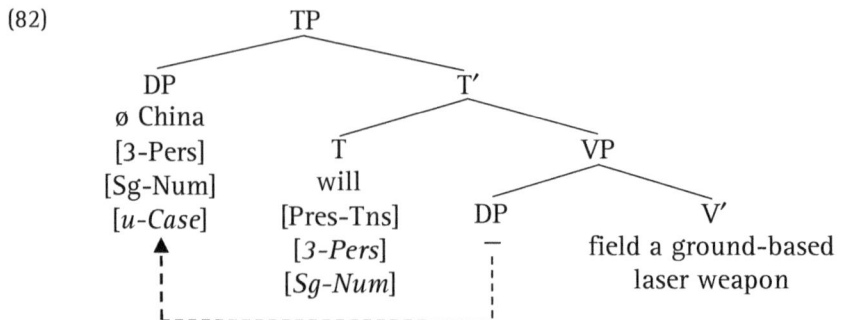

(82)

```
                              TP
              ┌───────────────┴───────────────┐
             DP                               T′
           ø China               ┌────────────┴────────────┐
           [3-Pers]              T                         VP
           [Sg-Num]            will              ┌──────────┴──────────┐
           [u-Case]          [Pres-Tns]         DP                    V′
              ▲               [3-Pers]           ⊤         field a ground-based
              ┆               [Sg-Num]           ┆              laser weapon
              └─────────────────────────────────┘
```

On the assumption made earlier that all finite clauses are CPs, the resulting TP will be merged with a null finite complementiser carrying an interpretable indicative mood feature, and uninterpretable (and unvalued) person and number features. The complementiser will agree with (and assign nominative case to) the DP *ø China*, so deriving the CP below:

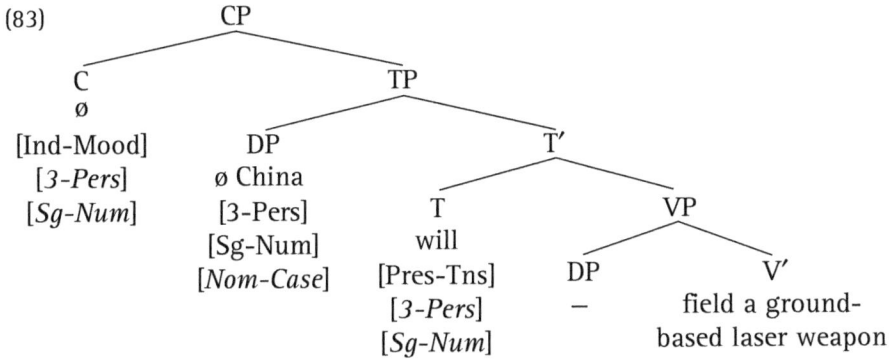

(83)

```
                        CP
          ┌──────────────┴──────────────┐
          C                             TP
          ø              ┌───────────────┴───────────┐
     [Ind-Mood]          DP                          T′
      [3-Pers]         ø China           ┌────────────┴──────────┐
      [Sg-Num]         [3-Pers]          T                       VP
                       [Sg-Num]         will          ┌──────────┴──────────┐
                      [Nom-Case]     [Pres-Tns]        DP                   V′
                                      [3-Pers]         –            field a ground-
                                      [Sg-Num]                     based laser weapon
```

However, given the impoverished nature of English morphology, the case/agreement features italicised in (83) will have no overt phonetic spellout at PF (although those on the subject and auxiliary are visible in a sentence like '*She is* fielding a laser weapon').

The derivation then continues by merging the CP in (83) as the complement of the adjective *likely*, forming an AP which is subsequently merged as the complement of the verb BE, forming a VP. This VP is then merged with a null present tense affix (= *Af*), forming the T-bar shown in simplified form below:

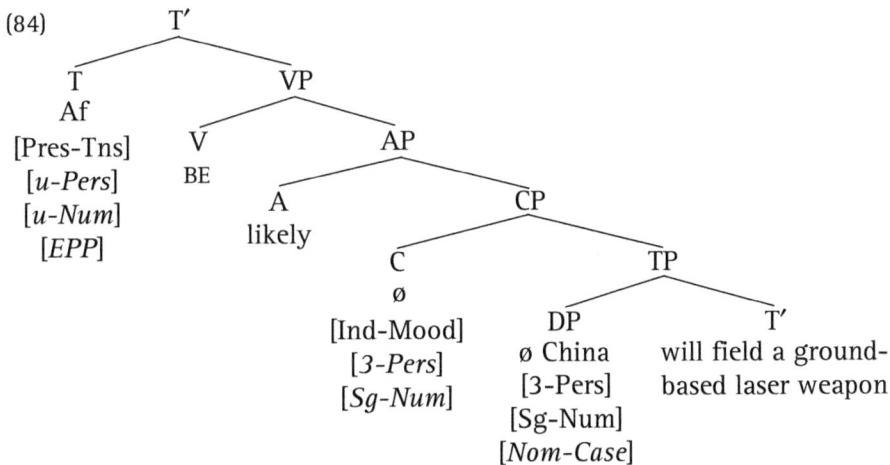

(84)

```
              T′
     ┌─────────┴─────────┐
     T                   VP
     Af          ┌────────┴────────┐
  [Pres-Tns]     V                 AP
   [u-Pers]     BE          ┌───────┴────────┐
   [u-Num]                  A                CP
    [EPP]               likely     ┌──────────┴──────────┐
                                   C                     TP
                                   ø            ┌─────────┴─────────┐
                              [Ind-Mood]        DP                  T′
                               [3-Pers]       ø China      will field a ground-
                               [Sg-Num]       [3-Pers]     based laser weapon
                                              [Sg-Num]
                                             [Nom-Case]
```

At the stage of derivation in (84), the tense affix (T-*Af*) is active as a probe by virtue of its unvalued person and number features, and searches for an active goal to value these; likewise, the EPP feature on T-*Af* searches for the closest XP goal that it agrees with in person to attract to spec-TP. So, what we might expect to happen at this point is for T-*Af* to agree with (and attract) the DP goal *ø China*. However, neither operation (Agreement or Attraction) is possible, for two reasons. Firstly, the DP *ø China* occupies a position below the null complementiser, and so the Impenetrability Condition (78) prevents this DP from agreeing with or being attracted by the tense affix (because the affix is positioned above the CP headed by the null complementiser). And secondly, the DP *ø China* is inactive (for either Agreement or A-Movement) when we reach the stage of derivation in (84), because its case feature was valued as nominative at the earlier stage of derivation in (83). Since a goal can only be active for Agreement or A-Movement if it has an unvalued case feature, it follows that the nominative DP *ø China* is unable to agree with the tense affix in (84), and unable to move to become its specifier either. This means that the derivation in (84) crashes because the person/number features on the tense affix can't be valued, and because the EPP feature on T is unable to do its work and so can't be deleted – and both are illegible at the PF and LF interfaces. So, on the assumptions made here, (79a) *China is likely will field a ground-based laser weapon* is underivable, and hence predicted to be ungrammatical. However, the problem this poses is that (as data like 79 and 80 above show), such sentences do actually occur in some varieties of English; and this raises the question of how cross-clausal agreement (also termed long-distance agreement) is licensed in those varieties. Below, I'll suggest an answer to this question.

The constituent which effectively blocks the tense affix in (84) from agreeing with and attracting the DP *ø China* is the intervening null complementiser, because on the one hand this induces an impenetrability violation, and on the other hand it inactivates the DP *ø China* by assigning it nominative case. This raises the possibility that (in varieties which allow sentences like 79 and 80 above) the complement clause *will field a ground-based laser weapon* is a defective clause which projects only as far as TP, and contains no CP projection at all. Let's take a closer look at the effect that this would have on the derivation.

Suppose that the derivation proceeds as before, until we have formed the TP in (82) above. Suppose, too, that this TP is then merged with the adjective *likely* to form an AP, and that the resulting AP is subsequently merged with the verb BE to form a VP, and that this VP is in turn merged with a tense-affix to form the T-bar shown in simplified form in (85) below:

(85)

```
              T′
        ┌─────┴─────┐
        T           VP
        Af      ┌────┴────┐
    [Pres-Tns]  V         AP
      [u-Pers]  BE    ┌────┴────┐
      [u-Num]        A          TP
       [EPP]       likely   ┌────┴────┐
                           DP         T′
                         ø China   will field a ground-
                         [3-Pers]  based laser weapon
                         [Sg-Num]
                         [u-Case]
```

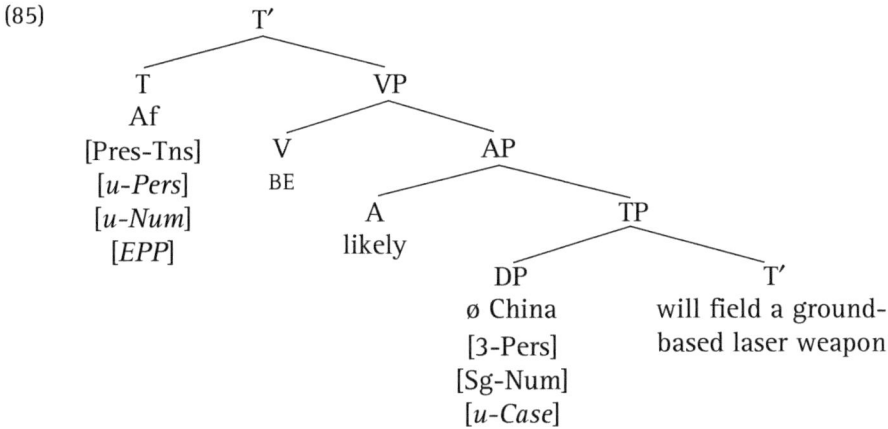

The unvalued person/number features on the tense affix/T-*Af* make it active as a probe for Agreement and A-Movement, so T-*Af* searches for an XP goal that can value these. The closest such goal is the DP *ø China*, which is active by virtue of its unvalued case feature. Being φ-complete, the DP *ø China* can value the unvalued φ-features on T-*Af* as third person singular. The EPP feature on T-*Af* attracts the closest goal that it agrees with in person (= the DP *ø China*) to move to spec-TP (as shown by the arrow below), and the EPP feature is thereafter stripped from T-*Af*, because it is illegible at the PF and LF interfaces. This gives rise to the TP in (86) below:

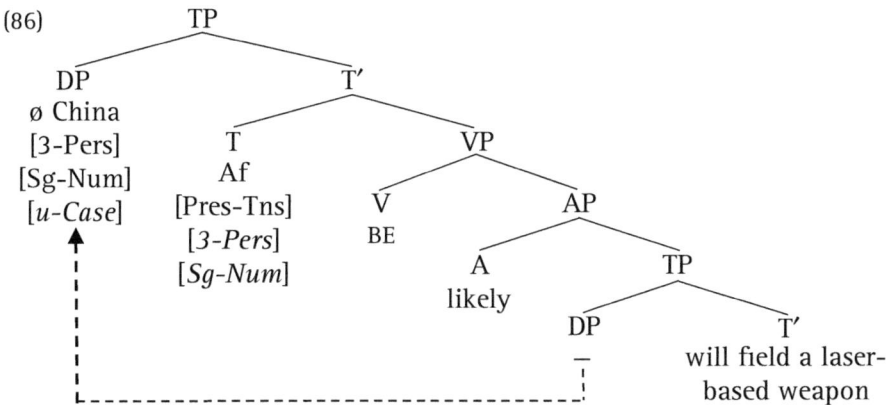

(86)

```
              TP
       ┌───────┴───────┐
      DP               T′
    ø China       ┌────┴────┐
   [3-Pers]       T         VP
   [Sg-Num]       Af    ┌────┴────┐
   [u-Case]   [Pres-Tns] V        AP
      ▲        [3-Pers]  BE   ┌────┴────┐
      ┊        [Sg-Num]      A          TP
      ┊                    likely   ┌────┴────┐
      ┊                            DP         T′
      ┊                             —     will field a laser-
      └─────────────────────────────┘     based weapon
```

In addition, V-BE adjoins to T-*Af* via Head Movement (arrowed in 87 below):

(87)

```
                        TP
          ┌──────────────┴──────────────┐
        DP                              T′
      ø China            ┌──────────────┴──────────────┐
     [3-Pers]           T                              VP
     [Sg-Num]      ┌─────┴─────┐           ┌────────────┴────────────┐
     [u-Case]     V          Af           V                         AP
                  BE     [Pres-Tns]       ─                ┌─────────┴─────────┐
                  ▲      [3-Pers]                         A                   TP
                  ┊      [Sg-Num]                       likely        ┌────────┴────────┐
                  └───────────────────────────────┘                 DP               T′
                                                                      ─      will field a laser-
                                                                             based weapon
```

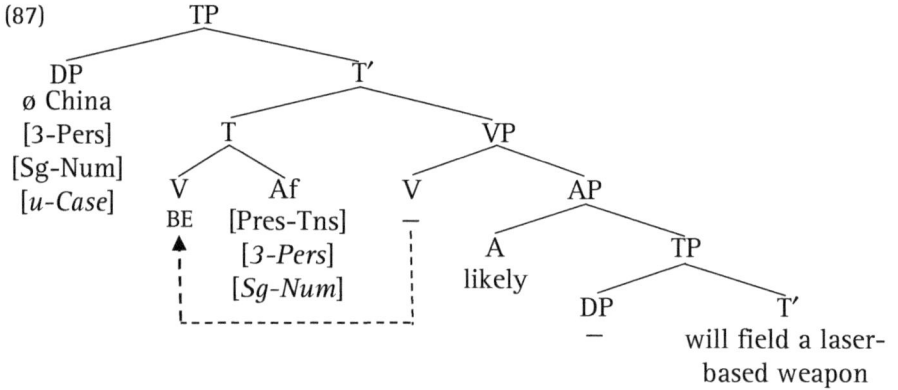

The resulting TP is merged with a null complementiser to form the CP in (88) below:

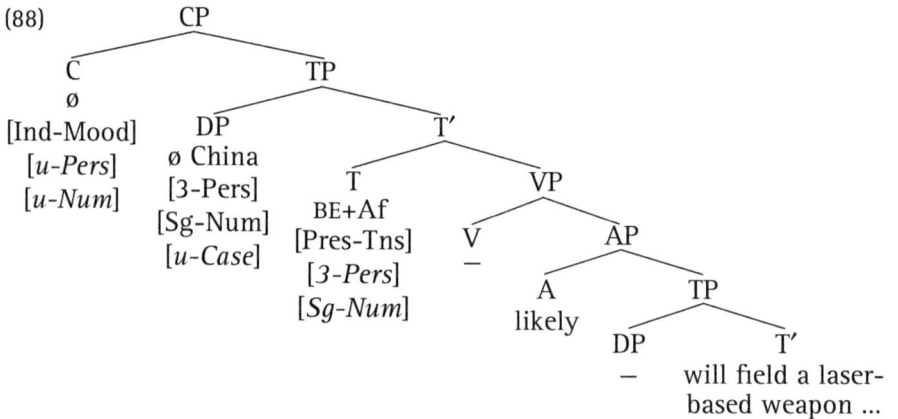

(88)

```
                    CP
        ┌───────────┴───────────┐
       C                        TP
       ø            ┌───────────┴───────────┐
   [Ind-Mood]      DP                       T′
    [u-Pers]     ø China         ┌──────────┴──────────┐
    [u-Num]      [3-Pers]        T                     VP
                 [Sg-Num]      BE+Af          ┌─────────┴─────────┐
                 [u-Case]    [Pres-Tns]      V                   AP
                             [3-Pers]        ─         ┌──────────┴──────────┐
                             [Sg-Num]                 A                      TP
                                                    likely          ┌────────┴────────┐
                                                                    DP               T′
                                                                     ─      will field a laser-
                                                                            based weapon ...
```

The null complementiser in (88) is active as a probe for Agreement and Case-marking by virtue of its unvalued person and number features, and searches for an XP goal which can value these. The closest such goal c-commanded by the complementiser is the DP ø China, which is active by virtue of its unvalued case feature. Since this DP carries both person and number features and is therefore φ-complete, it can value the unvalued person and number features on the complementiser as third person singular. Since the null complementiser is finite (by virtue of being indicative in mood) and φ-complete (in that it carries both person and number), it can in turn value the unvalued case feature on the DP ø China as nominative in accordance with the Nominative Case Condition (11i), so resulting in the final derived syntactic structure in (89) below:

(89)

```
                          CP
              ┌───────────┴───────────┐
              C                       TP
              ø              ┌────────┴────────┐
        [Ind-Mood]          DP                 T′
         [3-Pers]         ø China      ┌───────┴───────┐
         [Sg-Num]         [3-Pers]     T               VP
                          [Sg-Num]   BE+Af      ┌───────┴───────┐
                         [Nom-Case] [Pres-Tns]  V               AP
                                     [3-Pers]   ─        ┌───────┴───────┐
                                     [Sg-Num]   likely   A               TP
                                                               ┌─────────┴─────────┐
                                                              DP                   T′
                                                               ─    will field a laser-
                                                                    based weapon
```

The resulting structure satisfies the requirement imposed by the Legibility Condition for all features to be valued at the end of a derivation, and is ultimately spelled out at PF as (79a) *China is likely will field a ground-based laser weapon.*

   The overall conclusion to come out of our discussion here is that cross-clausal Subject Raising/A-Movement in sentences like *China is likely will ...* is ungrammatical in standard varieties of English, and this follows from the assumption that the complement clause (= the *will*-clause) is a CP (as in 84 above), since the head C of the relevant CP inactivates the complement clause subject (by assigning it nominative case), and makes the subject impenetrable to a probe in the main clause. By contrast, for speakers who accept sentences like (79a), the complement *will*-clause is a defective clause which has the status of a TP that does not project further into a CP (as in 85 above), so the complement clause subject is not inactivated, and is not impenetrable to a higher probe. The difference between the two varieties reduces to the following: in standard varieties, all finite clauses are CPs, and consequently finite complement clauses do not allow their subjects to agree with or be attracted by a higher T-probe; but in some (non-standard) varieties, the complement of a Raising predicate (or passive participle) can be a finite TP, and this allows a T probe in a higher clause to agree with and trigger A-Movement of the complement clause subject in sentences like (79, 80) above.

   The analysis of cross-clausal A-Movement outlined in (86) above has interesting implications for case assignment. Under the analysis of nominative case-marking in (11i), a finite C assigns nominative case to (and thereby inactivates) the subject of its clause: the assumption that the *will*-clause is a defective clause which projects only up to TP and hence contains no C to case-mark its subject allows the subject of *will* to remain active for the A-Movement operation arrowed in (86) above.

3.4.2   Agreement across a finite CP

The key assumption made in the previous section (§3.4.1) is that cross-clausal agreement and A-Movement are only possible out of a finite complement clause that is defective (and has the status of TP), not out a complete clause that projects into CP. However, the empirical basis of this claim is cast in doubt by sentences such as the following (which are used by a minority of speakers only):

(90)   a.   There **appear** <u>that</u> there are *no major differences* ... (researcherslinks. com)

   b.   There **appear** <u>that</u> there are *many users having this issue* ... (support. mozilla.org)

   c.   There **appear** <u>that</u> there were *17 articles* published or broadcast from July through November (clearinghouse.net)

   d.   We must push boundaries to succeed and continue pushing boundaries even where there **seem** <u>that</u> there are *no more* to push (sethresnik.com)

   e.   There **seem** <u>that</u> there are *many people* that are having problems with TI requirements (forum.thaivisa.com)

   f.   There **is** likely <u>that</u> there will be *less suffering* in those areas where humans are the direct cause or recipient of suffering ... (forum. effectivealtruism.org)

   g.   There **was** felt <u>that</u> there was not *as tight a control as there should be* ... (thespacereview.com)

   h.   There **was** rumoured <u>that</u> there would be *a 6th single called 'Higher Ground'* ... (discogs.com)

In these expletive *there* sentences, a (bold-printed) verb in a higher clause agrees with an italicised associate in a complement clause introduced by the underlined complementiser *that*. Moreover, we find two copies of expletive *there* – one as the subject of the main clause, and another as the subject of the *that*-clause. What is going on here? A potential answer can be offered in relation to (90a) above, if we suppose that this is derived as follows.

The verb BE first-merges with the (negative) QP complement *no major differences* and second-merges with expletive *there* to form the VP *there BE no major differences*. This VP is then merged with a present-tense affix, forming the T-bar below:

(91)

```
                          T′
              ┌───────────┴───────────┐
              T                       VP
              Af              ┌────────┴────────┐
           [Nf-Tns]          DP                 V′
           [u-Pers]         there        ┌──────┴──────┐
           [u-Num]        [3-Pers]       V             QP
            [EPP]         [u-Case]       BE    no major differences
                                               [3-Pers]
                                               [Pl-Num]
                                               [u-Case]
```

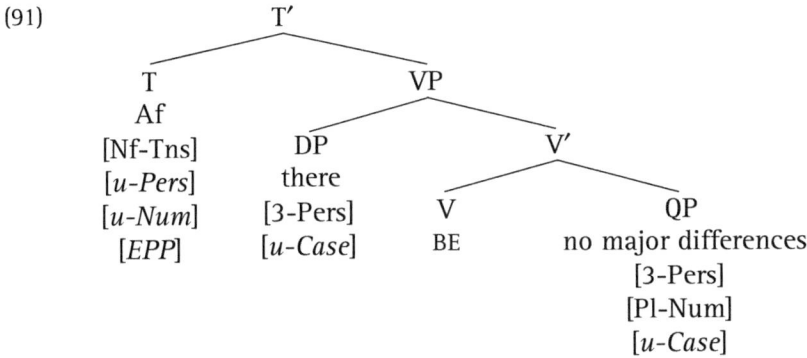

The tense affix/T-*Af* is active as a probe at this point (because of its unvalued person and number features), and it searches for the minimal goal set that can value these. The closest goal c-commanded by T-*Af* is expletive *there* (active by virtue of its unvalued case feature), but this is a defective goal by virtue of lacking number (so not being φ-complete), and thus it cannot value any φ-features on T-*Af* on its own. Accordingly, T-*Af* probes deeper into the structure to find the next closest goal, locating the QP *no major differences*. Since this QP has both person and number and so is φ-complete, and since it is active through its unvalued case feature, it can enter into a multiple agreement relation with T-*Af*. As a result, the third-person features on the QP and DP goals (*no major differences* and *there*) jointly value the unvalued person feature on T-*Af* as third person, and the plural number feature on the QP goal values the unvalued number feature on the T-*Af* probe as plural. At the same time, the EPP feature on T-*Af* attracts the closest goal that it agrees with in person (= *there*) to move to spec-TP (with the EPP feature thereafter being stripped/removed from the derivation). In addition, the (auxiliary-like) verb BE adjoins to the tense affix in T, via Head Movement. The resulting TP is then merged with the complementiser *that*, forming the CP below (with the gaps – representing the positions out of which *there* and BE move):

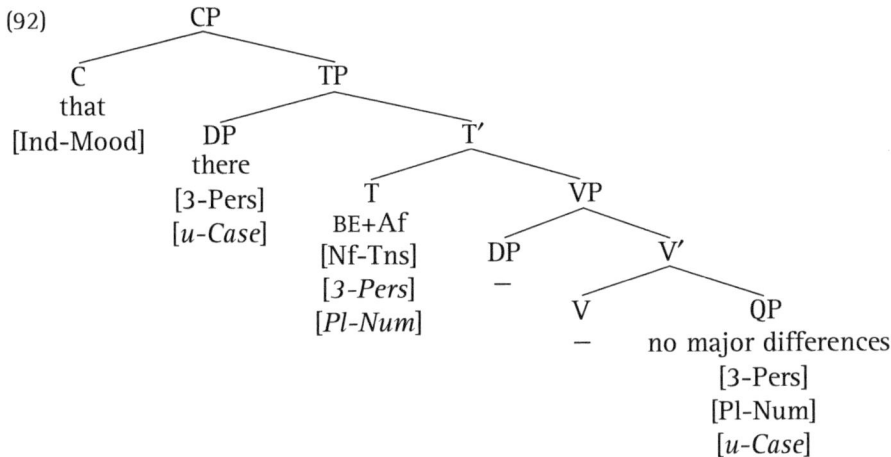

(92)

```
              CP
      ┌───────┴───────┐
      C               TP
     that     ┌───────┴───────┐
  [Ind-Mood]  DP              T′
             there    ┌───────┴───────┐
            [3-Pers]  T               VP
            [u-Case]  BE+Af    ┌──────┴──────┐
                    [Nf-Tns]   DP            V′
                    [3-Pers]    −      ┌──────┴──────┐
                    [Pl-Num]          V             QP
                                      −    no major differences
                                            [3-Pers]
                                            [Pl-Num]
                                            [u-Case]
```

Let's suppose that the complementiser *that* in (92) carries indicative mood, but is defective in respect of lacking agreement features (and hence lacking the ability to assign case, since the Completeness Condition 6ii requires case assigners to be φ-complete); this means that expletive *there* and its associate remain active at this point, since both have unvalued case features.

The derivation then continues by merging the *that*-clause structure in (92) as the complement of the verb *appear*, forming a VP which is in turn merged as the complement of a tense affix/T-Af, so generating the T-bar below:

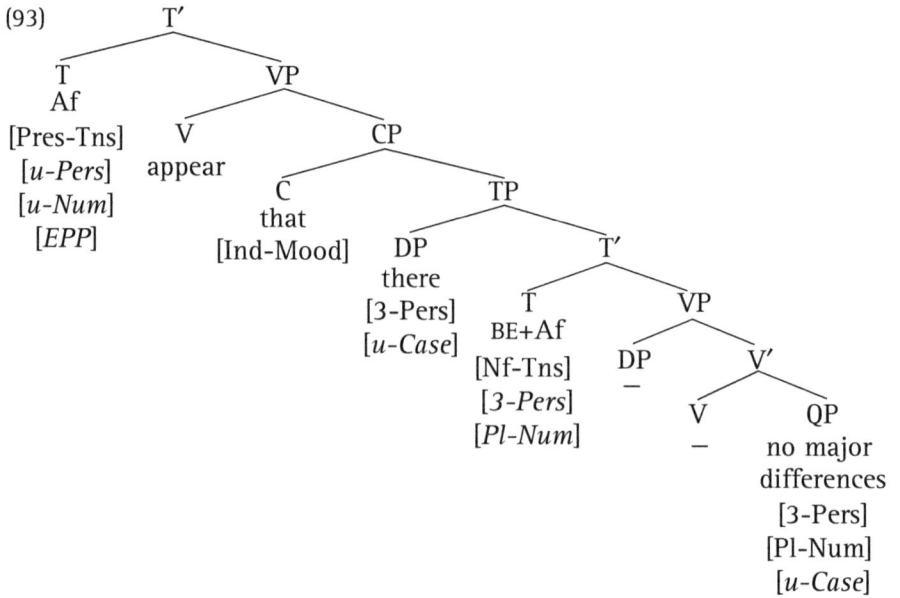

(93)

```
                    T′
         ┌──────────┴──────────┐
         T                      VP
         Af          ┌──────────┴──────────┐
      [Pres-Tns]      V                     CP
       [u-Pers]     appear        ┌─────────┴─────────┐
       [u-Num]                    C                   TP
        [EPP]                    that        ┌────────┴────────┐
                             [Ind-Mood]      DP               T′
                                            there      ┌──────┴──────┐
                                           [3-Pers]    T             VP
                                           [u-Case]  BE+Af     ┌──────┴──────┐
                                                     [Nf-Tns]  DP           V′
                                                     [3-Pers]   —     ┌──────┴──────┐
                                                     [Pl-Num]         V            QP
                                                                      —         no major
                                                                              differences
                                                                               [3-Pers]
                                                                               [Pl-Num]
                                                                               [u-Case]
```

The tense affix/T-Af in the higher clause (at the top of the tree) is active as a probe by virtue of its unvalued person and number features, and it searches for any goal(s) that can value these. The closest goal c-commanded by T-Af is expletive *there*, whose unvalued case feature makes it active; however, *there* is a defective goal (lacking number), so cannot (on its own) value any of the φ-features on the tense affix. Consequently, T-Af probes deeper into the structure, locating the QP *no major differences* as the next closest goal (active by virtue of its unvalued case feature); since this QP is φ-complete, multiple agreement can take place at this point between the probe T-Af and its two goals (expletive *there* and its QP associate *no major differences*). Accordingly, the third-person features on the expletive and its associate jointly value the unvalued person feature on T-Af as third-person, and the plural-number feature on the *no*-QP values the unvalued number feature on T-Af as plural. In addition, the EPP feature on T-Af attracts the closest goal that it agrees with in person (= expletive *there*) to move to spec-TP (and the EPP feature is thereafter stripped from T-*Af*), and the resulting TP is merged with a null complementiser to form the CP in (94) below (with the arrow showing A-Movement of *there* from spec-TP in the complement clause to spec-TP in the main clause):

(94)

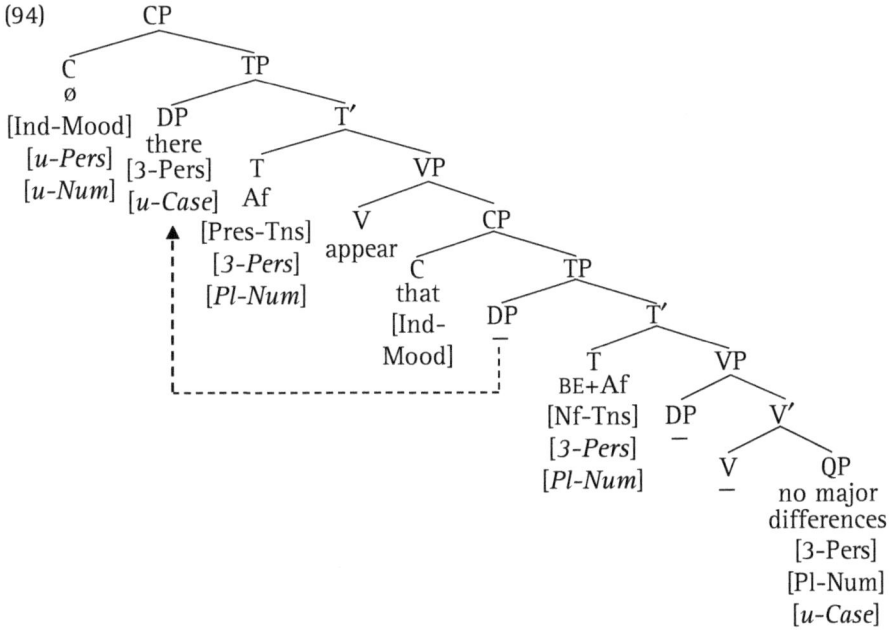

At this point, the null complementiser (C-ø) at the top of the tree is active as a probe (by virtue of its unvalued person and number features), and searches for a goal set that can value them. The closest goal c-commanded by C-ø is expletive *there*, whose unvalued case feature makes it active; but *there* is a defective goal (lacking number), so cannot value the unvalued φ-features on C-ø. Accordingly, C-ø probes deeper into the structure, locating the QP *no major differences* as the next closest goal (active by virtue of its unvalued case feature). Since this *no*-QP is φ-complete, it can also serve as a controller for agreement. Consequently, multiple agreement takes place, and the third-person feature carried by *there* and by the *no*-QP jointly value the unvalued person feature on C-ø as third-person, and the plural-number feature on the *no*-QP values the unvalued number feature on C-ø as plural. At the same time, the (finite and φ-complete) complementiser C-ø values the unvalued case features on expletive *there* and its *no*-QP associate as nominative, so deriving the structure below:

(95)

```
              CP
          /        \
         C           TP
         ø        /      \
   [Ind-Mood]  DP          T'
     [3-Pers]  there    /      \
     [Pl-Num]  [3-Pers]  T        VP
               [Nom-    Af     /     \
                Case]  [Pres-Tns]  V    CP
                       [3-Pers]  appear  /    \
                       [Pl-Num]       C      TP
                                  that    /     \
                                  [Ind-  DP      T'
                                  Mood]   —    /     \
                                           T       VP
                                         BE+Af   /    \
                                         [Nf-Tns] DP    V'
                                         [3-Pers]  —   /    \
                                         [Pl-Num]    V     QP
                                                     —   no major
                                                         differences
                                                         [3-Pers]
                                                         [Pl-Num]
                                                         [Nom-Case]
```

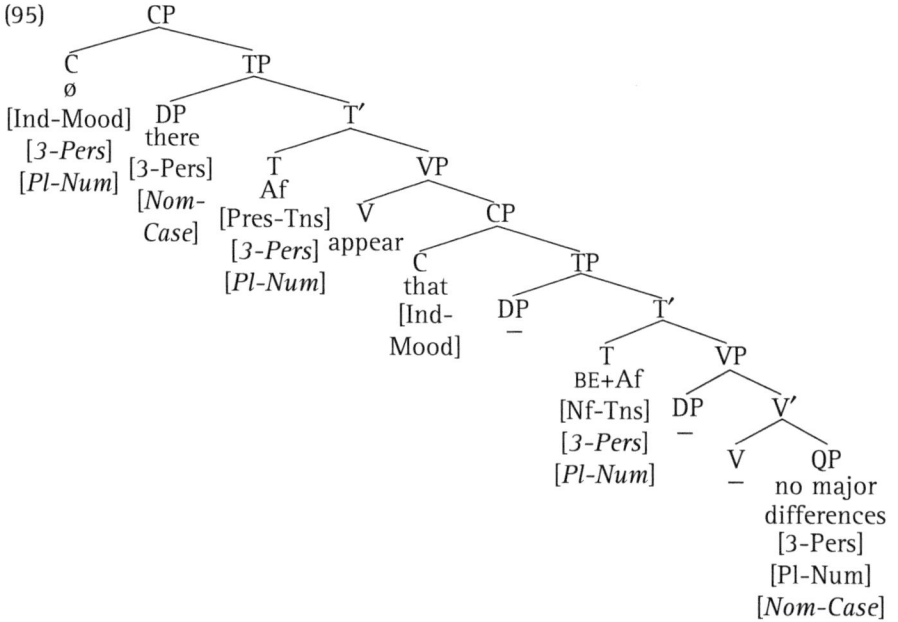

When the structure in (95) is transferred to the PF component, the lower
T-head in the complement clause (comprising BE+*Af*) is spelled out as the
third person plural present tense form *are*; in addition, the T-affix in the
main clause is lowered onto the verb *appear* (by Affix Hopping in the PF
component), and the resulting complex V-head (of the form V+*Af*) is spelled
out as the third person plural present tense form *appear*. The overall structure would be expected to be spelled out as in (96a) below; but instead, we
find the double-*there* structure in (96b):

(96)   a. *There appear that − are no major differences
        b. There appear that *there* are no major differences

It would seem that when expletive *there* undergoes the Raising/A-Movement
operation arrowed in (94), instead of leaving behind a null copy of *there*
as in (96a), it leaves behind an <u>overt</u> copy of *there* immediately following
the complementiser *that* in (96b). For obvious reasons, the type of Raising
found in (96b) has become known as Copy Raising (because the raised
constituent leaves an overt copy of itself behind). Why should *there* leave
a copy behind when it raises?

   A plausible answer is this. Following the idea put forward by Ross
(1967) that constraints on extraction apply only to gap-creating movement
operations (i.e. to movement operations which leave a gap/null copy behind), let's suppose that what rules out (96a) is that it creates the structure
shown in simplified form below:

(97)   *There* appear [$_{CP}$ [$_C$ that] [$_{TP}$ ~~there~~ [$_T$ are] no major differences]]

It would then follow that a structure like (97) is ruled out because it violates the Impenetrability Condition, in that a null copy of *there* (= ~~there~~) is positioned below the complementiser *that,* and its antecedent (= *there*) is positioned above the CP headed by *that* – leading to an impenetrability violation. Additionally, we can suppose that a structure like (97) violates the Minimality Condition, if this requires a trace/gap/null copy in an A-position to be bound by (i.e. have as its antecedent) a constituent on the edge of the minimal/closest clausal functional projection above it; and since constituents in an A-position can either move to the edge of TP via A-Movement or to the edge of CP by A-bar Movement, this means that a trace in an A-position must be bound within the closest TP or CP above it. If so, there would be a minimality violation in (97) because *~~there~~* is not bound by a constituent on the edge of the CP immediately above the TP containing *~~there~~*.

Furthermore, (97) would also violate a filter (devised by Chomsky & Lasnik 1977: 451) which was given the following formulation in §1.5.2:

(98)   **COMP-Trace Filter/CTF**
       Any structure at the end of a syntactic derivation in which an overt
       COMP/complementiser is immediately adjacent to and c-commands a
       trace (i.e. a gap/null copy left behind by a moved constituent) is filtered
       out as ill-formed

The CTF violation arises because the overt complementiser *that* c-commands and immediately precedes a null copy of the raised subject *there.* We could then hypothesise that use of an overt (italicised) copy of *there* after *that* in (96b) is a rescue strategy designed to avoid the Impenetrability/Minimality/ COMP-Trace violations which would ensue if a gap/null copy were used as in (96a). On this view, spelling out the copy of *there* following *that* overtly provides a way to repair the structure (i.e. to ensure that it does not violate the Impenetrability/Minimality/COMP-Trace Conditions). By hypothesis, repair mechanisms are only used as a last resort, where required in order to avoid a derivation crashing.

The Copy Raising analysis sketched above for *there appear(s) that there ...* structures can arguably be extended to cases like the following:

(99)   a.   There **look** <u>like</u> there might be *some interesting changes ...*
            (ffteducationdatalab.org.uk)
       b.   There **look** <u>like</u> there have been *some problems* (Radford 2004b: 317)
       c.   There **look** <u>like</u> there were *a few that didn't make it*
            (marineacquariumssa.com)
       d.   There **looks** <u>like</u> there is *a massive leak ...* (autospies.com)
       e.   There **looks** <u>like</u> there has been *a high turnout* (expressandstar.com)
       f.   There **looks** <u>like</u> there was *a crowd of young people ...*
            (manchestereveningnews.co.uk)

(100)   a.   There **sound** <u>like</u> there are *some interesting developments* ...
             (gibbonedu.org)

        b.   There **sound** <u>like</u> there were *some significant differences* too
             (mumsnet.com)

        c.   There **sound** <u>like</u> there have been *quite a lot of changes* ...
             (homebrewtalk.com)

        d.   There **sounds** <u>like</u> there is going to be *a fun event* ... (salisburyjournal.
             co.uk)

        e.   There **sounds** <u>like</u> there has been *a lot of sadness* ... (unexplained-
             mysteries.com)

        f.   There **sounds** <u>like</u> there was *a game* last night (imdb.com)

Rogers (1974: 53), Rooryck (2000: 48), López-Couso & Méndez-Naya (2012),
and Kanda & Honda (2018: 141–42) treat *like* as a complementiser in this
use (and they propose a similar treatment for *as if/as though*). If so, using
an overt copy of *there* following *like* could be a repair strategy designed to
avoid Impenetrability/Minimality/COMP-Trace violations.

3.4.3   Copy Raising with non-expletive subjects

It might seem as if the Copy Raising analysis outlined in §3.4.2 for sentences with expletive subjects can be extended in a relatively straightforward fashion to handle sentences like those in (101) below with italicised
non-expletive personal pronouns as their subjects:

(101)   a.   *I* appear that *I* may have accidentally mis-represented the 802.3
             position (grouper.ieee.org)

        b.   We KNOW that we need at least 6 players but *we* appear that *we*
             MIGHT get one (unitedlounge.com)

        c.   Do *you* appear that *you*'re lying, even when you're telling the truth?
             (TopLawyerCoach.com)

        d.   *He* appears that *he* is unable to deal with disappointment (autism.org.
             uk)

        e.   *She* appears that *she* doesn't want to budge at all (cnn.com)

        f.   *They* appear that *they* are planning to bring mischief to DCI
             (dancecentral.fandom.com)

However, a complication that arises with a Copy Raising analysis of sentences
like (101) above is that when the (italicised) main clause subject is nominal,
the (bold-printed) complement clause subject is a personal pronoun:

(102)   a.   *The president* seems <u>that</u> **he**'s having fun (today.com)

        b.   *Boris Johnson* looks <u>like</u> **he**'ll win big (theliberal.ie)

        c.   *Your other trouble* sounds <u>like</u> **it** may be a one-time glitch (vlab.ncep.
             noaa.gov)

    d. When faced with the task, *many students* appear <u>as if</u> **they** do not know where to begin (Gasper 2014: 1)

    e. *Boris* looks <u>as though</u> **he**'s survived the Cummings lockdown road trip (politicalbetting.com)

    f. *Baroness Thatcher* was announced <u>that</u> **she** had died (Danny Savage, BBC Radio 5 Live)

    g. *The police* have been found <u>that</u> *they* can be held accountable (Listener, BBC Radio 5 Live)

In other words, if sentences like (102) involve Copy Raising, we have to say that the copy left behind by raising the italicised subject out of the *that/ like/as if/as though*-clause is not a full copy of the raised DP/QP, but rather a pronominal copy. Sentences like (102) have been argued to involve movement, because idiomatic nominals like those italicised below can occur in this type of structure:

(103)   a. *The shit* looks <u>like</u> it's gonna hit the fan (Rogers 1974: 154)

    b. *All hell* sounds <u>like</u> it's breaking loose under the hood (wranglertjforum.com)

    c. *Some headway* looks <u>like</u> it could be made in the near future (agriculture.com)

    d. *Close tabs* sound <u>as if</u> **they** are being kept on the CIA

    e. *The fur* seems <u>like</u> it's gonna fly

    f. *Dirty tricks* look <u>like</u> **they** are being played on the opposition

    g. *The wool* looks <u>like</u> it's been pulled over his eyes

The premise of the idiom argument for movement is that (e.g. in 103g) the DP *the wool* originates as the complement of the verb *pull* in the idiom *pull the wool over someone's eyes*, and hence must undergo Copy Raising in order to become the subject of the *looks* clause. However, if sentences like those in (103) do indeed involve Copy Raising, the question arises as to why the lower copy is spelled out as a pronoun (rather than as a full copy of the raised italicised subject).

    One answer which could be given to this question is in terms of economy of spellout (i.e. a desire to minimise the amount of overt material pronounced). Reasoning along these lines, we might suppose that only the person/number/gender/case features of the copy of the raised subject following the underlined complementiser are spelled out/lexicalised (not its other features), and this can most economically be done by using a personal pronoun to spell out the relevant bundle of person/number/gender/case features. An alternative (syntactic) approach is to suppose that the italicised raised nominal is underlyingly contained within an XP shell headed by the pronoun (so that the nominal and its pronominal copy underlyingly form a single phrase/XP), and that raising moves only the nominal, leaving the pronoun behind. We can provide an informal illustration of the difference between these two approaches in relation to (102a) *The president seems that he's having fun.*

Under the spellout approach, the DP *the president* undergoes Copy Raising, resulting in the superficial syntactic structure shown in highly simplified form below:

(104)   *The president* seems that **the president** is having fun

In the PF component, only the person/number/gender/case features on the bold-printed copy following *that* are spelled out, with the result that the bold-printed copy is lexicalised as the third person masculine singular nominative pronoun *he.*

By contrast, under the shell approach, the DP *the president* originates inside an XP headed by the pronoun *he*, and the DP *the president* undergoes movement on its own, resulting in the syntactic structure in (105) below, where the pronoun *he* is stranded as the subject of the complement clause:

(105)   *The president* seems that [**he** ~~the president~~] is having fun

Both approaches are problematic in a number of ways: for example, the spellout solution in (104) in effect allows the PF component to introduce a new word (the pronoun *he*) into the derivation; and the shell analysis in (105) (in extracting *the president* out of a larger XP *he the president* which has moved from being the specifier of *having* to becoming the specifier of *is*) leads to violation of constraints on movement (e.g. the Constraint on Extraction Domains which bars movement out of a specifier, and the Freezing Principle which bars extraction out of a moved constituent).

One way of avoiding technical problems in accounting for how a raised constituent can leave behind a pronominal copy is to adopt an alternative binding approach developed in work dating back to Lappin (1983, 1984). The key assumption underlying the binding analysis is to suppose that sentences like those in (102) involve two separate (i.e. independently generated) subjects, with the main clause subject binding (i.e. serving as the antecedent of) the pronoun which functions as the complement clause subject. Let's look briefly at how such an analysis (if adapted to the framework used here) would handle a sentence like (102b) *Boris Johnson looks like he'll win big.* Let's suppose that *like* is a finite complementiser which merges with the TP *he'll win big* and assigns nominative case to the pronoun *he.* Suppose too that the CP *like he'll win big* is merged as the complement of *look*, forming the V-bar *look like he'll win big.* In addition, suppose that this V-bar is then merged with *Boris Johnson* (which we can take to be a DP headed by a null determiner, with the overall DP being paraphrasable informally as 'the specific individual Boris Johnson'), to form a VP which is in turn merged with a present-tense affix to form the T-bar below:

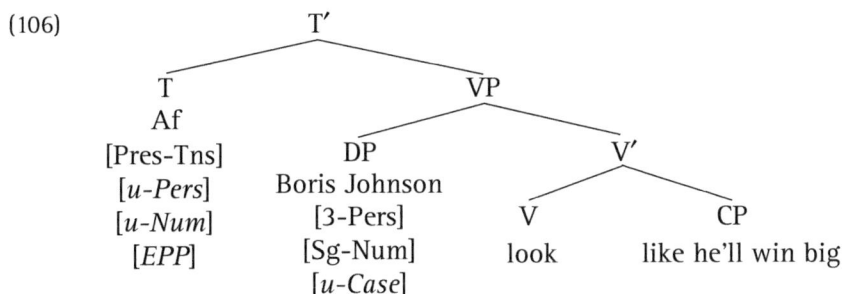

(106)

```
                    T′
          ┌─────────┴─────────┐
          T                   VP
          Af          ┌───────┴───────┐
      [Pres-Tns]      DP              V′
       [u-Pers]   Boris Johnson  ┌────┴────┐
       [u-Num]     [3-Pers]      V         CP
        [EPP]      [Sg-Num]     look   like he'll win big
                   [u-Case]
```

The tense affix/*Af* is active as a probe by virtue of its unvalued person and number features, and it searches for any active goal(s) that can value these. The only active goal c-commanded by T-*Af* is the DP *Boris Johnson* (whose unvalued case feature makes it active), since all constituents inside the complement clause CP are inactive at this point. Accordingly, the person/number features on the DP *Boris Johnson* value the unvalued person/number features on T-*Af* as third person singular. In addition, the EPP feature on T-*Af* attracts (a copy of) the closest goal that it agrees with in person (= the DP *Boris Johnson*) to move to spec-TP (and the EPP feature is thereafter stripped from T-*Af* and thereby removed from the derivation). Subsequently, the resulting TP is merged with a null complementiser to form the CP in (107) below (with the arrow showing A-Movement of the DP *Boris Johnson* from spec-VP to spec-TP in the main clause):

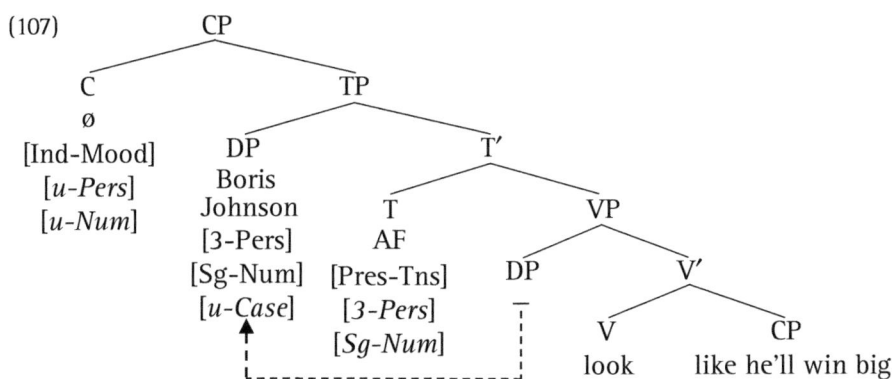

(107)

```
                    CP
          ┌─────────┴─────────────┐
          C                       TP
          ∅              ┌─────────┴─────────┐
      [Ind-Mood]         DP                 T′
       [u-Pers]         Boris      ┌─────────┴─────────┐
       [u-Num]         Johnson     T                  VP
                       [3-Pers]   AF          ┌────────┴────────┐
                       [Sg-Num]  [Pres-Tns]   DP              V′
                       [u-Case]   [3-Pers]    ┬         ┌──────┴──────┐
                         ↑        [Sg-Num]    ┊         V            CP
                         ┊                    ┊        look    like he'll win big
                         └────────────────────┘
```

At this point, the null complementiser at the top of the tree is active as a probe (by virtue of its unvalued person and number features), and searches for any active goal(s) that can value them. The only active goal c-commanded by the complementiser is the DP *Boris Johnson* (whose unvalued case feature makes it active); accordingly, this DP values the unvalued φ-features on the complementiser as third person singular. At the same time, the complementiser (being both finite and φ-complete) also values the unvalued case feature on the DP *Boris Johnson* as nominative, so deriving the structure in (108) below:

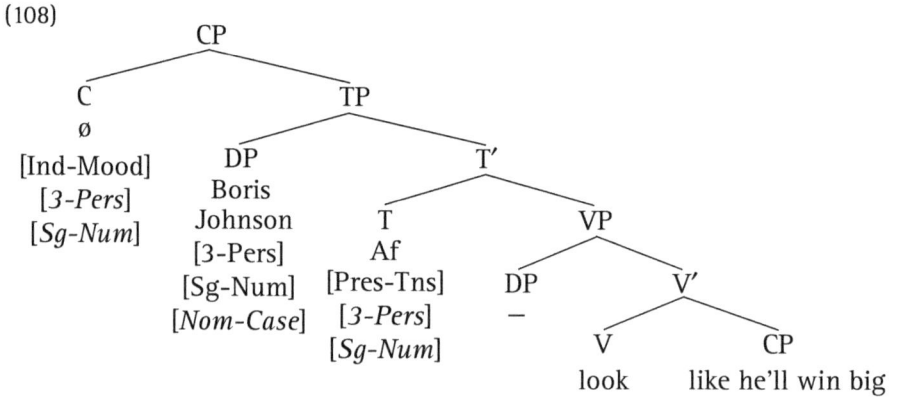

(108)

```
                        CP
              ┌─────────┴─────────┐
              C                   TP
              ø          ┌────────┴────────┐
        [Ind-Mood]      DP               T′
         [3-Pers]      Boris        ┌─────┴─────┐
         [Sg-Num]     Johnson       T           VP
                      [3-Pers]      Af      ┌────┴────┐
                      [Sg-Num]  [Pres-Tns]  DP        V′
                     [Nom-Case]  [3-Pers]   −     ┌───┴───┐
                                 [Sg-Num]         V       CP
                                               look   like he'll win big
```

When this structure is handed over to the PF component, the present tense affix is lowered from T onto the verb *look* by Affix Hopping, and the resulting complex V-head *look+Af* is spelled out as *looks* (and the overall sentence as *Boris Johnson looks like he'll win big*).

More interesting is the question of what happens when the structure in (108) is processed in the semantic component. On the assumption that *look* (in this use) is a verb which does not theta-mark its subject (which is why *look* allows an expletive *there* subject, as we saw earlier), it follows that the DP *Boris Johnson* will not be assigned a theta role by the verb *look*. However, since this DP is not an expletive (and occupies an A-position), it must be assigned a theta role somehow, or else the derivation will crash. But how? The answer suggested by Lappin (1984: 245) is that in such structures 'The matrix subject inherits its theta role from the pronoun which it binds in the complement.' This means that if the DP *Boris Johnson* is interpreted as binding the complement clause subject *he*, then *Boris Johnson* will inherit the theta role of *he* (and hence will be interpreted as the AGENT argument of *win*). This binding is possible because the pronoun *he* requires a third person masculine singular antecedent, and the DP *Boris Johnson* satisfies this requirement (although gender is not shown in the simplified structure of 108).

A potential problem might at first sight appear to be that this binding relation applies across the edge of an intervening CP (= across the edge of the CP headed by *like*), so appears to violate the Impenetrability Condition. However, this is unproblematic, since a (bold-printed) pronominal like *he* can freely be bound (across an intervening CP boundary) by an (italicised) antecedent in a higher clause, as we see from (109) below:

(109)   *Boris* didn't know [$_{CP}$ that/whether/if **he** was behind in the polls]

Consequently, any such objection to the derivation in (106–108) is spurious.

What is interesting about the derivations sketched in this section from a theoretical point of view is that they suggest that a non-thematic position (like the specifier position in a VP headed by a verb like *seem/appear/look* etc.) can either be filled by an expletive (as in our discussion of sentences like *there seems/appears/looks* ...), or by a non-expletive constituent that is construed as binding a pronoun which originates in a thematic position within a complement clause (thereby enabling the relevant pro/nominal to inherit the theta role of the pronoun that it binds).

To summarise: in Module 3.4 we have looked at cases of cross-clausal Agreement, A-Movement and Case-marking. I began by discussing sentences like (79a) *China is likely will field a ground-based laser weapon*, where *China* is raised from being the subject of *will* to becoming the subject of *is*, and is thereby extracted out of a finite *will*-clause. I argued that in such cases, the finite complement clause is defective (in the sense that it is a TP, not a CP), and that the absence of a complementiser to case-mark the subject of *will* means that the subject is active and can (via A-Movement) be raised to become the subject of *is*. I went on to discuss sentences like (90a) *There appear that there are no major differences*, where Agreement (between *appear* and *no major differences*) applies across an intervening CP headed by *that*. I sketched a Copy Raising account on which expletive *there* (via A-Movement across the intervening complementiser *that*) raises from being the subject of *are* to becoming the subject of *appear*, leaving behind an overt copy of *there*, in order not to induce an Impenetrability/Minimality/COMP-Trace violation. I went on to discuss sentences like (102b) *Boris Johnson looks like he'll win big*, arguing that these involve directly generating *Boris Johnson* in a non-thematic position as the subject of *look*, and *he* in a thematic position as the subject (and AGENT argument) of *win*, with *Boris Johnson* binding (and thereby inheriting the theta role of) *he*: on this view, such sentences do not involve cross-clausal Agreement, A-Movement or Case-marking.

You should now be able to tackle Exercise 3.4.

3.5 Summary

In this chapter, we have looked at the syntax of Agreement, A-Movement, and Case-marking. In Module 3.1 we saw that subject-verb Agreement involves a relation between a finite T-probe and a nominal or pronominal XP goal which it c-commands: the T-probe is made active by unvalued (person/number) φ-features which it carries when it enters the derivation, and its (pro)nominal goal is made active by its unvalued case feature. More generally, the probe and goal enter the derivation carrying a set of valued inherent/interpretable features, and a set of unvalued contextual/uninterpretable features, and the unvalued features are valued by operations like Agreement and Case-marking in the course of the derivation. We also saw that Case-marking is contingent on a person/number agreement relation between probe and goal, and that A-Movement involves a T probe attracting the closest goal that it agrees with in person to become its specifier. I argued that Agreement, A-Movement and Case-marking are subject to the following conditions governing their application:

(5)   **Activity Conditions**

    (i)   A head can only be an active probe for Agreement or A-Movement or Case-marking if it carries some unvalued φ-feature/s, and becomes inactive once its φ-feature/s have been valued (**Probe Condition**)

    (ii)   An XP can only be an active goal for Agreement, A-Movement, or Case-marking if it has an unvalued case feature, and becomes inactive once its case feature is valued (**Goal Condition**)

    (iii)   If a constituent is part of a movement chain at a given point in a derivation, only the highest copy in the chain can be active for operations like Agreement, A-Movement or Case-marking (**Highest Copy Condition**)

(6)   **Feature Valuation Conditions**

    (i)   When an active probe like T c-commands an active XP goal, each unvalued φ-feature on the probe will be valued by the goal – that is, assigned a value which is a copy of the corresponding feature value on the goal (**Agreement**)

    (ii)   Only a φ-complete XP (i.e. one with person and number) can serve as a goal valuing unvalued features on a probe, and conversely only a φ-complete probe (i.e. one with person and number) can value unvalued features on a goal (**Completeness Condition**)

    (iii)   Each feature on a constituent must be valued (i.e. assigned a single, appropriate value) in order for the constituent to be legible at the PF/LF interfaces; if not, the derivation will crash (**Legibility Condition**)

(7)   **EPP Condition**

An EPP feature on a probe T attracts the closest XP goal that T agrees with in person to undergo A-Movement to spec-TP, and the EPP feature is stripped from T (and removed from the derivation) once the movement has taken place

(11)   **Case Conditions**

A φ-complete case-assigning probe values an unvalued case feature on an XP goal that it agrees with in respect of one or more φ-features, and assigns the goal a case value that depends on the nature of the probe – namely:

(i)   *nominative* if the probe is a finite C with a TP complement (where a finite C is one that is indicative, subjunctive or imperative in mood)
(ii) *null* if the probe is an intransitive infinitival C with a TP complement
(iii) *accusative* if the probe is transitive

In Module 3.2, we looked at the syntax of clauses with an expletive subject. I argued that expletive *it* enters the derivation with inherently valued third-person and singular-number features and an unvalued case feature, and that its person/number features value those of the auxiliary HAVE in sentences such as *It has transpired that he was cheating*, while the unvalued case feature on *it* is valued by (abstract/invisible) agreement with the (overt or null) complementiser introducing the relevant clause. I further argued that expletive subjects (like other subjects) are quasi-arguments that originate within VP, and from there are attracted by the EPP feature on T to move to spec-TP. I went on to claim that expletive *there* (in existential clauses) enters the derivation with an inherently valued third person feature and an unvalued case feature, and is initially merged as the specifier of an existential predicate which has the associate of the expletive as its complement. Expletive *there* and its associate jointly value the unvalued features on the auxiliary (or affix) in T via multiple agreement. The unvalued case features on expletive *there* and its associate are in turn valued via (abstract) agreement with the complementiser introducing the relevant clause. I suggested that expletives are subject to the following conditions on their use:

(45)   **Expletive Conditions**
       (i)   <u>External Argument Condition</u>
       An expletive can only be merged as the highest argument of a verb with no external argument
       (ii) <u>Indefiniteness Condition</u>
       Existential *there* can only be merged as the specifier of an existential verb with an indefinite (pro)nominal complement
       (iii) <u>Inactivity Condition</u>
       Expletive *it* can only be merged with a constituent which does not contain an active nominal or pronominal (i.e. one carrying an unvalued case feature)

In Module 3.3, we looked at the syntax of Agreement, A-Movement and Case-marking in infinitive clauses. I argued that infinitival *to* (although not overtly inflecting for agreement) enters the derivation carrying an unvalued person feature which (in conjunction with the EPP feature on infinitival *to*) serves to attract the clause subject to undergo A-Movement from its initial position inside VP to its derived position in spec-TP as the subject of infinitival *to*. If the resulting *to*-infinitive TP is subsequently embedded as the complement of an item which is not a case-assigner (like the Raising verb *seem* in 'There do **seem** *to have been some problems*' or the passive participle *believed* in 'He is **believed** *to be telling the truth*'), the subject will continue to move until it ends up in a position within the domain of a case-assigner. However, if the infinitival TP is embedded as the complement of a case-assigner (e.g. an ECM verb like *believe* in 'We **believe** *him to be telling the truth*', or a complementiser like *for* in 'We are anxious **for** *the agreements to be ratified*'), the subject in spec-TP will be case-marked by the relevant case assigner (in conformity with the Case Conditions in 11 above), and will thereafter become inactive for further A-operations.

In Module 3.4, we looked at cases of cross-clausal Agreement, A-Movement and Case-marking. I began by discussing sentences like (79a) *China is likely will field a ground-based laser weapon*, where *China* is raised from being the subject of *will* to becoming the subject of *is*. I argued that in such cases, the finite complement clause is defective (in that it is a TP rather than a CP), and that the absence of a complementiser to case-mark the subject of *will* means that the complement clause subject is active and can be raised up to become the subject of *is* by A-Movement. I then went on to discuss sentences like (90a) *There appear that there are no major differences*, where Agreement (between *appear* and *no major differences*) applies across an intervening CP headed by *that*. I sketched a Copy Raising account on which expletive *there* (via A-Movement across the defective intervening complementiser *that*) raises from being the subject of *are* to becoming the subject of *appear*, leaving behind an overt copy of *there*, in order to avoid violations of the Impenetrability/Minimality/COMP-Trace conditions. I went on to discuss sentences like (102b) *Boris Johnson looks like he'll win big*, arguing that these involve base-generating *Boris Johnson* in a non-thematic position as the subject of *look*, and *he* in a thematic position as the subject (and AGENT argument) of *won*, with *Boris Johnson* binding (and thereby inheriting the theta role of) *he*: on this view, such binding structures do not involve Copy-Raising (and likewise do not involve cross-clausal Agreement, A-Movement or Case-marking).

3.6   Bibliographical notes

On **agreement typology** (i.e. a cross-linguistic survey of agreement patterns in a wide range of languages), see Corbett (2006); for an overview of the treatment of agreement in Minimalism, see Fuß (2005), Baker (2008),

Miyagawa (2010), Preminger (2012, 2014), and Smith et al. (2020). Note that this chapter is specifically concerned with agreement in the verbal domain, setting aside **Concord** in the nominal domain (e.g. between determiners, adjectives and the nouns they modify): on Concord, see Norris (2014). Also set aside here are other phenomena which are taken by some to involve agreement, such as Negative Concord (Zeijlstra 2004), or sequence of tense restrictions (Zeijlstra 2012; Kauf & Zeijlstra 2018; see also Armenante & Braun 2022).

The probe-goal account of Agreement sketched in Module 3.1 is loosely based on Chomsky (1998, 1999, 2001): for a critique of this approach, see Danon (2011); and for a critique of the Activity Condition, see Nevins (2005), and Bošković (2007). The assumption about **feature valuation** made in Chomsky (1998, 1999) that features which enter the derivation valued are interpretable and those which enter the derivation unvalued are uninterpretable is called into question in work by Pesetsky & Torrego (2004, 2007); they argue for the two additional possibilities that features can also enter the derivation (i) uninterpretable but valued, and (ii) interpretable but unvalued. In much the same vein, Bošković (2011b) argues that gender features on nouns with arbitrary gender in languages like Serbo-Croation enter the derivation valued, in spite of arbitrary gender being an uninterpretable feature. Chomsky (2007, 2008) and Miyagawa (2005, 2006a, 2010) argue that agreement features originate on C and are 'handed down' to T; for a challenge to this view, see Carstens (2003), and Haegeman & van Koppen (2012). On so-called **semantic agreement** in British English structures like *The government are ruining the country*, see den Dikken (2001), Sauerland & Elbourne (2002), and Smith (2017). On **complementiser agreement**, see Bayer (1984b), Haegeman (1992), Zwart (1993, 1997, 2006), Shlonsky (1993), Bennis & Haegeman (1994), Hoekstra & Smits (1999), Carstens (2003, 2016), Fuß (2004, 2008, 2014), Barbiers et al. (2005), van Koppen (2005, 2017), Weiß (2005), Gruber (2008), Mayr (2010), Diercks (2010, 2013), Haegeman & van Koppen (2012), Boef (2013), Lewis (2013), Deal (2015), and Diercks et al. (2020).

The idea that **nominative case** is assigned by a finite C dates back to Chomsky (2001). However, much other research follows earlier work by Iatridou (1993) and Chomsky (1998, 1999) in taking a tensed T/INFL to be the constituent that assigns nominative case to clause subjects under agreement. A variant of this view is to see nominative case as the reflex of a tense feature on T (Varlokosta 1994, Alexiadou & Anagnastopoulou 1999, Uchibori 2000, Pesetsky & Torrego 2001, 2004, 2007). On languages which show overt agreement between verbs and constituents to which they assign **accusative case**, see Bárány (2015), and Smith (2020); however, note that overt object agreement in some languages may be restricted to objects with a certain type of property, such as definiteness or specificity. It should also be noted that a number of researchers have argued that case-marking can be independent of agreement: see Uchibori (2000), Woolford (2006), Baker (2008), Bobaljik (2009), Dalrymple & Nikolaeva (2011), Ussery (2009, 2012), Petersen (2011), and Preminger (2012, 2014).

On the nature of the **EPP feature** of T which attracts the closest appropriate goal to move to become its specifier (and whether it is possible to dispense with it), see Chomsky (1982, 1995, 1998, 1999, 2001), Rothstein (1983), Alexiadou & Anagnastopoulou (1998), Martin (1999), Déprez (2000), Grohmann et al, (2000), Holmberg (2000), Sabel (2000), Goodall (2001), Kiss (2001), Lasnik (2001), Bošković (2002, 2007), Roberts & Roussou (2002), Rosengren (2002), Svenonius (2002a), Haeberli (2003), Richards (2003), Epstein et al. (2005), Goldshlag (2005), Miyagawa (2005, 2006a, 2010), van Craenenbroeck & den Dikken (2006), Epstein & Seely (2006), Sheehan (2006), Landau (2007), Sifaki & Sitaridou (2007), Boeckx (2008), Castillo et al. (2009), Roberts (2010), Sigurðsson (2010), Lin (2011), Cable (2012), Chapman (2013), Chomsky (2015), Richards (2016), and Fernández-Salgueiro (2020).

On the syntax of **expletive pronouns/structures**, see Jenkins (1975), Bolinger (1977), Milsark (1977), Breivik (1983), Williams (1984, 2006), Postal & Pullum (1988), Inoue (1991), Lasnik (1992, 1995, 2003), Abbott (1993), den Dikken (1995), Groat (1995, 1999), Rothstein (1995), Law (1996), Moro (1997, 2006), Sobin (1997), Chomsky (1998, 1999, 2000, 2001), Schütze (1999), Koster & Zwart (2000), Felser & Rupp (2001), Bowers (2002), Han (2004), Hazout (2004a, 2004b), Sobin (2004), Rupp (2005), Moro (2006), Rezak (2006), Henry & Cottell (2007), Hornstein (2007), Biberauer (2008), Hartmann (2008), Kallulli (2008), Deal (2009), Light (2015), Kayne (2016), Haider (2017, 2019), Greco et al. (2017), and van Craenenbroeck (2020). On structures such as *There were three fish caught in the lake*, see Chomsky (1999), Bowers (2002), Caponigro & Schütze (2003), and Rezak (2006). On agreement in structures like *There's lots of people in the room*, see Sobin (1997), Schütze (1999), and den Dikken (2001). On **multiple agreement** in expletive structures, see Chomsky (2001, 2008), Hiraira (2001, 2005), and Henderson (2006).

The claim made in Module 3.3 that **infinitival *to*** carries EPP and person features follows the analysis proposed in Chomsky (1999) for defective infinitive clauses; but note that (contrary to what is proposed here), much work assumes that *to* in Control clauses carries both person *and number* features. On infinitives which overtly inflect for person/number agreement in European Portuguese, see Raposo (1987), Ambar (2007), and Gonçalves et al. (2014). Not touched on in our discussion here are non-standard *for-to* infinitives (as in *He is likely for to get injured*) in some varieties of English, including Belfast English (Henry 1992, 1995), Ottowa Valley English (Carroll 1983), Ozark English (Elgin & Haden 1991), and Smoky Mountain English (Montgomery & Hall 2004).

The phenomenon discussed in Module 3.4 of Raising subjects out of finite clauses in structures like *China is likely will field weapons* has potential parallels with Raising out of certain types of finite complement clause in languages like Brazilian Portuguese, Greek, Romanian, and Bantu (a phenomenon sometimes termed **Hyper-Raising**): see Grosu & Horvath (1984), Harford Perez (1985), Rivero (1989), Iatridou (1993), Watanabe (1993), Ura (1994), Varlokosta (1994), Alexiadou & Anagnastopoulou (1999), Ferreira (2004, 2009), Rodriguez (2004), Martins & Nunes (2005, 2009), Zeller (2006), Nunes (2008), Landau (2009), Alexiadou et al. (2012), Carstens & Diercks (2013), Petersen & Terzi (2015), Yuan (2016), Fong (2018), and Zyman (2018a).

Copy Raising is a phenomenon briefly noted in Postal (1971: 162–63, 1974: 200), and analysed in more detail in Rogers (1971, 1972, 1974), Joseph (1976), Perlmutter & Soames (1979), Horn (1981), Lappin (1983, 1984), Déprez (1992), Heycock (1994: 272ff), Ura (1994, 1995), Gisbourne (1996, 2010), Groat (1997), Moore (1998), Terada (2000), Potsdam & Runner (2001), Matushansky (2002), Asudeh (2002, 2004, 2011b, 2012), Rezak (2004, 2011), Fujii (2005, 2007), Asudeh & Toivonen (2006, 2007, 2012), Landau (2009, 2011), Mack (2010), Takano (2013), Kim (2014), Ziegler (2014), Doran (2015), Frazier & Clifton (2015), Brook (2016, 2018), Poortvliet (2016), den Dikken (2017, 2018), Camilleri (2018), Kanda & Honda (2018), Kobayashi (2018) and Rudolph (2019).

On **cross-clausal/long-distance agreement**, see Bruening (2001), Branigan & McKenzie (2001), Polinsky & Potsdam (2001, 2006), Polinsky (2003), Hazout (2004a), Legate (2005), Frank (2006), Bošković (2007), Alexiadou et al. (2012), Petersen & Terzi (2015), Branan (2018), Ostrove (2018), Bjorkman & Zeijlstra (2019), Wurmbrandt (2019), and Börjeson & Müller (2020).

A technical issue not touched on in this chapter concerns **the locus of agreement**, and more specifically whether (as assumed here) Agreement is an operation taking place in the syntax and dependent on syntactic relations like c-command, or whether it is a post-syntactic operation which takes place in the PF component (Bobaljik 2009) – or indeed whether it involves two suboperations – one which sets up an agreement link between probe and goal in the syntax, and another that copies the relevant φ-features in the PF component (Benmamoun et al. 2009; Arregi & Nevins 2012; Bhatt & Walkow 2013; Smith 2015, Kalin 2020).

3.7 Workbook

In the exercises below, an [M] after an example sentence indicates that a model answer is provided in the free-to-download *Students' Answerbook* (and in the *Teachers' Answerbook* as well). You will find it helpful to look at this model answer before attempting to tackle other examples in the exercise. Some other exercise examples have an [S] after them, indicating that they are for self-study: this means that after reading the relevant module (and those preceding it), and looking at the helpful hints and model answer associated with the exercise, students should be able to analyse these self-study examples on their own, and then compare their answers with those provided in the *Students' Answerbook*. The remaining exercise examples (i.e. those not marked with [M] or [S] after them) are intended for teachers to use as the basis for hands-on problem-solving work in seminars, classes, or assignments: answers to all of these non-self-study examples are provided in the *Teachers' Answerbook*. Note that Exercise 3.1 tests you on Module 3.1, Exercise 3.2 on Module 3.2, and so on; and that each exercise in a given chapter presupposes familiarity with material covered in earlier chapters and in earlier modules of the same chapter. Unparenthesised numbers like 4 refer to material in the exercises, whereas parenthesised numbers like (22) refer to examples and conditions in the main text of the book.

EXERCISE 3.1

This exercise is designed to be attempted after reading Module 3.1 and the chapters preceding it.

Discuss how Agreement, Case-marking and A-Movement work in the following sentences, focusing in each case on the syntax of the italicised (pro)nominal constituents and the bold-printed (auxiliary/main) verbs:

1   *He* **is** telling the truth [M]
2   *No traces of any DNA* **were** found [S]
3   *We workers* **are** being exploited
4   *Several new candidates* **have** emerged [S]
5   *The economy* **has** grown considerably
6   *The guards* **deny** *they* **tortured** the prisoners

Helpful hints
Bear in mind the discussion of the VP-Internal Subject Hypothesis (and the syntax of unaccusative/passive predicates) in the previous chapter, and the role played by the Activity Conditions (5) in the main text/

summary Module 3.5, the Feature Valuation Conditions (6) in the main text/summary, the EPP Condition (7) in the main text/Summary, and the Case Conditions (11) in the main text/summary. In dealing with agreement, concern yourself with the case, agreement, and movement properties of goals, but not their internal structure: for example, take *several new candidates* in 4 to be a QP, but don't concern yourself with its internal structure. In the case of complex QPs or DPs, assume that the case/agreement properties of the overall phrase are those of its head, since phrases are projections of their heads. For the purposes of this exercise, make the simplifying assumption that finite auxiliaries originate in the head T position of TP (setting aside the possibility that they may originate in a lower auxiliary projection and from there move to T via Head Movement). In the case of 5, assume that *considerably* is an ADVP which adjoins to the VP headed by *grown* to form a larger VP.

EXERCISE 3.2

This exercise is designed to be attempted after reading Module 3.2 and the module and chapters preceding it.

Account for the (un)grammaticality of the following expletive sentences, paying particular attention to the syntax of Agreement and Case-marking:

1 It is said that he was taking bribes [M]
2 *There is said that he was taking bribes [M]
3 There has emerged a new strain of the virus [S]
4 *It has emerged a new strain of the virus [S]
5 It was raining heavily [S]
6 *There was raining heavily [S]
7 It does not matter that he lied
8 *There does not matter that he lied
9 There have been some changes to on-street parking
10 There has been some changes to on-street parking (darlington.gov.uk)
11 In her whole life, there has been only me (M. A. Graham, *A Golden Forever*, Google Books, 2009: 94)
12 *In her whole life, there have been only I
13 It appears there was some unrest

Helpful hints
Bear in mind the VP-Internal Subject Hypothesis (and the syntax of unaccusative predicates), and the role played by conditions like the Activity Conditions, Valuation Conditions, EPP Condition, and Case

Conditions outlined in (5), (6), (7) and (11) in the main text/Summary in regulating how Agreement and Case-marking apply. For the purposes of this exercise, make the following assumptions (but don't concern yourself with the internal structure of the relevant XPs): in 1, 2, 7, 8, the *that*-clause is a CP; in 5, 6, *heavily* is an ADVP which adjoins to the VP headed by *raining* to form an even larger VP; in 7, 8 *not* is an ADVP which serves as the specifier of a NEGP with a null NEG head; in 9, 10, *some changes to on-street parking* is a QP; and in 11, 12, *in her whole life* is a PP directly merged in spec-CP. Note that the use of *has* in 10 is generally taken to be non-standard (with Standard English preferring to use *have*, as in 9): consider the possibility that people who produce non-standard sentences like 10 may treat expletive *there* as inherently third person singular. In relation to 10–12, bear in mind that the verb BE can seemingly assign accusative case to its complement in sentences like 'If you were *me*, what would you do?' Bear in mind, too that (as noted in the book) a phrase like *only me* can function as a third person singular expression in a sentence like 'Only me is working in the office at present' (where *only me* is paraphrasable as 'nobody but/except me').

In dealing with agreement, concern yourself with the overall case and agreement properties of goals, but not with their internal structure: for example, in the case of complex QPs or DPs, assume that the case/agreement properties of the overall phrase are those of its head, since phrases are projections of their heads. For the purposes of this exercise, make the simplifying assumption that finite auxiliaries originate in the head T position of TP (setting aside the possibility that they may originate in a lower auxiliary projection and from there move to T via Head Movement).

Bear in mind the following assumptions about expletive clauses made in Module 3.2:

- expletive *it* enters the derivation with inherently valued third-person and singular-number features and an unvalued case feature; its person/number features value those of an affix/auxiliary in T
- expletive *there* enters the derivation with an inherently valued third person feature and an unvalued case feature; the expletive and its associate jointly value the unvalued features on an affix/auxiliary in T
- expletive subjects (like other subjects) originate within VP, and from there are attracted by the EPP feature on T to move to spec-TP.
- case on an expletive subject (and any associate it has) is valued via agreement with a complementiser

EXERCISE 3.3

This exercise is designed to be attempted after reading Module 3.3 and the modules and chapters preceding it.

Discuss the syntax of the infinitive structures in the sentences below, focusing on the syntax of the constituents involved in Agreement, A-Movement and Case-marking:

1 The suspect is expected to be charged [M]
2 They haven't decided whether to charge the suspect [S]
3 *The suspect was decided to be charged (intended to be synonymous with 'It was decided to charge the suspect') [S]
4 They don't want it to rain [S]
5 It was said to be raining [S]
6 The enquiry found there to be no evidence of any malpractice [S]
7 There was found to be no evidence of any malpractice
8 He was thought to be the ringleader
9 *The chairman has been impossible for to attend the meeting (intended to be synonymous with 'It has been impossible for the chairman to attend the meeting')
10 It/*There is unlikely for there/*it to be any protests
11 There needs to be some changes (James Moore, CTVnews.ca)
12 They were hoping for there to be some changes

In the case of 12 set aside the agreement-based account of movement and case-marking outlined in the book, and instead follow the alternative (agreement-free) account of movement and case-marking sketched in the helpful hints below.

Helpful hints

In relation to the sentences in 1–11, say how the derivation of these sentences would proceed if we adopt the agreement-based account of Case-marking and A-Movement outlined in this chapter. Accordingly assume (as claimed in Module 3.3) that infinitival *to* enters the derivation carrying an interpretable nonfinite tense feature [Nf-Tns], an uninterpretable (and unvalued) person feature [*u-Pers*], and an EPP feature which attracts the closest XP goal it agrees with in person to move to spec-TP, and is subsequently stripped from T-*to* (and thereby removed from the derivation entirely) because it is illegible at the PF and LF interfaces. Bear in mind the VP-Internal Subject Hypothesis (and the syntax of unaccusative and passive predicates), and the role played by conditions like the Activity Conditions, Valuation Conditions, EPP Condition, and

Case Conditions outlined in (5), (6), (7) and (11) in the main text/Summary in regulating how Agreement and Case-marking apply. In the case of 2, concern yourself only with the syntax of the infinitival *whether*-clause. In relation to 11, note that the use of the singular form *needs* is generally taken to be non-standard (with Standard English preferring to use the plural form *need*); see the suggestions about singular agreement in sentences where *there* has a plural associate in the helpful hints for example 10 in Exercise 3.2. In dealing with agreement, concern yourself with the overall case and agreement properties of goals, but not with their internal structure. For the purposes of this exercise, make the simplifying assumption that finite auxiliaries originate in the head T position of TP (setting aside the possibility that they may originate in a lower auxiliary projection and from there move to T via Head Movement).

In relation to the sentence in 12 consider how its derivation would work if we reject the agreement-based account of movement and case-marking in the book (because it leads to a panoply of abstract agreement features and operations which have no overt manifestation and thus little empirical rationale), and instead explore an alternative agreement-free account of movement and case-marking based on the revised assumptions outlined in 13, 14 below:

13   A-Movement is triggered not by person agreement nor by an EPP feature on T, but rather by an [Attr-Pers] feature on a T-head, meaning 'Attract the closest XP goal with a person feature'. This attraction feature is stripped from T (and thereby removed from the derivation entirely) once it has done its work, because it is illegible at PF and LF

14   Case-marking does not involve agreement, but rather a case-assignment feature on a probe such as [Ass-Nom]/[Ass-Acc]/[Ass-Null] meaning 'Assign nominative/accusative/null case to any local/nearby XP goal(s) with an unvalued case feature'; this case-assignment feature is stripped (i.e. removed from the derivation) once it has done its work, because it is illegible at PF and LF

EXERCISE 3.4

This exercise is designed to be attempted after reading Module 3.4 and the modules and chapters preceding it.

Discuss the syntax of the sentences in 1–8 below, saying why 2, 3, 4, 5, 8 are considered non-standard; in addition, discuss the case-marking of the italicised items in the bracketed finite clauses in 9, 10:

1   It seems there were no arrests [M]
2   There seem were some problems ... (forums.autodesk.com)

3 There seem there are two extremes (freethoughtblogs.com) [S]

4 There seems there are two parts (sanfrancisco.granicus.com)

5 You seem that are still missing the point (instructables.com)

6 The mayor looks like he has been re-elected [S]

7 Everybody looks like they have passed the exam

8 Certain groups are likely for to be under-represented (issuu.com) [S]

9 He is someone [*who/whom* I think is making progress] [S]

10 I think [*he/*him* is making progress]

Helpful hints

Examples 1–8 are all complex sentences comprising a main clause and a complement clause; in relation to these, consider the following three issues:

(i)   Is the complement clause a TP or a CP? If it is a CP, is the complementiser heading the CP defective or non-defective?

(ii) Does the subject undergo Raising from spec-TP in the complement clause into spec-TP in the main clause, and if so does the subject leave behind an overt copy (and if so, how and why?). Or do the main and complement clauses have separate subjects?

(iii) How do Agreement, A-Movement and Case-marking work in these structures?

Bear in mind that while for most speakers, expletive *there* is specified for (third) person but unspecified for number, some speakers can treat it as inherently third person singular. In relation to 6, 7, assume that perception verbs like *look* are ambiguous between a thematic and non-thematic use. In its thematic use, *look* theta-marks its subject and has an appearance interpretation (so that 6 has a meaning paraphrasable as 'The mayor has an appearance suggesting he has been re-elected' – for example, the mayor has a broad smile on his face). By contrast, in its non-thematic use, *look* does not theta-mark its subject (so allows an expletive subject as in '*It* looks like there are problems', or an idiomatic subject as in '*Close tabs* look like they are being kept on the FBI') and has a probability interpretation (so that 6 is paraphrasable as 'It looks like/It is probable that the mayor has been re-elected'). For the purposes of this exercise, assume that *like* in 6, 7 is a complementiser, and adopt the binding analysis of *look like* structures outlined in the book (adapted from Lappin 1984). In 8, take *certain groups* to be a QP headed by the quantifier *certain*, and consider whether *for* is a (defective or non-defective?) complementiser, or whether (in the relevant variety) it is fused with the infinitive particle *to*, forming the complex infinitive particle (i.e. infinitival T-head) *forto*.

In relation to the bracketed relative clauses in 9, 10, set aside the agreement-based account of movement and case-marking outlined in the book, and instead make the following assumptions (outlined in the helpful hints for Exercise 3.3):

11 A-Movement is triggered not by person agreement nor by an EPP feature on T, but rather by an [Attr-Pers] feature on a T-head, meaning 'Attract the closest XP goal with a person feature'. This attraction feature is stripped from T (and thereby removed from the derivation entirely) once it has done its work, because it is illegible at PF and LF

12 Case-marking does not involve agreement, but rather a case-assignment feature on a probe such as [Ass-Nom]/[Ass-Acc]/[Ass-Null] meaning 'Assign nominative/accusative/null case to any local/nearby XP goal(s) with an unvalued case feature'; this case-assignment feature is stripped (i.e. removed from the derivation) once it has done its work, because it is illegible at PF and LF

In addition, in 9 assume that *who* originates as the subject of *making progress*, then becomes subject of *is*, then moves to the edge of the CP in the *making*-clause (shown as CP_1 below), and finally to the edge of the CP in the *think*-clause (= CP_2) – leaving behind copies in the positions italicised below (where *Af* denotes a present-tense affix):

13 He is someone

$[_{CP2}$ who $[_{C2}$ ø$]$ $[_{TP}$ I $[_T$ Af$]$ think $[_{CP1}$ *who* $[_{C1}$ ø$]$ $[_{TP}$ *who* $[_T$ is$]$ *who* making progress]]]]

Assume that C_1 and C_2 carry an [Attr-Wh] feature enabling them to attract an XP containing a wh-word to become their specifier, and that this feature (being illegible at the PF and LF interfaces) is stripped from C (and removed from the derivation entirely) once it has triggered Wh-Movement. Consider the possibility that C_1 may carry an optional [Ass-Nom] case feature which (if present) assigns nominative case to the subject of the clause it introduces, and that the verb *think* can carry an optional [Ass-Acc] feature which (if present) enables *think* to assign accusative case to a local/nearby XP with an unvalued case feature. Take *who* to be a relative wh-pronoun (a pronominal DP) which enters the derivation carrying the features [3-Pers, Sg-Num, u-Case] – plus an additional feature marking it as animate in gender (in contrast to inanimate *which*), though you can ignore this gender feature in your discussion, as it plays no role in agreement. Account for why the subject of *is making progress* can be spelled out as either nominative *who* or accusative *whom* in 9, but only as nominative *he* (not as accusative *him*) in 10.

4 | The clause periphery

4.0 Overview

As we saw in Chapter 1, the classic analysis of clauses in the 1980s took them to comprise a VP headed by a lexical verb, and assumed that on top of VP there were two different types of functional projection: a TP containing a tense-marked auxiliary/affix/infinitive particle and its subject, and a CP containing a complementiser and other peripheral constituents (e.g. fronted constituents, clausal modifiers and so on). However, more recent research has suggested CP and TP should each be 'split' into a number of distinct functional projections. In this chapter and the next, we look at evidence that the clause periphery (i.e. that part of the clause structure above TP which is traditionally labelled CP) can be split up into a range of different types of projection, including force phrase/FORCEP, topic phrase/TOPP, focus phrase/FOCP, modifier phrase/MODP and finiteness phrase/FINP projections. In Chapter 6, we'll look at evidence that the clause subperiphery (i.e. the TP constituent housing a T auxiliary/affix/infinitive particle and its subject) can likewise be split up into a number of different functional projections. This approach has been termed 'Cartographic', since its aim is to devise a 'map of the left periphery' (Rizzi 1997: 282).

4.1 The Cartographic approach

The key insight underlying the Cartographic approach to splitting up the clause periphery into a number of distinct types of projection is that each different type of peripheral constituent occupies a unique position on the edge of a dedicated functional projection (i.e. a functional projection which is dedicated to housing a constituent of the relevant type on the edge of the projection). This implies (inter alia) that a peripheral topic will appear on the edge of a topic projection, a peripheral focused constituent on the edge of a focus projection, a peripheral relative constituent on the edge of a relative projection … and so on. Rizzi (2014b) argues that the postulation of a range of different types of peripheral head hosting different types of constituent gains cross-linguistic support from structures in other

languages like those bracketed below which contain a bold-printed peripheral head with an italicised specifier (where Q denotes a question particle,
TOP denotes a topic particle, FOC denotes a focus particle, REL denotes a
relative particle, and EXCL denotes an exclamative particle):

(1)   a. Ik   weet   niet   [*wie*   **of**   [Jan   gezien   heeft]]
           I   know   not   who   Q   Jan   seen   has
           'I don't know who Jan has seen'
           (Dutch, Haegeman 1994)

       b. Un   sè   do   [*dan*   *lo*   **yà**   [Kofi   hu   i]]
           I   heard that   snake the   TOP   Kofi   killed it
           'I heard that the snake, Kofi killed it'
           (Gungbe, Aboh 2004)

       c. Un   sè   do   [*dan*   *lo*   **wè**   [Kofi   hu]]
           I   heard that   snake the   FOC   Kofi   killed
           'I heard that the snake, Kofi killed'
           (Gungbe, Aboh 2004)

       d. Der   Mantl [*den*   **wo**   [dea   Hons   gfundn   hot]]
           The   coat   which REL   the   Hans   found   has
           'The coat which Hans has found'
           (Bavarian, Bayer 1984b)

       e. [*Che*   *bel*   *libro*   **che**   [ho   letto]]!
           What   nice   book   EXCL   I.have read
           'What a nice book I read!'
           (Italian, Rizzi 2014b)

In each case the head of the relevant bracketed peripheral projection is the
bold-printed particle, the italicised constituent preceding the head is its specifier, and the bracketed constituent following the head is its complement.

The head of each peripheral projection assigns its specifier (if any) and
complement a specific interpretation at the semantics interface: for instance, the head of the topic projection tells the semantic component that
'my specifier is to be interpreted as the topic, and my complement as the
comment' (Cinque & Rizzi 2010a: 51). In a similar way, a focus head 'assigns the focus interpretation to its specifier, and the presupposition interpretation to its complement' (Cinque & Rizzi 2010a), where the focus
constitutes 'new information, information assumed not to be shared by the
interlocutor' (Rizzi 2014b: 8). A key assumption in this approach is that (in
conformity with the Linear Correspondence Axiom of Kayne 1994), no peripheral projection can have more than one specifier. For obvious reasons,
this has been dubbed the 'split CP' analysis, because it involves splitting
what had previously been treated as a single type of peripheral constituent

(= CP) into a number of different types of projection (a topic phrase, focus phrase etc.), each housing a different type of peripheral constituent.

Under this Cartographic approach, the head of each peripheral projection is dedicated to housing a particular type of constituent on the edge of its projection. This assumption follows from a featural uniqueness principle posited by Cinque & Rizzi (2008), which can be outlined informally as follows (where an interpretable feature is one which contributes to semantic interpretation/meaning):

(2)   **One Feature One Head Principle**
        Each functional head carries only one interpretable feature

It follows from (2) that no head can mark (for example) both force and topic, or both focus and finiteness.

Constituents occupying the specifier position of a peripheral projection do so in order to satisfy a requirement for them to occupy a criterial position in a spec–head relation with a matching head (Rizzi 1997: 282): for example, a peripheral topic must occupy the specifier position in a topic projection in order to be in a spec–head relation with a topic head. Once a constituent is in its criterial position, it is thereby frozen in place in consequence of a constraint termed the Criterial Freezing Condition in Rizzi (2005, 2006a, 2010, 2014a, 2014b) and Rizzi & Shlonsky (2006, 2007). For present purposes, these requirements can be subsumed within the following condition:

(3)   **Criterial Freezing Condition/CFC**
        (i) A peripheral constituent must occupy a criterial position to be
             interpretable at LF
        (ii) A constituent which occupies its criterial position is frozen in place

Condition (3i) tells us that (for example) a peripheral constituent must end up (at the end of the syntactic derivation) as the specifier of a topic projection in order to be interpretable as a topic in the semantic component; and (3ii) specifies that any constituent occupying its criterial position is frozen in place (and cannot move).

By way of an introduction to this approach, we'll start by looking at the rationale for positing Force and Topic projections.

4.1.1 Force and topic projections

As a starting point for our discussion, consider the structure of the bracketed clause produced by speaker B in the dialogue below:

(4)   SPEAKER A: The demonstrators have been looting shops and setting fire
                    to cars
        SPEAKER B: They must know [*that this kind of behaviour*, we will not
                    tolerate it]

Here, the italicised phrase *this kind of behaviour* is the topic of the bracketed embedded clause in (4B), where a topic is a constituent which tells us what the clause is about, and conveys old/familiar information known to the speaker and hearer. In this case, the italicised topic refers back to the activity of looting shops and setting fire to cars which is old/familiar information by virtue of having been mentioned earlier by speaker A. But whereabouts is the topic positioned within its containing clause?

Since topics can be phrases (e.g. the topic *this kind of behaviour* is a DP in 4B) and since phrases can be specifiers, a plausible analysis is that topics occupy the specifier position in a peripheral projection which is positioned above the TP headed by *will* but below the CP headed by *that*. But what is the nature of this peripheral projection? One possibility is that it is a CP, and hence that the topic occupies spec-CP. However, since the italicised topic in (4B) is contained within a projection headed by the complementiser *that*, a CP analysis requires us to assume that the bracketed embedded clause contains two separate CP projections – an outer one containing the complementiser *that*, and an inner one containing the topic *this kind of behaviour*. On this view, the bracketed embedded clause will involve CP recursion (i.e. one CP stacked on top of another), and the embedded clause bracketed in (4B) will have the structure shown in simplified form below:

(5)

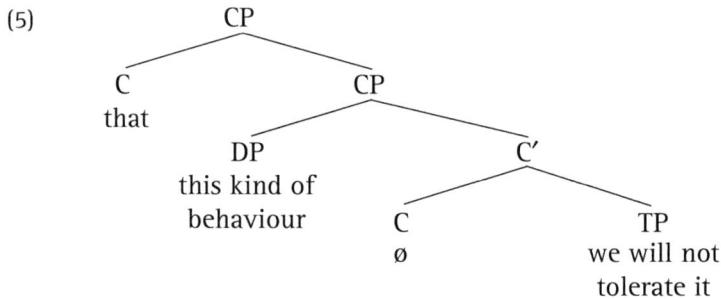

The advantage of a CP recursion analysis is that it accommodates topic structures within the traditional CP+TP+VP model of clause structure, without the need to posit additional types of projection. The disadvantage, however, is that in treating the projection containing the complementiser *that* and the projection containing the topic *this kind of behaviour* as exactly the same type of CP projection, the CP recursion analysis fails to recognise important differences between the two types of CP. For example, the higher CP headed by *that* has the semantic function of marking the embedded clause as declarative in force/type, while the lower CP serves to mark its specifier *this kind of behaviour* as the topic of the sentence.

Moreover, (contrary to what a CP recursion analysis might lead us to expect), the two CPs are not interchangeable, in that the CP containing the topic cannot be positioned above the CP containing *that* – as we see from the ungrammaticality of:

(6)   *They must know [cp this kind of behaviour [cp that [tp we will not tolerate it]]]

These differences suggest that the two peripheral projections labelled CP in (5) above are not simply two different instances of the same CP projection, but rather constitute two distinct types of projection.

One way of capturing this (pioneered in influential Cartographic work by Luigi Rizzi in the mid-1990s cited in the Bibliographical notes) is to split CP up into a number of different types of functional projection. On this 'split CP' approach, the projection housing the complementiser *that* (which serves to mark the clause as declarative in force and thus having the force of a statement) is categorised as a force phrase (FORCEP), and its head complementiser *that* is categorised as a FORCE head. By contrast, the projection which serves to mark the DP *this kind of behaviour* as a topic is categorised as a topic phrase (= TOPP), and is headed by a null topic particle (= TOP). On this alternative approach, the embedded clause bracketed in (4B) does not have the CP recursion structure in (5) above, but rather the split projection structure in (7) below (so called because CP has been split into distinct FORCEP and TOPP projections):

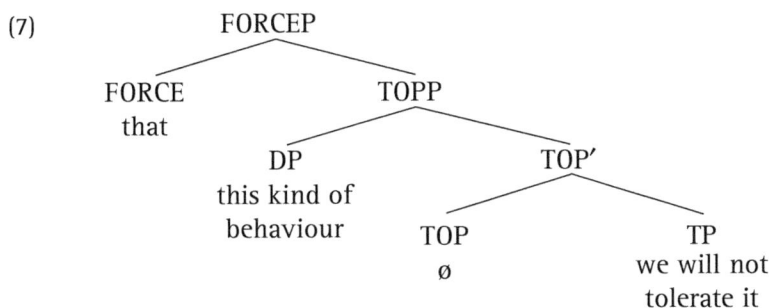

(7)

```
                    FORCEP
              _____/_____
           FORCE          TOPP
           that       ___/\___
                    DP          TOP'
               this kind of  __/\__
                 behaviour  TOP        TP
                             ø     we will not
                                   tolerate it
```

The idea that the phrase housing the topic is a topic projection headed by a topic particle (albeit one which is null in English) gains cross-linguistic plausibility from the observation that there are a number of languages which have an overt topic particle which is positioned after a topic – including Gungbe, as we saw in (1b) above. This adds cross-linguistic plausibility to the idea that topics are the specifiers of a topic phrase (= TOPP) projection that is headed by a topic particle which is overt in languages like Gungbe, but null in languages like English.

4.1.2   In situ and ex situ topics

In a split projection structure like (7) above, the constituent which serves as the specifier of the TOPP projection functions as a topic on which the TP constituent makes a relevant comment. Since the topic is directly merged in situ as the specifier of a TOPP projection, we can refer to it as an <u>in situ</u> topic. In (7), the relevance of the comment to the topic is ensured by using the resumptive pronoun *it* to 'resume' or 'reprise' (i.e. refer back to) the topic *this kind of behaviour*, so ensuring that the comment in TP is relevant to the topic in TOPP: accordingly, we can refer to this as a <u>resumptive</u> topic structure. In topic structures containing a resumptive pronoun, the topic is conventionally said to be <u>dislocated</u>, and a structure like (4B, 7) where the topic is to the left of the comment is said to be an instance of <u>Left Dislocation</u>.

Although our example in (4B) involves a topic in spec-TOPP being reprised by a resumptive personal pronoun (*it*), examples like those in (8) below show that a variety of other types of (bold-printed) resumptive expression can be used to reprise an (italicised) in situ topic:

(8)   a. *High speed corners with a dry line*, **that**'ll burn your tyres out (Martin Brundle, BBC1 TV)

  b. *The Everton fans*, there's lots of different opinions **here** (Danny Kelly, talkSPORT Radio)

  c. *Any Premier League team*, take the three best players out of **the team** and they're gonna struggle (Dan Walker, BBC Radio 5)

  d. *Many of them*, I have no idea where **these teams** are (Danny Kelly, talkSPORT Radio)

  e. *The Championship*, one of the greatest things about **that league** is that it's the most unpredictable league around (Listener, BBC Radio 5)

Thus, it would be more accurate to say that Topicalisation involves an in situ topic reprised by a resumptive nominal or pronominal constituent.

Alongside resumptive topic structures like (4B, 8), we also find topic structures like (9B) below which have a *gap* (marked by −) in the position occupied by resumptive *it* in (4B):

(9)   SPEAKER A: The demonstrators have been looting shops and setting fire to cars

  SPEAKER B: They must know [that *this kind of behaviour*, we will not tolerate −]

There is a gap in (9B) in the sense that the transitive verb *tolerate* has no complement/object immediately following it; in fact, it is the topic *this kind of behaviour* which is interpreted as the object of *tolerate*. Since gaps can arise via movement, a plausible analysis of (9B) is to suppose that the DP *this kind of behaviour* originates as the thematic complement of *tolerate* and then (in order to mark it as a topic) moves to become the specifier of a TOPP projection in the clause periphery. On this view, Topicalisation in the embedded clause in (9B) involves the Topic Fronting operation arrowed below:

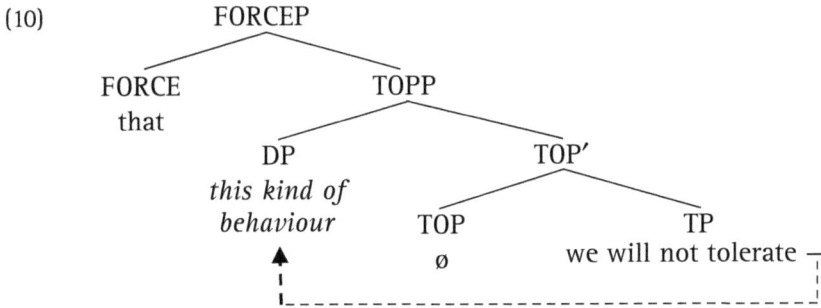

(10)

```
                    FORCEP
              _____
         FORCE                 TOPP
         that            _____
                      DP                   TOP′
                 this kind of         _____
                  behaviour       TOP                   TP
                      ↑            ø          we will not tolerate —
                      |_____|
```

We can then suppose that topics are <u>ex situ</u> (i.e. displaced/fronted) constituents which move to spec-TOPP in gap-containing topic structures like (9B, 10), but are <u>in situ</u> constituents directly merged in spec-TOPP in gapless topic structures like (4B, 7). The overall complement clause is typed as declarative in force by virtue of being a FORCEP headed by the indicative complementiser *that*.

There is independent evidence that ex situ topic structures (= those containing gaps) involve movement, whereas in situ topic structures do not. One such piece of evidence comes from the observation that ex situ/gap structures are subject to the Island Constraint of Ross (1967, 1986), whereas in situ/gapless structures are not. Ross's constraint can be characterised informally as follows, where an <u>island</u> is a structure resistant to extraction by movement operations which leave a gap behind, a <u>gap</u> is a null copy of a moved constituent, and the <u>antecedent</u> of a gap is the moved constituent which leaves the null copy behind:

(11)   Island Constraint
        No gap inside an island can have an antecedent outside the island

As we saw in §1.5.1, Ross identified a number of different types of constituent as islands, including complex NPs (comprising an NP with a clause embedded inside it). In the light of the assumption that complex NPs are islands, consider the following contrast (where a bracketed relative clause CP is contained inside a bracketed NP; a detail that has been set aside below is that the *laws*-NP is modified by a null quantifier which denotes 'an unspecified number of'):

(12)   a. *Violent criminals*, we need [NP laws [CP that send — to prison for life]]
        b. *Violent criminals*, we need [NP laws [CP that send **them** to prison for life]]

On the assumption that the gap-containing topic structure in (12a) involves movement (with the italicised topic originating in the gap position marked – and subsequently moving from there to the italicised specifier position in TOPP), we correctly predict that (12a) will be ungrammatical because the moved topic has left behind an illicit gap inside the bracketed complex NP island (i.e. inside a CP contained within an NP). Conversely, on the assumption that no movement is involved in the resumptive structure (12b) (because both the italicised topic and the bold-printed resumptive pronoun are directly merged in situ), we correctly predict that resumptive topic structures like (12b) will be grammatical, because there is no gap inside the bracketed complex NP in (12b).

Thus far, we have seen two different types of topic structure: in situ structures where the topic is associated with a resumptive, and ex situ structures where the topic is associated with a gap. However, in colloquial English, we also find a third type of topic structure involving an <u>orphaned</u> topic which is not associated with any resumptive or gap – as the examples in (13) below illustrate (where the orphaned topic is italicised):

(13)   a. *England*, I agree with you completely on Capello (Listener, BBC Radio 5)
        b. *Wales*, it's just gonna rain all day (Lisa O'Sullivan, talkSPORT Radio)
        c. *Your pension*, you've been told you've got to pay more (Interviewee, BBC Radio 5)
        d. *Defoe*, even I could have scored that goal (Alan Green, BBC Radio 5, boasting that even he could have scored a goal that Defoe missed)
        e. *Germany*, I think Portugal were unlucky (Alan Brazil, talkSPORT Radio, commenting on a match where Portugal were unlucky to be beaten by Germany)

The examples in (13) contain an italicised topic in the periphery of the clause, but the comment TP (after the comma) contains no resumptive or gap linked to the topic. The topic typically has an *as for* interpretation: for example, the topic *England* in (13a) has the paraphrase '*As for England, I agree with you completely on Capello*'. The crucial requirement in topic clauses is that the comment made in the TP following the topic should be relevant to the topic: one way of ensuring relevance is by use of a resumptive or gap in the TP commenting on the topic; however, it is clear from examples like those in (13) that relevance does not require the use of a resumptive or gap (at least, in colloquial English).

On the assumptions made here, gap-containing topic structures like (10) above involve movement, but gapless topic structures like (8, 13) do not. Further evidence in support of this claim comes from case-marking – as can be illustrated in relation to the replies given by speaker

B in the dialogue below (where capitals mark contrastive stress, and strikethrough marks ellipsis):

(14)   SPEAKER A: What do you think about John and Mary?
       SPEAKER B: (i)   SHE, I don't think [$_{CP}$ [$_C$ ø] – is guilty]]
                    (ii) But HIM, I suspect [$_{CP}$ [$_C$ that] *he* probably is ~~guilty~~]

Since case is preserved under movement (in the sense that a moved constituent retains any case that it was assigned before it moved), it follows that the topic *she* in the gap-containing structure in (14Bi) carries the nominative case it received in the gap position from the null complementiser before moving to become the specifier of a topic phrase projection in the clause periphery. By contrast, the fact that the topic *him* in (14Bii) carries a different (accusative) case from that carried by the nominative resumptive pronoun *he*, provides empirical evidence that no movement is involved in gapless topic structures. On one (widespread) assumption, an in situ topic like *him* in (14Bii) receives default case – that is, the case assigned to a (pro)-nominal constituent which occupies a position where it does not fall within the domain of any case assigner. The default case in English is accusative (though in some other languages like German and Arabic, for example, it is nominative). For present purposes, we can characterise this phenomenon for English as follows:

(15)   **Default Case Assignment**
       A (pro)nominal which does not fall within the domain of (i.e. which
       is not c-commanded by) a local (i.e. nearby) case assigner receives
       accusative case by default

Other types of constituent which have been argued to be assigned accusative case by default include those italicised below:

(16)   a. Who wants an ice-cream? – *Me*!
       b. She's a bit taller than *me*
       c. It was *me* that reported the incident
       d. If you were *me*, what would you do?
       e. *Me* cheat on you? No way!
       f. *Me* being lazy, I ordered a takeaway

For more detailed discussion of default case, see Schütze (2001).

4.1.3   Multiple topic structures

All of the topic structures we have looked at so far have contained only a single topic. However, sentences can in principle contain more than one topic, as the following authentic examples of double topic structures illustrate (where the first topic is bold-printed and the second is italicised):

(17)   a. You just get the feeling that **Arsenal**, *the way they keep the ball*, it's particularly clever (Steve Claridge, BBC Radio 5)
        b. **Everton**, *Saha*, he did look quite sharp (Danny Mills, BBC Radio 5)
        c. **A good friend of mine**, *his daughter*, I promised to go and say hello to her today (Alan Brazil, talkSPORT Radio)
        d. **The people on the street**, *the demands we are aware of*, they have a legitimacy (Alistair Burt, BBC Radio 5)

If each topic is housed in a separate topic projection, sentences like (17) will involve TOPP recursion (i.e. a structure in which the periphery of a single clause contains more than one TOPP projection). On this view, the periphery of the *that*-clause in (17a) will have the following structure (where *Arsenal* is a DP headed by a null D, and indeed the club is sometimes referred to as *the Arsenal*):

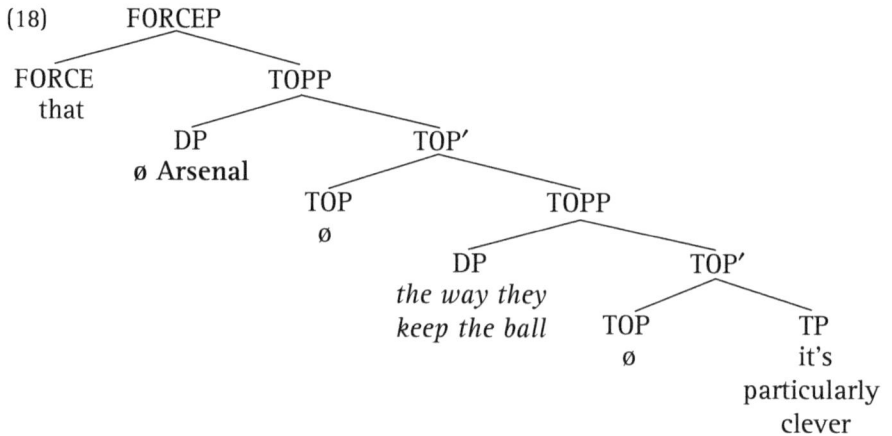

(18)

```
            FORCEP
          /        \
    FORCE            TOPP
    that            /    \
            DP           TOP'
          ø Arsenal     /    \
                   TOP        TOPP
                    ø        /    \
                        DP          TOP'
                   the way they    /    \
                   keep the ball  TOP      TP
                                   ø       it's
                                           particularly
                                           clever
```

Both topics highlighted in (18) are directly merged in situ (and assigned accusative case by default), and both are reprised by a resumptive pronoun – the higher topic *Arsenal* being reprised by *they*, and the lower topic *the way they keep the ball* being reprised by *it*.

The TOPP recursion analysis of multiple topic structures gains independent motivation from the observation by Rizzi (2012) that languages like Abidji which allow topic recursion use a separate topic particle (bold-printed below and glossed as TOP) to mark each (italicised) topic – as in double topic sentences such as the following, where either highlighted topic can be positioned in front of the other:

(19)   a. *kòfí* **ɛ́kɛ́** *òkókò* *ɛ́* **ɛ́kɛ́** è pìpjé nì
           Kofi TOP banana the TOP he peel it
           'Kofi, the banana, he peeled it'
        b. *òkókò* *ɛ́* **ɛ́kɛ́** *kòfí* **ɛ́kɛ́** è pìpjé nì
           banana the TOP Kofi TOP he peel it
           'The banana, Kofi, he peeled it'

This makes it plausible to suggest that English multiple topic structures like (18) also involve TOPP recursion (i.e. they involve projecting more than one topic phrase constituent within the periphery of a single clause).

However, while gapless multiple topic structures like (18) above are grammatical, by contrast gap-containing/ex situ multiple topic structures are ungrammatical – as illustrated by the contrasts below (attributed to Rachel Nye and Ian Roberts in Rizzi 2013a: 214):

(20)   a. *John*, I convinced – to buy your car
        b. *Your car*, I convinced John to buy –
        c. *John, **your car**, I convinced – to buy –
        d. *Your car, **John**, I convinced – to buy –

As we see from (20a, 20b), either *John* or *your car* can freely be topicalised by being moved into the specifier position in a topic projection. However, we can't topicalise both *John* and *your car*, as we see from the ungrammaticality of (20c, 20d). Why should this be? The answer lies in a constraint (mentioned in §1.5.1) which was formulated by Abels (2012: 247) as follows (where *likes* denote 'constituents which are alike' – that is, constituents of the same type):

(21)   **Intervention Condition**
        Likes cannot cross likes

From this perspective, what goes wrong in (20c, 20d) is that one (bold-printed) topic moves to the edge of an inner TOPP projection, and then another (italicised) topic moves to the edge of an outer TOPP projection, and in the process the (italicised) outer topic crosses the (bold-printed) inner topic, in violation of the Intervention Condition (21). On this view, one moved topic cannot cross another moved topic.

A further constraint which may cause structures like (20c, 20d) to be degraded is the Distinctness Condition of Richards (2010: 5), which we can characterise informally as follows (where non-distinct constituents are constituents which are alike, and 'at PF' means 'at the end of the syntactic derivation, at the point where syntactic structures are inputted into the PF component for processing'):

(22)   **Distinctness Condition**
        Any structure at PF which contains a sequence of two non-distinct
        constituents <α, α> is degraded

It follows from the constraint in (22) that the succession of two highlighted topicalised DPs in (20c, 20d) leads to degraded grammaticality.

Emonds (2004: 107) claims (on the basis of contrasts like that shown in slightly adapted form below) that the clause periphery can contain two different types of topic (an in situ and an ex situ topic), but that when the two co-occur, an (italicised) in situ topic must precede a bold-printed ex situ/fronted topic:

(23)   a. *My mother*, **a man like that**, I don't think she would hire –
        b. **A man like that*, **my mother**, I don't think she would hire –

This restriction can again be argued to follow from the Intervention Condition. In (23a) the italicised outer topic is directly generated in situ, and so does not move across the (bold-printed) inner topic. By contrast, in (23b) the italicised ex situ topic moves across the bold-printed in situ inner topic, and the resulting movement of one topic across another leads to an intervention violation (though for me at least, the violation feels stronger where one <u>fronted</u> topic crosses another <u>fronted</u> topic, as in 20c and 20d; this suggests that the topics are more alike if both are fronted, rather than if one is fronted and the other is not).
    You should now be able to tackle Exercise 4.1.

4.2   Focus projections

In Module 4.1, we saw that the clause periphery can comprise two distinct projections, one housing a complementiser (FORCEP), and another housing a topic (TOPP). In this module, we will see that the clause periphery can also contain a third type of functional projection – namely a focus phrase/ FOCP projection containing a focus (i.e. focused/focalised constituent) as its specifier.

4.2.1   Peripheral focused constituents

From a discourse perspective, a focused constituent represents new information (i.e. information not previously mentioned in the discourse and assumed to be unfamiliar to the hearer). Because focusing introduces new information and wh-questions are typically used to ask for new information (e.g. *Who did you see?* asks for the identity of the person you saw), focusing can be used in replies to wh-questions. By way of illustration, consider the following dialogue:

(24)   SPEAKER A: How many goals did Cristiano Ronaldo score for Real
                    Madrid?
        SPEAKER B: Would you believe [that *451 goals* he scored – in 438
                    games]?!

Here, the italicised phrase produced by speaker B originates in the gap position as the complement of the verb *scored*, and is then moved to the periphery of the bracketed clause, in order to focus it (i.e. mark it as conveying new information). Some authentic examples of focusing (which I recorded from a variety of radio and TV programmes) are given below, where the focused constituent is italicised:

(25) a. We told you there were going to be goals, and *goals* there were (Jake Humphreys, BT Sport TV) (21)
    b. *Straight up the other end* Crusaders went (Ian Abrahams, talkSPORT Radio)
    c. *Another good cross* he delivers (Rob Palmer, Sky Sports TV)
    d. *Excellent football* that was (Ray Wilkins, Sky Sports TV)
    e. *Very relaxed* they were in the interview, as far as I could see (Sir Ming Campbell, BBC Radio 5)

But whereabouts in the clause periphery are focused constituents positioned, and how do they get there?

A relevant observation to make in this regard is that there are languages in which a focused peripheral constituent is followed by an overt focus particle – as we see from the examples in (26) below (where the focused constituent is italicised, and the focus particle is bold-printed and glossed as FOC; note that PRT denotes a particle, AGR an agreement marker, and PERF a perfect aspect marker):

(26) a. Ùn lɛ́n   ɖɔ   *wémà* lɔ   **wɛ**   Séna xìá.
      I   think-PERF that book the FOC Sena read-PERF
      'I think that it is *the book* that Sena has read'
      (Gungbe, Aboh 2004: 238)
    b. *Gà mālàm* **nē** na maid   dà   littāfin
      to teacher FOC I   return PRT book
      'It was *to the teacher* that I returned the book'
      (Hausa, Green 2007: 62)
    c. *Ekitabu* **kyo** Kambale   a-asoma
      book   FOC   Kambale   AGR-read
      'It was *the book* that Kambale read'
      (Kinande, Schneider-Zioga 2007: 412)

This makes it plausible to suggest that peripheral focused constituents are the specifiers of a focus phrase (= FOCP) projection which is headed by an overt (bold-printed) focus particle in languages like Gungbe, Hausa and

Kinande, but by a null focus particle in languages like English. On this view, the *that*-clause in a sentence like (24B) above will be derived as shown below (where *451 goals* is treated as a NUMP/numeral phrase, and the internal structure of TP is not shown):

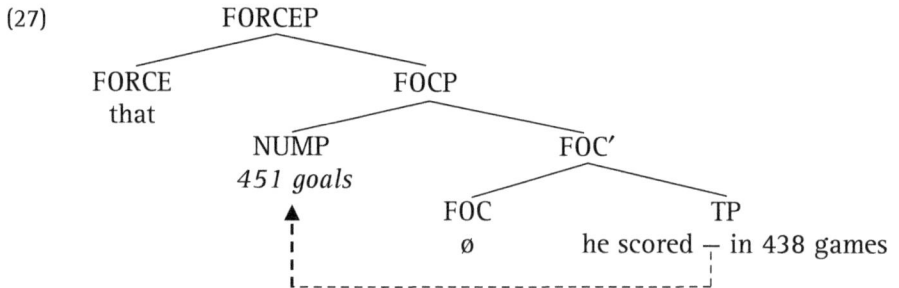

(27)

```
                    FORCEP
              _____|_____
           FORCE          FOCP
           that      _____|_____
                  NUMP            FOC'
                 451 goals    _____|_____
                    ▲       FOC          TP
                    ┊       ø        he scored — in 438 games
                    ┊                            ┊
                    └────────────────────────────┘
```

Since this is a gap structure (i.e. a structure in which there is a gap – internally within TP), we can suppose that the italicised focused constituent originates within TP in the position marked by the gap and from there moves to the edge of the focus phrase projection in the clause periphery, as shown by the arrow in (27). It would seem that Focusing always involves movement, whereas (as we saw earlier) topics can either be directly merged in situ in spec-TOPP or moved there.

The assumption that clauses can contain peripheral topic and focus projections raises the question of whether the periphery of a given clause can contain both topicalised and focused constituents. The answer is 'yes', as we see from authentic examples such as the following:

(28)   a. **Fernando Alonso**, *189 points* <u>he</u>'ll have – (David Croft, BBC Radio 5)
       b. **Kevin Pietersen**, *five* <u>he</u> was out for – (George Reilly, BBC Radio 5)
       c. **The goal**, *none more important* he has scored – than <u>that one</u> (Gary Neville, Sky Sports TV)
       d. **Harry Kane**, *100* <u>he</u> scores (Banner in Liverpool's Anfield Stadium, celebrating Harry Kane scoring his 100th goal)
       e. **Stuart Broad**, *a fantastic piece of bowling* that was – in the last test match (Elliot Cook, talkSPORT Radio)

The bold-printed constituent on the periphery of each of the clauses in (28) is an in situ topic (directly merged in spec-TOPP), reprised by the underlined resumptive constituent within the main body of the clause in (28a–28d), but unreprised in (28e). The italicised constituent is focused and appears to have been fronted (i.e. positioned at the front of the clause by movement), since it leaves a gap behind lower down in the clause (marked by –). Given these assumptions (and the further assumption that clauses canonically contain a FORCEP projection marking clause type), the clause periphery in (28a) will have the following structure:

(29)

```
                    FORCEP
              ┌───────────┴───────────┐
          FORCE                      TOPP
            ø              ┌───────────┴───────────┐
                          DP                      TOP′
                        Fernando          ┌────────┴────────┐
                         Alonso          TOP              FOCP
                                          ø         ┌───────┴───────┐
                                                  NUMP            FOC′
                                                189 points    ┌─────┴─────┐
                                                    ▲        FOC         TP
                                                    ¦         ø      he'll have ─
                                                    └─────────────────────────┘
```

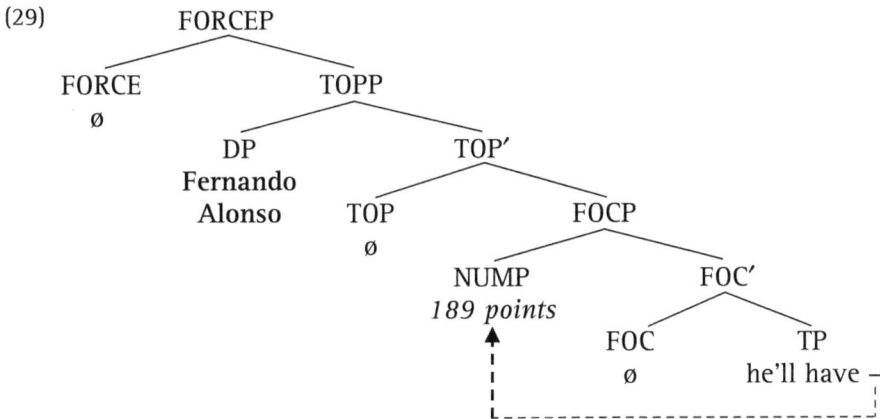

The null indicative FORCE head of FORCEP in (29) serves to type the relevant clause as declarative in force. The TOPP projection below FORCEP contains an (in situ) topic *Fernando Alonso* which is directly merged in spec-TOPP, and reprised by the resumptive pronoun *he* in spec-TP. The focused NUMP/numeral projection *189 points* originates as the complement of the verb *have* and moves from its initial position to become the specifier of the focus phrase/FOCP projection below TOPP, as shown by the arrow in (29).

Although in sentences like (28) above, the bold-printed topic precedes the italicised focused constituent, the converse order (in which an italicised focused constituent precedes a bold-printed in situ topic) is also possible – as we see from sentences such as the following:

(30) a. *189 points*, **Fernando Alonso**, he now has –
      b. *Five*, **Kevin Pietersen**, he was out for –, not fifty-five
      c. *Anything Messi can do*, **Ronaldo**, he can do – even better

Sentences like (28, 30) are in keeping with the claim made by Rizzi (1997: 291) that 'A focus and one or more topics can be combined in the same structure. In that case, the focal constituent can be both preceded and followed by topics.'

4.2.2 Comparing topic and focus

An important question arising from the postulation of separate topic and focus projections in the clause periphery is what differences there are between topicalised and focused constituents. One important difference lies in their semantic properties: topics represent old/familiar information and tell us what a sentence is about, and are often paraphrasable by 'As for … '. By contrast, focused constituents represent new/unfamiliar information, and are often paraphrasable by a cleft or pseudo-cleft sentence. Consequently, (28a) can be paraphrased as follows: 'As for Fernando

Alonso, what he'll have is 189 points'. Topicalised and focused constituents also differ in that there is typically a slight pause immediately after a topic (marked by the comma after the bold-printed topics in 28), but not necessarily after a focused constituent (like those italicised in 25). Furthermore, a topic can be positioned on the edge of a clause either by Move or by Merge (and a topic merged in situ in the clause periphery may or may not be reprised by a resumptive expression internally within the clause), whereas a focused constituent can only get into the clause periphery by movement (and so is always associated with a gap internally within the main body of the clause, and cannot be reprised by a resumptive constituent).

A further difference between topicalised and focused constituents is that topics (by virtue of referring to a specific entity assumed to be familiar to the hearer) are referential expressions, and consequently non-referential/non-specific pronouns like *something/someone/somebody, anything/anyone/anybody*, or *everything/everyone/everybody* can only be focused, not topicalised – as we see from the ungrammaticality which results from using a (bold-printed) referential resumptive pronoun (i.e. the kind of pronoun used to reprise a topic) to reprise a fronted non-specific pronoun in sentences such as:

(31)   a. *Everything*, the tanks destroyed (*it)
        b. *Something*, I think (*it) must have upset him
        c. *Anything*, people are willing to confess to (*it) under torture

If the italicised constituents in (31) were topics, it ought to be possible for them to be reprised by a (bold-printed) resumptive pronoun; the fact that this is not possible suggests that non-specific expressions are not possible topics, and hence that the italicised constituents in (31) are focused.

An additional difference between focused and topicalised constituents is that although clauses can contain more than one topic, they cannot contain more than one focused constituent – as we see from the impossibility of focusing both *something* and *everyone* in (32b) below:

(32)   a. You must give something to everyone at Christmas
        b. **Everyone*, **something** you must give – to – at Xmas

The ungrammaticality of multiple-focus structures like (32b) results from violation of the Intervention Condition (21), in that (32b) involves illicit movement of one fronted focused QP (*everyone*) across another fronted focused QP (*something*), thereby inducing an intervention violation.

The numerous differences outlined above between peripheral topicalised and focused constituents make it plausible to posit that the two serve as the specifiers of different types of functional head (a peripheral topic serving as the specifier of a TOP head, and a peripheral focused constituent serving as the specifier of a FOC head).

You should now be able to tackle Exercise 4.2.

4.3 Modifier and finiteness projections

In this module, we will see that in addition to FORCEP, TOPP and FOCP constituents, the clause periphery can also contain one or more modifier projections/MODP, and a finiteness projection/FINP.

4.3.1 Modifier projections

In addition to complementisers, topics and focused constituents, the periphery can also contain one or more clausal adjuncts. These are constituents (like those italicised below) which serve to modify the particular clause (bracketed below) in whose periphery they are situated:

(33) a. I suspect [that *in spite of the rain* the game will go ahead]
b. I wonder [if *during the holidays* you could find time to read my dissertation]
c. I have heard [that *tomorrow* he will fly to Paris]
d. I know [that *occasionally* he plays poker]
e. I would think [that *if it rains* we should abandon the game]
f. I'd suggest [that *when he comes home* you should talk to him]

Such adjuncts typically provide information about the circumstances (e.g. time, place, manner, conditions etc.) under which the event described in the modified clause takes place, and so they are termed circumstantial. Typical circumstantial peripheral constituents include prepositional phrases (as in 33a, 33b) above, or adverbials (as in 33c, 33d), or clauses introduced by subordinating conjunctions (as in 33e, 33f). Circumstantial modifiers like these don't give rise to intervention effects, as we see from the fact that in sentences like (34) below, a (bold-printed) topicalised constituent can move out of the gap position in which it originates into the clause periphery across an intervening (italicised) modifier:

(34) a. I must warn you that **this kind of behaviour**, *in this kind of town*, people will not tolerate –
b. I must say that **the government's response**, *in the present crisis*, I find – wholly unacceptable
c. **Cheese**, *often* people have strong feelings about – (Davison 1984: 807)
d. **Wine**, *in some restaurants*, you have to pay a small fortune for –

This suggests that the italicised modifiers are directly merged in situ in the position they occupy in the clause periphery. Since they serve to modify the clause containing them, this raises the possibility that they serve as specifiers of a modifier projection/MODP in the clause periphery. If so, the *that*-clause in a sentence like (34a) above will have the structure shown in simplified form below, with the fronted topic *this kind of behaviour* crossing the intervening in situ PP modifier *in this kind of town* without inducing any intervention effect:

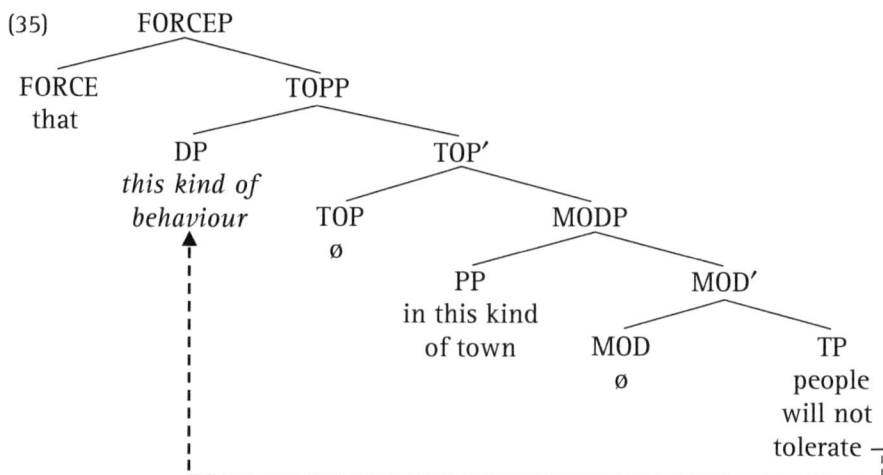

(35)

```
            FORCEP
           /      \
      FORCE        TOPP
      that        /    \
              DP          TOP'
      this kind of       /    \
      behaviour      TOP       MODP
        ▲            ø        /     \
        |                  PP         MOD'
        |              in this kind   /    \
        |              of town     MOD      TP
        |                          ø      people
        |                                 will not
        |                                 tolerate —
        └----------------------------------------------┘
```

MODP projections can occupy a wide range of different positions in the clause periphery, as illustrated by the authentic examples below (which I recorded from a variety of live, unscripted radio and TV programmes), where the italicised constituents are modifiers, the bold-printed constituents are dislocated topics, and the underlined constituents are resumptive pronouns:

(36) a. That tells you that *at the highest level*, **the big teams**, <u>they</u> don't fancy it (Darren Lewis, talkSPORT Radio)

  b. *At the end of the day*, **the players**, <u>they</u>'re in there to win things (Listener, talkSPORT Radio)

  c. **Fabio Capello**, *whether we like it or not*, <u>he</u>'s still part of the England team (Adrian Durham, talkSPORT Radio)

  d. **The director tonight**, *if we had extra time*, <u>he</u> would hang, draw and quarter me (Dotun Adebayo, BBC Radio 5)

  e. You have to say that **Higuain**, *normally* <u>he</u> would have hit the target (Jon Driscoll, Sky Sports TV)

Moreover, as sentences like those in (37) below illustrate, the periphery of a single clause can contain multiple (italicised) modifiers (following a bold-printed dislocated topic in the case of 37b):

(37)   a. *Last week, in Paris, after a hard day's work*, he met his agent again
          (Haegeman 2012: 73)
        b. I just felt that **Roy Hodgson**, *a few weeks ago, when Liverpool lost to*
          Everton, he was in a minority of one (John Motson, BBC Radio 5)

This suggests that modifiers can (in general) be freely positioned between other constituents within the periphery. If each MODP projection contains only one clausal modifier, this in turn means that the periphery of a given clause can optionally contain one or more MODP projections (giving rise to MODP recursion – i.e. clauses whose periphery contains more than one MODP).

Our discussion so far leads to the more general conclusion that each XP in the clause periphery is housed in (and serves as the specifier of) a dedicated functional projection (i.e. a functional projection which only allows a specific type of specifier). Thus, a topic serves as the specifier of a topic projection/TOPP, a focused constituent as the specifier of a focus projection/FOCP, and a clausal modifier as the specifier of a modifier projection/MODP. Note in particular that this approach to clausal modifiers treats them as specifiers contained in a separate MODP projection of their own, rather than (as in earlier work discussed in Chapter 1) as adjuncts which adjoin to a TP or CP to form an even larger TP or CP.

4.3.2   Finiteness projections

A further type of peripheral projection identified by Rizzi (1997) is a finiteness projection/FINP that is positioned below all other peripheral projections and immediately above TP, and serves to mark whether the clause containing it is finite or nonfinite. One type of (nonfinite) FIN head found in English is the infinitival complementiser *for*, for example, in sentences such as:

(38)   She never intended **for** *him* to get hurt

As would be expected if *for* is the head FIN constituent of a FINP projection which is positioned below all other peripheral projections and immediately above TP, *for* is positioned below other (italicised) constituents in the periphery of the same clause and immediately above the (underlined) clause subject in spec-TP:

(39)   a. What's critical is [*if people saw the helicopter*, **for** them to contact us]
          (Police spokeswoman, BBC Radio 5)
        b. We would not want [*in a game like the one tomorrow*, **for** any
          spectators to get hurt]
        c. The police advice was [*on no account* **for** any member of the public
          to approach the escaped convict]

In these examples, infinitival *for* is preceded by an (italicised) clausal modifier contained within a MODP projection – the modifier being a conditional *if*-clause in (39a), and a PP in (39b, 39c). Assuming that *for* is in FIN, such examples are consistent with FINP being the lowest projection in the clause periphery, hence positioned immediately above the TP housing the (underlined) subject of the clause. If case-marking by a transitive head like *for* requires the transitive head to c-command and be immediately adjacent to the constituent it case-marks, it follows that the FIN head *for* in (39) will have to immediately precede the underlined infinitive subject (and not be able to precede the italicised modifier). This will be the case if *for* is in FIN, and FINP is the lowest projection in the periphery, so that FINP is positioned immediately above the subject in spec-TP.

Given the assumption that the head FIN constituent of FINP marks whether a clause is finite or nonfinite, we might expect English to have a finiteness marker which is the finite counterpart of the infinitival FIN constituent *for*. In this connection, it is interesting to observe double-*that* clauses such as those bracketed below:

(40)   a. And now we're told [**that**, *for a further two years*, **that** <u>we</u>'re going to have that pay restraint] (Dave Prentice, BBC Radio 4)

   b. He knows [**that**, *at the end of the summer*, *whether we do anything at the Euros or not*, **that** <u>he</u>'s going to be going] (Adrian Durham, talkSPORT Radio)

   c. The party opposite said [**that** *if we cut 6 billion from the budget* **that** <u>it</u> would end in catastrophe] (David Cameron, Prime Minister's Questions, BBC Radio 5)

   d. My hope is [**that**, *by the time we meet*, **that** <u>we</u>'ll have made some progress] (Barack Obama, Press conference, BBC Radio 5)

The bracketed clauses in these examples contain an initial occurrence of *that*, then one or two (italicised) modifying adjunct phrases/clauses, then a second occurrence of *that*, and then the (underlined) clause subject. The first occurrence of *that* in a sentence like (40d) can plausibly be taken to occupy the head FORCE position of FORCEP (marking the clause it introduces as indicative in mood and declarative in force), but where is the second occurrence positioned? It might at first sight seem as if the second *that* could occupy the head MOD position of the MODP containing the clausal modifier *by the time we meet*. However, any such structure would fall foul of a filter posited by Chomsky & Lasnik (1977), which was given the following informal characterisation in §1.5.2:

(41)   **Doubly Filled COMP Filter**
   At the end of a syntactic derivation, any structure in which the edge of a projection headed by an overt complementiser is doubly filled (i.e. contains some other overt constituent) is filtered out as ungrammatical

One way of avoiding any violation of the filter in (41) is to take the second occurrence of *that* to occupy the head FIN position of FINP. If so, the periphery of the clause bracketed in (40d) will have the structure shown below:

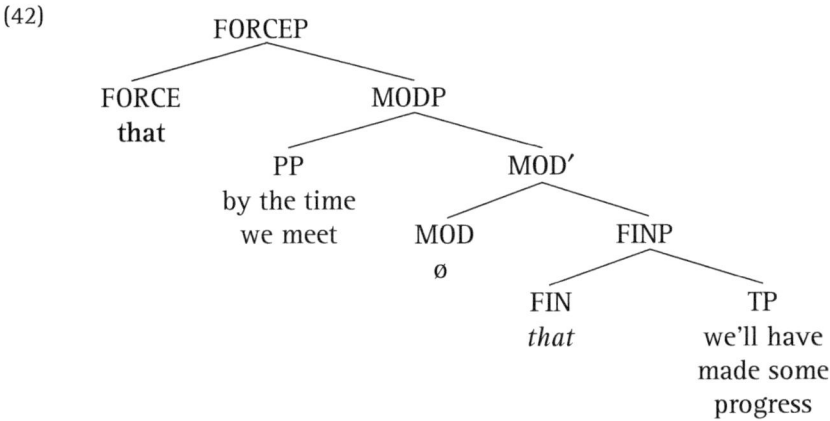

(42)

```
                    FORCEP
              ┌────────┴────────┐
          FORCE              MODP
          that          ┌──────┴──────┐
                       PP           MOD′
                   by the time    ┌────┴────┐
                   we meet      MOD        FINP
                                 ø      ┌────┴────┐
                                      FIN         TP
                                      that     we'll have
                                               made some
                                               progress
```

This would mean that, in spoken English, the particle *that* in an indicative clause can either be used to spell out a FORCE head (as with the bold-printed occurrence of *that* in 42), or can be used to spell out a FIN head (as with the italicised occurrence of *that* in 42). We can suppose that in the same way as a transitive infinitival FIN head like *for* assigns accusative case to its subject, so too the finite FIN head *that* in (42) serves to assign nominative case to its subject *we* – whereas other peripheral heads (including the FORCE head *that*) are not case assigners. The assumption that FIN is a case assigner would mean that the Case Conditions presented in §3.1.2 need to be revised along the lines specified below, by replacing mention of C as a case assigner by FIN in (43i):

(43)   **Case Conditions**
        A case-assigning probe values an unvalued case feature on an XP goal
        and assigns the goal a case value that depends on the nature of the
        probe – namely:
        (i)   *nominative* if the probe is a finite FIN with a TP complement (where
               a finite FIN is one that is indicative, subjunctive or imperative in
               mood)
        (ii)   *null* if the probe is an intransitive infinitival FIN with a TP
               complement
        (iii) *accusative* if the probe is transitive

The claim embodied in (43) that FIN (not FORCE) is the case assigner in the clause periphery has interesting consequences for a clause such as that bracketed in (44a) below, which we can take to have the peripheral structure shown in simplified form in (44b):

(44)   a.   I must admit [that me too, I hate garlic]

b.

```
                    FORCEP
              ┌───────────┴───────────┐
          FORCE                     TOPP
          that              ┌─────────┴─────────┐
                           DP                 MOD′
                         me too        ┌────────┴────────┐
                                     MOD              FINP
                                      ø         ┌───────┴───────┐
                                               FIN            TP
                                                ø        I hate garlic
```

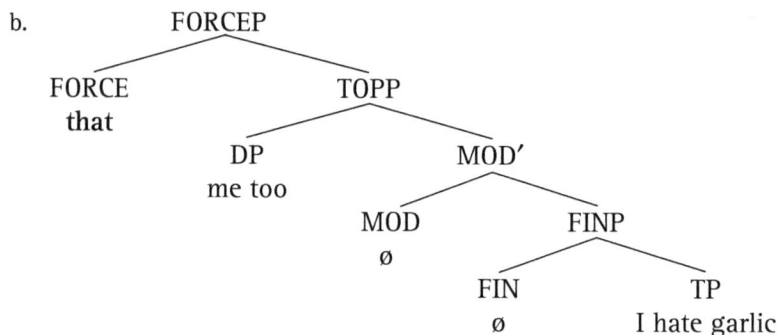

On the assumptions made in (43), the null FIN head *ø* in (44b) assigns nominative case to the subject *I* (because FIN is finite, FIN c-commands *I*, and FIN is the closest case-assigner c-commanding *I*), but the FORCE head *that* is not a case assigner – hence it does not assign nominative case to the immediately subjacent topic *me too*. Instead, the topic receives accusative case by default by virtue of not falling within the domain of a local case assigner: see the Default Case Assignment Condition in (15) above, and the discussion of (14, 16).

You should now be able to tackle Exercise 4.3.

4.4   Complete and truncated clauses

In this module, we'll see that some clauses have a more complex peripheral structure than others. More specifically, we'll see that some are complete clauses which include both FINP and FORCEP projections (and can optionally include other projections like TOPP, FOCP and MODP positioned between FORCEP and FINP), whereas others are truncated clauses which project only as far as FINP, and thus lack the FORCEP projection found in complete clauses (as well as lacking TOPP and FOCP projections).

4.4.1   Complete clauses

An interesting theoretical issue arising from the split projection view of the clause periphery concerns how long/cross-clausal movement works in the case of complete clauses (i.e. movement out of one complete clause into another). In this connection, consider how Topicalisation works in the structure below:

(45)   SPEAKER A: The demonstrators have been looting shops and setting fire to cars

SPEAKER B: *This kind of behaviour*, they must know [that, with the full force of the law, we will crack down on –]

Let's suppose that all root clauses are complete clauses (since they require a FORCEP projection to mark their illocutionary force), and that clauses introduced by the indicative complementiser *that* are likewise complete clauses (because indicative *that* clauses are declarative in force). Given these assumptions, (45B) will involve movement out of one complete clause into another. More specifically, the italicised topic *this kind of behaviour* originates in the gap position (as the complement of the preposition *on*) and from there moves across the edge of the *that*-clause to the specifier position in a topic projection at the front of the main clause. But how does this movement take place?

Locality constraints require long/cross-clausal movement to take place one clause at a time, so that a constituent moving out of one clause into another transits through the edge of the highest projection in the lower clause before moving into the higher clause. One of these locality constraints is Chomsky's (1998) Impenetrability Condition (discussed in §1.5.1), which we can adapt from the CP framework to the split projection framework by reformulating it as:

(46)   **Impenetrability Condition**
        Anything below the head H of the highest projection HP in a complete
        clause is impenetrable to anything above HP

Above/below here mean 'c-commanding/c-commanded by', and a complete clause is one containing a FORCEP projection. Let's therefore suppose that the topic transits through the highest peripheral projection in the complement clause, and thus moves into spec-FORCEP in the *that*-clause, before subsequently going on to move into its criterial position in spec-TOPP in the main clause. On this view, the topic first undergoes the movement arrowed below in the complement clause:

(47)

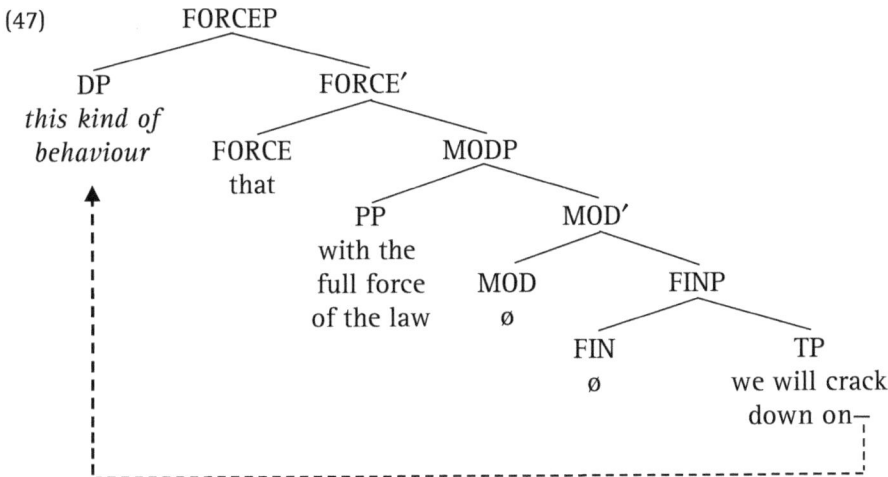

The arrowed movement will not violate the Impenetrability Condition/IC outlined in (46) above, since IC bars direct movement from a position below a FORCE head to one above/outside FORCEP (and the fronted topic in 47 moves from a position below the FORCE head *that* into a specifier position <u>inside</u> the FORCEP headed by *that*).

Once it has moved to the edge of the FORCEP projection in the complement clause, the fronted topic can then move from there into the specifier position of a TOPP projection in the main clause, as shown by the arrow below:

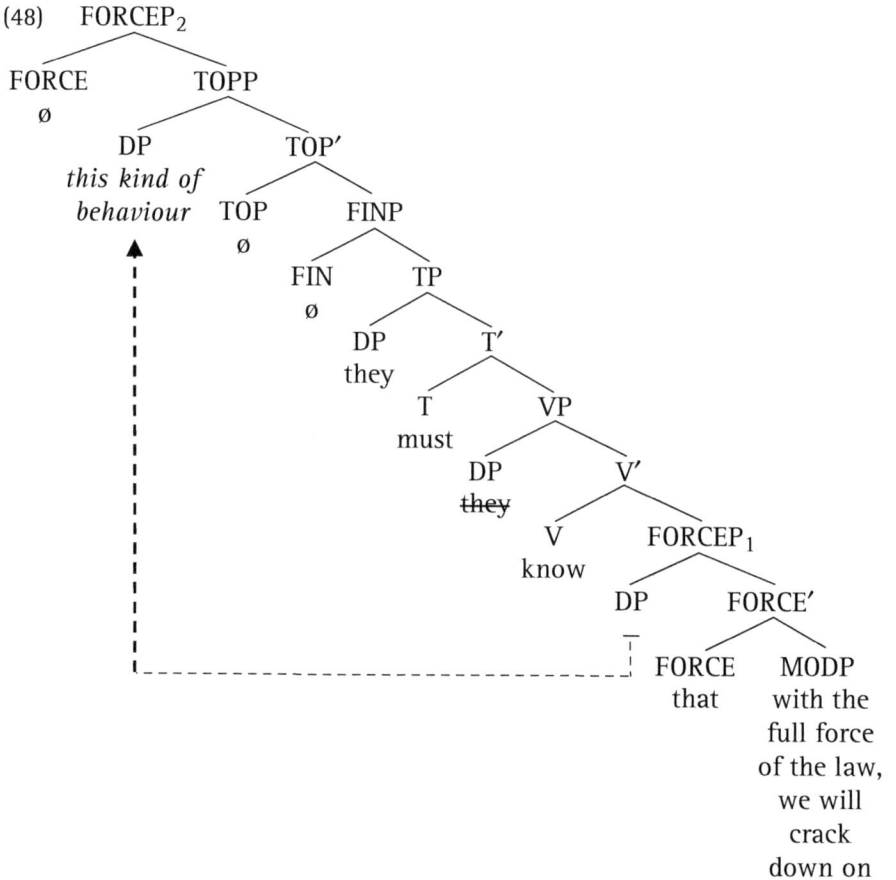

(48)   FORCEP$_2$

```
        FORCEP₂
       /        \
   FORCE        TOPP
     Ø          /    \
          DP          TOP'
      this kind of    /    \
       behaviour    TOP    FINP
                     Ø     /    \
                        FIN      TP
                         Ø      /    \
                            DP        T'
                           they      /    \
                                   T        VP
                                  must     /    \
                                        DP        V'
                                       they      /    \
                                              V      FORCEP₁
                                            know     /      \
                                                  DP        FORCE'
                                                          /       \
                                                      FORCE       MODP
                                                       that      with the
                                                                 full force
                                                                 of the law,
                                                                 we will
                                                                 crack
                                                                 down on
```

Since the topic moves from a position on the edge of highest projection (FORCEP$_1$) in the periphery of the lower clause to a position within the periphery of the higher clause, the arrowed movement in (48) does not violate the Impenetrability Condition (46). Since spec-FORCEP is not the criterial position for a topic (but rather is simply a transit position through which any XP constituent moving out of the complement clause can transit), the movement arrowed in (48) will not incur any violation of the Criterial Freezing Condition (3) either.

4.4.2   Truncated clauses

In addition to complete clauses which have the status of FORCEP projections able to house a full range of peripheral constituents (e.g. topics and/or focused constituents), there is also a class of truncated clauses whose periphery projects only as far as the FINP projection. Rizzi & Shlonsky (2007) and Rizzi (2014a) posit that bare declarative complement clauses (i.e. those not introduced by the overt complementiser *that*) are truncated at the FINP level (in the sense that they project only as far as FINP): accordingly, Rizzi (2014a: 30) claims that 'finite clauses with null complementisers in English involve truncation of the higher structure of the C system, of FORCE (hence the absence of the declarative force-marker *that*) and of the topic-focus system' and thus contain only 'a vestigial presence of the C-system' comprising a projection of 'the lowest head, FIN'.

The difference between complete and truncated (i.e. incomplete/defective) clauses can be illustrated by the contrast below:

(49)   a.   John believes [**that** Mary wrote this book]
         b.   John believes [**that** *this book*, Mary wrote]

(50)   a.   John believes [Mary wrote this book]
         b.   *John believes [*this book*, Mary wrote]

Given Rizzi's assumptions, the bracketed *that*-clauses in (49) will be complete clauses projecting up to FORCEP, and consequently the FORCE head *that* allows a TOPP complement containing the fronted topic *this book* in (49b). By contrast, the bare complement clauses bracketed in (50) are truncated clauses that project only as far as FINP, and since a FIN head does not allow a TOPP complement, topicalisation of the italicised DP *this book* is not possible in (50b).

In this connection, it is interesting to note that *for*-infinitives don't allow a peripheral topic like that italicised in (51a) below or a peripheral focused constituent like that italicised in (51b), or a peripheral FORCE head like interrogative *whether* in (51c):

(51)   a.   *He is anxious [*the inheritance dispute* **for** us to settle it amicably]
         b.   *He is anxious [*everything* **for** them to thrash out in detail]
         c.   *He is wondering [*whether* **for** us to have a staycation this summer]

One way of ruling out structures like (51) would be to suppose that *for*-infinitives are truncated clauses which project only as far as FINP. Such an analysis could also be extended to Control infinitives with a PRO subject like that bracketed in (52a) below, since such clauses do not allow a peripheral focus constituent (like that italicised in 52b), or a peripheral dislocated topic (like that italicised in 52c):

(52)   a. He decided [PRO to leave everything to his children]
        b. *He decided [*everything* PRO to leave to his children]
        c. *He decided [*his children* PRO to leave everything to them]

By contrast, interrogative Control infinitives like those bracketed below have the status of complete clauses, since they require a FORCEP projection to house the italicised interrogative operator and type the clause as a question:

(53)   a. I didn't know [*whether* PRO to laugh or cry]
        b. I didn't know [*what* PRO to say]
        c. I didn't know [*who* PRO to contact]

In sentences like (52, 53), we can suppose that PRO is assigned null case by a null, intransitive infinitival FIN head; by contrast, in *for*-infinitives the infinitive subject is assigned accusative case by the transitive FIN head *for*.

Thus, some verbs/predicates select a FORCEP complement (and allow other peripheral constituents like a topic or focus), whereas others select a (smaller) FINP complement (and do not allow other peripheral constituents). Still, this picture is seemingly challenged by clauses like those bracketed below:

(54)   a. And I'm hoping [*on Friday night* **that** we can turn up and get the points] (Dean Saunders, BBC Radio 5)
        b. The problem we've got is [*in an ideal world*, **that** all patients would be on single-sex wards] (Hospital spokesperson, BBC Radio 5)
        c. I'm sure [*behind the scenes* **that** he's got the backing] (Steve McClaren, BBC1 TV)
        d. Arsène Wenger said [*if a defensive midfield player becomes available*, **that** they will be in for him] (Mark Chapman, BBC Radio 5)
        e. I'm not sure [*going into the Premier League*, **that** their squad's that strong] (Jason Burt, talkSPORT Radio)

Here, the bracketed complement clauses are bare (in the sense that they do not begin with the overt complementiser *that*) and thus, on the assumption that a declarative FORCE head is always lexicalised as *that*) must have the status of FINP rather than FORCEP. But if so, how come they allow an italicised PP or subordinate clause in their periphery? A plausible answer comes from the suggestion made by Rizzi (2014a) that natural language grammars allow FINP recursion structures of the form FINP+MODP+FINP (where MODP is a projection which houses circumstantial clause modifiers). On this view, the V-bar headed by the verb *hoping* in (54a) above would have the FINP recursion structure below:

(55)

```
                        V'
            ┌───────────┴───────────┐
            V                      FINP₂
         hoping          ┌──────────┴──────────┐
                        FIN₂                   MODP
                         ø          ┌──────────┴──────────┐
                                    PP                    MOD'
                                 on Friday      ┌──────────┴──────────┐
                                   night       MOD                   FINP₁
                                                ø          ┌──────────┴──────────┐
                                                          FIN₁                   TP
                                                          that                 we can
                                                                            turn up and
                                                                           get the points
```

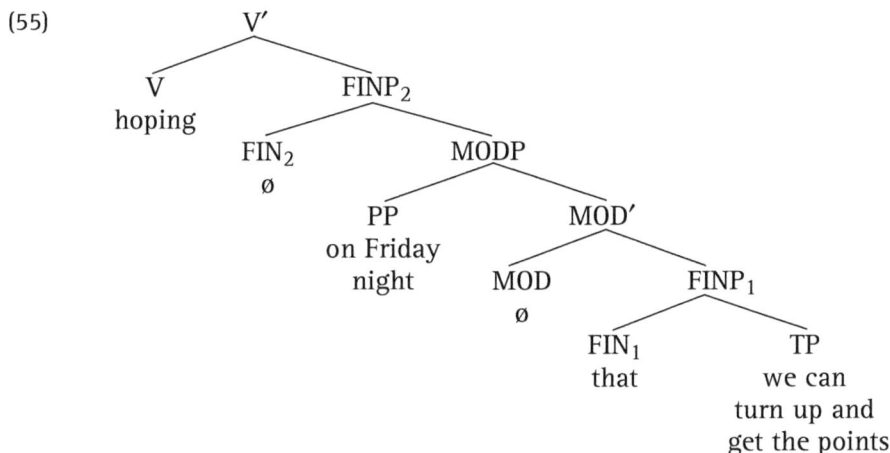

If an overt complementiser like *that* serves to mark the upper or lower boundary of the clause periphery (and hence can either spell out the highest FORCE head or the lowest FIN head in the periphery), then it follows that only the lower FIN head (FIN_1) will be lexicalised as *that*. (It should be noted, however, that some speakers do not like sentences in which FIN is spelled out as *that*.)

The key assumptions made about clause structure in this module can be summarised as follows:

(56)   **Assumptions about the clause periphery**
    (i)   Clauses which can contain peripheral topic or focus constituents are complete clauses which have FORCEP as the highest and FINP as the lowest projection in the periphery (with any other peripheral projections being positioned between FORCEP and FINP)
    (ii)   Clauses which cannot contain peripheral force-marking, topicalised or focused constituents are truncated clauses which have a periphery that projects only as far as FINP
    (iii)   FINP recursion allows for FINP+MODP+FINP structures

You should now be able to tackle Exercise 4.4.

4.5 Summary

In this chapter, we have seen that the clause periphery (traditionally analysed as containing one or more CP projections) has been split up in recent Cartographic work into a number of distinct projections (including FORCEP, TOPP, FOCP, MODP and FINP). In Module 4.1, I argued that all (non-defective) clauses contain a FORCEP projection which serves to specify the illocutionary force of the clause (e.g. whether it is declarative, interrogative or imperative in force); I noted that a declarative FORCE head in a complement clause can be spelled out as the complementiser *that*. I went on to argue that the criterial position for a peripheral topic constituent is as the specifier of a TOPP projection below FORCEP, and that clauses can contain one or more TOPP projections. I distinguished between two different types of topic: <u>in situ</u> topics which are directly merged in spec-TOP and may be reprised by a resumptive constituent lower down in the structure; and <u>ex situ</u> topics which originate in some position within TP and from there move into spec-TOPP, leaving a gap behind. I noted that the two types of topic differ in that ex situ topics are case-marked in the position which they originate in (and obey constraints on movement), whereas in situ topics are assigned accusative case by default, and are not subject to movement constraints.

In Module 4.2, I argued that peripheral focused constituents move to their criterial position in spec-FOCP from a position within TP, leaving a gap behind in the position which they move from. I noted that a FOCP constituent can either precede or follow any TOPP constituent in the same clause, but that the two types of constituent differ in three ways: (i) focused constituents always result from movement into their criterial position and always leave a gap behind, whereas topicalised constitituents can either be generated in situ in their criterial position, or be moved there; (ii) the periphery of a given clause can only contain a single FOCP, but can contain multiple TOPP constituents; (iii) non-specific pronouns like *something/someone/somebody, anything/anyone/anybody,* or *everything/everyone/everybody* can only be focused, not topicalised.

In Module 4.3, I noted that in addition to a force-marking complementiser, a focus, and one or more topics, the clause periphery can also contain one or more circumstantial modifiers: these are typically PP, ADVP, or subordinate clause constituents which provide information about the circumstances (e.g. time, place, manner, conditions etc.) under which the event described in the modified clause takes place. I argued that these circumstantial modifiers are directly merged in situ as the specifiers of MODP projections, and that the MODP containing them can occupy a range of periphery-medial positions between the highest and lowest peripheral projections in a given clause. I went on to argue that the periphery of a clause also contains a FINP projection (in the lowest position in the periphery, immediately above TP) whose head serves to mark its containing clause as finite or nonfinite, and to case-mark the subject (e.g. the infinitival complementiser *for* is a FIN head which serves to mark its clause as infinitival, and serves to case-mark the subject of the *for*-clause as accusative).

In Module 4.4, I outlined the claim made by Rizzi that although complete clauses have the status of FORCEP projections which can house a full range of peripheral constituents (e.g. topics and/or focused constituents), there is also a class of truncated clauses whose periphery projects only as far as the FINP projection (and so do not allow peripheral topic or focus constituents). I took a brief look at how cross-clausal movement works when an XP moves out of one complete clause into another, and argued that (in order to satisfy locality constraints on movement such as the Impenetrability Condition), a constituent which moves out of one clause into another has to transit through the edge of the highest peripheral projection in the lower clause (FORCEP) before moving into the periphery of the higher clause. I then went on to look at the structure of truncated clauses, arguing that these include declarative complement clauses not introduced by the overt complementiser *that* as their first word, and *for*-infinitives. I noted that Rizzi allows for the possibility that the periphery of truncated clauses may contain a MODP constituent, and handles this in terms of FINP recursion structures of the form FINP+MODP+FINP.

Thus, the overall picture which our discussion in this module leads us to is that the periphery of a complete clause comprises FORCEP and FINP projections between which there can optionally be TOPP, FOCP and MODP projections; but by contrast, the periphery of truncated clauses projects only as far as FINP, though the mechanism of FINP recursion allows for FINP+MODP+FINP structures.

Constructs and assumptions which have played a key role in our discussion in this chapter include the following:

(2)   **One Feature One Head Principle**
        Each functional head carries only one interpretable feature

(3)   **Criterial Freezing Condition/CFC**
        (i) A peripheral constituent must occupy a criterial position to be
            interpretable at LF
        (ii) A constituent which occupies its criterial position is frozen in place

(11)   **Island Constraint**
        No gap inside an island can have an antecedent outside the island

(15)   **Default Case Assignment**
        A (pro)nominal which does not fall within the domain of (i.e. which
        is not c-commanded by) a local (i.e. nearby) case assigner receives
        accusative case by default

(21)   **Intervention Condition**
        Likes cannot cross likes

(22)   **Distinctness Condition**
        Any structure at PF which contains a sequence of two non-distinct
        constituents <α, α> is degraded

(41) **Doubly Filled COMP Filter**
      At the end of a syntactic derivation, any structure in which the edge
      of a projection headed by an overt complementiser is doubly filled (i.e.
      contains some other overt constituent) is filtered out as ungrammatical

(43) **Case Conditions**
      A case-assigning probe values an unvalued case feature on an XP goal
      and assigns the goal a case value that depends on the nature of the
      probe – namely:
      (i)   *nominative* if the probe is a finite FIN with a TP complement (where
            a finite FIN is one that is indicative, subjunctive or imperative in
            mood)
      (ii) *null* if the probe is an intransitive infinitival FIN with a TP
            complement
      (iii) *accusative* if the probe is transitive

(46) **Impenetrability Condition**
      Anything below the head H of the highest projection HP in a complete
      clause is impenetrable to anything above HP

(56) **Assumptions about the clause periphery**
      (i)   Clauses which can contain peripheral topic or focus constituents
            are complete clauses which have FORCEP as the highest and FINP
            as the lowest projection in the periphery (with any other peripheral
            projections being positioned between FORCEP and FINP)
      (ii) Clauses which cannot contain peripheral force-marking, topicalised
            or focused constituents are truncated clauses which have a
            periphery that projects only as far as FINP
      (iii) FINP recursion allows for FINP+MODP+FINP structures

4.6   Bibliographical notes

The **Cartographic approach** to the periphery has been developed in work by
Luigi Rizzi over several decades (see Rizzi 1996, 1997, 2000a, 2000b, 2001,
2004a, 2004b, 2005, 2006a, 2006b, 2006c, 2007, 2010, 2011, 2012, 2013a,
2013b, 2013c, 2014a, 2014b, 2015a, 2015b, 2016a, 2016b, 2017, 2018,
2020; Rizzi & Shlonsky 2006, 2007; Cinque & Rizzi 2008, 2010a, 2010b;
Rizzi & Cinque 2016; Rizzi & Bocci 2017), and built on by numerous other
researchers, including Aboh (2004, 2005, 2006, 2007, 2010, 2016), Aboh
& Pfau (2010), Badan (2007), Badan & Del Gobbo (2010), Baltin (2010),
Belletti (2004a, 2004b, 2009), Benincà (2001, 2006, 2010, 2012a, 2012b),
Benincà & Cinque (2010), Benincà & Munaro (2010), Benincà & Poletto

(2004), Bianchi & Cruschina (2016), Bianchi & Frascarelli (2010), Bianchi et al. (2016), Biloa (2013), Bocci (2004, 2007, 2009, 2013), Brugé et al. (2012), Cardinaletti (2004, 2009), Cardinaletti et al. (2014), Cinque (2002, 2023), Cruschina (2006, 2008, 2010a, 2010b, 2011a, 2011b, 2012), Cruschina & Remberger (2008, 2017), Danckaert (2011, 2012), Demonte & Fernández Soriano (2009, 2013, 2014), Durrleman (2008), Endo (2007a, 2007b, 2014, 2015a, 2015b, 2017, 2018), Franco (2009), Frascarelli (2000), Frascarelli & Hinterhölzl (2007), Frascarelli & Puglielli (2007), Garzonio (2005), Giusti (1996, 2012), Grewendorf (2002), Grewendorf & Poletto (2009), Haegeman (2000a, 2003, 2004, 2006a, 2006b, 2007a, 2007b, 2009, 2010, 2012, 2013, 2017, 2019, 2021), Haegeman & Hill (2014), Jayaseelan (2003, 2008), Jiménez-Fernández (2011, 2015), Krapova (2002), Krapova & Cinque (2008), Laenzlinger (1999), Legate (2002), Munaro (2003), Nye (2013), Paoli (2003, 2007), Paul (2005, 2014), Pearce (1999), Poletto (2000), Puskás (2000), Roberts (2004), Roussou (2000), Salvi (2005), Shlonsky (1997, 2010, 2014), Shlonsky & Soare (2011), Shlonsky & Bocci (2019), Speas & Tenny (2003), Torrence (2013), Tsai (2008), Villa-García (2010, 2011a, 2011b, 2012a, 2012b, 2012c, 2015), and Villalba (2000). For overviews of the Cartographic approach, see Cinque & Rizzi (2008, 2010a), Shlonsky (2010), Rizzi (2013a), Rizzi & Cinque (2016), Rizzi & Bocci (2017), and Shlonsky & Bocci (2019). It should be noted that much Cartographic research posits a far wider range of types of peripheral projection than that assumed here; however, to simplify exposition I have consciously limited the number of different types of peripheral head utilised here.

On **topics**, see Gruber (1967), Ross (1967, 1973), Lakoff (1969), Neubauer (1970), Emonds (1970, 1976, 2004), Postal (1971, 1972), Higgins (1973), Hirschbühler (1973, 1974, 1975), Rodman (1974, 1997), van Riemsdijk & Zwarts (1974, 1997), Gundel (1975, 1985, 1988), Contreras (1976), Keenan & Schieffelin (1976a, 1976b), Chomsky (1977), Cinque (1977, 1983), Rivero (1978, 1980), Prince (1981a, 1981b, 1984, 1997), Reinhart (1981), Vat (1981), Kitagawa (1982), van Haaften et al. (1983), Greenberg (1984), Pesetsky (1989), Demirdache (1991), Ward & Prince (1991), Authier (1992), Geluykens (1992), Lasnik & Saito (1992), Watanabe (1993), Lambrecht (1994), Ziv (1994), Büring (1997, 1999, 2003), Grohmann (1997, 2000, 2003, 2006), Zaenen (1997), Birner & Ward (1998a, 1998b), Portner & Yabushita (1998), Maki et al. (1999), Cormack & Smith (2000), Frascarelli (2000), Gregory & Michaelis (2001), Platzack (2001, 2004), Grewendorf (2002), Boeckx (2003, 2012), Belletti (2004a), Benincà & Poletto (2004), Casielles-Suárez (2004), Frey (2004, 2005), Shaer & Frey (2004), Boeckx & Grohmann (2005), Grohmann (2006), Samek-Lodovici (2006, 2009), Féry (2007), Frascarelli & Hinterhölzl (2007), Manetta (2007), Bianchi & Frascarelli (2010), Ott (2012a, 2012b, 2014, 2015), Constant (2014), Villa-García (2015), Bayer & Dasgupta (2016), Büring

(2016), Miyagawa (2017a), and Radford (2018). Some researchers argue for there being more than one type of topic projection: for discussion, see Belletti (2004a), Benincà & Poletto (2004), Bianchi & Frascarelli (2010), Frascarelli & Hinterhölzl (2007), and Samek-Lodovici (2006, 2009).

On **Left Dislocation**, see van Riemsdisk & Zwarts (1974, 1977), Rodman (1974, 1977), Gundel (1975), Cinque (1977), Vat (1981), van Haaften et al. (1983), Greenberg (1984), Prince (1984), Anagnastopoulou et al. (1997), Grohmann (1997), Gregory & Michaelis (2001), Grewendorf (2002), Frey (2004, 2005), Boeckx & Grohmann (2005), and Manetta (2007).

On **focus**, see Schachter (1973), Akmajian (1979), Prince (1981a), Culicover & Rochemont (1983), Taglicht (1984), Erteschik-Shir (1986), Brody (1990), Kiss (1995, 1998), Rooth (1985, 1992, 1996), Horvath (1986, 1995, 2000, 2007), Rochemont (1986), König (1991, 2017), Rizzi (1996, 1997, 2013c), Büring (1997, 2009), Kiss (1998), Lahiri (1998), Romero (1998), Zubizaretta (1998, 2009), Ambar (1999), Kidwai (1999), Pearce (1999), Cormack & Smith (2000), Frascarelli (2000), Benincà (2001), Szendröi (2001), Kim (2002, 2006), Drubig (2003), Green & Jaggar (2003), Benincà & Poletto (2004), Brunetti (2004), Futagi (2004), Lee (2004), Park (2005), Cruschina (2006, 2012), Féry & Samek-Lodovici (2006), Samek-Lodovici (2006, 2009), Aboh (2007), Eckardt (2007), Frascarelli & Puglielli (2007), Green (2007), Jayaseelan (1996, 2003, 2008), Hartman & Ai (2009), Badan & Del Gobbo (2010), Fanselow & Lenertová (2010), Miyagawa (2010), Dehé et al. (2011), Cheng & Downing (2012), M. Wagner (2012), Ortega-Santos (2013), Rizzi (2013c, 2016a), Dominguez (2014), Irani (2014), Wierzba (2014, 2019), De Cesare (2015), Jiménez-Fernández (2015), Arregi (2016), Authier & Haegeman (2016), Bianchi & Cruschina (2016), Bianchi et al. (2016), van der Wal (2016), Cruschina & Remberger (2017), Erlewine (2017b), Badan & Crocco (2019), and Borise (2019).

On **finiteness**, see Lasser (1997), Klein (1998, 2006), Bianchi (2003), Landau (2004), Adger (2007), Anderson (2007), Nikolaeva (2007), Radford (2008), Amritavalli (2013), Kissock (2013), Ritter & Wiltschko (2014), O'Neill (2015), Cowper (2016), Eide (2016), Goodall (2017), Manzini & Savoia (2018), Lowe (2019), and Manzini & Roussou (2019).

On **intervention** effects, see Starke (2001), Kim (2002, 2006), Boeckx & Jeong (2004), Rizzi (2006b), Beck (2006), Beck & Kim (2006), Boeckx & Lasnik (2006), Endo (2007a), Friedmann et al. (2009), Abels (2012), Haegeman (2012), and Haegeman et al. (2014).

On the **Doubly Filled COMP Filter**, see Chomsky & Lasnik (1977), Seppänen & Trotta (2000), Koopman (2000), Koopman & Szabolsci (2000), Zwicky (2002), Collins (2007), Bayer & Brandner (2008), Baltin (2010), Schönenberger (2010), Bayer (2015, 2016), Collins & Radford (2015), and Radford (2013, 2018).

4.7   Workbook

In the exercises below, an [M] after an example sentence indicates that a model answer is provided in the free-to-download *Students' Answerbook* (and in the *Teachers' Answerbook* as well). You will find it helpful to look at this model answer before attempting to tackle other examples in the exercise. Some other exercise examples have an [S] after them, indicating that they are for self-study: this means that after reading the relevant module (and those preceding it), and looking at the helpful hints and model answer associated with the exercise, students should be able to analyse these self-study examples on their own, and then compare their answers with those provided in the *Students' Answerbook*. The remaining exercise examples (i.e. those not marked with [M] or [S] after them) are intended for teachers to use as the basis for hands-on problem-solving work in seminars, classes, or assignments: answers to all of these non-self-study examples are provided in the *Teachers' Answerbook*. Note that Exercise 4.1 tests you on Module 4.1, Exercise 4.2 on Module 4.2, and so on; and that each exercise in a given chapter presupposes familiarity with material covered in earlier chapters and in earlier modules of the same chapter. Unparenthesised numbers like 4 refer to material in the exercises, whereas parenthesised numbers like (22) refer to examples and conditions in the main text of the book.

EXERCISE 4.1

This exercise is designed to be attempted after reading Module 4.1 and the chapters preceding it.

Discuss the structure of the periphery of the clauses in the sentences below (in the case of sentences 1–3, concerning yourself only with the bracketed clauses):

1   I must admit [that us republicans, we don't trust you democrats] [M]
2   I think [that Red Bull, one of their spotters actually got arrested] (David Coulthard, BBC1 TV)
3   I don't know [whether this high tempo, we can sustain (it) for a full season] [S]
4   This particular case, the FBI, they solved (it) very quickly [S]
5   Diesel cars, the pollution they cause, people underestimate (it)
6   The flat tyre, John explained that there had been nails on the ground (after Rodman 1997: 38)
7   Hillary Clinton, her husband Bill Clinton, his advisor was a Ku Klux Klan member (Political commentator, BBC Radio 5)

8   The assignments, most of *(them) are fine [S]
9   This statue, the top of *(it), someone has vandalised

In 8 and 9, the notation *(*them*)/*(*it*) means that the sentence is grammatical
if *them/it* is used, but ungrammatical if it is not.

Helpful hints

In each of the sentences, concern yourself with the structure of the
clause periphery; do not concern yourself with the internal structure
of TPs below the periphery. In the case of sentences 1–3, contrast CP
recursion and Cartographic analyses; but for the remaining sentences,
present only Cartographic analyses. Take nominal constituents in
the periphery to be topics, and bear in mind that a topic can be (i) a
fronted/ex situ topic which leaves behind a gap when it moves, or (ii)
an in situ topic reprised by a resumptive pronoun like *it/them*, or (iii)
an in situ topic which is unreprised. Take the phrases *us republicans,
you democrats, Red Bull, this high tempo, this particular case, the FBI,
the pollution they cause, the flat tyre, Hillary Clinton, her husband Bill
Clinton, his adviser, the assignments, this statue,* and *the top of it* to be
DPs headed by an overt or null D, but don't concern yourself with their
internal structure. In addition, take *one of their spotters* to be a NUMP,
and *diesel cars* to be a QP headed by a null quantifier (meaning 'an
unspecified number of'), but don't concern yourself with the internal
structure of these phrases. In 3, take *whether* to be an interrogative
complementiser which has a null yes–no operator Op_{YNQ} as its specifier,
and take this operator to be an ADVP.

In arriving at your analysis, consider the possible role played by
conditions like the following in relevant examples:

10   **Constraint on Extraction Domains/CED** (from §1.5.1)
Only complements allow material to be extracted out of them, not
specifiers or adjuncts

11   **Freezing Principle** (from §1.5.1)
The constituents of a moved phrase are frozen internally within (and so
cannot be extracted out of) the moved phrase

12   **Impenetrability Condition** (= 46)
Anything below the head H of the highest projection HP in a complete
clause is impenetrable to anything above HP

13   **Intervention Condition** (= 21)
Likes cannot cross likes

14   Clause Typing Conditions (from §1.4.3):
   (i) A clause is interpreted as being of a given type (interrogative or exclamative etc.) if it contains a peripheral clause-typing specifier of the relevant type
   (ii) An indicative clause is interpreted as declarative in type by default if it does not contain a peripheral clause-typing specifier

EXERCISE 4.2

This exercise is designed to be attempted after reading Module 4.2 and the module and chapters preceding it.

Discuss the structure of the periphery of the clauses in the sentences below (concentrating on the bracketed clauses alone in the case of 1a–1c):

1a I doubt [that anyone at all, you would dare complain to about my cooking] [M]
1b I doubt [that my cooking, anyone at all, you would dare complain to about it] [M]
1c *I doubt [that anyone at all, my cooking, you would dare complain to about] [M]
2a Everything else, I hereby bequeath to my wife [S]
2b My wife, everything else, I hereby bequeath to her [S]
2c *Everything else, my wife, I hereby bequeath to [S]
3a Something special, he gave to everyone
3b Everyone, he gave something special to
3c *Something special, everyone, he gave to
4a Everything possible he has done for his sick mother
4b His sick mother, everything possible he has done for her
4c *Everything possible, his sick mother, he has done for
5a The rumours about everything else, he flatly denied [S]
5b ??Everything else, he flatly denied the rumours about [S]
5c *Everything else, the rumours about he flatly denied [S]
6a Everything about the president, I thoroughly dislike
6b The president, everything about him, I thoroughly dislike
6c *The president, everything about, I thoroughly dislike

Helpful hints
In each of the above sentences, concern yourself with the structure of the clause periphery, but do not concern yourself with the internal

structure of TPs below the periphery. Treat *my cooking, my wife, his sick mother, the president*, and *the rumours about everything else* as DPs, but do not attempt to analyse their internal structure; and treat *anyone at all, something special, everyone, everything else, everything possible*, and *everything about the president/him* as QPs, but do not attempt to analyse their internal structure. In 5 and 6, treat the *about*-phrase as an adjunct to the expression it modifies (so that in *the rumours about him*, the PP *about him* is an adjunct to the NP *rumours*: this idea gains support from *one*-pronominalisation in 'Which rumours? The *ones* about Prince Androgen?').

In relevant sentences, consider the role played by one or more of the following:

7　　**Distinctness Condition** (adapted from Richards 2010: 5)
　　At PF, any sequence <α, α> of two adjacent non-distinct constituents is degraded

8　　**Intervention Condition** (Abels 2012: 247)
　　Likes cannot cross likes

9　　**Path Containment Condition** (Pesetsky 1982a: 309)
　　If two paths overlap, one must contain the other (NB: paths = movement paths)

10　　**Constraint on Extraction Domains/CED** (adapted from Huang 1982)
　　Only complements allow material to be extracted out of them, not specifiers or adjuncts

11　　**Specificity Condition** (adapted from Fiengo & Higginbotham 1981)
　　Specific nominals are opaque domains for extraction (i.e. nominals introduced by specific expressions such as *the/this/that/my/your/his* etc. are resistant to having anything extracted out of them)

12　　**Freezing Principle** (adapted from Wexler & Culicover 1980)
　　The constituents of a moved phrase are frozen internally within (and so cannot be extracted out of) the moved phrase

Note that many of these conditions/principles/constraints are not discussed in this chapter (although some were introduced in §1.5.1), and two – 9 and 11 – are introduced for the first time here, to test your ability to determine how constraints which are unfamiliar to you block illicit derivations.

EXERCISE 4.3

This exercise is designed to be attempted after reading Module 4.3 and the modules and chapters preceding it.

Discuss the structure of the periphery of the clauses in the sentences below (concentrating on the bracketed clauses alone in sentences containing these):

1   I doubt [if Lord Scumme-Bagge, in his will, anything at all, he left to charity] [M]
2   I know [that, generally, the FBI, in cases like this, they find the killer] [S]
3   Everton, if it wasn't for their goalkeeper, Arsenal, they could have scored eight (Darren Gough, talkSPORT Radio)
4   I feel [that the president, his supporters, everything possible they have done]
5   Do you think [that Paris Saint-Germain, with the money they have behind them, that they're the new powerhouse in French football]? (Alan Brazil, talkSPORT Radio) [S]
6   I wonder [if, one Thursday, that you wouldn't mind coming into the studio] (Andy Goldstein, talkSPORT Radio)
7   It means that they can be enticed, [because sometimes, then, that they have less of a bond with their home country] (Tim Vickery, BBC Radio 5) [S]
8   All of a sudden, in the big interviews with football journalists, that Sir Alex has changed his tune (Neil Ashton, talkSPORT Radio)

Note that the use of *that* in sentences like 6–8 is non-standard, and some speakers also don't like the second occurrence of *that* in sentences like 5 – though I have recorded numerous examples of structures like 5 and several of structures like 6–8 from live, unscripted radio and TV broadcasts (see Radford 2018).

Helpful hints
In the clauses you analyse, concern yourself with the structure of the clause periphery, but not with the internal structure of TPs below the periphery. Treat *Lord Scumme-Bagge, the FBI, Everton, Arsenal, Paris Saint-Germain, the president,* and *his supporters* as DPs, but do not attempt to analyse their internal structure; treat *everything possible* as a QP, but do not attempt to analyse its internal structure; and treat *one Thursday* as a PP (headed by a null preposition – perhaps a null counterpart of *on*) and likewise treat *all of a sudden* as a PP (perhaps with *all* being in spec-PP), but do not concern yourself with the internal structure of these PPs. Treat the *if*-clause in 3 and the *because*-clause in

7 as a projection of the CONJ/subordinating conjunction *if/because* and hence a CONJP, but do not concern yourself with the internal structure of the *if*-clause in 3. However, treat *if* in 1 and 6 as an interrogative complementiser/FORCE head, and assume that it has a null yes–no question operator Op_{YNQ} as its specifier (and that this is an ADVP). For the purposes of this exercise, treat *sometimes/then* in 7 as ADVP constituents (though they could more abstractly be taken to be PP constituents headed by a null preposition).

EXERCISE 4.4

This exercise is designed to be attempted after reading Module 4.4 and the modules and chapters preceding it.

Discuss the structure of the periphery of the clauses in the sentences below (concentrating on the bracketed clauses alone in the case of sentences containing these):

1 Some cases, I suspect that the FBI, they never solve [M]
2 The president, everyone says that *(he) is stubborn
3 The key file, he found that several parts of *(it), they had redacted [S]
4 I don't think [that for the sake of your own well-being, that if you are in a bilingual classroom, that once you have completed the homework in one language, that you should have to do it all over again in the second one] (example which Eiichi Iwasaki tells me that Jim McCloskey informed him that Chris Potts devised)
5 He is now planning, in the next few months, to run marathons for charity [S]
6 An expensive diamond ring like this, a man like that, I don't think would ever buy for his wife (Radford 2018: 65) [S]
7 I think [previously, that in trying to protect his off stump, he flicked the ball to the on side] (Ian Chappell, BBC Radio 5 Live Sports Extra)
8 I just think [Arsenal, honestly, that they are gonna fall behind if they don't sign a striker] (John Cross, talkSPORT Radio)
9 It is not impossible [for in future for Google's G-mail to crash] (forum.telus. com) [S]
10 It's time [for now Rooney to go] (Darren Gough, talkSPORT Radio)

Note that the notation *(he)/*(it) in 2, 3 means that the sentence is grammatical if *he/it* is used, but ungrammatical if *he/it* is omitted. Note too that the use of the complementisers *that/for* in sentences 7–10 is non-standard: say what is odd about their use.

Helpful hints

In each of the relevant clauses, concern yourself with the structure of the clause periphery, and with how nominals in the periphery are case-marked; do not concern yourself with the internal structure of TPs below the periphery. Make the following assumptions about the status of various constituents, but don't attempt to analyse their internal structure: *the FBI, the president, the key file, Arsenal* are DPs headed by an overt or null D; *some cases, everyone, several parts of (it)* are QPs headed by a quantifier; *for the sake of your own well-being, now, in the next few months, in trying to protect his off stump,* and *in future* are PPs headed by an overt or null preposition (with *now* paraphrasable as 'at the present time'); the subordinate clauses *if there is a problem, if you are in a bilingual classroom,* and *once you have completed the homework in one language* are CONJP constituents (i.e. projections of a subordinating conjunction/CONJ like *if/once*); *an expensive diamond ring like this* and *a man like that* are ARTP constituents; *honestly* and *previously* are ADVP constituents.

Bear in mind the following assumptions made about the clause periphery in Module 4.4:

11   **Assumptions about the clause periphery** (= 56)
   (i)   Clauses which can contain peripheral topic or focus constituents are complete clauses which have FORCEP as the highest and FINP as the lowest projection in the periphery (with any other peripheral projections being positioned between FORCEP and FINP)
   (ii) Clauses which cannot contain peripheral force-marking, topicalised or focused constituents are truncated clauses which have a periphery that projects only as far as FINP
   (iii) FINP recursion allows for FINP+MODP+FINP structures

In addition, in relevant clauses, consider the role played by the following:

12   **Default Case Assignment** (= 15)
   A (pro)nominal which does not fall within the domain of (i.e. which is not c-commanded by) a local (i.e. nearby) case assigner receives accusative case by default

13   **Criterial Freezing Condition/CFC** (= 3)
   (i)   A peripheral constituent must occupy a criterial position to be interpretable at LF
   (ii) A constituent which occupies its criterial position is frozen in place

14   **Intervention Condition** (= 21)
   Likes cannot cross likes

15   **Impenetrability Condition** (= 46)
      Anything below the head H of the highest projection HP in the periphery
      of a complete clause (i.e. one containing FORCEP) is impenetrable to
      anything above HP

16   **Constraint on Extraction Domains/CED** (from §1.5.1)
      Only complements allow material to be extracted out of them, not
      specifiers or adjuncts (adapted from Huang 1982)

17   **Freezing Principle** (from §1.5.1)
      The constituents of a moved phrase are frozen internally within (and so
      cannot be extracted out of) the moved phrase (adapted from Wexler &
      Culicover 1980)

18   **Doubly Filled COMP Filter** (= 41)
      At the end of a syntactic derivation, any structure in which the edge
      of a projection headed by an overt complementiser is doubly filled (i.e.
      contains some other overt constituent) is filtered out as ungrammatical

19   **COMP-Trace Filter/CTF** (from §1.5.2)
      Any structure at the end of a syntactic derivation in which an overt
      COMP/complementiser is immediately adjacent to and c-commands a
      trace (i.e. a gap/null copy left behind by a moved constituent) is filtered
      out as ill-formed

20   **Distinctness Condition** (= 22)
      Any structure at PF which contains a sequence of two non-distinct
      constituents $\langle \alpha, \alpha \rangle$ is degraded

In relation to 19, assume that (for the purposes of CTF) two constituents are
immediately adjacent if one precedes the other, and there is no overt constituent intervening between them.

5 | More peripheral constituents

5.0   Overview

In this chapter we turn to look at what positions in the clause periphery are occupied by a range of different types of peripheral constituent which were not discussed in the previous chapter, including fronted negative constituents, wh-constituents of various kinds, and inverted auxiliaries. We'll see that these can be accommodated within a Cartographic model in which the clause periphery canonically comprises FORCEP and FINP projections, with optional TOPP, FOCP and MODP constituents positioned between them.

However, two notes of caution should be sounded at the outset. The first of these is that inter-speaker variation means that some sentences which are fine for me may not be fine for some other native English speakers. By way of illustration, I note that Emonds (1970) argued that some syntactic operations are restricted to applying in root/main clauses, and consequently do not apply in complement clauses. One such operation, Emonds claimed, is (Subject–Auxiliary) Inversion, which (by virtue of being a root operation) can apply in root/main clauses like those in (1a, 1b) below, but not in italicised complement clauses like (1c, 1d) (the examples and judgements being from Emonds 1970: 6–7):

(1)   a. Never in my life have I spoken to him
       b. When is he coming, and where is he from?
       c. *John thought that Bill hadn't come and *that neither had Mary*
       d. *Mary doesn't know why Susan in leaving, and we don't know *why is she* either

In these examples, Inversion is triggered by a peripheral negative constituent (*never in my life/neither*) in (1a, 1c), and so I'll refer to the phenomenon as Negative Inversion. By contrast in (1b, 1d) Inversion is triggered by a peripheral interrogative constituent (*when/where/why*), and so I'll refer to the phenomenon as Interrogative Inversion. In Emonds's, (American) variety of English, both Negative Inversion and Interrogative Inversion are restricted to occurring in root clauses. By contrast, in my own (British) variety, Interrogative Inversion is restricted to applying in root clauses, but Negative Inversion is not. Thus, for me, the italicised auxiliary-inverted negative complement clause in (1c) is perfectly grammatical, but the italicised auxiliary-inverted interrogative complement clause in (1d) is not. In the discussion in this chapter, some of the illustrative examples I use (which are – naturally enough – based on my own variety of English) will involve Negative Inversion in a complement clause: bear in mind that speakers who treat Negative Inversion as a root phenomenon will find such sentences (like those in 2c, 2d, 5, 7e, 15, 26, 27b, 29, 62, 66, and 69 below) degraded. Note that this does not undermine the argumentation put forward here, since theories of grammar (and grammars of English) have to be able to account for the full range of structures found in all varieties of English (including mine!).

A second note of caution is the following. In this module, I shall be seeking to establish what combinations of different types of peripheral projection (e.g. FORCEP, TOPP, FOCP, MODP, FINP) are possible, and what kinds of conditions/constraints rule out combinations that are not possible. This means that some of the example sentences below have an extremely complex periphery, and may feel somewhat contrived. This inevitably means that they cause parsing difficulties, especially where they involve constituents moving to the periphery across other constituents moving to the periphery, and where anyone parsing the sentence has to establish where each moved peripheral constituent originated prior to movement. In the case of structures with a complex periphery that is difficult to parse, many speakers reject the sentences as unacceptable (perhaps because parsing such sentences imposes a heavy memory load). However, the (unasterisked) complex structures illustrated in this chapter are grammatical for me, especially if read with a clear pause between each peripheral constituent.

5.1   Negative and Interrogative Inversion

In this module, we look at the syntax of Negative and Interrogative Inversion, and attempt to determine the position occupied by the fronted negative or interrogative constituent on the one hand, and the inverted auxiliary on the other. Please bear in mind the cautionary note in Module 5.0 that my variety of English allows Negative Inversion to apply in root and non-root clauses alike, whereas some speakers restrict Negative Inversion to applying in root clauses only.

5.1.1   Negative Inversion

We'll begin by examining the position in the clause periphery occupied by fronted negative constituents and inverted auxiliaries in a type of structure (illustrated below) traditionally said to involve Negative Inversion:

(2)   a. *Nothing* **would** I ever do to upset you

   b. *On no account* **should** you leave the country

   c. I can assure you [that *at no time* **did** he misbehave in any way]

   d. He was adamant [that *not a single drop of alcohol* **had** he touched]

Such structures contain an (italicised) fronted negative XP followed by a (bold-printed) inverted auxiliary. But what position in the clause periphery do the negative constituent and the inverted auxiliary occupy, and how do they get there?

Rizzi (1997) and Haegeman (2012) argue that Negative Inversion involves focusing of the fronted negative constituent. One reason for thinking this is that (as we saw in §4.2.2), non-referential/non-specific pronouns like *something/anything/everything* can be focused (but not topicalised) in English, and this suggests that fronting of the non-referential pronoun *nothing* in (2a) is the result of focusing rather than topicalisation. This assumption would also account for why *nothing* cannot be reprised by a (bold-printed) resumptive pronoun in a sentence like (3) below:

(3)   *Nothing* would I ever do (***it**) to upset you

Since only topicalised (and not focused) constituents can be reprised by a resumptive pronoun, the ungrammaticality of sentences like (3) when they contain a resumptive is consistent with the peripheral negative constituent *nothing* being focused.

A further reason for thinking that peripheral negative constituents are focused is that (like typical focused constituents) they can be used to supply new information in reply to a question, as in the dialogue below:

(4)   SPEAKER A: How much alcohol have you had?

   SPEAKER B: *Not a single drop* have I touched in the past 6 months

A third reason for treating peripheral negative constituents as focused is that they can contain a focus marker like *only* or *even*, as in:

(5)   a. It is unfortunate [that *only one of the hostages* have they released]

   b. It is unfortunate [that *not even one of the hostages* have they released]

For reasons such as these, Rizzi and Haegeman suppose that the peripheral negative constituent in such structures occupies spec-FOCP. Accordingly, in a sentence like (2a) '*Nothing* would I ever do to upset you', the pronominal QP *nothing* moves to spec-FOCP from its initial position as the thematic complement of the verb *do* by Focus Movement (a subtype of A-bar Movement).

It seems clear that Auxiliary Inversion in Negative Inversion structures is triggered by the focusing of a negative constituent, since we find Inversion in structures like (2, 4B, 5) with a focused negative constituent, but not in structures where other kinds of constituent are focused (as we saw in Module 4.2). Moreover, there is no Auxiliary Inversion in structures like those below which contain an unfocused peripheral negative constituent occupying the specifier position in a peripheral MODP projection:

(6)   a. *In no time at all*, the fire reached the outskirts of the town
        b. *For no apparent reason*, the dam burst
        c. *With no money*, it is difficult to make ends meet
        d. *Not long ago*, they discovered a new Inca temple using Lidar

Rizzi and Haegeman account for this triggering effect by supposing that the fronted auxiliary moves to the edge of the same FOCP projection as the focused negative constituent, so that FOC attracts an auxiliary to adjoin to FOC when FOC attracts a focused negative constituent to become its specifier.

However, sentences such as the following (illustrating a phenomenon termed non-adjacent inversion by Haegeman 2000b) cast doubt on the assumption that the inverted auxiliary moves to FOC in clauses containing a preposed negative constituent:

(7)   a. *Nothing at all*, <u>when questioned</u>, **did** he say
        b. *On no account*, <u>during the vacation</u>, **would** I go into the office
           (Haegeman 2000b: 133)
        c. *Under no circumstances*, <u>however desperate I was</u>, **would** I ask her for money
        d. *Not one of the wounded soldiers*, <u>hard though the surgeons tried</u>, **could** they save
        e. He prayed that *never again* <u>atrocities like these</u> **would** he witness
           (Haegeman 2012: 48, fn. 46)
        f. *On very few occasions*, <u>people like him</u>, **do** they get the credit they deserve

The reason is that the italicised fronted negative constituent (in spec-FOCP) is separated from the bold-printed inverted auxiliary by a variety of other (underlined) peripheral constituents: these include a prepositional phrase (in spec-MODP) in (7b), a subordinate clause (again in spec-MODP) in (7a, 7c, 7d), a fronted topic (in spec-TOPP) in (7e), and a dislocated topic (again in spec-TOPP) in (7f). Sentences like those in (7) provide evidence that the inverted auxiliary must be the head of a lower peripheral projection than that containing the focused negative constituent. But what precisely is the projection containing the inverted auxiliary?

Since the inverted auxiliary immediately precedes the subject *I/he/they* in (7), and since FINP is the projection immediately above the TP containing the subject, a plausible answer is that the inverted auxiliary moves from T to FIN via Head Movement. Evidence in support of this comes from the observation that the inverted auxiliary and its subject cannot be separated by intervening constituents, as we see from the ungrammaticality which results if we re-position the underlined peripheral constituents in (7) between the (bold-printed) inverted auxiliary and its (italicised) subject, as in (8) below:

(8) a. *Nothing at all **did**, <u>when questioned</u>, *he say*

b. *On no account **would**, <u>during the vacation</u>, *I* go into the office

c. *Under no circumstances **would**, <u>however desperate I was</u>, *I* ask her for money

d. *Not one of the wounded soldiers **could**, <u>hard though the surgeons tried</u>, *they* save

e. *He prayed that never again **would**, <u>atrocities like these</u>, *he* witness

f. *On very few occasions, **do**, <u>people like him</u>, *they* get the credit they deserve

Sentences such as (7, 8) thus suggest that a fronted negative constituent moves to the specifier position in FOCP, whereas a fronted auxiliary moves to the head FIN position of FINP.

However, this conclusion raises the question of why a fronted negative constituent moving to spec-FOCP should trigger movement of an auxiliary from T to FIN, when FOCP and FINP are two separate peripheral projections. A plausible answer is that a focused negative constituent transits through spec-FINP on its way to spec-FOCP, and that (at the point where it is in spec-FINP) it attracts an auxiliary in T to move to adjoin to FIN. On this view, (7a) above would have the derivation shown below, if we take *when questioned* to be a CONJP projection headed by the CONJ/subordinating conjunction *when* (perhaps an elliptical variant of *when he was questioned*):

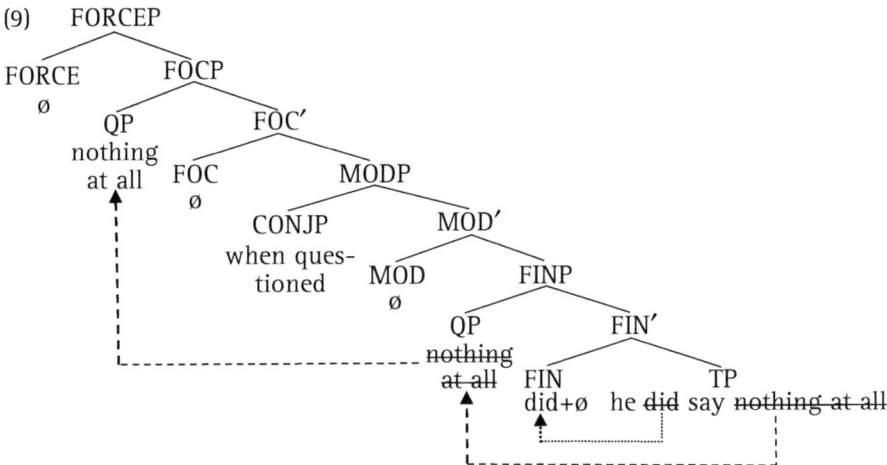

(9)   FORCEP

FORCE   FOCP
  ∅
       QP   FOC'
     nothing
      at all   FOC   MODP
               ∅
                    CONJP   MOD'
                   when ques-
                     tioned   MOD   FINP
                               ∅
                                    QP   FIN'
                                  nothing
                                  at all   FIN   TP
                                          did+∅   he did say nothing at all

The focused negative QP *nothing at all* originates as the thematic complement of the verb *say*, and from there initially moves to become the specifier of a null FIN head *ø* which concomitantly attracts the auxiliary *did* to move from T to adjoin to FIN-*ø*. Subsequently, the focused negative QP moves into its criterial position in spec-FOCP, and lower copies of the focused QP and the inverted auxiliary receive a null spellout (marked by strikethrough above).

5.1.2   Interrogative Inversion

A further type of context in which we find Auxiliary Inversion is in wh-questions like those below, illustrating a phenomenon traditionally termed Interrogative Inversion:

(10)   a. *Which dress* **was** she wearing?
        b. *Who* **have** they arrested?
        c. *How many cars* **does** he own?
        d. *At what time* **are** they arriving?

Rizzi (1997, 2001) and Haegeman & Guéron (1999) argue that the fronted (italicised) wh-XPs in Interrogative Inversion structures are focused and move to spec-FOCP. From a semantic perspective, such an analysis is far from implausible: interrogative wh-constituents ask for new information, and in this respect they fulfil a similar role to other focused constituents (which provide new information). Moreover, a focus analysis is also plausible from a typological perspective, since in some languages an (italicised) fronted interrogative constituent can be followed by a (bold-printed) focus particle, as the examples below illustrate (where FOC denotes a focus particle, and AGR an agreement affix):

(11)   a. *Manwa*   **ad**   izra   hassan?
            who   FOC   saw   hassan
            'Who was it that Hassan saw?'
            (Berber, Alami 2011)
        b. *Inā*   **nè**   sukà   jē?
            Where   FOC   have   go?
            'Where is it that they have gone?'
            (Hausa, Green 2007: 84)
        c. *Iyondi*   **yo**   Kambale   a-alangira?
            who   FOC   Kambale   AGR-saw
            'Who is it that Kambale saw?'
            (Kinande, Schneider-Zioga 2007: 412)

It is plausible to take the italicised fronted wh-constituent to be the specifier of the bold-printed focus particle in such sentences, and to treat the focus particle as the head FOC constituent of a FOCP projection.

Further evidence in support of claiming that interrogative wh-constituents move to spec-FOCP in Interrogative Inversion structures comes from the ungrammaticality of sentences like the following:

(12)   a. *What <u>to whom</u> did he say?
        b. *What <u>to nobody</u> did he say?

If, as claimed here, fronted negative and interrogative XPs are focused in clauses where Auxiliary Inversion takes place, then the ungrammaticality of sentences like (12) can be attributed to them violating the constraint that there can be no more than one FOCP projection in the periphery of a given clause.

Let's now turn to the question of where the inverted auxiliary is positioned in Interrogative Inversion structures. There is evidence that (as in the case of Negative Inversion) the inverted auxiliary does not move into the head FOC position of FOCP, but rather moves into the head position in a lower FINP projection. Such an assumption would predict that other peripheral constituents can be positioned between the focused interrogative constituent and the inverted auxiliary – and this prediction is borne out by sentences such as those in (13) below, where an italicised interrogative constituent is separated from a bold-printed inverted auxiliary by an underlined peripheral constituent which is a PP modifier in (13a–13d), a reduced subordinate clause in (13e), and a dislocated topic in (13f):

(13)   a. *What* <u>at present</u> **do** you need? (fgcquaker.org)
        b. *How long*, <u>in the light of this promotion</u>, **will** you stay here? (Ross 1967: 31)
        c. *What else*, <u>with no money to speak of</u>, **could** he possibly have done? (Kayne 1998: 155, fn. 66)
        d. *Under what circumstances*, <u>during the holidays</u>, **would** you go into the office? (Sobin 2003: 193)
        e. *Why*, <u>when asked</u>, **did** all the students I interviewed say they would take 'study drugs' again? (unibathtime.co.uk)
        f. *How often*, <u>that book</u>, **has** he praised it in public? (Kayne 1998: 155, fn. 66)

Such sentences suggest that Interrogative Inversion can be treated in much the same way as Negative Inversion. If so, the fronted wh-constituent will first move into spec-FINP (at that point, triggering the head FIN constituent of FINP to attract a finite auxiliary to move from T to adjoin to FIN), and thereafter move on its own to spec-FOCP. On this view, (13a) will have the derivation shown below:

(14)

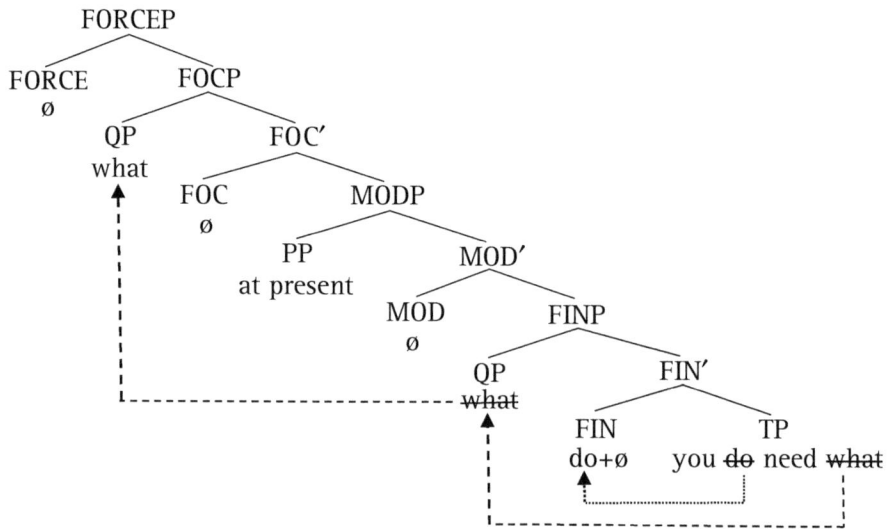

We can handle Auxiliary Inversion here in the same way as for Negative Inversion if we suppose that a null FIN head which attracts a focused negative or interrogative XP to become its specifier also attracts a T auxiliary to adjoin to FIN (as shown by the dotted arrow in 14). Spec-FINP being simply a transit position, the focused QP *what* in (14) subsequently moves from spec-FINP into its criterial position in spec-FOCP.

An interesting property of focus structures is that (as we see from the clause whose structure is shown in highly simplified form in 15 below) a TOPP containing an (italicised) peripheral topic can be positioned between a FORCEP containing a (bold-printed) force-marking complementiser and a FOCP containing an (underlined) focused constituent:

(15)   He prayed [FORCEP **that** [TOPP *atrocities like those* [FOCP never again [FINP would [TP he witness]]]]] (Radford 2004a: 329)

Accordingly, a prediction made by the analysis of Interrogative Inversion sketched in (14) above is that in front of the focused interrogative wh-constituent we should be able to have an (in situ or ex situ) topic – and this prediction is borne out by sentences like those below (where an underlined topic is positioned in front of an italicised focused interrogative constituent):

(16)   a. A book like this, *to whom* would you give? (Delahunty 1983)
        b. That kind of pen, *what* can you use it for? (Radford 1988: 532)

   c. <u>Tom</u>, *why* would anyone want to meet? (Bianchi 1999: 179)

   d. <u>Tottenham</u>, *where* do they go from here? (Ronnie Irani, talkSPORT Radio)

   e. <u>This kind of performance</u>, *how* do you think the fans will react to it? (Mark Chapman, BBC Radio 5)

   f. <u>Agbonlahore</u>, *how sharp* was he? (Jason Cundy, talkSPORT Radio)

On the assumptions made here, a sentence like (16a) will have the structure shown in highly simplified form below:

(17)   [$_{FORCEP}$ ø [$_{TOPP}$ a book like this [$_{FOCP}$ to whom [$_{FINP}$ would [$_{TP}$ you give]]]]]

On this view, the TOPP projection containing the topic *a book like this* is positioned immediately below FORCEP, and the FOCP containing the focused interrogative phrase *to whom* is positioned between TOPP and FINP.

   Although a structure like (17) in which two different phrases (the ARTP *a book like this* and the PP *to whom*) are both moved to the periphery by A-bar Movement aren't too bad for me (perhaps because I am an experienced linguist used to parsing structures with a complex periphery), many speakers find don't find them acceptable. One reason may be that they violate the following constraint (from Abels 2012: 247) introduced in §1.5.1:

(18)   **Intervention Condition/IC**
    Likes cannot cross likes

The putative IC violation arises because one A-bar moved argument crosses another (in that the fronted ARTP *a book like this* crosses the intervening fronted ARTP *to whom*, and both phrases are arguments of the verb *give*). Another reason may be that they violate the following condition devised by Pesetsky (1982a: 309), where the term 'paths' denotes 'movement paths':

(19)   **Path Containment Condition/PCC**
    If two paths overlap, one must contain the other

The constraint in (19) bars movement paths from cutting across each other – a condition clearly violated in (16a), as shown schematically below:

(20)

[$_{FORCEP}$ ø [$_{TOPP}$ *a book like this* [$_{FOCP}$ **to whom** [$_{FINP}$ would [$_{TP}$ you give — —]]]]]

However, if the topic is generated in situ and reprised by a resumptive pronoun like *it* (as in 16b '<u>That kind of pen</u>, *what* can you use it for?'), no intervention or path containment violation arises.

   The examples discussed above all involve short (clause-internal) movement of an interrogative wh-constituent to spec-FOCP. But what about cases such as the following, which involve long (cross-clausal) movement of an interrogative wh-constituent:

(21)   Where is it thought [that he will go]?

Let's suppose that *where* is a wh-PP with a meaning paraphrasable as 'to what place'. In (21), *where* originates as the complement of the verb *go* in the bracketed complement clause, and ultimately ends up in spec-FOCP in the main clause. But what positions does the wh-PP transit through? Locality considerations restrict long-moved constituents to moving one clause at a time – that is, first to the periphery of the closest clause containing the wh-QP, then to the periphery of the next closest clause, and so on. In part, this is the consequence of the Impenetrability Condition, which was given the following formulation in §4.4.1 (where above/below mean 'c-commanding'/'c-commanded by', and a complete clause is one whose periphery contains FORCEP):

(22)   **Impenetrability Condition/IC**
        Anything below the head H of the highest projection HP in a complete clause is impenetrable to anything above HP

The condition in (22) rules out movement across the edge of FORCEP, because this is the highest projection in the periphery and so IC would prevent *where* from moving into the periphery of the main clause without transiting through the edge of the FORCEP projection in the complement clause. Thus, (22) would rule out the movement represented by the lower (dotted) arrow below:

(23)
[$_{FORCEP}$ ∅ [$_{FOCP}$ where ∅ [$_{FINP}$ ~~where~~ is [$_{TP}$ it ~~is~~ thought

[$_{FORCEP}$ that [$_{FINP}$ he will go ~~where~~]]]]]]

This is because *where* illicitly moves across the edge of the complement clause FORCEP projection headed by *that*, in violation of the Impenetrability Condition (22). However, this locality violation can be avoided if *where* transits through the edge of the complement clause FORCEP, as shown below:

(24)
[$_{FORCEP}$ ∅ [$_{FOCP}$ where ∅ [$_{FINP}$ ~~where~~ is [$_{TP}$ it ~~is~~ thought

[$_{FORCEP}$ ~~where~~ that [$_{FINP}$ he will go ~~where~~]]]]]]

On this view, *where* moves first into spec-FORCEP in the complement clause (as shown by the dotted arrow), then into spec-FINP in the main clause (where it triggers Auxiliary Inversion), and finally into its criterial position in spec-FOCP in the main clause. There is no locality violation in (24), since *where* moves <u>through</u> the edge of FORCEP in the complement clause, and not (illicitly) <u>across</u> the edge of FORCEP.

You should now be able to tackle Exercise 5.1.

5.2   Wh-questions without Interrogative Inversion

In this module, we examine the syntax of wh-questions used without Auxiliary Inversion. We look at two types of these: on the one hand, embedded wh-questions (e.g. wh-question clauses embedded as the complement of some predicate), and on the other hand *how come* questions (which have the idiosyncratic property that for most speakers, they don't allow Auxiliary Inversion even in main/root clauses).

5.2.1   Embedded wh-questions

Given the arguments in Module 5.1 that root wh-questions involve moving an interrogative wh-XP into spec-FOCP, it might at first sight seem plausible to suppose that embedded wh-questions like those bracketed below have a parallel syntax, with the italicised interrogative wh-XP occupying spec-FOCP:

(25)   a. I wonder [*where* she **has** gone]
        b. He enquired [*which apartment* she **was** living in]
        c. He asked [*how much time* the test **would** take]
        d. He was dying to find out [*what hotel* she **was** staying in]

However, there are a number of reasons for thinking that the italicised wh-XPs are not focused in such structures. For one reason, if they were, we would expect them to trigger Auxiliary Inversion in the same way as they do in root/main clause questions like (10) above. After all, negative constituents which are focused in embedded clauses trigger Auxiliary Inversion (in varieties of English like mine), as we see from structures like those bracketed in (26) below:

(26)   a. I reiterated [that *under no circumstances* **would** I accede to his demands]
        b. He swore [that *never again* **would** he get involved in family disputes]
        c. Boris maintained [that *in no way* **had** he acted improperly]

The fact that there is no Auxiliary Inversion in embedded questions like those bracketed in (25) makes it implausible that the fronted wh-constituent is focused.

Further evidence in support of the conclusion that embedded wh-questions don't involve wh-focusing comes from the observation that they can themselves contain an (italicised) focused constituent, as we see from structures such as:

(27)   a.   He asked [why *absolutely everyone* the police had detained –]
         b.   He asked [why *nobody at all* had the police detained –]

The italicised QPs in (27) exhibit characteristics typical of focused constituents: for instance, they are associated with a gap in the comment TP, and cannot be reprised by a resumptive pronoun – as we see from the ungrammaticality of:

(28)   a.   *He asked [why *absolutely everyone* the police had detained <u>them</u>]
         b.   *He asked [why *nobody at all* had the police detained <u>them</u>]

Furthermore, the fronted QP *nobody at all* in (27b) has the further property (typical of focused negative constituents) of triggering Auxiliary Inversion (in varieties of English like mine). Since the italicised constituents in (27) are focused and since the clause periphery can only contain one FOCP constituent, it follows that the peripheral interrogative constituent *why* cannot be focused in embedded questions like (27) if the italicised constituent following it is focused. (It should be noted that speakers who treat Auxiliary Inversion as a root operation won't accept sentences like 27b; and that parsing problems caused by sentences which involve A-bar Movement of multiple XPs to the periphery will further reduce the acceptability of sentences like 27 because they involve both Focus Movement of *absolutely everyone/nobody at all*, and Wh-Movement of *why* – though both sentences are OK for me).

But if *why* is not in spec-FOCP in (27), where is it positioned? A reasonable supposition is that *why* is positioned on the edge of the leftmost projection in the bracketed clause (i.e. on the edge of FORCEP) – and indeed this is what is claimed by Rizzi (1997) and Haegeman (2000b). This assumption would predict that a wide range of other constituents can be positioned below/after the FORCEP constituent containing the interrogative wh-XP – and this prediction is borne out (for speakers like me who don't restrict Auxiliary Inversion to applying in root clauses), as we see from the (heavily contrived) embedded wh-question structure shown in highly simplified form below (which needs to be read with pauses between the different peripheral constituents, to facilitate parsing):

(29)   We must question [$_{FORCEP}$ why [$_{MODP}$ in a civilised society [$_{TOPP}$ drug addicts [$_{MODP}$ when they ask for help [$_{FOCP}$ only rarely [$_{FINP}$ do [$_{TP}$ they get get it]]]]]]]]

The assumption that interrogative wh-constituents in embedded questions are in spec-FORCEP is plausible from a semantic perspective, since the main function of FORCEP is to mark a clause as declarative/interrogative/exclamative/imperative etc. in force/type. And in §1.4.3, we saw that the following conditions determine how clauses are typed:

(30)   **Clause Typing Conditions**
    (i) A clause is interpreted as being of a given type (interrogative or exclamative etc.) if it contains a peripheral clause-typing specifier of the relevant type
    (ii) An indicative clause is interpreted as declarative in type by default if it does not contain a peripheral clause-typing specifier

It follows from condition (30i) that positioning *why* in spec-FORCEP in (29) will type the bracketed complement clause as a wh-question.

A further argument in support of positing that interrogative wh-constituents occupy spec-FORCEP in embedded questions can be formulated in relation to the selectional properties of predicates. Question-asking predicates (like *ask, enquire, wonder* etc.) select an interrogative clause as their complement. Given the assumptions made here, this means that the complement of an interrogative predicate must be a projection with an interrogative specifier. This selectional requirement will be met in a structure like that bracketed in (29) above if *why* is positioned on the edge of the highest (FORCEP) projection in the embedded clause, and if *why* thereby immediately follows the predicate *question*.

The assumption that a wh-XP in an embedded wh-question occupies spec-FORCEP and that FORCEP has to be the highest projection in an embedded clause in order to satisfy selectional requirements predicts that no other constituents will be able to precede an interrogative wh-XP in an embedded wh-question. So, although (as discussed earlier in relation to 16 above) a topic can precede an interrogative wh-XP in a main clause question, the same (*topic+wh*) order is ungrammatical in embedded questions like those bracketed in (31b, 32b) below:

(31)   a. I'm curious [$_{FORCEP}$ *why* [$_{TOPP}$ <u>politicians</u> [$_{FINP}$ people mistrust them]]
        b. *I'm curious [$_{TOPP}$ politicians [$_{FORCEP}$ *why* [$_{FINP}$ people mistrust them]]

(32)   a. I'm unsure [$_{FORCEP}$ *why* [$_{FOCP}$ <u>absolutely everyone</u> [$_{FINP}$ he mistrusts]]
        b. *I'm unsure [$_{FOCP}$ <u>absolutely everyone</u> [$_{FORCEP}$ *why* [$_{FINP}$ he mistrusts]]

According to Rizzi (1997: 301), FORCEP has to be the highest projection in embedded clauses (not TOPP or FOCP) because 'verbs select for declaratives or questions, not for clauses with or without topic (or focus)'. In more general terms, this selectional requirement can be seen as the consequence of a condition such as the following:

(33)   **Selection Condition**
A selector and its selectee (e.g. a verb and its complement) must be as close as possible (ideally, immediately adjacent); the further apart they are, the more degraded the structure becomes

The conclusion to be drawn from our discussion of wh-questions in this section and the last is that in root/main-clause/direct speech wh-questions, the fronted interrogative wh-XP is focused, and moves through spec-FINP (where it triggers Auxiliary Inversion) into its criterial position in spec-FOCP. By contrast, in embedded wh-questions, the interrogative wh-XP is unfocused and moves directly into a different criterial position in spec-FORCEP. This suggests the following generalisation about the syntax of interrogative wh-XPs:

(34)   **Interrogative Generalisation**
(i) A peripheral interrogative XP that triggers Auxiliary Inversion moves through spec-FINP (with FIN attracting a finite auxiliary to adjoin to it) into its criterial position in spec-FOCP
(ii) The criterial position for a peripheral interrogative XP that does not trigger Auxiliary Inversion is spec-FORCEP

It should be noted, however, that (34) is simply a descriptive stipulation, and not a theoretical principle.

5.2.2   *How come* questions

Our discussion has so far neglected a somewhat idiosyncratic type of wh-question illustrated below:

(35)   a. *How come* we can't get things through Congress? (Barack Obama, cited in merriam-webster.com)
b. *How come* you're not at work today? (macmillamdictionary.com)
c. *How come* you told him? (collinsdictionary.com)
d. *How come* you've ended up here? (ldoceonline.com)

Such questions are introduced by *how come*, and have a number of idiosyncratic properties. One of these is that (in most varieties) *how come* doesn't trigger Auxiliary Inversion (unlike *why* in e.g. *Why can't we get things through Congress?*). Another is that *how* and *come* seem to have become fused together to form a single word – and indeed, they are sometimes written as such, as in the following conversation (from the online *urbandictionary*):

(36)   Dave: yo, u hungry?   Todd: no, u?   Dave: howcome?

There are good reasons for taking *how come* to function as a single word in present-day English. Firstly, *how come* is invariable, in the sense that *how* cannot be substituted by other wh-words (as we see in 37a below), and *come* cannot be substituted by other forms of the same verb (as we see in 37b):

(37)   a. *How/*However/*When/*Where* come he resigned?
        b. How *come/*comes/*came/*coming* he resigned?

Secondly, the string *how come* is indivisible, in the sense that no other constituents (like those italicised below) can intrude between the two items:

(38)   How (*in your view,) (*Charles,) come he resigned?

Thirdly, *come* cannot be deleted via an ellipsis operation like Sluicing (leaving *how* on its own) in a sentence like (39) below (from Kim & Kim 2011: 4):

(39)   You're always grinning about something. *How come/*How?*

The fact that the string *how come* is invariable and indivisible is consistent with it having become a single word in present-day English. (An important caveat to note, however, is that the observations made about *how come* above and below hold for most but not for all speakers: there is a great deal of variation between speakers in how they use *how come*, discussed at length in Radford 2018: 216–92.)

Having established that *how come* functions as a single word in colloquial English, let's ask what category it belongs to. Collins (1991) argues that it functions as a complementiser in contemporary English. However, categorising *how come* as a complementiser proves problematic in certain respects. For one thing, *how come* differs from typical interrogative complementisers like *if/whether* in being able to occur in main/root/principal/independent clauses like:

(40)   **How come**/*If/*Whether Boris has resigned?

Moreover, unlike typical complementisers (but like typical wh-words), *how come* allows Sluicing/ellipsis of its complement in sentences such as:

(41)   I suspected he had left, but I wasn't sure **why/how come**/*whether/*if ~~he had left~~

Furthermore, like the adverb *why* (but unlike the complementisers *whether/if*), *how come* can be modified by the adverb *exactly*, for example, in:

(42)   I have no idea **how come exactly/why exactly**/*whether exactly/*if exactly the server is working

In addition, *how come* can be coordinated with other wh-adverbs, as we see from the internet-sourced examples below:

(43)   a. I don't know *why, or where, or how come*, but about 6 years ago my dad decided we didn't need 'The Weasley's' in our life (fanfiction.net)

     b. I spend many hours on the computer assessing *why, when and how come* – Jose did not care (M. Sampedro-Iglesia, *The Heroes Among Us*, WestBow Press, 2011: 32)

Thus, there are numerous respects in which *how come* behaves more like the adverb *why* than like the complementisers *whether/if*. Let's therefore take it to be an ADVP.

But whereabouts in the clause periphery is *how come* positioned? An interesting property of *how come* questions is that (as illustrated below) *how come* can be followed by a range of other peripheral constituents:

(44)   a. **How come** *in the daylight* we can only see the sky but when it's night time you can see space? (helium.imascientist.org.au)

     b. **How come**, *if this is such a huge problem*, that there isn't more useful and legit information on how to overcome it? (nextscientist .com)

     c. **How come** *the things you did last night*, you can't remember them? (Radford 2018: 247)

     d. **How come** *at no point, even when asked to, did* he apologise? (Radford 2018: 243)

Thus, in (44a) *how come* precedes a MODP projection containing the peripheral PP *in the daylight*; in (44b) *how come* precedes a MODP containing an *if*-clause and a FINP containing *that*; in (44c), *how come* precedes the topic DP *the things you did last night*; and in (44d), *how come* precedes a FOCP containing the focused negative PP *at no point*, a MODP containing the reduced subordinate clause *even when asked to*, and a FINP containing the inverted auxiliary *did*. Why does *how come* precede other peripheral constituents in sentences like (44)?

Since *how come* marks the clause it introduces as interrogative in force, and since FORCEP is the highest projection in the clause periphery, a plausible answer is to suppose that *how come* occupies spec-FORCEP – that is, the specifier position in FORCEP. On this assumption, (44d) would have the peripheral structure shown in simplified form below (if we take *how come* to be an ADVP, and treat *even when asked to* as a CONJP headed by the CONJ/subordinating conjunction *when*):

(45)

```
                    FORCEP
           ┌──────────┴──────────┐
        ADVP                   FORCE'
        how          ┌───────────┴───────────┐
        come      FORCE                     FOCP
                    ø            ┌───────────┴───────────┐
                                PP                      FOC'
                               at no          ┌──────────┴──────────┐
                               point        FOC                   MODP
                                ▲            ø          ┌───────────┴──────────┐
                                ┊                     CONJP                   MOD'
                                ┊                   even when       ┌──────────┴──────────┐
                                ┊                   asked to      MOD                    FINP
                                ┊                                  ø          ┌──────────┴──────────┐
                                ┊                                            PP                    FIN'
                                ┊                                             ▲          ┌──────────┴──────────┐
                                └┄┄┄┄┄┄┄┄┄┄┄┄┄┄┄┄┄┄┄┄┄┄┄┄┄┄┄┄┄┄┄┄┄┄┄┄┄┄┄┄┄┄┄┄┄┘         FIN                   TP
                                                                                        ┊ did+ø                he did
                                                                                        └┄┄┄┄┄┄┄┄┄┄ at no point
                                                                                                     apologise
```

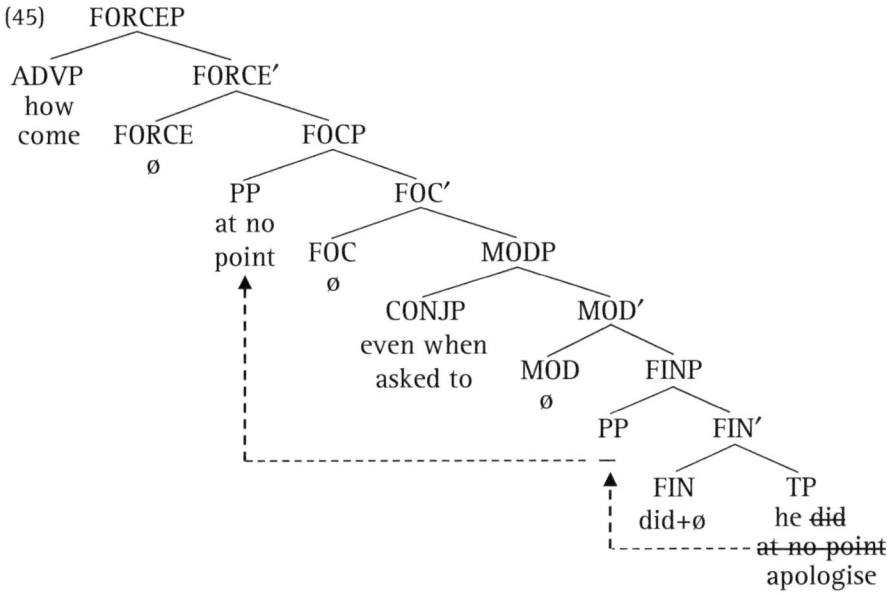

Here, the null FIN head *ø* attracts the focused negative PP *at no point* to become its specifier, and at the same time also attracts the T auxiliary *did* to adjoin to it. Subsequently, the FOC head attracts the focused PP *at no point* to move to its criterial position in spec-FOCP. The overall clause is typed as a wh-question by virtue of its periphery containing the interrogative clause-typing ADVP *how come* in spec-FORCEP.

The FORCEP analysis of *how come* in (45) accounts for *how come* generally being the highest constituent in the periphery of the clause containing it. For example, in the complement clause bracketed below, *how come* precedes the dislocated topic *my passport* and the PP modifier *at the airport* and cannot follow them:

(46) a. It is unclear [how come, *at the airport*, *my passport*, they didn't stamp it]

  b. *It is unclear [*at the airport*, *my passport*, how come they didn't stamp it]

This follows from the assumption that *how come* is in spec-FORCEP, since FORCEP is canonically the highest projection in the clause periphery (in embedded clauses, at least: but see the discussion of 48 below).

A second property accounted for under the FORCEP analysis is that root *how come* questions (unlike other root wh-questions) don't trigger Auxiliary Inversion – as we see from sentences like (35) above. This can be accounted for if we suppose that *how come* is directly merged in situ in spec-FORCEP, and that only an interrogative XP which is focused and transits through spec-FINP triggers Auxiliary Inversion. (Accordingly, Inversion of the auxiliary *did* in 45 above is not triggered by *how come* but rather by the focused negative PP *at no point* transiting through spec-FINP on its way to spec-FOCP.)

A third property which can be accounted for if *how come* is directly merged in situ in spec-FORCEP is that (as observed by Collins 1991) *how come* always has scope over the clause it introduces, never over an embedded clause. In this respect, it differs from *why* – as illustrated below:

(47)   a. *Why* did John say Mary left?

        b. *How come* John said Mary left?

In (47a), *why* can either question the reason for John saying what he said, or the reason for Mary leaving. This ambiguity can be accounted for if *why* can originate either as an adjunct to the VP in the *left*-clause, or as an adjunct to the VP in the *say*-clause: in either eventuality, *why* moves through spec-FINP in the main clause (triggering Auxiliary Inversion) into spec-FOCP. By contrast, in (47b) *how come* questions the reason for John saying what he said, not the reason for Mary leaving. This follows if *how come* is directly merged in spec-FORCEP in the main clause and can only have scope over the clause in which it originates (not over a lower clause). Furthermore, because *how come* is directly generated in spec-FORCEP (and does not move there from spec-FINP), it will not trigger Auxiliary Inversion.

However, a potential complication arising from the claim that *how come* is directly merged in spec-FORCEP is posed by the observation that in root clauses, *how come* can be preceded by peripheral constituents like those italicised below:

(48)   a. *Before you go to bed, after you've had a shower,* **how come** you check your email? (Radford 2018: 244)

        b. *On Thursday,* **how come** there were no lectures? (Radford 2018: 247)

        c. *The mistakes we made when we were young,* **how come** we repeat them when we are old? (Radford 2018: 244)

        d. *The mayor of Trumpton, after campaigning so hard,* **how come** he didn't get re-elected?

Thus, *how come* is preceded by two MODPs containing subordinate clauses introduced by *before/after* in (48a), by a MODP containing the PP *on Thursday* in (48b), by a TOPP containing the dislocated topic *the mistakes we made when we were young* in (48c), and by a TOPP containing the dislocated topic *the mayor of Trumpton* and a MODP containing *after campaigning so hard* in (48d). Moreover, as we see from the (highly contrived) example below, *how come* can be both preceded and followed by other peripheral constituents within the same clause:

(49)   *Humpty Dumpty, if he was so popular,* **how come** his friends, at no
         point, even after he fell off the wall, did they rally round him?

Here, *how come* is preceded by a TOPP containing the dislocated topic
Humpty Dumpty, and a MODP containing a subordinate clause introduced
by *if*; at the same time, *how come* is also followed by a TOPP containing
the dislocated topic *his friends*, a FOCP containing the focused negative PP
at no point, a MODP containing the subordinate clause *even after he fell
off the wall*, and a FINP containing the inverted auxiliary *did*. Of course,
the periphery of (49) is so complex that, to facilitate parsing, the sentence
needs to be read with a pause between successive peripheral constituents –
and even then, parsing such a complex structure remains difficult because
of the memory load required.

The question posed by our discussion above is how we can account for
this seemingly idiosyncratic behavior of *how come*. A plausible answer is to
maintain the FORCEP analysis of *how come*, but to posit that FORCEP is only
required to be the highest peripheral projection in complement clauses like
those bracketed in (46) because of requirement imposed by the Selection Condition (33) for selector and selectee to be as close as possible – more specifically,
because the predicate *unclear* selects a complement headed by an interrogative
FORCEP. We can then suppose that in root/main clauses (since they are not selected by any higher predicate), certain peripheral projections (including TOPP
and MODP projections) can be projected above FORCEP, leading to sentences
like (48) and (49) above. On this view, a sentence like (50a) below would have
the structure in (50b) (simplified by not showing the internal structure of FINP,
or the position within FINP in which *at no point* originates):

(50)   a. Humpty Dumpty, how come, at no point did anyone help him?
         b.

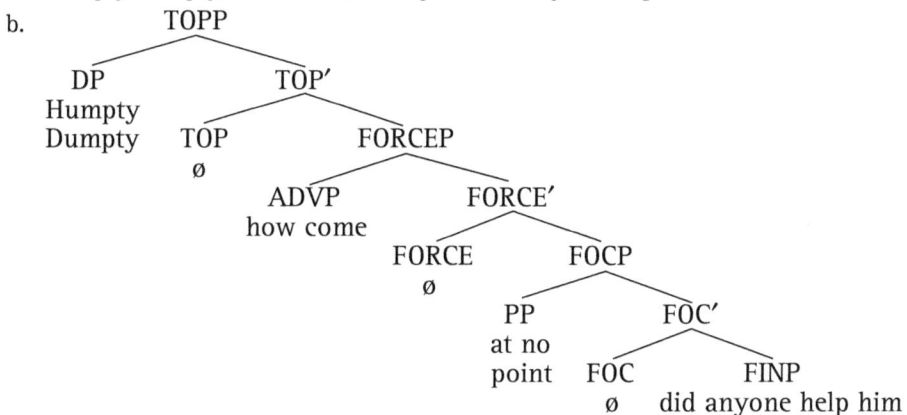

The overall sentence would be interpreted as interrogative in force in accordance with the Clause Typing Condition in (30i) by virtue of containing the
interrogative clause-typing specifier *how come* in its periphery.

However, an alternative approach to accounting for data like (44–49) above is offered by Shlonsky & Soare (2011). They argue that *how come* is directly merged in situ as the specifier of an INTP/interrogative phrase which is a medial peripheral projection (in the sense that it is positioned between FORCEP and FINP): INTP allows one or more TOPP and MODP constituents to be positioned above or below it, and also allows a FOCP and a FINP projection below it. On this view, the order of the peripheral projections in (49) above is as shown in highly simplified form below (where ø is a null FORCE head):

(51)   [$_{FORCEP}$ ø [$_{TOPP}$ Humpty Dumpty [$_{MODP}$ if he was so popular [$_{INTP}$ how come [$_{TOPP}$ his friends [$_{FOCP}$ at no point [$_{MODP}$ even after he fell off the wall [$_{FINP}$ did [$_{TP}$ they rally round him]]]]]]]]]

However, there are two potential problems posed by the INTP analysis. One is that it fails to account for why (even for speakers like me who allow Auxiliary Inversion in non-root clauses) a structure like (51) can't be embedded as the complement of a predicate like *unclear* which selects an interrogative FORCEP complement – as we see from the ungrammaticality of:

(52)   *It is unclear [Humpty Dumpty, if he was so popular, how come his friends, at no point, even after he fell off the wall, did they rally round him]

After all, under the INTP analysis in (51), the predicate *unclear* would indeed select an interrogative FORCEP as its complement. By contrast, under the FORCEP analysis of *how come* in (50), what's wrong with (52) is that *unclear* has a TOPP complement, and not the interrogative FORCEP complement that it requires.

The second potential problem with the INTP analysis of *how come* is that it is not in accordance with the Interrogative Generalisation in (34) above, repeated as (53) below:

(53)   **Interrogative Generalisation**
         (i) A peripheral interrogative XP that triggers Auxiliary Inversion moves through spec-FINP (with FIN attracting a finite auxiliary to adjoin to it) into its criterial position in spec-FOCP
         (ii) The criterial position for a peripheral interrogative XP that does not trigger Auxiliary Inversion is spec-FORCEP

The INTP analysis in (51) is clearly inconsistent with (53ii), which specifies that the criterial position for interrogative XPs that do not trigger Interrogative Inversion is spec-FORCEP. So, from this perspective at least, it can be argued that the FORCEP analysis of *how come* in (45, 50b) is preferable.

You should now be able to tackle Exercise 5.2.

5.3   Yes–no questions

The analyses of root and embedded wh-questions outlined in §5.1.2 and §5.2.1 respectively raise the question of what happens in root and embedded yes–no questions – an issue taken up in this module.

5.3.1   Root yes–no questions

There is evidence (outlined more fully in Radford 2016: 259–65, and Radford 2020: 220–25) that root yes–no questions contain an abstract/null/silent yes–no question operator, and that this operator is responsible for triggering Auxiliary Inversion. The null question operator analysis gains plausibility from the observation that Shakespearean English had main clause yes–no questions containing an inverted auxiliary preceded by the adverbial yes–no question operator *whether*, as illustrated below:

(54)   a.   *Whether* **had** you rather lead mine eyes or eye your master's heels?
           (Mrs Page, *The Merry Wives of Windsor*, III.ii)
        b.   *Whether* **dost** thou profess thyself a knave or a fool? (Lafeu, *All's Well that Ends Well*, IV.v)

The postulation of an adverbial operator which received an overt spellout as *whether* in earlier varieties of English but which has a null spellout in present-day English raises the possibility that yes–no questions have a parallel syntax to that of wh-question operators (like *who, what, where, when* etc.). If so, this would mean that in root yes–no questions, the yes–no question operator (which I will abbreviate as Op_{YNQ}, and treat as an ADVP) is focused, and moves from spec-FINP (where it triggers Auxiliary Inversion) into its criterial position in spec-FOCP. On this view, the periphery of a sentence like:

(55)   Last night, did he go out?

would have the derivation below (where *last night* is treated as a PP headed by a null temporal preposition with a meaning similar to *on/during*, and the sentence is paraphrasable as 'Is it the case that last night he went out?'):

(56)   FORCEP
       /   \
  FORCE   FOCP
    ø   /   \
        ADVP   FOC'
        Op_YNQ   /   \
              FOC   MODP
               ø   /   \
                    PP   MOD'
                   last   /   \
                   night MOD   FINP
                           ø   /   \
                              ADVP   FIN'
                              Op_YNQ   /   \
                                     FIN   TP
                                     did+ø   he did go out

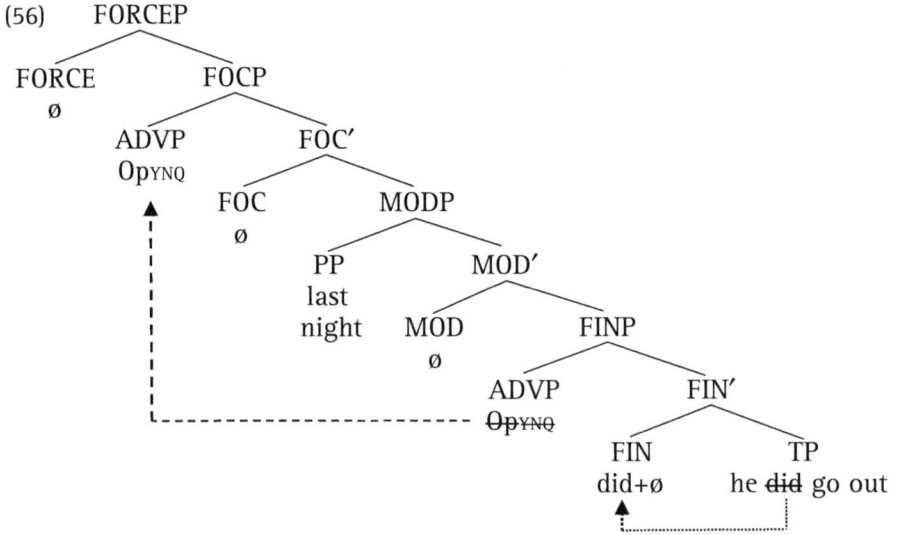

Let's make the following assumption about Auxiliary Inversion:

(57)   **Auxiliary Inversion**
        A null FIN head which has a focused interrogative/negative XP as its specifier attracts a finite auxiliary in T to adjoin to FIN

On this view, FIN (at the point where it has the interrogative operator ADVP *Op*$_{YNQ}$ as its specifier) attracts the T auxiliary *did* to adjoin to the null FIN head. Subsequently, the yes–no question operator (being focused) moves to its criterial position in spec-FOCP. The resulting structure is then spelled out at PF as (55), *Last night, did he go out?* (A possibility that I will set aside here is that the MODP containing *last night* may alternatively occupy a position above FOCP – or perhaps even above FORCEP.)

At first sight, it might seem implausible to suppose that a focused constituent can be null. However, American Sign Language allows null interrogative wh-operators (Petronio & Lillo-Martin 1997). Likewise (as noted by Yamakoshi 2002), wh-drop in questions occurs in Child English (illustrated by the first utterance in 58a below produced by a two-year-old girl), and in colloquial adult Bavarian (illustrated by the omission of *was* 'what' in 58b, where 2PL denotes second person plural, and PRT a discourse particle – and angle brackets indicate constituents present in the syntax but unpronounced in the phonology):

(58)   a.   <What> the porcupine doing? What the porcupine doing?
             (Claire, 2;1; Hill 1983)
        b.   <Was>   dea-ts-n   es   do?
             what   do-2PL-PRT   you   (t)here
             'What are you guys doing (t)here?'
             (Bayer 2010: 32)

The fact that we find null operators in contexts which require a focused interrogative wh-operator adds plausibility to the idea that a null question operator can be focused.

A key claim made in the analysis in (56) above is that the yes–no question operator originates as the specifier of FINP (in which position, it triggers Auxiliary Inversion) and from there moves to its criterial position in spec-FOCP. Such an analysis predicts that the yes–no question operator can only have scope over the clause containing it, not over a lower clause. This claim is borne out by the observation that a question like *Did John say Mary left?* can only question whether John said something, not whether Mary left. This means that the null yes–no question operator is like *how come* in (47b) in respect of only being able to have scope over the clause containing it – but unlike *why* in (47a), in that *why* can originate in a clause below that in which it ends up.

A piece of evidence in support of the focused interrogative operator analysis of yes–no questions is distributional in nature. As we saw in our earlier discussion of wh-questions, an interrogative wh-operator can only be focused (and trigger concomitant Auxiliary Inversion) in a root clause question, not in an embedded question like that bracketed in (59a) below; and as expected under the focused yes–no question operator analysis, yes–no questions show the same restriction against Auxiliary Inversion in embedded questions, as we see in (59b):

(59)   a. *The FBI finally discovered [*where* **had** the hostages been held]
        b. *The FBI finally discovered [Op_{YNQ} **had** the hostages been held in a cave]

This can be accounted for if we suppose that Interrogative Inversion involves focusing of an interrogative operator and is restricted to root clauses. Embedded questions, by contrast, contain an unfocused interrogative operator in spec-FORCEP, and this operator (since it is not focused) does not trigger Auxiliary Inversion – as we see from the (bold-printed) uninverted auxiliary in:

(60)   The FBI finally discovered [*where* the hostages **had** been held]

But what of the syntax of embedded yes–no questions?

5.3.2   Embedded yes–no questions

Embedded yes–no questions are introduced by the complementisers *whether/if*, which have been argued to have an abstract yes–no question operator as their specifier (see e.g. Radford 2016: 263–65, or Radford 2020: 223–35). If we treat embedded yes–no questions in the same way as embedded wh-questions, they will contain a null interrogative operator in spec-FORCEP; and (as illustrated below) this operator will not trigger Inversion of the bold-printed auxiliary because the (italicised) operator is not focused:

(61)   The FBI were hoping to discover [Op_{YNQ} if/whether the hostages **had** been held in a cave]

Since FORCEP can be followed by a wide range of other peripheral constituents (including TOPP, FOCP and MODP), we would expect to find that embedded yes–no questions can contain a wide range of peripheral constituents following *if/whether*. And as the (heavily contrived) embedded question structure bracketed below illustrates, this is indeed the case:

(62)   We all need to probe deep into our consciences and constantly keep asking [$_{FORCEP}$ Op_{YNQ} whether [$_{MODP}$ in a civilised society [$_{TOPP}$ people like that [$_{MODP}$ when they are in trouble [$_{FOCP}$ never ever [$_{FINP}$ should [$_{TP}$ we turn our back on them]]]]]]]]

On this view, embedded yes–no questions contain a null yes–no question operator in spec-FORCEP which serves to type the clause as a yes–no question. (Two caveats should be noted here, however. Firstly, speakers who treat Auxiliary Inversion as a root phenomenon will not accept structures like 62; and secondly, the extreme complexity of the periphery of 62 makes it difficult to parse, and for this reason many speakers will find it unacceptable: to aid parsing, it needs to be read with an audible pause between successive peripheral constituents.)

The analysis outlined here accounts for why other peripheral constituents cannot be positioned between a predicate and a *whether/if*-clause that it selects as its complement – as we see from the contrasts below:

(63)   a. The weather forecasters are now *unsure* [**if** it will snow at Xmas]
         b. *The weather forecasters are now *unsure* [at Xmas **if** it will snow]

(64)   a. I'm *curious* [**whether** the second attack, anyone else witnessed it]
         b. *I'm *curious* [the second attack, **whether** anyone else witnessed it]

In (63a, 64a) the adjectives *unsure/curious* immediately precede the *if/whether* projection that serves as their complement, in accordance with the locality requirement (imposed by the Selection Condition 33) for a selector to be as close as possible to its selectee. By contrast, in (63b) an underlined PP modifier (and in 64b an underlined topic) are positioned between the selector (*unsure/curious*) and its selectee (the *if/whether* projection), in violation of the locality requirement on selection.

Considerations such as those outlined above suggest that the complementisers *if/whether* occupy the head FORCE position of FORCEP in embedded yes–no questions, and have an abstract yes–no question operator as their specifier. This operator can serve to block extraction out of an embedded FORCEP, for example, in a structure such as the following (where *how* is construed as modifying *react*):

(65)   *How* did you wonder [$_{FORCEP}$ Op$_{YNQ}$ [$_{FORCE}$ whether] he would react –]?

The presence of the yes–no question operator in the bracketed spec-FORCEP prevents *how* from moving out of the gap position and transiting through spec-FORCEP in the complement clause and spec-FIN in the main clause, on its way to the italicised spec-FOCP position in the main clause. So, the only option is for *how* to 'jump across' FORCEP and move directly through spec-FINP into spec-FOCP in the main clause, violating both locality requirements (since *how* illicitly moves across the edge of FORCEP in violation of the Impenetrability Condition 22), and the Intervention Condition (18) (since one interrogative operator crosses another).
    You should now be able to tackle Exercise 5.3.

5.4   Exclamative and relative clauses

Having looked at the syntax of wh-questions, we now turn to look at the syntax of two other types of clause that involve Wh-Movement – namely exclamatives on the one hand, and relatives on the other.

5.4.1   Exclamative clauses

Let's begin by looking at the syntax of exclamative wh-clauses. Rizzi (1997: 283) takes a FORCEP projection to serve the function of typing a clause as declarative/interrogative/exclamative, etc. Accordingly, Radford (2004a: 332) suggests that 'exclamative wh-expressions ... move into the specifier position within FORCEP', and thereby type the clause as exclamative. What this would lead us to expect is that when a predicate selects an exclamative clause as its complement, the locality requirement on selection will mean that the exclamative FORCE head will be the highest head in the periphery of the clause, and hence the exclamative wh-constituent will precede any topic, focus or modifier in the periphery of the clause. And indeed, this claim seems to be borne out by an (admittedly contrived) sentence structure such as the following (which needs to be read with a pause between adjacent peripheral projections, as an aid to parsing):

(66)   It's amazing [$_{FORCEP}$ *in how many countries* [$_{TOPP}$ that kind of behaviour [$_{FOCP}$ under no circumstances at all [$_{FINP}$ would [$_{TP}$ it be tolerated]]]]]

Here, *amazing* is a predicate which selects an exclamative clause as its complement. Given the adjacency requirement on selection imposed by the Selection Condition (33), this means that *amazing* must be immediately followed by an exclamative FORCEP – as indeed it is in (66). The exclamative FORCEP is in turn followed by a TOPP projection containing the dislocated topic *that kind of behaviour*; this TOPP is itself followed by a FOCP containing the focused negative PP *under no circumstances at all*; FOCP is followed by a FINP containing the inverted auxiliary *would*; and FINP is followed by a TP containing the subject *it*. (An important point to note is that 66 will be unacceptable to speakers for whom Auxiliary Inversion is a root phenomenon, and to speakers for whom its complex periphery makes the sentence difficult to parse.)

Note that positioning some other constituent between the selecting predicate *amazing* and the selected exclamative FORCEP containing *in how many countries* results in degradation, as illustrated below:

(67)   a. *It's amazing [$_{TOPP}$ that kind of behaviour [$_{FORCEP}$ *in how many countries* [$_{FOCP}$ under no circumstances at all [$_{FINP}$ would [$_{TP}$ it be tolerated]]]]]

        b. *It's amazing [$_{FOCP}$ under no circumstances at all [$_{TOPP}$ that kind of behaviour [$_{FORCEP}$ *in how many countries* [$_{FINP}$ would [$_{TP}$ it be tolerated]]]]]

This is because sentences like (67) violate the Selection Condition (33), in that the selector (*amazing*) is separated from the selectee (the exclamative FORCEP containing the exclamative PP *in how many countries*) by one or more intervening peripheral projections (by TOPP in 67a, and by FOCP and TOPP in 67b). By contrast, in a root exclamative clause (which, by its nature, is not selected by a higher predicate), there is no selectional requirement for FORCEP to be the highest projection in the periphery – and hence a structure such as the following is fine as a root/main clause (if read with a pause between adjacent peripheral projections, as an aid to parsing):

(68)   [$_{TOPP}$ That kind of behaviour [$_{FORCEP}$ *in how many countries* [$_{FOCP}$ under no circumstances at all [$_{FINP}$ would [$_{TP}$ it be tolerated]]]]]

In (68), the dislocated topic *that kind of behaviour* can be positioned above the exclamative FORCEP containing *in how many countries* precisely because there is no higher predicate like *amazing* which requires the exclamative FORCEP to be the highest projection in the periphery of the clause containing it. (Of course, a familiar caveat needs to be made about 68, namely that it will be unacceptable to speakers for whom its complex periphery makes the sentence difficult to parse.)

5.4.2   Relative clauses

Having examined the structure of the clause periphery in interrogative and exclamative clauses so far in this chapter, let's conclude by taking a look at the periphery of (restrictive) relative clauses. Rizzi (1997: 289) maintains that 'relative operators occupy the highest specifier position, the spec of FORCE'. If FORCEP is indeed the highest/leftmost projection in the periphery of a relative clause, it follows that other peripheral constituents (e.g. topic, focus, or modifier constituents) will follow the FORCEP housing the relativiser, as illustrated by the bracketed relative clause in the (heavily contrived) sentence below:

(69)   A university is the kind of place [*where*, **that kind of behaviour**, <u>under no circumstances</u>, *despite pressure from students*, **will** the authorities tolerate it]

As would be expected if FORCEP is the highest projection in a relative clause, the FORCEP containing the italicised relative wh-XP *where* precedes a (bold-printed) topic *that kind of behaviour*, an (underlined) focused negative phrase *under no circumstances*, an (italicised) PP modifier *despite pressure from students*, and a bold-printed inverted auxiliary *will*. On this view, the bracketed relative clause in (69) will have the peripheral structure shown in skeletal form below:

(70)   A university is the kind of place [$_{FORCEP}$ where [$_{TOPP}$ that kind of behaviour [$_{FOCP}$ under no circumstances [$_{MODP}$ despite pressure from students [$_{FINP}$ will [$_{TP}$ the authorities tolerate it]]]]]]

We can then suppose that the FORCEP projection housing relative *where* serves to mark the overall clause as relative in type, as well as marking the clause as declarative in force. (Of course, the caveat should be made about 69/70 that it will be unacceptable to speakers for whom Auxiliary Inversion is a root phenomenon, and to speakers for whom its complex periphery imposes a heavy processing load which makes the sentence extremely difficult to parse.)

However, the FORCEP analysis of relative clauses proves problematic in certain respects. For one thing, it is at variance with the following principle posited by Cinque & Rizzi (2008), introduced in Module 4.1:

(71)   **One Feature One Head Principle**
         Each functional head carries only one interpretable feature

The principle in (71) rules out the possibility of an analysis in which a FORCE head marks both relative clause type and declarative force.

An additional problem with positing that relative clauses are projections of a FORCE head which marks both the relative type and the declarative force of the clause is that not all relative clauses are declarative in force. For example, the bracketed relative clauses in (72) below are interrogative in force:

(72)   a. Mike's leadership was second to none, [without which how else could six novices laugh our way through ten days at minus 40?] (polarchallenge.org)
        b. It's one of them situations now [where Harry, what does he do?] (Ray Parlour, talkSPORT Radio)
        c. Then you launched these podcasts, [which, how many times have these been downloaded]? (Richard Bacon, BBC Radio 5)
        d. This is a vital piece of evidence [which how come the police overlooked?]

Likewise, the relative clauses bracketed in (73) below are imperative in force:

(73)   a. The top speed [which please don't try to reach] is 220 miles an hour (Ferrari test driver, BBC Radio 5)
        b. You will please correct the false statement made last week in your next issue, [after which please don't handle my name at all] (Robin Sterling 2013, *Tales of Old Blount County, Alabama*, Google Books, p. 278)
        c. You will start with completing their application form, [which please be careful to triple check …] (interviewarea.com)
        d. Just a couple of comments, Peter. One regards the spelling of Kanté, [on which see the attached screenshot] (email from me to Peter Trudgill)

And those bracketed in (74) below are exclamative in force:

(74)   a. We were put up in a hotel [where, when we arrived, what a lovely surprise there was waiting for us!]
        b. It was a war [in which, what unspeakable acts of brutality people committed in the name of freedom!]
        c. It was a time [when, how happy people were to lead a simple life!]
        d. It was something [which, how often he had dreamt about!]

Such examples suggest that relative clauses can be not only declarative in force, but alternatively interrogative, imperative or exclamative; this leads us to the conclusion that force and type are different features which (under the One Feature One Head Principle) must be realised on different heads.

    One way of implementing this idea is to suppose that on top of the FORCEP constituent which marks a relative clause as declarative/interrogative/imperative etc. in force, there is a separate projection marking the clause as relative in type, which I will denote as RELP; and indeed this is the position argued for in more recent work by Rizzi (2005, 2013a, 2015a) and Radford (2019). This RELP constituent will be the highest projection in the periphery of a relative clause (in order to be adjacent to its antecedent in non-extraposed restrictive relatives), and will house a wh-XP which serves to type the clause as relative. If so, relative operators like *who/which/where/when* will not be positioned on the edge of FORCEP, but rather on the edge of RELP – as shown in skeletal form for (74a) above in (75) below:

(75)   We were put up in a hotel [$_{RELP}$ where [$_{MODP}$ when we arrived [$_{FORCEP}$ what a lovely surprise [$_{FINP}$ there was waiting for us!]]]]

Although the (italicised) relative operator is often overt (like *which* in 76a below), the edge of RELP can sometimes contain a null relative operator (below shown as Op_{REL}) in place of an overt wh-operator like *which*, as in (76b). Likewise, the (bold-printed) head REL constituent of RELP can either be spelled out overtly (as with *that* in 76b below) or receive a null spellout as ø (as in 76a):

(76)   a. It was something [$_{RELP}$ *which* [$_{REL}$ **ø**] how often he had dreamed about!]
         b. It was something [$_{RELP}$ Op_{REL} [$_{REL}$ **that**] how often he had dreamt about!]

On the assumptions made here, the relative clauses bracketed in (76) above will have the peripheral structure shown in simplified form in (77) below (where – represents the gap left behind by movement of the relative operator *which*/Op_{REL} to spec-FORCEP, and the relative operator is treated as a pronominal DP (like the relative pronoun *lequel* 'the.which' in French):

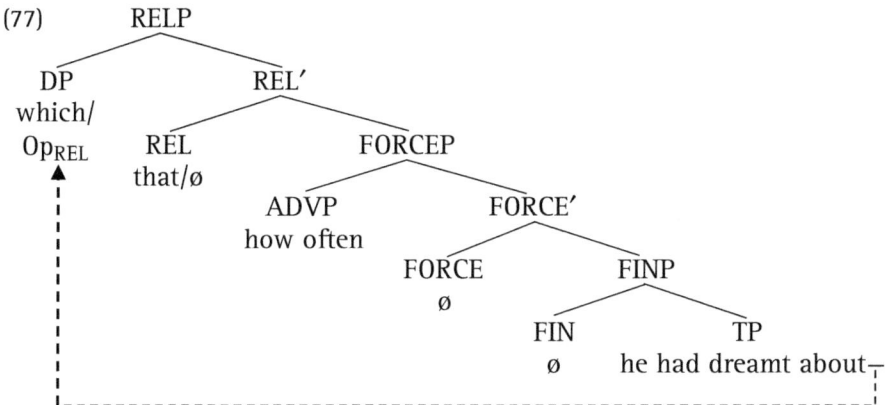

(77)

RELP
├─ DP (which/Op_{REL})
└─ REL'
   ├─ REL (that/ø)
   └─ FORCEP
      ├─ ADVP (how often)
      └─ FORCE'
         ├─ FORCE (ø)
         └─ FINP
            ├─ FIN (ø)
            └─ TP (he had dreamt about—)

The relative operator in spec-RELP can be either overt or null, and serves to type the overall structure as a relative clause. The REL head can likewise either be spelled out as the overt complementiser *that*, or as a null head ø.

However, RELP cannot have both an overt specifier and an overt head, as we see from the ungrammaticality of:

(78)   *It was something [$_{RELP}$ *which* **that** [$_{FORCEP}$ how often he had dreamed about!]]

A structure like (78) is ruled out because it violates a filter introduced in §1.5.2, where it was given the following formulation:

(79)   **Doubly Filled COMP Filter/DFCF**
At the end of a syntactic derivation, any structure in which the edge of a projection headed by an overt complementiser is doubly filled (i.e. contains some other overt constituent) is filtered out as ungrammatical

The DFCF violation arises in (78) because the overt relative complementiser *that* has the overt specifier *which*, leading to the ungrammatical collocation *which that.

An issue which arises from the structure in (77) relates to the movement of the relative operator (either *which* or its null counterpart) from being the complement of *about* to becoming the specifier of the REL head. One question which arises is whether the arrowed Relative Movement operation in (77) satisfies locality requirements on movement, such as the Impenetrability Condition in (22) above, repeated as (80) below:

(80)   **Impenetrability Condition**
Anything below the head H of the highest projection HP in a complete clause is impenetrable to anything above HP

The assumption embodied in (80) allows *which* (or its null operator counterpart) to move directly to spec-RELP across the edge of FINP and across the edge of FORCEP, without violating any locality requirement: the edge of FORCEP and FINP are not barriers to movement in (77) because neither is the highest projection in the periphery (the highest peripheral projection being RELP).

A second question which arises in relation to the derivation in (77) is whether the relative operator (in crossing the exclamative phrase *how often*) violates the following constraint (repeated from 22 above):

(81)   **Intervention Condition**
Likes cannot cross likes

We might expect some kind of intervention effect, since if *how often* moves to the periphery from some position internally within TP, this would mean that one fronted wh-constituent (*which*) moves across another (*how often*). Still, for me at least, the intervention effect is not particularly strong here: this may be because the two types of wh-constituent are different (e.g. *which* is relative, and *how often* is exclamative; and *which* is an argument but *how often* is an adjunct).

The relative clause structures we have looked at so far can be termed gap relatives, since they all involve an ex situ relative operator moving to spec-RELP from some position within TP, leaving a gap behind in the position out of which it moves. However, alongside gap relatives we also find resumptive relatives in which an (overt or null) relative operator is reprised by an (underlined) resumptive pronoun, so resulting in relative clauses like those bracketed below:

(82)   a. King Kong is a movie [*which* you'll laugh yourself sick if you see <u>it</u>] (Ross 1967: 433)

   b. There really may be a lot of interaction [*which* the kid doesn't hear any of <u>it</u>] (Prince 1995: 4)

   c. We were first introduced by a friend [*who*, we will try to protect <u>her</u> privacy] (Prince Harry, BBC Radio 5)

   d. This is a girl [*who*, in real life, you'd never let <u>her</u> have the keys to your house, right?] (Jeremy Clarkson, BBC2 TV)

   e. I really liked flying in an airplane [*that* I understand how <u>it</u> works] (Bever et al. 1976: 150)

   f. We're afraid of things [*that* we don't know what <u>they</u> are] (Ferreira & Swets 2005: 263)

   g. He's a guy [<u>he</u>'s got an incredible knowledge of the game] (Steve Smith, talkSPORT Radio)

   h. Dimitar Berbatov, he's the kind of player [<u>he</u> scores those fancy lobs] (Connor MacNamara, BBC Radio 5)

If we treat such structures in a parallel fashion to the in situ resumptive topic structures discussed in §4.1.2, they will involve an overt or null relative wh-operator directly merged in situ in spec-RELP being reprised by an underlined resumptive pronoun within TP. In (82a–82d) the edge of RELP comprises an overt relative operator (*which/who*) which is the specifier of a null REL head; in (82e–82h) the edge of RELP comprises a null relative operator which is the specifier of a REL head which is spelled out as the overt relative complementiser *that* in (82e, 82f), and as a null relative complementiser in (82g, 82h). Thus, the RELP projections in (82a, 82c, 82e, 82g) will have the structures shown in highly simplified form below:

(83)   a. ... a movie [$_{RELP}$ *which* [$_{REL}$ ø] you'll laugh yourself sick if you see <u>it</u>]

   b. ... a friend [$_{RELP}$ *who* [$_{REL}$ ø] we will try to protect <u>her</u> privacy]

   c. ... an airplane [$_{RELP}$ *Op$_{REL}$* [$_{REL}$ **that**] I understand how <u>it</u> works]

   d. ... a guy [$_{RELP}$ *Op$_{REL}$* [$_{REL}$ ø] <u>he</u>'s got an incredible knowledge of the game]

Where an overt relative operator is used, it is spelled out in its default form (e.g. the relative operator is spelled out as *who* in 82c and 82d because WHO is spelled out as *whose* if genitive, *whom* if accusative in formal styles, and *who* otherwise). For a monograph-length treatment of the syntax of relative clauses in everyday English, see Radford (2019).

You should now be able to tackle Exercise 5.4.

5.5   Summary

This chapter began in Module 5.1 by looking at the phenomenon of Negative Inversion (in structures like *No evidence did they offer*) and Interrogative Inversion (in sentences like *What evidence did they offer?*). I argued that the fronted negative/interrogative XP is focused in both types of structure: it originates internally within TP (here, as the complement of *offer*), and is attracted by a FIN head to transit through spec-FINP (with the FIN head concomitantly triggering Auxiliary Inversion and attracting a finite T auxiliary to adjoin to FIN), before subsequently being attracted by a FOC head to move to its criterial position in spec-FOCP.

In Module 5.2, I looked at wh-questions that don't trigger Auxiliary Inversion. I started by examining complement clause questions (like that italicised in 'I wonder *what evidence they offered*'), and I argued that in such cases, the wh-QP *what evidence* originates within TP (here, as the complement of *offered*) and from there moves directly into spec-FORCEP, where it types the relevant clause as a wh-question. I went on to look at (main and embedded clause) *how come* questions like *How come you were late?* I suggested that these involve *how come* functioning as an ADVP which is directly merged in situ in spec-FORCEP, and does not move there from spec-FINP (so does not trigger Auxiliary Inversion).

In Module 5.3, I turned to look at the syntax of yes–no questions. I started by looking at root yes–no questions with Auxiliary Inversion (like *Did they offer any evidence?*), and argued that these involve a focused (but silent) yes–no operator/Op_{YNQ} which originates in spec-FINP (where it triggers Auxiliary Inversion) and from there moves into its criterial position in spec-FOCP. I went on to discuss embedded yes–no questions like that italicised in 'I wonder *if/whether they offered any evidence.*' I argued that these are FORCEP constituents headed by the interrogative complementiser *if/whether*, and that they contain a null yes–no question operator in spec-FORCEP.

In Module 5.4, I examined exclamative and relative clauses. I began by looking at exclamatives (like *How little evidence they offered!*), and I argued that these involve a FORCE head attracting an exclamative wh-XP (like *how little evidence*) to move from its initial position inside TP (here, as the complement of *offer*) into its criterial position in spec-FORCEP, where it serves to type the clause as exclamative in force. I then turned to look at relative clauses, and I argued that these are RELP constituents which contain within them a separate FORCEP constituent which is usually declarative in force, but can alternatively be interrogative, exclamative or imperative. I argued that the head REL constituent of RELP contains an overt or null complementiser, and that REL has an XP specifier which contains an overt or null relative operator that serves to type the clause as relative, and to link the relative clause to its antecedent. This relative operator moves into spec-RELP from its initial position within TP in gap relatives like that italicised in 'He's someone *who very few people like* – '; but the relative operator is generated in situ in and reprised by a (bold-printed) resumptive constituent in resumptive relatives like 'He's someone *who very few people like* **him**'.

Constructs and operations which have played an important role in our discussion in this chapter include the following:

(18)   **Intervention Condition/IC**
         Likes cannot cross likes

(19)   **Path Containment Condition/PCC**
         If two [movement] paths overlap, one must contain the other

(22)   **Impenetrability Condition**
         Anything below the head H of the highest projection HP in a complete clause is impenetrable to anything above HP

(30)   **Clause Typing Conditions**
         (i) A clause is interpreted as being of a given type (interrogative or exclamative etc.) if it contains a peripheral clause-typing specifier of the relevant type
         (ii) An indicative clause is interpreted as declarative in type by default if it does not contain a peripheral clause-typing specifier

(33)   **Selection Condition**
         A selector and its selectee (e.g. a verb and its complement) must be as close as possible (ideally, immediately adjacent); the further apart they are, the more degraded the structure becomes

(34)   **Interrogative Generalisation**
         (i) A peripheral interrogative XP that triggers Auxiliary Inversion moves through spec-FINP (with FIN attracting a finite auxiliary to adjoin to it) into its criterial position in spec-FOCP
         (ii) The criterial position for a peripheral interrogative XP that does not trigger Auxiliary Inversion is spec-FORCEP

(57)   **Auxiliary Inversion**
A null FIN head which has a focused interrogative/negative XP as its specifier attracts a finite auxiliary in T to adjoin to FIN

(71)   **One Feature One Head Principle**
Each functional head carries only one interpretable feature

(79)   **Doubly Filled COMP Filter/DFCF**
At the end of a syntactic derivation, any structure in which the edge of a projection headed by an overt complementiser is doubly filled (i.e. contains some other overt constituent) is filtered out as ungrammatical

5.6   Bibliographical notes

On **Negative Inversion** in standard varieties of English see Hooper & Thompson (1973), Radford (1988, 2009a, 2009b), Authier (1992), Haegeman (1995, 2000c), Sobin (2003), Büring (2004), Jacobsson (2007), Maekawa (2007), de Clerk (2010), Haegeman (2012), Collins & Postal (2014), Radford & Iwasaki (2015), Francis (2017), Jiménez-Fernández (2018), and Martín (2019).

On **wh-questions** see Chomsky (1957, 1968, 1972, 1973, 1975, 1977, 1980, 1981, 1986a), Katz & Postal (1964), Jacobs & Rosenbaum (1968), Baker (1970), Emonds (1970), Bresnan (1970, 1972, 1976, 1979), Chomsky & Lasnik (1977), Baltin (1982, 2010), Erteschik-Shir (1986), Pesetsky (1989), Lasnik & Saito (1992), Henry (1995), Jayaseelan (1996, 2003), Hallman (1997), Rizzi (1996, 1997, 2000a, 2000b, 2001, 2004a, 2004b, 2005, 2006a, 2006b, 2006c, 2010, 2011, 2012, 2013a, 2013b, 2013c, 2014a, 2014b, 2015a, 2015b), Haegeman & Guéron (1999), Koopman (2000), Haegeman (2000b, 2012), Sobin (2003), Rizzi & Shlonsky (2006, 2007), Cable (2007, 2008, 2010a, 2010b), Cinque & Rizzi (2008, 2010a), Goedegebuure (2009), Shlonsky & Soare (2011), Bayer (2014, 2015, 2016), Rizzi & Cinque (2016), Endo (2014, 2015a, 2015b, 2017, 2018), Rizzi & Bocci (2017), Radford (2018), and Badan & Crocco (2019). On *how come* questions, see Zwicky & Zwicky (1971), Collins (1991), Ochi (2004), Fitzpatrick (2005a), Conroy (2006), Kim & Kim (2011), Shlonsky & Soare (2011), Claridge (2012), Endo (2014, 2015a, 2015b, 2017, 2018), and Radford (2018). On **yes–no questions**, see Katz & Postal (1964), Bresnan (1970), Larson (1985), Grimshaw (1993), Roberts (1993a), den Dikken (2006), Haegeman (2012), and Bianchi & Cruschina (2016).

On **exclamatives** see Elliot (1974), Milner (1978), Grimshaw (1979), Oomen (1979), Gérard (1980), Radford (1980, 1982, 1989, 1997c, 2016, 2020), Huddleston (1993), Obenauer (1994), Benincà (1995, 1996), Michaelis & Lambrecht (1996), Portner & Zanuttini (2000), Zanuttini & Portner (2000, 2003), Gutiérrez-Rexach (2001, 2008), Michaelis (2001), Villalba (2001,

2003, 2008), Ambar (2002), d'Avis (2002, 2016), Beijer (2002), Munaro (2003), Collins (2004), Castroviejo (2006, 2007, 2008, 2010, 2019), Lipták (2006), Miró (2006, 2008), Ono (2006), Ono & Fujii (2006), Sæbø (2006, 2010), Abels (2007, 2010), Marandin (2008), Beyssade (2009), Brandner (2010), Delsing (2010), Jónsson (2010), Yamato (2010), Honda (2011), Kalinina (2011), Chernilovskaya et al. (2012), Rett (2012), Zevakhina (2013), Chernilovskaya (2014), Delfitto & Fiorin (2014), Badan & Cheng (2015), Nouwen & Chernilovskaya (2015), Siemund (2015), Bosque (2017), Zubi-aguirre Sebastián (2017), Palacios Roman (2018), Trotzke & Giannakidou (2019), Vishenkova & Zevakhina (2019), Al-Bataineh (2020), and de Moraes Sieiro (2020).

On **relative clauses** see Quirk (1957), Kuroda (1968), Morgan (1972), Vergnaud (1974), Hirschbühler (1976), Carlson (1977), Bresnan & Grimshaw (1978), Emonds (1979), Erdmann (1980), Ihalainen (1980), Weisler (1980), Harris & Vincent (1980), Cornilescu (1981), Groos & van Riemsdijk (1981), McCawley (1981), Shnukal (1981), Shorrocks (1982), Hirschbühler & Rivero (1983), Borer (1984), Kekalainen (1985), Safir (1986b, 1999), Heim (1987), Kjellmer (1988, 2010), Miller (1988), Kameshima (1989), Fabb (1990), Lebeaux (1991), Borsley (1984, 1992, 1997, 2001), de Vries (1993), Åfarli (1994), Doherty (1994), Jacobsson (1994), Rooryck (1994), Guy & Bayley (1995), Keenan (1985), Prince (1995), Seppänen & Kjellmer (1995), Grosu (1996, 2003), Dubinsky (1997), Reid (1997), Sag (1997), Seppänen (1997), Sigley (1997), Tottie (1997a, 1997b), Geisler (1998), Grosu & Landman (1998), Newbrook (1998), Sauerland (1998, 1999, 2003), Wiltschko (1998), Bianchi (1999, 2000), Comrie (1999, 2002), Khalifa (1999), Alexiadou et al. (2000), Citko (2000, 2001, 2002, 2004, 2008), Zwart (2000), Izvorski (2001), Munaro (2001), Akiyama (2002), Bhatt (2002, 2015), Caponigro (2002, 2004), de Vries (2002, 2006), Tagliamonte (2002), Aoun & Li (2003), Benincà (2003, 2012a, 2012b), del Gobbo (2003), Herrmann (2003, 2005), Loock (2003, 2005, 2007a, 2007b, 2010), Arnold (2004, 2007), Authier & Reed (2005), Adger & Ramchand (2005), Cable (2005), Cecchetto (2005), Heycock (2005), Donati (2006), Hulsey & Sauerland (2006), van Riemsdijk (2006), Fiorentino (2007), Inada (2007), Kayne (2007, 2015), Parry (2007), Cinque (2008, 2011, 2013, 2017b, 2020), Herdan (2008), Sportiche (2008, 2015, 2017), Caponigro & Pearl (2008, 2009), Castillo (2009), Yang (2009), Berizzi (2010), Berizzi & Rossi (2010), Cecchetto & Donati (2010, 2015), Donati & Cecchetto (2011), Benincà & Cinque (2010, 2014), Bertollo & Cavall (2012), Hackl & Nissenbaum (2012), Simonin (2012), Sistrunk (2012), Boef (2013), Caponigro et al. (2013), Suárez-Gómez (2014), Collins (2015), Collins & Radford (2015), Haegeman et al. (2015), Hinrichs et al. (2015), Kalivoda & Zyman (2015), Sportiche (2015, 2017), Deal (2016), Douglas (2016), Patterson & Caponigro (2016), Radford (2016, 2019), Burke (2017), and Wen (2020).

On **resumptive relatives** (and the use of resumptives more generally), see Kroch (1981), Chao & Sells (1983), Sells (1984, 1987), Engdahl (1985), Prince (1990, 1995), Demirdache (1991), Contreras (1991), Erteschik-Shir (1992), Shlonsky (1992), Bondaruk (1995), Dickey (1996), Suñer (1998), McDaniel & Cowart (1999), Sharvit (1999), Aoun (2000), Aoun et al. (2001), McKee & McDaniel (2001), Alexopoulou & Keller (2002, 2007), Cresswell (2002), McCloskey (2006a, 2017a, 2017b), Rouveret (2002, 2011), Boeckx (2003), Asudeh (2004, 2011a, 2012), Merchant (2004b), Cann et al. (2005), Ferreira & Swets (2005), Grolla (2005), Szczegielniak (2005), Šímová (2005), Alexopoulou (2006, 2010), Salzmann (2006, 2011), Bianchi (2008), Bošković (2009), Friedmann et al. (2009), Nakamura (2009), Omaki & Nakao (2010), Heestand et al. (2011), Keffala (2011), Keffala & Goodall (2011), Clemens et al. (2012), Han et al. (2012), Beltrama (2013), Hofmeister & Norcliffe (2013), Polinsky et al. (2013), Ackerman et al. (2014), Müller (2014), Sichel (2014), Cerron-Palomino (2015), Francis et al. (2015), Hladnik (2015), Beltrama & Xiang (2016), Blythe (2016), Guz (2017), Keshev & Meltzer-Asscher (2017), Morgan & Wagers (2018), Checa-Garcia (2019), Radford (2019), and Loss & Wicklund (2020).

5.7 Workbook

In the exercises below, an [M] after an example sentence indicates that a model answer is provided in the free-to-download *Students' Answerbook* (and in the *Teachers' Answerbook* as well). You will find it helpful to look at this model answer before attempting to tackle other examples in the exercise. Some other exercise examples have an [S] after them, indicating that they are for self-study: this means that after reading the relevant module (and those preceding it), and looking at the helpful hints and model answer associated with the exercise, students should be able to analyse these self-study examples on their own, and then compare their answers with those provided in the *Students' Answerbook*. The remaining exercise examples (i.e. those not marked with [M] or [S] after them) are intended for teachers to use as the basis for hands-on problem-solving work in seminars, classes, or assignments: answers to all of these non-self-study examples are provided in the *Teachers' Answerbook*. Note that Exercise 5.1 tests you on Module 5.1, Exercise 5.2 on Module 5.2, and so on; and that each exercise in a given chapter presupposes familiarity with material covered in earlier chapters and in earlier modules of the same chapter. Unparenthesised numbers like 4 refer to material in the exercises, whereas parenthesised numbers like (22) refer to examples and conditions in the main text of the book.

EXERCISE 5.1

This exercise is designed to be attempted after reading Module 5.1 and the chapters preceding it.

Discuss the structure of the periphery of the clauses in the sentences below (in the case of sentences containing a bracketed clause, concerning yourself only with the periphery of the bracketed clause):

1   I must admit [that a scene as grotesque as that, never before, in all my life, have I witnessed] [M]
2   Nothing at all, even under duress, did he say [S]
3   I'm sure [that a player like that, no way, under any circumstances, would they sell to a rival team]
4   That painting, how much, in the end, did you sell *(it) for? [S]
5   How much, in an average year, of your salary do you lose in tax?
6   At no point, for any reason, would, under any circumstances, the men give up
7   What, when you met him, did he say that on no account, at the meeting, should you do? [S]
8   What did Mary claim that they stole? [S]
9   What did Mary claim did they steal? (Belfast English, Henry 1995: 108)
10 What now do you think you are? (diablo.fandom.com)

Note that the notation *(it) in 4 means 'the sentence is grammatical if *it* is used, but ungrammatical if *it* is omitted'.

Helpful hints

Assume that all the structures in 1–8 are grammatical – as they are in my own variety of English (though speakers who treat Auxiliary Inversion as a root phenomenon, or who find sentences with a complex periphery hard to parse may find some of the sentences degraded). In each example, concern yourself only with the structure of the peripheral projections in the relevant clauses, not with the internal structure of the TP beneath these. In 2 take *nothing at all* to be a QP and *even under duress* to be a PP; in 3 take *a player like that* to be an ARTP, and *no way* to be a PP headed by a null variant of *in*; in 4 take *how much* to be a QP (perhaps an elliptical form of *how much money*); in 5 take *how much of your salary* to originate as a QP which is the complement of *lose*, and bear in mind the possibility of split/discontinuous spellout (and the spellout rules in 14 and 15 below); in 7 take *when you met him* to be a CONJP headed by the subordinating conjunction/CONJ *when*. In all these cases, don't concern yourself with the internal structure of the relevant QP/ARTP/PP/CONJP constituents, or with the internal structure of TP constituents. In relation to 6, note that most speakers find it unacceptable (why do you think this is?), though it is OK for me: bear in mind the possibility that FINP recursion can give rise to FINP+MODP+FINP structures. Note that 9 is an example of interrogative Inversion in Belfast English, and that the complement of *claim* in this sentence cannot be introduced by the complementiser *that*, so might be a truncated clause which projects only as far as FINP.

Where relevant, consider the possible role played by one or more of the following:

11   **Intervention Condition** (= 18)
     Likes cannot cross likes

12   **Impenetrability Condition** (= 22)
     Anything below the head H of the highest projection HP in the periphery of a complete clause is impenetrable to anything above HP

13   **Path Containment Condition** (= 19)
     If two movement paths overlap, one must contain the other

14   **Low Spellout Rule** (from §2.3.3)
     A KP/PP/CP which is the lowest/rightmost constituent of a larger phrase that undergoes movement can be spelled out on a lower copy of the moved phrase

15   **Default Spellout Rule/DSR** (from §1.4.1)
     For a constituent whose spellout is not determined in some other way, the highest copy of the constituent is overtly pronounced, and any lower copies are silent

EXERCISE 5.2

This exercise is designed to be attempted after reading Module 5.2 and the module and chapters preceding it.

Discuss the structure of the periphery of the interrogative clauses in the sentences below (analysing only the bracketed complement clauses in examples so marked):

1   I wonder [where, the homeless, in times of crisis, they go] [M]
2   He was unaware [what kind of food, on no account, if you are diabetic, should you eat] [S]
3   Capello has to know [who, when the chips are down, that he can trust] (Graham Taylor, BBC Radio 5) [S]
4   I wonder [how many other clubs, if their entire first team is on that kind of money] (Bob Beech, talkSPORT Radio)

5 Why, at no point, despite being ill, did he call a doctor?

6 You never know [life, where it takes you] (Ray Parlour, talkSPORT Radio) [S]

7 He protested [that where else, at the time, could he have gone?]

8 How come, in spite of subsidies, that the bank collapsed? [S]

9 How come Humpty Dumpty, after the fall, they couldn't mend?

10 How come at no point, even after the scandal, did they investigate him? [S]

11 The alibi he gave, how come at no point, in spite of requests, did anyone check *(it)?

12 (*I wonder) during the trial, the main defence witness, how come the DA didn't cross-examine him?

Say which structures are non-standard, and why: note that speakers who treat Auxiliary Inversion as a root phenomenon, or who find sentences with an extremely complex periphery hard to parse may find some of the sentences degraded. Note too that the use of the complementiser *that* in 3, 8 is accepted by some speakers (including me) but not by most, that 4 is highly marked (i.e. strikes most speakers – including me – as weird), and that the word order in the bracketed clause in 6 likewise strikes many speakers (including me) as very odd. The notation *(it) in 11 means 'the sentence is grammatical with *it*, but ungrammatical without *it*'; the notation (*I wonder) in 12 means 'the sentence is ungrammatical with *I wonder*, but grammatical without it.' The phrase 'when the chips are down' in 3 means 'when things are going badly'.

Helpful hints

Concern yourself only with the structure of the peripheral projections in each relevant clause, not with that of the TPs beneath these. Make the following assumptions about the categorial status of various peripheral constituents, but don't concern yourself with their internal structure: *what kind of food*, *who*, and *how many other clubs* are QPs; *the homeless*, *Humpty Dumpty*, *the alibi he gave*, *the main defence witness* and *life* are DPs (headed by an overt or null determiner); *why, where, where else, despite being ill*, and *even after the scandal* are PPs (headed by an overt or null preposition); *if you are diabetic* and *when the chips are down* are CONJPs/subordinate clause projections headed by the CONJ/subordinating conjunction *if/when*. In addition, in relevant sentences, consider the role played by one or more of the following:

13   **Interrogative Generalisation (= 34)**
         (i) A peripheral interrogative XP that triggers Auxiliary Inversion moves from spec-FINP (with FIN attracting a finite auxiliary to adjoin to it) into its criterial position in spec-FOCP
         (ii) The criterial position for a peripheral interrogative XP that does not trigger Auxiliary Inversion is spec-FORCEP

14   **Intervention Condition** (= 18)

Likes cannot cross likes

15   **Minimality Condition** (from §1.3.2)

A moved constituent must move to the minimal/closest potential landing site above it

16   **Selection Condition** (= 33)

A selector and its selectee (e.g. a verb and its complement) must be as close as possible (ideally, immediately adjacent); the further apart they are, the more degraded the structure becomes

EXERCISE 5.3

This exercise is designed to be attempted after reading Module 5.3 and the modules and chapters preceding it.

Discuss the structure of the periphery of the interrogative clauses in the sentences below (in the case of sentences 6–9, concerning yourself only with the periphery of the bracketed complement clause):

1   During the demonstration, the police, did they arrest anyone? [M]
2   The president, if you need support, can you count on *(him)? [S]
3   At any point, did anyone threaten you? [S]
4   Did at any point did anybody ever point a gun at you? (courtlistener.com)
5   Crisp, yummy and delicious potato chips, do you want to eat? (pinterest)
6   He asked [if, the team captain, under no circumstances, at the end of the season, would they sell to a rival]
7   I wonder [whether, at some stage, that Graham Potter might think the guile and invention of Adam Lallana might pay dividends today] (Darren Fletcher, Sky Sports TV) [S]
8   It worries me now [that Terry, does he really want to play for England?] (Martin Keown, BBC Radio 5)
9   *It's unclear [any of the suspects if the police arrested] [S]

Say what is unusual/noteworthy about some of the sentences and what challenges (if any) they pose to the description of yes–no questions given in Module 5.3: note that 4, 7, 8 are non-standard structures, and for me, 5 feels odd. Note also that speakers who treat Auxiliary Inversion as a root phenomenon, or who find sentences with a complex periphery hard to parse may find some of the sentences degraded. The notation *(him) in 2 means that the sentence is grammatical if *him* is used, but ungrammatical without *him*.

Helpful hints

Concern yourself only with the structure of the peripheral projections in the relevant clause, not with the internal structure of the TP beneath these. Make the following assumptions about the categorial status of various peripheral constituents, but don't concern yourself with their internal structure: in 2, take *if you need support* to be a CONJP/projection of the subordinating CONJ/conjunction *if*; in 5, take *crisp, yummy and delicious potato chips* to be a QP headed by a null quantifier meaning 'an unspecified quantity of'; in 6 take *the team captain* to be a DP; in 8 take *Terry* to be a DP headed by a null determiner; and in 9 take *any of the suspects* to be a QP. Bear in mind the following assumptions/conditions:

10   Intervention Condition (= 18)

        Likes cannot cross likes

11   Path Containment Condition (= 19)

        If two [movement] paths overlap, one must contain the other

12   Impenetrability Condition (= 22)

        Anything below the head H of the highest projection HP in the periphery
        of a complete clause is impenetrable to anything above HP

13   Selection Condition (= 33)

        A selector and its selectee (e.g. a verb and its complement) must be as
        close as possible (ideally, immediately adjacent); the further apart they
        are, the more degraded the structure becomes

14   Auxiliary Inversion (= 57)

        A null FIN head which has a focused interrogative/negative XP as its
        specifier attracts a finite auxiliary in T to adjoin to FIN

EXERCISE 5.4

This exercise is designed to be attempted after reading Module 5.4 and the modules and chapters preceding it.

Discuss the structure of the periphery of the exclamative/relative clauses in the sentences below (in the case of sentences containing a bracketed clause, concerning yourself only with the periphery of the bracketed clause):

1   We all know [what a job that Luis Suarez has done since he's been at the club] (Micky Gray, talkSPORT Radio) [M]

2   Look [how close, on the corners, that Valentino is] (Julian Ryder, BT Sports TV = 'Look how close moto GP champion Valentino Rossi is to the edge of the track when he rides round corners')

3   Aaron Ramsey, again, what a season that he's having! (Ray Parlour, talkSPORT Radio)

4   *(To) how many people, nothing at all, at Xmas, did Scrooge give! [S]

5   It's something [that, off the pitch, that we've got to help the players deal with] (Football executive, BBC Radio 5)

6   They need to be solid at the back against a Spanish team [that what a goal they scored!] (Ray Parlour, talkSPORT Radio) [S]

7   Joe Hart has come out to look at the wall, [which, Negredo, is he gonna join?] (Clive Tyldesley, Sky Sports TV)

8   I am growing chillies this year which is something [never have I grown before] (luxurycolumnist.com) [S]

9   As Liverpool chase the game, there may be more room [in which for Manchester United to manoeuvre] (Clive Tyldesley, Sky Sports TV)

Say what is unusual/noteworthy about some of the sentences and what challenges (if any) they pose to the assumptions made in Module 5.4. Note that the use of *that* in 1–3 and the second occurrence of *that* in 5 is generally regarded as non-standard, as is the *for*-infinitive structure in 9. Note also that speakers who treat Auxiliary Inversion as a root phenomenon, or who find sentences with a complex periphery hard to parse may find relevant sentences degraded. The notation *(to)* in 4 means that the sentence is grammatical if *to* is used, but ungrammatical without *to*.

Helpful hints

Concern yourself only with the structure of the peripheral projections in the relevant exclamative or interrogative clauses, not with the internal structure of the TP beneath these. Make the following assumptions about the categorial status of various peripheral constituents, but don't concern yourself with their internal structure: the phrases *what a job*, *what a season*, *what a goal*, and *how many people* are exclamative QPs, *how close* is an exclamative AP, and *nothing at all* is a negative QP; proper names like *Aaron Ramsey* and *Negredo* are DPs; *never* is a PP headed by a null preposition, paraphrasable as 'at no time'; and likewise *again* is a PP with a more abstract structure paraphrasable as 'on another occasion'. Bear in mind the assumptions in 10 and 11 below made in Module 5.4, and the further assumptions/conditions in 12–19:

10   Exclamative clauses are FORCEP constituents which involve an exclamative XP moving from some position within TP into its criterial position in spec-FORCEP, where it serves to type the relevant clause as exclamative in force

11 Relative clauses are RELP constituents whose specifier is an overt or null relative XP (e.g. the overt DP *which* or the null relative DP operator Op_{REL}) and whose head is an overt complementiser like *that*, or a null complementiser. In resumptive relatives, the relative wh-XP is generated in situ in spec-RELP; in gap relatives, the relative wh-XP moves from a position within TP to spec-RELP, leaving a gap behind. Beneath RELP, there is a FORCEP which marks the relative clause as for example, interrogative, exclamative, imperative, or declarative etc. in force.

12 **Auxiliary Inversion** (= 57)
A null FIN head which has a focused interrogative/negative XP as its specifier attracts a finite auxiliary in T to adjoin to it

13 **Minimality Condition** (from §1.3.2)
A moved constituent must move to the minimal/closest potential landing site above it

14 **Intervention Condition** (= 18)
Likes cannot cross likes

15 **Path Containment Condition** (= 19)
If two [movement] paths overlap, one must contain the other

16 **Impenetrability Condition** (= 22)
Anything below the head H of the highest projection HP in the periphery of a complete clause is impenetrable to anything above HP

17 **Selection Condition** (= 33)
A selector and its selectee (e.g. a verb and its complement) must be as close as possible (ideally, immediately adjacent); the further apart they are, the more degraded the structure becomes

18 **Doubly Filled COMP Filter** (revised version of 79)
At the end of a syntactic derivation, a structure is filtered out as ungrammatical if it contains a clause whose periphery includes an overt complementiser c-commanded by some other overt constituent within the periphery of the same clause

19 **Distinctness Condition** (from §4.1.3)
At PF, any sequence <α, α> of two adjacent non-distinct constituents is degraded

6 | The subperiphery

6.0 Overview

Under the traditional CP+TP+VP analysis of clause structure, the periphery of the clause is analysed as a CP projection, and the subperiphery (i.e. that part of the clause structure positioned between the CP periphery and the VP core) is analysed as a TP projection. But in this chapter, we'll look at evidence that the subperiphery has a more articulated/complex structure, and comprises a number of distinct projections, with each projection housing a different kind of subperipheral constituent (e.g. an auxiliary, or subject, or adverbial modifier, or floating quantifier, and so on). The term subperiphery used here corresponds broadly to the term 'middle field' used in Germanic Linguistics.

6.1 Auxiliary and subject projections

Under the classic CP+TP+VP analysis of clause structure, finite clauses can contain an auxiliary occupying the head T position of TP, with the subject of the auxiliary occupying spec-TP. In this module, however, we'll look at evidence suggesting that auxiliaries and their subjects are housed in separate projections.

6.1.1 Auxiliary projections

Evidence from sentences such as the following suggests that the subperiphery can contain other (italicised) auxiliaries in addition to (a bold-printed) finite auxiliary in T:

(1)   He **might** *have been being* held in solitary (confinement)

Here, the clause contains the modal auxiliary *might*, the perfect auxiliary *have*, the progressive auxiliary *been*, and the passive voice auxiliary *being*. Superficially, the auxiliary *might* occupies the head T position of TP, since (like a typical finite T auxiliary), it can undergo Inversion (i.e. T-to-C movement) in sentences like:

(2)   *Might* he have been being held in solitary?

If we assume that, in the same way as *might* heads a TP projection of its own, so too the perfect aspect auxiliary *have* heads a PERFP projection, the progressive aspect auxiliary *been* heads a PROGP projection, and the passive voice auxiliary *being* heads a VOICEP projection, the subperiphery of the sentence in (1) will have the following structure:

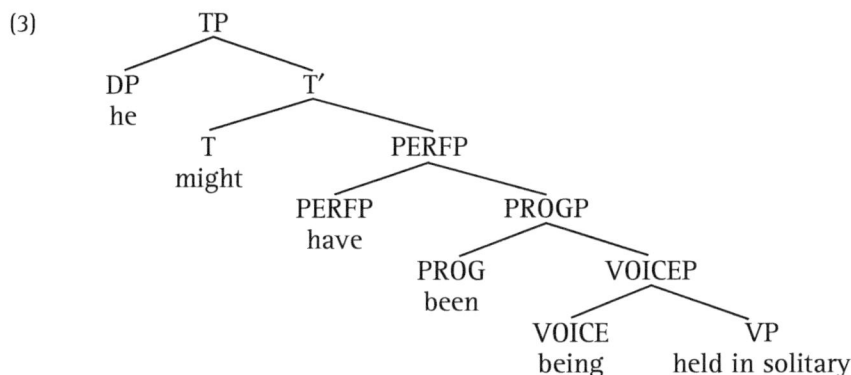

(3)

```
                    TP
            ┌───────┴───────┐
           DP               T′
           he        ┌──────┴──────┐
                     T           PERFP
                   might    ┌──────┴──────┐
                          PERFP         PROGP
                          have      ┌─────┴─────┐
                                   PROG       VOICEP
                                   been    ┌────┴────┐
                                         VOICE       VP
                                         being   held in solitary
```

(Since the focus here is on the subperiphery, for the sake of expository simplicity, I generally omit any representation of the clause periphery in tree diagrams in this chapter.)

Some evidence in support of the structure in (3) comes from ellipsis. An auxiliary typically allows its complement to undergo ellipsis in an appropriate discourse setting. And, just as the analysis in (3) predicts, the T auxiliary *might* allows ellipsis of its complement (marked by strikethrough below) in the utterance produced by the second speaker in (4a) below, so does the PERF auxiliary *have* in (4b), the PROG auxiliary *been* in (4c), and the VOICE auxiliary *being* in (4d):

(4)　　FIRST SPEAKER:　　Do you think he might have been being held in solitary?
　　　SECOND SPEAKER:　a.　Yes, he **might** ~~have been being held in solitary~~
　　　　　　　　　　　　b.　Yes, he might **have** ~~been being held in solitary~~
　　　　　　　　　　　　c.　Yes, he might have **been** ~~being held in solitary~~
　　　　　　　　　　　　d.　Yes, he might have been **being** ~~held in solitary~~

In accordance with Grice's (1975) conversational maxim 'Be concise', a more concise response like (4a) is preferred to a more repetitious response like (4d) – and in addition, the string *been being* in (4d) feels awkward, perhaps because it falls foul of an Anti-Iteration Filter which renders a string of two or more words which are similar in form degraded (and the same filter makes 1 ungainly as well).

However, an interesting issue which arises in relation to the structure in (3) concerns the morphosyntax of the auxiliary *might*. This marks both modality (more specifically, possibility) and past tense. There are two reasons for treating *might* as the past tense of *may*. Firstly, *might* ends in the same past tense suffix -*t* as irregular past tense verbs like *sent/kept/bought/felt/ left/lost/meant* etc. And secondly, when the present tense modal *may* is used in direct speech (as in 5a below), it is transposed into the past tense form *might* in indirect/reported speech after a past tense verb like *said* (as in 5b):

(5)   a. 'I **may** be free tomorrow morning', Sam said
        b. Sam said that she **might** be free the following morning

We can therefore conclude that *might* marks both modality and past tense.

   This is significant because Cinque & Rizzi (2008) argued for a featural uniqueness principle which was outlined in Module 4.1 as follows (where interpretable features are those contributing to meaning):

(6)   **One Feature One Head Principle**
        Each functional head carries only one interpretable feature

The principle in (6) entails that since tense and modality are different interpretable features, they must originate on separate heads (tense on a T/tense head, and modality on an M/modal head). In the case of our sentence (1), this means that *may* originates as the head M constituent of an MP/modal projection, and then (via Head Movement) adjoins to a past tense affix/*Af* in T, in the manner shown by the arrow below (where the internal structure of PERFP is not shown, because our concern here is with the modal):

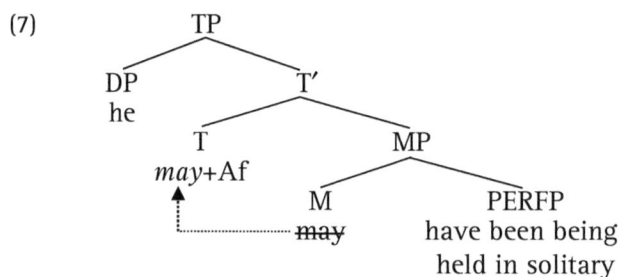

(7)
```
                    TP
              _____|_____
            DP             T′
            he        _____|_____
                    T             MP
                 may+Af       ____|____
                   ↑        M           PERFP
                   └┄┄┄┄┄┄ may      have been being
                                    held in solitary
```

If the affix in T is present tense, the *may+Af* complex in T will be spelled out as *may* in the PF component; if the affix is past tense, *may+Af* will be spelled out as *might*.

   The analysis in (7) has implications for other finite auxiliaries. For example, consider the syntax of the auxiliaries italicised below:

(8)   a. He *has* been held in solitary
        b. He *is* being held in solitary
        c. He *was* held in solitary

In (8a), *has* marks both present tense and perfect aspect. Thus, the One Feature One Head Principle in (6) would suggest that *have* originates as a PERF head marking perfect aspect, and from there moves to adjoin to a present-tense affix in T, in the manner shown by the arrow below:

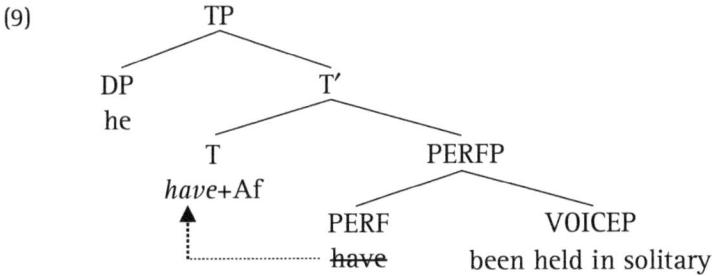

(9)

```
                    TP
           ┌─────────┴─────────┐
          DP                   T'
          he          ┌────────┴────────┐
                      T               PERFP
                   have+Af      ┌────────┴────────┐
                      ↑       PERF            VOICEP
                      ┊····················· have    been held in solitary
```

If (as here) the affix is present tense and has a third person singular subject, it will be spelled out at PF as -s, and this affix will be attached to a contracted stem form *ha-* of the perfect auxiliary HAVE to form *has*. In much the same way, the italicised progressive aspect auxiliary BE in (8b) will originate as a PROG head which raises to attach to a (present) tense affix in T; and the passive voice auxiliary BE in (8c) will originate as a VOICE head which raises to attach to a (past) tense affix in T (and thus is spelled out as *was*). So, on this view, finite auxiliaries have a complex (split projection) structure, and originate as the head of a lower auxiliary projection MP/PERFP/PROGP/VOICEP, and from there raise to adjoin to a (past or present) tense affix in T. (A potential exception is the auxiliary *do*; if this marks only present/past tense, it can be taken to originate in T.)

The split projection analysis of finite auxiliaries outlined above has interesting implications for the syntax of *need* in negative sentences such as:

(10) a. He *need* **not** worry about anything (englishforums.com)
      b. Globalisation *need* **not** mean deregulation (ft.com)
      c. A conventional kitchen layout *need* **not** be boring (raymunnkitchens.co.uk)
      d. He *need* **not** have been concerned (yourdictionary.com)
      e. Tax *need* **not** be taxing (Her Majesty's Revenue and Customs)

In these sentences, *need* is a present tense modal auxiliary expressing necessity, as we see from the fact that (like other modals such as *may/can/must/will*), it does not carry the suffix -s when used with a third person singular subject. But there are two other properties of *need* which are interesting here. Firstly, *need* is a narrow scope modal, in the sense that it falls within the scope of (i.e. is modified by) the negative adverb *not* in sentences like (10): hence (10a) is paraphrasable as 'It is **not** *necessary* for him to worry about anything' (and not as 'It is *necessary* for him **not** to worry about anything'). And secondly, *need* (when used as an auxiliary) is a polarity item which must originate in a position where it is within the scope of a negative (or interrogative, or conditional) constituent – hence the ungrammaticality of a sentence such as *He need worry about everything.*

Such considerations suggest that the modal *need* originates in (10) as the head M/modal constituent of an MP/modal phrase projection positioned below the NEGP constituent containing *not*, and that the modal *need* raises from M to adjoin to a present tense affix in T. On this view, (10a) will be derived as follows. The verb *worry* first-merges with the PP *about anything* and second-merges with the pronominal DP *he* to form the VP *he worry about anything.* This VP is then merged with the M/modal head *need* to form the MP/modal projection *need he worry about anything.* The resulting MP is merged with a null NEG head which has the ADVP *not* as its specifier to form the NEGP below (simplified by not showing the internal structure of the VP, because this is not at issue here):

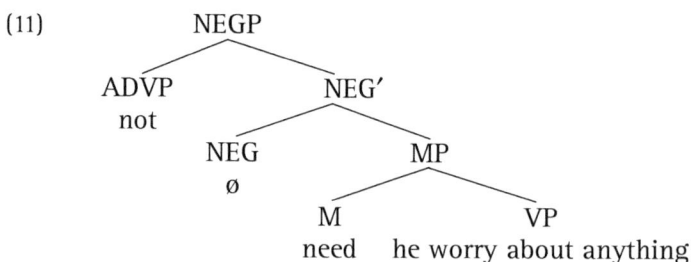

(11)

```
              NEGP
            /      \
        ADVP       NEG′
        not       /    \
                NEG      MP
                 ø      /   \
                       M     VP
                     need  he worry about anything
```

The negative ADVP *not* here c-commands *need*, thereby accounting for *not* having scope over *need*, and for *not* licensing the use of the polarity item *need* (and also licensing the additional polarity item *anything*).

The NEGP in (11) is then merged with a present tense affix/*Af* in T. This affix attracts the modal stem *need* to adjoin to it; and in addition, the EPP feature on T attracts *he* to raise to spec-TP, so deriving the structure below:

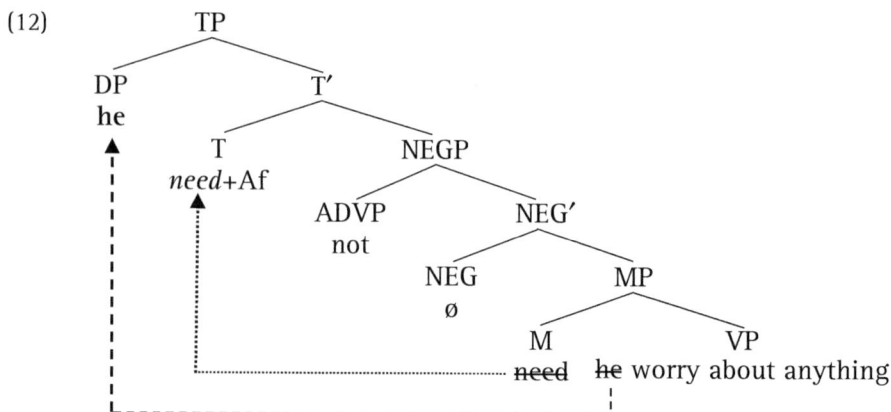

(12)

```
                    TP
                  /    \
             DP          T′
             he        /    \
              ▲      T        NEGP
              ┆   need+Af    /    \
              ┆     ▲     ADVP     NEG′
              ┆     ┆     not     /    \
              ┆     ┆          NEG      MP
              ┆     ┆           ø      /   \
              ┆     ┆                 M     VP
              ┆     ┆·············· need  he worry about anything
              └ ─ ─ ─ ─ ─ ─ ─ ─ ─ ─ ─ ─ ─ ─ ─ ┘
```

Since a present tense affix attached to a modal has a null spellout in English, the *need+Af* complex in T will be spelled out as *need* at PF; and the overall structure will be spelled out as the sentence 10a *He need not worry about anything.* The important point illustrated here is that we have to posit that *need* originates in M and moves (across *not*) into T in order to account for *not* having scope over *need* at LF in spite of *need* preceding *not* at PF. (A point of detail to note is that I have assumed in 12 that *need* moves directly to adjoin to the tense affix in T, and does not transit through NEG because NEG does not contain any inflectional affix that the auxiliary needs to attach to.)

However, while the assumption in (12) that *need* originates in an MP projection below NEGP holds for a narrow scope modal like *need* (i.e. one interpreted as falling within the scope of *not*), it does not hold for a wide scope modal (i.e. one interpreted as having scope over *not*) like *may* in:

(13)   He may not have said anything

Here, the modal *may* has scope over *not*, as we see from the paraphrase 'It *may* be the case that he did **not** say anything.' What this means is that the modal *may* originates above *not* here, so that (13) has the derivation below:

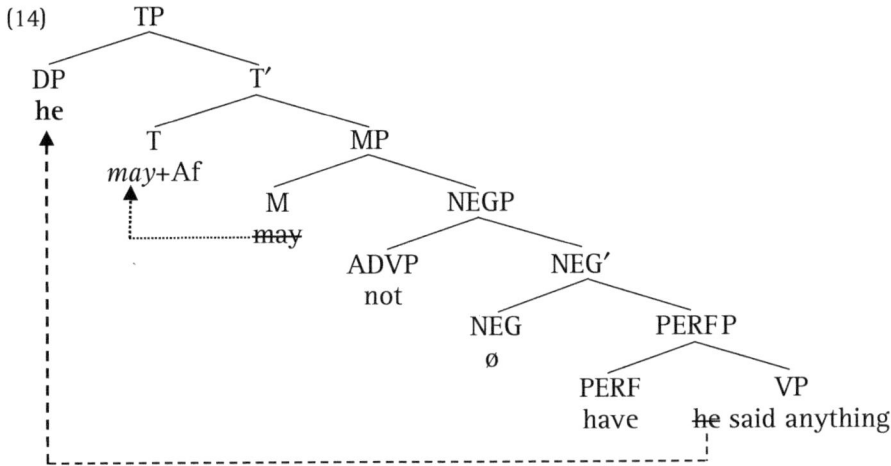

(14)

TP

DP *he*

T'

T *may+Af*

MP

M *may*

NEGP

ADVP *not*

NEG'

NEG ∅

PERFP

PERF *have*

VP *he said anything*

Since the modal *may* originates in an M position c-commanding *not* in (14), it follows that *may* will have scope over *not*. The modal raises to adjoin to a tense affix/*Af* in T, and will be spelled out as *may* if the tense affix marks present tense, but as *might* if the tense affix marks past tense.

Overall, the key assumption underlying the analyses in (7, 9, 12, 14) is that auxiliaries originate in a dedicated auxiliary projection below T and from there (if finite) move to adjoin to a tense affix in T.

6.1.2   Subject projection

Under the classic CP+TP+VP analysis of clause structure, the criterial position for subjects is spec-TP: thus, subjects originate internally within VP, and from there move to their criterial position in spec-TP. This can be illustrated by the reply given by speaker B in the dialogue below:

(15)   SPEAKER A :   What did John tell you?

SPEAKER B :   **That** *he* <u>does</u> not like garlic

If we adopt the classic CP+TP+VP model of clause structure, the clause produced by speaker B in (15) above will have the structure shown below (simplified by not showing the internal structure of NEGP):

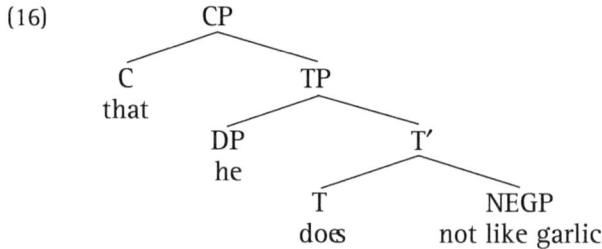

(16)

```
                        CP
              ┌─────────┴─────────┐
              C                   TP
            that          ┌───────┴───────┐
                          DP              T′
                          he        ┌─────┴─────┐
                                    T          NEGP
                                  does    not like garlic
```

Under the analysis in (16), the subject ends up in its criterial position as the specifier of the tense head T (here containing the present tense auxiliary *does*). Such an analysis provides a straightforward account of the subject *he* immediately preceding *does*.

However, the spec-TP analysis of subjects raises the question of how to deal with sentences like those in (17) below where an italicised subject is separated from its associated bold-printed auxiliary by some underlined intervening constituent:

(17)   a. *Its polymorphic nature* <u>almost certainly</u> **has** allowed the selection of variants that have helped humankind survive the scourge of malaria (pubmed.ncbi.nlm.nih.gov)

b. *They* <u>very occasionally</u> **can** spread to either nearby lymph nodes or internal organs (peachskinclinic.co.uk)

c. *My dad* <u>on occasions</u> **would** send me to the co-op with an even longer list (brigstockcouncil.org.uk)

d. *The defendant* <u>during the trial</u> **had** taken the stand in his defense (openjurist.org)

e. *The accused*, <u>when he took the oath of an American officer</u>, **was** not given a license to slaughter unarmed men, women and children (asser.nl)

f. And I am sure that *everyone*, <u>although tired</u>, **had** had a most enjoyable day (semvc.com)

g. *They* <u>almost all</u> **will** suffer gearbox pinion bearing wear/failure at some point (pistonheads.com)

h. *The men* <u>both</u> **were** charged and are awaiting trial (*Gettysburg Times*, 27 July 1988)

A range of different types of (underlined) constituent can intervene between subject and auxiliary, including an ADVP in (17a, 17b), a PP in (17c, 17d), a full or reduced CONJP (i.e. clause headed by a subordinating conjunction/ CONJ) in (17e, 17f), and a floating QP in (17g, 17h). And indeed there can be multiple constituents intervening between subject and auxiliary, whether of the same or different types – as illustrated by the examples below:

(18) a. *I* <u>simply</u> <u>eventually</u> <u>probably</u> <u>just</u> **wouldn't** care anymore (forum. charltonlife.com)

   b. I've learned that *HR,* <u>historically,</u> <u>probably</u> <u>really</u> **has** been in sore need of improvement (thriveglobal.com: HR = Human Resources)

   c. My guess is that *it* <u>probably</u> <u>already</u> **has** peaked (eurogamer.net)

   d. *I* <u>frankly</u> <u>really</u> **couldn't** care less about the political parties in Britain (bbs.boingboing.net)

   e. *They* <u>clearly</u> <u>all</u> **can** sing very well (foodscienceinstitute.com)

   f. *They* <u>definitely</u> <u>both</u> **should** medal (winnipegfreepress.com)

So, for example, the underlined intervenors are multiple ADVP constituents in (18a–18d), and an ADVP followed by a floating QP in (18e, 18f). If the subject and auxiliary are positioned on the edge of the same TP constituent (as with *he* and *does* in 16 above), how are we to account for constituents like those underlined in (17, 18) above being able to be positioned in between a subject and its associated auxiliary?

At first sight, it might seem plausible to treat the underlined constituents as adjuncts. Since adjuncts of the same kind can be recursively stacked on top of each other, we could then suppose that the subperiphery of a sentence like (18a) would have the simplified structure below (where *n't* originates as the head of NEGP, and encliticises onto/attaches to the end of *would*):

(19)

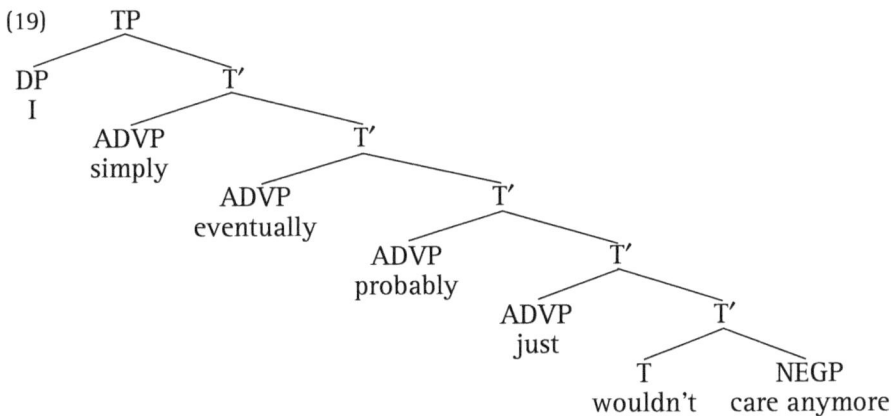

Each adverbial would adjoin to a T-bar constituent to project it into an even larger T-bar. The assumption made in (19) that the adverbs are ADVP constituents (and not just ADV heads) is borne out by the observation that they can be substituted by larger ADVPs (e.g. *simply* can be substituted by *quite simply* and *probably* by *more likely than not*). Analysing the relevant adverbials as T-bar adjuncts would enable us to maintain the traditional assumption that a finite auxiliary and its subject are positioned on the edge of the same TP projection, with the auxiliary being in head-TP (i.e. occupying the head T position of TP), and its subject in spec-TP.

However, the T-bar adjunct analysis runs into theoretical problems. This is because it violates a putatively universal constraint on adjunction (dating back to Baltin 1978/1982 and Chomsky 1986b) which can be characterised informally as follows:

(20)   **Like-Adjoins-to-Like Constraint**
        Adjunction can only adjoin like to like

The likeness constraint on adjunction in (20) allows one head X to be adjoined to another head Y, or one maximal projection XP to be adjoined to another maximal projection YP, but does not allow an ADVP to be adjoined to a T-bar (as in 19), because this involves illicitly adjoining a maximal projection to an intermediate projection (and the two are not likes, because they are different types of projection). Of course, the likeness violation is even clearer where the status of the adjunct as a maximal projection is self-evident – for example, where the supposed T-bar adjunct is a PP like *during the trial* in (17d), or a CONJP/subordinate clause like *when he took the oath of an American officer* in (17e).

But if the T-bar adjunction analysis of intervening adverbials in (19) is ruled out by a universal constraint on adjunction, what alternative do we have? A plausible answer is to reject the traditional assumption that the auxiliary and its subject are contained within the same TP projection, and to suppose instead that subject and auxiliary are contained in different projections – and more specifically, to suppose that a tensed auxiliary is contained within a TP/tense phrase projection, whereas its subject is contained within a separate SUBJP/subject phrase projection. Let's suppose that spec-SUBJP is the criterial position for a subject, and extend the Criterial Freezing Condition outlined in Module 4.1 to apply not only to constituents in the periphery, but also those in the subperiphery. This we can do by adding the condition italicised below:

(21)   **Criterial Freezing Condition/CFC**
        (i) A peripheral *or subperipheral* constituent must occupy a criterial
            position to be interpretable at LF
        (ii) A constituent which occupies its criterial position is frozen in place

On one implementation of this idea, the subperipheral structure of the clause in (18a) would not be as in (19) above, but rather as shown in simplified form below:

(22)

```
        SUBJP
       /     \
     DP      SUBJ'
     I      /     \
        SUBJ       TP
         Ø        /   \
              ADVP     TP
             simply   /   \
                  ADVP     TP
                eventually /   \
                       ADVP     TP
                     probably  /   \
                           ADVP     TP
                            just   /   \
                                  T     NEGP
                              wouldn't  care
                                       anymore
```

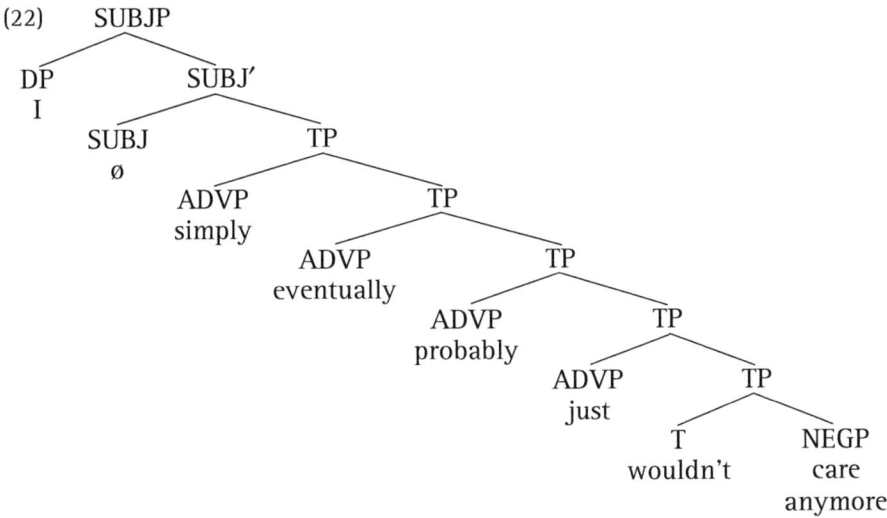

Under the analysis in (22), the auxiliary *wouldn't* is the head of a TP projection, and the subject *I* would be the specifier of a separate SUBJP projection (with a null head). The adverbial constituents would each be analysed as TP adjuncts which adjoin to a TP to form an even larger TP. Since in each case adjunction involves one maximal projection adjoining to another (i.e. ADVP adjoining to TP), the Like-Adjoins-to-Like Constraint in (20) is satisfied by the analysis in (22). Hence, theoretical considerations relating to the likeness constraint on adjunction in (20) favour the analysis in (22) over that in (19).

The assumption that subjects are contained in a separate SUBJP projection raises the question of what the function of SUBJP is. Rizzi (2005: 213) argues that spec-SUBJP is the criterial position for subjects, and that it is 'a position dedicated to a special interpretive property of the scope-discourse kind ("aboutness")'.

However, there is also a further potential rationale for the postulation of separate tense and agreement projections from morphological considerations. There is a widespread view that (in the same way as T is the locus of tense), the head which is here labelled as SUBJ is the locus of agreement with the clause subject; for this reason, in much work in the 1980s we find the label AGR$_S$ (denoting subject agreement) used instead, to mark a head which agrees in person and number with the clause subject.

One piece of evidence adduced in support of the claim that SUBJ is the locus of agreement comes from north Italian dialects which use an (italicised) subject clitic to 'double' (i.e. copy features of/mark agreement with) the subject in a finite clause such as the following (from Belletti 2001: 499):

(23)   La   Maria   *la*   parla
        The   Mary   she   speaks
        'Mary is speaking'

Subject clitic doubling is found in dialects spoken in Florence and Trento (Brandi & Cordin 1989), Padua and other areas of northern Italy (Poletto 1993), and also in Franco-Provençal (Roberts 1993b). One way of handling the phenomenon is to suppose that the subject DP *la*_{the} *Maria*_{Mary} occupies spec-SUBJP, and the clitic *la*_{she} (which agrees in person, number and gender with the subject) occupies the head SUBJ position of SUBJP. Of course, since English does not have clitic doubling, we can suppose that the head of SUBJP in the English counterpart of this type of structure contains an abstract person/number agreement affix which ends up attached to the finite verb (in much the same way as a finite T carries a tense affix). This would mean that SUBJ in finite clauses carries an agreement affix, and T a tense affix. This approach can be justified on universalist grounds, in that in more highly inflected languages, tense and agreement are marked by morphologically distinct affixes (e.g. the French verb form *chanterai* 'will sing' comprises the verb stem *chant-*, the future tense affix *-er*, and the first person singular agreement affix *-ai*). There's much more that could be said about this, but I won't pursue the issue any further here.

You should now be able to tackle Exercise 6.1.

6.2   Subperipheral adverbs

Although adverbial modifiers have been treated as adjuncts hitherto, in this module we will see that there is evidence for treating them as specifiers of dedicated functional heads (with each functional projection serving to house a particular type of ADVP as its specifier).

6.2.1   Analysing ADVPs as specifiers

As we see from the analysis in (22) above, adverbs positioned between a subject and auxiliary can be treated as adjuncts to the TP headed by the auxiliary. However, in sentences such as those below, there is a close semantic relationship between the italicised adverb and the bold-printed auxiliary, in that they denote similar concepts:

(24)   a. Ageing can be cured – and, in part, it *soon* **will** be (economist.com)
      b. He *now* **is** feeling empathy for her (E. McKinney, *A Rose for Liliana*, iUniverse, 2008: 278)
      c. But there is no reason why this *necessarily* **must** be so (isca.ox.ac.uk)
      d. I think he *possibly* **may** have a storage unit somewhere too (pistonheads.com)
      e. Authorities investigating a child abuse report *legally* **may** disclose to parents that a report was made (careinnovations.org)

f. Experts say everyone should assume they *already* **have** been exposed to the virus at this point (huffpost.com)

g. I don't think they *yet* **have** accepted the fact that there were only Democrats voting with me in 1993 (Bill Clinton, Public Papers of the Presidents of the United States, US Government Publishing Office, June 13, 1998, p. 964, govinfo.gov)

So, for example, in (24a) the auxiliary *will* (denoting future time) is modified by the immediately preceding adverb *soon* (also denoting future time). In (24b) the auxiliary *is* (denoting present tense) is modified by the immediately preceding adverb *now* (denoting present time). In (24c), the auxiliary *must* (denoting necessity) is modified by the immediately preceding adverb *necessarily* (also denoting necessity). In (24d), the auxiliary *may* (denoting possibility) is modified by the immediately preceding adverb *possibly* (also denoting possibility). In (24e), the auxiliary *may* (here denoting permission) is modified by the immediately preceding adverb *legally* (denoting the kind of permission). In (24f/24g) the auxiliary *have* (used to denote present tense and perfect aspect) is modified by an immediately preceding adverb (*already/yet*) which is semantically related (because *yet* means 'until now' and *already* means 'before now'). The close semantic relationship between the auxiliary and the adverb modifying it in cases like (24) raises the question of whether the two are on the edge of the same projection and in a specifier-head relationship, and whether the adverb should be analysed as occupying spec-TP and functioning as the specifier of the auxiliary.

If we adopt this approach and treat the italicised adverbs in (24) as occupying spec-TP, the string *it soon will be* in (24a) would have the subperipheral structure shown in simplified form in (25) below, where the VP headed by *cured* undergoes ellipsis, marked by strikethrough; note that for the sake of expository simplicity, here and elsewhere below, I set aside the claim made in §6.1.1 that a finite auxiliary originates as the head of an auxiliary projection below T and from there raises to adjoin to an affix in T:

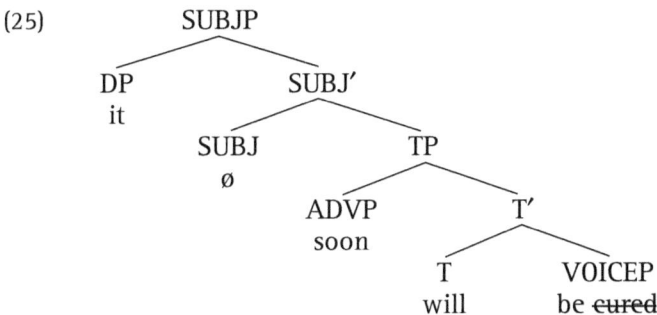

(25)

```
              SUBJP
           ╱        ╲
        DP            SUBJ′
        it         ╱        ╲
               SUBJ            TP
                Ø          ╱       ╲
                      ADVP            T′
                      soon        ╱      ╲
                               T          VOICEP
                              will      be c̶u̶r̶e̶d̶
```

Since the ADVP *soon* is the specifier of *will* in (25) we can account for the close relation between them, since both mark future time, and both are positioned on the edge of the same TP projection. On this view, each subperipheral adverbial is the specifier of a semantically related auxiliary head: for ease of reference, let's refer to this as the spec-AUX analysis of subperipheral adverbs.

However, the spec-AUX analysis runs into a number of empirical problems. For one thing, the adverb modifying the auxiliary in sentences like (24) can equally be positioned <u>after</u> the auxiliary – as illustrated below:

(26)   a. It **will** *soon* be cured
      b. He **is** *now* feeling empathy for her
      c. But there is no reason why this **must** *necessarily* be so
      d. I think he **may** *possibly* have a storage unit somewhere too
      e. Authorities **may** *legally* disclose to parents that a report was made
      f. Everyone should assume they **have** *already* been exposed to the virus
      g. I don't think they **have** *yet* accepted that only Democrats voted with me in 1993

It is clear that the italicised adverb can't (superficially, at least) be the specifier of the bold-printed auxiliary in sentences like (26), because the adverb follows the auxiliary (whereas specifiers precede their heads). We might therefore be tempted to conclude that sentences like (26) undermine the spec-AUX analysis of subperipheral adverbs.

And yet, we can continue to maintain the spec-AUXP analysis if we posit that the ADVP+AUX order in a structure like (25) is reversed in sentences like (26) because the auxiliary raises from T to SUBJ. On this (Auxiliary Raising) view, the subperiphery of the sentence in (26a) *It will soon be cured* will have the derivation shown below (where VOICEP is a projection headed by the passive voice auxiliary *be*):

(27)

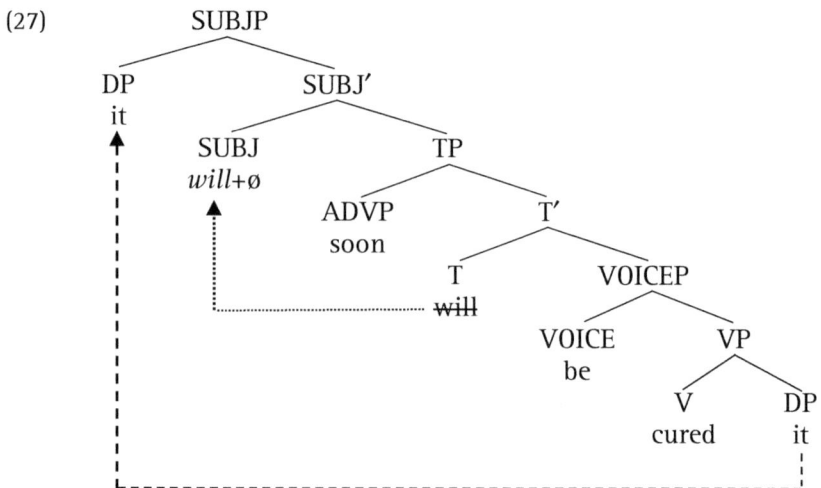

Under the analysis in (27), the auxiliary *will* undergoes Head Movement from T to SUBJ and thereby comes to move in front of the ADVP *soon*, so reversing the underlying ADVP+AUX order. (A complication set aside here arises if *will* originates in an AUXP below T, and then moves from AUX to adjoin to a tense affix in T, and then the resulting *will+Af* complex adjoins to the null SUBJ head.)

However, the assumption that a subperipheral adverb serves as the specifier of a semantically related auxiliary is called into question by the observation that (for example) an adverb like *possibly* is not restricted to modifying a modal auxiliary like *may* expressing possibility, but rather can modify a wide range of other auxiliaries with very different semantic properties, like those bold-printed below:

(28)   a. The market *possibly* **is** feeling the absence of previous powerful constructive speculative leadership (*The San Francisco Examiner*, 25 July 1934)

b. The volcano *possibly* **has** been active during the past 10,000 years (volcanodiscovery.com)

c. Greg Jennings *possibly* **will** return to practice Sunday (profootballtalk.nbcsports.com)

d. I think it *possibly* **would** have been helpful for this to have been a bit higher (euansguide.com)

e. I *possibly* **shall** start off on a trip the end of next week (Letter from G. C. Marshall to Mrs J. J. Winn, May 24, 1943, marshallfoundation.org)

f. This group *possibly* **should** be screened (medscape.com)

g. The second transaction *possibly* **must** wait until the first transaction reaches syncpoint (ibm.com)

h. However, we have a sneaking suspicion that Levein will play as defensively as he *possibly* **dare** (betting.betfair.com)

Such sentences appear at first sight to undermine any attempt to claim that the adverb serves as the specifier of a semantically related functional head that is dedicated to licensing the adverb as its specifier.

However, Cinque (1999) outlines a way of defending the claim that adverbs function as specifiers of dedicated functional heads. He argues that in cases like (28), the adverb *possibly* does not serve as the specifier of the auxiliary, but rather as the specifier of a separate functional projection above the auxiliary: this functional projection has a null modal head which itself expresses possibility, so that specifier and head are semantically related to each other. More generally, Cinque (1999: 77) claims that 'each adverb class enters into a special spec/head relation with one particular functional head, and vice-versa'; and Cinque (2004) refers to this as the 'functional specifier' approach. On this view, (28f) *This group possibly should be screened* will have the structure shown in simplified form below (where F_{MOD} denotes a functional head expressing modality):

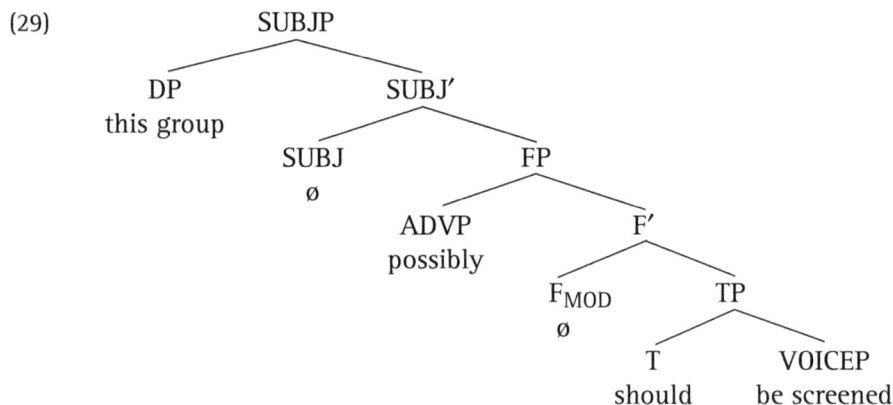

(29)

```
                        SUBJP
            ┌─────────────┴─────────────┐
           DP                         SUBJ′
        this group          ┌───────────┴───────────┐
                          SUBJ                       FP
                           ø              ┌──────────┴──────────┐
                                        ADVP                   F′
                                      possibly         ┌────────┴────────┐
                                                     F_MOD               TP
                                                       ø          ┌───────┴───────┐
                                                                  T             VOICEP
                                                               should        be screened
```

A structure like (29) enables us to maintain that a subperipheral adverb functions as the specifier of a dedicated functional head/F. (An incidental detail set aside in 29 is that under the analysis of finite auxiliaries in §6.1.1, *should* will originate as the head of a lower modal projection and from there raise into the T position that it occupies in 29.)

To illustrate how the analysis works, let's look at some specific claims about adverbs made by Cinque (1999: 84–107). Speech act adverbs like *frankly, honestly, sincerely* etc. are generated as specifiers of a speech act mood head. Evaluative adverbs like *(un)fortunately, luckily, regrettably, surprisingly, strangely/oddly (enough), (un)expectedly* etc. are generated in the specifier position of an evaluative mood head. Evidential adverbs (like *allegedly, reportedly, apparently, obviously, clearly, evidently,* etc.) are generated in the specifier position of an evidential mood head. Epistemic adverbs (like *probably, presumably, supposedly* etc.) are generated as specifiers of an epistemic modal head, and *perhaps* as the specifier of an irrealis mood head. Habitual adverbs like *usually, habitually, generally, regularly* etc. are generated as specifiers of a habitual aspect head, frequentative adverbs like *often* as specifiers of a frequentative aspect head, continuative adverbs like *still* as the specifiers of a continuative aspect head, completive adverbs like *completely* as the specifiers of a completive aspect head ... and so on. In each case, the relevant mood/modal/aspectual heads can be (and typically are) null in English.

But what is the motivation for treating ADVPs as functional specifiers rather than adjuncts? There are two main reasons. One is theoretical in nature: namely, that if we reanalyse adverbial modifiers as specifiers rather than adjuncts, we can eliminate phrasal adjuncts from our theory of Universal Grammar, since all phrasal adjuncts will be reanalysed as specifiers, and this will lead to a more restrictive/tightly constrained theory.

The other reason is empirical in nature (relating to word order), in that the functional specifier analysis provides a more principled account of word order – for example, the relative ordering of ADVPs in clauses containing multiple ADVPs (as we will see in §6.2.2 below), and the variable positioning of ADVPs with respect to auxiliaries on the one hand (discussed in §6.3.1) and with respect to subjects on the other (discussed in §6.3.2).

6.2.2   Relative ordering of multiple ADVPs

Our discussion of adverbs in §6.2.1 was simplified by considering sentences which contain only one subperipheral ADVP. However, sentences can frequently contain two or more ADVPs within the subperiphery, as the examples in (18) above illustrate. Nevertheless, there are restrictions on the relative ordering of multiple subperipheral ADVPs in such cases, as we see from the positions of the italicised ADVPs below:

(30) a. He *already completely* has annihilated the opposition
      b. *He *completely already* has annihilated the opposition

(31) a. He *still almost* can't stop himself
      b. *He *almost still* can't stop himself

(32) a. He *once intentionally* had crashed his car
      b. *He *intentionally once* had crashed his car

(33) a. He *frankly unfortunately* has always been careless with money
      b. *He *unfortunately frankly* has always been careless with money

(34) a. The car *sometimes abruptly* would come to a halt
      b. *The car *abruptly sometimes* would come to a halt

How can we account for such restrictions on the relative ordering of ADVPs?

If the italicised adverbials were adjuncts (e.g. TP adjuncts as in 22 above), we would expect that they could be stacked on top of each other in any order, and hence the ungrammaticality of the (b) examples in (30–34) above would remain unaccounted for. For example, under the adjunct analysis, (34a) would have the structure shown in simplified form below:

(35)

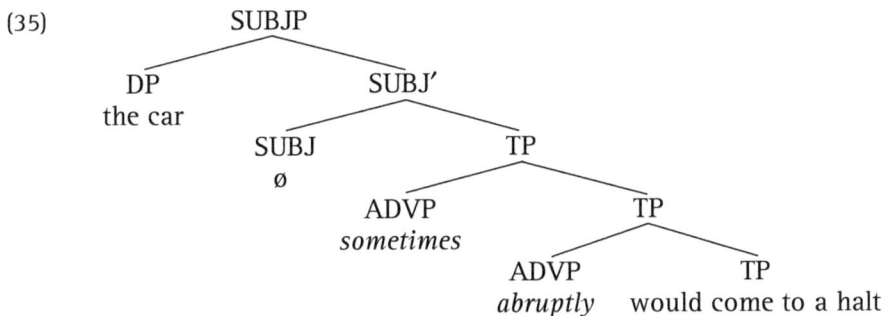

Under this analysis, the italicised adverbial modifiers *sometimes* and *abruptly* are each analysed as TP adjuncts (i.e. as constituents which adjoin to a TP to form a larger TP with the same head). Thus, the ADVP *abruptly* adjoins to the TP *would come to a halt* to form the larger TP *abruptly would come to a halt*; and the ADVP *sometimes* then adjoins to this larger TP to form the even larger TP *sometimes abruptly would come to a halt*. However, a problem which arises in relation to this analysis is that since adjuncts of the same kind can be stacked on top of the constituents they modify in any order, we would expect it to be equally possible to adjoin *sometimes* to the TP *would come to a halt* to form the larger VP *sometimes would come to a halt*, and then adjoin *abruptly* to this larger VP to form the even larger VP *abruptly sometimes would come to a halt*. However, the resulting sentence (34b) *'The car *abruptly sometimes* would come to a halt' is ungrammatical, and the TP-adjunct analysis offers us no account of why this should be.

By contrast, under the functional specifier analysis, the relative ordering of adverbial modifiers can be handled in terms of the familiar head-complement selection mechanism by which heads impose restrictions on the types of complement which they do and don't select/allow. Let's see how.

Cinque (1999: v) maintains that there is a 'fixed universal hierarchy of functional projections', and that clausal projections housing adverbs occur in the order specified below, where each italicised adverb functions as the specifier of a capitalised functional head (with MOD denoting a modality head, ASP an aspect head, and T a tense head, and some adverbials are able to occupy two different positions in the hierarchy, denoted by the subscripts $_{(I)}$ and $_{(II)}$ respectively):

(36)   **Adverb Hierarchy**

[*frankly* MOD$_{\text{speech act}}$ [*fortunately* MOD$_{\text{evaluative}}$ [*allegedly* MOD$_{\text{evidential}}$
[*probably* MOD$_{\text{epistemic}}$ [*once* T$_{\text{past}}$ [*then* T$_{\text{future}}$ [*perhaps* MOD$_{\text{irrealis}}$
[*necessarily* MOD$_{\text{necessity}}$ [*possibly* MOD$_{\text{possibility}}$ [*usually* ASP$_{\text{habitual}}$
[*again* ASP$_{\text{repetitive(I)}}$ [*often* ASP$_{\text{frequentative(I)}}$ [*intentionally* MOD$_{\text{volitional}}$
[*quickly* ASP$_{\text{celerative(I)}}$ [*already* T$_{\text{anterior}}$ [*no longer* ASP$_{\text{terminative}}$
[*still* ASP$_{\text{continuative}}$ [*always* ASP$_{\text{perfect(?)}}$ [*just* ASP$_{\text{retrospective}}$
[*soon* ASP$_{\text{proximative}}$ [*briefly* ASP$_{\text{durative}}$
[*characteristically*(?) ASP$_{\text{generic/progressive}}$ [*almost* ASP$_{\text{prospective}}$
[*completely* ASP$_{\text{completive(I)}}$ [*well* VOICE [*fast/early* ASP$_{\text{celerative(II)}}$
[*again* ASP$_{\text{repetitive(II)}}$ [*often* ASP$_{\text{frequentative(II)}}$ [*completely* ASP$_{\text{completive(II)}}$

What the Adverb Hierarchy specifies is that (e.g.) a functional head denoting speech act mood (and allowing an ADVP like *frankly* as its specifier) can select as its complement a functional projection whose head denotes evaluative mood (and which allows an ADVP like *fortunately* as its specifier) ... and so on.

How this works in more concrete terms can be illustrated for (34a) above, which will have the structure in (37) below under the functional specifier analysis of ADVPs, where F_{FREQ} denotes a functional head which licenses a frequency adverb like *sometimes* as its specifier, and F_{MANN} denotes a functional head which licenses a manner adverb like *abruptly* as its specifier:

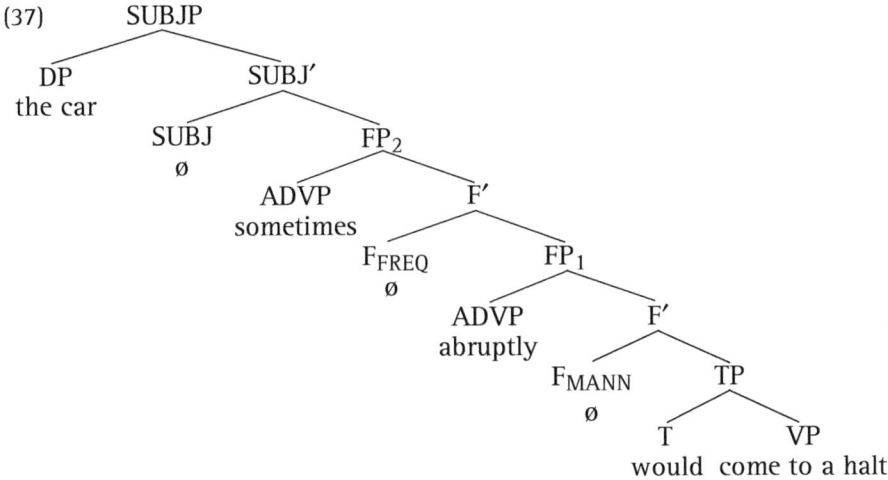

(37)

```
              SUBJP
            /       \
         DP          SUBJ'
      the car       /      \
               SUBJ          FP₂
                 ∅          /    \
                       ADVP       F'
                    sometimes    /   \
                             F_FREQ    FP₁
                               ∅      /    \
                                  ADVP      F'
                                abruptly   /   \
                                      F_MANN    TP
                                         ∅     /   \
                                             T      VP
                                          would come to a halt
```

Adverb order in (34/37) then follows if F_{FREQ} can select a complement headed by F_{MANN}, but F_{MANN} cannot select a complement headed by F_{FREQ}. I leave you to verify for yourself that the ordering of adverbs in (30–33) above likewise conforms to the ordering in the Adverb Hierarchy in (36) above.

The analysis outlined in this section presupposes that 'ADVPs occupy the specifier position of distinct functional projections' (Cinque 1999: 29). Cinque (1999: 44) notes that an important theoretical advantage of the functional specifier analysis of adverbials over the more traditional adjunct analysis outlined in (22) above is that it enables us to dispense with phrasal adjuncts (i.e. XPs which adjoin to YPs to form even larger YPs), since all phrasal adjuncts (e.g. *sometimes* and *abruptly* in 37 above) are reanalysed as specifiers.

You should now be able to tackle Exercise 6.2.

6.3   Word order variation

In §6.2.2, we saw that the relative ordering of adverbial modifiers with respect to each other can be accounted for in a principled fashion under the functional specifier analysis. In this module, we will see that the analysis can also account for the variable order which ADVPs show with respect to other constituents in the clause – including auxiliaries and subjects.

6.3.1 ADVPs and auxiliaries

The variable position of ADVPs with respect to auxiliaries can be illustrated by the following examples (which are the English counterparts of a set of Italian examples used to illustrate this variability in Cinque 1999: 49):

(38) a. Gianni *then perhaps wisely* **had** decided not to go
      b. Gianni *then perhaps* **had** *wisely* decided not to go
      c. Gianni *then* **had** *perhaps wisely* decided not to go
      d. Gianni **had** *then perhaps wisely* decided not to go

If we adopted the traditional adjunct analysis of adverbial modifiers, the three adverbs *then*, *perhaps* and *wisely* that precede *had* in (38a) would be treated as TP adjuncts, adjoined to a TP headed by *had*. And yet, if they are all TP adjuncts, we would predict that the auxiliary *had* cannot be positioned in front of any of them. But this prediction is false, as we see from the grammaticality of (38b–38d).

By contrast, under the functional specifier analysis of adverbial modifiers, (38a) will have the subperipheral structure shown in simplified form below (where F_1, F_2 and F_3 are functional heads which each license a different kind of adverbial specifier):

(39)
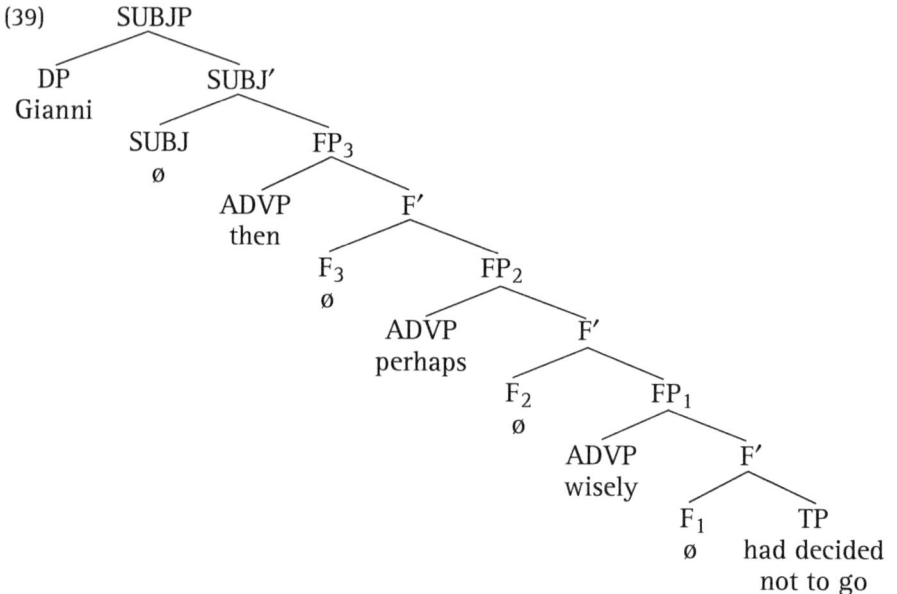

In (39), *had* occupies the head T position of TP, and each modifying ADVP is housed in a separate dedicated functional projection above TP. But how do we account for the different positions occupied by *had* in (38b–38d)? The answer given by Cinque is that the auxiliary *had* can optionally raise to adjoin to any of the functional head positions between T and its subject.

On this view, (38b) *Gianni then perhaps* **had** *wisely decided not to go* involves the auxiliary *had* raising to adjoin to the F_2 head between *perhaps* and *wisely* in (39); sentence (38c) *Gianni then* **had** *perhaps wisely decided not to go* involves the auxiliary *had* raising to adjoin to the F_3 head between *then* and *perhaps*; and sentence (38d) *Gianni* **had** *then perhaps wisely decided not to go* involves the auxiliary *had* raising to adjoin to the SUBJ head between *Gianni* and *then*. If we assume that locality constraints require a moved head to adjoin to the closest accessible head above it each time it moves, this means that (38d) will involve the four separate Auxiliary Raising operations arrowed below:

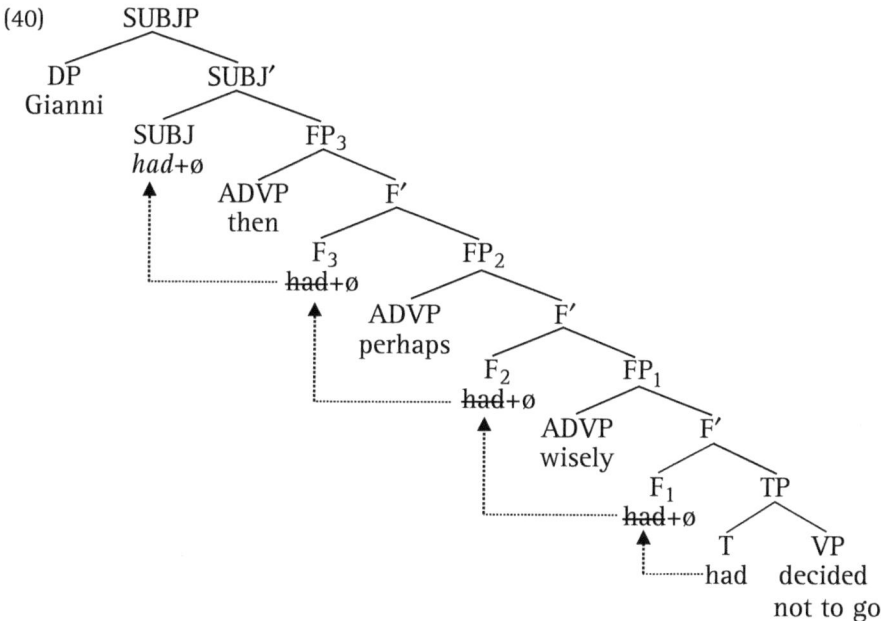

(40)

```
        SUBJP
       /     \
     DP       SUBJ'
   Gianni    /     \
          SUBJ      FP3
          had+ø    /    \
               ADVP      F'
               then     /    \
                      F3      FP2
                    had+ø    /    \
                          ADVP     F'
                        perhaps   /    \
                                F2      FP1
                              had+ø    /    \
                                    ADVP     F'
                                   wisely   /    \
                                          F1      TP
                                        had+ø    /   \
                                              had    T      VP
                                                  decided
                                                  not to go
```

On these assumptions, the subperipheral adverbs (and the subject) must be specifiers of (null) functional heads in order to account for how the auxiliary *had* can come to be positioned between them. The auxiliary *had* will remain in situ in T in (38a), but raise up to F_2 in (38b), up to F_3 in (38c) and up to SUBJ in (38d).

6.3.2 ADVPs and subjects

In the same way as adverbs can occupy variable positions with respect to auxiliaries (as illustrated in 38 above), so too they can occupy variable positions with respect to subjects – as illustrated by Cinque (1999: 109) in relation to the variable position occupied by the adverb *probably* in relation to the subject *George* in the following sentences:

(41) a. George *probably* will have read the book

b. *Probably* George will have read the book

Rather than assume that the adverb *probably* occupies two different positions in each of these sentences (on the edge of a functional projection immediately above TP in 41a, and above SUBJP in 41b), Cinque suggests that the adverb occupies a fixed position, and that the variant word orders 'involve the movement of the subject DP ... around the ADVP'. He does not add further detail, but a plausible implementation of this idea is as follows.

Let us suppose that (41a) has the subperipheral structure below (simplified for expository purposes by setting aside the possibility that *will* originates as the head of a lower auxiliary projection and from there raises to adjoin to T):

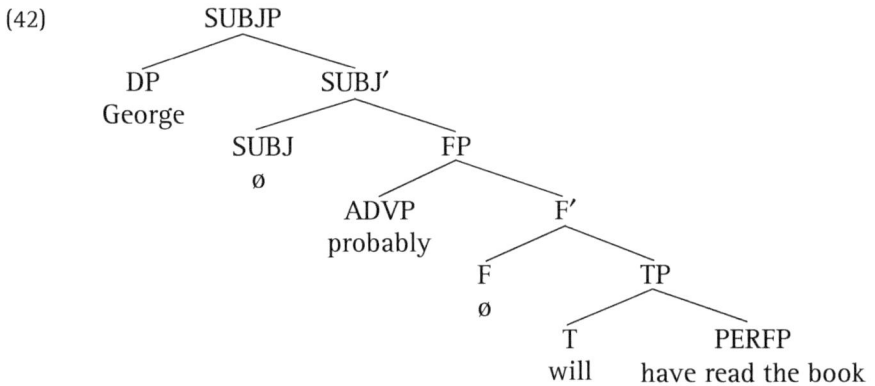

(42)

```
                    SUBJP
              ┌───────┴───────┐
             DP             SUBJ′
           George       ┌─────┴─────┐
                      SUBJ          FP
                       ∅       ┌─────┴─────┐
                             ADVP          F′
                           probably    ┌────┴────┐
                                       F         TP
                                       ∅      ┌───┴────┐
                                              T       PERFP
                                             will   have read the book
```

Given the VP-Internal Subject Hypothesis, the DP *George* will originate as the thematic subject of *read the book*, and from there raise to the specifier position of SUBJP. Under the Auxiliary Raising analysis in §6.1.1, the auxiliary *will* originates as the head of a lower auxiliary projection (not shown above), and from there raises to T. The ADVP *probably* will serve as the specifier of a functional projection/FP with an abstract epistemic modal head (see 36 above), and occupy an intermediate position between SUBJP and TP.

Now consider (41b). Let's suppose that once again the adverb *probably* is housed in a functional projection positioned between SUBJP and TP, but that this time, the subject *George* (which originates as the specifier of *read the book*) raises only as far as spec-TP, resulting in the structure below:

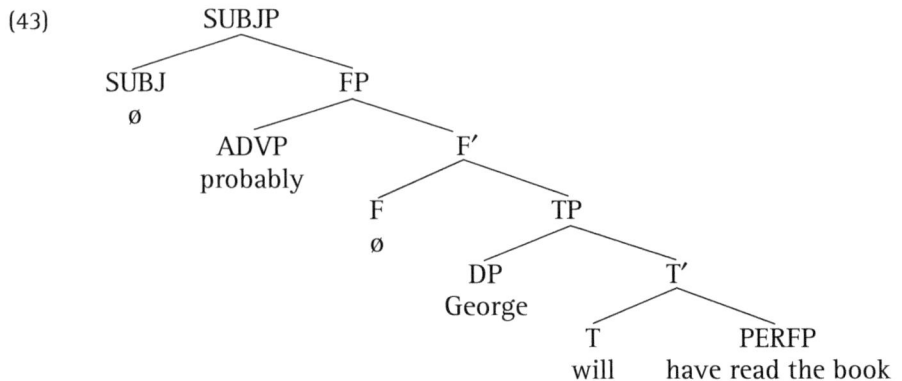

(43)

```
                    SUBJP
              ┌───────┴───────┐
            SUBJ              FP
             ∅          ┌──────┴──────┐
                      ADVP            F′
                    probably     ┌─────┴─────┐
                                 F           TP
                                 ∅      ┌─────┴─────┐
                                       DP           T′
                                     George    ┌─────┴─────┐
                                               T          PERFP
                                              will    have read the book
```

The structure (43) will then be spelled out at PF as the sentence (43b) *Probably George will have read the book*. On this view, the relative order of subject and adverb is accounted for not in terms of variation of the position of the adverb, but rather in terms of variation in the position of the subject (i.e. whether the subject raises out of its initial VP-internal position to the edge of TP, or to the edge of SUBJP).

One consequence of this kind of approach is that it assumes that the subject can occupy variable positions within the clause – for example, spec-SUBJP in (42) but spec-TP in (43). One way of accounting for this might be to suppose that either T or SUBJ can carry an EPP feature allowing it to attract a subject to become its specifier. Still, the assumption that the subject only raises as far as spec-TP in a structure such as (43) is potentially problematic in a framework which posits that spec-SUBJP is the criterial position for a subject. After all, since *George* is in spec-TP in (43), how can it be interpreted as the clause subject if spec-SUBJP is the criterial position for a subject? And if SUBJP does not house the subject in (43), what function does the SUBJP projection serve? One answer might be to suppose that the SUBJ head serves the PF function of housing a subject agreement affix (which lowers onto T in structures containing a finite auxiliary in T), and SUBJ serves the LF function of attracting the subject to move from spec-TP to spec-SUBJP in the semantic/LF component, thereby enabling *George* to be interpreted as the clause subject at LF in (43) because it is in spec-SUBJP at LF. Note, however, that this involves positing that movement operations can apply not only in the syntax but also in the LF component (e.g. raising a constituent from a non-criterial to a criterial position).

6.3.3   Postmodifying ADVPs

The overall conclusion which emerges from our discussion in this module so far is that subperipheral ADVPs can be analysed (within a more articulated model of syntax) as specifiers of dedicated functional heads. However, since specifiers are always the leftmost constituents within the projection housing them, what this predicts is that subperipheral modifiers will always be positioned to the left of the constituents that they modify. And yet a complication which arises from this assumption is that some subperipheral modifiers can not only precede the constituents they modify, but can alternatively follow them – as illustrated by the dual position of the adverb *once* below:

(44)   a. He probably **once** *had been in love with her*
         b. He probably *had been in love with her* **once**

In (44a), *once* is a premodifying ADVP in the sense that it precedes the italicised TP that it modifies (*had been in love with her*). By contrast, in (44b) *once* is a postmodifying ADVP, in that it follows the TP that it modifies. Under the traditional TP adjunct analysis of subperipheral adverbs (illustrated in 22 above), the dual position of *once* can be accounted for straightforwardly, since adjuncts can (in principle) be adjoined either to the left or right of constituents they modify: hence (under the adjunct analysis), *once* is adjoined to the left of the TP *had been in love with her* in (44a), but to the right of it in (44b). But how can we account for the dual position of *once* under the functional specifier analysis?

Sentence (44a) in which *once* precedes the TP *had been in love with her* can be analysed under the functional specifier analysis of ADVPs as follows:

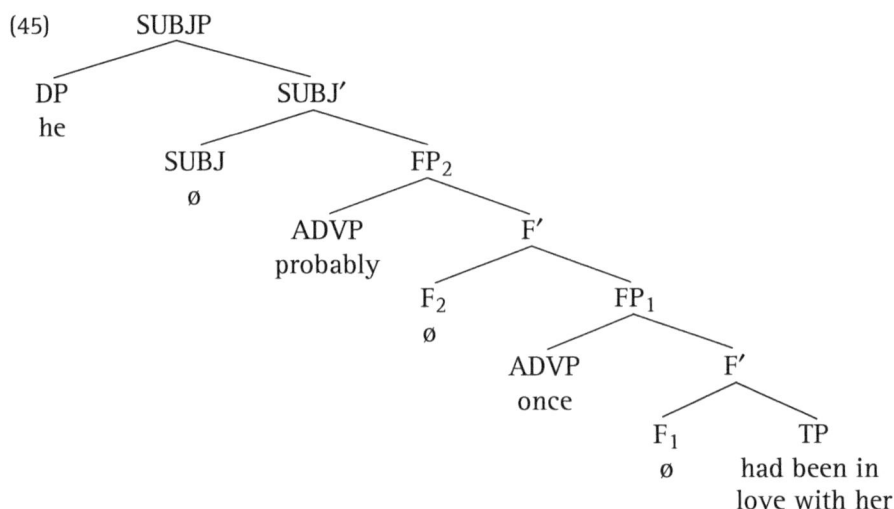

(45)

```
                    SUBJP
             ┌────────┴─────────┐
            DP                SUBJ′
            he          ┌────────┴─────────┐
                       SUBJ              FP₂
                        ø         ┌───────┴──────┐
                                ADVP           F′
                               probably  ┌──────┴───────┐
                                        F₂           FP₁
                                        ø      ┌──────┴──────┐
                                             ADVP          F′
                                             once     ┌─────┴─────┐
                                                     F₁          TP
                                                     ø       had been in
                                                             love with her
```

Here, F_1 is a functional head which allows a temporal adverb such as *once* as its specifier, and F_2 is a functional head which allows a modal adverb like *probably* as its specifier. As we would expect from their specifier status, each of the two adverbs precedes the TP that they modify (*had been in love with her*).

But now consider how we can account for the clause-final position of *once* in (44b) *He probably had been in love with her once*. Since specifiers are always the leftmost constituents of the projections containing them, how does *once* end up to the right of the TP *had been in love with her* in (44b)? The answer suggested by Cinque is that adverb-final order is the result of moving the constituent which is the complement of the projection housing the adverb to a position where it is the specifier of a functional projection immediately above that housing the adverb. More concretely, in the case of a structure like (45) above, the TP *had been in love with her* moves to become the specifier of a functional projection (denoted as FP$_2$ below) which is immediately above the FP$_1$ projection containing the adverb *once*. The relevant movement operation is shown by the arrow below:

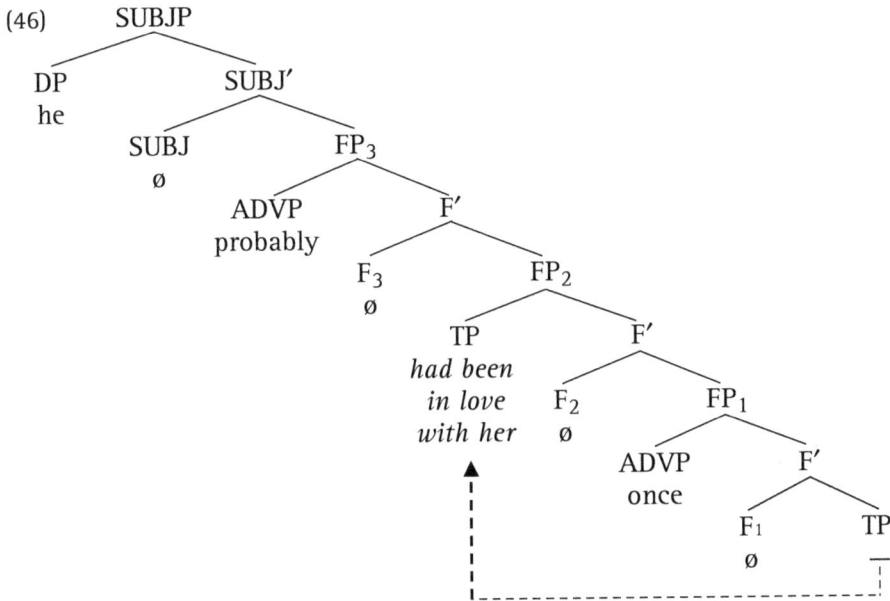

(46)

```
        SUBJP
       /      \
     DP        SUBJ'
     he       /     \
         SUBJ        FP₃
          ∅        /     \
               ADVP       F'
             probably    /   \
                       F₃     FP₂
                       ∅     /    \
                          TP       F'
                      had been    /   \
                      in love   F₂     FP₁
                      with her   ∅    /    \
                            ▲     ADVP      F'
                            ┊     once     /   \
                            ┊            F₁     TP
                            ┊             ∅     ┬
                            ┊                   ┊
                            └───────────────────┘
```

We can refer to this type of movement operation as Complement Raising, because it involves raising the TP complement of the functional projection FP$_1$ housing the adverb *once* to become the specifier of a higher functional projection FP$_2$ positioned immediately above FP$_1$.

As our discussion here illustrates, the functional specifier analysis of subperipheral adverbs brings with it the potential complication that adverbial postmodifiers involve positing an additional movement operation and an additional functional projection (to house the moved constituent). Clearly, even more abstract structures and even more movement operations will be required in sentences involving multiple postmodifying constituents.

Moreover, a further potential complication posed by the Complement Raising analysis in (46) can be illustrated by a sentence such as the following:

(47)   *Which of the two sisters* had he probably been in love with once?

Here, the italicised interrogative wh-phrase *which of the two sisters* originates as the complement of the preposition *with*, and from there moves through spec-FINP into spec-FOCP in the clause periphery via Wh-Movement/A-bar Movement. However, if the TP *had been in love with which of the two sisters* moves into the spec-FP$_2$ position in (46), and Wh-Movement subsequently extracts *which of the two sisters* out this fronted TP, the resulting derivation will violate the following two constraints (outlined in §1.5.1):

(48)   **Constraint on Extraction Domains/CED**
Only complements allow material to be extracted out of them, not specifiers or adjuncts (Cattell 1976, Cinque 1978, and Huang 1982)

(49)   **Freezing Principle/FP**
The constituents of a moved phrase are frozen internally within (and so cannot be extracted out of) the moved phrase (Wexler & Culicover 1980: 119)

The CED violation arises because *which of the two sisters* is extracted out of a TP which occupies a specifier position (spec-FP$_2$) in (46); and the freezing violation arises because *which of the two sisters* is extracted out of a TP which has already undergone the movement arrowed in (46). Thus, the Complement Raising analysis in (46) would seemingly make the incorrect prediction that sentences such as (47) should be ungrammatical – unless constraints like (48) and (49) are modified in some way (see Bošković 2020 for discussion of this kind of problem).

To summarise: in Module 6.3, we have looked at the variable position of adverbs, auxiliaries and subjects. I noted Cinque's claim that this variation can be accounted for by supposing that adverbs occupy a fixed position within the clause, and that word order variation can be attributed to movement of other constituents – for example, auxiliaries raising to a range of functional head positions above T, subjects raising either to spec-TP or to spec-SUBJP, and the complement of a functional head raising to become the specifier of a superordinate/higher functional projection.

You should now be able to tackle Exercise 6.3.

6.4   Other subperipheral constituents

Although our discussion in Module 6.2 and Module 6.3 dealt specifically with subperipheral ADVPs, in this module, we will see that it can be generalised from these to other types of subperipheral XP which function as modifiers.

6.4.1   PPs and subordinate clauses

As we see from the sentences below (repeated from 17c–17h above), in addition to ADVPs, a range of other types of XP (underlined below) can be positioned in the subperiphery between the italicised subject and the bold-printed auxiliary:

(50)   a. *My dad* <u>on occasions</u> **would** send me to the co-op with an even longer list (brigstockcouncil.org.uk)

b. *The defendant* <u>during the trial</u> **had** taken the stand in his defense (openjurist.org)

c. *The accused,* <u>when he took the oath of an American officer,</u> **was** not given a license to slaughter unarmed men, women and children (asser.nl)

d. And I am sure that *everyone,* <u>although tired,</u> **had** had a most enjoyable day (semvc.com)

e. *They* <u>almost all</u> **will** suffer gearbox pinion bearing wear/failure at some point (pistonheads.com)

f. *The men* <u>both</u> **were** charged and are awaiting trial (*Gettysburg Times,* 27 July 1988)

In (50a, 50b), the underlined subperipheral constituent is a PP, in (50c, 50d) it is a CONJP (i.e. clause headed by the subordinate conjuction/CONJ *when/ although*), and in (50e, 50f) it is a floating QP. A range of different constituents can co-occur within the subperiphery of a single clause, as we see from the highlighted constituents below:

(51)   They **probably,** *while at uni,* <u>at some point</u> had done drugs

Thus in (51) we find the adverb *probably,* the reduced CONJP/subordinate clause *while at uni,* and the PP *at some point* all positioned between the subject *they* and the auxiliary *had.* There are parallels between PPs and ADVPs which suggest that the two should be treated in the same way (i.e. as specifiers of dedicated functional heads): for example, the ADVP *probably* in (51) can be substituted by the PP *in all probability,* and conversely the PP *on occasions* in (50a) can be substituted by the ADV *occasionally;* and many of the items treated as ADVPs in our earlier discussion could be given a more abstract analysis as PPs headed by a null preposition (e.g. *then* in 40 is paraphrasable as 'at that time'). Moreover, CONJP constituents (i.e. clauses introduced by a subordinating conjunction/CONJ) are similar in many ways to PPs, and indeed prepositions like *before/after/since/until* can be used to introduce subordinate clauses. If we treat all subperipheral ADVPs, PPs and CONJPs in the same way (as specifiers of dedicated functional heads), a sentence like (51) above will have the subperipheral structure below (if *while at uni* is a projection of the subordinating conjunction/CONJ *while* and is perhaps a reduced form of *while they were at uni*):

(52)

```
            SUBJP
          /        \
        DP          SUBJ'
        they       /      \
                 SUBJ       FP3
                  Ø        /    \
                        ADVP      F'
                        probably /    \
                                F3      FP2
                                Ø      /    \
                                  CONJP       F'
                                  while      /    \
                                  at uni   F2      FP1
                                           Ø      /    \
                                               PP        F'
                                               at some  /    \
                                               point   F1      TP
                                                       Ø      /    \
                                                            T       VP
                                                            had    done drugs
```

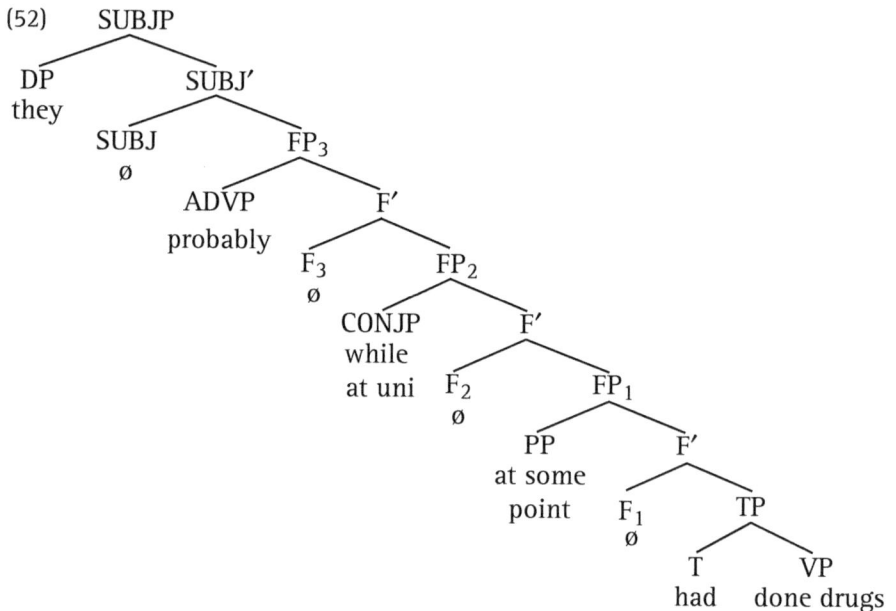

Such an analysis enables us to generalise Cinque's functional specifier analysis of adverbs as follows:

(53)   **Functional Specifier Hypothesis/FSH**

Each XP in the periphery or subperiphery of a clause is the specifier of a dedicated functional head

In conformity with FSH, each XP/maximal projection in the subperiphery in (52) is housed in a separate projection: DP *they* is in spec-SUBJP, ADVP *probably* is in spec-FP_3, CONJP *while at uni* is in spec-FP_2, and PP *at some point* is in spec-FP_1. Under FSH, XPs previously analysed as adjuncts are reanalysed as specifiers (so eliminating operations which adjoin one maximal projection to another). We might further suppose that each type of (sub)peripheral XP occupies a fixed position within the (sub)periphery, determined by the kind of selectional requirements embodied in a template like the Adverb Hierarchy in (36) above.

FSH (53) can arguably be subsumed within a broader generalisation along the following lines:

(54)   **Merge Hypothesis**

A maximal projection/XP can only be introduced into a structure containing it via (first- or second-) merge with a head

It follows from (54) that an XP can either be a complement (first-merged with a head) or a specifier (second-merged with a head), but cannot be an adjunct. This in turn would mean that the only kind of adjunction operation sanctioned by linguistic theory is adjunction of one head to another: this type of head-to-head adjunction appears to be independently required in order to handle cliticisation (e.g. of *n't* to *could* in *couldn't*).

6.4.2 Floating QPs: Stranded under movement

As illustrated in (50e, 50f) above, the subperiphery can also contain floating QPs. Interestingly, these can occupy a range of different positions in the subperiphery – as illustrated below:

(55)   a. The players should have *both* been fined
        b. The players should *both* have been fined
        c. The players *both* should have been fined

One way of accounting for the multiple positions they occupy is to suppose that floating quantifiers can be stranded in intermediate positions through which subjects transit: for succinctness, let's call this the stranding analysis. We can illustrate how it works in terms of the sentences in (55). Let's suppose that *both* originates as the head Q/quantifier of the QP *both the players*, and that this QP originates as the complement of the passive participle *fined*. Let's further suppose that in (55a), the QP *both the players* moves to become the specifier of the passive voice auxiliary *been*, and then the DP *the players* subsequently moves on its own to spec-SUBJP, leaving *both* stranded as the specifier of the VOICEP headed by *been*. Likewise, let's suppose that in (55b), the QP *both the players* moves to become the specifier of the perfect aspect auxiliary *have*, and then the DP *the players* moves on its own to spec-SUBJP, leaving *both* stranded as the specifier of the PERFP constituent headed by *have*. And finally, let's suppose that in (55c), the QP *both the players* moves to become the specifier of the auxiliary *should* in T, and then the DP *the players* moves on its own to spec-SUBJP, leaving *both* stranded as the specifier of the TP headed by *should*.

These assumptions would mean that the sentences in (55a/55b/55c) above would have the respective structures shown in highly simplified form in (56a/56b/56c) below (with the structures simplified by showing only maximal projections, and only overt items):

(56)   a. [$_{SUBJP}$ the players [$_{TP}$ should [$_{PERF}$ have [$_{VOICEP}$ *both* been [$_{VP}$ fined]]]]]
        b. [$_{SUBJP}$ the players [$_{TP}$ should [$_{PERF}$ *both* have [$_{VOICEP}$ been [$_{VP}$ fined]]]]]
        c. [$_{SUBJP}$ the players [$_{TP}$ *both* should [$_{PERF}$ have [$_{VOICEP}$ been [$_{VP}$ fined]]]]]

On this view, the floating quantifiers are stranded under movement of the subject through the edge of the various auxiliary projections, and end up as specifiers of the relevant auxiliaries. (Note that, for the sake of expository simplicity, I set aside the possibility that *should* originates as the head of a modal projection below TP and from there moves to adjoin to a past tense affix in T.)

Although the stranding analysis of floating quantifiers seems attractive at first sight, closer reflection suggests that it is potentially problematic in certain respects. For example, on the classic variant of the stranding analysis, 'leftward movement undergone by the subject over the quantifier proceeds through the specifier of QP' Shlonsky (1991: 159). This would mean that the derivation of (55c) *The players **both** should have been fined* would include the movement operations arrowed in the structure shown below (simplified by not showing the internal structure of T-bar):

(57)

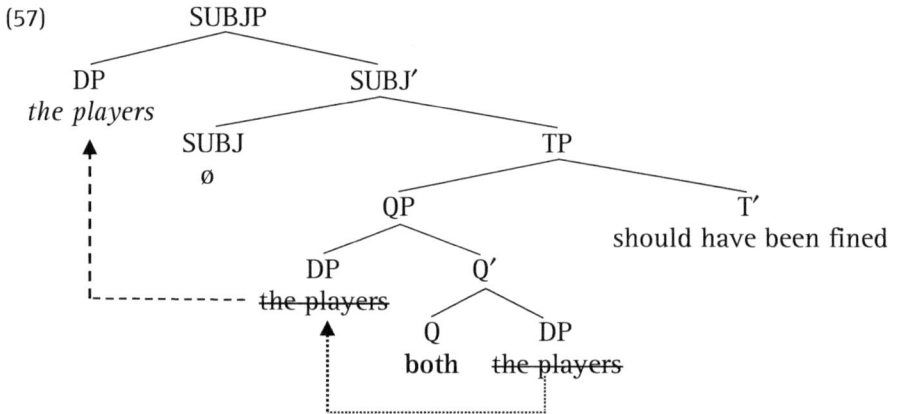

On this view, the DP *the players* moves from comp-QP (i.e. from being the complement of Q-*both*) to spec-QP, as shown by the lower/dotted arrow in (57); and subsequently the DP *the players* moves from spec-QP to spec-SUBJP, as shown by the higher/dashed arrow.

Unfortunately, however, the movements arrowed in (57) violate a number of constraints on movement. For example, movement of the DP *the players* from comp-QP to spec-QP violates an antilocality constraint which Boeckx (2007: 110) formulates as follows:

(58)   Antilocality Constraint
         'Movement internal to a projection counts as too local, and is banned'

The antilocality violation arises because the DP moves from complement to specifier position internally within the same QP projection. In addition, the second movement of the DP *the players* from spec-QP to spec-SUBJP violates the Constraint on Extraction Domains/CED (48), because CED bars extraction out of a specifier, and the QP out of which *the players* is extracted in (57) occupies spec-TP. Indeed, given the assumption that the relevant QP originates in spec-VP and from there moves to spec-TP, the DP movement operation arrowed in (57) will also violate the Freezing Principle/FP (49), because the DP *the players* is extracted out of a QP *both the players* that has moved from spec-VP to spec-TP.

Our discussion here leads to the conclusion that the particular implementation of the quantifier stranding analysis outlined in (57) runs into theoretical problems. However, these can potentially be overcome if we adopt an alternative implementation of the stranding analysis which makes use of the split spellout mechanism outlined in §2.3.3. On this alternative approach to stranding, all the variants of the sentences in (55) would involve fronting the whole QP *both the players*, and the differences between them would lie in whether the quantifier *all* is spelled out on the highest copy of the movement chain, or on some lower copy in the chain. On this split spellout account, (55c) would have the syntactic derivation below (simplified for expository purposes by ignoring the possibility that *should* originates as the head of a modal projection and from there moves to adjoin to a tense affix in T):

(59)

As indicated by the arrows in (59), the QP *both the players* originates as the complement of the passive participle *fined*, and then moves in successive-cyclic fashion through spec-VOICEP, spec-PERFP, and spec-TP into spec-SUBJP. In the PF component, only the highest copy of the DP *the players* (inside QP$_5$) can be spelled out overtly, in accordance with the Default Spellout Rule which was given the following formulation in §1.4.1:

(60)   **Default Spellout Rule/DSR**

For a constituent whose spellout is not determined in some other way, the highest copy of the constituent is overtly pronounced, and any lower copies are silent

But let's suppose that floatable quantifiers like *all/both/each* are subject to a special spellout rule of their own, which can be formulated as follows:

(61)   Floating Quantifier Spellout Rule/FQSR
         Floatable quantifiers can be spelled out on any non-initial link of an
         A-Movement chain in standard varieties of English

The qualification 'non-initial' is added to (61) in order to account for the ungrammaticality of sentences like that below:

(62)   *The players should have been fined *both*

In (62), the quantifier *both* is illicitly spelled out in its initial position (as the complement of *fined*), and this accounts for the ungrammaticality of the resulting sentence. A point to note in passing is that there is considerable variation in non-standard varieties of English with respect to the positions in which floating quantifiers can be spelled out: see Henry (2012) for an interesting discussion.

Under the spellout account in (61), we can make the following assumptions about where in the tree (59) Q-*both* is spelled out. In (55a) 'The players should have *both* been fined', Q-*both* is spelled out in spec-VOICEP; in (55b) 'The players should *both* have been fined', Q-*both* is spelled out in spec-PERFP; and in (55c) 'The players *both* should have been fined', Q-*both* is spelled out in spec-TP. And in (63) below, Q-*both* is spelled out in spec-SUBJP:

(63)   *Both* the players should have been fined

So, the split spellout account seemingly provides us with a mechanism for maintaining the stranding analysis of floating quantifiers.

However, although the split spellout variant of the stranding analysis accounts for the (un)grammaticality of quantifier stranding in sentences like those in (55) and (62) above, it proves problematic for sentences like those below:

(64)   a. *They* have **both** been vaccinated
         b. *Peter, Paul and Mary* have **all** been vaccinated
         c. *The patients* have **all three** been vaccinated

The reason is that the putative source QPs under the stranding analysis, (highlighted below) are ungrammatical:

(65)   a. *Both* *they* have been vaccinated
         b. *All* *Peter, Paul and Mary* have been vaccinated
         c. *All three* *the patients* have been vaccinated

Nor can the source QP be *both of them/all of Peter, Paul and Mary/all three of the patients*, since this would raise questions about where *of* has gone, and why in (64a) the subject is *they* and not *them*.

A further problem for the stranding account arises in clauses with a plural subject where the stranded quantifier is *each*, as in:

(66)   We have *each* been goading the other

Any suggestion that the underlying subject of *goading the other* is the QP *each we* poses the problem that this is ungrammatical; and to assume that the underlying subject is *each of us* raises not only the question of where *of* has gone, but also how the auxiliary *have* comes to be first person plural in (66), when a phrase like *each of us* requires third person singular agreement, as in (67) below:

(67)   Each of us *has* been goading the other

Moreover, the further question arises of how the subject comes to be nominative *we* in (66) when its supposed source in (67) contains accusative *us*.

An additional potential problem for the stranding analysis is posed by sentences where the (bold-printed) stranded quantifier has an (italicised) complement of its own, as in:

(68)   a. But they were, **all** *of them*, deceived, for another Ring was made (J.
             R. R. Tolkien, *The Fellowship of the Ring*, George Allen & Unwin,
             London, 1954)
          b. They have, **each** *of them* been allowed a bottle of beer a day
             (George Washington to William Pearce, 23 December 1793,
             founders.archives.com)
          c. They would **neither** *of them* have opposed that (J. Shattock & E.
             Jay, *The Selected Works of Margaret Oliphant, Part VI*, London,
             Routledge, 2021: 138)
          d. They should **none** *of them* have the tag in the query (discuss.elastic.co)
          e. They didn't **either** *of them* appreciate what had happened (basclub.org)
          f. They have **several** *of them* been widely reported both in the East and
             the West (rareamericana.com)

In cases like (68), it is hard to see how the quantifiers *all/each/neither/none/either/several* could be stranded by movement of the subject *they*, since the floating quantifier has a complement of its own – namely *of them*.

Nonetheless, care needs to be taken in evaluating sentences like (68), since they may not be instances of floating quantifiers, but rather may represent a different kind of structure in which a highlighted QP is right-dislocated. Some evidence in support of this view is that (like right-dislocated constituents but unlike typical floating quantifiers) the highlighted QPs in (68) can also occur at the end of the sentence. Moreover, the structure in (68) can contain quantifiers like *either/neither/several/none* which are otherwise unable to float, and the highlighted constituents seem to form a separate intonation group of their own (which can be marked by the use of a comma preceding and following the relevant constituent, as in 68a): this marks them out as different from typical floating quantifiers. If so, we should probably not treat sentences like (68) as providing us with evidence about the syntax of floating quantifiers.

Yet another potential problem which arises with the stranding analysis is the following. On the stranding account, floating QPs always occupy the specifier position of an auxiliary projection which the subject transits through. However, this assumption proves problematic for sentences like the following:

(69)   They allegedly *both* rarely do heed advice

It is difficult to argue that *both* is stranded as the specifier of an auxiliary in (69), since there is no auxiliary between the adverbs *allegedly* and *frequently*.

Overall, then, the considerations outlined in relation to (55–69) above call into question the twin ideas that (i) a floating quantifier is stranded under movement, and that (ii) superficially a floating quantifier occupies the specifier position of an auxiliary projection through which the subject transits. Consequently, in the next section, I explore the alternative possibility that a floating quantifier is directly generated in situ as the specifier of a dedicated functional projection which can occupy a variety of positions within the subperiphery.

6.4.3   Floating QPs: In a dedicated projection

A traditional assumption made in work in the 1980s was that floating quantifiers occupy much the same range of positions as adverbs – as we see from the potential parallel between the positions occupied by the floating quantifier *all* and the adverb *quietly* below:

(70)   a. The students *all* entered the room
        b. The students *quietly* entered the room

Moreover, as observed by Sag (1978), floating quantifiers pattern like adverbs (and unlike *not/n't*) in respect of not permitting VP ellipsis in structures like:

(71)   a. Otto has read this book, and my brothers have (*all/certainly*) read it, too
        b. Otto has read this book, and my brothers have (**all/*certainly*) ~~read it,~~ too
        c. Otto has read this book, but my brothers have (*n't/not*) ~~read it~~

This led to proposals that floating quantifiers should be treated in the same way as adverbs: on one implementation of this idea, both *all* and *quietly* would serve as adjuncts to the VP *entered the room* in (70). This is far from implausible at first sight, since a sentence like (72a) below containing the quantifier *most* can be closely paraphrased by a sentence like (72b) containing the adverb *mostly*:

(72)   a. *Most* students hate taking exams
        b. Students *mostly* hate taking exams

However, closer reflection suggests that floating quantifiers aren't adverbial in nature. For example, unlike *mostly* in (72b), floating quantifiers such as *both/all/each* don't allow the adverbial affix *-ly* to be attached to them; and conversely, *mostly* in (72b) has no floating quantifier counterpart (cf. **Students **most** hate taking exams*). Moreover (unlike adverbs) floating quantifiers have inherent number properties, and can only quantify subjects with matching number properties – as we see from:

(73)   a. *The two men* were **each/both/*all** feeling tired
        b. *The three men* were **each/all/*both** feeling tired

As these examples show, the quantifier *each* requires a subject denoting more than one entity, *both* requires a subject denoting two entities, and *all* requires a subject denoting more than two entities. By contrast, when used as a genuine adverb (paraphrasable as 'entirely'), the word *all* has no number properties and hence can be used with a singular subject, as in:

(74)   *The dog* was **all** wet

The contrast between (73) and (74) thus casts doubt on the assumption that floating quantifiers are adverbs. In addition, floating quantifiers and adverbs differ in their distribution, as illustrated below:

(75)   a. The students entered the room *quietly*
        b. *The students entered the room *all*

Thus, the adverb *quietly* in (75a) above can follow the VP *entered the room*, but the floating quantifier *all* in (75b) cannot.

    The considerations outlined above lead to the conclusion that while floating quantifiers resemble adverbs in some respects, they differ from them in others. This raises the possibility of treating them in much the same way as Cinque treats adverbial modifiers (namely as specifiers of dedicated functional heads), but with the difference that the relevant dedicated functional head licenses a QP rather than an ADVP as its specifier. On this functional specifier analysis, the subperiphery of a sentence like (69) 'They allegedly *both* rarely do heed advice' would have the structure shown in

(76) below (where $F_1/F_2/F_3$ denote dedicated functional heads which each license a different kind of specifier):

(76)   SUBJP

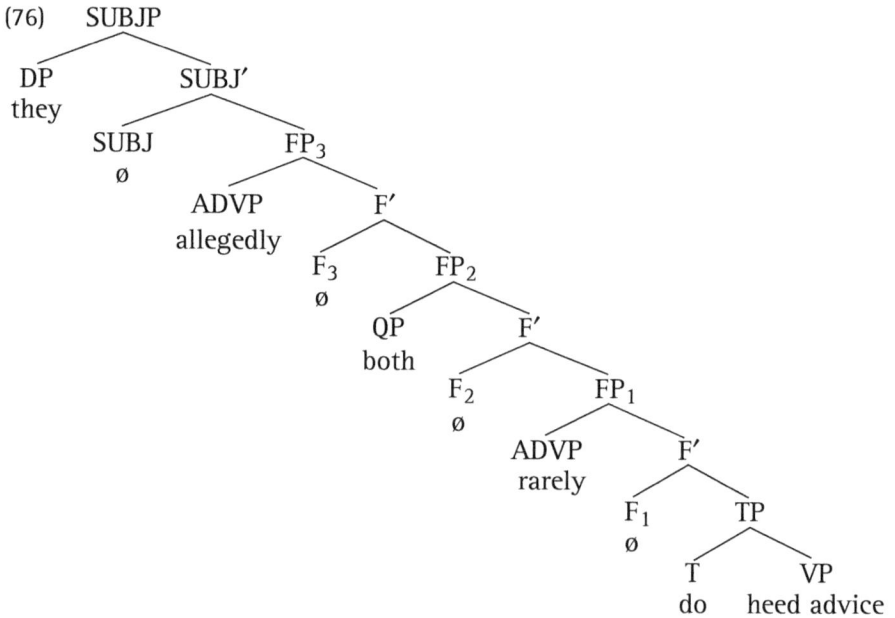

An incidental point of detail to note in relation to (76) is that I have made the simplifying assumption that the auxiliary *do* marks present tense but not aspect/modality, and hence can be taken to originate in T; but if we take *do* to mark habitual aspect as well as tense, then *do* will originate as the head of a habitual aspect projection/HABP below TP, and from there raise to adjoin to a present tense affix in T.

As for the range of positions which floating quantifiers can or can't occupy in sentences like (55/62), we can handle this by supposing that a functional projection housing a floating quantifier can in principle occupy any position in the subperiphery below the subject (i.e. any position below the edge of SUBJP but above the edge of VP). Moreover, we can handle structures in which a floating quantifier is positioned between two adverbs, as we see from (76) above. Furthermore, if we make the plausible assumption that a floating quantifier is construed as quantifying a subject with specific number properties, we can account for *each* requiring a subject denoting more than one entity, *both* requiring a dual subject (i.e. one denoting two entities), and *all* requiring a subject denoting three or more entities. I shall therefore assume henceforth that floating quantifiers are QPs which serve as specifiers of dedicated functional heads.

Although (as noted above) floating quantifiers behave like adverbs in certain respects, they also differ from them in other respects. One significant difference is that (as illustrated below) an adverb like *sometimes* can typically either precede or follow a constituent that it modifies, whereas a floating quantifier like *both* cannot function as a postmodifier – as illustrated below:

(77)   a. They *sometimes both* would order lobster
       b. They *both* would order lobster <u>sometimes</u>
       c. *They *sometimes* would order lobster <u>both</u>

In (77a), the ADVP *sometimes* and the floating QP *both* serve as premodifiers of the TP *would order lobster*. But while *sometimes* can also serve as a postmodifier in (77b), the floating QP *both* cannot – as we see from the ungrammaticality of (77c). Why should this be?

Under the functional specifier analysis of subperipheral modifiers outlined here, (77a) will have the structure shown in simplified form below:

(78)

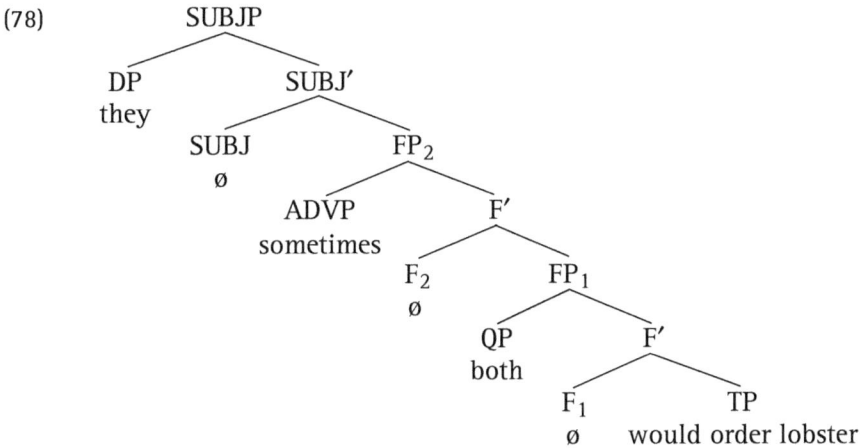

Given this assumption, (77b) will be derived by moving the FP_1 constituent *both would order lobster* to become the specifier of an additional functional projection above the FP_2 constituent housing *sometimes* – as shown below:

(79)

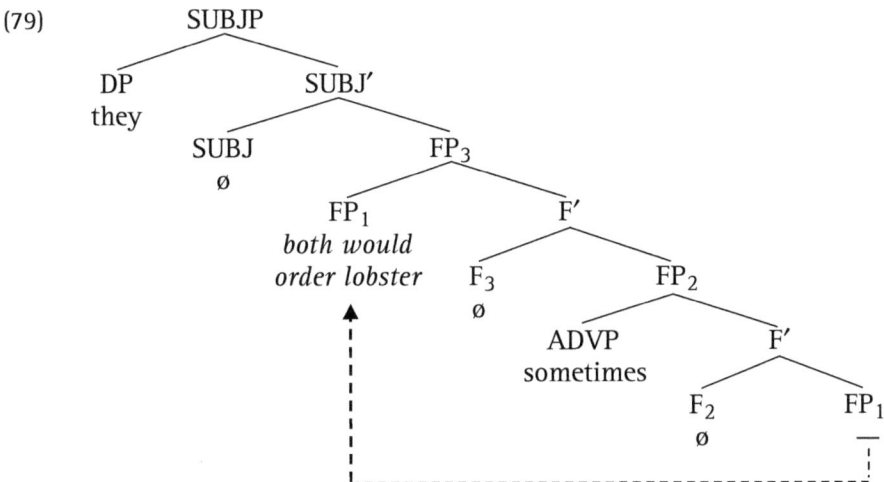

Although (as we see from 78 above) the ADVP *sometimes* originates as a premodifier to FP$_1$ *both would order lobster*, it comes to be positioned after FP$_1$ and stranded at the end of the sentence as a result of the Complement Raising operation arrowed in (79).

By contrast, the quantifier *both* cannot be stranded at the end of the sentence in the same way, as we see from the ungrammaticality of (77c). What this means in terms of the functional specifier analysis is that a floating quantifier doesn't allow the Complement Raising operation arrowed below:

(80)

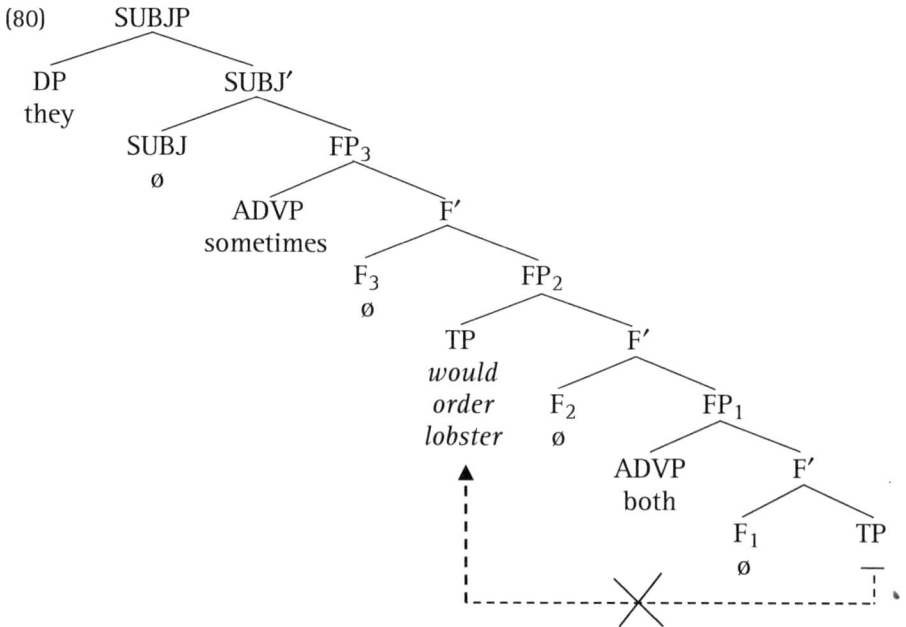

This means that an additional complication posed by the functional specifier analysis of modifiers is that some premodifiers allow a Complement Raising operation which in effect converts them into postmodifiers, whereas others do not. We can account for this by positing that the kind of functional head that allows a frequency adverbial like *sometimes* as its specifier can trigger raising of its complement, whereas the kind of functional head which allows a floating QP as its specifier cannot. Still, this leaves open the question of why this should be so.

To sum up: I have argued in Module 6.4 that, like adverbial modifiers, floating quantifiers also function as specifiers of dedicated functional heads, and I have shown that such an analysis accounts for how a floating quantifier can end up positioned between two adverbs. I noted, however, that the type of functional head which licenses a floating quantifier as its specifier does not trigger the Complement Raising operation by which functional heads which license an adverb as their specifier can trigger movement of their complement to become the specifier of a higher functional projection (contrast 79 and 80 above). The consequence of this is that floating quantifiers in English can only function as premodifiers, whereas adverbs can be either premodifiers or postmodifiers.

You should now be able to tackle Exercise 6.4.

6.5   Summary

This module has been concerned with the structure of the subperiphery of clauses – that is, that part of the structure positioned between the CP periphery and the VP core. In the classic CP+TP+VP model of clause structure, the subperiphery was analysed as a unitary TP constituent; however, in this module we have looked at evidence for the subperiphery being split into a number of separate projections, resulting in it having a more articulated/complex structure than traditionally assumed.

In Module 6.1, I noted that the subperiphery can contain multiple auxiliary projections, including not just a TP/tense projection, but also an MP/modal projection, PERFP/perfect aspect projection, PROGP/progressive aspect projection, and VOICEP/passive voice projection, in each case headed by a corresponding type of auxiliary. I argued that finite auxiliaries typically originate as the head of an auxilary projection (MP/PERFP/PROGP/VOICEP) below TP, and from there raise to adjoin to a (past or present) tense affix in T – though I noted that the auxiliary *do* (if we take it to mark tense alone) can be taken to be directly generated in T. I went on to argue that the traditional assumption that subjects are contained in the same TP projection as finite auxiliaries proves problematic for sentences which contain constituents intervening between subject and auxiliary, like the intervening ADVP *most definitely* in 'He <u>most definitely</u> **did** apologise.' I noted that earlier work had treated such intervening adverbials as T-bar adjuncts, but that such an analysis would violate a likeness constraint on adjunction proposed by Baltin (1978) to the effect that a maximal projection like *most definitely* can only adjoin to another maximal projection. I argued that this problem can be overcome if the auxiliary *did* is treated as heading the TP *did apologise*, and if the subject *he* is analysed as contained in a separate SUBJP projection; under the traditional analysis of adverbial modifiers as adjuncts, the ADVP *most definitely* can then be analysed as a maximal projection which adjoins to another maximal projection (i.e. to the TP *did apologise*).

However, in Module 6.2, I outlined Cinque's claim that adverbial modifiers should be reanalysed as specifiers of functional projections, each with a dedicated functional head that licenses a specific type of adverb as its specifier. I reported Cinque's claim that such a functional specifier analysis is preferable to the traditional adjunct analysis, in part because it enables us to dispense with phrasal adjuncts altogether, and in part because it enables us to account for the relative ordering of multiple subperipheral adverbials in terms of the familiar head-complement selection mechanism. I also noted Cinque's hypothesis that adverbs of a given type occupy a fixed position within the clause, and that the relative positions of different types of adverb can be captured by the putatively universal Adverb Hierarchy in (36).

In Module 6.3, I looked at the variable position of adverbs, auxiliaries and subjects. I noted Cinque's claim that this variation can be accounted for by supposing that adverbs occupy a fixed position within the clause, and that word order variation can be attributed to movement of other constituents – for example, auxiliaries raising to a range of functional head positions above T, subjects raising to either spec-TP or spec-SUBJP, and the complement of a functional head raising to become the specifier of a superordinate/higher functional projection.

In Module 6.4, I argued that other subperipheral constituents (including PPs, subordinate clauses/CONJPs, and floating QPs) can be analysed (within a more articulated model of syntactic structure) as specifiers of dedicated functional heads. But I noted that floating quantifiers differ from other subperipheral constituents in that they can occupy a wide range of subperipheral positions between the SUBJ head and the VP. I outlined the stranding analysis of floating quantifiers whereby they are stranded under movement of the subject through intermediate auxiliary projections, and I presented a split spellout account of this. However, I argued that the stranding analysis of floating quantifiers proves problematic in relation to sentences where a floating quantifier is stranded between two adverbs, and I outlined an alternative account under which floating quantifiers are housed within a dedicated functional projection that can occupy a range of positions within the subperiphery (between SUBJP and VP). I noted that floating quantifiers differ from adverbs in that they do not allow Complement Raising, and thus cannot function as postmodifiers.

Key constructs in our discussion this chapter include the following:

(6)   **One Feature One Head Principle**
        Each functional head carries only one interpretable feature

(20)   **Like-Adjoins-to-Like Constraint**
        Adjunction can only adjoin like to like

(36)   **Adverb Hierarchy**
        [*frankly* MOOD$_{\text{speech act}}$ [*fortunately* MOOD$_{\text{evaluative}}$ [allegedly MOOD$_{\text{evidential}}$
        [*probably* MOD$_{\text{epistemic}}$ [*once* T$_{\text{past}}$ [*then* T$_{\text{future}}$ [*perhaps* MOOD$_{\text{irrealis}}$

[*necessarily* MOD$_{necessity}$ [*possibly* MOD$_{possibility}$ [*usually* ASP$_{habitual}$

[*again* ASP$_{repetitive(I)}$ [*often* ASP$_{frequentative(I)}$ [*intentionally* MOD$_{volitional}$

[*quickly* ASP$_{celerative(I)}$ [already T$_{anterior}$ [*no longer* ASP$_{terminative}$

[*still* ASP$_{continuative}$ [*always* ASP$_{perfect(?)}$ [*just* ASP$_{retrospective}$ [*soon* ASP$_{proximative}$

[*briefly* ASP$_{durative}$ [*characteristically*(?) ASP$_{generic/progressive}$ [*almost* ASP$_{prospective}$

[*completely* ASP$_{completive(I)}$ [*well* VOICE [*fast/early* ASP$_{celerative(II)}$

[*again* ASP$_{repetitive(II)}$ [*often* ASP$_{frequentative(II)}$ [*completely* ASP$_{completive(II)}$

(53)　**Functional Specifier Hypothesis/FSH**
Each XP in the periphery or subperiphery of a clause is the specifier of a dedicated functional head

(54)　**Merge Hypothesis**
A maximal projection/XP can only be introduced into a structure containing it via (first- or second-) merge with a head

(61)　**Floating Quantifier Spellout Rule/FQSR**
Floatable quantifiers can be spelled out on any non-initial link of an A-Movement chain in standard varieties of English

6.6　Bibliographical notes

For more detailed textbook accounts of the claim made here that auxiliaries originate as the head of an **auxiliary projection** below T and from there (if finite) move to adjoin to a tense affix in T, see the discussion of **Auxiliary Raising** in Radford (2020: 236–60), or Radford (2004a, 2004b, 2009a, 2009b, 2016).

The **split TP analysis** (splitting TP into two separate projections, one which is the locus of tense, and another which is the locus of subjects/subject agreement) was known in earlier work as the split INFL hypothesis (in an era when INFL was treated as the locus of tense and agreement features in finite clauses). It dates back to work by Pollock (1989), Chomsky (1989, 1993), Belletti (1990, 2001), Speas (1994), Watanabe (1994), Giorgi & Pianesi (1997), Aygen-Tosun (1998), and Griffin (2003). It has been claimed that there is evidence supporting the hypothesis from language acquisition (Malamud-Makowski 1994; Ingham 1998; Hanson 1999; Guasti & Rizzi 2002; Deen 2002), and language disorders (Schaeffer 1994; Friedemann 1998; Friedmann & Grodzinsky 1997, 2000; Ferreiro 2003). For discussion of **SUBJP**, see Cardinaletti (1997, 2004), Rizzi & Shlonsky (2006, 2007), Haegeman (2002a, 2002b, 2007b, 2013, 2017, 2019, 2021), Haegeman & Danckaert (2017), and Haegeman & Starke (2021).

On the treatment of **adverbs** as specifiers of dedicated functional projections, see Cinque (1999, 2004, 2017a, 2023), and Rizzi & Cinque (2016): for a critical perspective, see Bobaljik (1999), Nilsen (2003), Meira (2004), Manninen (2005), Holmer (2013), Smit (2014), and Forsmo (2020). On similar approaches to Cinque's, see Laenzlinger (1993, 1996, 1999, 2000), and Alexiadou (1994, 1997). For a defence of the alternative (traditional) adjunct analysis of adverbs, see Costa (2000, 2004), Haider (2000, 2004), Rosengren (2000), Maienborn (2001), Ernst (2002, 2004), Williams (2002), and Svenonius (2002b).

On **floating quantifiers**, see Maling (1976), Klein (1977), Sag (1978), Haig (1980), Vater (1980), Jaeggli (1982), Nakamura (1983), Dowty & Brodie (1984), Sportiche (1986, 1988), Giusti (1990, 1991b), Junker (1990), Yatabe (1990), Fukushima (1991a, 1991b), Shlonsky (1991), Doetjes (1992, 1997), Hasegawa (1993), Akiyama (1994), Baltin (1995), Hoeksema (1996), Merchant (1996), Tonoike (1996), Torrego (1996), Hamamo (1997), Paunovic (1997), Brisson (1998, 2000), Abeillé & Godard (1999), Benmamoun (1999), Fox & Nissenbaum (1999), Haegeman & Guéron (1999), Ishii (1999), De Cat (2000), McCloskey (2000), Bošković (2001, 2004), Yoo (2001, 2002), Kang (2002), Bobaljik (2003), Kobuchi-Philip (2003, 2007), Puskás (2003), Terada (2003), Tsoulas (2003), Nakanishi (2004, 2008), Janke & Neeleman (2005), Fitzpatrick (2006), Miyagawa (2006b, 2017b), Endo (2007b), Miyagawa & Arikawa (2007), Roehrs (2008), Spector (2008, 2009), Tanaka (2008), Valmara (2008), Cirillo (2009, 2012), Kim & Kim (2009), Heejeong Ko (2010), Koopman (2010), Reed (2010), Rezak (2010), Rochman (2010), Simpson (2011), Harwood (2012), Henry (2012), Ko & Oh (2012), Ott (2012b), Jenks (2013), Osborne (2013), Fukuda & Polinsky (2014), Lacerda (2016), Otoguro & Snijders (2016), Chaiphet (2017), Kostopoulos (2017), Kitagawa (2018), Zyman (2018b), Al Khalaf (2019), Kim (2020), and Netkachev (2020).

6.7   Workbook

In the exercises below, an [M] after an example sentence indicates that a model answer is provided in the free-to-download *Students' Answerbook* (and in the *Teachers' Answerbook* as well). You will find it helpful to look at this model answer before attempting to tackle other examples in the exercise. Some other exercise examples have an [S] after them, indicating that they are for self-study: this means that after reading the relevant module (and those preceding it), and looking at the helpful hints and model answer associated with the exercise, students should be able to analyse these self-study examples on their own, and then compare their answers with those provided in the *Students' Answerbook*. The remaining exercise examples (i.e. those not marked with [M] or [S] after them) are intended for teachers to use as the basis for hands-on problem-solving work in seminars, classes, or assignments: answers to all of these non-self-study examples are provided in the *Teachers' Answerbook*. Note that Exercise 6.1 tests you on Module 6.1, Exercise 6.2 on Module 6.2, and so on; and that each exercise in a given chapter presupposes familiarity with material covered in earlier chapters and in earlier modules of the same chapter. Unparenthesised numbers like 4 refer to material in the exercises, whereas parenthesised numbers like (22) refer to examples and conditions in the main text of the book.

EXERCISE 6.1

This exercise is designed to be attempted after reading Module 6.1 and the chapters preceding it.

Discuss the syntax of the subperiphery of the sentences below (concerning yourself only with the bracketed complement clause in 2):

1   He probably need not worry about that (dallasnews.com) [M]
2   I know [what song I definitely really truly do not want played at my funeral], and that is Amazing Grace (yoru-yume.livejournal.com) [S]
3   He clearly couldn't do anything
4   He potentially may not have been telling the truth
5   What else could he possibly have done? [S]
6   What else could potentially he be doing? (Bret Baier, Fox News)

For the interrogative clauses in 2, 5, 6, consider also the structure of the periphery.

Helpful hints
For the purposes of this exercise, follow Module 6.1 and adopt the traditional analysis of adverbial modifiers as adjuncts to the constituent they modify. Don't concern yourself with the internal structure of verb phrases in any of the sentences. In 2, assume that *what song* is an interrogative QP, and that *not want played at my funeral* is a NEGP, but don't concern yourself with the internal structure of either. In 3, assume that *n't* is a clitic which originates as the head NEG of NEGP, and encliticises/attaches to the end of a tensed auxiliary (i.e. an auxiliary carrying an overt or null tense affix) in T: for present purposes, treat *could* as the past tense of *can* and assume that *could* spells out a *can+Af* structure, where *Af* is a past tense affix in T. In 4, treat *not* as an ADVP which is the specifier of a NEGP with a null NEG head; in addition, treat

have been telling the truth as a PERFP/perfect aspect phrase, but don't concern yourself with its internal structure. In 5 and 6 treat *what else* as an interrogative QP, but don't concern yourself with its internal structure. Discuss what role is played by the following (where relevant):

7   **One Feature One Head Principle** (= 6)
     Each functional head carries only one interpretable feature

8   **Like-Adjoins-to-Like Constraint** (= 20)
     Adjunction can only adjoin like to like

9   **Minimality Condition** (from §1.3.2)
     A moved constituent must move to the minimal/closest potential landing site above it

10   **Interrogative Generalisation** (from §5.2.1)
     (i) A peripheral interrogative XP that triggers Auxiliary Inversion moves from spec-FINP (with FIN attracting a finite auxiliary to adjoin to it) into its criterial position in spec-FOCP
     (ii) The criterial position for a peripheral interrogative XP that does not trigger Auxiliary Inversion is spec-FORCEP

EXERCISE 6.2

This exercise is designed to be attempted after reading Module 6.2 and the module and chapters preceding it.

Discuss the syntax of the subperiphery of the sentences below:

1   He perhaps already has hired someone [M]
2   He frankly usually doesn't completely trust anyone
3   They unfortunately couldn't afford it [S]
4   They probably will soon have finished it
5a   She doesn't often have time for lunch
5b   She often doesn't have time for lunch
6   He sadly wasn't fully paying attention [S]

Helpful hints

Compare the traditional CP+TP+VP model of clause structure in which subperipheral adverbs are treated as adjuncts with the alternative functional specifier analysis outlined in Module 6.2. In negative sentences, treat *n't* as the head NEG constituent of NEGP, and take it to be a clitic which (in the syntax) encliticises to (i.e. attaches to the end/

right of) a tensed auxiliary in T (i.e. an auxiliary inflected for present/
past tense). Concern yourself only with the structure of the subperiphery,
and do not attempt to analyse the internal structure of verb phrases. In
developing your analyses, discuss the role played by the following (where
relevant):

7   **One Feature One Head Principle** (= 6)
     Each functional head carries only one interpretable feature

8   **Like-Adjoins-to-Like Constraint** (= 20)
     Adjunction can only adjoin like to like (i.e. one head to another, or one
     maximal projection to another)

9   **Adverb hierarchy** (= 36)
     [*frankly* MOOD$_{speech\ act}$ [*fortunately* MOOD$_{evaluative}$ [*allegedly* MOOD$_{evidential}$
     [*probably* MOD$_{epistemic}$ [*once* T$_{past}$ [*then* T$_{future}$ [*perhaps* MOOD$_{irrealis}$
     [*necessarily* MOD$_{necessity}$ [*possibly* MOD$_{possibility}$ [*usually* ASP$_{habitual}$
     [*again* ASP$_{repetitive(I)}$ [*often* ASP$_{frequentative(I)}$ [*intentionally* MOD$_{volitional}$
     [*quickly* ASP$_{celerative(I)}$ [*already* T$_{anterior}$ [*no longer* ASP$_{terminative}$
     [*still* ASP$_{continuative}$ [*always* ASP$_{perfect(?)}$ [*just* ASP$_{retrospective}$ [*soon* ASP$_{proximative}$
     [*briefly* ASP$_{durative}$ [*characteristically*(?) ASP$_{generic/progressive}$ [*almost* ASP$_{prospective}$
     [*completely* ASP$_{completive(I)}$ [*well* VOICE [*fast/early* ASP$_{celerative(II)}$
     [*again* ASP$_{repetitive(II)}$ [*often* ASP$_{frequentative(II)}$ [*completely* ASP$_{completive(II)}$

10   **Functional Specifier Hypothesis/FSH** (= 53)
     Every XP in the periphery or subperiphery of a clause is the specifier of
     a dedicated functional head

11   **Merge Hypothesis** (= 54)
     A maximal projection/XP can only be introduced into a structure
     containing it via (first- or second-) merge with a head

EXERCISE 6.3

*This exercise is designed to be attempted after reading Module 6.3 and the
modules and chapters preceding it.*

Account for word order variation in the position of the italicised ADVPs/
PPs in the following sets of sentences:

1a I should have *probably* reported it *immediately* [M]
1b I should *probably* have reported it *immediately* [M]
1c *Probably* I should have reported it *immediately* [M]
1d I *probably* should have reported it *immediately* [M]

2a This is *possibly* the best outcome

2b *Possibly* this is the best outcome

2c This *possibly* is the best outcome

3a He must *surely still* be in his room

3b He *surely* must *still* be in his room

3c *Surely* he must *still* be in his room

4a He *usually* doesn't *at any point* interrupt her [S]

4b *Usually* he doesn't *at any point* interrupt her [S]

4c He doesn't *usually* interrupt her *at any point* [S]

5a They could *potentially entirely* reject the deal

5b They could *potentially* reject the deal *entirely*

5c *Potentially* they could reject the deal *entirely*

5d They *potentially* could *entirely* reject the deal

5e They *potentially* could reject the deal *entirely*

Helpful hints

Compare the adjunct analysis of ADVP/PP modifiers in the traditional CP+TP+VP model of clause structure with the alternative functional specifier account outlined in Module 6.3. Concern yourself only with the structure of the subperiphery (not with the periphery), and do not attempt to show the internal structure of verb phrases/VPs in any of the examples. In 2, bear in mind the traditional assumption that BE (in its use as a copula/linking verb) originates in V and from there moves to adjoin to a tense affix in T in indicative clauses. In 4, take *n't* to originate as the head NEG constituent of a NEGP constituent, and assume that it encliticises to (i.e. adjoins to the end/right of) a finite auxiliary in T. In developing your analyses, discuss what role (if any) is played in relevant examples by the principles/hypotheses/hierarchy outlined in 7–11 of Exercise 6.2.

EXERCISE 6.4

This exercise is designed to be attempted after reading Module 6.4 and the modules and chapters preceding it.

Discuss the syntax of the subperiphery in the sentences below:

1 The Brownlee brothers, in spite of leading the race, both were eventually overtaken [M]

2 They undoubtedly had both deeply regretted the decision

3 The men had evidently all blatantly disobeyed orders [S]

4 The fighters, throughout, although tired, had both gamely swapped punches

5   They allegedly each are still blaming the others

6   She probably hasn't at all (In reply to 'Has she heard from him?') [S]

Helpful hints

Compare the adjunct analysis of peripheral modifiers in the traditional CP+TP+VP model with the functional specifier account. Concern yourself only with the structure of the subperiphery of the sentences, and do not analyse the internal structure of the verb phrases they contain. In 1–5, consider whether floating quantifiers are (i) adjuncts, or (ii) stranded in the specifier position of an intermediate auxiliary projection through which the subject transits, or (iii) specifiers of a dedicated functional head which licenses a floating QP as its specifier. In 1, treat *the Brownlee brothers* as a DP, and *in spite of leading the race* as a PP but don't concern yourself with the internal structure of either phrase. In 4 treat *throughout* as a PP (paraphrasable as 'throughout the fight/event'), and treat *although exhausted* as a CONJP/subordinate clause (a reduced form of *although they were exhausted*, perhaps) – but do not concern yourself with the internal structure of these constituents. Treat 6 as involving a VP ellipsis operation whereby a VP present in the syntax can be given a null spellout in the PF component if its contents are recoverable (e.g. from an antecedent). Discuss the role played by the following (where relevant):

7   **One Feature One Head Principle** (= 6)
     Each functional head carries only one interpretable feature

8   **Like-Adjoins-to-Like Constraint** (= 20)
     Adjunction can only adjoin like to like (i.e. one head to another, or one maximal projection to another)

9   **Constraint on Extraction Domains/CED** (= 48)
     Extraction is only possible out of a complement, not out of a specifier or adjunct

10   **Freezing Principle** (= 49)
     The constituents of a moved phrase are frozen internally within (and so cannot be extracted out of) the moved phrase

11   **Adverb Hierarchy** (= 36)
     [*frankly* $\text{MOOD}_{\text{speech act}}$ [*fortunately* $\text{MOOD}_{\text{evaluative}}$ [*allegedly* $\text{MOOD}_{\text{evidential}}$
     [*probably* $\text{MOD}_{\text{epistemic}}$ [*once* T_{past} [*then* T_{future} [*perhaps* $\text{MOOD}_{\text{irrealis}}$
     [*necessarily* $\text{MOD}_{\text{necessity}}$ [*possibly* $\text{MOD}_{\text{possibility}}$ [*usually* $\text{ASP}_{\text{habitual}}$
     [*again* $\text{ASP}_{\text{repetitive(I)}}$ [*often* $\text{ASP}_{\text{frequentative(I)}}$ [*intentionally* $\text{MOD}_{\text{volitional}}$
     [*quickly* $\text{ASP}_{\text{celerative(I)}}$ [*already* $\text{T}_{\text{anterior}}$ [*no longer* $\text{ASP}_{\text{terminative}}$
     [*still* $\text{ASP}_{\text{continuative}}$ [*always* $\text{ASP}_{\text{perfect(?)}}$ [*just* $\text{ASP}_{\text{retrospective}}$ [*soon* $\text{ASP}_{\text{proximative}}$
     [*briefly* $\text{ASP}_{\text{durative}}$ [*characteristically*(?) $\text{ASP}_{\text{generic/progressive}}$ [*almost* $\text{ASP}_{\text{prospective}}$

[*completely* ASP$_{\text{completive(I)}}$ [*well* VOICE [*fast/early* ASP$_{\text{celerative(II)}}$
[*again* ASP$_{\text{repetitive(II)}}$ [*often* ASP$_{\text{frequentative(II)}}$ [*completely* ASP$_{\text{completive(II)}}$

12   **Functional Specifier Hypothesis/FSH (= 53)**
      Every XP in the periphery or subperiphery of a clause is the specifier of
      a dedicated functional head

13   **Merge Hypothesis (= 54)**
      A maximal projection/XP can only be introduced into a structure
      containing it via (first- or second-) merge with a head

14   **Default Spellout Rule/DSR (= 60)**
      For a constituent whose spellout is not determined in some other way,
      the highest copy of the constituent is overtly pronounced, and any lower
      copies are silent

15   **Floating Quantifier Spellout Rule/FQSR (= 61)**
      Floatable quantifiers can be spelled out on any non-initial link of an
      A-Movement chain in standard varieties of English

7 Abbreviated registers

7.0 Overview

In this module, we look at abbreviated registers of (spoken or written) English which allow certain types of constituent to be dropped (i.e. not overtly expressed), resulting in sentences which lack overt subjects, or auxiliaries, or articles, or objects, and so on. We will analyse different kinds of constituent drop found in different registers of English, and ask whether this is a syntactic phenomenon (whereby certain functional projections are missing in the syntax), or a phonological one (whereby material present in the syntax is given a null spellout in the phonology). We deal with Subject Drop in Module 7.1, Auxiliary Drop in Module 7.2, Article Drop in Module 7.3, Be Drop in Module 7.4, and Object Drop in Module 7.5.

7.1 Subject Drop

In abbreviated registers/styles of spoken English, we find a phenomenon which I will refer to as Sentence-Initial Ellipsis, whereby sentences can be abbreviated by allowing one or more constituents at the beginning of a sentence to be dropped. In this module, we examine one phenomenon of this kind (referred to here as Subject Drop) by which a subject can be dropped when it is the first word in a sentence.

7.1.1 The nature of Subject Drop

The phenomenon of Subject Drop can be illustrated by sentences like those below, in which the subject in <angle brackets> is 'dropped' in the sense that it is unpronounced:

(1)   a. SPEAKER A: Would you care for some tea?
          SPEAKER B: <I> wouldn't say no (Mackenzie 1998: 288)
    b. SPEAKER A: Am I invited to the party?
          SPEAKER B: <You> must be, surely (Weir 2012: 106)
    c. <I> just saw Bert. <He> looks like death warmed over (Zwicky & Pullum 1983: 159)

d. MONICA: Okay, everybody relax. This is not even a date. It's just
two people going out to dinner and not having sex.

CHANDLER: <It> sounds like a date to me (TV show *Friends*, Ozaki
2010: 39)

e. SPEAKER A: I saw Rachel yesterday. I brought her flowers and we
had a chat

SPEAKER B: <It> clearly did her a lot of good (Nariyama 2004: 252)

f.   <There> isn't much we can do about it (Thrasher 1977: 44).

g.   <It> turns out you can't do that in Texas (Schmerling 1973: 582).

As these examples illustrate, constituents which undergo Subject Drop are
typically personal pronouns (like those bracketed in 1a–1e), or expletive
pronouns like those bracketed in (1f, 1g). This may be because such pronouns have little or no lexical semantic content, and instead are functors (i.e. function words) essentially comprising bundles of grammatical
features.

There is empirical evidence in support of positing that sentences like
those in (1) have a <bracketed> subject which is present in the syntax, but
not pronounced in the phonology. One such piece of evidence comes from
the agreement morphology on the (bold-printed) finite auxiliary/verb in
sentences such as the following:

(2)   a.   <I> **am** not feeling too good this morning

b.   <You> **weren't** the only one, were you?

c. SPEAKER A: How's the veal today?

SPEAKER B: <It> **has** been better (Napoli 1982: 95)

d.   He's a wild card. <He> **flies** by the seat of his pants (dialogue from
the film *Top Gun*; Ito & Kashirara 2010: 21)

e. SPEAKER A: You want to use that?

SPEAKER B: <It> **depends** on how big a news day it is (dialogue
from film *Broadcast News*; Ito & Kashihara 2010: 28)

Since finite auxiliaries/verbs agree in person and number with their subjects, it's hard to see how we can (for example) account for use of the
first person singular form *am* in (2a) unless we posit that *am* has (a silent
counterpart of) the first person subject pronoun *I* as its subject; and similar
considerations hold for (2b–2e).

A second piece of evidence in support of positing that sentences like
those in (1) have syntactic subjects comes from tag sentences like those
below:

(3)   a.   <We> mustn't jump to conclusions, must **we**?

b.   <You> blew it, didn't **you**? (Kay 2002)

c.   <He> can't sing a note, can **he**? (Napoli 1982: 91)

d. <They> can't take everybody, can **they**? (Bailey 2011: 24)

e. <It> feels good to have them on again, doesn't **it**? (Shibata 2017: 2)

f. <There> isn't any pizza left by any chance, is **there**?

Tag sentences have the property that the tag (following the comma) contains a (bold-printed) pronominal copy of the main clause subject. Thus, the occurrence of the bold-printed pronoun *I* in the tag in (3a) provides evidence for claiming that the main clause must have a first person singular subject (albeit unpronounced). And a parallel logic can be applied to the examples in (3b–3f).

A third piece of evidence in support of positing that reduced sentences have syntactic subjects comes from sentences containing anaphors (and other expressions requiring a local antecedent) like those bold-printed below:

(4) a. <I> accidentally cut **myself** while shaving

b. <We/You/They> took **each other/one another** for granted

c. <She> ought to mind **her own** business

d. <They> shouldn't lose **their cool** in front of the children

Since the bold-printed expressions in (4) require a local antecedent with matching person/number/gender features, the grammaticality of the relevant sentences suggests that they have a syntactic subject with matching features. Moreover, a subject is required in order to bear the theta role assigned to it by the relevant predicate: for example, <I> is the EXPERIENCER argument of *cut* in (4a).

A claim implicit in the discussion of the examples in (1–4) above is that the missing subject is a pronoun, and not a full DP. Evidence that this is indeed the case comes from the following dialogue, where <?> indicates a missing subject whose precise identity is in question:

(5) SPEAKER A: What do you think of Dubai?

SPEAKER B: <?>'s a great place for a holiday

The use of the contracted third person singular copula *'s* here provides evidence that the missing subject is third person singular. But is the missing subject the pronominal DP *it* as in (6a) below, or the lexical DP *Dubai* as in (6b)?

(6) a. <It>'s a great place for a holiday

b. <Dubai>'s a great place for a holiday

A clue to the answer comes from the observation that the string *'s a* in (5B) has the phonetic spellout [sə], not [zə]. This can be accounted for in a straightforward fashion if the missing subject in (5B) is *it* as in (6a), since the word *it* ends in the voiceless consonant [t], and a contracted auxiliary assimilates to the last segment of the immediately preceding word it cliticises to in respect of voicing and hence is realised as voiceless [s] after the voiceless consonant [t]. By contrast, if the missing subject had been *Dubai* as in (6b), we would (wrongly) have predicted that the auxiliary would have been realised as the voiced segment [z], since this is the form of the contracted auxiliary required when it cliticises onto a word ending in a vowel/diphthong, like the diphthong [ai] in *Dubai*. Such considerations provide evidence that the 'missing' subject is a pronoun (like *it*) which has phonetic features of its own, and is not inherently null. In this respect, it differs from the inherently null subject of a coordinate clause like the *and*-clause in:

(7)   Muscat is in the Gulf of Oman *and's* only a stone's throw from the desert

In (7), the contracted auxiliary *'s* is pronounced [z], consistent with the view that the subject of *'s* is an empty category with no phonetic features of its own, with the result that *'s* undergoes progressive voice assimilation to the voiced final consonant [d] of *and*. (See Wilder 1994a, 1994b, and Haegeman & Starke 2021 for arguments that the subject of a coordinate clause is an empty category.)

Further evidence that the missing subject in Subject Drop structures is a pronoun comes from ellipsis in clausal idioms. Huang & Mendes (2019) note that where a clausal idiom undergoes VP Ellipsis, its subject can only be pronominal, not nominal – as illustrated by the following examples:

(8)   a. SPEAKER A: When the news got out, the shit hit the fan
             SPEAKER B: No *it*/**the shit* didn't

        b. SPEAKER A: It looks like the chickens have come home to roost
             SPEAKER B: Yes, I'm afraid *they*/**the chickens* have

Significantly, a VP-ellipsed clausal idiom allows a silent subject in (9B) below, where <?> denotes a mystery missing subject:

(9)   SPEAKER A: Did the shit hit the fan?
        SPEAKER B: <?> Sure did!

Given that (8a, 8b) tell us that a clausal idiom only allows VP Ellipsis if it has a pronominal subject, it follows that the mystery missing subject <?> in (9) must be the pronoun *it*, and not the nominal *the shit*.

Our discussion so far has led to the conclusion that Subject Drop involves sentences that have a pronominal subject which is present in the syntax, but is given a null/silent pronunciation in the phonology. A question which this assumption poses is: under what conditions/in what contexts can a subject be dropped? Two main conditions have been proposed governing the use of Subject Drop in spoken English. Firstly, it only applies in root/main clauses like those in (1) above, not in non-root clauses like those in square brackets below:

(10)   a. *I know [<you> gotta leave now] (Zwicky & Pullum 1983: 159)

       b. *[Because <it> was raining hard], we decided to stay at home

       c. *She is someone [that <we> know well]

       d. *There is more snow today [than <there> was yesterday]

       e. *The pitch was so flooded [that <they> had to call off the game]

       f. *[Clever though <he> is], he can't beat his 9-year-old son at chess

       g. *[Had <you> been there], you would really have enjoyed it

Thus, the subject cannot undergo ellipsis in a bracketed clause which is a complement clause as in (10a), an adverbial clause as in (10b), a relative clause as in (10c), a comparative clause as in (10d), a consecutive clause as in (10e), a concessive clause as in (10f), or a conditional clause with an inverted auxiliary as in (10g). Numerous studies have observed this restriction holding in spoken English: for example, Nariyama (2004: 245) reports that in his empirical study 'No subject ellipsis was found for subordinate clauses.'

A second widely reported condition on Subject Drop in spoken English is that it only applies where the missing subject is the first word in the sentence containing it. Accordingly, it is permitted in sentences like (1) above where this 'first word' requirement is met, but not in sentences like those in (11) below:

(11)   a. *Which pub did <you> go to?

       b. *Not a single word did <he> say

       c. *Have <you> seen any good movies lately? (Napoli 1982: 93)

       d. *What a great time <we> had!

       e. *Crying like a baby <he> was

The dropped subject is preceded by an (italicised) preposed interrogative wh-phrase and inverted auxiliary in (11a), a preposed negative phrase and inverted auxiliary in (11b), an inverted auxiliary in (11c), a preposed exclamative wh-phrase in (11d), and a fronted VP in (11e). Sentences like (11) are ruled out by the constraint that a subject can only be dropped when it is the first word in its sentence. (For discussion of apparent – but not real – exceptions to this first word condition, see Haegeman 2019.) Why should it be that Subject Drop in spoken English only affects sentence-initial subjects in root clauses? In the next section, we'll look an interesting answer provided by Luigi Rizzi, involving a mechanism termed Truncation.

7.1.2   A Truncation account of Subject Drop

Rizzi (1994, 1998, 2000a) argues that Subject Drop sentences have a syntactic structure which is truncated above SUBJP (in the sense that peripheral projections above SUBJP are not present in the syntax), leaving the subject as the highest constituent in the structure, and vulnerable to being deleted (i.e. given a silent spellout) in the phonology. More specifically, Rizzi argues that Subject Drop in spoken English can be handled in terms of a Truncation analysis which involves the assumptions below:

(12)   **Syntactic truncation account of Subject Drop**

(i) A sentence can have a truncated syntactic structure whose root is not FORCEP, but some lower projection such as SUBJP

(ii) The edge of the highest projection in a sentence structure can be unpronounced in the PF component, provided that it contains only phonetically weak material with recoverable semantic content

The edge of a given projection XP comprises its head X, and any other constituent of XP that c-commands X: in typical cases, this means that the edge of a projection XP includes the head of XP and any specifier that it may have. The 'provided that' condition in (12ii) is a reflection of the Recoverability Condition on deletion proposed in Chomsky (1964b: 41) and Katz & Postal (1964: 79) to the effect that material can only be unpronounced if its content is recoverable. In consequence of this condition, only functors (i.e. functional categories with no substantive lexical semantic content) can be unpronounced.

Having sketched the assumptions underlying the Truncation account, let's look at how this approach handles Subject Drop in colloquial English. Rizzi argues that this is the result of the root sentence structure being truncated above SUBJP, leaving SUBJP as the root/highest projection in the structure. In the light of this, consider the structure of speaker B's sentence in the dialogue below (slightly adapted from 1e above):

(13)   SPEAKER A: I saw Rachel yesterday. I brought her flowers and we had a chat

SPEAKER B: <It> clearly has done her a lot of good

On Rizzi's account, (13B) will have a truncated structure along the lines shown in simplified form below (with the functional head F being an evidential mood head under the analysis of adverbs like *clearly* in Cinque 1999, and the perfect aspect auxiliary *has* originating as a PERF head and from there raising to T):

(14)
```
                    SUBJP
              ┌───────┴───────┐
            DP              SUBJ'
            it        ┌───────┴───────┐
                    SUBJ              FP
                     ø         ┌───────┴───────┐
                             ADVP             F'
                            clearly    ┌───────┴───────┐
                                       F              TP
                                       ø        ┌───────┴───────┐
                                                T            PERFP
                                              has     done her a lot of good
```

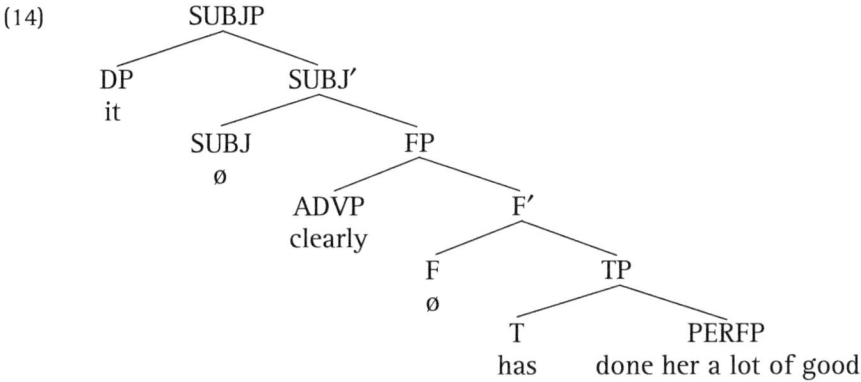

Because the pronoun *it* is on the edge of the root projection SUBJP, it can be unpronounced at PF (since it is phonetically weak, and it has no lexical semantic content), in accordance with (12ii). (An incidental point to note in passing is that here and elsewhere, I set aside the possibility that subjects transit through spec-TP on their way to spec-SUBJP.)

The assumption that Subject Drop sentences are truncated and project no peripheral constituents above SUBJP accounts for why Subject Drop is not found in sentences like those in (11) above, since it is clear that in each sentence in (11) there will be one or more projections above the SUBJP projection containing the unpronounced subject. For example, if root wh-questions involve an inverted auxiliary moving from SUBJ to FIN, and a focused wh-operator moving through spec-FINP into spec-FOCP (as argued in §5.1.2), a sentence like (11a) *Which pub did you go to?* will have the derivation below (simplified by not showing the internal structure of the VP constituent, and not showing movement of the subject *you* from inside VP to the edge of SUBJP, in order to reduce visual complexity):

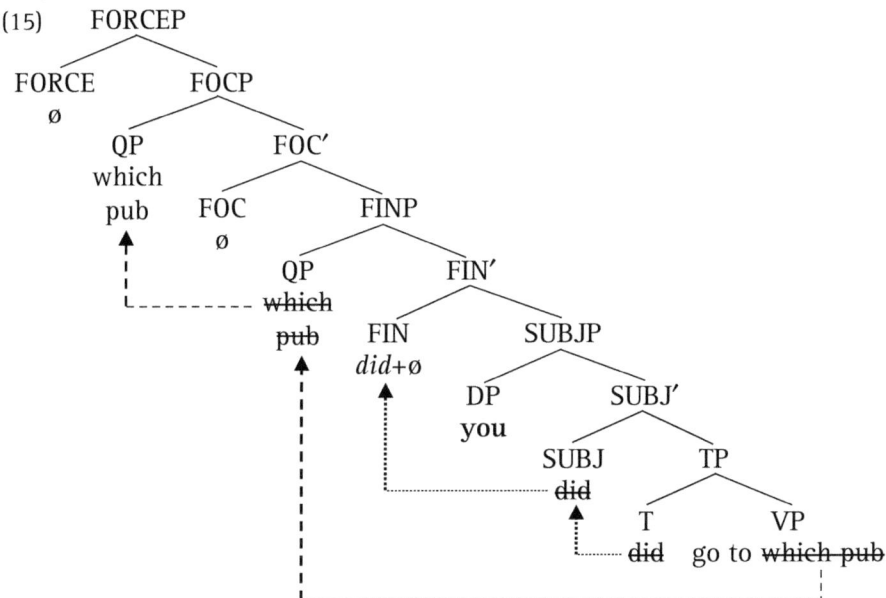

(15)
```
        FORCEP
    ┌──────┴──────┐
  FORCE         FOCP
    ø      ┌──────┴──────┐
          QP           FOC'
        which     ┌──────┴──────┐
         pub     FOC          FINP
          ↑       ø      ┌──────┴──────┐
          ┊             QP           FIN'
          └────────── which    ┌──────┴──────┐
                        pub    FIN         SUBJP
                         ↑    did+ø   ┌──────┴──────┐
                         ┊           DP          SUBJ'
                         ┊           you    ┌──────┴──────┐
                         ┊                SUBJ           TP
                         ┊············ did          ┌────┴────┐
                         ┊             ↑            T        VP
                         ┊             ┊········ did   go to which pub
                         └─────────────────────────────────────────┘
```

The outcome is a structure in which the (bold-printed) subject *you* is not on the edge of a root projection (since it is in spec-SUBJP, and the root projection is FORCEP). Consequently, the subject cannot be null/unpronounced via (12ii) – thereby accounting for the ungrammaticality of (11a) **Which pub did <you> go to?*

As we have seen, Rizzi argues that Truncation in abbreviated styles of spoken English can be handled by treating 'certain informal registers of English ... as allowing truncation' (Rizzi 1998: 28). By contrast, more formal registers of English do not allow ellipsis of subjects. Why should this be? Rizzi's answer is that more formal varieties don't allow truncation of the clause periphery, so that the counterpart of (14) in more formal styles is the untruncated FORCEP structure below:

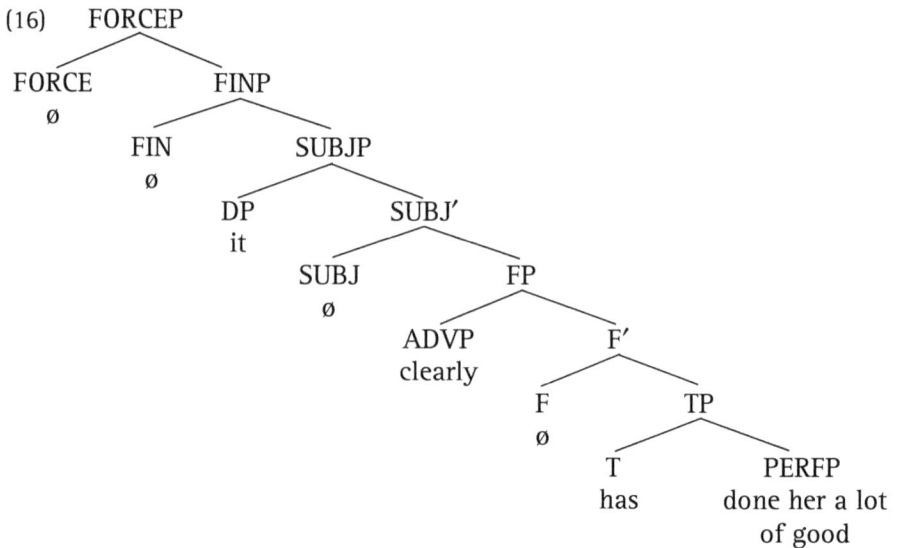

(16)   FORCEP
    ┌──────────┴──────────┐
  FORCE   FINP
    ∅   ┌────────┴────────┐
            FIN   SUBJP
             ∅   ┌──────┴──────┐
                    DP   SUBJ′
                    it   ┌──────┴──────┐
                          SUBJ   FP
                           ∅   ┌──────┴──────┐
                               ADVP   F′
                              clearly   ┌────┴────┐
                                        F   TP
                                        ∅   ┌────┴────┐
                                           T   PERFP
                                          has   done her a lot
                                                   of good

Since the pronoun *it* is not on the edge of a root projection in (16) (because *it* is in spec-SUBJP, and the root projection is FORCEP), *it* cannot receive a null spellout. On this view, the difference between informal registers of English which allow Subject Drop in root clauses and formal registers which don't is that informal registers allow truncated structures like (14) above in which there are no peripheral projections above SUBJP, whereas formal registers don't and instead require full/untruncated FORCEP structures like (16).

7.1.3   Subject+Auxiliary Drop

Although our discussion hitherto has centred on Subject Drop, the assumption that peripheral projections above SUBJP can be truncated enables us to account for sentences such as the following, where both a subject and an auxiliary following it can undergo sentence-initial ellipsis and be dropped at the beginning of a sentence.

(17)   a.   <I've> been waiting for over an hour
        b.   <I'm> not feeling too good at present
        c.   <There's> been a bit of a mix-up
        d.   <I'll> see you in the morning (Mackenzie 1998: 288)
        e.   <I'd> love to see you (forum.wordreference.com)
        f.   <It's> been a long time (Nariyama 2004: 247)

If we take such sentences to be truncated above SUBJP and the truncated subject and auxiliary to be on the edge of the same SUBJP projection (which is plausible, since the auxiliary cliticises onto the subject in 17), then a sentence like (17a) will have the truncated syntactic structure shown below (simplified by not showing the internal structure of TP, and not showing *have* raising from T into SUBJ):

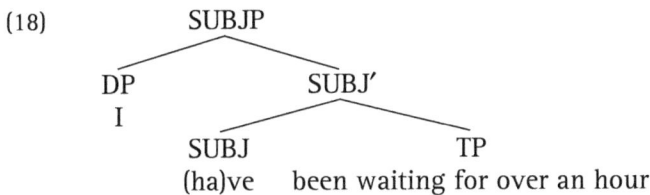

(18)   SUBJP
           ┌────────┴────────┐
          DP   SUBJ'
           I   ┌──────┴──────┐
                   SUBJ   TP
                  (ha)ve   been waiting for over an hour

Under the Truncation account, both the subject *I* and the auxiliary *have* can receive a null spellout at PF via (12ii), because they are phonetically weak, because they are functors with no lexical semantic content, and because they are on the edge of a root projection (by virtue of occupying the specifier/head positions of the root projection SUBJP).

The SUBJP analysis can also be extended to sentences such as the following, where only the subject undergoes ellipsis, not the auxiliary:

(19)   a.   <It> isn't raining much at present
        b.   SPEAKER A: How are you?
             SPEAKER B: <I> could be better (Napoli 1982: 94)
        c.   SPEAKER A: How's the veal today?
             SPEAKER B: <It> has been better (Napoli 1982: 95)

An analysis of (19a) consistent with the SUBJP analysis of Subject Drop outlined above is to suppose that the subject is on the edge of SUBJP, but that the negative auxiliary *isn't* is in T (where it is adjacent to the NEGP constituent in which the clitic *n't* originates). This would mean that (19a) has the structure shown in highly simplified form below:

(20)

```
              SUBJP
          ┌─────────────┐
        DP           SUBJ′
        it        ┌────────────┐
               SUBJ           TP
                ø        ┌──────────────┐
                        T              NEGP
                      isn't      raining much at present
```

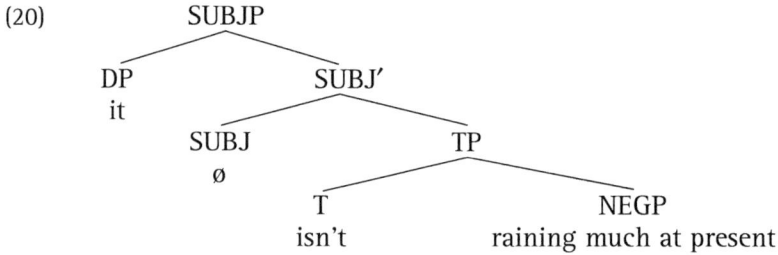

This would allow the subject *it* to be unpronounced in accordance with (12ii), since *it* is positioned on the edge of the root projection SUBJP.

Although this module has focused on spoken English, it should be noted that Subject Drop is also found in a wide variety of registers of written English. For example, Subject Drop is found in diary entries like (21a) below, encyclopedia entries (21b), biographies (21c), instructional materials (e.g. recipe books 21d, stage directions 21e, product labels 21f), postcards (21g), emails (21h), text/SMS messages (21i), social media (e.g. Facebook 21j, Twitter 21k), and telegrams (21l). In the examples below, the subject of each underlined (auxiliary or lexical) verb is omitted/dropped; (21a–21g) are from Haegeman (2019), and (21h–21l) are from the sources specified:

(21)   a. Sat there for 3/4 hours (*The Diary of Virginia Woolf* 1940: 334)

   b. Teeters hind part of body almost constantly, bobs head (entry for 'Common Sandpiper' in *Collins Nature Guide: Birds of Britain and Europe* 1994: 112)

   c. Exhibits paintings in a student art show at 2 the Dalmau Gallery, Barcelona. Experiments with cubism. (*Dali: The Salvador Dali Museum Collection*, Little, Brown & Co., Boston, 1991: 181; cited in Matushansky 1995).

   d. Serves four. If refrigerated, will keep a week to 10 days (E. Kennedy, *Things My Mother Told Me*, Branden Press, Boston, 1975: 105)

   e. Tosses the pencil. Starts on another (https://freedrama.net/deargod.html)

   f. Contains caffeine (label on a can of Coca Cola)

   g. Wish you were here (holiday postcard)

   h. Still have horrible cold (Scott 2010: 12)

   i. Can't believe it's that time of week already (Tagg 2009: 175)

   j. Hope you're happy in your new country (Deneys 2020: 99)

   k. Survived my first rugby match (Daeninck 2019: 83)

   l. Have been detained (Barton 1998: 51)

The register of written English which has attracted most attention in this respect is diary writing, and the dropping of constituents in diary entries has come to be known as Diary Drop. This phenomenon has been extensively researched, particularly by Liliane Haegeman and her colleagues (see inter alia Haegeman 1987a, 1990a, 1990b, 1997, 2000a, 2002b, 2007a,

2013, 2017, 2019, 2021; Haegeman & Ihsane 1999, 2001; Haegeman & Starke 2021). In Exercise 7.1 of the Workbook module, you can explore potential differences between Subject Drop in spoken English, and Subject Drop in the diary register of written English.

To summarise: Module 7.1 began by discussing the phenomenon of Subject Drop in spoken English, and went on to outline Rizzi's Truncation analysis of it. We saw that under his analysis, truncating peripheral projections above SUBJP in root clauses leaves the subject as a root specifier (hence the highest constituent present in the syntax), and this allows material on the edge of a root projection (its head and any specifier that it may have) to be unpronounced in the PF component. As we have seen, the Truncation analysis provides a principled syntactic account of why only the subjects of root clauses can generally undergo this kind of ellipsis in spoken English, and only when they are sentence-initial. The same Truncation analysis can also account for how both subject and auxiliary can undergo sentence-initial ellipsis and be dropped in sentences like (17).

The Truncation analysis outlined here provides a principled account of Subject Drop in spoken English: nonetheless, it runs into a number of potential problems. One such is the following: if FIN is the locus of finiteness/mood features in a clause, how does a finite T auxiliary like *has* in (14) acquire its indicative mood/finiteness feature if the clause is a truncated structure containing no FINP projection? Is a truncated clause assigned indicative mood by default? Likewise, if (as suggested in §4.3.2) the subject of a finite clause is assigned nominative case by a FIN head immediately above it, how does the subject *it* get case-marked in a structure like (14) if the truncated structure contains no FINP projection? After all, if (pro)-nominals must have case, the absence of a case assigner for the subject in a truncated structure like (14) will potentially cause the derivation to crash.

A second potential problem comes from the absence of FORCEP in a truncated structure such as (14). After all, since the function of FORCEP is to mark the force of a clause, the question posed by the truncation analysis is how a truncated SUBJP structure like (14) comes to be interpreted as declarative in force, if it contains no FORCE projection. A plausible answer is that an indicative clause structure like (14) is interpreted as declarative in force by default, in accordance with the clause-typing conditions below (from Module 1.1):

(22)   **Clause Typing Conditions**
    (i) A clause is interpreted as being of a given type (interrogative or exclamative etc.) if it contains a peripheral clause-typing specifier of the relevant type
    (ii) An indicative clause is interpreted as declarative in type by default if it contains no peripheral clause-typing specifier

Since (14) is an indicative clause containing no peripheral clause-typing specifier, it is interpreted as declarative by default via (22ii).

You should now be able to tackle Exercise 7.1.

7.2   Auxiliary Drop

In addition to Subject Drop, colloquial English also allows another type of sentence-initial ellipsis which I will refer to as Aux(iliary) Drop, whereby an inverted auxiliary can undergo ellipsis if it is the first word in its sentence. In this module, we look at this phenomenon and explore a range of alternative accounts.

7.2.1   A Truncation account of Auxiliary Drop

The phenomenon of Aux Drop in colloquial English can be illustrated by root/main clause yes–no questions such as the following:

(23)　　a.　<Does> anyone want a cup of tea? (Rühlemann 2012: 5)

　　　　b.　<Are> you not winning the game? (Schirer 2008: 37)

　　　　c.　<Have> you seen any good movies lately? (Zwicky & Zwicky 1981: 536)

Aux Drop sentences like (23) clearly can't be truncated SUBJP structures, if (as argued in Module 5.1) inverted auxiliaries are on the edge of FINP. Still, we might be able to preserve the spirit of the Truncation analysis if we supposed that sentences like (23) are truncated FINP structures which contain a null yes–no question operator in spec-FINP that attracts the inverted auxiliary to adjoin to FIN. This would mean that a sentence like (23a) involves the successive Head Movement operations arrowed in the structure below (simplified by not showing the internal structure of VP, nor the null heads that the inverted auxiliary adjoins to each time it moves):

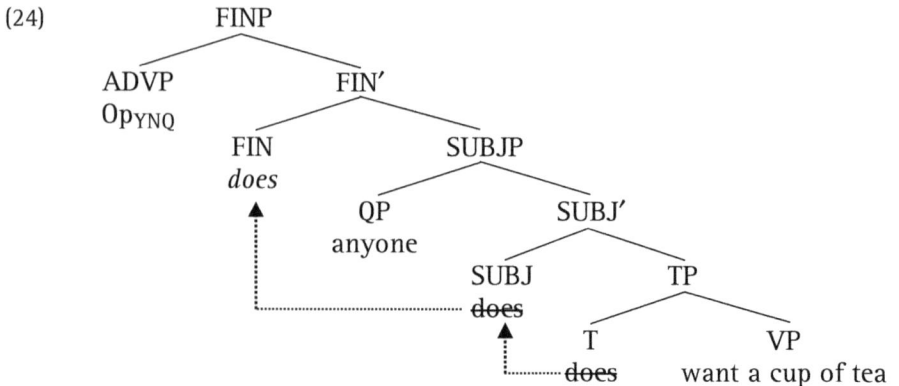

(24)

FINP
- ADVP
  Op$_{YNQ}$
- FIN′
  - FIN
    does ▲
  - SUBJP
    - QP
      anyone
    - SUBJ′
      - SUBJ
        ~~does~~ ▲
      - TP
        - T
          ~~does~~
        - VP
          want a cup of tea

The yes–no question operator in spec-FINP c-commands (and hence licenses use of) the polarity item *anyone*. The structure (24) is interpreted as a yes–no question via (22i) by virtue of containing a yes–no question operator in the clause periphery (here, in spec-FINP). Such a structure would allow for *does* to be unpronounced at PF via (12ii) because it is a weak functor/auxiliary with no lexical semantic content, and because it it is on the edge of the root projection FINP. Moreover, an analysis like (24) can account for why the verb *want* is in the infinitive form in (23a) – namely because *want* originates as the (head V of the VP) complement of the auxiliary *do* (which selects an infinitive complement); likewise *winning* in (23b) is in the progressive participle form because it originates as the complement of the progressive auxiliary *are*; and *seen* in (23c) is in the perfect participle form because it originates as the complement of the perfect auxiliary *have*.

A question arising from the analysis of Aux Drop outlined in (24) is why the non-modal auxiliaries *do/be/have* can have a silent spellout (as we see in 23 above), but modal auxiliaries generally can't – as illustrated by the examples below (showing judgements reported in Fitzpatrick 2005b):

(25)   a.   *<Can> anyone pick up John at the airport?
         b.   *<Will> anyone play the piano at the party tomorrow?
         c.   *<Could> anyone have picked up John at the airport yesterday?
         d.   *<Would> everyone be happier if classes were cancelled?
         e.   *<Should> everyone leave if the neighbours complain?

The answer to this question given by Schirer (2008: 18) is that 'Auxiliaries which cannot be deleted have semantic content which cannot be recovered, while the deletion-eligible auxiliaries *do*, *be*, and *have* do not.' This account appeals to the Recoverability Condition of Chomsky (1964b) and Katz & Postal (1964).

This same intuition is given a parsing implementation by Pesetsky in terms of the following principle:

(26)   **Principle of Unambitious Reverse Engineering (PURE)**
         When determining the identity of unpronounced material in the course
         of reverse-engineering a speaker's syntactic derivation, the language
         system of the hearer considers only the minimally semantically
         contentful possibilities compatible with the morphosyntactic
         environment (Pesetsky 2020: 5)

(The term 'reverse-engineering' means 'parsing the structure produced by a speaker in order to try and work out the identity of the missing constituent/s'. The term 'minimally semantically contentful possibilities' means

'constituents with as little semantic content as possible'.). So, when trying to identify the missing auxiliary in (23a) *Anyone want a cup of tea?*
the hearer conjectures that the missing auxiliary is *does*, because this is
the auxiliary with the least semantic content which allows a complement
headed by an infinitival verb like *want*, and also allows a third person
singular subject like *anyone*. Under the PURE account, the reason why the
auxiliaries *have/be/do* can be dropped but modals cannot is that modals
have too much semantic content to reverse-engineer.

And yet, sentences such as the following suggest that some modals can
sometimes be dropped:

(27)   a.   <Would> you like to go fishing this afternoon?
         b.   <Would> you mind if I went home early today?
         c.   <Will> tomorrow at four be okay? (after Carter & McCarthy
              1995: 147)

How come? A plausible answer is that modal drop is possible where the
overall content of the sentence gives sufficient clues to the nature of the
missing modal. So, for example, *would like to* is a frequent collocation,
so it's easy enough to infer that the missing modal in (27a) is *would*.
Similarly, since *would* is used in counterfactual conditionals like *I would
feel annoyed if he went home early*, once again it can readily be inferred
that the missing modal in (27b) is *would*. In much the same way, the
presence of the future expression *tomorrow at four* in (27c) enables the
inference to be drawn that the missing auxiliary is the future modal *will*.
On this view, all unstressed auxiliaries can in principle be dropped, but in
cases where a modal is dropped, hearers may struggle to reverse-engineer
(i.e. identify) the missing modal if the sentence contains insufficient clues
as to its identity.

However, the Truncation account of Aux Drop outlined in (24) above faces
a potential theoretical problem. Under the analysis of root/main clause
yes–no questions in §5.3.1, the interrogative operator in yes–no questions
is focused, and its criterial position is spec-FOCP. It therefore follows that
the truncated FINP structure in (24) above will crash at the LF interface,
because the operator is not in the criterial spec-FOCP position required for
the structure to be interpreted as a yes–no question. One potential way of
circumventing this problem while still maintaining that Aux Drop involves
Truncation would be to suppose that Aux Drop sentences are truncated
at FOCP. This would mean that an Aux Drop sentence like (23a) *<Does>
anyone want a cup of tea?* has the truncated FOCP structure in (28) below
(with the yes–no question operator raising to spec-FOCP, and the inverted
auxiliary *does* raising to FOC):

(28)

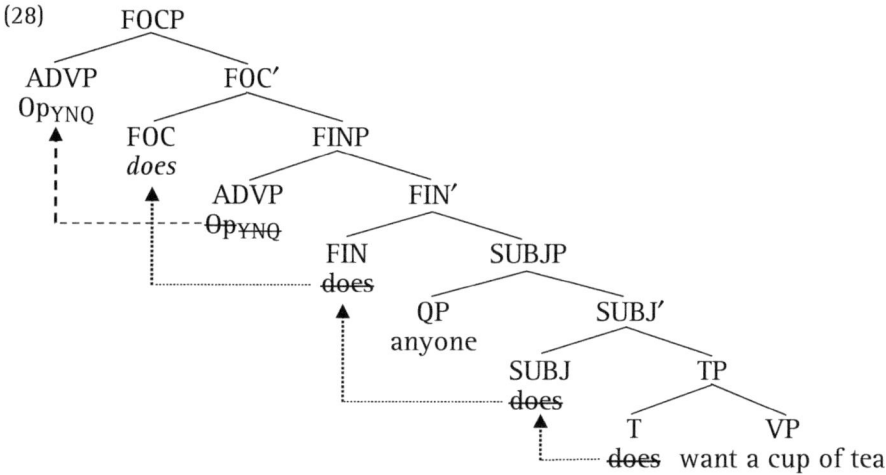

In the LF component, the structure will be interpreted as a yes–no question by virtue of containing a focused yes–no question operator in its criterial position in spec-FOCP. In the PF component, the operator and the inverted auxiliary can be unpronounced via (12ii), by virtue of being on the edge of the root projection (FOCP). The structure in (28) can thus be spelled out at PF as the Aux Drop structure (23a) *Anyone want a cup of tea?*

However, a potential empirical problem arising from the truncated FOCP analysis in (28) is that it requires us to suppose that the inverted auxiliary *does* raises from FIN to FOC, in order to get to the edge of FOCP and thus be eligible to be given a null spellout in the PF component. And yet, the analysis of questions in §5.1.2 presented empirical evidence from sentences like (29) below that inverted auxiliaries move only as far as FIN (and not into FOC) in root/main clause questions:

(29)   a. *What* <u>at present</u> **do** you need? (fgcquaker.org)

b. *How long*, <u>in the light of this promotion</u>, **will** you stay here? (Ross 1967: 31)

c. *What else*, <u>with no money to speak of</u>, **could** he possibly have done? (Kayne 1998: 155, fn. 66)

d. *Under what circumstances*, <u>during the holidays</u>, **would** you go into the office? (Sobin 2003: 193)

e. *Why*, <u>when asked</u>, **did** all the students I interviewed say they would take 'study drugs' again? (unibathtime.co.uk)

f. *How often*, <u>that book</u>, **has** he praised it in public? (Kayne 1998: 155, fn. 66)

On the assumption that the italicised interrogative XPs in (29) are in spec-FOCP, it follows that the bold-printed inverted auxiliaries cannot be in FOC, since the two are separated by underlined XPs which (under the

Functional Specifier Hypothesis) serve as the specifiers of some other peripheral projection. A more plausible analysis is that the italicised interrogative XPs in (29) are in spec-FOCP, the underlined intervening XPs are in spec-MODP in (29a–29e) and in spec-TOPP in (29f), and the bold-printed inverted auxiliaries occupy the head FIN position of FINP. If – contrary to what is suggested here – inverted auxiliaries moved to FOC, the bold-printed auxiliaries in (29) would (wrongly) be predicted to precede the underlined XP modifiers. See §5.1.2 for further evidence supporting the conclusion that inverted auxiliaries move to FIN, not to FOC.

But if the inverted auxiliary doesn't move to FOC in (28) and instead moves only as high as FIN, it would not be eligible for ellipsis, since it would not be on the edge of the root projection FOCP. The bottom line is that whichever version of the Truncation analysis we adopt (the FINP analysis in 24 or the FOCP analysis in 28), we run into theoretical or empirical problems (relating to the position of the operator, or of the inverted auxiliary) which undermine the analysis.

7.2.2   A Left Edge Ellipsis account

A further problem for the Truncation analysis of Auxiliary Drop outlined in §7.2.1 is posed by sentences such as the following, which involve both Aux Drop and Subject Drop:

(30)   a.   <Do you> mind if I smoke? (Mackenzie 1998: 288)

     b.   <Are you> going to be long? (Nariyama 2004: 255)

     c.   <Are there> any pears today? (Napoli 1982: 97)

     d.   <Is there> anybody else with a comment? (Rühlemann 2012: 5)

     e.   <Have you> ever been to Chicago? (Schmerling 1973: 580)

At first sight, such sentences might seem unproblematic for the Truncation account. After all, we might simply assume that they are truncated FINP structures, so that a sentence like (30a) has the syntactic derivation shown in simplified form below:

(31)

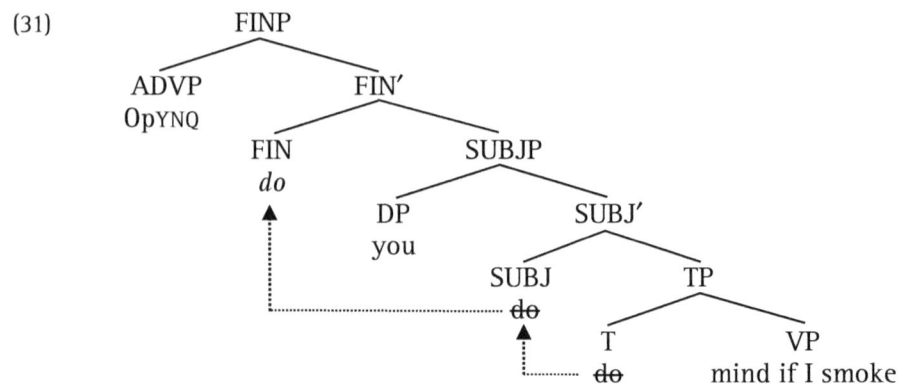

The null yes–no question operator will license the use of the polarity item *mind*, and trigger Inversion of the auxiliary *do*. We could then suppose that *do* (being on the edge of the root projection FINP) receives a null spellout in the PF component via (12ii). However, this would derive *You mind if I smoke?* And while this is perfectly grammatical, it leaves unanswered the question of how the pronoun *you* also comes to be dropped in (30a) *Mind if I smoke?* After all, *you* is on the edge of SUBJP, but SUBJP is not the root projection in the structure, so the ellipsis operation in (12ii) can't apply here. Similar problems arise if we suppose that *Mind if I smoke?* is a truncated FOCP structure with the operator and auxiliary on the edge of FOCP (as in 28 above): giving a null spellout to the edge of FOCP will still leave the subject intact on the edge of SUBJP.

But if we reject the assumption in (24, 28, 31) that root yes–no questions which show Auxiliary (+Subject) Drop have a syntactic structure which is truncated above FINP or FOCP, what alternative are we left with? An interesting answer is provided by Schirer (2008). He suggests that Truncation is a phonological rather than a syntactic phenomenon. More specifically, he proposes that Aux+Subject Drop sentences (i.e. sentences in which both auxiliary and subject have been dropped) have a full/untruncated syntactic structure which projects all the way up to FORCEP, but that in the PF component 'The phonology ... allows the deletion of material when it appears on the left edge of the sentence' (Schirer 2008: 15). Let's adopt the following implementation of his proposal (adapted to fit the framework used here):

(32)   **Left Edge Ellipsis account of Auxiliary (+Subject) Drop**
        (i) Reduced clauses have the same full syntactic structure as their
             unreduced counterparts
        (ii) The left edge of a continuous set of one or more projections at the
             top of a tree in a root clause can undergo ellipsis in the phonology

To see how this account works, consider the sentences below, where (33a) involves Aux Drop, and (33b) Aux+Subject Drop:

(33)   a. <Do> you need any help?
        b. <Do you> need any help?

Let's suppose that both sentences have the full syntactic structure below (simplified by not showing the internal structure or null constituents of TP):

(34)

```
                    FORCEP
                   /      \
             FORCE         FOCP
               ø          /    \
                      ADVP      FOC'
                      Op_YNQ    /    \
                         ↑   FOC     FINP
                         ┊    ø      /    \
                         ┊       ADVP      FIN'
                         └──────Op_YNQ    /    \
                                      FIN       SUBJP
                                       do      /     \
                                       ↑     DP        SUBJ'
                                       ┊     you      /     \
                                       ┊          SUBJ       TP
                                       └··········· do     need any help
```

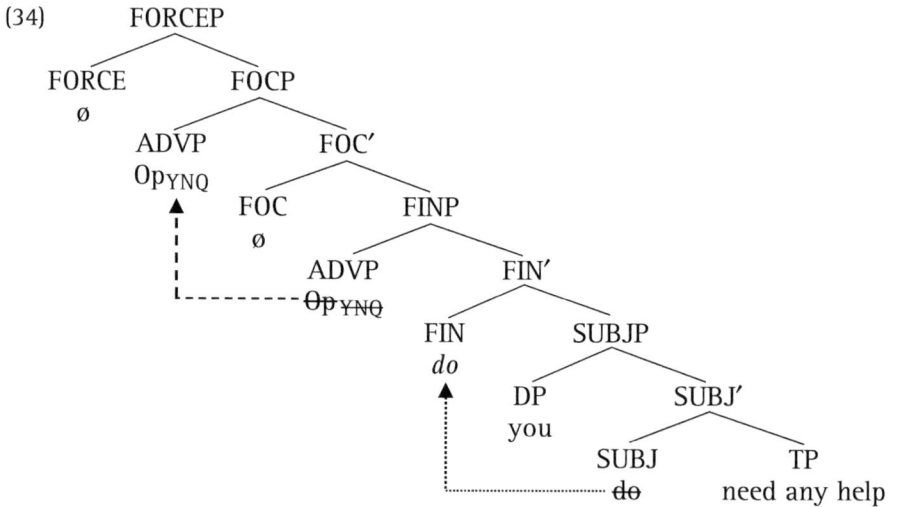

The structure in (34) will be handed over to the PF and LF components at the end of the syntactic derivation. In the LF component, (34) is interpreted as a yes–no question in accordance with (22i) by virtue of containing a yes–no question operator on the edge of FOCP. In the PF component, the Left Edge Ellipsis operation in (32ii) will allow a null spellout to be given to the left edge of FORCEP, or of FORCEP+FOCP (i.e. to the left edge of FORCEP as well as to the left edge of FOCP), or of FORCEP+FOCP+FINP … and so on. This raises the possibility that all the material on the left edge of the FORCEP+FOCP+FINP projections in (34) can receive a null spellout at PF, so deriving (33a) *You need any help?* An alternative possibility allowed for by (32ii) is that the left edge of the FORCEP+FOCP+FINP+SUBJP projections can receive a null spellout, so deriving (33b) *Need any help?* Thus, the Left Edge Ellipsis account in (32) can handle both Aux Drop sentences like (33a) and Aux+Subject Drop sentences like (33b) in a unitary fashion. Under this analysis, truncated projections are present in the syntax, but given a null spellout in the phonology. This contrasts with Rizzi's treatment of truncated constituents, in which they are not present at any level of the derivation (neither in the syntax, nor or in the phonology).

7.2.3   A prosodic account

Both the Truncation account outlined in §7.2.1 and the Left Edge Ellipsis account sketched in §7.2.2 attempt to characterise the deletion domain (i.e. the set of constituents which can undergo sentence-initial ellipsis) in purely structural terms as the left edge of one or more peripheral projections. However, there is evidence that the structural approach is potentially misguided, and that prosodic factors (involving stress and intonation patterns) play a pivotal role (as argued by Thrasher 1973; Napoli, 1982; Zwicky &

Pullum 1983; Gerken 1991, 1994; Sigurðsson & Maling 2007, 2010; and Weir 2008, 2009a, 2009b, 2012, 2016, 2017, 2018, 2022). To see why, consider the following sentences:

(35) a. Has the professor arrived yet?
      b. <Has> the professor arrived yet?
      c. <Has the> professor arrived yet?
      d. <Has the pro> 'fessor arrived yet? (Napoli 1982: 85)

Let's suppose that the sentences in (35) all have the (full/untruncated) syntactic structure below (simplified by not showing the internal structure of TP):

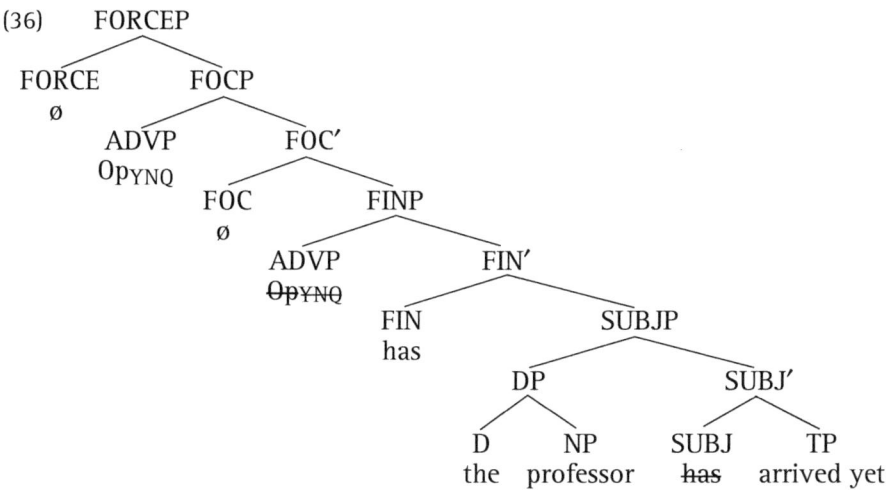

(36)

```
      FORCEP
     /      \
  FORCE    FOCP
    Ø      /    \
      ADVP       FOC'
      Oᴘʏɴǫ     /    \
          FOC      FINP
           Ø      /    \
             ADVP       FIN'
             O̶ᴘ̶ʏ̶ɴ̶ǫ̶   /     \
                  FIN        SUBJP
                  has       /     \
                        DP          SUBJ'
                       /  \        /     \
                      D    NP    SUBJ     TP
                     the professor  h̶a̶s̶   arrived yet
```

One possibility allowed for by the Left Edge Ellipsis account in (32) is that the left edge of the FORCEP+FOCP+FINP projections in (36) can be given a silent spellout at PF, so that only constituents of SUBJP get spelled out overtly at PF. This will derive (35b) *<Has> the professor arrived yet?*

But now consider what happens in (35c) *<Has the> professor arrived yet?* It might at first sight appear as if what is unpronounced here is the left edge of the FORCEP+FOCP+FINP+SUBJP projections; but the left edge of SUBJP includes the whole of the DP *the professor*, and yet only the first word of that DP (= *the*) is silent, not the whole of the edge of SUBJP. The same problem arises in (35d) *<Has the pro> 'fessor arrived yet?* where once again what is deleted is not the whole DP *the professor* on the edge of SUBJP, but rather the word *the* and the first syllable (*pro*) of the word *professor*. Napoli argues on the basis of such considerations that the domain of the relevant deletion operation cannot be identified in syntactic terms, because 'A syntactic deletion rule cannot delete part of a word' (Napoli 1982: 99). Instead, she concludes that in sentences like (35b–35d) 'a phonological deletion rule is operative' (Napoli 1982: 99). And she makes the following suggestions about the nature of the rule:

> The rule deletes unstressed (or lightly stressed) initial material. Dwight Bolinger (personal communication) suggests that if we ... divide the intonation contour of a sentence into the prehead (the part preceding the first main accent), the head (from the first main accent to the last main accent), and the post-head (the falling part after the last main accent), we could say that the rule deletes the prehead.   (Napoli 1982: 99)

She further notes Bolinger's suggestion that the rule can operate not only at the clause level, but also at the phrase level (so that the PP *of course* can be truncated to *course*), and at the word level (so that *because* can be truncated to *coz*).

Weir (2012: 106) characterises the relevant phenomenon as 'the result of a general process of weak syllable drop at the left edge of prosodic phrases, in order to satisfy a constraint requiring prosodic phrases to start with accented syllables'. He takes prosodic phrases to include clauses, maximal projections, and words. He formalises his approach in terms of Optimality Theory, but I will leave interested readers to read the technical details of his work for themselves (see Weir 2012: 110–19). For present purposes, I will characterise the phenomenon informally as follows:

(37)   **Prosodic account of Weak Syllable Drop**
         (i) Reduced clauses have the same full syntactic structure as their
              unreduced counterparts
         (ii) A continuous sequence of one or more weak syllables at the
              beginning of a prosodic phrase (e.g. a sentence) can undergo ellipsis
              at PF

In the case of a sentence like *Has the professor arrived?* the three syllables *has+the+pro* are weak; *has* is deleted on its own in (35b), *has+the* are deleted together in (35c), and *has+the+pro* are all three deleted in (35d).

The overall conclusion to be drawn from our discussion in this module and the last is that sentences involving Subject Drop and/or Auxiliary Drop in informal styles of spoken English have a full (untruncated) syntactic structure, but can be given an abbreviated spellout via an ellipsis operation in the PF component which is structural in nature under the Left Edge Ellipsis account (32), and phonological in nature under the Prosodic Account (37) – though only the latter approach can account for the types of reduced clause found in (35c, 35d).

You should now be able to tackle Exercise 7.2.

7.3 Article Drop

Thus far in this chapter, I have focused on structures in spoken English in which subjects and auxiliaries are dropped. However, in this module, I turn to look at a very different phenomenon (characteristic of certain written registers) which I shall refer to as Article Drop, since it involves omission of the definite/indefinite articles *the/a* (where *a* should be understood to include its variant *an* as well).

Article Drop is restricted to occurring in written English, and is found in many such registers: for example, a corpus of posts on the social media platform Twitter collected by Daeninck (2019) includes examples of Article Drop such as the following:

(38) a. *<The>* motive was rage fueled by rejection
b. *<The>* entire cast was on fire
c. *<The>* suspect planted blood in *<the>* RAV4 ...
d. If not used to these sorts of climbs maybe best to take her next time or not try her on *<the>* tallest mountain in England for *<the>* first try!

Although Article Drop is relatively infrequent in Daeninck's corpus of tweets (with only 6 per cent of articles in her corpus being dropped, by my calculations), there are other written registers where it is much more common. For example, Article Drop is pervasive (to the point of being the norm) in a very different kind of abbreviated register widely referred to as headlinese, found in the headlines of newspaper and magazine articles.

To illustrate this, I collected a sample of 390 front-page headlines in British newspapers over a six-week period from the beginning of April to mid-May in 2021. My sample showed a very high frequency of Article Drop in obligatory contexts – that is, contexts where an article would be required in unabbreviated registers (e.g. modifying an NP headed by a singular common noun which is countable). My sample contained 462 instances of Article Drop (290 of *the*-drop, 172 of *a*-drop); overall, articles were dropped in 96 per cent of obligatory contexts (the same figure as reported for Dutch newsflash headlines by Oosterhof & Rawoens 2017). There were frequently multiple instances of (the same or different) articles being omitted within a single sentence – as below:

(39) a. <The> Bank predicts <the> strongest year since <the> Second World War as Britain surges out of lockdown (*The Times*, 7 May)
b. <A> Tory peer victimised <a> female worker at <a> firm (*Daily Telegraph*, 14 April)

    c. <The> EU unveils <a> big push for <the> Pfizer vaccine (*Financial Times*, 15 April)

    d. <A> majority of Britons trust <the> Oxford jab, <a> poll shows (*The Times*, 9 April)

Unlike Subject Drop or Auxiliary Drop, Article Drop is not restricted to sentence-initial position, since (as we see from 38, 39 above) it can equally affect nominals which are subjects, direct objects or prepositional objects. Moreover, Article Drop is not restricted to root clauses, since it can also affect (italicised) articles in non-root clauses like those bracketed below:

(40)   a. <A> Court rules [Boris owes <*a*> £535 debt] (*Daily Mirror*, 13 May 21)

    b. <The> rota will mean [<*the*> Queen is not alone] (*Daily Mirror*, 19 April)

    c. Downing Street sources claim [<*the*> former chief adviser released <*the*> PM's messages out of spite] (*Daily Telegraph*, 23 April)

    d. <The> Queen says [<*the*> Duke's death 'has left a huge void' in her life] (*Daily Telegraph*, 12 April)

    e. Stocks retreat [after <*a*> US inflation surge sparks fears [<*the*> economy is overheating]] (*Financial Times*, 13 May)

    f. Starmer hits out [as <*the*> Tories reject <*the*> Labour call for <*a*> Commons inquiry into lobbying] (*Metro*, 16 April)

Articles are omitted because they are words with little informational content or impact, and headlines aim to be as concise, informative and impactful as possible.

Indeed, prescriptive manuals and style sheets that set out editing rules for composing headlines explicitly instruct subeditors to omit articles. For example, Williams (2013) outlines eight grammar rules for newspaper headlines, one of which is: 'Leave out articles (*a, an, the*).' In the same vein, Ghosh (2022) prescribes 'Avoid the use of articles like *a, an, the*.' Likewise, the St Petersburg College guide on 'How to write a news article: Headlines' (spcollege.libguides.com) specifies 'Do not use articles – *a, an, the*.' However, in the remainder of this module, I will argue that there are structural conditions on Article Drop which undermine any such simplistic prescriptive rule-based account. I will explore a number of possible syntactic accounts, starting with a Truncation account.

7.3.1 A Truncation analysis of Article Drop

A suggestion which might at first sight seem plausible is that Article Drop involves use of truncated nominals which contain no superordinate nominal functional projections (like DP, ARTP or QP), but rather are truncated NPs (i.e. NPs which don't project any functional nominal superstructure above NP). This would mean (for instance) that the complement of the verb *reject* in (40f) above is not the DP … ARTP structure in (41a) below (containing ellipsed articles), but rather the NP … NP structure in (41b) (not containing any articles):

(41)   a. [DP <the> [NP Labour call for [ARTP <a> [NP Commons inquiry into lobbying]]]]

   b. [NP Labour call for [NP Commons inquiry into lobbying]]

However, evidence against positing that all nominals in headlines are truncated NPs with no functional superstructure of any kind comes from the observation that many NPs in headlines (such as those underlined below) are modified by quantifiers and numerals like those bold-printed below:

(42)   a. Civil service staff <are> ordered to reveal **all** second jobs (*The Times*, 15 April)

   b. Minnesota <is> hit by **more** unrest (*Financial Times*, 14 April)

   c. Travel abroad <is> to become legal, but tests and quarantine will remain for **most** destinations (*Daily Telegraph*, 1 May)

   d. Free kits <are> to be available for **every** adult in England (*Daily Mirror*, 5 April)

   e. No end <is> in sight as Johnson says normal is **some** way off (*Daily Telegraph*, 6 April)

   f. **Only 14** breaches of lobbying rules <are> found in **two** years (*The i*, 16 April)

On the assumption that the highlighted nominals in (42) have the status of QP or NUMP (i.e. quantifier or numeral phrases), it is clearly untenable to maintain that all layers of functional superstructure above NP are truncated in headlinese.

   But could we instead maintain that nominals in headlinese show truncation of the highest (DP) layer of structure? This, too, seems to be too strong a claim, since possessive/genitive nominals like those underlined below are frequently found:

(43)   a. Northern Ireland's First Minister <is> toppled in <a> backlash over Brexit (*The i*, 29 April)

   b. Bozo's phone number <was> on the internet for 15 years (*Daily Star*, 1 May)

   c. Johnson's Mustique holiday <is> added to inquiries into potential rule breaches (*Financial Times*, 11 May)

   d. EY's Wirecard audits <are> slammed in <a> report (*Financial Times*, 19 April)

   e. Starmer's leadership <is> in crisis over <the> reshuffle move to demote Rayner (*The Guardian*, 10 May)

Moreover, (underlined) nominals with an (italicised) pronominal possessive modifier are also frequent in newspaper headlines:

(44) a. <The> young <are> turning *their* <u>backs</u> on learning to drive (*Daily Telegraph*, 26 April)

  b. <The> Duke planned *his* <u>funeral</u> with military precision (*Daily Telegraph*, 16 April)

  c. Cameron <is> told: *your* <u>reputation</u> is in tatters after Greensill lobbying (*The Guardian*, 14 May)

  d. Harry <is> set to miss *her* <u>95th birthday</u> (*Daily Mirror*, 19 April)

  e. <There are> 10 days to save *my* <u>life</u> (*Sunday People*, 2 May 21)

Under the analysis in Radford (2020: 201) nominal and pronominal possessives like *your car/the queen's car* are DPs with the skeletal structure below (with the possessive affix being spelled out as *-r* on *your*, and as *'s* on *the queen's*):

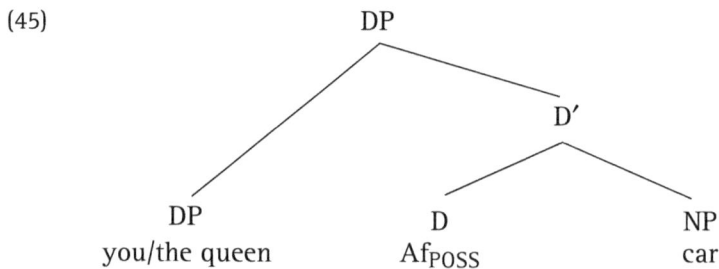

(45)

```
                        DP
                      /    \
                     /      \
                    /        D'
                   /        /  \
                  /        /    \
               DP         D      NP
            you/the queen  Af_POSS  car
```

If we adopt an analysis along similar lines, the frequent use of nominal/pronominal possessive structures like (43/44) in headlines undermines the claim that nominals in headlinese involve DP truncation.

  Instead, what seem to be systematically truncated are the articles *the/a*. Interestingly, Article Drop even occurs inside possessive DPs in structures like the following (where the bold-printed article in the specifier position of the DP in square brackets is truncated):

(46) a. <The> Queen says [<the> Duke's death] 'has left a huge void' in her life (*Daily Telegraph*, 12 April)

  b. [**<The>** Queen's final preparations] aim to steer <the> Royal family into calmer waters (*Daily Telegraph*, 16 April)

  c. Downing Street sources claim <the> former chief adviser released [**<the>** PM's messages] out of spite (*Daily Telegraph*, 23 April)

  d. [**<The>** BBC's Philip tributes] set <a> record for complaints (*The Guardian*, 13 April)

  e. [**<The>** Alawi sect's faith in Assad] <is> knocked by Syrian crises (*Financial Times*, 14 April)

In all thirteen such structures in my sample of headlines, the article was always deleted (i.e. my sample contained no DPs like *the Duke's death*). The bracketed possessive DP constituents in (46) have clearly not been truncated, and retain the affix *'s* which (on one view) would be the head D of the DP. If we were to adopt a Truncation approach, we would have to say that the specifier of the overall DP is truncated above NP, so that the bracketed DP in (46a) above has the structure below:

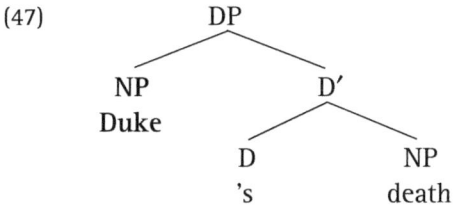

(47)

```
                DP
          ┌──────┴──────┐
        NP              D′
        Duke        ┌───┴────┐
                    D        NP
                    's      death
```

This would mean that the bold-printed specifier in (47) would not be the DP constituent required in non-abbreviated registers, but rather a truncated NP.

However, there are several reasons to be sceptical about the Truncation analysis of the specifier *Duke* in (47). For one thing, Truncation typically affects constituents on the left edge of a root projection; and yet (as we have seen) articles are omitted in a wide range of positions within headlines. Secondly, it is potentially inconsistent to posit that a nominal is truncated to NP when (as in 47) it is contained inside an untruncated nominal which projects all the way up to DP. Thirdly, the Truncation account fails to account for why the NP *Duke* receives the same interpretation as a definite DP like '*the* Duke', and not an indefinite interpretation like '*a* Duke'. Moreover, if we take *Duke* to be an unaccusative argument of the noun *death*, (47) also violates the DP Hypothesis argued for by Longobardi (1994, 1996, 2001) whereby definite arguments are required to be DPs. In addition, if articles are the locus of the number, person and case properties of nominals (with these features being transmitted to the NP below them via Concord), it could be argued that a truncated NP cannot receive number or case, so causing the derivation to crash. Moreover, absence of the article (and its φ-features) would then pose problems in accounting for subject-verb agreement in a (constructed) headline like *Sheep runs amok*.

7.3.2 Null article and article ellipsis accounts

One way of overcoming the objections to the Truncation approach outlined in §7.3.1 would be to suppose that the abbreviated nominal *Duke* in (46a) is an untruncated DP headed by a null article, so that the DP *Duke's death* has the structure below:

(48)

```
                    DP
            ┌────────┴────────┐
          DP                  D′
        ┌──┴──┐            ┌───┴───┐
        D     NP           D       NP
        ø     Duke         's      death
```

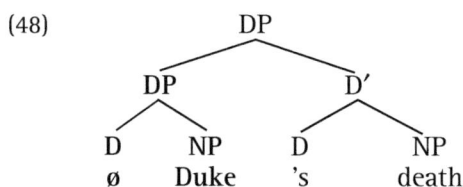

Such a structure is preferable to the NP analysis (47), firstly because it makes for structural continuity with unabbreviated registers (by treating the specifier *Duke* as a DP), and secondly because it conforms to the DP Hypothesis (in that the argument of the unaccusative noun *death* is the DP *ø Duke*). Under the analysis in (48), Article Drop in headlines is not the result of structural Truncation (i.e. non-projection of DP/ARTP), but rather the result of this register having a null article which is used in place of the overt articles *the/a*. (For an analysis positing null articles in headlines in German, see Lemke et al. 2017, and Reich 2017.)

However, the null article hypothesis raises the question of whether it is plausible to suppose that a register like headlinese could have developed a functor of its own (a null article) which is not found in unabbreviated (or spoken) registers of the same language. Moreover, it poses the learnability question of how such a null article could be acquired. Certainly not via the normal process of L1 acquisition, since infants acquiring their L1 can't read newspaper headlines. Nor via the normal process of L2 acquisition, since while transfer effects might lead an L2 learner whose L1 lacks articles to omit them, there are no such transfer effects at work in headlinese: on the contrary, headline writers omit articles which are obligatory in non-abbreviated registers of their native language.

A more plausible analysis would arguably be to suppose that the abbreviated nominal *Duke* in (46a) has the same syntactic structure (49) below as its untruncated counterpart *the Duke's death*:

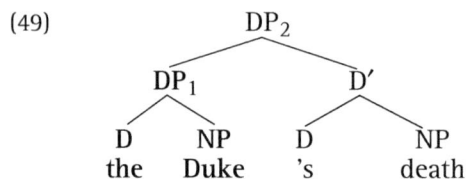

(49)

```
                       DP₂
            ┌──────────┴──────────┐
          DP₁                     D′
        ┌──┴──┐               ┌───┴───┐
        D     NP              D       NP
        the   Duke            's      death
```

That is to say, the definite article *the* would be present in the syntax, but (in the headlinese register) would undergo a type of ellipsis in the spellout component which can be characterised informally as follows:

(50)   **Article Drop**

An article which is the first word in the functional projection that it heads can be dropped

Saying here that an article can be 'dropped' means that an article present in the syntax can be given a null spellout/null printout. Since the article *the* in (49) is the first word of the DP_1 projection that it heads, it can be dropped, as in (46a) – and a parallel analysis can be proposed for (46b–46e).

The ellipsis account of Article Drop outlined in (50) above predicts that articles can only be dropped if they are the first word in a DP/ARTP containing them. This is true of every single one of the dropped articles in my own sample of headlines. But what about the following headlines (the first being internet-sourced, and the second being a spoof headline constructed by me), where the dropped article is not initial within the italicised nominals containing it?

(51)   a. Boris Johnson's 2020: A tumultuous year that upturned *all <the> PM's hopes* (*The Independent*, 29 December 2020)

        b. *Only <the> PM's allies* stand by him

If we suppose that the italicised nominals are QPs headed by the quantifiers *all/only*, the italicised strings in (51a/51b) will have the structure in (52a/52b):

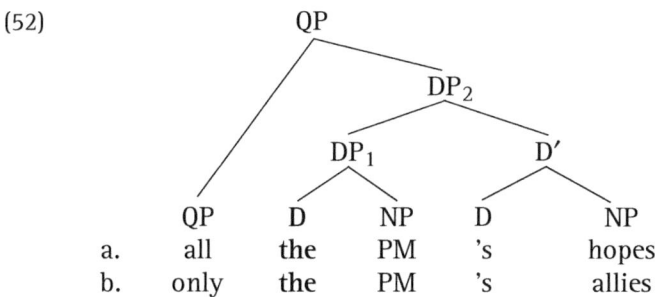

(52)

```
                      QP
                     /  \
                      DP₂
                    /      \
                 DP₁        D'
                /  \       /  \
        QP     D    NP    D    NP
   a.   all    the  PM    's   hopes
   b.   only   the  PM    's   allies
```

This means that although the article *the* is not initial within (i.e. is not the first word of) the QP (since it follows the Q *all/only*), it is initial within the DP_1 projection that it heads and thus can undergo the Article Drop operation in (50).

The condition that only an <u>initial</u> article can be dropped also accounts for my intuition that the (bold-printed) articles cannot be deleted in (constructed) headlines such as the following (an intuition shared by Andrew Weir, pc):

(53)   a. MEPs earn [*twice* **the** salary of MPs], report reveals

        b. [*What* **the** hell] is BoJo up to?

        c. [*What* **a** nasty piece of work] PM's aide turns out to be!

        d. Cummings creates [*quite* **a** stir]

If the bracketed nominals are DPs/ARTPs headed by *the/a*, it follows from the account of Article Drop in (50) that the bold-printed articles cannot be dropped in (53) because they are not initial within the (bracketed) DP/ARTP that they head, being preceded by the italicised items *twice/what/quite* (which, on one view, are specifiers of the articles).

The account of Article Drop outlined above (whereby it involves not pronouncing/printing articles which are present in the syntax) raises a number of questions in its wake, however. One (raised by an anonymous reviewer) is why an article can only be omitted when initial within its projection, and not when medial as in structures like (53). A plausible answer is to suppose that Article Drop is a subtype of Left Edge Ellipsis which involves giving a null spellout to the edge of a DP or ARTP (where the edge comprises the head and any specifier that it has). Where the left edge of the DP/ARTP comprises an article on its own, the Recoverability Condition of Chomsky (1964b) and Katz & Postal (1964) allows deletion of the article, because it is a functor with minimal semantic content. But where (as in the nominals bracketed in 53 above), the article has a specifier, the Recoverability Condition precludes deletion of the edge of the DP/ARTP because the specifier has substantive lexical semantic content. In more concrete terms, this means that in the DP *twice the salary of MPs* in (53a), the edge of the DP (= the string *twice the*) cannot be deleted because *twice* has semantic content which cannot be recovered if it is deleted.

Another question arising from the analysis in (50) is why, as observed by Mårdh (1980: 153), an article can't be deleted in a (constructed) headline such as:

(54)   Motorway speed limit to be reduced to fifty miles *an* hour in bad
        weather

A plausible answer is that the Recoverability Condition makes the article *an* undroppable in (54) because it functions as a distributive quantifier, and recoverability considerations prevent quantifiers from being dropped (because they are too contentful).

An interesting restriction on Article Drop observed in much work on headlines is that an article cannot be dropped from a direct object if the subject of the sentence contains an article. Stowell (1999) captured this generalisation in terms of a constraint which can be paraphrased informally as follows:

(55)   C-command Condition on Article Drop
        No nominal allows Article Drop if it is c-commanded by a nominal with
        an overt article

How this constraint works can be illustrated in terms of the following set of hypothetical headlines, where ø denotes a dropped article:

(56) a. A man bites a dog
      b. ø man bites a dog
      c. ø man bites ø dog
      d. *A man bites ø dog

In none of these headlines does the subject *a/ø man* violate the constraint, since the subject has no nominal constituent c-commanding it. Nor does the object *a dog* violate the constraint in (56a, 56b), because it has not undergone Article Drop. And although the object *ø dog* in (56c) has undergone Article Drop, it is c-commanded by a subject *ø man* which has also undergone Article Drop, so there is again no violation of the C-command Condition in (55). By contrast, the article-dropped object *ø dog* in (56d) does indeed violate the constraint, since it is c-commanded by the article-containing subject *a man*.

To summarise: in Module 7.3 we have looked at Article Drop, which is sporadic in some registers (e.g. social media like Twitter), but systematic in others (e.g. newspaper headlines). I argued that this involves a definite or indefinite article which is present in the syntax not being pronounced/printed if it is the first word of the projection that it heads.

You should now be able to tackle Exercise 7.3.

7.4 Be Drop

In this module, I turn to look at a further phenomenon characteristic of the headlinese register, which I will term Be Drop: by this, I mean omitting finite (indicative) forms of be in obligatory contexts (i.e. in contexts where adults would require the use of such a form of be in untruncated registers). Prescriptive guidelines on writing headlines often explicitly instruct sub-editors to omit (finite) forms of be. For example, Williams (2013) specifies 'Leave out *to be*', advising subeditors to say 'Residents unhappy about new road' rather than 'Residents *are* unhappy … '. Likewise, Ghosh (2022) recommends 'Avoid the use of *is, are, was, to be*, etc.' And in the same spirit, the Headline Writing Guidelines on pavilion.dinfos.edu (2020) instruct headline writers to 'Omit forms of the verb *to be* (*is, are, was, were*).' However, in this module, I will argue that any such prescriptive rule-based account is oversimplistic (in that it overlooks structural conditions on Be Drop), and I present (and evaluate) alternative syntactic accounts.

7.4.1 Characteristics of B̨ᴇ Drop

My sample of newspaper headlines contains 192 cases of Bᴇ Drop, 79 involving passive Bᴇ as in (57a) below, 64 involving copular Bᴇ as in (57b), 39 involving the future Bᴇ ᴛᴏ structure as in (57c), and 10 involving progressive Bᴇ as in (57d):

(57) a. Minnesota <is> hit by more unrest (*Financial Times* 14 April)
      b. Labour <is> in turmoil after Tories inflict huge defeats (*The Guardian*, 8 May)
      c. Europe <is> to welcome Brits (*The Sun*, 22 April)
      d. Glaciers **<are>** melting twice as fast as 20 years ago (*The Guardian*, 29 April)

Bᴇ Drop is not restricted to root clauses, but is also found in subordinate clauses like those bracketed below (where the relevant instance of Bᴇ Drop is bold-printed):

(58) a. <A> corrupt police officer <is> caught [when <a> gangster group **<is>** hacked] (*The Times*, 13 May)
      b. Angela Rayner <is> 'fired' [as Labour **<is>** gripped by post-poll rancour] (*The Observer*, 9 May)
      c. High streets feel the rush [as lockdown curbs **<are>** eased] (*The Guardian*, 13 April)
      d. Holiday sun <is> on <the> horizon [as restrictions **<are>** set to ease in June] (*The Times*, 9 April)

Bᴇ Drop is systematic, in that finite forms of Bᴇ are dropped in 97 per cent of obligatory contexts in my sample of headlines. Exceptional cases where (bold-printed) Bᴇ is not dropped fall into the types illustrated below:

(59) a. *Bozo is a buffoon* says <a> Tory (*Daily Star*, 4 April)
      b. Cameron <is> told: *your reputation is in tatters* after Greensill lobbying (*The Guardian*, 14 May)
      c. After <a> week of sun, it's <a> bank hol chiller … just as hot tubs boom (*Daily Star*, 3 April)
      d. Cummings <is> warned he isn't in <the> clear over <the> Chatty Rat leak (*Daily Telegraph*, 26 April)

In cases like (59a, 59b), the italicised clause is a direct quotation (albeit not enclosed in inverted commas), and if the speech is quoted verbatim, it will retain the copula *is* from the original. (59c, 59d) could fall under a constraint (discussed below) that personal pronoun subjects don't allow Bᴇ Drop, or alternatively could fall under a different condition, to the effect that Bᴇ can't be dropped on its own when part of a clitic cluster.

Since indicative forms of BE function as auxiliaries, and since we saw in Module 7.2 that the other two non-modal auxiliaries (HAVE/DO) can undergo left edge ellipsis, we might expect to find that HAVE and DO can also undergo ellipsis in headlines. However, my sample contains no examples of HAVE/DO Drop; on the contrary, finite forms of HAVE and DO are overtly spelled out, as in the examples below:

(60)   a. Seven **have** died from blood clots after 18 m AstraZeneca jabs, watchdog says (*Financial Times Weekend*, 3 April)
       b. Whitehall dismisses claim former aide **has** been cleared (*The Times*, 26 April)
       c. Queen says Duke's death '**has** left a huge void' in her life (*Daily Telegraph*, 12 April)
       d. Jez: Life of crime **does** pay (*Daily Star*, 11 May)

Hence, I have employed the narrower term BE Drop here, rather than the more general term Aux Drop.

An interesting constraint which appears to hold in my sample of headlines is that in all cases of BE Drop, the subject of BE is always a nominal, never a personal pronoun. This is puzzling, in view of the fact that a clause (like that bracketed in 61a below) in which BE undergoes Gapping allows a (bold-printed) personal pronoun subject – as does a clause like (61b) in African American Vernacular English, where a null copula/ø is used in a context where standard English would use the contracted copula*'s*:

(61)   a. If you were me and [I <were> you] – would you believe it, even if it were true? (J. L. Chalker, *The Return of Nathan Brazil*, Hachette UK, 2013)
       b. **He** ø fast in everything he do (Labov 1969: 717)

In my sample of headlines, (bold-printed) nominative personal pronouns only occur as subjects of (italicised) overt finite auxiliaries or finite verbs, as in:

(62)   a. <A> Senior Tory says Johnson should quit if **he** *broke* donation rules (*The Guardian*, 3 May)
       b. Harry: I *left* <the> UK to break <the> cycle of pain (*The Times*, 14 May)
       c. 14 years on, <the> McCanns tell <their> missing daughter: **We** *are* waiting for you (*Daily Mirror*, 13 May)
       d. On her 18th birthday ... Madeleine parents say **they**'*ll* never give up (*Daily Express*, 13 May)
       e. Cummings <is> warned **he** *isn't* in <the> clear over <the> Chatty Rat leak (*Daily Telegraph*, 26 April)
       f. Her majesty <is> to spend more time at Windsor Castle where **she** *is* 'most comfortable' (*Daily Express*, 14 April)

So how can we account for BE Drop sentences not allowing pronominal subjects?

One possible answer is a pragmatic one: BE is dropped in order to avoid the use of items with minimal semantic content and impact; and (as suggested by Mike Jones, pc) subject pronouns are not used because subjects in headlines announce new topics, and pronouns are not suited to this use. However, the assumption that BE is dropped purely because it has minimal content/impact fails to account for an important aspect of its distribution – namely that BE Drop is incompatible with Wh-Movement (more generally, with constituents undergoing A-bar Movement into peripheral positions) – as we see from the observation that my data don't contain any BE Drop headlines such as the following (and my intuition is that these are not well-formed as headlines):

(63)   a.   *What on earth <is> Bozo up to?
         b.   *What chaos Bozo <is> causing!

The absence of headlines like (63) suggests an alternative syntactic approach under which BE Drop headlines are truncated clauses with a truncated periphery.

In the next section, I explore possible ways of implementing such an approach.

7.4.2   Truncation accounts of BE Drop

One potential implementation of the Truncation analysis would be to suppose that BE Drop clauses have a truncated structure which projects only up to SUBJP. On one variant of this idea, (57a) *Minnesota hit by more unrest* would have a truncated structure along the lines below (simplified by not showing the internal structure of the VOICEP in which the passive auxiliary *is* originates before raising through T into SUBJ):

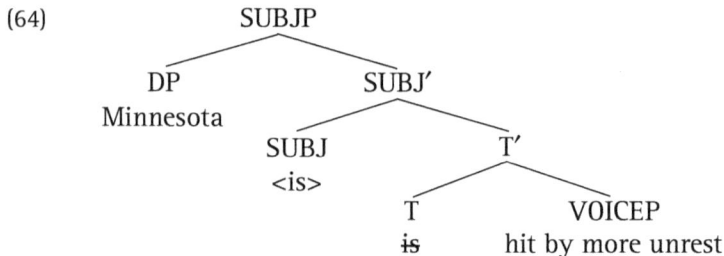

(64)

```
                    SUBJP
                  /       \
               DP          SUBJ'
            Minnesota     /      \
                      SUBJ        T'
                      <is>      /    \
                              T       VOICEP
                              i̶s̶    hit by more unrest
```

We can then suppose that (because of its minimal semantic content) BE can receive a <null spellout> in headlinese when it is the head of a root projection. Still, this analysis would have to be modified in some way in order to account for the observation made earlier that BE Drop is not restricted to root clauses, but rather can also apply to subordinate clauses like those bracketed in (58) above. Perhaps, then, we could suppose that Be Drop applies in truncated clauses (i.e. clauses which contain no peripheral FORCEP ... FINP projections).

Still, such an approach raises the question of which clauses can (and can't) be truncated (and why), and what the mechanism is by which BE comes to receive a null spellout. Under the analysis in (64), this can't be Left Edge Ellipsis, since this gives a null spellout to <u>all</u> constituents on the left edge of the highest projection in a clause – and this would lead us to expect that BE can only have a null spellout if its subject has a null spellout as well. But this is decidedly not the case: all Be Drop sentences in my data have overt subjects (and indeed in 64, the subject *Minnesota* receives an overt spellout).

One potential way of addressing this issue might be to suppose that BE raises to the head of SUBJP, whereas the subject (in the syntax, at least) raises only as far as spec-TP (an idea familiar from §6.3.1). This would mean that in place of (64) above, we have the revised truncated structure in (65) below:

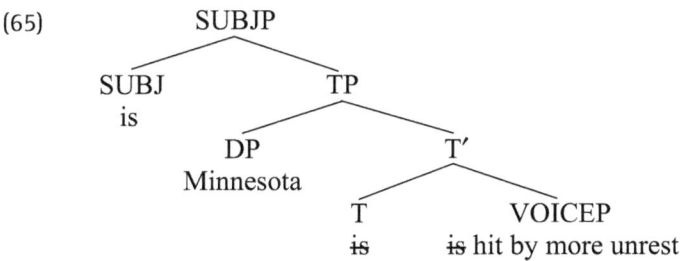

(65)

```
              SUBJP
          ╱         ╲
      SUBJ           TP
       is          ╱    ╲
               DP        T′
           Minnesota   ╱    ╲
                     T       VOICEP
                     i̶s̶    i̶s̶ hit by more unrest
```

In the PF component, *is* will receive a null spellout in SUBJ via the condition in (12ii) above that the left edge of the highest projection in a truncated clause can be unpronounced in the PF component. The overall structure will thus be spelled out as *Minnesota hit by more unrest*. The structure in (65) will be interpreted as declarative in force by the default Clause Typing Condition (22ii).

However, two important questions raise doubts about the plausibility of the derivation in (65). One is why the subject does not raise to the criterial position for subjects (spec-SUBJP). One possibility is that SUBJ in (65) carries a defective set of agreement features (e.g. perhaps number but not person), and this is enough for SUBJ to attract BE, but not enough for it to trigger raising of the subject to spec-SUBJP in the syntax (if subject raising is contingent on the presence of person). Still, this raises the further question of what interpretation SUBJP could receive in the LF component if it does not house the subject: one answer could be that the subject raises to spec-SUBJP in the semantic/LF component.

A second question raised by the derivation in (65) – and also by that in (64) – is why the subject in Be Drop sentences can't be nominative. A plausible answer is that if FIN is the locus of nominative case (in the sense that a finite FIN head assigns nominative case to subjects, as claimed in §4.3.2), truncating clauses at SUBJP would account for the absence of nominative pronouns like *she* as subjects in Be Drop headlines. If Be lacks one or more agreement features, it follows that unless it undergoes ellipsis, the derivation will crash at PF (because English has no spellout for a present tense form of Be with defective agreement features). On this view, ellipsis of Be serves to rescue a structure which would otherwise crash, since English has no overt spellout for a tensed verb with a defective set of agreement features. This would be in line with research dating back to Ross (1969) and Chomsky (1972) arguing that ellipsis operations can rescue derivations which would otherwise crash.

Since the subject is not within the domain of any case assigner (irrespective of whether we adopt the implementation of the SUBJP analysis in 65, or the variant of it in 64), we can suppose that the subject receives default accusative case via a Default Case Assignment Rule which was given the following informal characterisation in §4.1.2:

(66)   Default Case Assignment

A (pro)nominal which does not fall within the domain of (i.e. which is not c-commanded by) a local (i.e. nearby) case assigner receives accusative case by default

We could then suppose that in a (constructed) headline like (67) below, the italicised subject receives accusative case by default, via the case assignment condition (66) above:

(67)   *Us poor Brits* <are> victimised by Eurocrats ... again!

However, what remains to be accounted for under this story (as pointed out by Andrew Weir, pc) is why we don't find *?*Us victimised again!* (albeit this is not as bad as **We victimised again*). One possibility would be to invoke the pragmatic analysis offered by Mike Jones (pc) and mentioned earlier in §7.4.1, and suppose that subject personal pronouns are not used because subjects in headlines announce new topics, and personal pronouns are not suited to this use.

The assumption in (65) that Be Drop headlines are truncated clauses with defective agreement and defective subjects which raise only as far as spec-TP invites comparison with a phenomenon in Belfast English which Henry (1995) refers to as 'singular concord'. This involves *s*-forms of auxiliaries/verbs being used to spell out items which are specified for present tense but not for agreement. Consequently, singular concord clauses allow plural subjects as in:

(68)   a.   *The eggs* is cracked (Henry 1995: 16)
         b.   *These cars* goes very fast (Henry 1995: 16)

However, singular concord is incompatible with nominative subjects:

(69)   a. *They* is cracked (Henry 1995: 16)
        b. *They* **goes** very fast (Henry 1995: 16)

Furthermore, it is also incompatible with Auxiliary Inversion:

(70)   *Is the eggs* cracked? (Henry 1995: 16)

Alison Henry argues that in singular concord clauses, the subject 'moves only as far as SPEC/Tense' (Henry 1995: 17). Auxiliary Inversion is blocked in sentences like (70) because locality constraints require *is* to move through SUBJ into FIN, but *is* cannot move to SUBJ because it has no agreement features. In addition, subjects in singular concord clauses carry default (accusative) case:

(71)   *Us* and *them/*We* and *they* is always arguing (Henry 1995: 18)

Thus, the potential parallels between Be Drop in headlines and singular concord in Belfast English are suggestive.

    Returning now to headlines, it should be noted that something which is potentially problematic under the Left Edge Ellipsis account outlined in (65) above is why only be can be dropped in headlines, not other auxiliaries. After all, structures involving Left Edge Ellipsis allow ellipsis not only of be, but also of a range of other auxiliaries – as illustrated by the examples of Aux Drop below:

(72)   a. <Are> you not winning the game? (Schirer 2008: 37)
        b. <Does> anyone want a cup of tea? (Rühlemann 2012: 5)
        c. <Have> you seen any good movies lately? (Zwicky & Zwicky 1981: 536)
        d. <Will> tomorrow at four be okay? (after Carter & McCarthy 1995: 147)
        e. <Would> you like to go fishing this afternoon?

This asymmetry between the range of auxiliaries which can be dropped in Aux Drop structures like (72) on the one hand (where be, have, do and modals like will and would can be dropped) and headlines like (57) on the other (where only be can be dropped) poses a substantial challenge to the assumption that headlines undergo Left Edge Ellipsis. In terms of the analysis in (65), this amounts to asking why only be can raise to SUBJ (and thereby get into a position on the edge of a root projection where it can undergo Left Edge Ellipsis), and not other auxiliaries. Perhaps this is a reflex of the property that be is more mobile than other verbs (being the only verb that can raise out of VP in most varieties of English), and has a wider range of agreeing forms (*am/are/is/was/were*) than other verbs – and indeed some earlier work suggested that verbs with a rich set of overt agreement forms raise to a high position within clauses (e.g. Vikner 1995; Rohrbacher 1999). Still, this seems an implausible rationale if we are positing that SUBJ carries a defective set of agreement features in (65).

A further asymmetry is that whereas Aux Drop occurs only in main/root clauses like (72), BE Drop is found in root and non-root clauses like – for example, in subordinate clauses like the *when/as*-clauses in (58) above. An additional potential problem that arises with the analysis in (65) is that it is generally the case that an auxiliary only raises to SUBJ if its subject raises to spec-SUBJP, and this condition is violated in (65). Overall, then, a range of considerations argue against treating BE Drop clauses as truncated SUBJP structures with a SUBJ head with defective agreement features (perhaps carrying number but not person) which attracts BE (but not its subject) to raise to the edge of SUBJP, as in (65) above.

Accordingly, let's explore an alternative variant of the Truncation account of BE Drop which supposes that it is tense (not agreement) which is defective in BE Drop clauses (let's call this the Tense Deficit Hypothesis). This seems plausible, since Stowell (1999) reported that it is a characteristic of headlines that they often use present tense to report past events, as in the following example:

(73)   Minister of Defence White dies at 43 (de Lange 2008: 70)

It would seem that present tense serves as a default tense value in such cases.

One possible implementation of the Tense Deficit Hypothesis is to suppose that BE Drop clauses are truncated SUBJP+TP+VP structures in which T contains an affix which is unspecified for tense [*u-Tns*] in the syntax, and is assigned a discourse-determined tense value at LF, which will be [*Pres-Tns*] in the case of (57a) *Minnesota hit by more unrest* (though this would require us to abandon the Legibility Condition of §3.1.1, requiring all features to be valued at the end of the syntactic derivation). On this view, (57a) would be a truncated clause with the syntactic structure below, if BE raises to adjoin to the affix in T (with the structure being simplified by not showing the internal structure of VP):

(74)
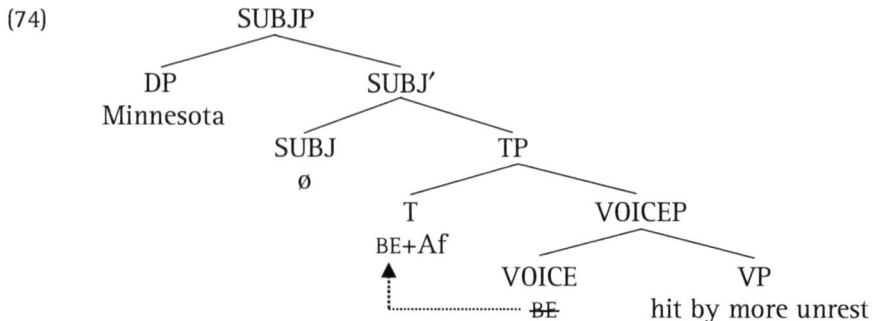

The resulting *BE+Af* head cannot be spelled out as an overt form of BE (since there is no overt spellout for forms of BE with an unvalued tense feature). Instead let's suppose that it receives a null spellout at PF, because BE has a null counterpart *ø* which is used as a default spellout in contexts where no overt form of BE is available – including in small clause structures like that bracketed below

(75)   I consider [this analysis *ø* potentially flawed]

We could then suppose that the *BE+Af* head in (74) receives the same default null spellout *ø* as is found in small clauses like that bracketed in (75) – and perhaps also in root clauses like that italicised in 'What? *John ø in prison?* No way!'

7.4.3   Bᴇ Drop and Article Drop

I now turn to touch on another characteristic of Bᴇ Drop headlines which appears to be empirically robust – namely that headlines which show Bᴇ Drop typically show Article Drop too, as illustrated by the examples below:

(76)   a.   *<A>* wife *<is>* fighting for life after *<a>* knife horror at *<a>* 2m
              country estate (*Daily Express*, 9 April)
         b.   Starmer *<is>* ejected from *<a>* pub by *<an>* angry landlord (*Daily
              Telegraph*, 20 April)
         c.   Cummings *<is>* to blame *<the>* PM for *<the>* Covid death toll
              (*Sunday Times*, 25 April)
         d.   *<The>* under-40s *<are>* to be offered *<an>* alternative to *<the>*
              Oxford jab (*The Independent*, 7 May)
         e.   *<An>* embryo *<is>* made from *<a>* monkey and *<a>* human (*The
              Times*, 16 April)
         f.   *<The>* UK *<is>* to use *<the>* presidency of *<the>* G7 to take on China
              (*Daily Telegraph*, 3 April)
         g.   *<The>* PM *<is>* *<the>* subject of *<a>* £535 county court order (*Daily
              Telegraph*, 13 May)

In my sample, 100 per cent of all subjects in Bᴇ Drop headlines showed Article Drop in obligatory contexts for articles, and 91 per cent of all non-subject constituents. Exceptions to this generalisation (i.e. Bᴇ Drop clauses containing highlighted non-subject nominals with overt articles) fall into the types illustrated below:

(77)   a.   India *<is>* braced for 500,000 infections **a** *day* (*Sunday Times*, 25 April)
         b.   Boris *<is>* painted into **a** *corner* (*Daily Mail*, 29 April)
         c.   Boris *<is>* on **the** *ropes* (*Daily Mail*, 27 April)
         d.   *<A>* Covid pill to take at home *<is>* on **the** *way* (*Daily Express*,
              21 April)

  e. Britain <is> on **the** *offensive* in <a> race with China for crucial minerals (*The Times*, 5 April)

  f. Cars and whisky <are> to **the** *fore* as Johnson chases <a> 'challenging' India trade deal (*Financial Times*, 16 April)

More specifically, they fall into two categories. In (77a), the article *a* has a distributive sense (paraphrasable as 'each'), and it has often been noted (in work dating back to Mårdh 1980) that articles which function as generic or distributive quantifiers can't be dropped (arguably for the same recoverability reasons that quantifiers like *each/every/any* can't be dropped). The remaining articles bold-printed in (77b–77f) are intrinsic parts of idioms/set phrases (*paint into a corner, on the ropes, on the way, on the offensive, to the fore*), and these are widely reported to be resistant to Article Drop. Still, it should be noted that my sample also contains some potential fixed phrases with dropped articles like 'on <the> brink of', 'in <the> wake of', 'in <the> pipeline', and 'on <the> way'; thus, it would appear that such phrases allow (but do not require) Article Drop.

 The question raised by the discussion above is what is the nature of the correlation between BE Drop and Article Drop. An intriguing question (raised by Giuliano Armenante, pc) is whether there could be some relation between Article Drop and BE Drop in headlines on the one hand, and the cross-linguistic observation made by Bošković (2012) that languages without articles typically also lack TPs on the other. For Bošković, nominals in languages without articles project only up to NP (not up to DP), and occur in clauses which lack TP and which also have subjects assigned default case. If personal pronouns like *him/her/it/them* are pronominal DPs, such an analysis would account for the absence of personal pronoun subjects in BE Drop sentences (if the latter have NP subjects).

 Still, a potential challenge to the claim that the subjects of BE Drop sentences do not allow DP subjects comes from the (spoof) headline in (67) above, repeated as (78) below:

(78) *Us poor Brits* <are> victimised by Eurocrats … again!

The problem which (78) poses is that it is a BE Drop sentence which has the seeming DP *us poor Brits* as its subject. However, it should be noted that this type of subject was not attested in my sample of BE Drop headlines (though of course this could have been an artefact of the relatively small sample size).

 Another potential challenge to the claim that BE Drop sentences don't allow DP subjects is posed by sentences like (43) above, repeated as (79) below:

(79) a. <u>Northern Ireland's First Minister</u> <is> toppled in <a> backlash over Brexit (*The i*, 29 April)

  b. <u>Bozo's phone number</u> <was> on the internet for 15 years (*Daily Star*, 1 May)

c. <u>Johnson's Mustique holiday</u> \<is> added to inquiries into potential rule breaches (*Financial Times*, 11 May)

d. <u>EY's Wirecard audits</u> \<are> slammed in \<a> report (*Financial Times*, 19 April)

e. <u>Starmer's leadership</u> \<is> in crisis over \<the> reshuffle move to demote Rayner (*The Guardian*, 10 May)

Here, the underlined subjects of the Be Drop sentences in question would appear to be DPs – at least if we adopt the DP analysis of possessive nominals in (45) above. Still, one way round this might be to follow Kayne (1994: 26) in supposing that possessors are not in spec-DP, but rather in a lower projection headed by the possessive affix *'s* (let's call this POSSP). On this view, we could suppose that the underlined constituents in (79) are defective (DP-less) nominals which project only up to POSSP, not up to DP. In more concrete terms, this would mean that the nominal *Starmer's leadership* in (79e) has the structure below:

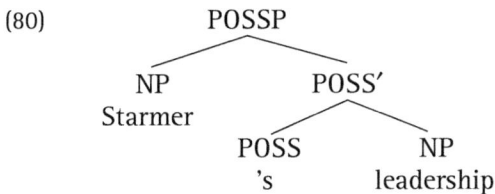

(80)

POSSP
- NP
  - Starmer
- POSS′
  - POSS
    - 's
  - NP
    - leadership

We could then maintain the view that nominals in Be Drop sentences lack the DP projection found in non-abbreviated registers.

Bošković (2012: 217) suggests that TP-less clauses contain a subject projection (which I will here take to be SUBJP), but no tense projection. If so, and if Be Drop clauses are truncated at SUBJP (as suggested in §7.4.2), a headline such as (76a) above could have a derivation along the simplified lines shown below:

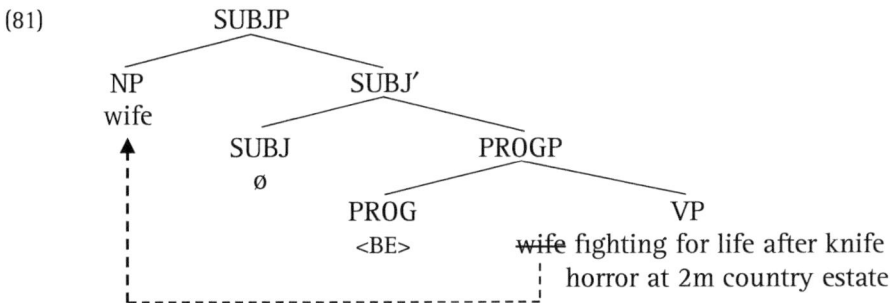

(81)

SUBJP
- NP
  - wife
- SUBJ′
  - SUBJ
    - ∅
  - PROGP
    - PROG
      - \<BE>
    - VP
      - ~~wife~~ fighting for life after knife horror at 2m country estate

On this view, the clause subject (*wife*) is an NP which raises from spec-VP to spec-SUBJP, and receives default accusative case via (66). The progressive auxiliary be cannot be assigned tense (because there is no TP projection), and will remain in PROG if SUBJ can only attract a tensed T-head to adjoin to it. If SUBJ contains an agreement affix which is lowered onto BE at PF, BE will end up marked for agreement but not tense. But since PF has no overt spellout for any (auxiliary or non-auxiliary) verb inflected for agreement but not tense, BE will be given a null spellout by default, and the overall structure in (81) is spelled out as *Wife fighting for life after knife horror at 2m country estate*.

An interesting technical issue arising from the 'no TP, no DP' derivation in (81) concerns how the subject NP *wife* raises to spec-SUBJP. Under the account of movement of subjects to spec-TP within the CP+TP+VP framework in §3.1.1, a T probe is said to attract the closest XP goal carrying a person feature to become its specifier (provided that the goal is active). If we transpose this account into the SUBJP analysis of subjects assumed here, this would mean that SUBJ attracts the closest XP carrying person to become its specifier. But if D is the locus of the person features of nominals, then SUBJ will be unable to attract the NP *wife* in (81) to become its specifier, because this NP is not projected further into DP, and so lacks person. One way round this would be to suppose that SUBJ attracts the closest XP that it agrees with in respect of one of more φ-features to become its specifier. We could then say that SUBJ in (81) carries a number feature which allows it to attract the NP *wife* to move to spec-SUBJP because the NP *wife* is specified as singular in number, and is active by virtue of its unvalued case feature.

Indeed, we might even go further and suppose that SUBJ in BE Drop headlines is a defective head which enters the derivation carrying an unvalued number feature, and attracts the closest XP carrying number to raise to spec-SUBJP: in the case of (81), this XP will be the NP *wife*. If SUBJ in BE Drop structures lacks a person feature, and if SUBJ can only attract an XP with person if SUBJ carries a person feature, it follows that the defective SUBJ in BE Drop structures (by virtue of carrying number but not person) cannot attract a DP carrying person to become its subject. This would provide a principled account of the observation reported above that BE Drop sentences don't have DP subjects (like *the queen* or *she*).

Under the approach outlined above, there are potential parallels between languages which lack DP and TP projections on the one hand, and headlines which exhibit BE Drop and Article Drop on the other. Still, a question arising from this approach concerns the exact nature of the inter-relation between DP and TP. Bošković (2012: 216) argues that TP is the clausal counterpart of the nominal constituent DP, so that 'the lack of DP in a language would imply the lack of its clausal counterpart, namely TP' (2012: 216) and hence 'article-less languages lack TP' (2012: 221). But why is there a correlation between articles and tense?

One possible answer (suggested by Giuliano Armenante, pc) can be offered in relation to work by Schwarz (2012) on the temporal properties of

DPs. I will present the key ideas in a highly simplified form here, for the sake of readers unfamiliar with work on formal semantics. In this connection, consider the interpretation of the articles *a/the* in the following examples:

(82)   a. A/the hostage is bleeding after being pistol-whipped
        b. A/the hostage is safe after being released

In (82a), the phrase *a/the hostage* means 'a/the person who *is* a hostage', whereas in (82b) it means 'a/the person who *was* a hostage' (but no longer is after being released). One way of accounting for this is to suppose that articles carry a tense which can either be bound by (i.e. interpreted as the same as) that of the finite verb/auxiliary in the containing clause (as in 82a), or can be contextually determined (as in 82b). This opens up the possibility that it is a tense deficit in the article which is at the root of Article Drop. Giuliano makes the following suggestion about tense-dropped (i.e. Be Drop) headlines:

> Tense-dropped headlines are not situated in a salient context (since a temporal reference is missing). This might explain why the article is dropped (It can't be bound, since its binder is dropped, and it can't be contextually evaluated either.) (Giuliano Armenante, pc)

The phrase 'It can't be bound, since its binder is dropped' can be paraphrased informally as 'It can't be interpreted as having the same tense as Be, since Be is tenseless.' One way of implementing this idea within the framework used here is to suppose that overt articles carry a tense feature which needs to be valued, and that in Be Drop clauses, this feature can't be valued by the tense feature on Be (since this is unspecified), and can't be contextually valued either (since the absence of tense on Be means there is insufficient contextual information). This entails that the use of overt articles in Be Drop clauses will cause the derivation to crash; and this results in the article receiving a null spellout by default (or forces the use of a null, tenseless article).

Still, while this analysis accounts for why Tense Drop (i.e. Be Drop) sentences like (76) above show Article Drop, it begs the question of why Article Drop is also found in clauses like those below which contain a (bold-printed) finite auxiliary or non-auxiliary verb which is either present tense (as in 83), or past tense (as in 84):

(83)   a. Jez: <A> life of crime **does** pay (*Daily Star*, 11 May)
        b. <A> mum **tells** of <an> encounter with <a> madman (*Sunday People*, 25 April)
        c. <A> cyber attack **shuts** down <a> US oil pipeline (*The i*, 10 May)

d. <The> PM **confirms** <a> huge easing of lockdown (*Metro*, 11 May)

e. <The> navy **heads** home but <the> dispute **rages** on (*The Independent*, 7 May)

(84)   a. <The> Tory party **paid** <the> bill for <a> 58,000 flat makeover (*Daily Mail*, 27 April)

b. <A> Tory peer **victimised** <a> female worker at <a> firm (*Daily Telegraph*, 14 April)

c. <A> terror victim **helped** <an> attacker catch <a> train (*Daily Telegraph*, 15 April)

d. <The> Duke **planned** his funeral with military precision (*Daily Telegraph*, 16 April)

e. <A> top Cameron mandarin **took** <a> job from Greensill (*The Times*, 14 April)

One possible answer is to suppose that Article Drop results from failing to mark nominal tense, and Be Drop from failing to mark clausal tense (on BE). It would then follow that Article Drop can occur irrespective of whether clausal tense is dropped (because there is no overt article on the nominal needing to be assigned a tense value), but that Tense Drop/Be Drop requires Article Drop, because the tense feature on overt articles can't be valued in the absence of clausal tense (for the reasons set out in the indented passage in the preceding paragraph).

An alternative account of the correlation is developed by Reich (2017). He argues that headlines are used to comment on some event *e* which is the topic of the headline. He maintains that headlines contain a null *e*-topic in spec-TOPP, and that this event topic binds (and thereby licenses) a null copula/NC, and can also bind (and license) a null article/NA on one or more nominals. Although I will not attempt to sketch his analysis here (since it requires familiarity with work in formal semantics), I note that it follows from his analysis that the use of a null article or null copula in headlines is subject to a condition to the effect that neither a null article nor a null counterpart of BE can be c-commanded by a nominal containing an overt article, or by an overt copula. This condition predict the pattern of (un)-grammaticality below (NA = null article; NC = null copula):

(85)   a. A policeman is awarded the Victoria Cross

b. NA policeman NC awarded NA Victoria Cross

c. NA policeman NC awarded the Victoria Cross

d. NA policeman is awarded the Victoria Cross

e. *NA policeman is awarded NA Victoria Cross

f. *A policeman NC awarded the Victoria Cross

g. *A policeman NC awarded NA Victoria Cross

Examples (85b–85d) satisfy the C-command Condition because no NA or NC is c-commanded by an overt copula or by a nominal headed by an overt article. By contrast, in (85e) the second NA violates the C-command Condition because it is c-commanded by the overt passive auxiliary *is*. In (85f), the use of NC violates the C-command Condition ·because it is c-commanded by a nominal headed by an overt article (*a policeman*). And in (85g) both NA and NC are c-commanded by a nominal headed by an overt article, in violation of the c-command requirement.

However, I would note that my own judgement is that (85e) is fine, and indeed my sample of headlines includes the following:

(86)   Navalny is moved to NA prison hospital (*Financial Times*, 20 April)

where the null article is c-commanded by the overt passive auxiliary *is*. This suggests that the C-command Condition needs to be modified, perhaps as below:

(87)   **Generalised C-command Condition on Article/Be Drop**
        Neither a null article nor a null counterpart of BE can be c-commanded
        by a nominal with an overt article

This yields the same grammaticality judgements for all the examples in (85), except (85e), which is predicted to be fine because neither null article is c-commanded by a nominal with an overt article.

Still, it seems odd that a seemingly arbitrary syntactic condition like (87) should govern the use of a null article/null BE in headlines. We might therefore wonder what the conceptual basis of this condition is. Since the c-commanding nominal which bars the use of a null article/null BE lower down in the clause is invariably the subject (hence the first constituent in the reduced clausal structure of headlines), (87) amounts (in layman's terms) to positing that if you start a headline with an overt article on the subject, you are thereby signalling that you are using a non-abbreviated register, and hence considerations of cohesion (i.e. continuity of style/ register) demand that you don't use null articles or null BE (which are characteristic of abbreviated registers) lower down in the clause. Note, however, that the converse doesn't appear to be the case: for example, in headines like (85c, 85d) you can start the sentence in an abbreviated register (by using a subject with a null article) and then switch to a non-abbreviated register and use an overt copula/overt article later/lower in the structure. This would suggest that there is a constraint on code-switching (more precisely, register-switching) to the effect that switching from a non-standard (abbreviated) register to a standard (unabbreviated) register is permitted, but the converse (i.e. switching from a standard unabbreviated register to a non-standard abbreviated one) is avoided.

To summarise: in Module 7.4 I have examined the phenomenon of BE Drop in headlines. I presented the two alternative accounts of BE Drop below:

(88)   **Agreement Deficit analysis of BE Drop**
        BE Drop clauses are truncated SUBJP constituents, headed by a SUBJ with defective agreement properties (e.g. with number but not person). SUBJ attracts BE to raise to adjoin to it, but (being defective) cannot attract the subject to move to spec-SUBJP; and since the clause lacks FIN, its subject cannot be assigned nominative case. Instead, the subject raises only as far as spec-TP, and is assigned accusative case by default. BE receives a null spellout by default at PF, because there is no overt spellout for defective forms of BE.

(89)   **Tense Deficit analysis of BE Drop**
        BE Drop clauses are truncated SUBJP constituents with a tense deficit, which means that BE receives a null spellout by default, and its subject receives default case. On one view, BE Drop clauses contain a TP whose head T contains an affix with an unvalued tense feature; on another view, they lack both TP and DP projections, and have NP subjects.

I also noted that BE Drop and Article Drop are correlated, and looked at accounts of this correlation, concluding that it can be described in terms of the Generalised C-command Condition in (87), which may ultimately be reducible to a constraint on register-switching, permitting switching from a non-standard (abbreviated) register to a standard (unabbreviated) register, but not from a standard (unabbreviated) register to a non-standard (abbreviated) one.
    You should now be able to tackle Exercise 7.4.

7.5   Object Drop

An interesting characteristic of certain abbreviated registers of written English is that they exhibit a phenomenon often referred to as Object Drop, because it involves an object being dropped. This is widely attested in instructional registers such as recipe books, maintenance or repair manuals, stage directions, product labels, and so on, but is also found in a range of informal written registers, such as diaries, SMS text messages, and social media posts. Typical examples I have gathered from the labels on a number of household products are shown below (with the dropped object shown as ø):

(90)   a. Don't stir ø. Don't thin ø. Brush ø on using light, even strokes in the direction of the grain, taking care to avoid overlap (*Instructions on a tin of woodstain*)

b. Heat ø on full power. Mix ø halfway through cooking ø and leave
   ø to stand for 1 minute. Stir ø before serving ø (*Instructions on a
   packet of frozen noodles*)

c. Shake ø gently before use. Store ø in the original container. Use ø
   within two months of first use. Do not store ø above 25˚C. Do not
   freeze ø. (*Instructions on a nasal spray*)

d. Pour ø into a low pressure sprayer or watering can or bucket and
   apply ø over the area to be cleaned. Allow the product 20 minutes to
   lift the dirt/moss/algae from the surface and then scrub ø with a firm
   brush. Finally wash ø off, preferably with a jet wash (*Instructions on
   a container of patio cleaner*)

e. Mix the sachet contents with the water in a small saucepan. Bring ø
   to the boil gently, stirring ø continuously. Simmer ø for 1–2 minutes,
   until the sauce is smooth and thickened (*Instructions on a packet of
   sauce mix*)

There are several reasons for positing that such sentences contain null
objects (in each of the positions marked ø) and that these objects are active
in the syntax. Thus, the null object can serve (for example) as the controller
of PRO in a sentence like (91a) below, or as the binder for a reflexive anaphor like *itself* in (91b), or as a constituent modified by secondary predicates as in (91c):

(91) a. Knead the dough and leave ø in a warm place [PRO to rise]
      b. Push the dough out and fold ø back on itself each fourth stroke (Neal
         1985: 47)
      c. Serve ø hot with lots of butter (Neal 1985: 35)

Massam & Roberge (1989: 135) note of the empty object/EO that 'EO
receives a specific interpretation, rather than, for example, an arbitrary
reference. The empty category need not have a particular linguistic antecedent; instead, its reference appears to be contextually defined.'

Massam & Roberge note (1989: 135–36) that the null/empty object is subject
to a constraint that it must appear in a position where it is theta-marked and
case-marked (more specifically, assigned accusative case) by the same transitive verb. This means that it can't occur as the subject of an ECM clause like
that bracketed in (92a) below, or as the object of a preposition like *with* in (92b):

(92) a. Put cake in oven. *Expect [ø to be done half an hour later]
      b. Mix the lemon juice and chopped parsley. *Then sprinkle scallops with ø

A further constraint to note is that the null objects are always interpreted
as third person referential/non-expletive pronouns – as is the case with the
null objects in (90) above. Thus, the empty object is a specific, thematic,
accusative, third person referential pronoun.

Key questions arising from the various observations above are: What is the nature of the null objects in sentences like (90) above, and how can we account for the constraints on their use? In this module, I compare and contrast three alternative accounts of null objects in instructional registers.

7.5.1   A Topic Drop analysis of null objects

An analysis which has been widely advocated in the relevant literature (dating back to Haegeman 1987a, 1987b) is one which claims that null objects in instructional registers are the result of Topic Drop. A number of different implementations of this analysis have been proposed in the literature, but for expository purposes, I'll present only one here, based on the following assumptions (with 93ii taken from the Truncation account of null subjects in 12ii above):

(93)   **Topic Drop analysis of null objects**
- (i) Null objects arise when a pronoun is topicalised and thereby moves to the edge of a TOPP projection at the root of a truncated clause
- (ii) The edge of the highest projection in a sentence structure can be unpronounced in the PF component, provided that it contains only phonetically weak material with recoverable semantic content

Let's look at how such an analysis might handle the use of null objects in a recipe instruction such as (90a) *Don't stir*. Let's suppose that imperatives have a null counterpart of *you* as their subject (below denoted as ~~you~~) in spec-SUBJP, and also contain a null imperator operator (Op_{IMP}) in spec-FORCEP (cf. Han 1998, 2000a, 2000b, 2001; Haegeman & Greco 2017: 9, fn. 4). In addition, let's posit that the missing object in (90a) *Don't stir* is the pronominal DP *it* (referring to a tin of woodstain) and that (via Topicalisation) *it* moves to become the specifier of a TOPP projection at the root of the clause. Given these assumptions (and others), the sentence will have the syntactic derivation below (simplified in numerous ways, including by not showing the internal structure of SUBJP):

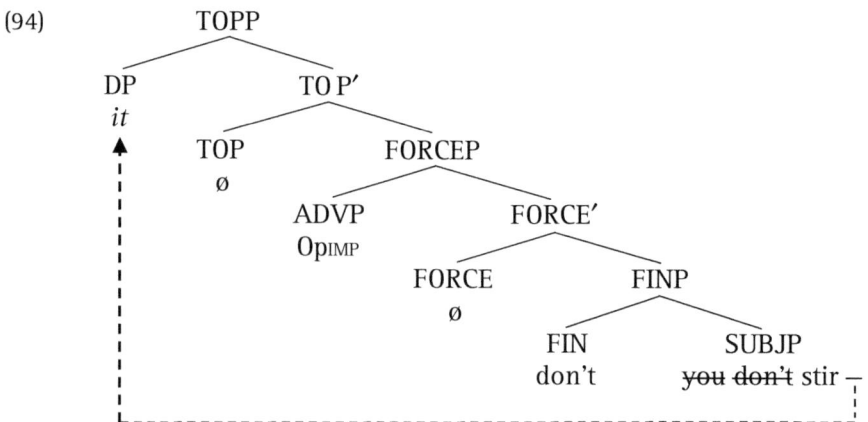

(94)

```
                        TOPP
                   ╱           ╲
                 DP             TOP'
                 it          ╱       ╲
                 ▲         TOP        FORCEP
                 ┆          ∅       ╱        ╲
                 ┆               ADVP         FORCE'
                 ┆               Op_IMP      ╱      ╲
                 ┆                       FORCE       FINP
                 ┆                         ∅       ╱      ╲
                 ┆                              FIN        SUBJP
                 ┆                             don't    you don't stir ─┐
                 ┆                                                       ┆
                 └───────────────────────────────────────────────────── ┘
```

When the structure in (94) is transferred to the PF component, the topic *it* is unpronounced in accordance with the Topic Drop spellout rule in (93ii) above, so deriving (90a) *Don't stir!*

Some of the assumptions made in (94) are worth expanding on. For one thing, I have assumed that although FORCEP is normally the highest projection in an embedded clause (in order to satisfy the selectional requirement for a predicate which selects e.g. an exclamative clause as its complement to be immediately adjacent to that complement), no such requirement holds in root clauses – hence a TOPP can be positioned on top of FORCEP in an exclamative root clause such as (95) below (where the italicised exclamative phrase is in spec-FORCEP under the analysis in §5.4.1):

(95)   [TOPP Cristiano Ronaldo, [FORCEP *what a fantastic career* he has had]]

A second assumption made in (94) is that *don't* undergoes Auxiliary Inversion in negative imperatives, and thereby ends up in FIN (preceding the subject in SUBJP) – an assumption which gains empirical support from the relative position of auxiliary and subject highlighted below:

(96)   *Don't* **you** dare contradict me!

A third assumption made in (94) is that the sentence contains a null imperative operator whose criterial position is the edge of FORCEP. This operator may well originate in a lower position (perhaps as the specifier of a FIN head which is imperative in mood, where it triggers Auxiliary Inversion before moving to spec-FORCEP), though this is not shown in (94). Interestingly, no Inversion takes place in positive imperatives, as we see from the fact that we find *You be careful!* rather than **Be you careful!* There is much more to be said about imperatives (see the references in the Bibliographical notes), but my concern here is with Topic Drop.

While the Topic Drop analysis in (94) offers the apparent theoretical advantage that it makes use of the same root ellipsis mechanism as was employed in the analysis of Subject Drop in (12ii), it turns out to be potentially problematic in several respects. For one thing, *it* is a weak pronoun – as we see from the fact that it can't be modified by the focus particle *even* as in (97a) below, it can't occur in focus position in a pseudo-cleft like (97b), and it can't be a topic in a sentence like (97c):

(97)   a. Even *this*/**Even it* didn't upset her
          b. What upset him was *this*/**it*
          c. *This*/**It*, I can't stand

Moreover, the Topic Drop analysis in (94) fails to account for why the null object in instructional registers (in sentences like 90 above) is always third person. After all, fronted overt topics can be first or second person, as illustrated by the fronted topics italicised in (98) below:

(98)   Me too/Us journalists/You guys, he would never talk to

The fact that overt fronted topics are not subject to person restrictions whereas null objects in instructional registers are restricted to being third person raises questions about the plausibility the Topic Drop analysis of null objects.

A further potential problem is that (as the examples below illustrate), fronting of an italicised topic in an imperative yields a degraded outcome:

(99)   a. *The weapons* leave − behind! (Jensen 2007)
         b. *This book*, leave − on the table! (Bianchi & Frascarelli 2010)

The low acceptability of sentences like (99) can be be attributed to an intervention effect, if imperatives contain a null imperative operator in their periphery, and if (as in 94 above) the fronted topic illicitly moves across the peripheral imperative operator in violation of the Intervention Condition which bars likes from crossing likes. On one view, an intervention violation would arise because a topic undergoing A-bar Movement into a peripheral position (spec-TOPP) crosses an imperative operator which also undergoes A-bar Movement into a peripheral position (e.g. if it moves from spec-FINP to spec-FORCEP). But if a null imperative operator is a barrier to fronting a topic, the Topic Drop analysis in (94) would wrongly predict that null objects would not occur: and yet null objects do indeed occur in imperatives, as we see from (90) above.

A final problem to note is that the Topic Drop analysis in (94) runs into potential problems in relation to contrasts such as the following (from Weir 2017):

(100)   a. Wait for ten minutes [before removing ø from oven]
         b. *The chicken*, wait for ten minutes [before removing − from the oven]

(101)   a. WARNING: [Placing ø into microwave] may cause damage
         b. *This dish*, [placing − into a microwave] may cause damage

As these examples illustrate, a null object can occur inside a bracketed clause which is an adjunct as in (100a), or a sentential subject (i.e. a clause used as the subject of another clause) as in (101a). However, no topic can be extracted out of an adjunct clause or a sentential subject, as we see from the ungrammaticality of (100b) and (101b), because any such movement would lead to violation of the Adjunct Island Constraint or Subject Island Constraint of Ross (1967). Thus, the Topic Drop analysis wrongly predicts that (100a, 101a) should not occur.

Given the objections outlined above to the Topic Drop analysis in (93), let's turn to look at an alternative analysis proposed by Weir (2017), under which Object Drop is taken to involve Article Drop.

7.5.2   An Article Drop analysis of null objects

The core assumptions underlying Weir's (2017) Article Drop analysis of null objects can be summarised informally as follows:

(102)   **Article Drop analysis of null objects**
Null objects are DPs headed by a null article with an NP complement which can optionally be unpronounced at PF (thereby giving rise to a null object)

On this view, Article Drop involves a DP headed by a null D which has an overt NP as its complement, whereas Object Drop involves a DP headed by a null D which has a null NP as its complement. This analysis provides an interesting perspective on the relation between pairs of sentences like those below:

(103)   a.   Wait for ten minutes [before removing *<the>* chicken from oven]
b.   Wait for ten minutes [before removing *ø* from oven] (=100a)

On one implementation of Weir's analysis, the article-dropped object in (103a) will have the structure in (104a) below, whereas the null object *ø* in (103b) will be a DP with the structure in (104b) below:

(104)   a.

```
            DP                              b.            DP
          /    \                                        /    \
        D        NP                                   D        NP
      <the>    chicken                              <the>   <chicken>
```

On this view, null objects have essentially the same DP structure as article-dropped objects, since both are DPs headed by a null determiner with an NP complement, and they differ only in respect of whether the relevant NP is overt as in (104a), or null as in (104b).

Potential evidence in support of the subsuming Object Drop within Article Drop comes from the observation that the two frequently occur together within the same sentences – as illustrated by the instructions below (taken from the labels on various household products), where I have italicised missing articles like *<the>* and bold-printed missing objects like *<**them/it**>*:

(105)   a.   Best before: see *<the>* side of *<the>* pack. Keep *<**them**>* frozen. If thawed, use *<**them**>* within 24 hours, and do not refreeze *<**them**>*. For *<the>* best results, cook *<**them**>* from frozen. If thawed, reduce *<the>* cooking time accordingly (*Cooking instructions on a packet of frozen pancakes*)

b. For <*the*> best results, cook <**them**> from frozen. If thawed, reduce <*the*> cooking time accordingly. Remove all <*the*> packaging before cooking <**them**>. To microwave <**them**>: Place <*the*> contents in a microwaveable container with 3 tbsp oil, cover <**them**> and vent <**them**>. Microwave <**them**> on full power for 20 minutes (*Instructions for frozen noodles*)

c. To open <**it**>, squeeze <*the*> cap and turn <**it**>. Pour 20 ml of undiluted mouthwash, rinse <**it**> around <*the*> teeth and gums for 30 seconds, then spit <**it**> out. Do not swallow <**it**>. To close <**it**>, turn <*the*> cap until it clicks. (*Instructions on a bottle of mouthwash*)

d. Squeeze <*the*> pouch gently to separate <*the*> rice grains. Tear or cut <*the*> top of <*the*> pouch by approx. 2 cm. Place <*the*> pouch upright in the microwave. Microwave <**it**> on full power for 2 minutes. Remove <*the*> pouch from <*the*> microwave, and tear <**it**> open (*Instructions on a packet of cooked rice*)

The co-occurrence of Article Drop and Object Drop within the same register is precisely what would be expected under Weir's analysis in which Object Drop is treated as involving Article Drop.

The Article Drop analysis of Object Drop in (102, 104) accounts for several properties of Object Drop. Firstly, both Article Drop and Object Drop are found only in written registers, not in the spoken language – hence neither results in a grammatical outcome in a conversation like that below:

(106)   SPEAKER A: What shall I do with the baking tray, honey?
        SPEAKER B: Put *the tray/it/*tray/*ø* over there, sweetie

Secondly, null objects denote specific entities (as we see from sentences like 90 above), in the same way as dropped articles typically have a specific interpretation. Thirdly, null objects are always third person, as noted earlier. This follows from the Article Drop analysis, since articles are inherently third person, as we see from the observation that an article-modified nominal requires third person agreement on a verb like that underlined below, and binds a third person anaphor like *himself/herself*:

(107)   *The/A true scholar* always <u>applies</u> *himself/herself* assiduously to research

A fourth property of null objects which follows from the Article Drop analysis is that null objects are never expletive: under the Article Drop analysis, this follows from the absence of expletive NPs in English.

A fifth property accounted for under the analysis in (102, 104) is that null objects can freely occur inside islands (as illustrated in 100a, 101a above), since the same is true of null articles like those italicised below:

(108)   a. Wait for ten minutes [before removing *<the>* chicken from *<the>* oven]

        b. WARNING: [Placing *<a>* metal container into *<a>* microwave] may cause damage

Overall, then, the null article analysis of Object Drop accounts for a wide range of properties of null objects.

However, although the idea of subsuming Object Drop under Article Drop is tempting, there are asymmetries between the two which potentially undermine the Article Drop analysis of null objects. One such asymmetry relates to the registers in which the two occur. For example, the sample of 390 newspaper headlines that I collected (discussed in §7.3.1) contained 462 instances of Article Drop, but not a single instance of Object Drop – a discrepancy hard to account for under an analysis like (102, 104) which treats Object Drop as a form of Article Drop. Moreover, in the (admittedly small) sample of product labels which I looked at, I found that some (like those in 105 above) involve both Object Drop and Article Drop, whereas others (like those in 90 above) show Object Drop but not Article Drop – suggesting that the two are different phenomena, and thus potentially undermining the symmetrical analysis in (104).

A further asymmetry between Object Drop and Article Drop concerns the syntactic environments in which they apply. As we saw in §7.3.1 (and illustrated below), Article Drop can apply to nominals in a wide range of positions:

(109)   a. <The> Bank predicts <the> strongest year since <the> Second World War as Britain surges out of lockdown (= 39a)

        b. <The> EU unveils <a> big push for <the> Pfizer vaccine (= 39c)

        c. <The> rota will mean [<the> Queen is not alone] (= 40b)

        d. Downing Street sources claim [<the> former chief adviser released <the> PM's messages out of spite] (= 40c)

        e. Starmer hits out [as *<the>* Tories reject *<the>* Labour call for *<a>* Commons inquiry into lobbying] (= 40f)

These examples show that Article Drop can apply to subjects (whether of main, complement, or adverbial clauses), to direct objects, to prepositional objects, to possessor/genitive nominals and so on. By contrast, only thematic objects of verbs can undergo Object Drop, not (as we saw in 92 above) objects of prepositions, or subjects of ECM clauses. The Article Drop analysis leaves this asymmetry unaccounted for (as Weir 2017 acknowledges).

Given the problems posed by the Article Drop analysis, in the next section, I will propose an alternative analysis, which (as far as I am aware) has not previously been proposed for Object Drop in instructional registers.

7.5.3   Null objects as instances of a null pronoun/*pro*

This section explores the possibility that dropped objects in instructional registers are instances of an inherently null, specific, thematic, accusative, third person referential pronoun (i.e. pronominal DP) *pro*. What this means in more concrete terms in that a sentence like (90a) *Don't stir* will have an analysis along the following lines (where the null object *pro* is assigned accusative case and theta-marked by the verb *stir*, and the null imperative subject is shown as ~~you~~):

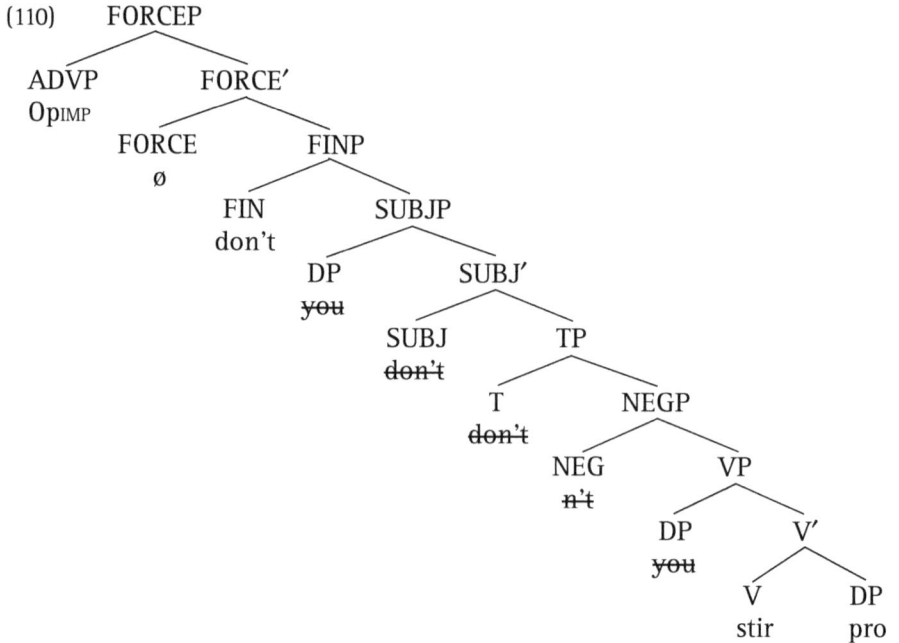

(110)   FORCEP

The tree diagram (110):

- FORCEP branches into ADVP (OpIMP) and FORCE'
- FORCE' branches into FORCE (Ø) and FINP
- FINP branches into FIN (don't) and SUBJP
- SUBJP branches into DP (~~you~~) and SUBJ'
- SUBJ' branches into SUBJ (~~don't~~) and TP
- TP branches into T (~~don't~~) and NEGP
- NEGP branches into NEG (~~n't~~) and VP
- VP branches into DP (~~you~~) and V'
- V' branches into V (stir) and DP (pro)

(I set aside here various questions of detail, including whether the imperative operator moves from some lower position – for example, from spec-FINP, thereby triggering FIN to attract the auxiliary *don't* to adjoin to it. I also set aside the question of whether the subject transits through spec-TP on its way to spec-SUBJP.) Analyses of null objects in standard language varieties in terms of *pro* have been proposed for a variety of languages, including Chamorro (Chung 1984), French (Zribi-Hertz 1984), Italian (Rizzi 1986), Imbabura Quechua, Korean and Thai (Cole 1987), Hungarian (Farkas 1987), Norwegian (Åfarli & Creider 1987), Brazilian Portuguese (Farrell 1990), and Catalan (Gavarrò 1991).

   Rizzi (1986) argues that null constituents need to be both licensed (via a local c-command relation with an appropriate kind of head) and identified. More specifically, Rizzi remarks that for any null constituent like *pro*, linguistic theory should:

specify (a) the conditions that formally license the null element (the conditions that allow it to occur in a given environment) and (b) the way in which the content of the null element (minimally, its phi-features) is determined or 'recovered' from the phonetically realized environment.

(Rizzi 1986: 518)

Accordingly, a question posed by the analysis in (110) is how the *pro* object of *stir* is licensed, and how it is identified.

As far as licensing is concerned, a potential answer is that the object *pro* found in instructional registers in English is licensed by being theta-marked and case-marked (more specifically, assigned accusative case) by a transitive verb which locally c-commands it (the licensing verb for the object *pro* being *stir* in 110). This will account for *pro* not being able to function as an ECM subject in (92a) *'Expect [*pro* to be done half an hour later]' because *pro* is assigned accusative case by the transitive verb *expect* but theta-marked by the passive participle *done*. It will also rule out use of *pro* as a prepositional object in a structure like (92b) 'Then sprinkle scallops with *pro*', because *pro* is neither case-marked nor theta-marked by a transitive verb. Furthermore, the requirement for *pro* to be theta-marked would account for why it can't be used as an expletive.

As for identification, this relates to the problem of determining what (person/number) φ-features *pro* carries. Farrell (1990) argues (in relation to Brazilian Portuguese) that *pro* can either be identified via agreement with an appropriate head (e.g. an auxiliary/verb richly inflected for person/number agreement can identify a *pro* subject), or by virtue of carrying intrinsic φ-features of its own. Following this approach, let us suppose that the *pro* found in Object Drop structures in instructional registers is an inherently third person referential pronoun which can be either singular or plural – for example, it is singular in (111a) below and hence substitutable by *it*, and plural in (111b) and hence substitutable by *them*:

(111) a. Place *pro* in the fridge on its own to cool
       b. Place *pro* in the fridge on their own to cool

Parallels can then be drawn with a different kind of *pro* found in English, namely the null *pro* subject found in imperative structures such as the following:

(112) a. Please *pro* keep yourself well wrapped up in winter!
       b. Please *pro* keep yourselves well wrapped up in winter!

On the assumptions made here, imperative *pro* subjects are inherently specified as second person singular/plural (singular in 112a, plural in

112b): hence I showed the null second person imperative subject as ~~you~~ in 110 above, to avoid confusion with the dropped object *pro*, which is inherently third person.

The key assumptions embodied in the *pro* analysis of null objects in the recipe register can be summarised as follows:

(113)   *Pro* analysis of null objects
         Null objects in instructional registers are instances of a null, specific, referential, thematic, third person, singular or plural, accusative pronominal DP *pro*

The *pro* analysis can account for significant differences between Article Drop and Object Drop. Since the two are distinct phenomena, it comes as no surprise that headlinese should allow Article Drop but not Object Drop; and conversely, it comes as no surprise that in some product labels like (90) above we should find Object Drop but not Article Drop. Similarly, it comes as no surprise that Article Drop can apply to prepositional objects (since this applies freely to an initial article in any nominal), but Object Drop cannot (since it only applies to pronominals which are theta-marked and case-marked by a transitive verb).

A further potential consideration in favour of the *pro* analysis of null objects is that it provides a principled account of why *pro* (being a pronoun) resembles an overt pronoun like *it* in being able to be used cataphorically (i.e. referring forward to a bracketed nominal following it) in a sentence such as the following:

(114)   Remove *it/ø* from heat immediately if [<the> omelette] starts to burn

Moreover, like the overt pronoun *them*, the null object pronoun *ø* can have split antecedents – as in the example below, where *ø* (like *them*) refers back to the two separate underlined constituents:

(115)   Sprinkle <u>the flour</u> over <u>the cold, cooked rice</u> in the mixing bowl and fold *ø/them* together gently (Ito 1993: 77, sourced from Neal 1985: 59)

Overall, then, the *pro* analysis accounts for a wide range of properties of null objects.

Still, it might be objected that the *pro* analysis is flawed from a theoretical perspective, in that it is inconsistent with the view that English has the typological characteristic that it is a 'no *pro*' language (i.e. one which lacks *pro* constituents). However, this typological claim is called into question by two observations. Firstly, imperatives allow second-person *pro* subjects (serving as the antecedent of the italicised expressions) in sentences such as (112) above, or (116) below:

(116)   a. Don't **pro** sell *yourself/yourselves* short!

　　　　 b. **pro** do it on *your own*!

Moreover, Collins (2021) argues at length that short passives (i.e. passives which have no overt agent *by*-phrase) contain a syntactically projected *pro* agent (paraphrasable somewhat awkwardly as 'by one' in 117a below) which can bind an anaphor like that italicised in (117a), or license a secondary depictive predicate like that italicised in (117b) (where we could alternatively have an overt agent like *by campers*):

(117)   a. Such privileges should be kept to *oneself* (Roberts 1987: 162)

　　　　 b. At the commune, breakfast is usually eaten *nude* (Collins 2005: 101)

In relation to (117b), it is interesting to note that the object object *pro* found in the recipe register can also license secondary predicates, as illustrated earlier in relation to (91c) 'Serve **pro** *hot with lots of butter.*' Thus, the claim that positing a null *pro* object in recipe registers creates a typological anomaly is undermined by the observation that there are other types of *pro* constituent found in English.

To summarise: Module 7.5 has been concerned with the null objects that occur in a range of registers of written English, particularly instructional registers. I began (in §7.5.1) by outlining a Topic Drop analysis under which Object Drop clauses are truncated TOPP structures which involve a topic being fronted and moved to spec-TOPP in the syntax, and then being given a null spellout in the phonology; I noted, however, that such an analysis provides no principled account of why null objects can occur inside syntactic islands. I then went on (in §7.5.2) to outline an alternative analysis under which Object Drop is treated as a particular instance of Article Drop, so that both article-dropped nominals and dropped objects are DPs headed by a null determiner, differing only in whether the NP complement of the determiner is overt or null. I noted, however, that there are significant distributional differences between Article Drop and Object Drop which call into question whether Object Drop can be subsumed under Article Drop: for example, Article Drop is pervasive in headlinese, but Object Drop is not; and Article Drop can freely apply to prepositional objects but Object Drop cannot. Finally (in §7.5.3), I outlined a third analysis, under which dropped objects in instructional registers are instances of an inherently null, specific, thematic, accusative, third person referential pronoun (i.e. pronominal DP) *pro*. I noted that the *pro* analysis accounts for significant differences between null objects and article-dropped nominals in respect of the registers and syntactic environments they occur in.

You should now be able to tackle Exercise 7.5.

7.6   Summary

This chapter has been concerned with structures which are abbreviated, in the sense that they involve dropping various kinds of constituent. I began in Module 7.1 by outlining Rizzi's Truncation analysis of **Subject Drop** in colloquial spoken English sentences like *<I> must have left my phone in the car*, under which truncating (i.e. not projecting) peripheral projections above SUBJP in root clauses leaves the subject *I* as a root specifier, and this allows material on the edge of a root projection to be unpronounced in the PF component.

In Module 7.2, we went on to look at **Auxiliary Drop** in spoken English sentences like *<Are> you feeling OK?* We saw that this is sometimes accompanied by Subject Drop in sentences like *<Are you> feeling OK?* I noted that sentences involving Aux+Subject Drop can't be handled in any straightforward way under a Truncation account, and can better be accounted for by supposing that such sentences have the same full (FORCEP) syntactic structure as their unreduced counterparts, but can be given an abbreviated spellout via an ellipsis operation in the PF component which gives a null spellout to the left edge of one or more peripheral projections at PF. I noted, however, that the Left Edge Ellipsis account can't handle abbreviated sentences like *<Has the pro>'fessor arrived yet?* and that this requires a prosodic account under which a string of one or more unstressed syllables at the beginning of a prosodic phrase (e.g. a sentence) can be unpronounced.

In Module 7.3, we looked at **Article Drop**, and saw that this is restricted to written registers, and is sporadic in some registers (e.g. social media like Twitter), but systematic in others (e.g. newspaper headlines). I argued that Article Drop involves a definite or indefinite article not being pronounced/printed if it is the first word in the functional projection which it heads, resulting in reduced sentences like *<The> government imposes <a> ban on <the> import of livestock.*

In Module 7.4, I discussed the phenomenon of Bᴇ **Drop** whereby in some abbreviated written registers such as headlinese, finite (indicative) forms of Bᴇ are systematically dropped, resulting in sentences like *BoJo <is> losing support.* I outlined two alternative Truncation analyses of these. Under one, Bᴇ Drop clauses are truncated SUBJP constituents, headed by a SUBJ with defective agreement properties (e.g. number but not person) which attracts Bᴇ to raise to adjoin to it, but (being defective) cannot attract the subject to raise to spec-SUBJP. Instead, the subject raises only as far as spec-TP (in the syntax, at least), and is assigned accusative case by default, and defective Bᴇ receives a null spellout by default at PF. An alternative account is that Bᴇ Drop clauses are truncated SUBJP constituents with a tense deficit which means that BE receives a null spellout, and its subject receives default case: on one implementation, they contain a TP whose head is unspecified for tense; on another view, they lack both TP and DP projections, and have NP subjects.

In Module 7.5, I discussed the phenomenon of **Object Drop** found in some registers of written English, especially instructional registers. I began by outlining a Topic Drop analysis under which Object Drop clauses are truncated TOPP structures which involve a topic being fronted and moved to spec-TOPP in the syntax, and then being given a null spell-out in the phonology. I went on to outline an alternative analysis under which Object Drop is treated as a particular instance of Article Drop, so that both article-dropped nominals and dropped objects are DPs headed by a null determiner, differing only in whether the NP complement of the determiner is overt or null. Finally, I outlined a third analysis, under which dropped objects are instances of an inherently null, specific, thematic, accusative, third person, singular/plural referential pronoun (i.e. pronominal DP) *pro*.

Key analyses, principles, conditions and hypotheses introduced in this chapter include the following:

(12)   **Syntactic truncation account of Subject Drop**
        (i) A sentence can have a truncated syntactic structure whose root is not FORCEP, but some lower projection such as SUBJP
        (ii) The edge of the highest projection in a sentence structure can be unpronounced in the PF component, provided that it contains only phonetically weak material with recoverable semantic content

(26)   **Principle of Unambitious Reverse Engineering (PURE)**
        When determining the identity of unpronounced material in the course of reverse-engineering a speaker's syntactic derivation, the language system of the hearer considers only the minimally semantically contentful possibilities compatible with the morphosyntactic environment (Pesetsky 2020: 5)

(32)   **Left Edge Ellipsis account of Auxiliary (+Subject) Drop**
        (i) Reduced clauses have the same full syntactic structure as their unreduced counterparts
        (ii) The left edge of a continuous set of one or more projections at the top of a tree in a root clause can undergo ellipsis in the phonology

(37)   **Prosodic account of Weak Syllable Drop**
        (i) Reduced clauses have the same full syntactic structure as their unreduced counterparts

(ii)   A continuous sequence of one or more weak syllables at the beginning of a prosodic phrase (e.g. a sentence) can undergo ellipsis at PF

(50)   **Article Drop**
An article which is the first word in the functional projection that it heads can be dropped

(87)   **Generalised C-command Condition on Article/Bᴇ Drop**
Neither a null article nor a null counterpart of Bᴇ can be c-commanded by a nominal with an overt article

(88)   **Agreement Deficit analysis of Bᴇ Drop**
Bᴇ Drop clauses are truncated SUBJP constituents, headed by a SUBJ with defective agreement properties (e.g. with number but not person). SUBJ attracts Bᴇ to raise to adjoin to it, but (being defective) cannot attract the subject to move to spec-SUBJP; and since the clause lacks FIN, its subject cannot be assigned nominative case. Instead, the subject raises only as far as spec-TP, and is assigned accusative case by default. Bᴇ receives a null spellout by default at PF, because there is no overt spellout for defective forms of Bᴇ.

(89)   **Tense Deficit analysis of Bᴇ Drop**
Bᴇ Drop clauses are truncated SUBJP constituents with a tense deficit, which means that Bᴇ receives a null spellout by default, and its subject receives default case. On one view, Bᴇ Drop clauses contain a TP whose head T contains an affix with an unvalued tense feature; on another view, they lack both TP and DP projections, and have NP subjects.

(93)   **Topic Drop analysis of null objects**
(i)   Null objects arises when a pronoun is topicalised and thereby moves to the edge of a TOPP projection at the root of a truncated clause
(ii)   The edge of the highest projection in a sentence structure can be unpronounced in the PF component, provided that it contains only phonetically weak material with recoverable semantic content

(102)   **Article Drop analysis of null objects**
Null objects are DPs headed by a null article with an NP complement which can optionally be unpronounced at PF (thereby giving rise to a null object)

(113)   ***Pro* analysis of null objects**
Null objects in instructional registers are instances of a null, specific, referential, thematic, third person, singular or plural, accusative pronominal DP *pro*

7.7 Bibliographical notes

On **registers and register variation**, see Ferguson (1982), Zwicky & Zwicky (1982), Biber (1995), Haegeman (2006c), Paesani (2006), and Massam & Stowell (2017). On more specific registers, see research on diary styles (Haegeman 1990a, 1990b, 1997, 2013, 2017, 2019; Matushansky 1995; Horsey 1998; Haegeman & Ihsane 1999, 2001), newspaper headlines (Simon-Vandenbergen 1981; Stowell 1990, 1991, 1996, 1999), recipe books and instruction manuals (Haegeman 1987a; Massam 1987; Massam & Roberge 1989; Culy 1996; Sigurðsson & Maling 2007; Paul & Massam 2020), note-taking (Janda 1985), telegrams and text messages (Barton 1998), telephone conversations (Hopper 1992), online blogs (Teddiman & Newman 2010), and emails/postcards (Nariyama 2006).

On **Subject Drop in spoken English** see Morgan (1973), Schmerling (1973), Thrasher (1973, 1974, 1977), Drachman (1974), Napoli (1982), Zwicky & Pullum (1983), Quirk et al. (1985), Akmajian et al. (1985), Ihalainen (1991), Hopper (1992), Rizzi (1994, 1998, 2000a), Cote (1996, 1997), Harvie (1998), Mackenzie (1998), Kay (2002), Nariyama (2004, 2006), Zwicky (2005), Oh (2005, 2006), Schirer (2008), Weir (2008, 2009a, 2009b, 2012, 2013, 2014, 2016, 2017, 2018, 2022), Mack & Fuerst (2009), Mack (2010), Bailey (2011), Mack et al. (2012), S. Wagner (2012, 2016), Torres Cacoullos & Travis (2014), Ikarashi (2015), Bae (2016), Sakamoto & Ikarashi (2017), Shibata (2017), and Lindstrom (2020).

Subject Drop in written English has been reported to occur in a wide range of registers, including informal writing (Zwicky & Zwicky 1981; Reiman 1994), diaries (Haegeman 1987b, 1990a, 1990b, 1997, 2000a, 2002b, 2007b, 2013, 2017, 2019; Matushansky 1995; Horsey 1998; Ihsane 1998, Haegeman & Ihsane 1999, 2001; Becquet 2000; Scott 2004, 2010; Newman & Teddiman 2010; Teddiman & Newman 2010; Nanyan 2013; Haegeman & Starke 2021), newspaper headlines (Straumann 1935; Mårdh 1980; Simon-Vandenbergen 1981; Stowell 1990, 1991, 1996, 1999; de Lange 2004, 2008; Weir 2009b, 2013, 2017), recipe books and instruction manuals (Haegeman 1987a; Massam 1987, 1989; Massam & Roberge 1989; Culy 1996; Sigurðsson & Maling 2007, 2010), note-taking (Janda 1985), telegrams (Barton 1998), text/ SMS messages (Crystal 2008; Tagg 2009; Cougnon & Fairon 2012), emails/ postcards/letters (Nariyama 2006), social media (Pérez-Sabatar 2012; Grant 2015; Daeninck 2019; Lansens 2019; Deneys 2020), TV dramas (Nariyama 2004), and cinema (Ito & Kashihara 2010).

On **Auxiliary Drop** in English, see Hendrick (1982), Andersen (1995), Fitzpatrick (2005b, 2006), Schirer (2008), Totsuka (2015, 2017), and Pesetsky (2020).

On **Article Drop** see Straumann (1935), Mårdh (1980), Simon-Vanden-bergen (1981), Bell (1991), Stowell (1990, 1991, 1996, 1999), de Lange (2004, 2008), de Lange & Avrutin (2009), Weir (2009b, 2012, 2013, 2014, 2017, 2018), Wiljergård (2011), Sato & Kim (2012), Horch & Reich (2016), Lemke et al. (2017), Oosterhof & Rawoens (2017), Paul (2017), Reich (2017), Moncomble (2018), Nemes (2019), Eilander (2020), and Tel (2020).

BE **Drop** is found not only in headlinese (see e.g. Reich 2017, and Kibsgaard 2019), but also in other varieties of English, most notably in English-based creoles and pidgins. It is a common feature of African American English/AAE, but note that in AAE, the present tense forms *is* and *are* are the only forms that can be null: see Labov (1969, 1995), Cukor-Avila (1999), Bender (2000), and Green (2002). Null copulas are also found in many other languages of the world (often restricted to present tense use): see Stassen (2013).

On **Object Drop in English** found, inter alia, in the instructional register (which includes recipes, instruction manuals, product labels and so on) see Sadock (1974), Allerton (1975), Fillmore (1986), Fitzpatrick et al. (1986), Haegeman (1987a, 1987b), Massam (1987, 1989, 1992), Massam & Roberge (1989), Ito (1993), Groefsema (1995), Culy (1996), Bender (1999), García Velasco & Portero Muñoz (2002), Cummins & Roberge (2004, 2005), Ohara (2007), Sigurðsson & Maling (2007, 2010), Ruppenhofer & Michaelis (2010), Wharton (2010), Ruda (2014, 2017), Massam et al. (2017), and Weir (2017). On **Object Drop in other languages**, see Chung (1984), Huang (1984, 1991), Zribi-Hertz (1984), Raposo (1986), Rizzi (1986), Åfarli & Creider (1987), Cole (1987), Farkas (1987), Authier (1988, 1989), Suñer & Yépez (1988), Bouchard (1989), Farrell (1990), Gavarrò (1991), Roberge (1991), Kato (1993), Landa (1995), Lambrecht & Lemoine (1996, 2005), Visser (1996), Cyrino (1997, 2004, 2021), Arteaga (1998), Hoji (1998), Keller & Lapata (1998), Li (1998), Kim (1999), Larjavaara (2000), Schwenter & Silva (2002), Xu (2003), Cummins & Roberge (2005), Schwenter (2006), Alamillo & Schwenter (2007), Sigurðsson & Maling (2007, 2010), Milambiling (2011), Erteschik-Shir et al. (2013), Paoli (2014), Panitz (2015), Cyrino & Matos (2016), Funakoshi (2017), Lee (2017), and Paul & Massam (2020).

On the syntax of **imperatives**, see Zwicky (1988), Beukema & Koopmans (1989), Zhang (1990), Platzack & Rosengren (1997), Potsdam (1998, 2018), Han (1998, 2000a, 2000b, 2001), Moon (2001), Flagg (2002), Jensen (2003, 2007), Rupp (1999, 2003), Portner (2004, 2007), Takahashi (2004), Mauck et al. (2005), Bennis (2006), Koopman (2007), van der Wurff (2007), Zanuttini (2008), Aikhenvald (2010), Kaufmann (2011), Medeiros (2013), Alcázar & Saltarelli (2014), Isac 2015, and Shormani (2021).

7.8   Workbook

In the exercises below, an [M] after an example sentence indicates that a model answer is provided in the free-to-download *Students' Answerbook* (and in the *Teachers' Answerbook* as well). You will find it helpful to look at this model answer before attempting to tackle other examples in the exercise. Some other exercise examples have an [S] after them, indicating that they are for self-study: this means that after reading the relevant module (and those preceding it), and looking at the helpful hints and model answer associated with the exercise, students should be able to analyse these self-study examples on their own, and then compare their answers with those provided in the *Students' Answerbook*. The remaining exercise examples (i.e. those not marked with [M] or [S] after them) are intended for teachers to use as the basis for hands-on problem-solving work in seminars, classes, or assignments: answers to all of these non-self-study examples are provided in the *Teachers' Answerbook*. Note that Exercise 7.1 tests you on Module 7.1, Exercise 7.2 on Module 7.2, and so on; and that each exercise in a given chapter presupposes familiarity with material covered in earlier chapters and in earlier modules of the same chapter. Unparenthesised numbers like 4 refer to material in the exercises, whereas parenthesised numbers like (22) refer to examples and conditions in the main text of the book.

EXERCISE 7.1

This exercise is designed to be attempted after reading Module 7.1 and the chapters preceding it.

Discuss the syntax of the dropped constituents in the following sentences from Helen Fielding's (1996) book *Bridget Jones's Diary* (these examples being cited by Haegeman & Ihsane 1999, 2001; I have added what I take to be the missing/dropped constituents in <angle brackets>):

1   <I> was worried that <we> might split (Fielding 1996: 227) [M]
2   <I> start to wonder whether <I> am <a> really good friend (Fielding 1996: 261)
3   <I> realise <I> was using <the> telly remote control by mistake (Fielding 1996: 153) [S]
4   <I> understand where <I> have been going wrong (Fielding 1996: 97)
5   <I> think <I> will cross that bit out as <it> contains <a> mild accusation (Fielding 1996: 25) [S]
6   <I> search for <my> hairbrush. <I> locate <it> in <my> handbag (Fielding 1996: 92) [S]
7   <I'm> feeling v. pleased with <my>self (Fielding 1996: 77; v. = very)

8   \<I\> suddenly start thinking of \<a\> former boyfriend Peter with whom \<I\>
     had \<a\> functional relationship for seven years, until \<we\> finished for \<a\>
     heart-felt agonizing reason \<I\> can no longer remember (Fielding 1996: 190)

Helpful hints

Extensive research (particularly by Liliane Haegeman and her
collaborators: Haegeman 1987b, 1990a, 1990b, 1997, 2000a, 2002b,
2007b, 2013, 2017, 2019, 2021; Haegeman & Ihsane 1999, 2001) has
shown that (especially in fictional varieties of the diary register) a much
wider range of constituents than just root/main clause subjects can be
dropped (e.g. subjects can be dropped in non-root as well as root clauses,
and some non-subject constituents can be dropped as well – e.g. articles
like *a/the*). The relevant register has come to be known as Diary Drop.
Compare the four different accounts of Diary Drop outlined below and
say which can best handle sentences 1–8: the analyses in 10–12 are not
covered in Module 7.1, and are designed to test your ability to compare
and contrast unseen analyses of a given set of phenomena.

9   **Subject Drop Truncation**
     (i) In the fictional diary register, a sentence can have a truncated
          syntactic structure which projects only as far as SUBJP
     (ii) The edge of the highest projection in a sentence can be
          unpronounced at PF

10   **Topic Drop Truncation**
     (i) In the fictional diary register, a sentence can have a truncated
          syntactic structure which projects only as far as TOPP
     (ii) Dropped constituents move to spec-TOPP in the syntax, and thereby
          (by virtue of being on the edge of the highest projection in the
          sentence) can be unpronounced at PF

11   **Left Edge Ellipsis**
     (i) In the fictional diary register, clauses have the same (untruncated)
          syntactic structure as in standard registers
     (ii) (A continuous string of one or more) weak items with little semantic
          content can be given a null spellout on the left edge of a clausal or
          nominal functional projection

12   **Editing account**
     Diary Drop sentences have the same (untruncated) syntactic structure
     as in standard registers, but the representation outputted by the PF
     component is edited by omitting personal pronouns and articles

In relation to 9, consider whether the restriction on Truncation only
applying in sentences (i.e. root clauses) may be relaxed in the Diary Drop
register, so allowing Truncation to apply in root and non-root clauses

as well. In relation to 11, assume that weak items include monosyllabic personal pronouns like for example, *I/you/he* and articles like *a/the*, and that Left Edge Ellipsis results in items which are present in the syntax being unpronounced in the phonology (or unprinted in written diary entries). The account in 12 differs from the others in that the analyses in 9–11 posit that Diary Drop is a natural (structure-dependent) operation, whereas the account in 12 assumes that it is an artificial (structure-independent) process which involves consciously editing out certain lexical items (personal pronouns and articles) which are weak and have minimal semantic content.

In analysing the relevant diary entries, don't try to draw tree diagrams for whole sentences which have a complex internal structure: instead, consider the internal structure of each of the component clauses separately. You might want to bear in mind the following:

13   **Clause Typing Conditions** (from §1.4.3)
  (i) A clause is interpreted as being of a given type (interrogative or exclamative etc.) if it contains a peripheral clause-typing specifier of the relevant type
  (ii) An indicative clause is interpreted as declarative in type by default if it contains no peripheral clause-typing specifier

14   **COMP-Trace Filter/CTF** (from §1.5.2)
  Any structure at the end of a syntactic derivation in which an overt COMP/complementiser is immediately adjacent to and c-commands a trace (i.e. a gap/null copy left behind by a moved constituent) is filtered out as ill-formed

15   **Intervention Condition** (from §1.5.1)
  Likes cannot cross likes

16   **Criterial Freezing Condition/CFC** (incorporating a modification from §6.1.2)
  (i) A peripheral or subperipheral constituent must occupy a criterial position to be interpretable at LF
  (ii) A constituent which occupies its criterial position is frozen in place

17   **Impenetrability Condition** (from §4.4.1)
  Anything below the head H of the highest projection HP in the periphery of a complete clause (i.e. one containing FORCEP) is impenetrable to anything above HP

18   **Island Constraint** (after Ross 1967)
  Any clause which is not the complement of a verb/adjective is an island (in the sense that it doesn't allow anything to be extracted out of it)

Note that it follows from 18 that adjunct/adverbial clauses, clauses which function as subjects or topics, and relative clauses etc. are islands/

barriers to extraction. Look at the model answer in the Answerbook before developing your analyses. To simplify your task, you might want to follow the suggestions made below.

In 2, analyse the *start* clause and the *whether* clause separately: in analysing the *start* clause, take *start to wonder whether I am a really good friend* to be a VP, but don't concern yourself with its internal structure; in analysing the *whether* clause, assume (as suggested in §5.3.2) that interrogative *whether* is a FORCE head which has an adverbial null yes–no question operator Op_{YNQ} as its specifier, and assume too that *am a really good friend* is a TP, but don't concern yourself with its internal structure. In 3, bear in mind the suggestion made in §4.4.2 that declarative complement clauses which are not introduced by *that* are FINP constituents; treat *was using the telly remote control by mistake* as a TP, but don't concern yourself with its internal structure. In 4, take *have been going wrong* to be a TP, but don't concern yourself with its internal structure; and take *where* to be a PP with a meaning paraphrasable as 'in what respect', but don't concern yourself with its internal structure. In 5, analyse the main+complement clause structure *I think I will cross that bit out* first: take *will cross that bit out* to be a TP, but don't concern yourself with its internal structure; and (following the analysis outlined in §4.4.2) assume that a *that*-less declarative complement clause (like the *cross* clause here) projects only as far as FINP. Then analyse the adjunct/adverbial clause headed by the subordinating conjunction *as*: for the reasons outlined in Radford (2018: 197–215), take it to be a CONJP headed by the CONJ/subordinating conjunction *as*, and take *it contains a mild accusation* to be a FORCEP. In 6, analyse each of the two sentences separately; in the second sentence, take *locate it in my handbag* to be a VP, but do not attempt to analyse its internal structure (because this is complex, and requires familiarity with work on split VPs which is not covered in this book). In 7, take *pleased* to be an adjective/A which has the PP *with myself* as its complement, and treat the ADVP *very* as its specifier; consider the internal structure of *myself*, and whether it may have a similar structure to a phrase like *my car* (with *my* and *self* seemingly being able to function as separate words in a phrase like *my old self*, in the same way as they do in *my old car*). In 8, analyse each of the four clauses in the sentence separately. First analyse the main clause *I suddenly start thinking of a former boyfriend Peter*: take *start thinking of a former boyfriend Peter* to be a VP, but don't concern yourself with its internal structure. Then, analyse the adjunct/adverbial/subordinate clause *until we finished for a heart-felt agonizing reason*: treat the *until*-clause in the same way as the *as*-clause in sentence 5 (see the guidance above), and take *finished for a heart-felt agonizing reason* to be a VP, but don't concern yourself with its internal structure. Next, analyse the relative clause *with whom I had a functional relationship for seven years*: take *had a functional relationship for seven years* to be a VP, but don't concern yourself with its internal structure. Finally, analyse the relative clause *I can no longer remember*. Follow the analysis in §5.4.2 under which relative clauses are RELP constituents in which an XP containing or comprising a relative pronoun/pronominal DP like *who/which* (or a null counterpart thereof) moves to spec-RELP from its original position (here, inside VP): assume that the REL head is null and has a FORCEP complement (for the reasons set out in §5.4.2).

EXERCISE 7.2

This exercise is designed to be attempted after reading Module 7.2 and the module and chapters preceding it.

Analyse the spoken English sentences below:

1a Did you ever visit Rome? [M]
1b You ever visit Rome? [M]
1c Ever visit Rome? [M]
2a A fine friend you turned out to be!
2b Fine friend you turned out to be! (Napoli 1982: 85)
3a I'm a bit ashamed of myself [S]
3b M'a bit ashamed of myself [S]
3c A bit ashamed of myself [S]
3d Bit ashamed of myself [S]
4a What time is it? [S]
4b Time is it? [S]
5   *Intended as replies to the question 'Do you play golf?':*
    a. Of course I do
    b. Course I do
    c. *Course do
6a Have you been exercising much lately? [S]
6b You been exercising much lately? [S]
6c Been exercising much lately? [S]
6d Exercising much lately? (adapted from Napoli 1982: 109) [S]
7a Has the cat got your tongue?
7b The cat got your tongue?
7c Cat got your tongue? (Napoli 1982: 85)
8a Have you any idea where she is?
8b You any idea where she is?

8c Any idea where she is?

8d Do you have any idea where she is?

8e You have any idea where she is?

8f Have any idea where she is?

Treat the shorter examples as reduced forms of the longer examples. In relation to 8, note that my own (British) variety of English allows all the sentences in 8; by contrast, Joseph Galasso and Jean Hannah (pc) tell me that their (American) varieties of English allow 8c–8f, but not 8a, 8b.

Helpful hints

Discuss how well each of the three alternative accounts of Subject/ Auxiliary Drop outlined below can handle the relevant reduced clauses in abbreviated registers of spoken English:

9   **Truncation account**

  (i) A reduced clause has a truncated syntactic structure whose root is not FORCEP, but some lower projection (e.g. TOPP, or FINP, or SUBJP).

  (ii) The edge of the root/highest projection in a sentence structure can be unpronounced in the PF component

10   **Left Edge Ellipsis account**

  (i) Reduced clauses have the same syntactic structure as their unreduced counterparts

  (ii) The left edge of a continuous set of one or more functional projections at the top of the tree in a root clause can undergo ellipsis in the PF component

11   **Prosodic account**

  (i) Reduced clauses have the same syntactic structure as their unreduced counterparts

  (ii) A continuous sequence of one or more weak syllables at the beginning of a prosodic phrase (e.g. a sentence) can undergo ellipsis (and be unpronounced) in the PF component

Under all three analyses, assume that only weak/unstressed material can undergo ellipsis and that ellipsis cannot give a null spellout to (the whole of) any word with substantive lexical content (in consequence of the Recoverability Condition requiring material undergoing ellipsis to be recoverable). In addition, assume that an indicative clause which contains no specifier in its periphery typing it as interrogative/exclamative etc. is interpreted as declarative in force by default.

   Make the following assumptions about the categorial status of relevant phrases, but don't concern yourself with their internal structure. In 2a, *a fine friend* is a focused ARTP/article phrase, and *you turned out to be* is a

SUBJP. In 3, *a bit ashamed of myself* is an AP comprising the head adjective *ashamed*, the KP complement *of myself*, and the ARTP specifier *a bit*. In 4, *what time* is a focused interrogative QP. In both 3 and 4, BE originates as the head V of VP, and from there can raise to T (and even higher to SUBJ) in a finite clause. In 5, *of course* is a KP which is a clause modifier, and is directly merged as the specifier of a MODP immediately below FORCEP. In 6, *exercising much lately* is a VP, and *been* is the head of a PROGP/progressive aspect projection. In 6, 7, *have* originates as the head of a PERFP/perfect aspect projection, and from there raises stepwise into FIN. In 8, *have* originates as the head V of the VP *you have any idea where she is* (with *any idea where she is* being a QP); in British (but not American) varieties, *have* can behave like an auxiliary and undergo Auxiliary Inversion and thereby raise into FIN (in a succession of short steps).

EXERCISE 7.3

This exercise is designed to be attempted after reading Module 7.3 and the modules and chapters preceding it.

Daeninck (2019) researches constituent drop on the social media platform Twitter, and reports the four main types of dropped constituent <bracketed> below:

1   **Subject Drop**

 1a <I> can't be bothered to go food shopping [M]

 1b <I> might just eat McDonald's for the rest of my life

 1c <I> wrote this in 2015 but it was my most read blog post in 2018

 1d <They> know everything about everyone

 1e <It> was a pleasure to meet you

2   **Subject+Aux Drop**

 2a <I'm> uploading a new video tonight

 2b <I've> just come off a long flight and on the plane I watched a 1990s classic I'd somehow never seen before

 2c <We'll> see how it goes

 2d <It was> so lovely meeting you

 2e <There's> no rest for the curious

3   **Aux Drop**

 3a <Does> anyone know if climbing Scafell Pike is dog friendly? [S]

 3b <Do> you ever talk to someone so much you start adopting their mannerisms and using their slang and you just sit back and think wtf is happening to me?

3c <Is> anyone else feeling really ... off?

3d <Are> you guys in?

4   Aux+Subject Drop

4a <Did you> miss my latest briefing?

4b <Do you> want to know what it was like for my team during my #MarsLanding?

4c <Does it> work for you?

4d <Have you> missed my nail-biting #MarsLanding?

4e <Are there> questions about my #MarsLanding?

(Note that *wtf* in 3b is an abbreviation of *what the fuck*; and the missing word shown as ... in 3c is presumably *pissed*.) Daeninck claims that the abbreviated tweets in her corpus obey the same constraints as operate in spoken English – namely that subjects and/or auxiliaries are only dropped in root clauses (and not in complement clauses or other subordinate clauses), and only when sentence-initial. Discuss the derivation of the first example in each set – that is, 1a, 2a, 3a and 4a – comparing alternative ways of analysing them (referring to other examples in each set where appropriate).

In addition to the four sentence types in 1–4 above, Daeninck's data include some tweets which potentially don't conform to the patterns in 1–4, including the following (where *Frozen 2* is the name of a film):

5a Shit, <I> guess I care about Frozen 2 now huh? [S]

5b <The> entire cast was on fire [S]

5c <It's the> last day here

5d If <she's> not used to these sorts of climbs <it's> maybe best to take her next time or not try her on <the> tallest mountain in England for <the> first try!

Say in what ways each of the sentences in 5 differs from the types of ellipsis found in 1–4, and how each might be analysed.

Helpful hints

Discuss the extent to which each of the sentences you analyse can be handled in terms of each of the three alternative accounts of ellipsis outlined in the helpful hints for Exercise 7.2 (namely, the Truncation, Left Edge Ellipsis, and Prosodic accounts); bear in mind too the possibility that the Twitter register may allow for a separate type of ellipsis involving the kind of Article Drop operation discussed in Module 7.3, whereby an article which is the first word in the projection that it heads can be null. For each set of sentences in 1–4, derive the first example from each set (i.e. 1a, 2a, 3a, 4a), and refer to other examples in the set (if appropriate) where they illustrate some relevant point. Which analysis handles the widest range of data in 1–5 overall?

In analysing 1a, for the purposes of the exercise, make the simplifying assumption that *can't* is an inherently negative auxiliary in T, and that *be bothered to go food shopping* is a VP, but don't concern yourself with the internal structure of this VP. In 2a, take *uploading a new video tonight* to be a VP, but don't concern yourself with its internal structure. In 3a, take *know if climbing Scafell Pike is dog friendly* to be a VP, but don't concern yourself with its internal structure. In 4a, take *miss my latest briefing* to be a VP, but don't concern yourself with its internal structure. In 5a, take *guess I care about Frozen 2 now* to be a VP (but don't concern yourself with its internal structure), and treat *shit* as an interjection projection/ INTJP which functions as the specifier of a speech act projection/ACTP which forms part of what we could call the superperiphery of the clause and hence is positioned above the FORCEP which is the highest projection in the periphery: for the purposes of the exercise, ignore the discourse particle *huh* at the end of the sentence. In 5b–5d, assume that the copula BE originates as the head V of VP, and from there raises to T (and can in principle raise further into SUBJ). In 5b, treat *the entire cast* as a DP headed by the determiner *the*, make the simplifying assumption that *entire cast* is an NP (though don't concern yourself with the structure of this NP). In 5c, treat *last day here* as an NP for the purposes of this exercise, but don't concern yourself with its internal structure. In the complex sentence in 5d, analyse the *if*-clause and the main clause (*<it's> maybe best to ...*) separately; treat the *if*-clause as a CONJP (headed by CONJ *if*) positioned on top of the main clause structure.

EXERCISE 7.4

This exercise is designed to be attempted after reading Module 7.4 and the modules and chapters preceding it.

Discuss how ellipsis of the <bracketed> items works in the headlines below (collected by me from British newspapers in April–May 2021, with the exception of Example 5:

1   <The> Tory party paid <the> bill for <a> 58,000 flat makeover (*Daily Mail*, 27 April) [M]
2   <The> rota will mean <the> Queen is not alone (*Daily Mirror*, 19 April)
3   <The> EU <is> hopeful of <a> Northern Ireland solution (*Financial Times*, 19 April) [S]

4   <The> young <are> turning their backs on learning to drive (*Daily Telegraph*, 26 April)

5   Me to blame for <the> Brexit fiasco, admits Boris (spoof headline, Mike Jones, pc) [S]

6   <We're> sick of his Bozwallop (*Daily Star*, 12 May)

7   <The> Prince is back. <He> Arrives in England ahead of <the> Duke's funeral (*The Sun*, 12 April) [S]

8   <Does> Anyone fancy a trip to the beer garden? (*Daily Telegraph*, 7 April) [S]

9   <Do you> Call this freedom? (*Daily Mail*, 6 April)

10   <Is it the> End of the nightmare? (*Sunday Express*, 2 May)

Note that *Bozwallop* in (6) is an invented noun meaning 'codswallop/nonsense characteristic of Bozo/Boris Johnson'.

Helpful hints

Bear in mind that more than one type of ellipsis may apply in some of these sentences (Article Drop, Bᴇ Drop, Subject Drop, Aux Drop: see the accounts of Subject/Aux Drop in the helpful hints for Exercise 7.2). Bear in mind, too, the following assumption made in the main text about Article Drop in headlinese:

11   **Article Drop**

An article which is the first word in the functional projection that it heads can be dropped

Say whether your analysis is in conformity with the following condition on Bᴇ Drop and Article Drop:

12   **Generalised C-command Condition on Article/Bᴇ Drop**

Neither a null article nor a null counterpart of ʙᴇ can be c-commanded by a nominal with an overt article

In relation to examples like 3 and 4, evaluate the following alternative accounts of Bᴇ Drop outlined in the main text:

13   **Agreement Deficit analysis**

Bᴇ Drop clauses are truncated SUBJP constituents, headed by a SUBJ with defective agreement properties (e.g. with number but not person). SUBJ attracts ʙᴇ to raise to adjoin to it, but (being defective) cannot attract the subject to move to spec-SUBJP; and since the clause lacks FIN, its subject cannot be assigned nominative case. Instead, the subject raises only as far as spec-TP, and is assigned accusative case by default. Bᴇ receives a null spellout by default at PF, because there is no overt spellout for defective forms of ʙᴇ.

14   Tense Deficit analysis

BE Drop clauses are truncated SUBJP constituents with a tense deficit, which means that BE receives a null spellout by default, and its subject receives default case. On one view, BE Drop clauses contain a TP whose head T contains an affix with an unvalued tense feature; on another view, they lack both TP and DP projections, and have NP subjects.

For the purposes of this exercise, make the simplifying assumption that complex nominals like *Tory Party, 58,000 flat makeover, EU, Brexit fiasco, Northern Ireland solution, beer garden* are NPs, but don't concern yourself with their internal structure. In 5, concern yourself only with the structure of the clause *Me to blame for <the> Brexit fiasco*. In 7, treat *ahead* as a P with a KP complement headed by the K/case particle *of*.

EXERCISE 7.5

This exercise is designed to be attempted after reading Module 7.5 and the modules and chapters preceding it.

Discuss the structure of the italicised clauses in the following extracts from authentic recipes in cookbooks:

1   Chill dough, *then roll to ¼″-thick* and *spread with date filling* and *turn over on itself* (¼″-thick = 'a quarter inch thick') [M]
2   Slice the mushrooms finely, and *put in a large bowl with the oil* [S]
3   Halve the avocado; scoop the flesh into a bowl, along with the lime juice, *then mash roughly*, and *season to taste*
4   Start ladling in the hot stock, letting each ladleful become absorbed *as you stir*, before adding the next one [S]
5   Spread the tortilla chips out on a foil-lined baking sheet and *sprinkle the cheese over*
6   Put the dish on the baking sheet in the oven for 30 minutes. *Let stand for 10 minutes* before serving, and make sure you scoop out the sauce beneath the sponge in the dish [S]
7   To serve the birds freshly stewed, let them stand 10 minutes *before cutting*
8   Make the compote, *if using*, by putting the berries into a small pan with the sugar and lemon juice (*if using* = 'if you are using it/the compote')

Example 1 is from Ruppenhofer & Michaelis (2010), example 7 from Bender (1999), and the remaining examples are from Ruda (2014), with all examples sourced from authentic cookbooks. In a couple of cases, I have shortened the sentences by omitting a few words (but not in ways that affect issues of concern here).

Helpful hints

Compare the following three accounts of Object Drop outlined in the book:

9   **Topic Drop account**
      (i) In the Recipe Register, a sentence/root clause can have a syntactic structure whose root (i.e. highest) projection is TOPP
      (ii) Dropped objects move to spec-TOPP in the syntax, and thereby (by virtue of being on the edge of the highest projection in the sentence) can be unpronounced at PF

10   **Null Article account**
      (i) Article Drop involves a DP/ARTP projection headed by a null article with an overt NP as its complement
      (ii) Dropped objects involve a DP/ARTP projection headed by a null article with a null NP as its complement

11   *Pro* **analysis of null objects**
      Null objects in the Recipe Register are instances of a null, specific, referential, thematic, third person, singular/plural, accusative pronominal DP *pro*

In addition, bear in mind a point not discussed in the main text, namely that a restricted number of verbs (and prepositions) in English allow an implicit null definite object (below denoted as an empty category/*ec*) – for example, *visit* in 12a below but not *see* in 12b, with *ec* paraphrasable as *her* in 12a and as *him* in 12b:

12a   She was feeling lonely, because nobody had **visited** *ec* for a long time
12b   *She missed her brother, because she hadn't **seen** *ec* for a long time

Let's call this kind of null object a 'lexically licensed null object', since only certain lexical items allow its use.

     Because many of the sentences in this exercise have long and complex structures, analyse the specific clause or phrase containing each dropped constituent separately, and avoid analysing the internal structure of verb phrases (because some of these are complex): in some cases, you may find it easier to use a labelled bracketing showing only key parts of the structure. Treat imperative clauses containing *and* as coordinate imperative root clauses, and analyse only clauses preceding/following *and*. For the purposes of this exercise, treat nominals following articles/ determiners as NPs (e.g. treat nominals like *lime juice/large bowl/tortilla chips* as NPs) and don't concern yourself with their internal structure. In relation to sentences like 4, 7, 8) bear in mind the following constraint due to Ross (1967):

13   **Adjunct Island Constraint**
      Adjuncts are islands – that is, they are structures out of which nothing can be extracted by any movement operation that leaves behind a gap (i.e. a null copy of the moved constituent)

In relation to 6 and 7, consider the implication of taking a phrase like *let the birds stand for 10 minutes* to involve a structure in which the transitive verb *let* takes a *to*-less infinitive complement – as below (where the sentence is paraphrasable as 'Ensure that the birds stand for 10 minutes'):

14   Let [*the birds/them* stand for 10 minutes]

Assume that the italicised infinitive subject in 14 is the thematic argument of *stand* (its complement if *stand* is an unaccusative predicate), but is assigned accusative case under c-command by the transitive verb *let*. In addition, bear in mind the discussion in the model answer in the Answerbook. In 8 consider whether *if using* is a reduced form of the finite clause *if you are using ø*, or whether it is a gerund clause with a PRO subject (*if PRO using ø*) – where *ø* is a null object of some kind.

Glossary and Abbreviations

Note: Bold print is used for headings, subheadings, and cross-references to other entries; §3.4.2 denotes Chapter 3, Module 4, Section 2.

A/AP Abbreviation for adjective/ adjectival phrase.

A-bar position/A-bar Movement See **A-position/A-Movement**.

abbreviated Abbreviated structures are structures in which certain functional categories are missing: for example, a newspaper headline like *<The> president <is> intending to host <a> peace conference*, where bracketed articles and a bracketed auxiliary are missing. **Abbreviated registers** are varieties which make systematic use of abbreviated structures. See Chapter 7.

Acc Abbreviation for accusative. See **case**.

accessible A constituent is accessible to a given operation if it is able to undergo the relevant operation without violating any constraints or other requirements.

A-chain See **A-position**.

active A constituent is active for (i.e. able to undergo) Agreement, A-Movement, or Case-marking if it satisfies a set of **Activity Conditions** which are given the following formulation in §3.1.1:

(i) A head can only be an active probe for Agreement or A-Movement or Case-marking if it carries some unvalued φ-feature/s, and becomes inactive once its φ-feature/s have been valued (**Probe Condition**)

(ii) An XP can only be an active goal for Agreement, A-Movement, or Case-marking if it has an unvalued case feature, and becomes inactive once its case feature is valued (**Goal Condition**)

(iii) If a constituent is part of a movement chain at a given point in a derivation, only the highest copy in the chain can be active for operations like Agreement, A-Movement or Case-marking (**Highest Copy Condition**)

Constituents which do not satisfy these conditions are **inactive** for the relevant operations. On a different use of *active* in relation to **active voice**, see **passive**.

adjoin See **adjunct**.

adjunct/adjunction An adjunct is a constituent which adjoins/ attaches to another to form a larger constituent of the same type via an operation termed **adjunction**. A **head adjunct** is a head which adjoins to another head to form a complex head. A **phrasal adjunct** is a phrase (more accurately: maximal projection) which adjoins to another phrase to form an even larger phrase of the same type: for example, a **VP adjunct** is a constituent which adjoins to a VP to form a larger VP; and a **T-bar adjunct** is a constituent which adjoins to a T-bar to form an even larger T-bar: see §1.2.3. The **Adjunct Island Constraint** specifies that adjuncts are islands which don't allow anything to be extracted out of them.

ADV The abbreviation ADV denotes an adverb, and **ADVP** denotes an adverbial phrase. Some linguists treat certain ADVP constituents as PPs headed by a null preposition: for example, *then* is traditionally taken to be an ADVP, but might be a PP with a more abstract structure paraphrasable as 'at that time'.

adverb hierarchy This refers to a template/schema used by Cinque (1999) to show the relative ordering within clauses of different functional projections housing adverbs. Part of the hierarchy is listed below (where higher adverbs precede lower ones):

[*frankly* MOOD$_{speech act}$
[*fortunately* MOOD$_{evaluative}$
[allegedly MOOD$_{evidential}$
[*probably* MOD$_{epistemic}$
[*once* T$_{past}$
[*then* T$_{future}$
[*perhaps* MOOD$_{irrealis}$
[*necessarily* MOD$_{necessity}$
[*possibly* MOD$_{possibility}$

[*usually* ASP$_{habitual}$
[*again* ASP$_{repetitive(I)}$
[*often* ASP$_{frequentative(I)}$
[*intentionally* MOD$_{volitional}$
[*quickly* ASP$_{celerative(I)}$
[already T$_{anterior}$
[*no longer* ASP$_{terminative}$
[*still* ASP$_{continuative ...}$

The full hierarchy is listed in (36) of §6.2.2.

ADVP See ADV.

Af See Affix.

affix/affixal The term **affix** (abbreviated to *Af*) is typically used to describe a grammatical **morpheme** which cannot stand on its own as an independent word, but which must be attached to a **host** word of an appropriate kind. An affix which attaches to the beginning of a word (e.g. *un-* in *unhappy*) is called a **prefix**: an affix which attaches to the end of a word (e.g. *-s* in *chases*) is called a **suffix**. An **affixal** head is one which behaves like an affix in needing to attach to a particular kind of host word. See also **clitic**. **Affix Hopping** is an operation in the PF component by which an unattached affix in T is lowered onto the closest auxiliary or non-auxiliary verb below T: see §1.3.1.

AGENT This is a term used to describe the semantic (= thematic) role which a particular type of argument plays in a given sentence. It typically denotes a person who wilfully causes some state of affairs to come about: hence for example, *John* plays the thematic role of AGENT argument of the verb *smashed* in a sentence such as 'John deliberately smashed the bottle.' See §2.2.2.

agreement An operation by which (e.g. in a sentence like *They are lying*) the person/number features of the auxiliary *are* come to be assigned the same values as those of its subject *they*, so that *are* is third person plural because it agrees in **person** and **number** with its third person plural subject *they*. A language has **rich agreement** if it uses a wide range of distinctive person/number inflections on verbs, and **poor agreement** if it does not: see Chapter 3.

Agreement Deficit Hypothesis This is an account of the syntax of Bᴇ **Drop** in newspaper headlines (outlined in **Module 7.4**) which makes the following assumptions:

Bᴇ Drop clauses are truncated SUBJP constituents, headed by a SUBJ with defective agreement properties (e.g. with number but not person). SUBJ attracts Bᴇ to raise to adjoin to it, but (being defective) cannot attract the subject to move to spec-SUBJP; and since the clause lacks FIN, its subject cannot be assigned nominative case. Instead, the subject raises only as far as spec-TP, and is assigned accusative case by default. Bᴇ receives a null spellout by default at PF, because there is no overt spellout for defective forms of Bᴇ.

A-Movement See A-position.

anaphor This is an item (like the **reflexive** anaphor *himself*) which cannot have independent reference, but which must be bound by (i.e. take its reference from) an appropriate antecedent that c-commands it within the same phrase or sentence. Hence, while we can say *John is deluding himself* (where *himself* refers back to *John*), we cannot say **For himself to have to wait would be unthinkable*, since the anaphor *himself* here has no antecedent.

animate The term animate is used to denote (the gender of) an expression which denotes a living being (e.g. a human being or animal), while the term **inanimate** is used in relation to an expression which denotes lifeless entities. For example, the **relative pronoun** *who* could be said to be animate in gender and the relative pronoun *which* inanimate – hence we say *someone who upsets people* and *something which upsets people*.

antecedent An expression which is referred to by another constituent (typically a pronoun or anaphor) of some kind. For example, in *John cut himself shaving*, *John* is the antecedent of the anaphor *himself*, since *himself* refers back to *John*. In a sentence such as *He is someone who we respect*, the antecedent of the **relative pronoun** *who* is *someone*.

Antilocality Constraint A constraint which (in the formulation of Boeckx (2007: 110) specifies that 'Movement internal to a projection counts as too local, and is banned.' This rules out (for example) movement from complement to specifier position internally within a given phrase.

AP Abbreviation for adjectival phrase.

A-position/A-Movement The difference between an **A-position** and an **A-bar position** can be illustrated in relation to a clause such as that produced by speaker B below:

SPEAKER A: What don't you understand?

SPEAKER B: [$_{CP}$ Why [$_{TP}$ you are blaming yourself]]

An A-position is one which can only be occupied by an **argument** (not by an adjunct), which can control **agreement**, and from which an **anaphor** can be bound; by contrast, an A-bar position is one which is not restricted to arguments (so can contain either an **adjunct** or an argument), but cannot control agreement or bind an anaphor. Given these criteria, the spec-TP position occupied by *you* in speaker B's utterance above is an A-position because the pronoun *you* that it contains is an argument (of the verb *blaming*), it controls/determines the agreement properties of the auxiliary *are*, and it serves as the antecedent of the anaphor *yourself*. By contrast, the spec-CP position occupied by *why* is an A-bar position because *why* is an adjunct, does not control agreement with *are*, and cannot bind an anaphor like *yourself*. **A-Movement** is movement to an A-position in the subperiphery (like spec-TP or spec-SUBJP); an **A-chain** is a movement chain formed by a constituent undergoing A-Movement. **A-bar Movement** is movement to an A-bar position (in effect, a specifier position in the clause periphery); an

A-bar chain is a movement chain formed by a constituent undergoing A-bar Movement; an **A-bar head** is the kind of head (like C) in the clause periphery which allows as its specifier either an argument or an adjunct expression.

argument This is a term borrowed by linguists from philosophy (more specifically, from predicate calculus) to describe the role played by particular constituents in the semantic structure of sentences. In a sentence such as 'John hit Fred', the overall sentence is said to be a **proposition** (a term used to describe the semantic content of a clause), and to consist of the **predicate** *hit* and its two arguments *John* and *Fred*. The two arguments represent the two participants in the act of hitting, and the predicate is the expression (in this case the verb *hit*) which describes the activity in which they are engaged. By extension, in a sentence such as 'John says he hates syntax' the predicate in the main clause is the verb *says*, and its two arguments are *John* and the clause *he hates syntax*; the argument *he hates syntax* is in turn a proposition whose predicate is *hates*, and whose two arguments are *he* and *syntax*. Since the complement of a verb is positioned internally within V-bar whereas the subject of a verb is positioned outside V-bar, complements are also referred to as **internal arguments**, and subjects as **external arguments**. The **argument structure** of a predicate provides a description of the set of **arguments** associated with the **predicate**, and the **theta role** which each fulfils in relation to the predicate. A **one-/two-/three-place predicate** is a predicate which has one/two/three arguments. See Module 2.2.

ART(icle)/ARTP The term **article** is used in traditional grammar to describe a particular subclass of determiner/quantifier: the word *the* is traditionally called the **definite article**, and the word *a(n)* is termed the **indefinite article**. In this book, I treat a phrase like *a book* as an **ARTP/article phrase** which is headed by the indefinite article, while treating a phrase like *the book* as a **determiner phrase/DP** headed by the determiner *the*. **Article Drop** denotes a phenomenon whereby definite and indefinite articles can be omitted in certain abbreviated registers of English – for example, newspaper headlines: it is characterised in Module 7.3 as involving an article which is the first word in the (DP/ARTP) projection that it heads being given a null spellout. The **C-command Condition on Article Drop** (devised by Stowell 1999) specifies that no nominal allows Article Drop if it is c-commanded by a nominal with an overt article: see Module 7.3 and Module 7.4.

articulated Work in the **Cartographic** model (outlined in **Chapters 4–6**) sees clauses as having a more articulated (i.e. more complex) structure than assumed in the traditional CP+TP+VP model of clause structure. Hence, the Cartographic model contains more functional projections than the traditional model: for example, CP is replaced by a set of functional projections including FORCEP, FINP and a range of (optional) additional projections such as TOPP, FOCP, and MODP.

aspect A term typically used to denote the duration of the activity described by a verb (e.g. whether the activity is ongoing or completed). In sentences such as:

(i)   He has taken the medicine
(ii) He is taking the medicine

the auxiliary *has* is said to be an auxiliary which marks **perfect aspect** (and hence to be a **perfect auxiliary**) in that it marks the perfection (in the sense of 'completion' or 'termination') of the activity of taking the medicine; for analogous reasons, *taken* is said to be a **perfect participle** verb form in (i) (though is sometimes referred to in traditional grammars as a 'past participle'). Similarly, *is* functions as an auxiliary which marks **progressive aspect** in (ii), because it relates to an activity which is ongoing or in progress; for this reason, *is* in (ii) is also referred to as a **progressive auxiliary**. In the same way, the verb *taking* in (ii) is said to be the **progressive participle** form of the verb (though is sometimes referred to in traditional grammars as a 'present participle').

associate An expression which represents the thematic argument in an expletive *there* construction, and which is associated with the expletive subject *there*: for example, *an unfortunate accident* in *There occurred an unfortunate accident.*

attract To say that a head H attracts
a constituent C is to say that H
triggers movement of C to some
position on the **edge** of HP (so that
C may move to adjoin to H, or to
become the specifier of H).

attribute See **value**.

AUX(iliary)/AUXP The term auxiliary
is used to categorise items such
as *will/would/can/could/shall/
should/may/might/must/ought* and
some uses of *have/be/do/need/
dare*. Such items have a number of
idiosyncratic properties, including
the fact that they can undergo
(Subject–Auxiliary) Inversion (e.g.
in questions like '*Can* you speak
French?'). An auxiliary projection/
AUXP is a phrase headed by an
auxiliary: see §6.1.1. **Auxiliary
Drop** (see Module 7.2) is a
phenomenon found in abbreviated
registers of English whereby an
auxiliary can be omitted if it is
the first word in a sentence – as in
<Are> you doing anything tonight?
Auxiliary selection relates to the
type of verb which a given auxiliary
selects as its complement: for
example, in many languages (the
counterpart of) BE when used as
a perfect auxiliary selects only a
complement headed by a verb with
no external argument, whereas
(the counterpart of) HAVE selects a
complement headed by a verb with
an external argument. See §2.3.2.

Auxiliary Inversion See **Inversion**.

Auxiliary Raising An operation by
which an auxiliary verb moves from
a lower to a higher head position
within a clause (e.g. moving from

being the head of an Auxiliary
Projection below T to adjoin to
an unattached tense affix in T,
as in §6.1.1; or moving from T
into a higher position within the
subperiphery, as in §6.2.1).

bar When used as a suffix attached
to a category label such as N,
V, P, T etc. (as in N-bar, V-bar,
P-bar, T-bar etc.), it denotes an
intermediate projection which is
larger than a word but smaller than
a phrase. Hence, in a phrase such
as *university policy on drugs*, we
might say that the string *policy
on drugs* is an N-bar, since it is a
projection of the head noun *policy*,
but is an intermediate projection
in that it has a larger projection
into the NP *university policy on
drugs*. For another use of bar in
the phrase 'A-bar position', see
A-position.

bare A bare noun phrase/nominal
is one used without any overt
quantifier or determiner to modify
it (e.g. *fish* in *Fish is expensive*). A
bare clause is one not introduced
by an overt complementiser (like
he was tired in *John said he was
tired*).

barrier A given structure is a barrier
to movement if it doesn't (readily)
allow other constituents to be
extracted/moved out of it. For
example, the bracketed *if*-clause
below is a barrier to extraction of
how in (ii):

(i) She will be annoyed [if he
     behaves *badly*]

(ii) **How* will she be annoyed [if he
      behaves –]?

In (ii), *how* originates in the gap position – that is, in the same position as *badly* occupies in (i) – and from there moves out of the bracketed *if*-clause to the front of the overall sentence. However, the *if*-clause is an **adjunct** to the main clause, and adjuncts are barriers to (i.e. resist) extraction, with the result that (ii) is ungrammatical.

Bᴇ Drop A phenomenon found in certain abbreviated registers of English (especially newspaper headlines) involving omission of indicative forms of Bᴇ – as in *Minnesota <is> hit by more unrest* (with omission of the bracketed auxiliary *<is>*). See Module 7.4.

binary A binary contrast is a two-way contrast (e.g. between a singular noun like *man* and its plural counterpart *men*). A binary-branching structure/tree diagram is one in which each non-terminal constituent (i.e. each constituent not at the foot/bottom of the tree) branches down into two other constituents immediately beneath it: see §1.2.2.

bind/bound To say that one constituent X binds another constituent Y (and conversely that Y is bound by X) is to say that X determines properties (usually, referential properties) of Y. For example, in a sentence such as *John blamed himself*, the reflexive anaphor *himself* is bound by *John* (equivalently, *John* binds *himself*), in the sense that the referential properties of *himself* are determined by *John* (i.e. *himself* refers back to *John*).

bottom-up To say that a syntactic structure is derived in a bottom-up fashion is to say that the structure is built up from bottom to top, with lower parts of the structure being formed before higher parts: see §1.2.2.

C Abbreviation for complementiser. See **complementiser**.

canonical A term used to mean 'usual', 'typical' or 'normal', as in 'The canonical word order in English is *specifier+head+complement*.'

Cartography/Cartographic An approach to syntax (associated with the work of Luigi Rizzi and his collaborators) which aims to devise a detailed 'map' of various types of syntactic structure (e.g. the clause periphery and subperiphery). The Cartographic model sees syntactic structures as containing many more functional projections than the traditional CP+TP+VP model. See Chapters 4–6.

case The different case forms of a pronoun are the different forms which the pronoun has in different sentence positions. It is traditionally said that English has three cases – **nominative** (abbreviated to NOM), **accusative** (= ACC, sometimes also referred to as objective), and **genitive** (= GEN). Personal pronouns typically inflect overtly for all three cases, whereas noun expressions overtly inflect only for genitive case. The different case forms of typical pronouns and noun expressions are given in the table below:

nominative	I	we	you	he	she	it	they	who	the king
accusative	me	us	you	him	her	it	them	who(m)	the king
genitive	my	our	your	his	her	its	their	whose	the
	mine	ours	yours		hers		theirs		king's

As is apparent, some pronouns have two distinct genitive forms: a weak (shorter) form used when they are immediately followed by a noun (as in 'This is *my car*'), and a strong (longer) form used when they are not immediately followed by a noun (as in 'This car is *mine*'). The null subject PRO found in **control** clauses is treated in this book as carrying **null case**: see §1.3.2.

case-marking Under the account of case marking in §3.1.2 (revised in §4.3.2 by replacing C by FIN), nominal and pronominal XP constituents are assigned case by an appropriate case assigner in accordance with the following **Case Conditions**: A case-assigning probe values an unvalued case feature on an XP goal and assigns the goal a case value that depends on the nature of the probe – namely:

(i)   *nominative* if the probe is a finite C/FIN with a TP complement (where a finite C/FIN is one that is indicative, subjunctive or imperative in mood)

(ii) *null* if the probe is an intransitive infinitival C/FIN with a TP complement

(iii) *accusative* if the probe is transitive

(Pro)nominal constituents which are in a position where they do not fall within the domain of any case assigner are assigned case by a **Default Case Assignment** operation which is given the following formulation in §4.1.2:

A (pro)nominal which does not fall within the domain of (i.e. which is not c-commanded by) a local (i.e. nearby) case assigner receives accusative case by default.

case particle Many linguists take *of* in structures like *destruction of the city* or *fond of him* to belong to the category K of 'case particle', and the *of*-phrase to be a KP/case phrase. The rationale for this is that *of* has to be used here because a noun like *destruction* and an adjective like *fond* are not case assigners, and hence the nominal *the city* and the pronominal *him* would be unable to be case-marked if the case particle *of* were not used to assign accusative case to them. The assumption here is all that (pro)-nominal constituents need to be assigned case in order to receive a **spellout** in the PF component: for example, the PF component needs to know whether a third person singular masculine pronoun has nominative, accusative or genitive case in order to determine whether to spell it out as *he*, *him* or *his*.

c-command In a structure containing two different constituents X and Y, X c-commands Y if X is independent of Y (i.e. if neither contains the other), and if the mother of X contains Y. The **C-command Condition on Article Drop** in newspaper headlines is a condition (devised by Stowell 1999 and discussed in **Module 7.3**) which specifies that no nominal allows Article Drop if it is c-commanded by a nominal with an overt article; this condition is generalised in **Module 7.4**.

CED Abbreviation for **Constraint on Extraction Domains**: see **extract**.

chain A set comprising a constituent and any traces/copies associated with it.

clause A clause is defined in traditional grammar as an expression which contains a **subject** and a **predicate**, and which may contain other types of constituent as well (e.g. one or more **complements** and/or **adjuncts**). In most cases, the predicate in a clause contains a lexical (= non-auxiliary) verb, so that there will be as many different clauses in a sentence as there are different lexical verbs. For example, in a sentence such as *She may think that you are cheating on her*, there are two lexical verbs (*think* and *cheating*), and hence two clauses. The *cheating* clause is *that you are cheating on her*, and the *think* clause is *She may think that you are cheating on her*, so that the *cheating* clause is one of the constituents of the *think* clause. More specifically, the *cheating* clause is the **complement** of the *think* clause,

and so is said to function as a **complement clause** in this type of sentence.

clause type/Clause Typing Conditions A clause is said to be declarative in type if used to make a statement, interrogative in type if used to ask a question, imperative in type if used to issue an order, etc. The **Clause Typing Conditions** outlined in §1.4.3 specify that:

(i) A clause is interpreted as being of a given type (interrogative or exclamative etc.) if it contains a peripheral clause-typing specifier of the relevant type

(ii) An indicative clause is interpreted as declarative in type by default if it contains no peripheral clause-typing specifier (where *peripheral* means 'within the clause periphery' – that is, within that part of the clause structure positioned above the subject).

cleft sentence A structure such as 'It was *syntax* that he hated most', where *syntax* is said to occupy **focus position** within the cleft sentence.

clitic(isation) The term **clitic** denotes an item which is a reduced form of another word, and which has the property that (in its reduced form) it must cliticise (i.e. attach itself to) an appropriate kind of **host** word. For example, we could say that the contracted negative particle *n't* is a clitic form of the negative particle *not*, and that the clitic *n't* attaches itself to a finite auxiliary verb, so giving rise to forms like *isn't, shouldn't, mightn't* etc. When a clitic attaches to the end of another word, it is said to be an **enclitic** (and to **encliticise** to the relevant word). A clitic differs from an **affix** in that a clitic is generally a reduced form of a full word, and has a corresponding full form (so that *'ll* is the clitic form of *will*, for example), whereas an affix (like noun plural *-s* in *cats*) has no full-word counterpart. **Clitic doubling** is a phenomenon which results in a structure containing a clitic copy of some other constituent (e.g. of a subject or object): see §6.1.2.

COMP/comp The label 'COMP' is an abbreviation for **complementiser**. By contrast, 'comp' is an abbreviation for **complement**, so comp-VP denotes 'the complement position in VP'.

complement This is a term used to denote a specific grammatical function (in the same way as the term **subject** denotes a specific grammatical function). A complement is a constituent which is directly **merged** with (and hence is the **sister** of) a head word, thereby projecting the head into a larger structure of essentially the same kind. For example, in *close the door*, *the door* is the complement of the verb *close*; in *after dinner*, *dinner* is the complement of the preposition *after*; in *good at physics*, *at physics* is the complement of the adjective *good*; in *loss of face*, *of face* is the complement of the noun *loss*. As these examples illustrate, complements typically follow their heads in English. The choice of complement (and the morphological form of the complement) is determined by properties of the head: for example, an auxiliary such as *will* requires as its complement an expression headed by a verb in the infinitive form (cf. 'He will *go/*going/*gone*'). Moreover, complements bear a close semantic relation to their heads (e.g. in *Kill him!* the word *him* is the complement of the verb *kill* and is an argument of the verb *kill*, representing the victim). Thus, a complement has a close morphological, syntactic and semantic relation to its head. A **complement clause** is a clause which is used as the complement of some other word (typically as the complement of a verb, adjective or noun). Thus, in a sentence such as *He never expected that she would come*, the clause *that she would come* serves as the complement of the verb *expected*, and so is a complement clause.

complementiser A particular category of clause-introducing word like *that/if/whether/for*, as used in sentences like 'I think [*that* you should apologise]', 'I don't know [*if/whether* she will agree]', 'They're keen [*for* you to show up]' where the italicised complementisers introduce the bracketed clauses. A **Complementiser Phrase/projection (CP)** is a clause headed by a complementiser. The term **complementiser** is abbreviated to **COMP** in earlier work and to

C in later work. **Complementiser agreement** is agreement between a complementiser and the subject of its clause (this being marked overtly in certain varieties of Flemish, German and Dutch): see §3.1.2.

complete clause A clause which has a periphery that includes a FORCEP projection. See §4.4.1.

Completeness Condition See **Feature Valuation Conditions.**

component A grammar is said to have three main components: a **syntactic component** which generates syntactic structures, a **semantic/LF component** which assigns each such syntactic structure an appropriate **semantic/LF representation** (= a representation of its **logical form**), and a **phonological/PF component** which assigns each syntactic structure generated by the syntactic component an appropriate **phonetic form/PF**.

COMP-Trace Filter A condition (introduced in §1.5.2) specifying that any superficial structure in which an overt complementiser immediately precedes and c-commands a trace (i.e. a gap/ null copy left behind by a moved constituent) is filtered out as ungrammatical at the end of the syntactic derivation.

concord A traditional term to describe an operation whereby a noun and any adjectives or determiners modifying it are assigned the same values for features such as number, gender and case.

condition See **constraint.**

conditional A term used to represent a type of clause which sets out

conditions – for example, '*If you should upset anyone*, I'll bar you', or '*Should you upset anyone*, I'll bar you', where the italicised are **conditional clauses.**

CONJ/CONJP/Conjunction The term conjunction denotes a word used to join two or more constituents together. In a sentence like *Although I was tired, I stayed up to watch the film*, *although* is a conjunction which links the subordinate clause *I was tired* to the main clause *I stayed up to watch the film* and so is termed a **subordinating conjunction** (abbreviated to SUB in some works, but to **CONJ** here, in order to avoid confusion with SUBJ/subject); consequently, subordinate clauses are treated as **CONJP** constituents here (but as SUBP constituents in some other works). In a sentence like *He stayed up and/but she went to bed*, the words *and/but* are **coordinating conjunctions** which conjoin/link the two main clauses *he stayed up* and *she went to bed*.

constraint A grammatical principle which prevents certain types of grammatical operation from applying to certain types of structure. The terms **condition** and principle are used in much the same way. See also specific constraints (e.g. the **Constraint on Extraction Domains**, listed under **Extract/ Extraction**).

content This term is generally used to refer to the semantic content (i.e. meaning) of a constituent (typically, of a word). However, it can also be used in a more general way to refer to the linguistic properties of an expression: for example, the expression **phonetic content** is used to refer to the phonetic form of (e.g.) a word: hence, we might say that **PRO** is a pronoun which has no phonetic content (meaning that it is a silent pronoun with no audible form).

contraction A process by which two different words are combined into a single word, with either or both words being reduced in form. For example, by contraction, *want to* can be reduced to *wanna, going to* to *gonna, he is* to *he's, they have* to *they've, did not* to *didn't*, etc. See also **clitic(isation)**.

control/controller In a nonfinite clause with a **PRO** subject which has an antecedent, the antecedent is said to be the **controller** of PRO (or to **control** PRO), and conversely PRO is said to be controlled by its antecedent; and the clause containing PRO is termed a **control clause**. So, in a structure like *John tried* [PRO *to quit*], the bracketed structure is a control clause, *John* is the controller of PRO, and conversely PRO is controlled by *John* (in the sense that PRO refers back to *John*). The term **control predicate/verb** denotes a word like *try* which takes an infinitive complement with a (controlled) PRO subject. See §2.5.2.

coordinate A **coordinate structure** is a structure containing two or more expressions joined together by a coordinating **conjunction** such as *and/but/or/nor* (e.g. *John and Mary* is a coordinate structure).

copula/copular verb A 'linking verb', used to link a subject with a non-verbal **predicate**. The main copular verb in English is BE (though verbs like BECOME, REMAIN, STAY etc. have much the same linking function). In sentences such as *They are lazy*, *They are fools* and *They are outside*, the verb *are* is said to be a copula (or copular verb) in that it links the subject *they* to the adjectival predicate *lazy*, or the nominal predicate *fools*, or the prepositional predicate *outside*.

copy The **Copy Theory of Movement** is a theory developed by Chomsky which maintains that a moved constituent leaves behind a copy of itself (called a **trace**) each time it moves, with the copy generally being given a null/silent spellout (and so being unpronounced) in the phonology. **Copy Raising** is a type of movement operation in which a raised constituent leaves an overt copy behind (e.g. in 'There look like *there* are no objections', where expletive *there* raises from being subject of the *are*-clause to becoming subject of the *look*-clause, and leaves an overt copy of itself behind). See §3.4.2 and §3.4.3.

coreferential Two expressions are coreferential if they refer to the same entity. For example, in *John cut himself while shaving, himself* and *John* are cofererential in the sense that they refer to the same individual.

count/countable A **count(able) noun** is a noun which can be counted. Hence, a noun such as *chair* is a count noun since we can say 'One

chair, two chairs, three chairs, …';
but a noun such as *furniture* is a
non-count/uncountable/mass noun
since we cannot say '*one furniture,
*two furnitures, …'.

CP **Complementiser Phrase**. See
Complementiser. On **CP recursion**,
see **recursion**.

crash A derivation is said to **crash**
if it violates some constraint/s or
interface condition/s, or results in
a structure which can't be assigned
a phonetic form and/or a semantic
interpretation. For example, if the
person or number features of HAVE
remain unvalued in a sentence
such as 'He HAVE left', the resulting
sentence will crash at the phonetics
interface, since the PF component
will be unable to determine whether
HAVE (if present tense) should be
spelled out as *have* or *has*.

Criterial Freezing Condition A
condition which is given the
following formulation in **Module
4.1** (with the italicised amendment
added in §**6.1.2**):

(i) A peripheral *or subperipheral*
constituent must occupy
a criterial position to be
interpretable at LF

(ii) A constituent which occupies
its criterial position is frozen in
place

cross-clausal Cross-clausal movement/
agreement is an operation that takes
place across an intervening clause
boundary. See Module 3.4.

D An abbreviation for **Determiner**.

declarative A term used as a
classification of the force
(or semantic type) of a clause
which is used to make a statement
(as opposed to a clause which is
interrogative, exclamative or
imperative in force).

dedicated To say that an adverb like
perhaps serves as the specifier of a
dedicated functional head (a head
expressing irrealis mood, according
to Cinque 1999: see §6.2.2) is to say
that it is the specifier of a functional
head which only allows adverbs
of the same type as *perhaps* as its
specifier.

default A default value or property is
one which obtains if all else fails
(i.e. if other conditions are not
satisfied). For example, if we say
that +*d* is the default past tense
inflection in English, we mean that
verbs which don't have an irregular
past tense form will form their past
tense by adding +*d* to their stem. On
Default Case Assignment, see **case
marking**. On the **Default Spellout
Rule**, see **spellout rules**.

definite Expressions containing
determiners like *the, this, that* etc.
are said to have **definite reference**
in that they refer to an entity
which is assumed to be known to
the addressee(s): for example, in a
sentence such as 'I hated the course',
the DP *the course* refers to a specific
course whose identity is assumed
to be known to the hearer/reader.
In much the same way, personal
pronouns like *he/she/it/they* etc. are
said to have definite reference. By
contrast, expressions containing the
article *a* are **indefinite**, in that (for
example) if you say 'I'm taking a

course', you don't assume that the hearer/reader knows what course you are taking.

degraded A sentence is said to be degraded if it is less than fully acceptable/less than fully grammatical.

deletion A type of operation by which a constituent present in the syntactic structure of a sentence is given a silent spellout (i.e. is unpronounced) in the phonological/PF component.

derive/derivation The derivation of a phrase or clause is the set of syntactic (e.g. merge, movement, adjunction, agreement, case marking etc.) operations used to form the relevant structure. To derive a structure is to say how it is formed (i.e. specify the operations by which it is formed).

determiner/D A word like *the/this/that* used to modify a noun or noun phrase is a determiner in the sense that it determines the referential properties of the noun (phrase). For example, *the* in a sentence like *Shall we take the car?* serves to indicate that the phrase *the car* is a definite referring expression, in the sense that it refers to a definite (specific) car which is assumed to be familiar to the hearer/addressee.

Determiner Phrase/DP A phrase like *the king of Utopia* which comprises a determiner *the* and a noun phrase complement *king of Utopia*. In work before the mid-1980s, a structure like *the king of Utopia* would have been analysed as a noun phrase (= NP), comprising the head noun *king*,

its complement *of Utopia* and its specifier *the*. Since Abney (1987), such expressions have been taken to have the status of DP/determiner phrase.

DFCF See **Doubly Filled COMP Filter**.

Diary Drop A register of written English used in diary entries whereby sentences are abbreviated by omitting various types of constituent, most notably subjects. See Module 7.1, and Exercise 7.1 of the Workbook module in **Chapter 7**.

direct object See **object**.

discontinuous spellout See **spellout**.

discourse Discourse factors are factors relating to the extrasentential setting in which an expression occurs (where extrasentential means 'outside the immediate sentence containing the relevant expression'). For example, to say that PRO has a **discourse controller** in a sentence such as *It would be wise* PRO *to prepare yourself for the worst* means that PRO has no antecedent within the sentence immediately containing it, but rather refers to some individual(s) outside the sentence (in this case, the person being spoken to).

dislocate/dislocation In sentences such as:

(i) *The mayor of Trumpton*, I doubt if he will win another term

(ii) I doubt if he will win another term, *the mayor of Trumpton*

the italicised constituent *the mayor of Trumpton* is said to be dislocated, because it is in a separate intonation group (set off by a comma) from the rest of the sentence. Where the dislocated constituent is to the left of the rest of the sentence as in (i), the phenomenon is termed **Left Dislocation**; where the dislocated constituent is to the right of the rest of the sentence as in (ii), it is termed **Right Dislocation**. See §4.1.2.

Distinctness Condition A condition devised by Richards (2010: 5), which is characterised informally as follows in §4.1.3:

Any structure at PF which contains a sequence of two non-distinct constituents <α, α> is degraded

The condition marks the sequence *who who* as degraded in a sentence such as **Who who was innocent would behave like that?*

distribution The distribution of a constituent denotes the range of positions that it can occupy in phrases/sentences.

domain The **domain** (or, more fully, **c-command domain**) of a head H is the set of constituents c-commanded by H – namely its sister and all the constituents contained within its sister. For example, the domain of C includes its TP complement and all constituents of the relevant TP.

Do-support This refers to the use of the dummy/meaningless auxiliary DO to form questions, negatives or tags in sentences which would otherwise contain no auxiliary. Hence, because a non-auxiliary verb like *want* requires Do-support in questions/negatives/tags, we have sentences such as '*Does* he want

some?', 'He *doesn't* want any', and 'He wants some, *does* he?'

Doubly Filled COMP Filter A condition specifying that at the end of a syntactic derivation, any structure in which the **edge** of a projection headed by an overt complementiser is doubly filled (i.e. contains some other overt constituent) is filtered out as ungrammatical: see §1.5.2.

DP Abbreviation for **determiner phrase**.

DP Hypothesis The hypothesis that all definite nominal and pronominal **arguments** have the status of DPs – not just nominals like *the president* which contain an overt determiner, but also proper names like *John*, and pronouns like *he*.

ECM See **Exceptional Case Marking**.

edge The edge of a given projection XP comprises the constituent(s) which are contained in XP but are not c-commanded by X (i.e. by the head of XP). Typically, the edge of XP will include its head X and any specifier it may have.

ellipsis/elliptical Ellipsis is an operation by which an expression is omitted in order to avoid repetition. In this book, an ellipsed constituent is taken to be present in the syntax, but given a silent pronunciation in the PF component. For example, in a sentence such as *I will do it if you will do it*, we can ellipse (i.e. give a silent pronunciation to) the second occurrence of the verb phrase/ VP *do it* to avoid repetition, and hence say *I will do it if you will*: this type of ellipsis is referred to as

VP ellipsis. An **elliptical** structure is one containing an 'understood' constituent which has undergone ellipsis (i.e. has been given a silent pronunciation). **Sentence-Initial Ellipsis** is a phenomenon found in abbreviated registers/styles of English whereby a constituent can be omitted at the beginning of a sentence, as with *<I> couldn't care less*, where the <bracketed> subject *I* is ellipsed: see Module 7.1.

embedded An embedded clause is one which is contained internally within another constituent. For example, in a sentence such as *He may suspect that I hid them*, the *hid*-clause (= *that I hid them*) is embedded within (and is the complement of) the verb phrase headed by the verb *suspect*. Likewise, in *The fact that he didn't apologise is significant*, the *that*-clause (*that he didn't apologise*) is an embedded clause in the sense that it is embedded within a noun phrase headed by the noun *fact*. A clause which is not embedded within any other expression is a **root clause** (see **root**) or **main clause**.

enclitic/encliticise See **clitic(isation)**.

EPP This was originally an abbreviation for the Extended Projection Principle, which posited that every T constituent must be projected into a TP which has a subject/specifier. In later work, the requirement for a T constituent like *will* to have a specifier is said to be a consequence of T carrying an EPP feature requiring it to project a specifier. The **EPP Condition** in

§3.1.1 specifies that an EPP feature on a **probe** T attracts the closest active XP **goal** that it agrees with in person to undergo A-Movement to spec-TP, and the EPP feature is stripped from T (and thereby removed from the derivation) once A-Movement has taken place.

Exceptional Case Marking/clause/ ECM Accusative subjects of infinitival complement clauses (like *him* in the clause italicised in 'I believe *him to be innocent*') are said to carry exceptional case, in the sense that the case of the accusative subject is assigned by the main clause verb *believe*, and it is exceptional for the case of the subject of one clause to be assigned by the verb in a higher clause. Transitive verbs (like *believe*) that take an infinitival TP complement with an accusative subject are said to be **ECM verbs**. The infinitive clause in such cases is said to be an **exceptional clause** or **ECM clause**. See §3.3.2.

exclamative A type of structure used to exclaim surprise, delight, annoyance, etc. In English syntax, the term is restricted largely to clauses beginning with an XP containing or comprising a wh-exclamative word like *What!* or *How!* – for example, '*What a fool I was!*' or '*How blind I was!*' See §5.4.1.

EXPERIENCER A term used in the analysis of semantic/thematic roles to denote an entity which experiences some emotional or cognitive state – for example,

John in *John felt unhappy*, or *John thought about his predicament.* See §2.2.2.

expletive An expletive pronoun is one with little or no inherent semantic content, such as *there* in sentences like *There is no truth in the rumour*, or impersonal *it* in sentences such as *It is unclear why he resigned.* These pronouns are non-referential and hence cannot be questioned by *where/what* (cf. **Where is no truth in the rumour?/*What is unclear why he resigned?*). In §3.2.3, the use of expletives is said to be subject to the following **Expletive Conditions:**

(i)   **External Argument Condition**
      An expletive can only be merged as the highest argument of a verb with no external argument

(ii) **Indefiniteness Condition**
      Existential *there* can only be merged as the specifier of an existential verb with an indefinite (pro)nominal complement

(iii) **Inactivity Condition**
      Expletive *it* can only be merged with a constituent which does not contain an active nominal or pronominal (i.e. one carrying an unvalued case feature)

For detailed discussion of the syntax of clauses with expletive subjects, see Module 3.2.

Extended Projection Principle See **EPP**.

external argument See **argument**. On the **External Argument Condition** on the use of expletives, see **expletive**.

extract/extraction Extract(ion) is another term for move(ment), and so denotes an operation by which one constituent is moved out of another. For instance, in a structure such as *Who do you think [he saw —]* the pronoun *who* has been extracted out of the bracketed clause (i.e. it is been moved out of the gap position marked —) and moved to the front of the overall sentence. The **extraction site** for a moved constituent is the position which it occupied before undergoing movement (e.g. the gap position in the above sentence). The **Constraint on Extraction Domains/CED** (introduced in §1.5.1) specifies that extraction is only possible out of a complement, not out of a specifier or adjunct.

extrapose/Extraposition In a structure where a constituent which is part of a larger phrase is detached from (and follows) the other constituents of the phrase, the detached constituent is said to have been extraposed or to have undergone Extraposition. So, for example, in:

(i)   *Scammers* often ring me [who claim to be from the bank]

the bracketed relative clause is separated from its antecedent *scammers* and positioned at the end of the sentence (and so is said to have been extraposed).

feature A device used to describe a particular grammatical property. For example, the personal pronoun *they* could be said to carry the features [third-person, singular-number, nominative-case]. See §1.1.3.

Feature Valuation Conditions A set of conditions which regulate agreement, case-marking and movement. These are given the following formulation in §3.1.1:

(i)   When an active probe like T c-commands an active XP goal, each unvalued φ-feature on the probe will be valued by the goal – that is, assigned a value which is a copy of the corresponding feature value on the goal (**agreement**)

(ii) Only a φ-complete XP (i.e. one with person and number) can serve as a goal valuing unvalued features on a probe, and conversely only a φ-complete probe (i.e. one with person and number) can value unvalued features on a goal (**Completeness Condition**)

(iii) Each feature on a constituent must be valued (i.e. assigned a single, appropriate value) in order for the constituent to be legible at the PF/LF interfaces; if not, the derivation will crash (**Legibility Condition**)

feminine This term is used in discussion of grammatical **gender** to denote pronouns like *she/her/hers* which refer to female entities.

filled To say that a given position in a structure must be filled is to say that it cannot remain empty but rather must be occupied (usually by an overt constituent of an appropriate kind).

filter This is a device which rules out superficial syntactic structures that fall foul of some grammatical requirement. For example, the **Doubly Filled COMP Filter** specifies that at the end of a syntactic derivation, any structure in which the edge of a projection headed by an overt complementiser is doubly filled (i.e. contains some other overt constituent) is filtered out as ungrammatical. This filter rules out the use of *that* in a clause like that bracketed in 'I wonder [$_{CP}$ *what* [$_c$ ø/*that] he did].'

FIN/FINP The abbreviation FIN denotes an (overt or null) particle used to mark a clause as finite or nonfinite, like the infinitival complementiser *for* in 'She's keen *for there to be a resolution.*' The italicised *for*-clause is analysed as a FINP/finiteness projection: see §4.3.2.

finite The term finite verb/finite clause denotes (a clause containing) an auxiliary or non-auxiliary verb which is inflected for tense/mood, and which can have a nominative subject like *I/we/he/she/they*. See §1.1.3.

floating quantifier A quantifier which is separated from (and follows) the expression that it quantifies. For example, in a sentence such as 'The students should *all* have passed their exams', *all* quantifies (but is separated from and follows) *the students*, so that *all* is a floating quantifier here. On one view, *all the students* moves from being the subject of *passed* to becoming the subject of *have*, and then *the students* moves on its own to become the subject of *should*, so leaving *all* stranded in front of *have* (hence the term **stranded quantifier** is often used in place of floating quantifier). See §6.4.2 and §6.4.3.

FOC/FOCP/focus(ed) A focused constituent is one which is marked (by its intonation/position) as containing new or unfamiliar information. Focus can often be signalled by moving a constituent to the front of a clause or sentence, as with the italicised constituents in the sentences produced by speaker B below:

SPEAKER A: What are the subjects you enjoy most and least?
SPEAKER B: *Syntax* I enjoy most. *Phonetics* I enjoy least

On one view, the italicised constituents move to occupy the specifier position in a FOCP/focus projection in the clause periphery, whose head FOC constituent is a focus particle which is overt in some languages, but null in English. See Module 4.2.

foot The foot of a (movement) chain is the constituent which occupies the lowest position in the chain.

FORCE/FORCEP The complementisers *that/if* in a sentence such as *I didn't know* [*that/if he was lying*] are said to indicate that the bracketed clauses are declarative/interrogative in force (in the sense that they have the force of a question/a statement). In work on the clause periphery by Luigi Rizzi (discussed in **Chapters**

4 and 5), such complementisers are said to constitute a **FORCE** head which can project into a **FORCEP**/force projection.

formal A formal speech style denotes a very careful and stylised form of speech (as opposed to the kind of informal colloquial speech style used in a casual conversation in a bar).

Freezing Principle A constraint specifying that the constituents of a moved phrase are frozen internally within (and so cannot be extracted out of) the moved phrase. See §1.5.1.

front/fronting See **preposing**.

functional category/functional head/ functor A word which has no descriptive content and which serves an essentially grammatical function is said to be a function word or functor. A functional category is a category whose members are function words: hence, categories such as complementiser, auxiliary, infinitive particle, case particle, and determiner are all functional categories – and so too are the expressions they head (e.g. C-bar/CP, T-bar/TP, D-bar/DP etc.).

Functional Specifier Hypothesis A hypothesis (derived from Cinque 1999) to the effect that every XP in the periphery or subperiphery of a clause is the specifier of a dedicated functional head. See §6.4.1.

gap An empty position in a given structure which results from a constituent undergoing ellipsis (as with the second occurrence of *ate* in *John ate an apple and Mary ~~ate~~ a pear*), or movement (as with *where* in *Where has he gone ~~where~~?*).

Gapping A form of **ellipsis** in which the head word is omitted from one (or more) conjoined clauses in a coordinate structure in order to avoid repetition. For example, the italicised second occurrence of *bought* can be gapped (i.e. omitted) in a sentence such as 'John bought an apple and Mary *bought* a pear', giving 'John bought an apple, and Mary a pear.'

gen In one use, an abbreviation for **genitive case**; in another, an abbreviation for **gender**.

gender A grammatical property whereby words are divided into different grammatical classes which play a role in **agreement/concord** relationships. In French, for example, nouns are intrinsically masculine or feminine in gender (e.g. *pommier* 'apple tree' is masculine, but *pomme* 'apple' is feminine), and articles inflect for gender, so that *un* 'a' is the masculine form of the indefinite article, and *une* is its feminine form. Articles in French have to agree in gender with the nouns they modify, hence we say *un pommier* 'an apple tree', but *une pomme* 'an apple'. In contemporary English, nouns don't have inherent gender properties, and their modifiers don't inflect for gender either. Only personal pronouns like *he/she/it* carry gender properties in present-day English, and these are traditionally said to carry **masculine/feminine/neuter** gender respectively (though the term **inanimate** is sometimes used in place of **neuter**).

generic To say that an expression like *eggs* in a sentence such as 'Eggs are fattening' has a generic interpretation is to say that it is interpreted as meaning 'eggs in general'.

genitive See **case**.

gerund When used in conjunction with the progressive aspect auxiliary *be*, verb forms ending in *-ing* are **progressive participles**; in other uses they generally function as **gerunds** (traditionally considered to be verbal nouns, by which is meant 'nouns derived from verbs'). In particular, *-ing* verb forms are gerunds when they can be used as subjects, or as complements of verbs or prepositions, and when (in literary styles) they can have a genitive subject like *my*. Thus *writing* is a gerund (verb form) in a sentence such as 'She was annoyed at [my *writing* to her mother]', since the bracketed gerund structure is used as the complement of the preposition *at*, and has a genitive subject *my*.

GOAL/goal The term GOAL is used in the analysis of semantic/thematic roles to denote the entity towards which something moves – for example, *Mary* in 'John sent *Mary* a letter': see §2.2.2. In a different sense, the term **goal** represents a constituent which agrees with, or is case-marked by, or is attracted by a higher head which serves as a **probe**: see §3.1.1. On the **Goal Condition**, see **active**.

head This term has two main uses. The head of a phrase is the key word which determines the syntactic and semantic properties of the phrase. So, in a phrase such as *fond of fast food*, the head of the phrase is the adjective *fond*, and consequently the phrase is an adjectival phrase (and hence can occupy typical positions associated with adjectival expressions – for example, as the complement of *is* in *He is fond of fast food*). In a different use of the same word, the head of a movement chain is the last-created/highest copy in the chain.

headlinese The register/style of language found in newspaper headlines.

Head Movement Movement of an item from one head position to another (e.g. movement of an auxiliary from T to C, or of the verb BE from V to T). See §1.4.3.

Highest Copy Condition See **active**.

identification/identify In a relative clause like that italicised in 'I'm looking for someone Op_{REL} I can trust' the null relative **operator** Op_{REL} can be used in place of the overt relative pronoun *whom* because the contents of the null operator can be identified by its antecedent *someone* (in the sense that the features carried by the operator will match those of its antecedent). On the identification of null objects in the recipe register of English, see Module 7.5.

illegible See **legible**.

impenetrable/Impenetrability Condition. The **Impenetrability Condition** is a grammatical principle (deriving from Chomsky 1998 and introduced in §1.5.1) specifying that anything below the head C of a CP is impenetrable to (i.e. cannot undergo a syntactic operation involving) anything above the CP. In §4.4.1, this is revised to say: 'Anything below the head H of the highest projection HP in a complete clause is impenetrable to anything above HP' (where a complete clause is one containing FORCEP).

imperative A term employed to classify a type of sentence used to issue an order (e.g. *Be quiet! Don't say anything!*), and also to classify the type of verb form used in an imperative sentence (e.g. *be* is a verb in the imperative **mood** in *Be quiet!*). Imperatives can begin with *please* (e.g. *Please be quiet!*).

inactive See **active**.

Inactivity Condition On this condition on the use of expletives, see **expletive**.

inanimate The term inanimate is used to denote (the gender of) an expression which denotes a lifeless entity. For example, the **relative pronoun** *which* could be said to be inanimate in gender, because it requires an inanimate **antecedent** – hence we say *something which upsets people* but not **someone which upsets people*.

Indefiniteness Condition On this condition on the use of expletives, see **expletive**.

indicative Indicative (auxiliary and main) verb forms are finite forms which are used (inter alia) in declarative and interrogative clauses (i.e. statements and questions). Thus, the italicised items are indicative in **mood** in the following sentences: 'He *is* teasing you', '*Can* he speak French?', 'He *had* been smoking', 'He *loves* chocolate', 'He *hated* syntax.' An **indicative clause** is a clause which contains an indicative (auxiliary or non-auxiliary) verb. See **mood**.

infinitive/infinitival The infinitive/infinitival form of a verb is the (uninflected) form which is used (inter alia) when the verb is the complement of a modal auxiliary like *can*, or of the infinitive particle *to*. Accordingly, the italicised verbs are infinitive/infinitival forms in sentences like 'He can *speak* French', and 'He's trying to *learn* French.' An infinitive/infinitival clause is a clause which contains a verb in the infinitive form. Hence, the bracketed clauses are infinitive clauses in: *He is trying [to help her]*, and *Why not let [him help her]*? (In both examples, *help* is an infinitive verb form, and *to* when used with an infinitive complement is said to be an **infinitive particle**.)

INFL A category devised by Chomsky (1981) whose members include finite auxiliaries (which are INFLected for tense/agreement), and the INFinitivaL particle *to*. INFL was abbreviated to **I** in Chomsky (1986b), and replaced by **T** (= tense marker) in later work.

in situ A constituent is said to remain in situ (i.e. 'in place') if it doesn't undergo movement.

interface levels Levels at which the grammar interfaces (i.e. connects) with speech and thought systems which lie outside the domain of grammar. **Phonetic Form** is the level at which the grammar interfaces with speech systems, and **Logical Form** is the level at which it interfaces with thought systems. **Interface conditions** are conditions which structures must meet in order to be processable by thought or speech systems.

intermediate projection See **project(ion)**.

internal argument See **argument**.

interpretable A feature is (semantically) interpretable if it contributes to meaning. For example, in the case of a pronoun like *they*, the features [third person, plural-number] are interpretable, but the feature [nominative-case] is not. See §3.1.3.

Interrogative Generalisation A generalisation (outlined in §5.2.1) specifying that:

(i) A peripheral interrogative XP that triggers Auxiliary Inversion moves from spec-FINP (with FIN attracting a finite auxiliary to adjoin to it) into its criterial position in spec-FOCP

(ii) The criterial position for a peripheral interrogative XP that does not trigger Auxiliary Inversion is spec-FORCEP

Interrogative Inversion A phenomenon whereby a focused interrogative constituent triggers

Subject–Auxiliary Inversion, as in *'What else* **would** you like?' See §5.1.2.

Intervention Condition A principle of grammar specifying that 'Likes cannot cross likes' (Abels 2012: 247) – that is, no constituent can move across an intervening constituent of the same kind. See §1.5.1.

INTP An interrogative projection in the clause periphery which Shlonsky & Soare (2011) claim allows *how come* as its specifier. See §5.2.2.

intransitive See **transitive**.

Inversion A term used to denote a movement process by which the relative order of two expressions is reversed. It is most frequently used in relation to the more specific operation by which an auxiliary verb comes to be positioned in front of its subject, for example, in questions such as *'Can* **you** speak Swahili?', where *can* is positioned in front of its subject *you*. In **Module 5.1**, **Auxiliary Inversion** is said to involve a null FIN head which has a focused interrogative/negative XP as its specifier attracting a finite auxiliary in T to adjoin to FIN.

irrealis An infinitive complement clause like that italicised in 'They would prefer (*for*) *you to abstain*' is said to denote an irrealis (a Latin word meaning 'unreal') event in the sense that the act of abstention is a hypothetical event which has not yet happened and may never happen.

island A structure out of which no subpart can be extracted by any movement operation. Island Constraints are a set of constraints devised by Ross (1967, 1986) specifying that no constituent inside an island can be extracted out of the island by any movement operation that leaves a gap behind. For example, coordinate structures like *William and Harry* are islands. Hence, in a sentence like *They sent William and Harry to Eton*, we can topicalise the whole coordinate structure *William and Harry* by moving it to the front of the overall sentence (as in '*William and Harry*, they sent to Eton'), but we cannot topicalise *Harry* alone (as we see from the ungrammaticality of **'Harry*, they sent William and to Eton'), nor *William* alone (cf. **'William*, they sent and Harry to Eton').

K/KP Case particle/case phrase. See **case particle**.

label A notational device used to represent linguistic (particularly categorial) properties of constituents. For example, if we say that the word *man* belongs to the category N of noun, we are using N as a label to indicate the categorial properties of the word *man* (i.e. to tell us what grammatical category *man* belongs to).

Left Edge Ellipsis A type of ellipsis found in abbreviated registers of English which is given the following characterisation in §7.2.2:

(i) Reduced clauses have the same full syntactic structure as their unreduced counterparts

(ii) The left edge of a continuous set of one or more projections at the top of a tree in a root clause can undergo ellipsis in the phonology

legible A structure is legible at the **PF interface** if it can be assigned an appropriate phonetic representation, and legible at the **LF interface** if it can be assigned an appropriate semantic representation (and conversely, **illegible** if not). On the **Legibility Condition**, see **Feature Valuation Conditions**.

lexical The word **lexical** is used in two different ways. Since a lexicon is a dictionary (i.e. a list of all the words in a language and their idiosyncratic linguistic properties), the term **lexical property** means 'property of some individual word(s)'. However, the word lexical is also used in a second sense, in which it is contrasted with functional (and hence means 'non-functional'). In this second sense, a **lexical category** is a category whose members are words with descriptive content: hence, categories such as noun, verb, adjective or adverb are lexical categories in this sense. So, for example, the term **lexical verb** means 'main verb' (i.e. a non-auxiliary verb like *go, find, hate, want* etc.).

lexicalise To say that (for example) a declarative FORCE head is lexicalised as *that* in a complement clause means that the FORCE head is spelled out/pronounced as *that*.

LF/Logical Form An **LF representation** is a representation of the logical form of some phrase or clause (i.e. of linguistic aspects of its meaning). The **LF component** of a grammar is the (semantic) component which converts syntactic structures into LF-representations. The **LF interface** is the point at which syntactic structures are transferred to the LF (i.e. semantic) component of the grammar.

license/licensing The licensing conditions for a given type of constituent specify the requirements that it needs to satisfy in order to be used. For example, to say that *not* licenses *any* in a sentence like *He has not made any comment* is to say that the presence of *not* allows *any* to be used – that is, *any* can only occur if a licenser like *not* is present (cf. **He has made any comment*). On the licensing conditions for the use of null objects in the recipe register of English, see Module 7.5.

Like-Adjoins-to-Like Constraint A constraint which specifies that likes can only adjoin to likes: hence adjunction can only involve one head adjoining to another, or one phrase/maximal projection adjoining to another. See §6.1.2.

linear/linearisation Linear ordering is the left-to-right ordering of words in a structure. On one view, **linearisation** is an operation by which unordered syntactic structures are assigned a linear ordering by linearisation conditions in the PF component.

link A constituent (or position) which is part of a movement **chain**.

local/locality A number of linguistic operations (e.g. Agreement, Case-marking, Movement etc.) are said to be local in the sense that they can only apply when one constituent is sufficiently close to another. For example, Auxiliary Inversion involves adjoining a T auxiliary to the closest head above it (i.e. to C/FIN). Locality requirements are imposed by constraints like the **Minimality Condition** and the **Impenetrability Condition**.

locative This is a term which denotes the semantic/thematic function of a constituent which denotes place: see §2.2.2. So, for example, *there/where* are locative pronouns in sentences such as 'I found it *there*?' or '*Where* did you find it?'

locus To say that T is the **locus** of tense is to say that the tense properties of (present or past tense) clauses originate on (an auxiliary/affix in) T.

Logical Form See **LF/Logical Form**.

long(-distance) movement Movement across an intervening clause boundary. See §2.4.2 and §2.4.3.

M M denotes a modal auxiliary which originates as the head of an MP/modal projection. See **modal**.

main clause See **root clause**.

main verb A non-auxiliary verb. See **auxiliary**.

marginal A marginal sentence is one which is of questionable grammaticality, marked by one or more preposed question marks (e.g. ?'I ought to apologise, shouldn't I?').

masc(uline) This term is used in discussions of grammatical **gender** to denote pronouns like *he/him/his* which refer to male entities. See **gender**.

matrix In a sentence such as 'I think *he lied*', the (italicised) *lied* clause is an **embedded/complement clause** (by virtue of being embedded as the complement of the verb *think*), and the *think* clause is the **matrix clause**, in the sense that it is the clause immediately containing the *lied* clause.

maximal projection See **projection**.

merge An operation by which two constituents are combined together to form a larger constituent: for example, by merging the P/preposition *to* with the QP/quantifier phrase *several people* we form the PP/prepositional phrase *to several people*. See §1.2.1. The **Merge Hypothesis** specifies that a maximal projection/XP can only be introduced into a structure containing it via (first- or second-) merge with a head: see §6.4.1.

Minimality Condition A constraint (termed the Relativised Minimality Condition in Rizzi 1990) specifying that a constituent can only enter into a syntactic relation with the minimal (= closest) constituent of the relevant type above/below it (where *above* means 'c-commanding', and *below* means 'c-commanded by'). See §1.3.2.

MOD/MODP Constituents in the clause periphery which modify the clause containing them (e.g. circumstantial adverbials) are treated as serving as specifiers of a MODP/modifier phrase projection with a null MOD/

modifier head under the analysis in §4.3.1.

modal/modality A modal item is one which expresses modality (i.e. notions such as possibility, futurity or necessity). The set of modal auxiliaries found in English is usually assumed to include *will/ would/can/could/shall/should/may/ might/must/ought*, and *need/dare* when followed by a 'bare' (*to*-less) infinitive complement. The set of modal adverbs found in English includes *possibly, perhaps, maybe, probably, conceivably, definitely* and *certainly*.

mood This is a term describing inflectional properties of finite verbs. Finite (auxiliary and non-auxiliary) verbs in English can be in the **indicative mood, subjunctive mood**, or **imperative mood**. Examples of each type of mood are given by the italicised verb forms in the following: 'He *hates* [= indicative] spaghetti'; 'The court ordered that he *be* [= subjunctive] detained indefinitely'; 'Please *keep* [= imperative] quiet!' The mood of the verb determines aspects of the interpretation of the relevant clause, so that for example, subjunctive verbs occur in **irrealis** clauses.

morpheme The smallest unit of grammatical structure. Thus, a plural noun such as *cats* comprises two morphemes, namely the stem *cat* and the plural suffix -*s*.

morphology/ morphological Morphology studies how **morphemes** are combined together to form words.

Morphological properties are properties relating to the form of words (e.g. relating to the inflections or affixes they carry). For example, it is a morphological property of regular count nouns that they have a plural form ending in -*s* (e.g. *cat* has the plural *cats*).

morphosyntactic A morphosyntactic property is a grammatical property, that is, a property which affects (or is affected by) relevant aspects of morphology and syntax. For instance, **case** is a morphosyntactic property in that (for example) pronouns have different morphological forms and occupy different syntactic positions according to their case: for example, the nominative form of the first person plural personal pronoun is *we* and its accusative form is *us*; the two occupy different syntactic positions in that the nominative form occurs as the subject of a finite verb (as in '*We* agreed'), whereas the accusative form occurs as the complement of a transitive verb or preposition (as in 'Join *us*').

MP A modal projection – that is, a phrase headed by a **modal** auxiliary: see §6.1.1.

multiple agreement Agreement between a **probe** and more than one **goal**. See §3.2.2, and §3.3.1.

N Abbreviation for **noun**.

native A native speaker of English is someone who has acquired and used English as a first language in an English-speaking environment from birth (or early childhood), and who speaks the language fluently.

A person's native language is a language which they have acquired and used from birth, and which they speak fluently.

natural language A language acquired in a natural setting by human beings (hence, excluding for example, computer languages, animal communication systems, etc.).

NEG See **NEGP**.

Negation A process or construction in which some proposition is said to be false. Negation involves the use of some negative item such as *not*, *n't*, *nobody*, *nothing*, *never*, etc. – though most discussions of negation in this book are about the *not/n't*: see **NEGP**.

Negative Inversion A phenomenon whereby a focused negative constituent triggers Subject–Auxiliary Inversion, as in '*Not a single word* **did** he utter'. See §5.1.1.

NEGP The abbreviation NEGP denotes a negative projection (i.e. a phrase whose edge contains *n't/not*). In this book, *n't* is treated as a clitic which originates as the head NEG constituent of NEGP and encliticises (i.e. attaches to the end of) a finite auxiliary in T; and *not* is treated as an ADVP occupying the specifier position in a NEGP with a null NEG head.

neuter See **gender**.

Nom An abbreviation for **nominative**. See **case**.

nominal This is the adjective associated with the word *noun*, so that a **nominal (constituent)** is one containing or comprising a noun.

However, the term is sometimes extended to mean 'expression containing or comprising a noun *or pronoun*'.

nominative See **case**.

non-auxiliary verb A lexical/main verb (like *want, try, hate, smell, buy* etc.) which requires **Do-support** to form questions, negatives and tags.

nonfinite See **finite**.

noun/N A category of word (whose members include items such as *boy/ friend/thought/sadness/computer*) which typically denotes an entity of some kind. In traditional grammar, a distinction is drawn between **common nouns** and **proper nouns**. Proper nouns are names of individual people (e.g. *Chomsky*), places (e.g. *Colchester, Essex, England*), dates (e.g. *Tuesday, February, Easter*), magazines (e.g. *Cosmopolitan*) etc. whereas common nouns (e.g. *boy, table, syntax* etc.) are nouns denoting general (non-individual) entities. Proper nouns have the semantic property of having unique reference, and the syntactic property that (unless themselves modified) they generally can't be modified by a determiner in English (cf. **the London*). On counts nouns, see **count**.

Noun Phrase/NP A phrase whose head is a noun. In work prior to the mid-1980s, a structure such as *the king of Utopia* was taken to be a noun phrase/NP comprising the head noun *king*, its complement *of Utopia*, and its specifier *the*. In more recent work, such expressions are taken to be **Determiner Phrases/DPs**

comprising the head determiner *the* and a noun phrase/NP complement *king of Utopia*, with the NP in turn comprising the head noun *king* and its complement *of Utopia*.

NP See **Noun Phrase**.

null A null constituent is one which is 'silent' or 'unpronounced' and so has no overt phonetic form. Such a constituent is said to receive a **null spellout** in the phonological component.

null case The case carried by **PRO**. See **case**.

null object See **Object Drop**.

null subject A subject pronoun which has grammatical and semantic properties but no overt phonetic form. There are a variety of different types of null subject, including the null **pro** subject which can be used in any finite clause in a language like Italian, the null counterpart of *you* found in English imperative clauses like *Look after yourself!*, the null **PRO** subject found in nonfinite **control** clauses like that bracketed in *The prisoners tried* [PRO *to escape*], and the null subject found in abbreviated sentences like *Can't find my pen. Must be on my desk at home.*

NUM An abbreviation for numeral. Hence a phrase like *ten people* is a **NUMP** (numeral projection) headed by the NUM/numeral constituent *ten*.

number A term used to denote the contrast between singular and plural forms. In English, we find number contrasts in nouns (cf. 'one *dog*', 'two *dogs*'), in some determiners (cf.

'*this* book', '*these* books'), in some pronouns (cf. *it/they*), and in finite (auxiliary or main) verbs (cf. 'It smells', 'They *smell*').

NUMP See NUM.

OBJ Abbreviation for **object** or object agreement affix.

object The complement of a transitive item (e.g. in *Help me!* the pronoun *me* is the object of the transitive verb *help*; and in *for me*, *me* is the object of the transitive preposition *for*). The term **object** is generally restricted to complements which carry accusative case – that is, to nominal or pronominal complements: hence, *nothing* would be the object (and complement) of *said* in *He said nothing*, but the clause *that he was tired* would be the **complement** (but not the object) of *said* in *He said that he was tired* – though some traditional grammars extend the term object to cover clausal complements as well as (pro)nominal complements. In sentences such as *She gave him them*, the verb *give* is traditionally said to have two objects, namely *him* and *them*: the first object (representing the recipient) is termed the **indirect object**, and the second object (representing the gift) is termed the **direct object**; the relevant construction is known as the **double object construction**. Where a verb has a single object (e.g. *nothing* in *He said nothing*), this is the direct object of the relevant verb.

Object Drop A phenomenon found in certain abbreviated registers of English (e.g. on product labels, in recipe books, in instruction manuals etc.) whereby a third person accusative pronoun such as *it/them* can be dropped/omitted – as in the following instructions on a nasal spray *Shake <it> gently before use* (where the third person pronoun *it* is omitted). See Module 7.5.

One Feature One Head Principle A principle which specifies that each functional head carries only one **interpretable** feature. See Module 4.1.

one-place predicate A predicate which has only one argument. See **argument**.

Op/operator This term is used in syntax to denote a constituent (e.g. negative, interrogative, relative, conditional, or imperative) whose semantic function is to convert a proposition into, for example, a negative or interrogative or relative or conditional or imperative clause. So, for example, a yes–no question like *Have you eaten anything?* can be analysed as containing a null/silent **yes–no question operator** (Op_{YNQ}) which types the clause as a yes–no question, which triggers **Auxiliary Inversion**, and which **licenses** the **polarity item** *anything*: see Module 5.3. Likewise, an interrogative word such as *what* in a sentence like *What has anyone ever done for me?* is a **wh-question operator**, since it types the relevant clause as a wh-question.

overt An expression is overt if it has an audible phonetic form, but **null**

if it has no phonetic content (and so is unpronounced/silent). Thus, in a structure such as:

(i)   He wants [PRO to leave]

he is an overt pronoun, but **PRO** is a null pronoun.

P Abbreviation of **preposition**.

participle A nonfinite verb form which encodes **aspect** or **voice**. English has three types of participle: **progressive participles** (ending in *-ing*) used in conjunction with the progressive aspect auxiliary BE in sentences like 'It is *raining*'; **perfect participles** (generally ending in *-d* or *-n*) used in conjunction with the perfect aspect auxiliary HAVE in sentences like 'The referee has *shown/showed* him a red card'; and **passive participles** (also generally ending in *-d* or *-n*) used in conjunction with the passive voice auxiliary BE in sentences like 'He was *shown/showed* a red card by the referee.'

particle/PRT This is an informal term used to describe a range of (typically monosyllabic) items which are invariable in form, and which don't fit easily into traditional systems of grammatical categories. For example, infinitival *to* (e.g. in *Try to be nice!*) is said to be an **infinitive particle**; *of* as used in expressions like *loss of face* is said to be a **case particle**; and *not* and *n't* are said to be **negative particles**. The term is sometimes extended to include prepositions used without a complement (e.g. *down* in *He fell down*).

passive/Passivisation A contrast is traditionally drawn between sentence pairs such as (i) and (ii) below:

(i)   The thieves stole the jewels
(ii) The jewels were stolen by the thieves

(i) is said to be an **active** clause (or sentence), and (ii) to be its **passive** counterpart; similarly, the verb *stole* is said to be an active verb (or a verb in the active **voice**) in (i), whereas the verb *stolen* is said to be a passive verb (or a verb in the passive voice – more specifically, a passive **participle**) in (ii); likewise, the auxiliary *were* in (ii) is said to be a passive **auxiliary. Passivisation** is a movement operation whereby (typically) an expression which is the complement of a verb in the passive participle form becomes the subject of the same clause (as in '*The jewels* were **stolen** – '). In cases of **long Passivisation**, the subject of a complement clause becomes the subject of a higher clause containing a passive participle (as in '*The minister* was **said** – to have lied to Parliament'). See Module 2.4.

past tense See **tense.**

PERF(ect)/PERFP The abbreviation PERF denotes an auxiliary marking perfect aspect, and PERFP denotes a phrase headed by a perfect aspect auxiliary (e.g. *have lied to her* in 'He may *have lied to her*'). See **aspect.**

periphery The periphery of a clause is that part of the clause structure which is positioned above/to the left of the subject. So, in a sentence like

'*Syntax, why do* <u>students</u> struggle to understand it?', all three italicised items that precede the underlined subject are positioned in the clause periphery. See Chapters 4 and 5.

Pers An abbreviation of **person.**

person In traditional grammar, English is said to have three grammatical persons. A **first person** expression (e.g. *I/we*) is one whose reference includes the speaker(s); a **second person** expression (e.g. *you*) is one which excludes the speaker(s) but includes the addressee(s) (i.e. the person or people being spoken to); a **third person** expression (e.g. *he/she/it/they*) is one whose reference excludes both the speaker(s) and the addressee(s) – that is, an expression which refers to someone or something other than the speaker(s) or addressee(s).

personal pronouns These are pronouns which carry inherent **person** properties – for example, first person pronouns such as *I/we*, second person pronouns such as *you*, and third person pronouns such as *he/she/it/they*. In the framework used here, personal pronouns are treated as pronominal DPs. See **person.**

PF/Phonetic Form A PF **representation** is a representation of the phonetic form of an expression. The **PF component** of a grammar is the component which converts the structures generated by the syntactic component of the grammar into PF representations, via a series of morphological and phonological operations. The **PF interface** is the point at which syntactic structures are transferred to the PF component of the grammar: the phrase 'at PF' means 'at the PF interface'.

phi-features/φ-features Person and number features. A **phi-complete** (or **φ-complete**) constituent is one which carries both person and number. See §3.1.1.

phonetic form See **PF** and **interface levels**.

phonetic representation See **representation**.

phrasal adjunct See **adjunct**.

phrase The term **phrase** is used to denote an expression larger than a word which is a **maximal projection**: see **projection**. In traditional grammar, the term refers strictly to non-clausal expressions (Hence, *reading a book* is a phrase, but *He is reading a book* is a clause, not a phrase). However, in the framework used here, clauses are analysed as types of phrases: for example, in the classic analysis of clause structure outlined in Chapter 1, *he will resign* is a tense phrase (TP), and *that he will resign* is a complementiser phrase (CP).

pied-piping A process by which a moved constituent drags one or more other constituents along with it when it moves. For example, if we compare a sentence like *Who were you talking to?* with *To whom were you talking?* we can say that in both cases the pronoun *who(m)* is moved to the front of the sentence, but that in the second sentence the preposition *to* is **pied-piped** along with the pronoun *whom*.

pl/plural A plural expression is one which denotes more than one entity (e.g. *these cars* is a plural expression, whereas *this car* is a singular expression).

polarity A polarity item/expression is a word/phrase (e.g. a word like *ever* or a phrase like *at all* or *care a damn*) which is restricted to occurring within the scope of a negative, interrogative or conditional constituent.

possessive/possessor/possessum A possessive structure is one which indicates possession, like *John's book*. In such structures, the person possessing the item in question (here, *John*) is termed the possessor, and the possessed object (here, *book*) is termed the possessum. On the structure of phrases like *John's book/your book* see §7.3.1.

PP See **prepositional phrase**.

pragmatics The study of how non-linguistic knowledge is integrated with linguistic knowledge in our use of language.

precede(nce) To say that one constituent precedes another is to say that it is positioned to its left (on the printed page) and that neither constituent contains the other. Precedence is left-to-right linear ordering.

predicate See **argument**.

premodifier A premodifier is a constituent which precedes and modifies some other constituent (e.g. *fervently* is a premodifier of the VP *believe in equality* in 'We all do fervently believe in equality').

prepose/preposing Preposing is an informal term to denote a movement operation by which a given expression is fronted – that is, moved to the front of some phrase, clause or sentence.

preposition/P A preposition is a word used to indicate notions such as direction (as in 'He went *to* Paris'), time (as in 'I met her *on* Friday'), place (as in 'She lives *in* a big house'), or means (as in 'He was killed *with* an axe'). In English, it is a characteristic property of prepositions that they are invariable, and that they can be modified by *straight/right* if they have an appropriate meaning (as in 'She went <u>straight</u> *to* the police'). Where a preposition has a nominal or pronominal complement, it is said to be **transitive**; in other uses, it is said to be **intransitive**. Hence *down* is a transitive preposition in *He fell down the stairs*, but an intransitive preposition in *He fell down*.

prepositional phrase/PP A phrase whose head is a preposition – for example, *in town, on Sunday, to the market, for someone else*, etc.

pres Abbreviation for present tense: See **tense**.

principle See **constraint**.

Principle of Unambiguous Reverse Engineering/PURE A principle devised by Pesetsky (2020: 5) specifying that 'When determining the identity of unpronounced material in the course of reverse-engineering a speaker's syntactic derivation, the language system of the hearer considers only the minimally semantically contentful possibilities compatible with the morphosyntactic environment': see §7.2.1.

PRO A null case pronoun (known informally as 'big PRO', because it is written in capital letters) which represents the understood subject of an infinitive complement of a **control** predicate, for example, in a structure such as *John decided* PRO *to leave*, where PRO refers back to *John*.

pro A null pronoun (known informally as 'little pro' because it is written in lower case letters). One type of *pro* is the understood null subject of a finite clause in an Italian sentence like '*pro* piovera domani' (= 'It will.rain tomorrow'). Another type of *pro* is the null third person object found in recipe registers, for example, 'Divide *pro* into four': see §7.5.3.

probe When a head is **active**, it serves as a probe which searches for a suitable goal within its complement (where the goal is a constituent which it can agree with, or case-mark, or attract to move to the edge of its projection): see §3.1.1. On the **Probe Condition**, see **active**.

PROG(ressive)/PROGP PROG denotes an auxiliary marking progressive aspect: PROGP denotes a progressive aspect phrase (like *be lying* in 'He may *be lying*'). See **aspect**; see also §6.1.1.

project(ion) A projection is a constituent containing or comprising a head word. For example, a noun phrase/NP such as *students of Linguistics* is a projection of its head noun *students* (equivalently, we can say that the noun *students* here projects into the NP *students of linguistics*). A **minimal projection** is a constituent which is not a projection of some other constituent: hence, heads (e.g. words) are minimal projections. An **intermediate projection** is a constituent which is larger than a word, but smaller than a full phrase (e.g. *is working* in *He is working*). A **maximal projection** is a constituent which is not contained within any larger constituent with the same head. So, for example, in a sentence like 'I've heard several *accounts of what happened*', the italicised noun phrase *accounts of what happened* is a maximal projection (an NP), since it is a projection of the noun *accounts* but is not contained within any larger projection of the noun *accounts* (if we assume that *several accounts of what happened* is a quantifier phrase/QP headed by the quantifier *several*). By contrast, in a sentence such as 'I've heard several *accounts*', the italicised noun *accounts* is both a minimal projection (by virtue of not being a projection of some other head) and a maximal projection (by virtue of not being contained within any larger structure which has the same head noun): hence *accounts* here can be analysed as an NP.

pronoun The word *pronoun* is composed of two morphemes – namely *pro* (meaning 'on behalf of') and *noun*: hence, a pronoun is traditionally said to be a word used in place of a noun expression. Pronouns differ from nouns in that they have no intrinsic descriptive content, and so are function words. There are a range of different types of pronoun found in English, including the pronominal NP *one(s)* used in sentences like *I'll take the red one(s)*, pronominal QPs like *any* in *I couldn't find any*, and pronominal DPs like *this* in *This is hard*. The term pronoun is most frequently used to indicate a class of items (like *he/him/his*) traditionally referred to as **personal pronouns** (though they are analysed in this book as pronominal DPs).

proposition This is a term used to describe the semantic content (i.e. meaning) of a sentence. For example, we might say that the sentence *Does John smoke?* questions the truth of the proposition that 'John smokes'. See **argument**.

prosodic account This is an account of abbreviated registers of English which (as outlined in **Module 7.2**) makes the following assumptions about reduced/abbreviated clauses:

(i) Reduced clauses have the same full syntactic structure as their unreduced counterparts

(ii) A continuous sequence of one or more weak syllables at the beginning of a prosodic phrase (e.g. a sentence) can undergo ellipsis at PF

pseudo-cleft sentence A sentence such as 'What he hated most was *syntax*', where *syntax* is said to occupy **focus position** within the overall sentence.

PURE An abbreviation of the **Principle of Unambitious Reverse Engineering.**

Q/QP See **quantifier.**

quantifier A quantifier/Q is a type of word used to denote quantity. Typical quantifiers include the universal quantifiers *all/both*, the free choice quantifiers *any/ whatever* (as in *You can choose any/whatever book you like*), the distributive quantifiers *each/every*, the partitive quantifiers *some/any*, etc. A **quantifier phrase/QP** is a phrase whose head is a quantifier – for example, an expression such as *many people*, or *few of the students*. The **QP Hypothesis** of §1.3.1 posits that all indefinite nominal arguments are QPs, headed by an overt or null quantifier. In this book, quantificational pronouns like *someone/anything/everyone* are taken to be pronominal QPs.

quantifier floating/stranding See **floating quantifier.**

question This refers to a type of sentence which is used to ask whether something is true, or to ask about the identity of some entity. See **yes–no question** and **wh-question.**

raising The term raising is used in two senses. In its most general sense, it denotes any movement operation which involves moving some constituent from a lower to a higher position in a structure. However, it also has a more specific sense, indicating a particular kind of

A-Movement operation (sometimes called **Subject Raising**) by which an expression is moved from being the subject of one clause to becoming the subject of another. The term **raising predicate** denotes a word like *seem* whose subject is raised out of subject position in an infinitival complement clause to become subject of the (TP constituent in the) *seem* clause. See Module 2.5.

realis A realis clause is one used to describe a real state of affairs, and typically contains an (auxiliary or non-auxiliary) verb which is **indicative** in **mood**, like the italicised verbs in 'He *cheats/cheated* at cards.'

Recoverability Condition This is a condition proposed in Chomsky (1964b: 41) and Katz & Postal (1964: 79) to the effect that a constituent which is present in the syntax can only be deleted/ellipsed/ unpronounced/null if its semantic content is recoverable.

recursion A structure involves recursion if it contains more than one instance of a particular category. For example, **CP recursion** structures are clauses which contain more than one CP projection in their periphery, like the clause italicised in 'He said [*that* [*unless she does as he says* [*that he will tell her father*]]]', which contains three bracketed CPs. See §4.1.1.

reduced See **abbreviated.**

reflexive See **anaphor.**

REL/relative/RELP In a sentence such as 'He's someone [*who you can trust*]', the bracketed clause is said to be a **relative clause** because it 'relates to' (i.e. modifies) the pronoun *someone*. The pronoun *who* which introduces the clause is said to be a **relative pronoun**, since it 'relates to' the expression *someone* (in the sense that *who* refers back to *someone*). **Restrictive relative clauses** serve the function of restricting the class of entities referred to by the antecedent to those which have the property described in the relative clause: for example, in a sentence like 'I need to work with people *who I can trust*', the italicised restrictive relative clause restricts the class of people referred to in the sentence to those trusted by me. Under the analysis in §5.4.2, a relative clause like that italicised in 'the film *which I watched*' is treated as a RELP/relative projection, with a REL head which has a relative operator (here, the relative pronoun *which*) as its specifier.

Relativised Minimality Condition See **Minimality Condition**.

representation A syntactic **representation** is a notation/device (typically, a tree diagram or labelled bracketing) used to represent the syntactic structure of an expression (i.e. the way in which it is structured out of words and phrases): a **semantic representation** is a representation of linguistic aspects of the meaning of an expression; a **PF representation** or **phonetic representation** is a representation of the phonetic form of an expression, specifying how it is pronounced.

restrictive relative clause See **relative clause**.

resumptive A sentence such as:

(i)   *Behaviour like that*, we simply cannot tolerate **it** in this school

involves an italicised **topic** followed by a comment. The relevance of the comment to the topic is ensured by using the **resumptive pronoun** *it* to 'resume' or 'reprise' (i.e. refer back to) the topic *this kind of behaviour*, so ensuring that the comment is relevant to the topic.

root The root of a tree is the topmost node in the tree. A **root clause** is a free-standing clause, that is, a clause which is not contained within another clause (or phrase). In traditional grammar, a root clause is termed a **principal clause**, **independent clause**, or **main clause**. By contrast, an **embedded clause** is a clause which is contained within some larger expression; and a **complement clause** is an embedded clause which is used as the complement of some item. So, in a sentence such as *I think he loves you*, the *think* clause (i.e. the expression *I think he loves you*) is a root clause, whereas the *loves* clause (i.e. the expression *he loves you*) is an embedded clause. Moreover, the *loves* clause is also a complement clause since it serves as the complement of the verb *think*.

scope The scope of an expression is the set of constituents which it modifies or which fall within (what we might informally call) its 'sphere of influence'. For example, a sentence like *He cannot be telling the truth* has a meaning paraphrasable as 'It is not possible that he is telling the truth', and in such a sentence the negative *not* is said to have scope over the modal auxiliary *can* (or to have **wide scope** with respect to *can*), and conversely *can* is said to fall within the scope of *not,* or to have **narrow scope** with respect to *not*. By contrast, a sentence such as *You mustn't tell lies* has a meaning paraphraseable as 'It is necessary that you not tell lies', and in such a sentence, the auxiliary *must* is said to have scope over the negative particle *n't* (or to have **wide scope** with respect to *n't*).

second person See **person.**

select(ion)/selectional/selector When a word has a particular type of complement, it is said to **select** (i.e. 'take' or 'allow') the relevant type of complement, and the relevant phenomenon is referred to as **(complement-) selection.** For example, we can say that the word *expect* has the **selectional property** that it can select an infinitive complement (e.g. in structures like 'They expect *to win*'). In this structure, the verb *expect* is the **selector** for the infinitive complement *to win*, in the sense that *expect* is the item which selects *to win* as its complement. **Selection restrictions** are restrictions which predicates impose on their choice of arguments: for example, the verb *think* requires an animate/rational subject.

semantics/semantic component
Semantics is the study of linguistic aspects of meaning. The **semantic component** of a grammar is the component which maps/converts syntactic structures into semantic representations. See **representation.**

sentence This term is usually used to denote a **root** <u>clause</u> – that is, a free-standing clause which is not contained within some larger expression. See **root.**

sg See **singular.**

silent See **null.**

singular A singular expression is one which denotes a single entity (e.g. *this car* is a **singular/sg** expression, whereas *these cars* is a **plural/pl** expression).

Sluicing A form of **ellipsis** in which the material following an interrogative wh-constituent is given a silent pronunciation – as with the material following *when* (marked by strikethrough) in 'I remembered that he was leaving, but forgot *when* ~~he was leaving~~.'

spec See **specifier.** Terms like **spec-CP/spec-TP** (etc.) denote the specifier of **CP/TP.**

specifier/spec The grammatical function fulfilled by certain types of constituent which precede the head of their containing phrase. For example, in a preposition phrase/PP such as *straight through the window*, the preposition *through* is the head of the PP, *the window* is the complement of *through*, and *straight* is the specifier of the (PP headed by the) preposition *through*.

spellout The pronunciation of an expression: for example, to say that an item has a **null spellout** is to say that it is 'silent' and so is unpronounced. **Discontinuous spellout** (also termed **split spellout**) is a phenomenon which arises when part of a moved phrase is spelled out on a lower copy of a moved constituent, and the remainder on the highest copy – as in '*How much do you believe of what he tells you?*', where the wh-phrase *how much of what he tells you* moves to the front of the sentence, with *how much* being spelled out in the position it moves to, and *of what he tells you* being spelled out in the position in which it originates. The **Default Spellout Rule** of §1.4.1 specifies that where the spellout of a constituent is not determined in some other way, the highest copy of the constituent is pronounced at PF, and any lower copies are silent. The **Low Spellout Rule** of §2.3.3 specifies that a KP/PP/CP which is the lowest/rightmost constituent of a larger phrase that undergoes movement can be spelled out on a lower copy of the moved phrase. The **Floating Quantifier Spellout Rule** of §6.4.2 specifies that floatable quantifiers can be spelled out on any non-initial link of an A-Movement chain in standard varieties of English.

split projection A split projection analysis is one in which a structure that was traditionally analysed as comprising a single phrase becomes reanalysed in subsequent work as comprising a number of separate phrases. For example, the traditional CP constituent is split up into (inter alia) FORCEP, TOPP, FOCP, MODP and FINP constituents in more recent **Cartographic** work. See Chapters 4–7.

split spellout See **spellout**.

stack/stacking Stacking is a process by which more than one constituent of the same type can be used to modify some other constituent. For example, an NP like *head of state* can be modified by numerous different APs/adjectival phrases in an expression like 'a *very sensitive, rather tall, really dark, incredibly handsome* head of state'. In this particular example, four different (italicised) APs are said to have been stacked on top of/to the left of the NP/noun phrase *head of state*.

stem The stem form of a word is the base form to which inflectional affixes are added. So, a verb form like *going* comprises the stem *go* and the inflectional suffix -*ing*.

stranded quantifier See **floating quantifier**.

string A continuous sequence of words contained within the same phrase or sentence. For example, in the sentence 'They hate syntax', the sequences *They hate, hate syntax* and *They hate syntax* are all strings – but *They syntax* is not.

Structure Dependence Principle A traditional grammatical principle (mentioned in §1.3.2) requiring that syntactic operations be sensitive to hierarchical relations between constituents – and to the relation **c-command** in particular.

SUBJ/SUBJP In work discussed in §6.1.2, the criterial position for a subject is taken to be the specifier position in a SUBJP/subject projection with an abstract SUBJ head.

subject The subject of a clause is a nominal or pronominal expression which is normally positioned between a complementiser and an (auxiliary or non-auxiliary) verb. Syntactic characteristics of subjects include the fact that they can trigger agreement with auxiliaries (as in 'The president **is** lying', where the auxiliary *is* agrees with the subject *the president*), and they can be inverted with auxiliaries in main clause questions (as in 'Is *the president* lying?', where the auxiliary *is* has been inverted with the subject *the president*).

Subject Drop A phenomenon whereby the subject of a finite clause can be dropped/omitted in abbreviated registers of English. For example, in spoken English, we frequently find sentences like *can't find my phone*, where the bracketed subject *I* is omitted. See Module 7.1.

subjunctive In a (formal style) sentence such as 'The judge ordered that he *be* detained indefinitely', the passive auxiliary verb *be* is traditionally said to be in the subjunctive **mood**, since although it has exactly the same form as the infinitive form *be* (e.g. in infinitive structures such as 'To *be* or not to *be* – that is the question'), it has a

nominative subject *he*, and hence is a **finite** verb form.

subperiphery/subperipheral The subperiphery of a clause comprises that part of the clause structure positioned above the verb phrase but below the periphery: in the traditional CP+TP+VP model of clause structure, it corresponds to the TP layer. A subperipheral constituent is one positioned in the subperiphery of the clause (i.e. on the edge of TP in the traditional CP+TP+VP model): see Chapter 6.

successive-cyclic movement Movement in a succession of short steps (e.g. one clause at a time). See §1.5.2.

suffix See **affix**.

T This denotes a tense-marking constituent containing either a tensed auxiliary, or an abstract tense affix, or a nonfinite tense particle like infinitival *to*. A phrase headed by a T constituent is labelled **TP. T-to-C Movement** is movement of an auxiliary verb from the head T position of TP into the head C position of CP – as with the italicised inverted auxiliary in '*Is* it raining?' See §1.4.3.

tag A string usually consisting of an auxiliary and a subject pronoun which is 'tagged' (i.e. added) onto the end of a sentence. Thus, the italicised string is the tag in the following: 'The president is working, *is(n't) he*?', and the overall sentence is known as a **tag question/tag sentence**. The tag usually contains a copy of the auxiliary in the main clause (which may or may not carry the negative suffix *n't*), and a pronominal copy of the subject.

tense/tensed (Auxiliary and main) verbs which are in the indicative **mood** in English show a binary (two-way) tense contrast, traditionally said to be between **present tense** forms and **past tense** forms. Thus, in 'John *hates* syntax', *hates* is a present tense verb form, whereas in 'John *hated* syntax', *hated* is a past tense verb form. This present/past tense distinction correlates with time reference, so that (for example) past tense verbs typically describe an event taking place in the past, whereas present tense verbs typically describe an event taking place in the present (or future). However, the correlation is an imperfect one, since for example, in a sentence such as 'If you *went* to Paris, you'd have a great time', the verb *went* carries the past tense inflection *-t* (found on past tense verbs like *left*) but does not denote past time (but instead denotes a hypothetical event). A tensed (auxiliary or non-auxiliary) verb form is one which carries (present/past) **tense** – for example, *is, could, hates, went,* etc. By extension, a tensed clause is one containing a tensed auxiliary or main verb.

Tense Deficit Hypothesis An account of BE **Drop** which (as outlined in §7.4.3) posits that:

BE Drop clauses are truncated SUBJP constituents with a tense deficit, which means that BE receives a null spellout by default, and its subject receives default case. On one view, BE Drop clauses contain a TP whose head T contains an affix with an unvalued tense feature; on another view, they lack both TP and DP projections, and have NP subjects.

THEME The name of a specific **theta role** (sometimes also termed PATIENT) representing the entity undergoing the effect of some action (e.g. *Harry* in 'William teased *Harry*'). See §2.2.2.

theta/θ A **theta role/θ-role/thematic role** is the semantic role played by an argument in relation to its predicate (e.g. AGENT, THEME, GOAL, etc.). For example, in a sentence like *William teased Harry*, the verb *tease* assigns the θ-role AGENT to its subject *William* and the theta role THEME to its complement *Harry*. A **theta-position/θ-position** is a position to which a theta role is assigned; a **theta-bar/θ-bar position** is a position to which no theta role is assigned. To say that a predicate **theta-marks** its arguments is to say that it determines the theta role played by each of its arguments. The **Theta Criterion/θ-Criterion** is a principle of Universal Grammar which specifies that each argument should bear one and only one theta role, and that each theta role associated with a given predicate should be assigned to one and only one argument. See Module 2.2.

third person See **person**.

TOP/TOPP TOP denotes a topic particle; TOPP denotes a topic

projection in the periphery of a
clause which contains a topic as its
specifier. See **topic**.

topic/Topicalisation/Topic Drop In a
dialogue such as the following:

SPEAKER A: I've been having
problems with the Fantasy
Syntax seminar
SPEAKER B: *That kind of course*, very
few students seem to get their
heads round

the italicised expression *that kind
of course* serves as the topic of the
sentence produced by speaker B, in
the sense that it refers back to *the
Fantasy Syntax seminar* mentioned by
the previous speaker: more generally,
an expression which represents 'old'
or 'familiar' information is said to be
a topic. **Topicalisation** is a movement
operation by which a constituent is
moved into the periphery of a clause
to mark it as a topic: see Module
4.1 and Module 4.2. **Topic Drop** is
an account of how a third person
pronoun can undergo Topicalisation
in the syntax and move into the
specifier position in a TOPP/topic
projection, and thereafter be given a
silent spellout in the phonology: see
§7.5.1.

TP Tense projection/tense phrase –
that is, a phrase headed by a tense-
marked auxiliary, or by an abstract
tense affix (*Af*), or by an infinitival
tense particle.

trace A **trace** of a moved constituent
is a (usually null) copy left behind
(as a result of movement) in each
position out of which a constituent
moves. See also **COMP-Trace Filter**.

transitive A word is traditionally
said to be transitive (in a given
use) if it assigns **accusative** case
to a noun or pronoun expression
which it immediately precedes and
c-commands: See **case**. So, *likes* in
'John *likes* him' is a transitive verb,
since it assigns accusative case
to its complement *him*. Likewise,
in is a transitive preposition in
'people have little faith *in* him'.
And similarly, infinitival *for* is a
transitive complementiser, since
it assigns accusative case to the
subject of its infinitive complement
(as in 'I'm keen [for *him* to
participate more actively]'). A verb
or complementiser is **intransitive**
(in a particular structure) if it
does not assign accusative case
to any constituent in the relevant
structure.

truncated/Truncation A truncated
clause is one which does not project
all the way up to FORCEP, but
rather only as far as (for example)
TOPP, or FINP, or SUBJP, and
consequently lacks one or more of
the peripheral projections found in
complete clauses (i.e. clauses that
contain FORCEP). In **Module 7.1**,
Truncation is given the following
characteristion (based on work by
Rizzi (1994, 1998, 2000a):

(i) A sentence can have a truncated
syntactic structure whose root
is not FORCEP, but some lower
projection such as SUBJP
(ii) The edge of the highest
projection in a sentence
structure can be unpronounced

in the PF component,
provided that it contains only
phonetically weak material with
recoverable semantic content

T-to-C movement See **T.**

two-place predicate A predicate which
has two arguments – for example,
tease in *William teased Harry* where
the two arguments of the predicate
tease are *William* and *Harry*. See
argument.

UG See **Universal Grammar.**

unaccusative An unaccusative
predicate is a word like *come* whose
superficial subject originates as its
complement. See Module 2.3.

unergative An unergative predicate is
a verb like *groan* in a sentence such
as 'He was *groaning*' which has an
AGENT subject but no overt object:
see §2.3.2.

**Uniform Theta Assignment
Hypothesis/UTAH** A hypothesis
(developed by Baker 1988) which
maintains that each theta role
assigned by a particular kind of
predicate is canonically associated
with a specific syntactic position:
for example, the complement
position is the canonical position
for a THEME argument. See §2.3.2.

uninterpretable Features are
uninterpretable if they have no
semantic content and hence play no
role in determining meaning. See
§3.1.3.

Universal Grammar/UG This term
denotes (a theoretical model of,
or the study of) those aspects of
grammar which are hypothesised to
be universal.

UTAH See **Uniform Theta Assignment
Hypothesis.**

V/VP See **verb/V** and **verb phrase/VP.**

value In relation to a feature such as
[Singular-Number], **number** is said
to be an **attribute** (and represents
the property being described) and
singular its value.

variety A particular (e.g. geographical
or social) form of a language.

verb/V A category of word which
has the morphological property
that it can carry a specific range of
inflections (e.g. the verb *show* can
carry past tense *-d*, third person
singular present tense *-s*, perfect *-n*
and progressive *-ing*, giving rise to
shows/showed/shown/showing), and
the syntactic property that it can
head the complement of infinitival
to (as in 'Do you want to *show* me?')

verb phrase/VP A phrase which is
headed by a verb – for example, the
italicised phrase in 'They will *help
you*'.

voice See **passive.** A VOICEP
constituent is a voice phrase headed
by a VOICE constituent like the
passive auxiliary BE: see §6.1.1.

VP See **verb phrase.** A VP-adverb is
an adverb which adjoins to a VP to
form an even larger VP (e.g. in *He
may have completely forgotten what
you asked*, the adverb *completely*
is adjoined to the VP *forgotten
what you asked*). On **VP Ellipsis**,
see **ellipsis.** On **VP adjunct**, see
adjunct.

**VP-Internal Subject Hypothesis/
VPISH** The hypothesis that subjects
originate internally within the verb
phrase, and from there move to the

criterial subject position (in spec-TP/ spec-SUBJP): see Module 2.1.

wh This is widely used as a feature carried by constituents which undergo Wh-Movement – for example, the relative pronoun *who* in *someone who I think is lying* can be described as a wh-pronoun, as can the interrogative pronoun *who* in *Who are you waiting for?* and the exclamative quantifier *what* in *What a great time we had!* See Chapter 5.

wh-constituent A constituent containing or comprising a **wh-word**.

Wh-Movement A type of movement operation whereby a **wh-constituent** is moved into the periphery of some clause (e.g. to the front of the overall sentence in '*Where* has he gone?').

wh-operator See **operator**.

wh-phrase A phrase containing a **wh-word** (e.g. *what kind of person* in *What kind of person is she?*).

wh-question A question which contains an interrogative **wh-word**, for example, *What are you doing?* On **wh-question operator**, see **operator**.

wh-word A word which begins with **wh** (e.g. *who/what/which/where/ when/why*), or which has a similar syntax to *wh*-words (e.g. *how*).

X A symbol used to denote any type of constituent which is a head (e.g. P, A, ADV, D, Q, T, C, etc.)

X-bar Syntax A theory of syntactic structure which posits that there are X-bar constituents larger than words but smaller than phrases: see **bar**.

XP A symbol used to denote any type of constituent which is a phrase/ maximal projection (e.g. PP, ADVP, AP, DP, QP, TP, CP, etc.).

yes–no question operator See **operator**.

YNQ An abbreviation of yes–no question. For example Op_{YNQ} denotes an abstract yes–no question operator: see **operator** and §1.4.3.

References

The references below include all items referred to in the book and the accompanying Answerbooks.

Abbott, B. 1993. A pragmatic account of the definiteness effect in existential sentences. *Journal of Pragmatics* 19: 39–55.

Abeillé, A. & Godard, D. 1999. A lexical approach to quantifier floating in French. In *Lexical and Constructional Aspects of Linguistic Explanation*, G. Webelhuth, J.-P. Koenig & A. Kathol (eds.) 81–96. Stanford, CA: CSLI Publications.

Abels, K. 2007. Deriving selectional properties of 'exclamative' predicates. In *Interfaces and Interface Conditions*, A. Späth (ed.) 115–40. Berlin: De Gruyter.

——2010. Factivity in exclamatives is a presupposition. *Studia Linguistica* 64: 141–57.

——2012. The Italian left periphery: A view from locality. *Linguistic Inquiry* 43: 229–54.

Abney, S. P. 1987. The English noun phrase in its sentential aspect. PhD diss. MIT.

Aboh, E. O. 2004 *The Morphosyntax of Complement-Head Sequences*. Oxford: Oxford University Press.

——2005. Deriving relative and factive constructions in Kwa. In *Proceedings of the XXX Incontro di Grammatica Generativa*,

L. Brugé, G. Giusti, N. Munaro, W. Schweikert & G. Turano (eds.) 265–85. Venice: Cafoscarina.

——2006. Complementation in Saramaccan and Gungbe: The case of C-type modal particles. *Natural Language and Linguistic Theory* 24: 1–55.

——2007. Focused versus non-focused wh-phrases. In *Focus Strategies in African Languages*, E. O. Aboh, K. Hartmann & M. Zimmermann (eds.) 287–314. Berlin: Mouton de Gruyter.

——2010. Information structuring begins with numeration. *Iberia* 2: 12–42.

——2016. Information structure: A Cartographic perspective. In *The Oxford Handbook of Information Structure*, C. Féry & S. Ishihara (eds.) 147–64. Oxford: Oxford University Press.

Aboh, E. & Pfau, R. 2010. What's a *wh*-word got to do with it? In *The Cartography of Syntactic Structures, Vol. 5: Mapping the left periphery*, P. Benincà & N. Munaro (eds.) 91–124. Oxford: Oxford University Press.

Ackema, P. 2010. Restrictions on subject extraction: A PF

interface account. In *Interfaces in Linguistics: New Research Perspectives*, R. Folli & C Ulbrich (eds.) 225–41. Oxford: Oxford University Press.

Ackema, P. & Neeleman, A. 2003. Context-sensitive spell-out. *Natural Language and Linguistic Theory* 21: 681–735.

Ackerman, L., Frazier, M. & Yoshida, M. 2014. Resumptive pronouns salvage island violations in forced-choice tasks. Poster presented to the 27th Annual CUNY Conference on Human Sentence Processing, Ohio State University, 14 March.

Adger, D. 2003. *Core Syntax: A minimalist approach*. Oxford: Oxford University Press.

——2007. Three domains of finiteness: A minimalist perspective. In *Finiteness: Theoretical and empirical foundations*, I. Nikolaeva (ed.) 23–58. Oxford: Oxford University Press.

Adger, D. & Ramchand, G. 2005. Merge and Move: Wh-dependencies revisited. *Linguistic Inquiry* 36: 161–93.

Åfarli, T. 1989. Passive in Norwegian and in English. *Linguistic Inquiry* 20: 101–8.

——1994. A promotion analysis of restrictive relative clauses. *The Linguistic Review* 11: 81–100.

Åfarli, T. & Creider, Ch. 1987. Nonsubject Pro-Drop in Norwegian. *Linguistic Inquiry* 18: 339–45.

Aikhenvald, A. Y. 2010. *Imperatives and commands*. New York: Oxford University Press.

Akiyama, M. 1994. On quantifier floating. *English Linguistics* 11: 100–22.

Akiyama, T. 2002. The infinitival relative clause in English: An analysis based on the British National Corpus. PhD diss. Lancaster University.

Akmajian, A. 1979. *Aspects of the Grammar of Focus in English*. New York: Garland.

Akmajian, A., Demers, R. A. & Harnish, R. H. 1985. *Linguistics*, 2nd ed. Cambridge, MA: MIT Press.

Alami, L. 2011. Word order, agreement and resumption in the Tashelhit variety of Berber. PhD diss. University of Essex.

Alamillo, A. R. & Schwenter, S. A. 2007. Null objects and neuter *lo*: A cross-dialectal variationist analysis. In *Selected Proceedings of the Third Workshop on Spanish Sociolinguistics*, J. Holmquist, A. Lorenzino & L. Sayahi (eds.) 113–21. Somerville, MA: Cascadilla Proceedings Project.

Al-Bataineh, H. 2020. Exclamatives are nonsententials: Evidence from Arabic and other languages. Ms. Memorial University of Newfoundland.

Alcázar, A. & Saltarelli, M. 2014. *The Syntax of Imperatives*. Cambridge: Cambridge University Press.

Alexiadou, A. 1994. Issues in the syntax of adverbs. PhD diss. University of Potsdam.

——1997. *Adverb Placement: A case study in asymmetric syntax*. Amsterdam: Benjamins.

Alexiadou, A. & Anagnastopoulou, E. 1998. Parametrizing Agr: Word-order, V-movement, and EPP-checking. *Natural Language and Linguistic Theory* 16: 491–539.

——1999. Raising without infinitives and the nature of agreement. *Proceedings of the West Coast Conference on Formal Linguistics* 18: 15–25.

——2001. The subject-in-situ generalization and the role of case in driving computations. *Linguistic Inquiry* 32: 193–231.

Alexiadou, A., Anagnostopoulou, E. & Schäfer, F. 2015. *External Arguments in Transitivity Alternations: A layering approach.* Oxford: Oxford University Press.

——2018. Passive. In *Syntactic Structures After 60 Years: The impact of the Chomskyan revolution in linguistics*, N. Hornstein, H. Lasnik, P. Patel-Grosz & C. Yang (eds.). Berlin: De Gruyter Mouton.

Alexiadou, A., Iordăchioaia, G. & Marchis, M. 2012. In support of long-distance agree. In *Local Modeling of Non-local Dependencies*, A. Alexiadou, G, Müller & T. Kiss (eds.) 55–81: Tübingen: Niemeyer.

Alexiadou, A., Law, P., Meinunger, A. & Wilder, C. (eds.) 2000. *The Syntax of Relative Clauses.* Amsterdam: Benjamins.

Alexiadou, A., & Schäfer, F. 2013. *Non-Canonical Passives.* Amsterdam: Benjamins.

Alexiadou, A. & Wilder, C. (eds.) 1998. *Possessors, Predicates and Movement in the Determiner Phrase.* Amsterdam: Benjamins.

Alexopoulou, T. 2006. Resumption in relative clauses. *Natural Language and Linguistic Theory* 24: 57–111.

——2010. Truly intrusive: Resumptive pronominals in questions and relative clauses. *Lingua* 120: 485–505.

Alexopoulou, T. & Keller, F. 2002. Resumption and locality: A crosslinguistic experimental study. *Chicago Linguistic Society Proceedings* 38: 1–14.

——2007. Locality, cyclicity and resumption: At the interface between the grammar and the human sentence processor. *Language* 83: 110–60.

Al Khalaf, E. 2019. Floating quantifiers are autonomous phrases: A movement analysis. *Glossa* 4(1): 89, 1–23.

Allerton, D. J. 1975. Deletion and proform reduction. *Journal of Linguistics* 11: 213–37.

Ambar, M. 1999. Aspects of the syntax of focus in Portuguese. In *The Grammar of Focus*, G. Rebuschi & L. Tuller (eds.) 23–54. Amsterdam: Benjamins.

——2002. Wh-questions and wh-exclamatives unifying mirror effects. In *Romance Languages and Linguistic Theory 2000: Selected papers from 'Going Romance 2000'*, C. Beyssade, R. Bok-Bennema, F. Drijkoningen, & P. Monachesi (eds.) 15–40. Amsterdam: Benjamins.

——2007. Verb Movement and tense: EPP and T-completeness. In

Proceedings of the XXXII Incontro di Grammatica Generativa, M. C. Picchi & A. Pona (eds.) 1–20. Alessandria: Edizioni dell'Orso.

Amritavalli, R. 2013. Separating tense and finiteness: Anchoring in Dravidian. *Natural Language & Linguistic Theory* 32: 283–306.

Anagnastopoulou, E., van Riemsdijk, H. & Zwarts, F. 1997 (eds.). *Materials on Left Dislocation*. Amsterdam: Benjamins.

Andersen, G. 1995. Omission of the primary verbs BE and HAVE in London teenage speech: A sociolinguistic study. MA thesis. University of Bergen.

Anderson, J. 1977. *On Case Grammar*. London: Croom Helm.

——2007. Finiteness, mood and morphosyntax. *Journal of Linguistics* 43: 1–32.

Angelopoulos, N., Collins, C. & Terzi, A. 2020. Greek and English passives and the role of *by*-phrases. *Glossa* 5: 90, 1–29.

Aoun, J. 2000. Resumption and last resort. *Documentação de Estudos em Lingüística Teórica e Aplicada* 16: 13–43.

Aoun, J., Choueiri, L. & Hornstein, N. 2001. Resumption, movement, and derivational economy. *Linguistic Inquiry* 32: 371–403.

Aoun, J. & Li, Y. A. 2003. *Essays on the Representational and Derivational Nature of Grammar*. Cambridge, MA: MIT Press.

Armenante, G. & Braun, J. 2022. Fake past in conditionals and attitude reports: A crosslinguistic correlation. In *Proceedings of Linguistic Evidence 2020: Linguistic theory enriched by experimental data*, R. Hörnig, S. von Weitersheim, A. Konietsko & S. Featherston (eds.). 519–40. Tübingen: University of Tübingen.

Arnold, D. J. 2004. Non-restrictive relative clauses in construction-based HPSG. In *Proceedings of the 11th International Conference on Head-Driven Phrase Structure Grammar*, S. Müller (ed.) 27–47. Stanford, CA: CSLI publications.

——2007. Non-restrictive relatives are not orphans. *Journal of Linguistic* 43: 271–309.

Arregi, K. 2016. Focus projection theories. In *The Oxford Handbook of Information Structure*, C. Féry & S. Ishihara (eds.) 185–202. Oxford: Oxford University Press.

Arregi, K. & Nevins, A. 2012. *Morphotactics: Basque auxiliaries and the structure of spellout.* Dordrecht: Springer.

Arteaga, D. 1998. On null objects in Old French. In *Romance Linguistics: Theoretical perspectives*, A. Schwegler, B. Tranel & M. Uribe-Etxebarria (eds.) 1–12. Amsterdam: Benjamins.

Asudeh, A. 2002. Richard III. *Chicago Linguistic Society Proceedings* 38: 31–46.

——2004. Resumption as resource management. PhD diss. Stanford University.

——2011a. Towards a unified theory of resumption. In *Resumptive Pronouns at the Interfaces*, A. Rouveret (ed.) 121–87. Amsterdam: Benjamins.

——2011b. Copy Raising and formal variation. Handout for talk at University of Edinburgh, 24 November.

——2012. *The Logic of Pronominal Resumption*. Oxford: Oxford University Press.

Asudeh, A. & Toivonen, I. 2006. Expletives and the syntax and semantics of Copy Raising. In *Proceedings of the LFG08 Conference*, M. Butt & T. H. King (eds.) 68–88. Stanford, CA: CSLI Publications.

——2007. Copy Raising and its consequences for perception reports. In *Architectures, Rules, and Preferences: Variations on themes* by Joan W Bresnan, A. Zaenen, J. Simpson, T. H. King, J. Grimshaw, J. Maling & C. Manning (eds.) 49–67. Stanford, CA: CSLI Publications.

——2012. Copy Raising and Perception. *Natural Language and Linguistic Theory* 30: 321–80.

Authier, J.-M. 1988. Null object construction in Kinande. *Natural Language and Linguistic Theory* 6: 19–37.

——1989. Arbitrary null objects and unselective binding. In *The Null Subject Parameter*, O. Jaeggli & K. Safir (eds.) 45–67. Dordrecht: Reidel.

——1992. Iterated CPs and embedded Topicalization. *Linguistic Inquiry* 23: 329–36.

Authier, J.-M. & Haegeman, L. 2016. On the syntax and semantics of Mirative Focus Fronting in French. Ms. Pennsylvania State University and Ghent University.

Authier, J.-M. & Reed, L. 2005. The diverse nature of non-interrogative Wh. *Linguistic Inquiry* 36: 635–47.

——2009. False negatives on Agentivity: The case of *get*-passives. Unpublished paper, Pennsylvania State University.

Aygen-Tosun, G. 1998. The split INFL hypothesis in Turkish. MA thesis. Boğaziçi University.

Badan, L. 2007. High and low periphery: A comparison between Italian and Chinese. PhD diss. University of Padua.

Badan, L. & Cheng, L. 2015. Exclamatives in Mandarin Chinese. *Journal of East Asian Linguistics* 24: 383–413.

Badan, L. & Crocco, C. 2019. Focus in Italian echo wh-questions: An analysis at syntax-prosody interface. *Probus* 31: 29–73.

Badan, L. & Del Gobbo, F. 2010. On the syntax of topic and focus in Chinese. In *The Cartography of Syntactic Structures, Vol. 5: Mapping the left periphery*, P. Benincà & N. Munaro (eds.) 63–90. Oxford: Oxford University Press.

Bae, T.-W. 2016. Subject ellipsis in spoken English. *SNU Working Papers in English Linguistics and Language* 14: 1–22.

Bailey, L. 2011. Null subjects in Northeast English. *Newcastle Working Papers in Linguistics* 17: 23–45.

Baker, C. L. 1970. Notes on the description of English questions: The role of an abstract question morpheme. *Foundations of Language* 6: 197–219.

Baker, M. 1988. *Incorporation*. Chicago: Chicago University Press.

——1997. Thematic roles and syntactic structure. In *Elements of Grammar*, L. Haegeman (ed.) 73–137. Dordrecht: Kluwer.

——2008. *The Syntax of Agreement and Concord*. Cambridge: Cambridge University Press.

Baker, M., Johnson, K. & Roberts, I. 1989. Passive arguments raised. *Linguistic Inquiry* 20: 219–51.

Baltin, M. 1978. Toward a theory of movement rules. PhD diss. MIT.

——1982. A landing site theory of movement rules. *Linguistic Inquiry* 13: 1–38.

——1995. Floating quantifiers, PRO and predication. *Linguistic Inquiry* 26: 199–248.

——2010. The nonreality of doubly filled Comps. *Linguistic Inquiry* 41: 331–5.

Banfield, A. 1982. *Unspeakable Sentences: Narration and representation in the language of fiction*. Boston: Routledge and Kegan Paul.

Bárány, A. 2015. Hungarian object agreement with personal pronouns. *Proceedings of the West Coast Conference on Formal Linguistics* 32: 208–17.

Barbiers, S., Bennis, H. & de Vogelaar, G. 2005. *Syntactic Atlas of the Dutch Dialects, Vol. 1*. Amsterdam: Amsterdam University Press.

Barton, E. 1998. The grammar of telegraphic structures: Sentential and nonsentential derivation. *Journal of English Linguistics* 26: 37–67.

Bayer, J. 1984a. Towards an explanation of certain *that-t* phenomena: The COMP node in Bavarian. In *Sentential Complementation*, W. de Geest & Y. Putseys (eds.) 23–32. Dordrecht: Foris.

——1984b. COMP in Bavarian syntax. *The Linguistic Review* 3: 209–74.

——2010. Wh-drop and recoverability. In *Structure Preserved: Studies in syntax for Jan Koster*, J. W. Zwart & M. de Vries (eds.) 31–40. Amsterdam: Benjamins.

——2014. Syntactic and phonological properties of wh-operators and wh-movement in Bavarian. In *Bavarian Syntax: Contributions to the theory of syntax*, G. Grewendorf & H. Weiss (eds.) 23–50. Amsterdam: Benjamins.

——2015. Doubly-filled Comp, wh-head movement, and derivational economy. In *Representing Structure in Phonology and Syntax*, M. van Oostendorp & H. van Riemsdijk (eds.) 7–40. Berlin: Mouton de Gruyter.

——2016. Doubly-filled comp, wh-head-movement, and the doubly-filled-comp-filter. Ms. Universität Konstanz.

Bayer, J. & Brandner, E. 2008. On wh-head-movement and the doubly-filled-comp-filter. *Proceedings of the West Coast Conference on Formal Linguistics* 26: 87–95.

Bayer, J. & Dasgupta, P. 2016. Emphatic topicalization and the structure of the left periphery: Evidence from German and Bangla. *Syntax* 19: 1–45.

Becquet, K. 2000. L'omission du sujet grammatical dans les journaux intimes. MA thesis. Université Charles de Gaulle, Lille.

Beijer, F. 2002. The syntax and pragmatics of exclamations and other expressive/emotional utterances. *Working Papers in Linguistics* 2: 1–22, Department of English, University of Lund.

Beck, S. 2006. Intervention effects follow from focus interpretation. *Natural Language Semantics* 14: 1–56.

Beck, S. & Kim, S.-S. 2006. Intervention effects in alternative questions. *Journal of Comparative German Linguistics* 9: 165–208.

Becker, M. 2006. There began to be a learnability puzzle. *Linguistic Inquiry* 37: 441–56.

Bell, A. 1991. *The Language of the News Media*. Oxford: Blackwell.

Belletti, A. 1990. *Generalized Verb Movement: Aspects of verb syntax*. Turin: Rosenberg and Sellier.

——2001. Agreement projections. In *The Handbook of Contemporary Syntactic Theory*, M. Baltin & C. Collins (eds.) 483–510. Oxford: Blackwell.

——2004a. Aspects of the low IP area. In *The Cartography of Syntactic Structures, Vol. 2: The structure of IP and CP*, L. Rizzi (ed.) 16–51. Oxford: Oxford University Press.

——2004b (ed). *The Cartography of Syntactic Structures, Vol. 3: Structures and beyond*. Oxford: Oxford University Press.

——2009. *Structures and Strategies*. London: Routledge.

Beltrama, A. 2013. Intrusive but not intruders. The processing of resumptive pronouns in Italian and English. Ms., University of Chicago.

Beltrama, A. & Xiang, M. 2016. Unacceptable but comprehensible: The facilitation effect of resumptive pronouns. *Glossa: A Journal of General Linguistics* 1: 1–24.

Bender, E. 1999. Constituting context: Null objects in English recipes revisited. *University of Pennsylvania Working Papers in Linguistics* 6: 53–68.

——2000. Syntactic variation and linguistic competence: The case of AAVE copula absence. PhD diss. Stanford University.

Benincà, P. 1995. Il tipo esclamativo. In *Grande Grammatica Italiana di Consultazione, Vol. 3*, L. Renzi, G. Salvi & A. Cardinaletti (eds.) 127–52. Bologna: Il Mulino.

——1996. La struttura della frase esclamativa alla luce del dialetto padovano. In *Italiano e Dialetti nel Tempo. Saggi di Grammatica per Giulio C. Lepschy*, P. Benincà, G. Cinque, T. De Mauro & N. Vincent (eds.) 23–43. Roma: Bulzoni.

——2001. The position of topic and focus in the left periphery. In *Current Studies in Italian Syntax: Essays Offered to Lorenzo Renzi*, G. Cinque & G. Salvi (eds.) 39–64. Amsterdam: Elsevier-North Holland.

——2003. La frase relativa in fiorentino antico. Paper presented to the *V° Incontro di Dialettologia*, University of Bristol, 26–27 September.

——2006. A detailed map of the left periphery of medieval Romance. In *Crosslinguistic Research in Syntax and Semantics: Negation, tense, and clausal architecture*, R. Zanuttini, H. Campos, E. Herburger & P. Portner (eds.) 53–86. Washington, DC: Georgetown University Press.

——2010. La periferia sinistra. In *Grammatica dell'Italiano Antico*, G. Salvi & L. Renzi (eds.) 27–59. Bologna: Il Mulino.

——2012a. Lexical complementisers and headless relatives. In *The Cartography of Syntactic Structures, Vol. 7: Functional heads*, L. Brugè, A. Cardinaletti, G. Giusti, N. Munaro & C. Poletto (eds.) 29–41. Oxford: Oxford University Press.

——2012b. Frasi relative e strutture copulari. In *Per Roberto Gusmani: Studi in ricordo*, V. Orioles & P. Borghello (eds.) 251–67. Udine: Forum editrice.

Benincà, P. & Cinque, G. 2010. La frase relativa. In *Grammatica dell'Italiano Antico*, G. Salvi & L. Renzi (eds.) 469–507. Bologna: Il Mulino.

——2014. Kind-defining relative clauses in the diachrony of Italian. In *Diachrony and Dialects*, P. Benincà, A. Ledgeway & N. Vincent (eds.) 257–78. Oxford: Oxford University Press.

Benincà, P. & Munaro, N. 2010 (eds.). *The Cartography of Syntactic Structures, Vol. 5: Mapping the left periphery.* Oxford: Oxford University Press.

Benincà, P. & Poletto C. 2004. Topic, Focus and V2: Defining the CP sublayers. In *The Cartography of Syntactic Structures, Vol. 2: The structure of IP and CP*, L. Rizzi. (ed.) 52–75. Oxford: Oxford University Press.

Benmamoun, E. 1999. The syntax of quantifiers and quantifier float. *Linguistic Inquiry* 30: 621–42.

Benmamoun, E., Bhatia, A. & Polinsky, M. 2009. Closest conjunct agreement in head-final languages. *Linguistic Variation Yearbook* 9: 67–88.

Bennis, H. 2006. Agreement, pro and imperatives. In *Arguments and Agreement*, P. Ackema, P. Brandt, M. Schloorlemmer & F. Weerman (eds.) 101–23. Oxford: Oxford University Press.

Bennis, H. & Haegeman, L. 1994. On the status of agreement and relative clauses in West Flemish. In *Sentential Complementation*, W. de Geest & Y. Putseys (eds.) 33–55. Dordrecht: Foris.

Berger, M. 2015. The subject position in Spanish nominalized infinitives. *University of Pennsylvania Working Papers in Linguistics* 21: 1–10.

Berizzi, M. 2010. Interrogatives and relatives in some varieties of English. PhD diss. University of Padua.

Berizzi, M. & Rossi, S. 2010. 'Something here what made me think.' Some new views on relative *what* in the dialects of English. *LangUE Proceedings* 2009: 14–26, University of Essex.

Bernstein, J. B. 1993. Topics in the syntax of nominal structures across

Romance. PhD diss. City University of New York.

——2001. The DP hypothesis: Identifying clausal properties in the nominal domain. In *The Handbook of Contemporary Syntactic Theory*, M. Baltin & C. Collins (eds.) 536–61. Oxford: Blackwell.

Bertollo, S. & Cavall, G. 2012. The syntax of Italian free relative clauses: An analysis. *Generative Grammar in Geneva* 8: 59–76.

Beukema, F. & Koopmans, P. 1989. A Government-Binding perspective on the imperative in English. *Journal of Linguistics* 25: 417–36.

Bever, T. G., Carroll, J. M. & Hartig, R. 1976. Analogy of ungrammatical sequences that are utterable and comprehensible are the origins of new grammars in language acquisition and linguistic evolution. In *An Integrated Theory of Linguistic Disability*, T. G. Bever, J. J. Katz & D. T. Langendoen (eds.) 149–82. New York: T. Y. Crowell Press.

Beyssade, C. 2009. Exclamation and presupposition. *MIT Working Papers in Linguistics* 60: 19–34.

Bhatt, R. 2002. The raising analysis of relative clauses: Evidence from adjectival modification. *Natural Language Semantics* 10: 43–90.

——2015. Relative clauses and correlatives. In *Syntax: Theory and analysis volume I*, T. Kiss & A. Alexiadou (eds.) 708–49. Berlin: De Gruyter.

Bhatt, R. & Walkow, M. 2013. Locating agreement in grammar: An argument from agreement in conjunctions. *Natural Language and Linguistic Theory* 31: 951–1013.

Bianchi, V. 1999. *Consequences of Antisymmetry: Headed Relative Clauses*. Berlin: Mouton de Gruyter.

——2000. The raising analysis of relative clauses: A reply to Borsley. *Linguistic Inquiry* 31: 123–40.

——2003. On finiteness as logophoric anchoring. In *Tense and Point of View*, J. Guéron & L. Tasmovski (eds.) 213–46. Nanterre: Université Paris X.

——2008. Resumptives and LF chains. Ms. University of Siena.

Bianchi, V., Bocci, G. & Cruschina, S. 2016. Focus fronting, unexpectedness and evaluative implicatures. *Semantics and Pragmatics* 9: 1–54.

Bianchi, V. & Cruschina, S. 2016. The derivation and interpretation of polar questions with a fronted focus. *Lingua* 170: 47–68.

Bianchi, V. & Frascarelli, M. 2010. Is topic a root phenomenon? *Iberia* 2: 43–88.

Biber, D. (1995) *Dimensions of Register Variation: A Cross-linguistic comparison*. Cambridge: Cambridge University Press.

Biber, D., Johansson, S., Leech, G., Conrad C. & Finegan E. 1999. *Longman Grammar of Spoken and Written English*. Harlow: Pearson.

Biberauer, T. 2008. Semi null-subject languages, expletives and expletive pro reconsidered. *Cambridge Occasional Papers in Linguistics* 4: 1–45.

Biloa, E. 2013. *The Syntax of Tuki: A Cartographic Approach*. Amsterdam: Benjamins.

Birner, B. J. & Ward, G. 1998a. *Information Status and Non-canonical Word Order in English*. Amsterdam: Benjamins.

——1998b. Discourse and information structure. Ms. Northwestern University, IL.

Bjorkman, B. & Zeijlstra, H. 2019. Checking up on (ϕ)-Agree. *Linguistic Inquiry* 50: 527–69.

Bloomfield, L. 1935. *Language*. London: George Allen and Unwin.

Blythe, H. 2016. Resumption in English: An investigation of usage and acceptability. *Cambridge Occasional Papers in Linguistics* 9: 156–83.

Bobaljik, J. 1999. Adverbs: The hierarchy paradox. *GLOT International* 4: 27–28.

——2003. Floating quantifiers: Handle with care. In *The Second GLOT International State-of-the-Article Book*, L. Cheng & R. Sybesma (eds.) 107–48. Berlin: Mouton de Gruyter.

——2009. Where's phi? Agreement as a post-syntactic operation. In *Phi-Theory: Phi-features across interfaces and modules*, D. Harbour, D. Adger & S. Béjar (eds.) 295–328. Oxford: Oxford University Press.

Bocci, G. 2004. Contrastive focalisation on topics and preverbal subjects in Italian. *Rivista di Grammatica Generativa* 29: 3–60.

——2007. Criterial positions and left periphery in Italian. *Nanzan Linguistics* 3: 35–70.

——2009. *On syntax and prosody in Italian*. PhD diss. University of Siena.

——2013. *The Syntax-Prosody Interface: A Cartographic perspective with evidence from Italian*. Amsterdam: Benjamins.

Boeckx, C. 2000. A note on contraction. *Linguistic Inquiry* 31: 357–66.

——2001. Scope reconstruction and A-movement. *Natural Language and Linguistic Theory* 19: 503–48.

——2003. *Islands and Chains: Resumption as derivational residue*. Amsterdam: Benjamins.

——2007. *Understanding Minimalist Syntax*. Oxford: Blackwell.

——2008. *Aspects of the Syntax of Agreement*. New York: Routledge.

——2012. *Syntactic Islands*. Cambridge: Cambridge University Press.

Boeckx, C. & Grohmann, K. K. 2005. Left dislocation in Germanic. In *Focus on Germanic Typology*, W. Abraham (ed.) 131–44. Berlin: Akadamie-Verlag.

Boeckx, C. & Hornstein, N. 2003. Reply to Control is not movement. *Linguistic Inquiry* 34: 269–80.

——2004. Movement under control. *Linguistic Inquiry* 35: 431–52.

——2006a. The virtues of control as movement. *Syntax* 9: 118–30.

——2006b. Control in Icelandic and theories of Control. *Linguistic Inquiry* 37: 591–606.

Boeckx, C. & Jeong, Y. 2004. The fine structure of intervention in syntax. In *Issues in Current Linguistic Theory: A Festschrift for Hong Bae Lee*, C. Kwon & W. Lee (eds.) 83–116. Seoul: Kyungjin.

Boeckx, C. & Lasnik, H. 2006. Intervention and repair. *Linguistic Inquiry* 37: 150–55.

Boef, E. 2013. Doubling in relative clauses: Aspects of morphosyntactic microvariation in Dutch. PhD diss. Meertens Instituut (KNAW), University of Utrecht.

Bolinger, D. 1977. *Meaning and Form.* London: Longman.

Bondaruk, A. 1995. Resumptive pronouns in English and Polish. In *Licensing in Syntax and Phonology,* E. Gussmann (ed.) 27–55. Lublin: Folium.

Borer, H. 1984. Restrictive relatives in modern Hebrew. *Natural Language and Linguistic Theory* 2: 219–60.

Borise, L. 2019. Phrasing is key: The syntax and prosody of focus in Georgian. PhD diss. Harvard University.

Börjeson, K. & Müller, G. 2020. Long-distance agreement and locality: A reprojection approach. In *Agree to Agree: Agreement in the minimalist program,* P. W. Smith, J. Mursell & K. Hartmann (eds.) 307–46. Berlin: Language Science Press.

Borsley, R. D. 1984. Free relatives in Polish and English. In *Contrastive Linguistics: Prospects and Problems,* J. Fisiak (ed.) 1–18. Berlin: Mouton.

——1992. More on the difference between English restrictive and non-restrictive relative clauses. *Journal of Linguistics* 28: 139–48.

——1997. Relative clauses and the theory of phrase structure. *Linguistic Inquiry* 28: 629–47.

——2001. More on the raising analysis of relative clauses. Ms. University of Essex.

——2010. On so-called transitive expletives in Belfast English.

English Language and Linguistics 13: 409–31.

Bošković, Z. 2001. Floating quantifiers and θ-role assignment. *Proceedings of the North East Linguistic Society* 31: 59–78.

——2002 A-Movement and the EPP. *Syntax* 5: 167–218.

——2004. Be careful where you float your quantifiers. *Natural Language and Linguistic Theory* 22: 681–742.

——2007. On the locality and motivation of Move and Agree: An even more minimal theory. *Linguistic Inquiry* 38: 589–644.

——2009. On relativization strategies and resumptive pronouns. In *Studies in Formal Slavic Phonology, Morphology, Syntax, Semantics, and Information Structure: Proceedings of Formal Description of Slavic Languages 7, Leipzig 2007,* G. Zybatow, U. Junghanns, D. Lenertová & P. Biskup (eds.) 79–93. Berlin: Peter Lang.

——2011a. Rescue by PF deletion, traces as (non)interveners, and the *that*-trace effect. *Linguistic Inquiry* 42: 1–44.

——2011b. On unvalued uninterpretable features. *Proceedings of the Annual Meeting of the North East Linguistics Society* 39: 109–20.

——2012. On NPs and clauses. In *Discourse and Grammar: From sentence types to lexical categories,* G. Grewendorf & T. E. Zimmerman (eds.) 179–242. Berlin: de Gruyter.

——2016. On the timing of labeling: Deducing Comp-trace effects, the Subject Condition, the Adjunct

Condition, and tucking in from labeling. *The Linguistic Review* 33: 17–66.

——2020. On smuggling, the freezing ban, labels and *tough*-constructions. In *Smuggling in Syntax*, A. Belletti & C. Collins (eds.) 53–95. Oxford: Oxford University Press.

Bosque, I. 2017 (ed.) *Advances in the Analysis of Spanish Exclamatives*. Columbus, OH: Ohio State University Press.

Bouchard, D. 1989. Null objects and the theory of empty categories. In *Studies in Romance Linguistics: Selected papers from the XVIIth linguistic symposium on Romance languages at Rutgers University*, C. Kirschner & J. Decesaris (eds.) 33–49. Amsterdam: Benjamins.

Bowers, J. 1973. Grammatical relations. PhD diss. MIT.

——2002. Transitivity. *Linguistic Inquiry* 33: 183–224.

Branan, K. 2018. Attraction at a distance: A'-movement and case. *Linguistic Inquiry* 49: 409–40.

Brandi, L. & Cordin, P. 1989. Two Italian dialects and the null subject parameter. In *The Null Subject Parameter*, O. Jaeggli & K. Safir (eds.) 111–43. Dordrecht: Kluwer.

Brandner, E. 2010. On the syntax of verb-initial exclamatives. *Studia Linguistica* 64: 81–115.

Branigan, P. 1992. Subjects and complementisers. PhD diss. MIT.

Branigan, P. & MacKenzie, M. 2001. Altruism, A'-movement, and object agreement in Innu-aimûn. *Linguistic Inquiry* 33: 385–407.

Breivik, L. E. 1983. *Existential there: A synchronic and diachronic study*. Bergen: Norwegian Research Council.

Bresnan, J. 1970. On complementizers: Toward a syntactic theory of complement types. *Foundations of Language* 6: 297–321.

——1972. Theory of complementation in English syntax. PhD diss. MIT (published as Bresnan 1979).

——1976. Evidence for a theory of unbounded transformations. *Linguistic Analysis* 2: 353–93.

——1979. *Theory of Complementation in English Syntax*. New York: Garland.

Bresnan, J. & Grimshaw, J. 1978. The syntax of free relatives in English. *Linguistic Inquiry* 9: 331–91.

Brillman, R. J. & Hirsch, A. 2016. An anti-locality account of English subject/non-subject asymmetries. *Chicago Linguistic Society Proceedings* 50: 73–88.

Brisson, C. M. 1998. Distributivity, maximality and floating quantifiers. PhD diss. Rutgers University.

——2000. Floating quantifiers as adverbs. In *Proceedings of the Fifteenth Eastern States Conference on Linguistics*, R. Daly & A. Riehl (eds.) 13–24. Ithaca, NY: Cornell University.

Brody, M. 1990. Some remarks on the focus field in Hungarian. *UCL Working Papers in Linguistics* 2: 1–25.

Brook, M. 2016. Syntactic categories informing variationist analysis: The case of English copy-raising. PhD diss. University of Toronto.

——2018. Taking it up a level: Copy-raising and cascaded tiers of morphosyntactic change. *Language Variation and Change* 30: 231–60.

Browning, M. A. 1996. CP recursion and *that-t* effects. *Linguistic Inquiry* 27: 237–55.

Brownlow, O. 2011. Towards a unified analysis of the syntax and semantics of *get* constructions. PhD diss. Queen Mary University of London.

Bruening, B. 2001. Syntax at the edge: Cross-clausal phenomena and the syntax of Passamaquoddy. PhD diss. MIT.

——2009. Selectional asymmetries between CP and DP suggest that the DP hypothesis is wrong. *University of Pennsylvania Working Papers in Linguistics* 15: 27–36.

——2013. By phrases in passives and nominals. *Syntax* 16: 1–41.

——2014. Precede and command revisited. *Language* 90: 342–88.

Bruening, B., Dinh, X. & Kim. L. 2015. Selection, idioms and the structure of nominal phrases with and without classifiers. Ms. University of Delaware.

Brugé, L., Cardinaletti, A., Giusti, G., Munaro, N. & Poletto, C. 2012. *Functional Heads*. Oxford: Oxford University Press.

Brunetti, L. 2004. *A Unification of Focus*. Padua: Unipress.

Büring, D. 1997. *The Meaning of Topic and Focus: The 59th Street Bridge accent*. London: Routledge.

——1999. Topic. In *Focus: Linguistic, cognitive and computational perspectives*, P. Bosch & R. van der Sandt (eds.) 142–65. Cambridge: Cambridge University Press.

——2003. On D-trees, beans and B-accents. *Linguistics and Philosophy* 26: 511–45.

——2004. Negative Inversion. Draft of paper presented to a meeting of the North East Linguistic Society. Ms. UCLA.

——2009. Towards a typology of focus realization. In *Information Structure*, M. Zimmermann & C. Féry (eds.) 177–205. Oxford: Oxford University Press.

——2016. (Contrastive) topic. In *The Oxford Handbook of Information Structure*, C. Féry & S. Ishihara (eds.) 64–85. Oxford: Oxford University Press.

Burke, I. 2017. Wicked *which*: The linking relative in Australian English. *Australian Journal of Linguistics* 37: 356–86.

Burton, S & Grimshaw, J. 1992. Coordination and VP-internal subjects. *Linguistic Inquiry* 23: 305–13.

Burzio, L. 1986. *Italian Syntax*. Dordrecht: Reidel.

Cable, S. 2005. Free relatives in Tlingit and Haida: Evidence that the mover projects. Ms. University of Massachusetts.

——2007. The grammar of Q: Q-particles and the nature of wh-fronting, as revealed by the wh-questions of Tlingit. PhD diss. MIT.

——2008. Question particles and the nature of *wh*-fronting. In *Quantification: A cross-linguistic perspective*, L. Matthewson (ed.) 105–78. Bingley: Emerald.

——2010a. *The Grammar of Q: Q-particles, Wh-Movement, and pied-piping*. Oxford: Oxford University Press.

——2010b. Against the existence of pied-piping: Evidence from Tlingit. *Linguistic Inquiry* 41: 563–94.

——2012. The optionality of movement and EPP in Dholuo. *Natural Language and Linguistic Theory* 30: 651–97.

Camilleri, M. 2018. On Raising and Copy Raising in Maltese. In *The Languages of Malta*, P. Paggio & A. Gatt (eds.) 171–201. Berlin: Language Science Press.

Cann, R., Kaplan, T. & Kempson, R. 2005. Data at the grammar-pragmatics interface: The case of resumptive pronouns in English. *Lingua* 115: 1551–78.

Capelle, B. 2005. Particle patterns in English: A comprehensive coverage. PhD diss. University of Leuven.

Caponigro, I. 2002. Free relatives as DPs with a silent D and a CP complement. In *Proceedings of WECOL 2000*, V. Samiian (ed.) 140–50. Fresno, CA: California State University.

——2004. The semantic contribution of *wh*-words and type shifts: Evidence from free relatives crosslinguistically. In *Proceedings of the 14th Semantics and Linguistic Theory Conference, SALT XIV*, R. B. Young (ed.) 38–55. Ithaca, NY: Cornell University.

Caponigro, I. & Pearl, L. 2008. Silent prepositions: Evidence from free relatives. In *The Syntax and Semantics of Spatial P*, A. Asbury, J. Dotlačil, B. Gehrke & R. Nouwen (eds.) 365–85. Amsterdam: Benjamins.

——2009. The nominal nature of *when, where*, and *how*: Evidence from free relatives. *Linguistic Inquiry* 40: 155–75.

Caponigro, I. & Schütze, C.T. 2003. Parameterizing passive participle movement. *Linguistic Inquiry* 34: 293–308.

Caponigro, I., Torrence, H. & Cisneros, C. 2013. Free relative clauses in two Mixtec languages. *International Journal of American Linguistics* 79: 61–96.

Cardinaletti, A. 1997. Subjects and clause structure. In *The New Comparative Syntax*, L. Haegeman (ed.) 33–63. London: Longman.

——2004. Towards a cartography of syntactic positions. In *The Structure of CP and IP*, L. Rizzi (ed.) 115–65. Oxford: Oxford University Press.

——2009 On a (wh-)moved topic in Italian, compared to Germanic. *Linguistics Today* 141: 3–40.

Cardinaletti, C., Cinque, G. & Endo, Y. (eds.). 2014. *On Peripheries: Exploring clause initial and clause final positions*. Tokyo: Hituzi Syobe Publishing.

Cardinaletti, A. & Starke, M. 1999. The typology of structural deficiency: A case study of the three classes of pronouns. In *Clitics in the Languages of Europe*, H. van Riemsdijk (ed.) 145–233. Berlin: Mouton de Gruyter.

Carlson, G. 1977. Amount relatives. *Language* 53: 520–42.

Carroll, S. 1983. On *for* and the constituency of infinitives. *Toronto Working Papers in Linguistics*, 4.

Carstens, V. 2003. Rethinking complementizer agreement: Agree with a case-checked goal. *Linguistic Inquiry* 34: 393–412.

——2016. Delayed valuation: A reanalysis of 'upwards' complementizer agreement and the mechanics of case. *Syntax* 19: 1–42.

Carstens, V. & Diercks, M. 2013. Parameterizing case and activity: Hyper-raising in Bantu. *Proceedings of the North East Linguistic Society* 40: 99–118.

Carter, R. & McCarthy, M. 1995. Grammar and the spoken language. *Applied Linguistics* 16: 141–58.

Casielles-Suárez, E. 2004. *The Syntax-Information Structure Interface: Evidence from Spanish and English.* New York: Routledge.

Castillo, C. 2009. English *to*-infinitive relative clauses. *Folia Linguistica Historica* 27: 135–53.

Castillo, J. C. C., Drury, J. E., & Grohmann, K. K. 2009. Merge over Move and the Extended Projection Principle: MOM and EPP revisited. *Iberia* 1: 53–114.

Castroviejo, M.E. 2006. Wh-exclamatives in Catalan. PhD diss. University of Barcelona.

——2007. A degree-based account of wh-exclamatives in Catalan. In *Proceedings of Sinn und Bedeutung*, E. Puig-Waldemüller (ed.) 134–49. Barcelona: Universitat Pompeu Fabra.

——2008. Deconstructing exclamations. *Catalan Journal of Linguistics* 7: 41–90.

——2010. An expressive answer: Some considerations on the semantics and pragmatics of wh-exclamatives. *Chicago Linguistic Society Proceedings* 44: 3–17.

——2019. On *wh*-exclamatives and gradeability. An argument from Romance. *Journal of Linguistics* 57: 41–82.

Cattell, R. 1976. Constraints on movement rules. *Language* 52: 18–50.

Cecchetto, C. 2005. Reconstruction in relative clauses and the copy theory of traces. *Linguistic Variation Yearbook* 5: 73–103.

Cecchetto, C. & Donati, C. 2010. On labelling: Principle C and Head Movement. *Syntax* 13: 241–78.

——2015. *(Re)labeling.* Cambridge, MA: MIT Press.

Cerron-Palomino, A. 2015. Resumption or contrast? Non-standard pronouns in Spanish relative clauses. *Spanish in Context* 12: 349–72.

Chaiphet, K. 2017. Aspects of quantifier float in Thai. MA thesis. City University of New York.

Chao, W. & Sells, P. 1983. On the interpretation of resumptive pronouns. *Proceedings of the North East Linguistic Society* 13: 47–61.

Chapman, C. 2013. A revised account of the EPP in French: A semantics-based analysis. *McGill Working Papers in Linguistics* 23: 1–23.

Chaves, R. 2012. On the grammar of extraction and co-ordination.

Natural Language and Linguistic Theory 30: 465–512.

——2013. An expectation-based account of subject islands and parasitism. *Journal of Linguistics* 49: 285–327.

Checa-García, I. 2019. Resumptive elements in Spanish relative clauses and processing difficulties: A multifactorial analysis. *Folia Linguistica* 53: 479–517.

Cheng, L. 1997. *On the Typology of Wh-Questions.* New York: Garland.

Cheng, L. & Downing, L. 2012. Against FocusP: Arguments from Zulu. In *Contrasts and Positions in Information Structure*, I. Kučerová & A. Neeleman (eds.) 247–66. Cambridge: Cambridge University Press.

Chernilovskaya, A. 2014. Exclamativity in discourse: Exploring the exclamative speech act from a discourse perspective. PhD diss. Utrecht University.

Chernilovskaya, A., Condoravdi, C. & Lauer, S. 2012. On the discourse effects of wh-exclamatives. *Proceedings of the West Coast Conference on Formal Linguistics* 30: 109–19.

Chomsky, N. 1955. *The Logical Structure of Linguistic Theory.* Mimeo, MIT (published as Chomsky 1975).

——1957. *Syntactic Structures.* The Hague: Mouton.

——1964a. The logical basis of linguistic theory. In *Proceedings of the Ninth International Congress of Linguists, Cambridge, Mass.,*

August 27–31, 1962. H. G. Lunt (ed.). The Hague: Mouton.

——1964b. *Current Issues in Linguistic Theory.* The Hague: Mouton.

——1965. *Aspects of the Theory of Syntax.* Cambridge, MA: MIT Press.

——1968. Noam Chomsky and Stuart Hampshire discuss the study of language. *The Listener*, 30 May, 79(2044): 687–91 .

——1970. Remarks on nominalization. In *Readings in English Transformational Grammar*, R. A. Jacobs & P. S. Rosenbaum (eds.) 184–221. Waltham, MA: Ginn.

——1972 *Language and Mind* (enlarged edition). New York: Harcourt Brace Jovanovich.

——1973. Conditions on transformations. In *A Festschrift for Morris Halle*, S. R. Anderson & P. Kiparsky (eds.) 232–86. New York: Holt, Rinehart and Winston.

——1975 *The Logical Structure of Linguistic Theory.* New York: Plenum Press.

——1977. On Wh-movement. In *Formal Syntax*, P. W. Culicover, T. Wasow & A. Akmajian (eds.) 71–132. New York: Academic Press.

——1980. On binding. *Linguistic Inquiry* 11: 1–46.

——1981. *Lectures on Government and Binding.* Dordrecht: Foris.

——1982. *Some Concepts and Consequences of the Theory of Government and Binding.* Cambridge, MA: MIT Press.

——1986a. *Knowledge of Language: Its nature, origin and use.* Praeger, New York.

——1986b. *Barriers*. Cambridge, MA: MIT Press.

——1989. Some notes on economy of derivation and representation. *MIT Working Papers in Linguistics* 10: 43–74. Reprinted as chapter 2 of Chomsky 1995.

——1993. A minimalist program for linguistic theory. In *The View from Building 20: Essays in honor of Sylvain Bromberger*, K. Hale & S. J. Keyser (eds.) 1–52. Cambridge, MA: MIT Press. Reprinted as chapter 3 of Chomsky 1995.

——1995. *The Minimalist Program*. Cambridge, MA: MIT Press.

——1998. Minimalist inquiries: The framework. *MIT Occasional Papers in Linguistics* 15. Republished as Chomsky 2000.

——1999. Derivation by phase. *MIT Occasional Papers in Linguistics* 18. Republished as Chomsky 2001.

——2000. *Minimalist inquiries: The framework*. In *Step by Step: Essays on minimalism in honor of Howard Lasnik*, R. Martin, D. Michaels & J. Uriagereka (eds.) 89–155. Cambridge, MA: MIT Press.

——2001. Derivation by phase. In *Ken Hale: A life in language*, M. Kenstowicz (ed.) 1–52. Cambridge, MA: MIT Press.

——2005. Three factors in language design. *Linguistic Inquiry* 36: 1–22.

——2007. Approaching UG from below. In *Interfaces+Recursion = Language?* U. Sauerland & H.-M. Gärtner (eds.) 1–29. Berlin: Mouton de Gruyter.

——2008. On phases. In *Foundational Issues in Linguistic Theory: Essays in honor of Jean-Roger Vergnaud*, R. Friedin, C. Otero & M.-L. Zubizarreta (eds.) 133–65. Cambridge, MA: MIT Press.

——2013. Problems of projection. *Lingua* 130: 33–49.

——2014. Minimal recursion: Exploring the prospects. *Studies in Theoretical Psycholinguistics* 43: 1–15.

——2015. Problems of projection: Extensions. In *Structures, Strategies, and Beyond: Studies in honour of Adriana Belletti*, E. Di Domenico, C. Hamann & S. Matteini (eds.) 3–16. Amsterdam: Benjamins.

——2021. Minimalism: Where are we now, and where can we hope to go? *Gengo Kenkyu* 160: 1–41.

Chomsky, N. & Lasnik, H. 1977. Filters and control. *Linguistic Inquiry* 8: 425–504.

——1993. The theory of principles and parameters. In *Syntax: An international handbook of contemporary research*, J. Jacobs, A. von Stechow, W. Sternefeld & T. Venneman (eds.) 506–69. Berlin: Mouton de Gruyter. Reprinted as chapter 1 of Chomsky 1995.

Chung, S. 1984. Identifiability and null objects in Chamorro. *Berkeley Linguistics Society Proceedings*: 10: 116–30.

Cinque, G. 1977. The movement nature of left dislocation. *Linguistic Inquiry* 8: 397–412.

——1978. Towards a unified treatment of island constraints. In *Proceedings of the Twelfth International Congress of Linguists*,

W. U. Dressler & W. Meid (eds.) 344–48. Innsbrücker Beiträge zur Sprachwissenschaft.

——1983. Topic constructions in some European languages and connectedness. *Tilburg Studies in Language and Literature* 4: 7–41. Reprinted in Anagnastopoulou, van Riemsdijk & Zwarts, 1997.

——1999. *Adverbs and Functional Heads*. Oxford: Oxford University Press.

——2002 (ed.) *The Cartography of Syntactic Structures, Vol. 1: The structure of DP and IP*. Oxford: Oxford University Press.

——2004. Issues in adverbial syntax. *Lingua* 114: 683–710.

——2008. Two types of non-restrictive relatives. *Empirical Issues in Syntax and Semantics* 7: 99–137.

——2011. On double-headed relative clauses. *Revista de Estudos Linguisticos da Universidade do Porto* 1: 67–91.

——2013. *Typological Studies: Word order and relative clauses*. Abingdon: Routledge.

——2017a. On the status of functional categories (heads and phrases). *Language and Linguistics* 18: 521–76.

——2017b. On the double-headed analysis of 'headless' relative clauses. Ms. University of Venice.

——2020. *The Syntax of Relative Clauses: A unified analysis*. Cambridge: Cambridge University Press.

——2023. *On Linearization: Toward a restrictive theory*. Cambridge, MA: MIT Press..

Cinque, G. & Rizzi. L. 2008. The cartography of syntactic structures. *Studies in Linguistics* 2: 42–58.

——2010a. The cartography of syntactic structures. In *The Oxford Handbook of Grammatical Analysis*, B. Heine & H. Narrog (eds.) 51–65. Oxford: Oxford University Press.

——2010b (eds.). *The Cartography of Syntactic Structures, Vol. 6: Mapping spatial PPs*. Oxford: Oxford University Press.

Cirillo, R. J. 2009. *The syntax of Floating Quantifiers: Stranding revisited*. Utrecht: LOT.

——2012. A fresh look at the debate on floating quantifiers. *Language and Linguistics Compass* 6: 796–815.

Citko, B. 2000. Parallel merge and the syntax of free relatives. PhD diss. State University of New York at Stony Brook.

——2001. Deletion under identity in relative clauses. *Proceedings of the North East Linguistic Society* 31: 131–45.

——2002. (Anti)reconstruction effects in free relatives: A new argument against the Comp account. *Linguistic Inquiry* 33: 507–11.

——2004. On headed, headless, and light-headed relatives. *Natural Language and Linguistic Theory* 22: 95–126.

——2005. On the nature of Merge: External Merge, Internal Merge, and Parallel Merge. *Linguistic Inquiry* 36: 475–96.

——2008. An argument against assimilating appositive relatives to coordinate structures. *Linguistic Inquiry* 39: 633–55.

Claridge, C. 2012. The origins of *how come* and *what ... for*. In *English Historical Linguistics 2010: Selected Papers from the Sixteenth International Conference on English Historical Linguistics*, I. Hegedüs & A. Fodor (eds.) 177–95. Amsterdam: Benjamins.

Clemens, L. E., Morgan, A. M., Polinsky, M. & Xiang, M. 2012. Listening to resumptives: An auditory experiment. Poster presented to the 25th Annual CUNY conference on Human Sentence Processing, City University of New York.

Cole, P. 1987. Null objects in Universal Grammar. *Linguistic Inquiry* 18: 597–612.

Collins, C. 1991. Why and how come. *MIT Working Papers in Linguistics* 15: 1–45.

——2005. A smuggling approach to the passive in English. *Syntax* 8: 81–120.

——2007. Home sweet home. *NYU Working Papers in Linguistics* 1: 1–34.

——2015. Relative clause deletion. *MIT Working Papers in Linguistics* 77: 57–69.

——2017. Merge(X,Y) = {X,Y}. In *Labels and Roots*, L. Bauke & A. Blümel (eds.) 487–68. Berlin: De Gruyter.

——2018. History of the *by*-phrase in generative syntax (1957 to 2005). *Ordinary Working Grammarian*. Blog. 17 September. https://bit.ly/3FQ5qHS

——2021. *Principles of Argument Structure: A Merge-based approach*. Ms. New York University.

Collins, C. & Postal, P. M. 2014. *Classical NEG Raising: An essay on the syntax of negation*. Cambridge, MA: MIT Press.

Collins, C. & Radford, A. 2015. Gaps, ghosts and gapless relatives in spoken English. *Studia Linguistica* 69: 191–235.

Collins, C. & Stabler, E. 2016. A formalization of minimalist syntax. *Syntax* 19: 43–78.

Collins, P. 2004. Exclamative clauses: A corpus-based account. *Word* 56: 1–17.

Comrie, B. 1999. Relative clauses: Structure and typology on the periphery of standard English. In *The Clause in English*, P. Collins & D. Lee (eds.) 81–91. Amsterdam: Benjamins.

——2002. Typology and language acquisition: The case of relative clauses. In *Typology and Second Language Acquisition*, A. G. Ramat (ed.) 19–37. Berlin: Mouton de Gruyter.

Conroy, A. 2006. The semantics of *how come*: A look at how factivity does it all. *University of Maryland Working Papers in Linguistics* 14: 1–24.

Constant, N. 2014. Contrastive topic: Meanings and realizations. PhD diss. University of Massachusetts, Amherst.

Contreras, H. 1976. *A Theory of Word Order with Special Reference to Spanish*. Amsterdam: North-Holland.

——1986. Spanish bare NPs and the ECP. In *Generative Studies in Spanish Syntax*, I. Bordelois, H. Contreras & K. Zagona (eds.) 25–49. Dordrecht: Foris.

——1987. Small clauses in Spanish and English. *Natural Language and Linguistic Theory* 5: 225–44.

——1991. On resumptive pronouns. In *Current Studies in Spanish Linguistics*, H. Campos & F. Martinez-Gil (eds.) 143–63. Washington, DC: Georgetown University Press.

Corbett, G. 2006. *Agreement*. Cambridge: Cambridge University Press.

Cormack, A. & Smith, N. 2000. Fronting: The syntax and pragmatics of 'focus' and 'topic'. *UCL Working Papers in Linguistics* 12: 387–416.

Cornilescu, A. 1981. Non-restrictive relative clauses: An essay in semantic description. *Revue Roumaine de Linguistique* 26: 41–67.

Costa, J. 2000. Adverbs as adjuncts to non-universal functional categories: Evidence from Portuguese. In *Adverbs and Adjunction*, A. Alexiadou & P. Svenonius (eds.) 103–122. Potsdam: Institut für Linguistik, Universität Potsdam.

——2004. A multifactorial approach to adverb placement: Assumptions, facts and problems. *Lingua* 114: 711–53.

Cote, S. 1996. Grammatical and discourse properties of null arguments in English. PhD diss. University of Pennsylvania.

——1997. Elaboration: A function and a form. Ms. University of Pennsylvania. Text of paper presented to the 23rd annual meeting of the Berkeley Linguistics Society.

Cougnon, L-A. & Fairon, C. (eds.) 2012. *SMS Communication: A linguistic approach*. Amsterdam: Benjamins.

Cowart, W. 1997 *Experimental Syntax: Applying objective methods to sentence judgments*. Thousand Oaks, CA: Sage Publications.

Cowper, E. 2016. Finiteness and pseudofiniteness: In *Finiteness Matters: On finiteness-related phenomena in natural languages*, K. M. Eide (ed.) 47–78. Amsterdam: Benjamins.

Craenenbroeck, J. van 2020. Expletives, locatives and subject doubling. In *Linguistic Variation: Structure and interpretation*, L. Franco & P. Lorusso (eds.) 661–90. Berlin: De Gruyter.

Craenenbroeck, J. van & den Dikken, M. 2006. Ellipsis and EPP repair. *Linguistic Inquiry* 37: 653–64.

Cresswell, C. 2002. Resumptive pronouns, wh-island violations, and sentence production. In *Proceedings of the 6th International Workshop on Tree-Adjoining Grammar and Related Frameworks (TAG+6)*, 101–9. Venice: Università di Venezia.

Cruschina, S. 2006. Informational focus in Sicilian and the left periphery. In *Phases of Interpretation*, M. Frascarelli (ed.) 363–85. Berlin: Mouton de Gruyter.

——2008. Discourse-related features and the syntax of peripheral positions: A comparative study of Sicilian and other Romance languages. PhD diss. University of Cambridge.

——2010a. Fronting as focalization in Sicilian. In *Syntactic Variation: The Dialects of Italy*. R. D'Alessandro, A. Ledgeway, I. Roberts (eds.) 247–60. Cambridge: Cambridge University Press.

——2010b. Aspetti morfologici e sintattici degli avverbi in siciliano. In *Quaderni di Lavoro ASIt n.11: Studi sui Dialetti della Sicilia*, J. Garzonio (ed.) 21–42. Padua: Unipress.

——2011a. On the syntactic status of sentential adverbs and modal particles. *Sprachtypologie und Universalienforschung (STUF)* 63: 345–57.

——2011b. Grammaticalization and the expression of evidentiality and epistemicity in Italian and in Sicilian. Unpublished handout, University of Manchester.

——2012. *Discourse-Related Features and Functional Projections*. Oxford: Oxford University Press.

Cruschina, S. & Remberger, E.-M. 2008. Hearsay and reported speech: Evidentiality in Romance. *Rivista di Grammatica Generativa* 33: 99–120.

——2017. Focus fronting. In *Manual of Romance Morphosyntax and Syntax*, E. Stark & A. Dufter (eds.) 502–35. Berlin: de Gruyter.

Crystal, D. 2008. *Txting: the Gr8 Db8*. Oxford: Oxford University Press.

Cukor-Avila, P. 1999. Stativity and copular absence in AAVE: Grammatical constraints at the subcategorical level. *Journal of English Linguistics* 27: 341–55.

Culicover, P. & Jackendoff, R. 2001. Control is not movement. *Linguistic Inquiry* 30: 483–512.

——2005. *Simpler Syntax*. Oxford: Oxford University Press.

——2006. Turn over control to the semantics. *Syntax* 9: 131–52.

Culicover, P. & Rochemont, M. 1983. Stress and focus in English. *Language* 59: 123–65.

Culy, C. 1996. Null objects in English recipes. *Language Variation and Change* 8: 91–124.

Cummins, S. & Roberge, Y. 2004. Null objects in French and English. In *Contemporary Approaches to Romance Linguistics*, J. Auger, C. Clements & B. Vance (eds.) 121–38. Amsterdam: Benjamins.

——2005. A modular account of null objects in French. *Syntax* 8: 44–64.

Cyrino, S. 1997. *O Objeto Nulo no Português Brasileiro: Um estudo sintático-diacrônico*. Londrina: Editora da UEL.

——2004. Null complement anaphora and null objects in Brazilian Portuguese. Ms. University of Campinas. https://www.researchgate.net/publication/242082650

——2021. On the syntax of null objects in Brazilian Portuguese. Handout for a conference on Null Objects from a Crosslinguistic and Developmental Perspective, University of Campinas.

Cyrino, S. & Matos, G. 2016. Null objects and VP Ellipsis in European and Brazilian Portuguese. In *The Handbook of Portuguese Linguistics*, W. L Wetzels, S. Menuzzi & J. Costa (eds.). London: Wiley-Blackwell.

Daeninck, B. 2019. Subject omission on Twitter: An explorative case study of the syntactic constraints of subject omission in finite clauses in English Twitter posts. MA thesis. Ghent University.

Dąbrowska, E. 2010. Naive v. expert intuitions: An empirical study of acceptability judgments. *The Linguistic Review* 27: 1–23.

Dalrymple, M. & Nikolaeva, I. 2011. *Objects and Information Structure*. Cambridge: Cambridge University Press.

Danckaert, L. 2011. On the left periphery of Latin embedded clauses. PhD diss. University of Ghent.

——2012. *Latin Embedded Clauses: The left periphery*. Amsterdam: Benjamins.

Danon, G. 2011. Agreement and DP-internal feature distribution. *Syntax* 14: 297–317.

Davies, W. D. & Dubinsky, S. 2004. *The Grammar of Raising and Control: A course in syntactic argumentation*. Oxford: Blackwell.

Davison, A. 1984. Syntactic markedness and the definition of the sentence topic. *Language* 60: 797–864.

d'Avis, F.-J. 2002. On the interpretation of wh-clauses in exclamative environments. *Theoretical Linguistics* 28: 5–31.

——2016. Different languages – different sentence types? On exclamative sentences. *Language and Linguistics Compass* 10: 159–75.

Deal, A.R. 2009. The origin and content of expletives: Evidence from 'selection'. *Syntax* 12: 285–323.

——2015. Interaction and satisfaction in φ-agreement. *Proceedings of the North East Linguistic Society* 45: 179–92.

——2016. Cyclicity and connectivity in Nez Perce relative clauses. *Linguistic Inquiry* 47: 427–70.

De Cat, C. 2000. Towards a unified analysis of French floating quantifiers. *Journal of French Language Studies* 10: 1–25.

De Cesare, A. M. 2015. Defining *focus modifiers* in a cross-linguistic perspective: A discussion based on English, German, French and Italian. In *Adverbs: Functional and diachronic aspects*, K. Pittner, D. Elsner & F. Barteld (eds.) 47–81. Amsterdam: Benjamins.

Déchaine, R.-M. & Wiltschko, M. 2002. Decomposing pronouns. *Linguistic Inquiry* 33: 409–42.

de Clerk, K. 2010. NEG-shift in English: Evidence from PP adjuncts. In *Proceedings of the 12th Seoul International Conference on Generative Grammar, 2010: Movement in minimalism*, D.-H. An & J. T. Kim (eds.) 231–51. Seoul: Hankuk.

Deen, K. U. 2002. The acquisition of Nairobi Swahili: The morphosyntax of inflectional prefixes and subjects. PhD diss. UCLA.

Dehé, N. 2002. *Particle Verbs in English: Syntax, information structure, and intonation.* Amsterdam: Benjamins.

Dehé, N., Feldhausen, I. & Ishihara, S. 2011. The prosody-syntax interface: Focus, phrasing, language evolution. *Lingua* 121: 1863–69.

Delahunty, G. 1983. But sentential subjects do exist. *Linguistic Analysis* 12: 379–98.

de Lange, J. 2004. Article omission in child speech and headlines. In *OTS Yearbook 2004*, A. Kerkhoff, J. de Lange & O.S. Leicht (eds.) 109–19. Utrecht Institute of Linguistics.

——2008. Article omission in headlines and child language: A processing approach. PhD diss. Utrecht University.

de Lange, J. & Avrutin, S. 2009. Reading between the (head)lines: A processing account of article omissions in newspaper headlines and child speech. *Lingua* 119: 1523–40.

Delfitto, D. & Fiorin, G. 2014. Exclamatives: Issues of syntax, logical form and interpretation. *Lingua* 152: 1–20.

del Gobbo, F. 2003 Appositives at the interface. PhD diss. University of California, Irvine.

Delsing, L.-O. 2010. Exclamatives in Scandinavian. *Studia Linguistica* 64: 16–36.

Demirdache, H. 1991. Resumptive chains in restrictive relatives, appositives, and dislocation structures. PhD diss. MIT.

Demonte, V. & Fernández Soriano, O. 2009. Force and finiteness in the Spanish complementizer system. *Probus* 21: 23–49.

——2013. El *que* citativo en español y otros elementos de la periferia oracional: Variación inter e intralingüística. In *Autour de 'que'*, D. Jakob & K. Plooj (eds.) 47–69. Frankfurt: Peter Lang.

——2014. Evidentiality and illocutionary force: Spanish matrix *que* at the syntax-semantics interface. *Linguistics Today* 214: 217–51.

Deneys, A.-S. 2020. Subject omission on Facebook: A quantitative study of subject omission in finite clauses in English Facebook posts. MA thesis. Ghent University.

Déprez, V. 1992. Raising constructions in Haitian Creole. *Natural Language and Linguistic Theory* 10: 191–231.

——2000. Parallel (a)symmetries and the internal structure of negative expressions. *Natural Language and Linguistic Theory* 18: 253–342.

de Vries, L. 1993. *Forms and Functions in Kombai, an Awyu Language of Irian Jaya.* Pacific Linguistics series B-108, Australian National University, Canberra.

de Vries, M. 2002. *The Syntax of Relativization.* Utrecht: LOT.

——2006. The syntax of appositive relativization: On specifying co-ordination, false free relatives and promotion. *Linguistic Inquiry* 37: 229–70.

Dickey, M. W. 1996. Constraints on the sentence processor and the distribution of resumptive pronouns. In *University of Massachusetts Occasional Papers in Linguistics* 19: 157–92.

Diercks, M. 2010. Agreement with subjects in Lubukusu. PhD diss. Georgetown University.

——2013. Indirect Agree in Lubukusu Complementizer Agreement. *Natural Language and Linguistic Theory* 31: 357–407.

Diercks, M., van Koppen, M., & Putnam, M. 2020. Agree probes down: Anaphoric feature valuation and phase reference. In *Agree to Agree: Agreement in the minimalist program*, P. W. Smith, J. Mursell & K. Hartmann (eds.) 347–89. Berlin: Language Science Press.

Dikken, M. den 1995. Binding, expletives and levels. *Linguistic Inquiry* 26: 347–54.

——2001. Pluringulars, pronouns and quirky agreement. *The Linguistic Review* 18: 19–41.

——2006. *Either* float and the syntax of co-*or*-dination. *Natural Language and Linguistic Theory* 24: 689–749.

——2017. Predication in the syntax of hyperraising and copy raising. *Acta Linguistica Academica* 64: 3–43.

——2018. Secondary predication and the distribution of raising to object. *Acta Linguistica Academica* 65: 87–117.

Di Sciullo, A. M., & Isac, D. 2008. The asymmetry of Merge. *Biolinguistics* 2: 260–90.

Doetjes, 1992. J.S. Rightward quantifiers float to the left. *The Linguistic Review* 9: 313–32.

——1997. *Quantifiers and selection: On the distribution of quantifying expressions in French, Dutch and English.* Utrecht: LOT.

Doherty, C. 1994. The syntax of subject contact relatives. *Chicago Linguistic Society Proceedings* 29: 55–65.

Dominguez, L. 2014. *Mapping Focus: The syntax and prosody of focus in Spanish.* Boston: Proquest.

Donati, C. 2006. On *wh*-head movement. In *Wh-Movement: Moving on*, L. Cheng & N. Corver (eds.) 21–46. Cambridge, MA: MIT Press.

Donati C. & Cecchetto, C. 2011. Relabeling Heads: A unified account for relativization structures. *Linguistic Inquiry* 42: 519–60.

Doran, D. 2015. The semantics of copy raising. MA thesis. McMaster University.

Dowty, D. & Brodie, B. 1984. A semantic analysis of floating quantifiers in transformationless grammar. *Proceedings of the West Coast Conference on Formal Linguistics* 3: 75–90.

Douglas, J. 2016. The syntactic structures of relativization. PhD diss. University of Cambridge.

——2017. Unifying the *that*-trace and anti-*that*-trace effects. *Glossa* 2: 1–28.

Drachman, G. 1974. The syntax of casual speech. *Salzburger Beiträge zur Linguistik* I: 273–95.

Drubig, H. B. 2003. Toward a typology of focus and focus constructions. *Linguistics* 41: 1–50.

Dubinsky, S. 1997. Infinitival relative clauses in English: An antisymmetric approach to discontinuous constituency. *Proceedings of the Eastern States*

Conference on Linguistics 96: 82–93. Ithaca, NY: Cornell University.

Duffield, N. 2015. Where not to put why, and why not? *The Journal of Konan University Faculty of Letters* 165: 57–68.

Durrleman, S. 2008. *The Syntax of Jamaican Creole: A Cartographic perspective.* Amsterdam: Benjamins.

Eckardt, R. 2007. Inherent focus on wh-phrases. *Sinn und Bedeutung* 11: 209–28.

Eide, K. M. 2016. Introduction. In *Finiteness Matters: On finiteness-related phenomena in natural languages,* K. M. Eide (ed.) 1–44. Amsterdam: Benjamins.

Eilander, S. 2020. Front page information: Article omission in Italian headlines in light of information density. MA thesis. Utrecht University.

Elenbaas, M. 2009. *The Synchronic and Diachronic Syntax of the English Verb-Particle Combination.* Utrecht: LOT.

Elgin, S. H. & Haden, R. 1991. *A Celebration of Ozark English.* Huntsville, AR: OCLS Press.

Elliot, D. E. 1974. Toward a grammar of exclamations. *Foundations of Language* 11: 231–46.

Embick, D. 1998. Voice systems and the syntax-morphology interface. *MIT Working Papers in Linguistics* 32: 41–72.

Emonds, J. 1970. Root and structure-preserving transformations. PhD diss. MIT.

——1976. *A Transformational Approach to English Syntax.* New York: Academic Press.

——1979. Appositive relatives have no properties. *Linguistic Inquiry* 10: 211–43.

——2004. Unspecified categories as the key to root constructions. In *Peripheries: Syntactic Edges and their Effects,* D. Adger, C. de Cat & G. Tsoulas (eds.) 75–120. Dordrecht: Kluwer.

Endo, Y. 2007a. *Locality and Information Structure. A Cartographic approach to Japanese.* Amsterdam: Benjamins.

——2007b. Locality and floating quantifiers. *Generative Grammar in Geneva* 5: 35–50.

——2014. *Why, what ... for, how come and why the hell. Papers from the International Spring Forum of the English Linguistic Society of Japan* 7: 10–16.

——2015a. Two ReasonPs: What are(*n't) you coming to the US for? In *The Cartography of Syntactic Structures, Vol. 10: Beyond functional sequence,* U. Shlonsky (ed.) 220–31. Oxford: Oxford University Press.

——2015b. *Why, what ... for, how come and why the hell. Papers from the International Spring Forum of the English Linguistic Society of Japan,* 7: 10–16.

——2017. Inter-speaker variation and subject-drop in *how come* questions in English. In *The Syntax-Morphology Interface in Generative Grammar,* C. Yim (ed.) 99–114. Seoul National University.

——2018 Variation in wh-expressions asking for a reason. *Linguistic Variation* 18: 299–314.

Engdahl, E. 1985. Parasitic gaps, resumptive pronouns, and subject extraction. *Linguistics* 23: 3–44.

Epstein, S. D., Kitahara, H. & Seely, T. D. 2015. From *Aspects*' 'daughterless mothers' (aka delta nodes) to *POP*'s 'motherless sets' (aka non-projection): A selective history of the evolution of simplest Merge. *MIT Working Papers in Linguistics* 77: 99–112.

Epstein, S. D., Pires, A. & Seely, T. D. 2005. EPP in T: More controversial subjects. *Syntax* 8: 65–80.

Epstein, S. D & Seely, T. D. 2006. *Derivations in Minimalism*. Cambridge: Cambridge University Press.

Erdmann, P. 1980. On the history of subject contact relatives in English. *Folia Linguistica Historica* 1: 139–70.

Erlewine, M. Y. 2014. Why the null complementizer is special in the English *that*-trace effect. Ms. MIT. https://ling.auf.net/lingbuzz/002029

——2017a. Why the null complementizer is special in complementiser-trace effects. *MIT Working Papers in Linguistics* 80: 371–80.

——2017b. Vietnamese focus particles and derivation by phase. *Journal of East Asian Linguistics* 26: 325–49.

Ernst, T. 1991. On the scope principle. *Linguistic Inquiry* 22: 750–56.

——2002. *The Syntax of Adjuncts*. Cambridge: Cambridge University Press.

——2004. Principles of adverbial distribution in the lower clause. *Lingua*: 114: 755–77.

Erteschik-Shir, N. 1986. Wh-questions and focus. *Linguistics & Philosophy* 9: 117–49.

——1992. Resumptive pronouns in islands. In *Island Constraints: Theory, Acquisition and Processing*, H. Goodluck & M. Rochemont (eds.) 89–108. Dordrecht: Kluwer.

Erteschik-Shir, N., Ibnbari, L., & Taube, S. 2013. Missing objects as topic drop. *Lingua* 136: 145–69.

Fabb, N. 1990. The difference between English restrictive and non-restrictive clauses. *Journal of Linguistics* 26: 57–78.

Fanselow, G. & Lenertová, D. 2010. Left peripheral focus: Mismatches between syntax and information structure. *Natural Language and Linguistic Theory* 29: 169–209.

Farkas, D. 1987. DO pro in Hungarian. In *Approaches to Hungarian, Vol. 2: Theories and analyses*, I. Kenesei (ed.) 191–211. Szeged: JATE.

Farrell, P. 1990. Null objects in Brazilian Portuguese. *Natural Language and Linguistic Theory* 8: 325–46.

Fassi-Fehri, A. 1980. Some complement phenomena in Arabic, the complementizer phrase hypothesis, and the Non-Accessibility Condition. *Analyse/Théorie* 54–114. Paris: Université de Paris, Vincennes.

Felser, C. & Rupp, L. 2001. Expletives as arguments: Germanic existential sentences revisited. *Linguistische Berichte*, 187: 289–324.

Ferguson, C. A. (1982) Simplified registers and linguistic theory.

In *Exceptional Language and Linguistics*, L. K. Obler & L. Menn (eds.) 49–66. New York: Academic Press.

Fernández-Salgueiro, G. 2020. On EPP effects and the properties of core functional categories. *Glossa: A Journal of General Linguistics* 5(1): 36.

Ferreira, F. & Swets, B. 2005. The production and comprehension of resumptive pronouns in relative clause 'island' contexts. In *Twenty-First Century Psycholinguistics: Four cornerstones*, A. Cutler (ed.) 263–78. Mahway, NJ: Lawrence Erlbaum Associates.

Ferreira, M. 2004. Hyperraising and null subjects in Brazilian Portuguese. *MIT Working Papers in Linguistics* 47: 57–85.

——2009. Null subjects and finite control in Brazilian Portuguese. *Linguistics Today* 142: 17–49.

Ferreiro, S. M. 2003. Verbal inflectional morphology in Broca's aphasia. MA thesis. Universitat Autònoma de Barcelona.

Féry, C. 2007. The prosody of topicalization. In *On Information Structure: Meaning and form*, K. Schwabe & S. Winkler (eds.) 69–86. Amsterdam: Benjamins.

Féry, C. & Samek-Lodovici, V. 2006. Focus projection and prosodic prominence in nested foci. *Language* 82: 131–50.

Fielding, H. (1996). *Bridget Jones's Diary*. Oxford: Picador.

Fiengo, R. & Higginbotham, J. 1981. Opacity in NP. *Linguistic Analysis* 7: 347–73.

Fillmore, C. J. 1968. The case for case. In *Universals in Linguistic Theory*, E. Bach & R. T. Harms (eds.) 1–88. New York: Holt Rinehart & Winston.

——1970. Subjects, speakers and roles. *Semantics of Natural Language* 21: 251–74.

——1986. Pragmatically controlled zero anaphora. *Berkeley Linguistics Society Proceedings* 12: 95–107.

Fiorentino, G. 2007. European relative clauses and the uniqueness of the relative pronoun type. *Rivista di Linguistica* 19: 263–91.

Fitzpatrick, E., Bachenko, J. & Hindle, D. 1986. The status of telegraphic sublanguages. In *Analyzing Language in Restricted Domains: Sublanguage description and processing*, R. Grishman & R. Kittredge (eds.) 39–51. Hillsdale, NJ: Erlbaum.

Fitzpatrick, J. 2005a. The *whys* and *how comes* of presupposition and NPI licensing in questions. *Proceedings of the West Coast Conference on Formal Linguistics* 24: 138–45.

——2005b. Anybody seen the auxiliary? *MIT Working Papers in Linguistics* 50: 71–91.

——2006. The syntactic and semantic roots of floating quantification. PhD diss. MIT.

Flagg, E. 2002. Interface issues in the English imperative. PhD diss. MIT.

Fong, S. 2018. Featural definition of syntactic positions: Evidence from hyper-raising. *Proceedings of the Linguistic Society of America* 3(2): 1–15.

Forsmo, M. G. 2020. The order of adverbs: Comparing Cinque and Ernst. Bachelor's project, Norwegian University of Science and Technology.

Fox, D. 2000. *Economy and Semantic Interpretation*. Cambridge, MA: MIT Press.

Fox, D. & Grodzinsky, Y. 1998. Children's passive: A view from the *by*-phrase. *Linguistic Inquiry* 29: 311–32.

Fox, D. & Nissenbaum, J. 1999. Extraposition and scope: A case for overt QR. *Proceedings of the West Coast Conference on Formal Linguistics* 18: 132–44.

——2004. Condition A and scope reconstruction. *Linguistic Inquiry* 35: 475–85.

Francis, E. J., Lam, C., Zheng, C. C., Hitz, J. & Matthews, S. 2015. Resumptive pronouns, structural complexity, and the elusive distinction between grammar and performance: Evidence from Cantonese. *Lingua* 162: 56–81.

Francis, N. 2017. Modal scope in Negative Inversion constructions. *Proceedings of the West Coast Conference on Formal Linguistics* 34: 214–21.

Franco, I. 2009. Verbs, subjects and stylistic fronting: A comparative analysis of the interaction of CP properties with verb movement and subject positions in Icelandic and Old Italian. PhD diss. University of Siena.

Frank, R. 2006. Phase theory and tree-adjoining grammar. *Lingua* 116: 145–202.

Frank, R. & Vijay-Shanker, K. 2001. Primitive c-command. *Syntax* 4: 164–204.

Frascarelli, M. 2000. *The Syntax-Phonology Interface in Focus and Topic Constructions in Italian*. Dordrecht: Springer.

Frascarelli, M. & Hinterhölzl, R. 2007. Types of topics in German and Italian. In *On Information Structure, Meaning and Form*, S. Winkler & K. Schwabe (eds.) 86–116. Amsterdam: Benjamins.

Frascarelli, M. & Puglielli, A. 2007. Focus in the Force-Fin system: Information structure in Cushitic Languages. In *Focus Strategies: Evidence from African Languages*, E. Aboh, K. Hartmann & M. Zimmermann (eds.) 161–84. Berlin: Mouton de Gruyter.

Fraser, J. B. 1965. An examination of the verb-particle construction in English. PhD diss. MIT.

Frazier, L. & Clifton, C. 2015. Without his shirt off he saved the child from almost drowning: Interpreting an uncertain input. *Language, Cognition & Neuroscience* 30(6): 635–47.

Freidin, R. & Vergnaud, J. R. 2001. Exquisite connections: Some remarks on the evolution of linguistic theory. *Lingua* 111: 639–66.

Frey, W. 2004. Notes on the syntax and pragmatics of German left dislocation. In *The Syntax and Semantics of the Left Periphery*, H. Lohnstein & S. Trissler (eds.) 163–209. Berlin: Mouton de Gruyter.

——2005. Pragmatic properties of certain German and English left peripheral constructions. *Linguistics* 43: 89–129.

Friedemann, N. 1998. Functional categories in agrammatic production. PhD diss. Tel-Aviv University.

Friedmann, N., Belletti, A. & Rizzi, L. 2009. Relativized minimality: Types of intervention in the acquisition of A-bar dependencies. *Lingua* 119: 67–88.

Friedmann, N. & Grodzinsky, Y. 1997. Tense and agreement in agrammatic production: Pruning the syntactic tree. *Brain and Language* 56: 397–425.

——2000. Split inflection in neurolinguistics. In *The Acquisition of Syntax: Studies in comparative developmental linguistics*, M.-A. Friedmann & L. Rizzi (eds.) 84–101. London: Longman.

Friedmann, N., Novogrodsky, R., Szterman, R. & Preminger, O. 2009. Resumptive pronouns as a last resort when movement is impaired: Relative clauses in hearing impairment. In *Current Issues in Generative Hebrew Linguistics* 7: 267–90.

Fujii, T. 2005. Cycle, linearization of chains, and multiple case checking. In *Proceedings of Console XIII*, S. Blaho, L. Vicente & E. Schoorlemmer (eds.) 39–65. University of Leiden: Student Organization of Linguistics in Europe.

——2007. Cyclic chain reduction. In *The Copy Theory of Movement*, N.

Corver & J. Nunes (eds.) 291–326. Amsterdam: Benjamins.

Fukuda, S. & Polinsky, M. 2014. Licensing of floating nominal modifiers and unaccusativity in Japanese. *Proceedings of the West Coast Conference on Formal Linguistics* 31: 189–98.

Fukui, N. 1986. A theory of category projection and its application. PhD diss. MIT.

——2011. Merge and Bare Phrase Structure. In *The Oxford Handbook of Linguistic Minimalism*, C. Boeckx (ed.) 73–95. Oxford: Oxford University Press.

Fukui, N. & Speas, M. 1986. Specifiers and projection. *MIT Working Papers in Linguistics* 8: 128–72.

Fukushima, K. 1991a. Phrase structure grammar, Montague semantics, and floating quantifiers in Japanese. *Linguistics and Philosophy* 14: 581–628.

——1991b. Generalized floating quantifiers. PhD diss. University of Arizona.

Funakoshi, K. 2017. Disjunction and Object Drop in Japanese. *Florida Linguistics Papers* 4: 11–20.

Fuß, E. 2004. Diachronic clues to pro-drop and Complementiser Agreement in Bavarian. In *Diachronic Clues to Synchronic Grammar*, E. Fuß & C. Trips (eds.) 59–100. Amsterdam: Benjamins.

——2005. *The Rise of Agreement: A formal approach to the syntax and grammaticalization of verbal inflection*. Amsterdam: Benjamins.

——2008. Multiple agreement and the representation of inflection in the c-domain. *Linguistische Berichte* 213: 77–106.

——2014. Complementizer Agreement (in Bavarian): Feature inheritance or feature insertion? In *Bavarian Syntax: Contributions to the Theory of Syntax*, G. Grewendorf & H. Weiß (eds.) 51–82. Amsterdam: Benjamins.

Futagi, Y. 2004. Japanese focus particles at the syntax-semantics interface. PhD diss. Rutgers University.

García Velasco, D. & Portero Muñoz, C. 2002. Understood objects in Functional Grammar. In *Working Papers in Functional Grammar 76*. University of Amsterdam.

Garzonio, J. 2005. Struttura informazionale e soggetti nulli in russo: Un approccio cartografico. PhD diss. University of Padua.

Gasper, S. 2014. An editing framework guiding students towards self-correcting errors in writing. MA thesis. Rowan University.

Gavarrò, A. 1991. A note on Catalan clitics. *Catalan Working Papers in Linguistics* 1: 65–73.

Geisler, C. 1998. Infinitival relative clauses in spoken discourse. *Language Variation and Change* 10: 23–41.

Gelderen, E. van 2009. Renewal in the left periphery: Economy and the complementiser layer. *Transactions of the Philological Society* 107: 131–95.

Geluykens, R. (1992) *From Discourse Process to Grammatical Construction: On left dislocation in English*. Amsterdam: Benjamins.

Gérard, J. 1980. *L'Exclamation en Français*. Tübingen: Niemeyer.

Gerken, L. 1991. The metrical basis for children's subjectless sentences. *Journal of Memory and Language* 30: 431–51.

——1994. Young children's representation of prosodic phonology: Evidence from English-speakers' weak syllable productions. *Journal of Memory and Language* 33: 19–38.

Ghosh, P. 2022. 12 news writing rules used by subeditors for compelling headlines. shareyouressays.com.

Ginzburg, J. & Sag, I. 2000. *Interrogative Investigations: The form, meaning, and use of English interrogatives*. Stanford, CA: CSLI Publications.

Giorgi, A. & Pianesi, T. F. 1997. *Tense and Aspect: From semantics to morphosyntax*. Oxford: Oxford University Press.

Gisbourne, N. 1996. English perception verbs. PhD diss. University College London.

——2010. *The Event Structure of Perception Verbs*. Oxford: Oxford University Press.

Giusti, G. 1990. Floating quantifiers, scrambling and configurationality. *Linguistic Inquiry* 21: 633–41.

——1991a. The categorial status of quantified nominals. *Linguistische Berichte* 136: 438–452.

——1991b. The syntax of floating *alles* in German. In *Issues in German Syntax*, W. Abraham, W. Kosmeijer & E. Reuland (eds.) 327–50. The Hague: Mouton.

——1996. Is there a FocusP and a TopicP in the Noun Phrase? *University of Venice Working Papers in Linguistics* 6: 105–28.

——1997. The categorial status of determiners. In *The New Comparative Syntax*, L. Haegeman (ed.) 94–113. Cambridge: Cambridge University Press.

——2012. On force and case, fin and num. In *Enjoy Linguistics: Papers Presented to Luigi Rizzi on the Occasion of his 60th Birthday*, V. Bianchi & C. Chesi (eds.) 205–17. Siena: CISCL Press.

Goedegebuure, P. 2009. Focus structure and Q-word questions in Hittite. *Linguistics* 47: 945–69.

Goldshlag, E. 2005. The EPP, nominative case and expletives. MA thesis. Tel Aviv University.

Gonçalves, A., Santos, A. L. & Duarte, I. 2014. (Pseudo-) inflected infinitives and control as *Agree*. In *Selected Papers from Going Romance, Leuven 2012*, K. Lahousse & S. Marzo (eds.) 161–80. Amsterdam: Benjamins.

Goodall, G. 1997. Theta-alignment and the *by*-phrase. *Proceedings of the Chicago Linguistics Society* 33: 129–39.

——2001. The EPP in Spanish. In *Objects and Other Subjects: Grammatical functions, functional categories, and configurationality*, W. D. Davies & S. Dubinsky (eds.) 193–223. Dordrecht: Kluwer.

——2017. Finiteness contrasts without tense? A view from Mandarin Chinese. *Journal of East Asian Linguistics* 26: 259–99.

Grant, H. (2015). Tumblinguistics: Innovation and variation in new forms of written CMC. MA thesis. University of Glasgow.

Greco, C., Haegeman, L. & Phan, T. 2017. Expletives and speaker-related meaning. In *Order and Structure in Syntax II: Subjecthood and argument structure*, M. Sheehan & L. R. Bailey (eds.) 69–93. Berlin: Language Science Press.

Green, L. J. 2002. *African American English: A linguistic introduction*. Cambridge: Cambridge University Press.

Green, M. 2007. *Focus in Hausa*. Oxford: Blackwell.

Green, M. & Jaggar, P. 2003. Ex-situ and in-situ focus in Hausa: Syntax, semantics and discourse. In *Research in Afroasiatic Grammar II*, J. Lecarme (ed.) 187–213. Amsterdam: Benjamins.

Greenberg, G. 1984. Left dislocation, topicalization, and interjections. *Natural Language and Linguistic Theory* 2: 283–87.

Gregory, M. & Michaelis, L. 2001. Topicalization and left dislocation: A functional opposition revisited. *Journal of Pragmatics* 33: 1665–1706.

Grewendorf, G. 2002. Left dislocation as movement. *Georgetown University Working Papers in Theoretical Linguistics* 2: 31–81.

Grewendorf, G. & Poletto, C. 2009. The hybrid complementizer system of Cimbrian. *Studies in Linguistics* 3: 181–94.

Grice, H. P. 1975. Logic and conversation. In *Syntax and*

Semantics 3: Speech Acts, P. Cole & J. Morgan (eds.) 41–58. New York: Academic Press.

Griffin, W. E. 2003. The split-INFL hypothesis and AgrsP in Universal Grammar. In *The Role of Agreement in Natural Languages: TLS 5 Proceedings*, W. E. Griffin (ed.) 25–36. Munich, Lincom Europa.

Grimshaw, J. 1979. Complement selection and the lexicon. *Linguistic Inquiry* 10: 279–326.

——1993. Minimal projection, heads, and optimality. Ms. Rutgers University.

Groat, E. 1995. English expletives: A minimalist approach. *Linguistic Inquiry* 26: 354–65.

——1997. A derivational program for syntactic theory. PhD diss. Harvard University.

——1999. Raising the case of expletives. In *Working Minimalism*, S. D. Epstein & N. Hornstein (eds.) 27–43. Cambridge, MA: MIT Press.

Groefsema, M. 1995. Understood arguments: A semantic/pragmatic approach. *Lingua* 96: 139–61.

Grohmann, K. K. 1997. On left dislocation. *Groninger Arbeiten zur Germanistischen Linguistik* 40: 1–33.

——2000. Prolific peripheries: A radical view from the left. PhD diss. University of Maryland.

——2003. *Prolific Domains*. Amsterdam: Benjamins.

——2006. Top issues in questions: Topics – Topicalization – Topicalizability. In *Wh-Movement: Moving On*, L. Cheng & N. Corver

(eds.) 249–88. Cambridge, MA: MIT Press.

Grohmann, K. K., Drury J. & Castillo, J. C. 2000. No more EPP. *Proceedings of the West Coast Conference on Formal Linguistics* 19: 153–66.

Grohmann, K. K. & Haegeman, L. 2002. Resuming reflexives. https://ling .auf.net/lingbuzz/000140

Grolla, E. 2005. Resumptive pronouns as last resort: Implications for language acquisition. *Penn Working Papers in Linguistics* 11: 71–84.

Groos, A. & van Riemsdijk, H. 1981. Matching effects in free relatives: A parameter of core grammar. In *Theory of Markedness in Generative Grammar*, A. Belletti, L. Brandi & L. Rizzi (eds.) 171–216. Pisa: Scuola Normale Superiore.

Grosu, A. 1996. The proper analysis of missing-P free relative constructions. *Linguistic Inquiry* 27: 257–93.

——2003. A unified theory of standard and transparent free relatives. *Natural Language and Linguistic Theory* 21: 247–331.

Grosu, A. & Horvath, J. 1984. The GB theory and Raising in Rumanian. *Linguistic Inquiry* 15: 348–53.

Grosu, A. & Landman, F. 1998. Strange relatives of the third kind. *Natural Language Semantics* 6: 125–70.

Gruber, B. 2008. Complementizer Agreement: New evidence from the Upper Austrian variant of Gmunden. MA thesis. University of Vienna.

Gruber, J. S. 1965. Studies in lexical relations. PhD diss. MIT.

——1967. Topicalization in child language. *Foundations of Language* 3: 37–65.

——1976. *Lexical Structures in Syntax and Semantics*. Amsterdam: North Holland.

Guasti, M. T. & Rizzi, L. 2002. Agreement and tense as distinct syntactic positions: Evidence from acquisition. In *Functional Structure in DP and IP*, G. Cinque (ed.) 167–94. Oxford: Oxford University Press.

Guilfoyle, E., Hung, H. & Travis, L. 1992. Spec of IP and spec of VP: Two subjects in Austronesian languages. *Natural Language and Linguistic Theory* 10: 375–414.

Gundel, J. K. 1975. Left dislocation and the role of topic-comment structure in linguistic theory. *Ohio State Working Papers in Linguistics* 18: 72–131.

——1985. Shared knowledge and topicality. *Journal of Pragmatics* 9: 83–107.

——1988. Universals of topic-comment structure. In *Studies in Syntactic Typology*, M. Hammond, E. A. Moravcsik & J. Werth (eds.) 209–42. Amsterdam: Benjamins.

Gutiérrez-Rexach, J. 2001. Spanish exclamatives and the interpretation of the left periphery. In *Romance Languages and Linguistic Theory 1999*, Y. D'hulst, J. Rooryck, & J. Schroten (eds.) 167–94. Amsterdam: Benjamins.

——2008. Spanish root exclamatives at the syntax/semantics interface. *Catalan Journal of Linguistics* 7: 117–33.

Guy, G. R. & Bayley, R. 1995. On the choice of relative pronouns in English. *American Speech* 70: 148–62.

Guz, W. 2017. Resumptive pronouns in Polish *co* relative clauses. *Journal of Slavic Linguistics* 25: 95–130.

Gwynne, N. M. 2013. *Gwynne's Grammar: The ultimate introduction to grammar and the writing of good English*. London: Ebury press.

Ha, S. 2010. A prosody analysis of the comp-trace effect. *English Language and Linguistics* 16: 109–33.

Haaften, T. van, Smits, R. & Vat, J. 1983. Left dislocation, connectedness and reconstruction. *Linguistics Today* 3: 133–54.

Hackl, M. & Nissenbaum, J. 2012. A modal ambiguity in *for*-infinitival relative clauses. *Natural Language Semantics* 20: 59–81.

Haeberli, E. 2003. Categorial features as the source of EPP and abstract case phenomena. In *New Perspectives on Case Theory*, E. Brandner & H. Zinsmeister (eds.) 89–126. Stanford, CA: CSLI publications.

Haegeman, L. 1985. The *get* passive and Burzio's generalization. *Lingua* 66: 53–77.

——1987a. Complement ellipsis in English: Or, how to cook without objects. In *Studies in Honour of René Derolez*, A. M. Simon-Vandenbergen (ed.) 248–61. Ghent: University of Ghent.

——1987b. Register variation in English: Some theoretical

observations. *Journal of English Linguistics* 20: 230–48.

——1990a. Non-overt subjects in diary contexts. In *Grammar in Progress*, J. Mascaró & M. Nespor (eds.) 167–74. Dordrecht: Foris.

——1990b. Understood subjects in English diaries. *Multilingua* 9: 157–99.

——1992. *Theory and Description in Generative Syntax*. Cambridge: Cambridge University Press.

——1994. *Introduction to Government and Binding Theory*, 2nd edition. Oxford: Blackwell.

——1995. *The Syntax of Negation*. Cambridge: Cambridge University Press.

——1997. Register variation, truncation, and subject omission in English and in French. *English Language and Linguistics* 1: 233–70.

——2000a. Adult null subjects in non *pro*-drop languages. In *The Acquisition of Syntax*, M.-A. Friedemann & L. Rizzi (eds.) 129–69. London: Addison, Wesley and Longman.

——2000b. Inversion, non-adjacent inversion and adjuncts in CP. *Transactions of the Philological Society* 98: 121–60.

——2000c. Negative preposing, Negative Inversion and the split CP. In *Negation and Polarity: Syntactic and semantic perspectives*, L. Horn & Y. Kato (eds.), 21–62. Oxford: Oxford University Press.

——2002a. Sentence-medial NP-adjuncts in English. *Nordic Journal of Linguistics* 25: 79–108.

——2002b. Non-overt subject pronouns in written English. In *Language, Context and Cognition: Papers in honour of Wolf Dietrich Bald's 60th birthday*, S. Sybil, M. Klages, E. Hantson, & U. Römer (eds.) 135–49. Munich: Langenscheidt-Longman.

——2003. Notes on long adverbial fronting in English and the left periphery. *Linguistic Inquiry* 34: 640–49.

——2004. Topicalization, CLLD and the left periphery. In *Proceedings of the Dislocated Elements Workshop*, B. Shaer, W. Frey & C. Maienborn (eds.) 157–92. Berlin: ZAS.

——2006a. Argument fronting in English, Romance CLLD and the left periphery. In *Crosslinguistic Research in Syntax and Semantics: Negation, tense, and clausal architecture*, R. Zanuttini, H. Campos, E. Herburger & P. H. Portner (eds.) 27–52. Washington, DC: Georgetown University Press.

——2006b. Conditionals, factives and the left periphery. *Lingua* 116: 1651–69.

——2006c. Register variation: Core grammar and periphery. In *Encyclopedia of Language and Linguistics: 2nd edition*, K. Brown (ed.) 468–74. Elsevier Science.

——2007a. Operator movement and topicalization in adverbial clauses. *Folia Linguistica* 18: 485–502.

——2007b. Subject omission in present-day written English: On the theoretical relevance of peripheral data. *Rivista di Grammatica Generativa* 32: 91–124.

——2009. The movement analysis of temporal adverbial clauses. *English Language and Linguistics* 13: 385–408.

——2010. The internal syntax of adverbial clauses. *Lingua* 120: 628–48.

——2012. *Adverbial Clauses, Main Clause Phenomena, and Composition of the Left Periphery.* Oxford: Oxford University Press.

——2013. The syntax of registers: Diary subject omission and the privilege of the root. *Lingua* 130: 88–110.

——2017. Unspeakable sentences: Subject omission in written registers – A Cartographic analysis. *Linguistic Variation* 17: 229–50.

——2019. Register-based subject omission in English and its implication for the syntax of adjuncts. *Anglophonia* 28. https://doi.org/10.4000/anglophonia.2873.

——2021. The decomposition of subjects and the role of SubjP. Ms. Ghent University.

Haegeman, L. & Danckaert, L. 2017. Variation in English subject extraction: The case of hyperactive subjects. In *Studies on Syntactic Cartography*, F. Si (ed.) 302–35. Beijing: China Social Sciences Press.

Haegeman, L. & Greco, C. 2017. Initial adverbial clauses and West Flemish V3. Ms. University of Ghent.

Haegeman, L. & Guéron, J. 1999. *English Grammar: A Generative perspective.* Oxford: Blackwell.

Haegeman, L. & Hill, V. 2014. Vocatives and speech-act projections: A case study in West Flemish. In *On Peripheries: Exploring clause initial and clause final positions*, C. Cardinaletti, G. Cinque & Y. Endo (eds.) 209–36. Tokyo: Hituzi Syobe Publishing.

Haegeman, L. & Ihsane, T. 1999. Subject ellipsis in embedded clauses in English. *Journal of English Language and Linguistics* 3: 117–45.

——2001 Adult null subjects in the non-pro drop languages: Two diary dialects. *Language Acquisition* 9: 329–46.

Haegeman, L., Jiménez-Fernández, Á. & Radford, A. 2014. Deconstructing the Subject Condition in terms of cumulative constraint violation. *The Linguistic Review* 31: 73–150.

Haegeman, L. & van Koppen, M. 2012. Complementizer agreement and the relation between T and C. *Linguistic Inquiry* 43: 441–54.

Haegeman, L., & Starke, E. 2021. Register-specific subject omission in English and French and the syntax of coordination. In *Continuity and Variation in Germanic and Romance*, S. Wolfe & C. Meklenborg (eds.) 15–43. Oxford: Oxford University Press.

Haegeman, L., Weir, A, Danckaert, L., D'Hulster, T. & Buelens, L. 2015. Against the root analysis of subject contact relatives in English. *Lingua* 163: 61–74.

Haider, H. 2000. Adverb placement: Convergence of structure and licensing. *Theoretical Linguistics* 26: 95–134.

——2004. Pre- and post-verbal adverbials in OV and VO. *Lingua* 114: 779–807.

——2005. How to turn German into Icelandic – and derive the OV-VO contrasts. *Journal of Comparative Germanic Linguistics* 8: 1–53.

——2017. In the absence of a subject. *Wiener Linguistische Gazette* 82: 87–98.

——2019. On absent, expletive and non-referential subjects. In *Semantic and Syntactic Aspects of Impersonality*, P. Herbeck, B. Pöll, & A. Wolfsgruber (eds.) 11–46. Hamburg: Helmut Buske Verlag.

Haig, J. 1980. Some observations on quantifier floating in Japanese. *Linguistics* 18: 1065–83.

Hallman, P. 1997. Reiterative syntax. In *Clitics, Pronouns and Movement*, J. R. Black & V. Motapayane (eds.) 87–131. Amsterdam: Benjamins.

Hamamo, S. 1997. On Japanese quantifier floating. In *Directions in Functional Linguistics*, A. Kamio (ed.) 173–97. Amsterdam: Benjamins.

Han, C.-H. 1998. The structure and interpretation of imperatives: Mood and force in Universal Grammar. PhD diss. University of Pennsylvania.

——2000a. The evolution of *do*-support in English imperatives. In *Diachronic Syntax: Models and mechanisms*, S. Pintzuk, G. Tsoulas & A. Warner (eds.) 275–95. Oxford: Oxford University Press.

——2000b. *The Structure and Interpretation of Imperatives: Mood and force in Universal Grammar.* London: Psychology Press.

——2001. Force, negation and imperatives. *The Linguistic Review* 18: 289–325.

Han, C., Elouazizi, N., Galeano, C., Görgülü, E., Hedberg, N., Jeffrey, M., Kim, K. & Kirby, S. 2012. Processing strategies and resumptive pronouns in English. *Proceedings of the West Coast Conference on Formal Linguistics* 30: 153–61.

Han, H.-S. 2004. *There* as an existential operator. *Language Research* 40: 451–64.

Hankamer, J. 1971. Constraints on deletion in syntax. PhD diss. Yale University.

Hankamer, J. & Sag, I. 1976. Deep and surface anaphora. *Linguistic Inquiry* 7: 391–428.

Hanson, R. 1999. Split INFL and the acquisition of Neg and Aux. *Calgary Working Papers in Linguistics* 21: 2–13.

Hardt, D. 1993. Verb phrase ellipsis: Form, meaning and processing. PhD diss. University of Pennsylvania.

Harford Perez, C. 1985. Aspects of complementation in three Bantu languages. PhD diss. University of Wisconsin–Madison.

Harris, M. & Vincent, N. 1980. On zero relatives. *Linguistic Inquiry* 11: 805–807.

Hartmann, J. M. 2008. *Expletives in existentials: English there and German da.* Utrecht: LOT.

Hartman, J. & Ai, R. R. 2009. A focus account of Swiping. In *Selected*

Papers from the 2006 Cyprus Syntaxfest, K. K. Grohmann & P. Panagiotidis (eds.) 92–122. Newcastle: Cambridge Scholars Publishing.

Harvie, D. 1998. Null subject in English: Wonder if it exists. *Cahiers Linguistiques d'Ottowa* 26: 15–25.

Harwood, W. 2012. There are several positions available: English intermediate subject positions. *Proceedings of ConSOLE* 19: 215–39.

Hasegawa, N. 1993. Floating quantifiers and bare NP expressions. In *Japanese Syntax in Comparative Grammar*, N. Hasegawa (ed.) 115–45. Tokyo: Kuroshio.

Hawkins, J. A. 2001. Why are categories adjacent? *Journal of Linguistics* 37: 1–34.

Hazout, I. 2004a. Long-distance agreement and the syntax of *for-to* infinitives. *Linguistic Inquiry* 3: 338–43.

——2004b. The syntax of existential constructions. *Linguistic Inquiry* 35: 393–430.

Heejeong Ko, E. O. 2010. A hybrid approach to floating quantifiers: Experimental evidence. *Linguistic Research* 29: 69–106.

Heffer, S. 2011. *Strictly English: The correct way to write ... and why it matters*. London: Windmill Books.

Heestand, D., Xiang, M. & Polinsky, M. 2011 Resumption still does not rescue islands. *Linguistic Inquiry* 42: 138–52.

Heim, I. 1987. Where does the definiteness restriction apply?

Evidence from the definiteness of variables. In *The Representation of (In)definiteness*, E. J. Reuland & A. ter Meulen (eds.) 21–42. Cambridge, MA: MIT Press.

Heim, I. & Kratzer, A. 1998. *Semantics in Generative Grammar*. Oxford: Blackwell.

Hellan, L. 1986. The headedness of NPs in Norwegian. In *Features and Projections*, P. Muysken & H. van Riemsdijk (eds.) 89–122. Dordrecht: Foris.

Henderson, B. 2006. Multiple agreement and inversion in Bantu. *Syntax* 9: 275–89.

Hendrick, R. 1982. Reduced questions and their theoretical implications. *Language* 58: 800–19.

Henry, A. 1992. Infinitives in a *for-to* dialect. *Natural Language and Linguistic Theory* 10: 279–301.

——1995 *Belfast English and Standard English: Dialect variation and parameter-setting*. Oxford: Oxford University Press.

——2012. Phase edges, quantifier float and the nature of (micro-) variation. *Iberia* 4: 23–39.

Henry, A. & Cottell, S. 2007. A new approach to transitive expletives: Evidence from Belfast English. *English Language and Linguistics* 11: 279–99.

Herdan, S. 2008. *Degrees and Amounts in Relative Clauses*. Proquest: Google Books.

Herrmann, T. 2003. Relative clauses in dialects of English: A typological approach. PhD diss. Albert-Ludwigs-Universität, Freiburg.

——2005. Relative clauses in English dialects of the British Isles. In *A Comparative Grammar of British English Dialects*, B. Kortmann, T. Herrmann, L. Pietsch & S. Wagner (eds.) 21–124. Berlin: Mouton.

Heycock, C. 1994. *Layers of Predication*. New York: Garland.

——2005. On the interaction of adjectival modifiers and relative clauses. *Natural Language Semantics* 13: 359–82.

Higgins, F. R. 1973. On J. Emonds' analysis of Extraposition. In J. Kimball (ed.) *Syntax and Semantics* 2: 149–95. New York: Academic Press.

Hill, J. A. C. 1983. *A computational model of language acquisition in the two-year-old*. Indiana University Linguistics Club, Bloomington, IN.

Hinrichs, L., Smzrecsanyl, B. & Bohmann, A. 2015. Which-hunting and the Standard English relative clause. *Language* 91: 806–36.

Hiraira, K. 2001. Multiple agree and the Defective Intervention Constraint. *MIT Working Papers in Linguistics* 40: 67–80.

——2005. Dimensions of symmetry in syntax: Agreement and clausal architecture. PhD diss. MIT.

Hirschbühler, P. 1973. La dislocation à gauche en français. *Le Langage et l'Homme* 23: 19–125.

——1974. La dislocation à gauche comme construction basique en français. In *Actes du Colloque Franco-Allemande de Grammaire Transformationelle*, C. Rohrer & N.

Ruwet (eds.) vol. 1, 9–17, Tübingen: Max Niemeyer Verlag.

——1975. On the source of lefthand NPs in French. *Linguistic Inquiry* 6: 155–65.

——1976. Two analyses of free relatives in French. *Proceedings of the North East Linguistic Society* 6: 137–52.

Hirschbühler, P. & Rivero, M. L. 1983. Remarks on free relatives and matching phenomena. *Linguistic Inquiry* 14: 505–19.

Hladnik, M. 2015. *Mind the gap: Resumption in Slavic relative clauses*. Utrecht: LOT.

Hoeksema, J. 1996. Floating quantifiers, partitives and distributivity. In *Partitives: Studies on the syntax and semantics of partitive and related constructions*, J. Hoeksema (ed.) 57–106. Berlin: Mouton de Gruyter.

Hoekstra, E. & Smits, C. 1999. Everything you always wanted to know about Complementizer Agreement. In *Proceedings of WECOL 10*, E. van Gelderen & V. Samiian (eds.) 189–200.

Hoffmann, T. 2011. *Preposition Placement in English*. Cambridge: Cambridge University Press.

Hofmeister, P. & Norcliffe, E. 2013. Does resumption facilitate sentence comprehension? In *The Core and the Periphery: Data-driven perspectives on syntax inspired by Ivan A. Sag*, P. Hofmeister & E. Norcliffe (eds.) 225–46. Stanford, CA: CSLI Publications.

Hoji, H. 1998. Null object and sloppy identity in Japanese. *Linguistic Inquiry* 29: 127–52.

Holmberg, A. 2000. Scandinavian stylistic fronting: How any category can become an expletive. *Linguistic Inquiry* 31: 445–83.

Holmer, A. 2013. Evidence from Formosan for a unified theory of adverb ordering. *Lingua* 122: 902–21.

Honda, M. 2011. Wh-exclamatives, factivity, and topicalization revisited. *Studies in Language Sciences* 17: 87–117.

Hooper, J. B. & Thompson, S. A. 1973. On the applicability of root transformations. *Linguistic Inquiry* 4: 465–97.

Hopper, R. 1992. *Telephone Conversation*. Bloomington, IN: Indiana University Press.

Horch, E. & Reich, I. 2016. On 'Article Omission' in German and the 'Uniform Information Density Hypothesis'. In *Proceedings of the 13th Conference on Natural Language Processing*, S. Dipper, F. Neubarth & H. Zinsmeister (eds.) 125–27. Bochum.

Horn, G. 1981. A pragmatic approach to certain ambiguities. *Linguistics and Philosophy* 4: 321–58.

Hornstein, N. 1995. *Logical Form: From GB to minimalism*. Oxford: Blackwell.

——1999. Movement and Control. *Linguistic Inquiry* 30: 69–96.

——2001. *Move: A minimalist theory of construal*. Oxford: Blackwell.

——2003. On control. In *Minimalist Syntax*, R. Hendrick (ed.) 6–81. Oxford: Blackwell.

——2007. Pronouns in a minimalist setting. In *The Copy Theory of Movement*, N. Corver & J. Nunes (eds.) 351–85. Amsterdam: Benjamins.

——2009. *A Theory of Syntax: Minimal operations and Universal Grammar*. Cambridge: Cambridge University Press.

Hornstein, N. & Nunes, J. 2008. Adjunction, labeling, and bare phrase structure. *Biolinguistics* 2: 57–86.

Horsey, R. 1998. Null arguments in English registers: A minimalist account. BA thesis. La Trobe University.

Horvath, J. 1986. *Focus in the Theory of Grammar and the Syntax of Hungarian*. Dordrecht: Foris.

——1995. Structural focus, structural case and the notion of feature assignment. In *Discourse-Configurational Languages*, K. É. Kiss (ed.) 28–64. Oxford: Oxford University Press.

——2000. Interfaces vs. the computational system in the syntax of focus. In *Interface Strategies*, H. Bennis, M. Everaert & E. Reuland (eds.) 183–206. Amsterdam: KNAW publications.

——2007. Separating 'focus movement' from focus. In *Clausal and Phrasal Architecture: Syntactic derivation and interpretation*, S. Karimi, V. Samiian & W. K. Wilkins (eds.) 108–45. Amsterdam: Benjamins.

Householder, F. W. 1987. Some facts about *me* and *I*. *Language Research* 23: 163–84.

Huang, C.-T. J. 1982. Logical relations in Chinese and the theory of grammar. PhD diss. MIT.

——1984. On the distribution and reference of empty pronouns. *Linguistic Inquiry* 15: 531–74.

——1991. Remarks on the status of the null object. In *Principles and Parameters in Comparative Grammar*, R. Freidin (ed.) 56–76. Cambridge, MA: MIT Press.

——1993. Reconstruction and the structure of VP: Some theoretical consequences. *Linguistic Inquiry* 24: 103–38.

Huang, N. & Mendes, G. 2019. On pronominalisation and clausal idioms. Ms. University of Maryland.

Huddleston, R. 1993. On exclamatory-inversion sentences. *Lingua* 90: 259–69.

Huddleston, R. & Pullum, G. K. 2002. *The Cambridge Grammar of the English Language.* Cambridge: Cambridge University Press.

Hulsey, S. & Sauerland, U. 2006. Sorting out relative clauses. *Natural Language Semantics* 14: 111–37.

Iatridou, S. 1993. On nominative case assignment and a few related things. *MIT Working Papers in Linguistics* 19: 175–96.

Ihalainen, O. 1980. Relative clauses in the dialect of Somerset. *Neuphilologische Mitteilungen* 81: 187–96.

——1991. The grammatical subject in educated and dialectal English: Comparing the London-Lund corpus and the Helsinki corpus of modern English dialects. In *English Computer Corpora: Selected papers and research guide*, S. Johansson & A.-B. Stenström (eds.) 201–14. Berlin: Mouton de Gruyter.

Ihsane, T. 1998. The syntax of diaries: Grammar and register variation. Mémoire de licence, University of Geneva, Department of English.

Ikarashi, K. 2015. A functional approach to English constructions related to evidentiality. PhD diss. University of Tsukuba.

Inada, S. 2007. Towards a syntax of two types of relative clauses. *Linguistic Research* 23: 1–41.

Ingham, R. 1998. Tense without agreement in early clause structure. *Language Acquisition* 7: 51–81.

Inoue, I. 1991. On the genesis of *there*-constructions. *English Linguistics* 8: 34–51.

Irani, A. 2014. Focusing in Hindi Syntax. MA thesis. Georgetown University.

Isac, D. 2006. In defense of a quantificational account of definite DPs. *Linguistic Inquiry* 37: 275–88.

——2015. *The Morphosyntax of Imperatives.* Oxford: Oxford University Press.

Ishii, Y. 1999. A note on floating quantifiers in Japanese. In *Linguistics: In search of the human mind*, M. Muraki & E. Iwamoto (eds.) 236–67. Tokyo: Kaitakusha.

Ito, T. 1993. Object ellipsis in subjectless nonfinite clauses in English. *English Linguistics* 10: 75–94.

Ito, T. & Kashihara, Y. 2010. Studies on English literature and linguistics with the aid of personal computers. *Kawasaki Journal of Medical Welfare* 16: 19–33.

Izvorski, R. 2001. Free adjunct free relatives. *Proceedings of the West*

Coast Conference on Formal Linguistics 19: 232–45.

Jackendoff, R. S. 1972. *Semantic Interpretation in Generative Grammar*. Cambridge, MA: MIT Press.

——1974. Introduction to the X-bar convention. Indiana University Linguistics Club.

——1977a. *X-bar Syntax: A study of phrase structure*. Cambridge, MA: MIT Press.

——1977b. Constraints on phrase structure rules. In *Formal Syntax*, P. W. Culicover, T. Wasow & A. Akmajian (eds.) 249–83. New York: Academic Press.

Jackendoff, R. S. & Culicover, P. W. 2003. The semantic basis of control in English. *Language* 79: 517–56.

Jacobs, R. A & Rosenbaum, P. S. 1968. *English Transformational Grammar*. Waltham, MA: Blaisdell Publishing Co.

Jacobsson, B. 1994. Nonrestrictive relative *that*-clauses revisited. *Studia Neophilologica* 66: 181–95.

——2007. A new look at Negative and Correlative Subject–Auxiliary Inversion in English. *Studia Neophilologica* 79: 35–44.

Jaeggli, O. 1982. *Topics in Romance Syntax*. Dordrecht: Foris.

——1986. Passive. *Linguistic Inquiry* 17: 587–622.

Janda, R. J. 1985. Note-taking English as a simplified register. *Discourse Processes* 8: 437–54.

Janke, V. & Neeleman, A. 2005. Floating quantifiers and English VP structure. Ms. University College London.

Jayaseelan, K. A. 1996. Question-word movement to focus and scrambling in Malayam. *Linguistic Analysis* 26: 63–83.

——2003. Question words in focus positions. *Linguistic Variation Yearbook* 3: 69–99.

——2008. Topic, focus and adverb positions in clause structure. *Nanzan Linguistics* 4: 43–68.

Jenkins, L. 1975. *The English Existential*. Tübingen: Narr.

Jenks, P. 2013. Quantifier float, focus and scope in Thai. *Berkeley Linguistic Society Proceedings* 39: 90–107.

Jensen, B. 2003. Syntax and semantics of imperative subjects. *Nordlyd* 31: 150–64.

——2007. In favour of a truncated imperative clause structure: Evidence from adverbs. *Working Papers in Scandinavian Syntax* 80: 163–85.

Jiménez-Fernández, Á. 2011. On the order of multiple topics and discourse-feature inheritance. *Dilbilim Araştırmaları* 2011: 5–32.

——2015. Towards a typology of focus: Subject position and microvariation at the discourse-syntax interface. *Ampersand* 2: 49–60.

——2018. Negative Preposing: Intervention and parametric variation in complement clauses. *Atlantis* 40.1.01.

Johnson, K. 1991. Object positions. *Natural Language and Linguistic Theory* 9: 577–636.

——2001. What VP-ellipsis can do, and what it can't, but not why. In *The Handbook of Contemporary*

Syntactic Theory, M. Baltin & C. Collins (eds.) 439–79. Oxford: Blackwell.

Jones, M. A. 1994. *Sardinian Syntax*. London: Routledge.

Jónsson, J. G. 2010. Icelandic exclamatives and the structure of the CP layer. *Studia Linguistica* 64: 37–54.

Joseph, B. D. 1976. Raising in modern Greek: A copy process? *Harvard Studies in Syntax* 2: 241–81.

Junker, M.-O. 1990. Floating quantifiers and distributivity. *Cahiers Linguistiques d'Ottowa* 18: 13–42.

Jurka, J. 2010 The importance of being a complement: CED effects revisited. PhD diss. University of Maryland.

Jurka, J., Nakao, C. & Omaki, A. 2011. It's not the end of the CED as we know it: Revisiting German and Japanese Subject Islands. *Proceedings of the West Coast Conference on Formal Linguistics* 28: 124–32.

Kalinina, E. 2011. Exclamative clauses in the languages of the North Caucasus and the problem of finiteness. In *Tense, Aspect, Modality and Finiteness in East-Caucasian Languages*, G. Authier & T. Maisak (eds.) 161–201. Bochum: Brockmeyer.

Kalin, L. 2020. Opacity in agreement. In *Agree to Agree: Agreement in the minimalist program*, P. W. Smith, J. Mursell & K. Hartmann (eds.) 149–77. Berlin: Language Science Press.

Kalivoda, N. & Zyman, E. 2015. On the derivation of relative clauses

in Teotitlán del Valle Zapotec. *Berkeley Linguistic Society Proceedings* 41: 219–43.

Kallulli, D. 2008. There is secondary predication in *there*-existentials. *Proceedings of the West Coast Conference on Formal Linguistics* 26: 279–87.

Kameshima, N. 1989. The syntax of restrictive and nonrestrictive relative clauses in Japanese. PhD diss. University of Wisconsin-Madison.

Kanda, Y. & Honda, M. 2018. A predication approach to Copy Raising from the perspective of evidentiality. *Tsukuba English Studies* 37: 141–55.

Kandybowicz, J. 2006. Comp-trace effects explained away. *Proceedings of the West Coast Conference on Formal Linguistics* 25: 220–28.

Kang, B. M. 2002. Categories and meanings of Korean floated quantifiers – with some reference to Japanese. *Journal of East Asian Linguistics* 11: 375–98.

Kato, M. A. 1993. The distribution of pronouns & null elements in object position in Brazilian Portuguese. In *Linguistic Perspectives on Romance Languages*, W. J. Ashby, M. Mithun & G. Perissinotto (eds.) 225–35. Amsterdam: Benjamins.

Katz, J. J. & Postal, P.M. 1964. *An Integrated Theory of Linguistic Descriptions*. Cambridge, MA: MIT Press.

Kauf, C. & Zeijlstra, H. 2018. Towards a new explanation of sequence of tense. *Semantics and Linguistic Theory* 28: 59–77.

Kaufmann, M. 2011. *Interpreting Imperatives.* Berlin: Springer.

Kay, P. 2002. English subjectless tagged sentences. *Language* 78: 453–81.

Kayne, R. S. 1981. Unambiguous paths. In *Levels of Syntactic Representation*, R. May & J. Koster (eds.) 143–83. Dordrecht: Foris.

——1984. *Connectedness and Binary Branching.* Dordrecht: Foris.

——1989. Null subjects and clitic climbing. In *The Null Subject Parameter*, O. Jaeggli & K. Safir (eds.) 239–59. Dordrecht: Kluwer.

——1991. Romance clitics, verb movement, and PRO. *Linguistic Inquiry* 22: 647–86.

——1994. *The Antisymmetry of Syntax.* Cambridge, MA: MIT Press.

——1998. Overt vs covert movement. *Syntax* 1: 128–91.

——2007. Some thoughts on grammaticalization: The case of *that.* Talk delivered at XVIII Conférence Internationale de Linguistique Historique, UQAM, Montreal.

——2015. A note on some even more unusual relative clauses. Ms. New York University. https://ling.auf .net/lingbuzz/002835

——2016. The unicity of *there* and the definiteness effect. Ms. New York University.

——2019. Notes on expletive there. *The Linguistic Review* 37: 209–30.

Keenan, E. 1985. Relative clauses. In *Language Typology and Syntactic Description. Vol. II: Complex constructions*, T. Shopen (ed.) 141–70. Cambridge: Cambridge University Press.

Keenan, E. & Schieffelin, B. 1976a. Foregrounding referents: A reconsideration of left dislocation in discourse. *Berkeley Linguistic Society Proceedings* 2: 240–57.

——1976b. Topic as a discourse notion: A study of topic in the conversations of children and adults. In *Subject and Topic*, C. N. Li (ed.) 335–84. New York: Academic Press.

Keffala, B. 2011. Resumption and gaps in English relative clauses: Relative acceptability creates an illusion of saving. *Berkeley Linguistics Society Proceedings* 37: 140–54.

Keffala, B. & Goodall, C. 2011. Do resumptive pronouns ever rescue illicit gaps? Poster presented at 24th annual CUNY conference on Human Sentence Processing, Stanford, CA.

Kekalainen, K. 1985. Relative clauses in the dialect of Suffolk. *Neuphilologische Mitteilungen* 86: 353–57.

Keller, F. & Lapata, M. 1998. Object Drop and discourse accessibility. *Proceedings of the West Coast Conference on Formal Linguistics* 17: 362–74.

Keshev, M. & Meltzer-Asscher, A. 2017. Active dependency formation in islands: How grammatical resumption affects sentence processing. *Language* 93: 549–68.

Khalifa, J.-C. 1999. A propos des relatives appositives: Syntaxe, sémantique, pragmatique. *Anglophonia* 6: 7–29.

Kibsgaard, M. K. M. 2019. Murder suspect seen on video. BA thesis.

Norwegian University of Science and Technology.

Kidwai, A. 1999. Word order and focus positions in Universal Grammar. In *The Grammar of Focus*, G. Rebuschi & L. Tuller (eds.) 213–44. Amsterdam: Benjamins.

Kim, J.-B. 2014. English copy raising constructions: Argument realization and characterization condition. *Linguistics* 52: 167–203.

Kim, K.-S. 2020. On the distribution of floating quantifiers. Ms. Hankuk University of Foreign Studies.

Kim, S.-S. 2002. Intervention effects are focus effects. *Japanese/Korean Linguistics* 10: 615–28.

——2006. Intervention effects are focus effects. *Harvard Studies in Korean Linguistics* 11: 520–33.

Kim, S. 1999. Sloppy/strict identity, empty objects, and NP ellipsis. *Journal of East Asian Linguistics* 8: 255–84.

Kim, J.-B. & Kim, J. S. 2009. English floating quantifier constructions: A non-movement approach. *Language and Information* 13: 57–75.

Kim, J.-B. & Kim, O. 2011. English *how come* construction: A double life. Paper presented to the Arizona Linguistics Circle 5, 28–30 October.

Kiss, K. É. 1995. Introduction. In *Discourse-Configurational Languages*, K. É. Kiss (ed.) 3–27. Oxford: Oxford University Press.

——1998. Identificational focus versus informational focus. *Language* 74: 245–73.

——2001. The EPP in a topic-prominent language, In *Subjects, Expletives and the EPP*, P.

Svenonius (ed.) 107–24. Oxford: Oxford University Press.

Kissock, M. J. 2013. Evidence for 'finiteness' in Telugu. *Natural Language & Linguistic Theory* 32: 1–30.

Kitagawa, C. 1982. Topic construction in Japanese. *Lingua* 57: 175–214.

——1986. Subjects in English and Japanese. PhD diss. University of Massachusetts.

——1994. *Subjects in Japanese and English*. New York: Garland.

——2018. Floating quantifiers in Japanese passives and beyond. *Journal of Japanese Linguistics* 34: 245–79.

Kjellmer, G. 1988. Conjunctional/adverbial *which* in substandard English. *Studia Anglica Posnaniensia* 21: 125–37.

——2010. And *which*: A note on (more or less) coordinated relatives. *English Studies* 91: 457–66.

Klein, S. 1977. A base analysis of the floating quantifier in French. *Proceedings of the North East Linguistic Society* 7: 147–63.

Klein, W. 1998. Assertion and finiteness. In *Issues in the Theory of Language Acquisition: Essays in honor of Jürgen Weissenborn*, N. Dittmar & Z. Penner (eds.), 225–45. Bern: Peter Lang.

——2006. On finiteness. In *Semantics in Acquisition*, V. van Geenhoven (ed.) 245–72. New York: Springer.

Klima, E. S. 1964. Negation in English. In *The Structure of Language*, J. A. Fodor & J. J. Katz (eds.) 246–323: Englewood Cliffs, NJ: Prentice-Hall.

Ko, H. & Oh, E. 2012. A hybrid approach to floating quantifiers. *Linguistic Research* 29: 69–106.

Kobayashi, K. 2018. A note on copy raising constructions in English. Ms. Kanto Gakuin University.

Kobuchi-Philip, M. 2003. Distributivity and the Japanese floating numeral quantifier. PhD diss. City University of New York.

——2007. Floating numerals and floating quantifiers. *Lingua* 117: 814–31.

König, E. 1991. *The Meaning of Focus Particles*. London: Routledge.

——2017. Syntax and semantics of additive focus markers from a cross-linguistic perspective. In *Focus on Additivity: Adverbial modifiers in Romance, Germanic and Slavic languages*, A. M. de Cesare Greenwald & C. Andorno (eds.) 23–44. Amsterdam: Benjamins.

Koopman, H. 2000. *The Syntax of Specifiers and Heads*. London: Routledge.

——2007. Topics in imperatives. In *Imperative Clauses in Generative Grammar: Studies in honour of Frits Beukema*, W. van der Wurff (ed.) 153–80. Amsterdam: Benjamins.

——2010. On Dutch *allemaal* and West Ulster English *all*. In *Structure Preserved*, W. Zwart & J. van de Vries (eds.) 267–76. New York: Academic Press.

Koopman, H. & Sportiche, D. 1991. The position of subjects. *Lingua* 85: 211–58.

Koopman, H. & Szabolsci, A. 2000. *Verbal Complexes*. Cambridge, MA: MIT Press.

Koppen, M. van 2005. One probe – two goals: Aspects of agreement in Dutch dialects, PhD diss. University of Leiden.

——2017. Complementizer Agreement. In *The Wiley-Blackwell Companion to Syntax*, 2nd edition, M. Everaert & H. van Riemsdijk (eds.) 923–62. London: Wiley-Blackwell.

Kostopoulos, E. E. 2017. Revising floating quantifiers: The syntax of Modern Greek *ola*. MA thesis. University of York.

Koster, J. & Zwart, J.-W. 2000. Transitive expletive constructions and the object shift parameter. *Linguistics in the Netherlands* 17: 159–70.

Krapova, I. 2002. On the left periphery of the Bulgarian sentence. *University of Venice Working Papers in Linguistics* 12: 107–28.

Krapova, I. & Cinque, G. 2008. On the order of *wh*-phrases in Bulgarian multiple *wh*-fronting. In *Formal Description of Slavic Languages*, G. Zybatow, L. Szucsich, U. Junghanns, & R. Meyer (eds.) 318–36. Frankfurt am Main: Peter Lang.

Kroch, A. 1981. On the role of resumptive pronouns in amnestying island constraint violations. *Chicago Linguistic Society Proceedings* 17: 125–35.

Kuno, S. 1981. Functional Syntax. *Syntax and Semantics* 13: 117–35.

Kuroda, S.-Y. 1968. English relativization and certain related problems. *Language* 44: 244–66.

——1988. Whether we agree or not. *Lingvisticae Investigationes* 12: 1–47.

Labov, W. 1969. Contraction, deletion and the inherent variability of the English copula. *Language* 45: 715–62.

——1995. The case of the missing copula: The interpretation of zeroes in African-American English. In *An Invitation to Cognitive Science*, L. Gleitman & M. Liberman (eds.) 25–54. Cambridge, MA: MIT Press.

Lacerda, R. 2016. Rebel without a case: Quantifier floating in Brazilian Portuguese and Spanish. In *The Morphosyntax of Portuguese and Spanish in Latin America*, M. A. Kato & F. Ordóñez (eds.) 78–106. Oxford: Oxford University Press.

Laenzlinger, C. 1993. Principles for a formal and computational account of adverbial syntax. MA thesis. University of Geneva.

——1996. Adverb syntax and phrase structure. In *Configurations: Essays on structure and interpretation*, A. M. Di Sciullo (ed.) 99–127. Somerville, MA: Cascadilla Press.

——1999. *Comparative Studies in Word Order Variation: Adverbs, pronouns, and clause structure in Romance and Germanic*. Amsterdam: Benjamins.

——2000. More on adverb syntax and phrase structure. In *Adverbs and Adjunction*, A. Alexiadou & P. Svenonius (eds.) 103–22. Potsdam: Institut für Linguistik, Universität Potsdam.

Lahiri, U. 1991. Embedded interrogatives and predicates that embed them. PhD diss. MIT.

——1998. Focus and negative polarity in Hindi. *Natural Language Semantics* 6: 57–123.

Lakoff, G. 1969. On derivational constraints. *Chicago Linguistic Society Proceedings* 5: 117–39.

Lambrecht, K. 1994 *Information Structure and Sentence Form*. Cambridge: Cambridge University Press.

Lambrecht, K. & Lemoine, K. 1996. Vers une grammaire des compléments zéro en français parlé. In *Absence de Marques et Représentation de l'Absence*, J. Chuquet & M. Frid (eds.) 279–309. Rennes: Presses Universitaires de Rennes.

——2005. Definite null objects in (spoken) French: A construction-grammar account. In *Grammatical Constructions: Back to the roots* M. Fried & H. C. Boas (eds.) 13–55. Amsterdam: Benjamins.

Landa, M. A. 1995. Conditions on null objects in Basque Spanish and their relation to leísmo and clitic doubling. PhD diss. University of Southern California, Los Angeles.

Landau, I. 2004. The scale of finiteness and the calculus of Control. *Natural Language and Linguistic Theory* 22: 811–77.

——2006. Severing the distribution of PRO from case. *Syntax* 9: 153–70.

——2007. EPP extensions. *Linguistic Inquiry* 38: 485–523.

——2009. This construction looks like a copy is optional. *Linguistic Inquiry* 40: 343–46.

——2011. Predication vs. aboutness in copy raising. *Natural Language and Linguistic Theory* 29: 779–813.

Lansens, E. 2019. Subject ellipsis on social media: Analyzing extralinguistic variables 'age' and 'motive' in relation to first person subject ellipsis in finite clauses on Twitter. Ms, Ghent University.

Lappin, S. 1983. Θ-roles and NP-movement. *Proceedings of the North East Linguistics Society* 13: 121–28.

——1984. Predication and raising. *Proceedings of the North East Linguistics Society* 14: 236–52.

Larjavaara, M. 2000. *Présence ou Absence de l'Objet: Limites du possible en français contemporain.* Helsinki: Academia Scientiarum Fennica.

Larsen, D. 2014. Particles and particle-verb constructions in English and other Germanic Languages. PhD diss. University of Delaware.

Larson, B. 2014. Russian comitatives and the ambiguity of adjunction. *Journal of Slavic Linguistics* 22: 11–49.

Larson, R. K. 1985. On the syntax of disjunction scope, *Natural Language and Linguistic Theory* 3: 217–64.

Lasnik, H. 1981. Restricting the theory of transformations. In *Explanation in Linguistics*, N. Hornstein & D. Lightfoot (eds.) 152–73. London: Longman.

——1992. Case and expletives revisited: Notes towards a parametric account. *Linguistic Inquiry* 23: 381–405.

——1995. Verbal Morphology: *Syntactic Structures* meets the minimalist program. In *Evolution and Revolution in Linguistic Theory*, H. Campos & P. Kempchinsky (eds.) 251–75.

Washington, DC: Georgetown University Press.

——1998. Some reconstruction riddles. in *Penn Working Papers in Linguistics* 5: 83–98.

——1999. Chains of arguments. In *Working Minimalism*, S. D. Epstein & N. Hornstein (eds.) 189–215. Cambridge, MA: MIT Press.

——2001. A note on the EPP. *Linguistic Inquiry* 32: 356–62.

——2003. *Minimalist Investigations in Linguistic Theory.* London: Routledge.

——2006. Conceptions of the cycle. In *Wh-Movement: Moving On*, L. Cheng & N. Corver (eds.) 197–216. Cambridge, MA: MIT Press.

Lasnik, H. & Saito, M. 1992. *Move α: Conditions on its application and output.* Cambridge, MA: MIT Press.

Lasnik, H. & Sobin, N. 2000. The *who/whom* puzzle: On the preservation of an archaic feature. *Natural Language and Linguistic Theory* 18: 343–71.

Lasser, I. 1997. Finiteness in adult and child German. PhD. diss. City University of New York.

Law, P. 1996. Remarks on the verb *be* and the expletive *there* in English. *Linguistische Berichte* 166: 492–529.

Lebeaux, D. 1991. Relative clauses, licensing and the nature of derivation. In *Syntax and Semantics 25: Perspectives on phrase structure*, S. Rothstein (ed.) 209–39. New York: Academic Press.

——1995. Where does Binding Theory apply? *University of Maryland*

Working Papers in Linguistics 3: 63–88.

Lee, P. C.-W. 2017. Anaphoric object drop in Chinese. In *Order and Structure in Syntax II: Subjecthood and argument structure*, M. Sheehan & L. R. Bailey (eds.) 329–38. Berlin: Language Science Press.

Lee, Y. 2004. The syntax and semantics of focus particles. PhD diss. MIT.

Legate, J. A. 2002. Warlpiri: Theoretical implications. PhD diss. MIT.

——2005. Phases and cyclic agreement. *MIT Working Papers in Linguistics* 49: 234–53.

——2014. *Voice and v: Lessons from Achenese*. Cambridge, MA: MIT Press.

Lemke, R., Horch, E. & Reich, I. 2017. Optimal encoding: Information Theory constrains article omission in newspaper headlines. In *Proceedings of the 15th Conference of the European Chapter of the Association for Computational Linguistics: Volume 2, Short papers*, 131–35. Valencia: Association for Computational Linguistics.

Lewis, R. E. 2013. Complementiser agreement in Najdi Arabic. MA thesis. University of Kansas.

Li, G. 1998. Null object and VP Ellipsis in Chinese? *Proceedings of the North American Conference on Chinese Linguistics* 9: 155–72. Los Angeles: GSIL.

Light, C. 2015. Expletive *there* in West Germanic. In *Syntax Over Time: Lexical, morphological, and information-structural interactions*, T. Biberauer & T. Walkden (eds.)

17–35. Oxford: Oxford University Press.

Lin, T.-H. J. 2011. Finiteness of clauses and raising of arguments in Mandarin Chinese. *Syntax* 14: 48–73.

Lipták, A. 2006. Word order in Hungarian exclamatives. *Acta Linguistica Hungarica* 53: 343–91.

Lindstrom, A. M. 2020. *Unexpressed Subjects in English: An empirical analysis of narrative and conversational discourse*. Washington, DC: Rowman & Littlefield.

Llinàs-Grau, M. & Fernández-Sánchez, J. F. 2013. Reflexiones en torno a la supresión del complementante en inglés, español y catalán. *Revista Española de Lingüística* 43: 55–88.

Lobeck, A. 1995. *Ellipsis: Functional heads, licensing and identification*. Oxford: Oxford University Press.

Löbel, E. 1989. Q as a functional category. In *Syntactic Phrase Structure Phenomena*, C. Bhatt, E. Löbel, & C. Schmidt (eds.) 133–58. Amsterdam: Benjamins.

Lohndal, T. 2009. Comp-*t* effects: Variation in the position and features of C. *Studia Linguistica* 63: 204–32.

Longobardi, G. 1994. Reference and proper names. *Linguistic Inquiry* 25: 609–66.

——1996. The syntax of N-raising: A minimalist theory. *OTS Working Papers no 5*. Utrecht: Research Institute for Language and Speech.

——2001. The structure of DPs: Some principles, parameters and problems. In *The Handbook of*

Contemporary Syntactic Theory, M. Baltin & C. Collins (eds.) 562–603. Oxford: Blackwell.

Loock, R. 2003. Les fonctions des propositions subordonnées relatives appositives en discours. *Anglophonia* 12: 113–31.

——2005. Appositive relative clauses in contemporary written and spoken English: Discourse functions and competitive structures. PhD diss. University of Lille III.

——2007a. Appositive relative clauses and their functions in discourse. *Journal of Pragmatics* 39: 336–62.

——2007b. Are you a good which or a bad which? The relative pronoun as a plain connective. In *Connectives as Discourse Landmarks*, A. Celle & R. Huart (eds.) 71–87. Amsterdam: Benjamins.

——2010. *Appositive Relative Clauses in English: Discourse functions and competing structures*. Amsterdam: Benjamins.

López-Couso, M. J. & Méndez-Naya, B. 2012. On the use of *as if, though,* and *like* in present-day English complementation structures. *Journal of English Linguistics* 40: 172–95.

Loss, S. S. & Wicklund, M. 2020. Is English resumption different in appositive relative clauses? *Canadian Journal of Linguistics* 65: 25–51.

Lowe, J. J. 2019. The syntax and semantics of nonfinite forms. *Annual Review of Linguistics* 5: 309–28.

Lyons, C. 1999. *Definiteness*. Cambridge: Cambridge University Press.

Mack, J. E. 2010. Information structure and the licensing of English subjects. PhD diss. Yale University.

Mack, J. E., Clifton, C. Jr., Frazier, L. & Taylor, P. V. 2012. (Not) hearing optional subjects: The effects of pragmatic usage preferences. *Journal of Memory and Language* 67: 211–23.

Mack, J. E. & Fuerst, Y. 2009. English optional expletives and the pragmatics of judgments. Paper presented to the 45th annual meeting of the Chicago Linguistic Society, 17 April.

Mackenzie, J. L. 1998 The basis of syntax in the holophrase. In *Functional Grammar and Verbal Interaction*, M. Hannay & A. M. Bolkestein (eds.) 267–96. Amsterdam: Benjamins.

Maekawa, T. 2007. The English left periphery in linearisation-based HPSG. PhD diss. University of Essex.

Mahajan, A. 1994. Active passives. *Proceedings of the West Coast Conference on Formal Linguistics* 23: 286–301.

Maienborn, C. 2001. On the position and interpretation of locative modifiers. *Natural Language Semantics* 9: 191–240.

Maki, H., Kaiser, L. & Ochi, M. 1999. Embedded topicalization in English and Japanese. *Lingua* 109: 1–14.

Malamud-Makowski, M. 1994. The structure of IP: Evidence from acquisition data. Paper presented at the 18th Annual Boston University Conference on Language Development, Boston, MA.

Maling, J. 1976. Notes on quantifier postposing. *Linguistic Inquiry* 7: 708–18.

Marandin, J.-M. 2008. The exclamative clause type in French. In *Proceedings of the HPSG08 Conference*, S. Müller (ed.) 436–56. Stanford, CA: CSLI Publications.

Marantz, A. 1984. *On the Nature of Grammatical Relations*. Cambridge, MA: MIT Press.

Manetta, E. 2007. Unexpected left dislocation: An English corpus study. *Journal of Pragmatics* 39: 1029–35.

Manninen, S. 2005. Review of Cinque (1999). *Journal of Linguistics* 41: 452–57.

Manzini, M. R. & Roussou, A. 2000. A minimalist approach to A-movement and control. *Lingua* 110: 409–47.

——2019. Morphological and syntactic (non)finiteness: A comparison between English and Balkan languages. *Working Papers in Linguistics and Oriental Studies* 5: 195–229.

Manzini, M. & Savoia, L. M. 2018. Finite and nonfinite complementation, particles and control in Aromanian, compared to other Romance varieties and Albanian. *Linguistic Variation* 18: 215–64.

Mårdh, I. 1980. *Headlinese: On the grammar of English front page headlines*. Malmö: CWK Gleerup.

Martín, L. M. 2019. Negative Inversion in standard English. *Odisea* 20: 91–116.

Martin, R. 1996. A minimalist theory of PRO and control. PhD diss. University of Connecticut, Storrs.

——1999. Case, the extended projection principle, and minimalism. In *Working Minimalism*, S. D. Epstein & N. Hornstein (eds.) 1–26. Cambridge, MA: MIT Press.

——2001. Null case and the distribution of PRO. *Linguistic Inquiry* 32: 141–66.

Martins, A. M. & Nunes, J. 2005. Raising issues in European and Brazilian Portuguese. *Journal of Portuguese Linguistics* 4: 53–77.

——2009. Syntactic change as chain reaction: The emergence of hyper-raising in Brazilian Portuguese. In *Historical Syntax and Linguistic Theory*, P. Crisma & G. Longobardi (eds.) 144–57. Oxford: Oxford University Press.

Massam, D. 1987. Middles, tough, and recipe context constructions in English. *Proceedings of the North East Linguistics Society* 18: 315–32.

——1989. Null objects and non-thematic subjects in middles and tough constructions. *Toronto Working Papers in Linguistics*, 10: 95–118.

——1992. Null objects and non-thematic subjects. *Journal of Linguistics* 28: 115–37.

Massam, D., Bamba, K. & Murphy, P. 2017. Obligatorily null pronouns in the instructional register and beyond. *Linguistic Variation* 17: 272–91.

Massam, D. & Roberge, Y. 1989. Recipe context null objects in English. *Linguistic Inquiry*, 20: 134–39.

Massam, D. & Stowell, T. (eds.) 2017. *Register Variation and Syntactic Theory*. Amsterdam: Benjamins.

Matushansky, O. 1995. Le sujet nul dans les propositions à temps fini en anglais. Maîtrise paper, University of Paris VIII.

——2002. Tipping the scales: The syntax of scalarity in the complement of *seem*. *Syntax* 5: 219–76.

Mauck, S., Pak, M., Portner, P. & Zanuttini, R. 2005. Imperative subjects: A cross-linguistic perspective. *Georgetown University Working Papers in Theoretical Linguistics* 4: 135–52.

Mayr, C. 2010. Ç. In *The Complementiser Phase: Subjects and wh-dependencies*, P. Panagiotidis (ed.) 117–42. Oxford: Oxford University Press.

McCawley, J. D. 1981. The syntax and semantics of English relative clauses. *Lingua* 53: 99–149.

——1993. Gapping with shared operators. *Berkeley Linguistic Society Proceedings* 19: 245–54.

McCloskey, J. 1997. Subjecthood and subject positions. In *Elements of Grammar*, L. Haegeman (ed.) 197–235. Dordrecht: Kluwer.

——2000. Quantifier Float and Wh-Movement in an Irish English. *Linguistic Inquiry* 31: 57–84.

——2006a. Resumption, successive cyclicity, and the locality of operations. In *Derivations in Minimalism*, S. D. Epstein & T. D. Seely (eds.) 184–226. Cambridge: Cambridge University Press.

——2006b. Questions and questioning in a local English. In *Negation, Tense and Clausal Architecture: Cross-linguistic Investigations*, R. Zanuttini, H. Campos, E. Herburger & P. Portner (eds.) 86–126. Washington, DC: Georgetown University Press.

——2017a. Observations and speculations on resumption (in Irish). Ms. University of California, Santa Cruz.

——2017b. Resumption. In *The Wiley-Blackwell Companion to Syntax*, 2nd edition, M. Everaert & H. van Riemsdijk (eds.) 3809–38. Hoboken, NJ: John Wiley & Sons.

McDaniel, D. & Cowart, W. 1999. Experimental evidence of a minimalist account of English resumptive pronouns. *Cognition* 70: B15–B24.

McKee, C. & McDaniel, D. 2001. Resumptive pronouns in English relative clauses. *Language Acquisition* 9: 113–56.

McNally, L. 1992. VP-coordination and the VP-internal subject hypothesis. *Linguistic Inquiry* 23: 336–41.

Medeiros, D. J. 2013. Approaches to the syntax and semantics of imperatives. PhD diss. University of Michigan.

Meira, B. J. 2004. Review of Cinque (1999). *Cadernos de Estudos Lingüísticos* 46: 283–90.

Meltzer-Asscher, A. 2012. Verbal passives in English and Hebrew: A comparative study. In *The Theta System: Argument structure at the interface*, M. Everaert, M. Marelj & T. Siloni (eds.) 280–307. Oxford: Oxford University Press.

Merchant, J. 1996. Object scrambling and quantifier float in German. *Proceedings of the North East Linguistic Society* 26: 179–93.

——1999. The syntax of silence: Sluicing, islands, and identity in ellipsis. PhD diss. University of California, Santa Cruz.

——2001. *The Syntax of Silence: Sluicing, Islands and Identity in Ellipsis*. Oxford: Oxford University Press.

——2002. Swiping in Germanic. In *Studies in Comparative Germanic Syntax*, W. Abraham & J.-W. Zwart (eds.) 295–321. Amsterdam: Benjamins.

——2003. Sluicing. Ms. University of Chicago.

——2004a. Fragments and ellipsis. *Linguistics and Philosophy* 27: 661–738.

——2004b. Resumptivity and non-movement. *Studies in Greek Linguistics* 24: 471–81.

——2008a. Variable island repair under ellipsis. In *Topics in Ellipsis*, K. Johnson (ed.) 132–53. Cambridge: Cambridge University Press.

——2008b. An asymmetry in voice mismatches in VP ellipsis and pseudogapping. *Linguistic Inquiry* 39: 169–79.

——2013a. Diagnosing ellipsis. In *Diagnosing Syntax*, L. Cheng & N. Corver (eds.) 537–42. Oxford: Oxford University Press.

——2013b. Polarity items under ellipsis. In *Diagnosing Syntax*, L. Cheng & N. Corver (eds.) 441–62. Oxford: Oxford University Press.

——2014. 'Some definitions'. Ms. University of Chicago.

——2019. 'Roots don't select, categorial heads do: Lexical-selection of PPs may vary by category. *The Linguistic Review* 36: 325–41.

Michaelis, L. 2001. Exclamative constructions. *Language Typology and Language Universals* 2: 1038–50.

Michaelis, L. & Lambrecht, K. 1996. The exclamative sentence type in English. In *Conceptual Structure, Discourse and Language*, A. Goldberg (ed.) 375–89. Stanford, CA: CSLI.

Milambiling, L. 2011. Null object constructions in Tagalog. *Proceedings of the Canadian Linguistics Association* 2011.

Miller, J. 1988. *That*: A relative pronoun? In *Edinburgh Studies in the English Language*, J. M. Anderson & M. Macleod (eds.) 113–19. Edinburgh: John Donald.

Milner, J.-C. 1978. *De la Syntaxe à l'Interprétation: Quantités, insultes, exclamations*. Paris: Éditions du Seuil.

Milsark, G. 1977. Toward an explanation of certain peculiarities of the existential construction in English. *Linguistic Analysis* 3: 1–29.

Miró, E. C. 2006. 'Wh'-exclamatives in Catalan. PhD diss. Universitat de Barcelona.

——2008. Deconstructing exclamations. *Catalan Journal of Linguistics* 7: 41–90.

Miyagawa, S. 2005. On the EPP. *MIT Working Papers in Linguistics* 49: 201–36.

——2006a. Moving to the edge. In *Proceedings of the 2006 KALS-KASELL International Conference on English and Linguistics*, 3–18. Busan: Pusan National University.

——2006b. Locality in syntax and floated numeral quantifiers in Japanese and Korean. *Japanese/Korean Linguistics* 14: 270–82.

——2010. *Why Agree? Why Move? Unifying agreement-based and discourse-configurational languages.* Cambridge, MA: MIT Press.

——2017a. Topicalization. Ms. MIT/University of Tokyo.

——2017b. Numeral quantifiers. In *Handbook of Japanese Syntax*, M. Shibatani, S. Miyagawa & H. Noda (eds.) 581–610. Berlin: De Gruyter Mouton.

Miyagawa, S. & Arikawa, K. 2007. Locality in syntax and floating numeral quantifiers. *Linguistic Inquiry* 38: 645–70.

Moncomble, F. 2018. The deviant syntax of headlines and its role in the pragmatics of headlines. *E-rea* 15(2). https://doi.org/10.4000/erea.6124

Montgomery, M. & Hall, J. S. 2004. *Dictionary of Smoky Mountain English*. Knoxville, TN: University of Tennessee Press.

Moon, G. G.-S. 2001. Grammatical and discourse properties of the imperative subject in English. PhD diss. Harvard University.

Moore, J. 1998. Turkish copy-raising and A-chain locality. *Natural Language and Linguistic Theory* 16: 149–89.

de Moraes Sieiro, P. L. 2020. Sentential wh-exclamatives in Brazilian Portuguese. MA diss. University of Brazil, Brasilia.

Morgan, A. M., & Wagers, M. 2018. English resumptive pronouns are more common where gaps are less acceptable. *Linguistic Inquiry* 49: 1–24.

Morgan, J. 1972. Some aspects of relative clauses in English and Albanian. In *The Chicago Which Hunt: Papers from the Relative Clause Festival*, P. M. Peranteau, J. N. Levi & G. C. Phares (eds.) 63–72. Chicago: Chicago Linguistic Society.

——1973. Sentence fragments and the notion 'sentence'. In *Issues in Linguistics: Papers in honor of Henry and Renee Kahane*, B. B. Kachru (ed.) 719–51. Urbana, IL: University of Illinois Press.

Moro, A. 1997. *The Raising of Predicates*. Cambridge: Cambridge University Press.

——2006. Existential sentences and expletive *there*. In *The Blackwell Companion to Syntax: vol.2*, M. Everaert & H. van Riemsdijk (eds.) 210–36. Oxford: Blackwell.

Müller, G. 2010. On deriving CED effects from the PIC. *Linguistic Inquiry* 41: 35–82.

——2014. Resumption by buffers: German relative clauses. *Linguistische Berichte* 239: 267–95.

——2015. Algorithms, representations, and ATR ratios. Ms. Universität Leipzig. https://ling.auf.net/lingbuzz/002551

——2017. Structure removal: An argument for feature-driven Merge. *Glossa* 2(1): 28.

Munaro, N. 2001. Free relatives as defective *wh* elements: Evidence from the NorthWestern Italian Dialects. In *Romance Languages and Linguistic Theory 1999*, Y. D'Hulst, J. Rooryk & J. Schroten (eds.) 281–306. Amsterdam: Benjamins.

——2003. On some differences between exclamative and interrogative wh-phrases in Bellunese: Further evidence for a split-CP hypothesis. In *The Syntax of Italian Dialects*, C. Tortora (ed.) 137–51. Oxford: Oxford University Press.

Muñoz Pérez, C., Verdecchia, M. & Carranza, F. 2021. Prosodic constraints on wh-extraction from infinitival clauses. Talk presented at the Linguistic Symposium on Romance Languages (LSRL 51), University of Illinois at Urbana-Champaign. Slides available online at http://bit.ly/3viAc7t

Nakajima, H. 2006. Adverbial cognate objects. *Linguistic Inquiry* 37: 674–84.

Nakamura, M. 1983. A nontransformational approach to quantifier floating phenomena. *Studies in English Linguistics* 11: 1–10.

Nakamura, T. 2009. Headed relatives, free relatives, and determiner-headed free relatives. *English Linguistics* 26: 329–55.

Nakanishi, K. 2004. Domains of measurement: Formal properties of non-split/split quantifier constructions. PhD diss. University of Pennsylvania.

——2008. Syntax and semantics of floating numeral quantifiers. In *Oxford Handbook of Japanese Linguistics*, S. Miyagawa & M. Saito (eds.) 287–319. Oxford: Oxford University Press.

Namai, K. 2000. Gender features in English. *Linguistics* 38: 771–79.

Nanyan, V. 2013. Subject omission in English diaries. MA thesis. Ghent University.

Napoli, D. J. 1982. Initial material deletion in English. *Glossa* 16: 85–111.

Nariyama, S. 2004. Subject ellipsis in English. *Journal of Pragmatics* 36: 237–64.

——2006. Pragmatic information extraction from subject ellipsis in informal English. *Proceedings of the 3rd Workshop on Scalable Natural Language Understanding*, 1–8. New York: Association for Computational Linguistics.

Neal, W. F. 1985. *Bill Neal's Southern Cooking*. Chapel Hill, NC: University of North Carolina Press.

Neeleman, A. 1994. Complex predicates. PhD diss. University of Utrecht.

Nemes, M. 2019. The syntax of English news headlines: A truncation approach. BA thesis. Eötvös Loránd University.

Netkachev, I. 2020. Are there floating quantifiers in Indonesian? Research paper no. WP BRP 105, Moscow: HSE University.

Neubauer, P. 1970. On the notion chopping rule. *Chicago Linguistic Society Proceedings* 6: 400–07.

Nevins, A. 2005. Derivations without the Activity Condition. *MIT Working Papers in Linguistics* 49: 287–310.

Newbrook, M. 1998. Which way? That way? Variation and ongoing changes in the English relative clause. *World Englishes* 17: 43–59.

Newman, J & Teddiman, L. 2010. First person pronouns in online diary writing. In *Handbook of Research on Discourse Behavior and Digital Communication: Language structures and social interaction*, vol. 1, R. Taiwo (ed.) 281–95. Hershey, PA: Information Science Reference.

Newmeyer, F. J. 2003. Grammar is grammar and usage is usage. *Language* 79: 682–707.

——2005. A reply to the critiques of 'Grammar is grammar and usage is usage'. *Language* 81: 229–36.

——2006a. On Gahl and Garnsey on grammar and usage. *Language* 82: 399–404.

——2006b. Grammar and usage: A response to Gregory R. Guy. *Language* 82: 705–6.

Nikolaeva, I. 2007 (ed). *Finiteness: Theoretical and empirical foundations.* Oxford: Oxford University Press.

Nilsen, Ø. 2003. *Eliminating positions: Syntax and semantics of sentence modification.* Utrecht: LOT.

Nomura, T. 2006. *ModalP and Subjunctive Present.* Tokyo: Hituzi Syobo.

Norris, M. 2014. A theory of nominal concord. PhD diss. University of California, Santa Cruz.

Nouwen, R. & Chernilovskaya, A. 2015. Two types of wh-exclamatives. *Linguistic Variation* 15: 201–24.

Nunes, J. 1995. The copy theory of movement and linearization of chains in the minimalist program. PhD diss. University of Maryland.

——1999. Linearization of chains and phonetic realization of chain links. In *Working Minimalism*, S. D. Epstein & N. Hornstein (eds.) 217–49. Cambridge, MA: MIT Press.

——2001. Sideward movement. *Linguistic Inquiry* 32: 303–44.

——2004. *Linearization of Chains and Sideward Movement.* Cambridge, MA: MIT Press.

——2008. Inherent case as a licensing condition for A-movement: The case of Hyper-Raising constructions in Brazilian Portuguese. *Journal of Portuguese Linguistics* 7: 83–108.

Nunes, J. & Uriagereka, J. 2000. Cyclicity and extraction domains. *Syntax* 3: 20–43.

Nye, R. 2013. How complement clauses distribute: Complementiser-*how* and the case against clause-type. PhD diss. University of Ghent.

Obenauer, H.-G. 1994. Aspects de la syntaxe A-barre: Effets d'intervention et mouvement des quantifieurs. PhD diss. University of Paris VIII.

Ochi, M. 2004. *How come* and other adjunct *wh*-phrases: A cross-linguistic perspective. *Language and Linguistics* 5: 29–57.

Oh, S.-Y. 2005. English zero anaphora as an interactional resource. *Research on Language and Social Interaction* 38: 267–302.

——2006. English zero anaphora as an interactional resource II. *Discourse Studies* 8: 817–46.

Ohara, M. 2007. Object drop in English and Japanese. *Annals of Foreign*

Studies 67: 69–80. Kobe City University of Foreign Studies.

Olsen, S. 1989. AGR(eement) in the German noun phrase. In *Syntactic Phrase Structure Phenomena*, C. Bhatt, E. Löbel, & C. Schmidt (eds.) 39–49. Amsterdam: Benjamins.

Omaki, A. & Nakao, C. 2010. Does English resumption really help to repair island violations? *Snippets* 21: 11–12.

O'Neil, J. 1995. Out of control. *Proceedings of the North East Linguistics Society* 25: 361–71.

O'Neill, T. E. 2015. The domain of finiteness: Anchoring without tense in copular amalgam sentences. PhD diss. City University of New York.

Ono, H. 2006. An investigation of exclamatives in English and Japanese: Syntax and sentence processing. PhD diss. University of Maryland.

Ono, H. & Fujii, T. 2006. English wh-exclamatives and the role of T-to-C in wh-clauses. *University of Maryland Working Papers in Linguistics* 14: 163–87.

Oomen, U. 1979. Structural properties of English exclamatory sentences. *Folia Linguistica* 13: 159–74.

Oosterhof, A. & Rawoens, G. 2017. Register variation and distributional patterns in article omission in Dutch. *Linguistic Variation* 17: 205–28.

Ortega-Santos, I. 2013. Corrective focus at the right edge in Spanish. *Lingua* 131: 112–35.

Osborne, T. 2013. The distribution of floating quantifiers: A dependency grammar analysis. *Proceedings of the Second International Conference on Dependency Linguistics*, 272–81. Prague: Matfyzpress.

Ostrove, J. 2018. When φ-agreement targets topics: The view from San Martín Peras Mixtec. PhD diss. University of California, Santa Cruz.

Otoguro, R. & Snijders, L. 2016. Syntactic, semantic and information structures of floating quantifiers. In *Proceedings of the Joint 2016 Conference on Head-Driven Phrase Structure Grammar and Lexical-Functional Grammar*, D. Arnold, M. Butt, B. Crysmann, T.H. King & S. Müller (eds.) 478–98. Stanford, CA: CSLI Publications.

Ott, D. 2012a. Movement and ellipsis in contrastive left-dislocation. *Proceedings of the West Coast Conference on Formal Linguistics* 30: 281–91.

——2012b. *Local Instability: Split topicalization and quantifier float in German*. Berlin: de Gruyter.

——2014. An ellipsis approach to contrastive left-dislocation. *Linguistic Inquiry* 45: 269–303.

——2015. Connectivity in left-dislocation and the composition of the left periphery. *Linguistic Variation* 15: 225–90.

Ozaki, S. 2010. Subjectless sentences in English. *Nagoya Bunri University Working Papers in Linguistics* 10: 35–46.

Öztürk, B. 2005. *Case, Referentiality, and Phrase Structure*. Amsterdam: Benjamins.

Paesani, K. 2006. Extending the non-sentential analysis: The case of special registers. In *The Syntax of Non-sententials*, L. Progovac, K. Paesani, E. Casielles & E. Barton (eds.) 147–82. Amsterdam: Benjamins.

Palacios Roman, M. 2018. English and Spanish exclamatives: A comparative study of the left periphery. Bachelor thesis. Leiden University.

Panitz, E. J. 2015. Null objects in Brazilian Portuguese, revisited. *Caderno de Squibs* 1: 25–34.

Paoli, S. 2003. COMP and the left periphery: Comparative evidence from Romance. PhD diss. University of Manchester.

——2007. The fine structure of the left periphery: COMPs and subjects: Evidence from Romance. *Lingua* 117: 1057–79.

——2014. Defective object clitic paradigms and the relation between language development and loss. *Journal of Linguistics* 50: 143–83.

Park, B.-S. 2005. Focus, parallelism, and identity in ellipsis. PhD diss. University of Connecticut, Storrs.

Parry, M. 2007. La frase relativa (con antecedente) negli antichi volgari dell'Italia nord-occidentale. *LabRomAn* 1: 9–32.

Patterson, G. & Caponigro, I. 2016. The puzzling degraded status of *who* free relative clauses in English. *English Language and Linguistics* 20: 341–52.

Paul, I. (2017). Reduced structure in Malagasy headlines. *Linguistic Variation* 17: 292–308.

Paul, W. 2005. Low IP area and left periphery in Mandarin Chinese. *Recherches Linguistiques de Vincennes* 33: 111–34.

——2014. *New Perspectives on Chinese Syntax*. Berlin: De Gruyter.

Paul, I. & Massam, D. 2020. Recipes in Malagasy and other languages. *Proceedings of Austronesian Formal Linguistics Association* 27: 98–112. National University of Singapore.

Paunovic, Z. 1997. Some notes on floating quantifiers. MA thesis. University of Essex.

Pearce, E. 1999. Topic and focus in a head-initial language: Maori. *Toronto Working Papers in Linguistics* 16: 249–63.

Pérez-Sabater, C. 2012. The linguistics of social networking: A study of writing conventions on Facebook. *Linguistik Online* 56: 81–93.

Perlmutter, D. M. 1968. Deep and surface structure constraints in syntax. PhD diss. MIT.

——1970. The two verbs *begin*. In *Readings in English Transformational Grammar*, R. A. Jacobs & P. S. Rosenbaum (eds.) 107–19. Waltham, MA: Ginn.

——1971. *Deep and Surface Structure Constraints in Syntax*. New York: Holt, Rinehart & Winston.

Perlmutter, D. & Soames, S. 1979. *Syntactic Argumentation and the Structure of English*. Berkeley, CA: University of California Press.

Pesetsky, D. 1982a. Paths and categories. PhD diss. MIT.

——1982b. Complementiser-trace phenomena and the Nominative Island Condition. *The Linguistic Review* 1: 297–343.

——1989. Language-particular processes and the Earliness Principle. Ms. MIT.

——2016. Complementizer-trace effects. Ms. MIT. https://ling.auf .net/lingbuzz/002385

——2020. Lack of ambition as explanation when a clause is reduced. Ms. MIT. Text of paper presented to the 13th Brussels Conference on Generative Linguistics, December.

——2021. Exfoliation: Towards a derivational theory of clause size. Ms. MIT. https://ling.auf.net/ lingbuzz/004440

Pesetsky, D. & Torrego, E. 2001. T-to-C movement: Causes and consequences. In *Ken Hale: A life in language*, M. Kenstowicz (ed.) 355–426. Cambridge MA: MIT Press.

——2004. Tense, case, and the nature of syntactic categories. In *The Syntax of Time*, J. Guéron & J. Lecarme (eds.) 495–537. Cambridge, MA: MIT Press.

——2007. The syntax of valuation and the interpretability of features. *Linguistics Today* 101: 262–94.

Petersen, C. 2011. The licensing of null subjects in Brazilian Portuguese. MA thesis. University of Sao Paolo.

Petersen, C. & Terzi, A. 2015. Hyper-Raising and locality: A view from Brazilian Portuguese and Greek. *Chicago Linguistic Society Proceedings* 50: 365–79.

Petronio, K. & Lillo-Martin, D. 1997. Wh Movement and the position of Spec-CP: Evidence from American Sign Language. *Language* 73: 18–57.

Phillips, C. 1996. Order and structure. PhD diss. MIT.

——2003. Linear order and constituency. *Linguistic Inquiry* 34: 37–90.

Pierce, A. E. 1992. *Language Acquisition and Syntactic Theory*. Dordrecht: Kluwer.

Platzack, C. 2001. Multiple interfaces. In *Cognitive Interfaces: Constraints on linking cognitive information*, U. Nikanne & E. van der Zee (eds.) 21–53. Oxford: Oxford University Press.

——2004. Cross-linguistic word order variation at the left periphery: The case of object-first main clauses. *Studies in Natural Language and Linguistic Theory* 59: 191–210.

Platzack, C. & Rosengren, I. 1997. On the subject of imperatives: A minimalist account of the imperative clause. *Journal of Comparative Germanic Linguistics* 1: 177–224.

Poletto, C. 1993. *La Sintassi del Soggetto nei Dialetti Italiani Settentrionali*. Padua: Unipress.

——2000. *The Higher Functional Field: Evidence from Northern Italian Dialects*. Oxford: Oxford University Press.

Polinsky, M. 2003. Non-canonical agreement is canonical. *Transactions of the Philological Society* 101: 279–312.

Polinsky, M., Clemens, L. E., Morgan, A. M., Xiang, M. & Heestand, D. 2013. Resumption in English. In *Experimental Syntax and Island Effects*, J. Sprouse & N. Hornstein (eds.) 341–59. Cambridge: Cambridge University Press.

Polinsky, M. & Potsdam, E. 2001. Long-distance agreement and topic in Tsez. *Natural Language and Linguistic Theory* 19: 583–646.

——2006. Expanding the scope of control and raising. *Syntax* 9: 171–92.

Pollock, J.-Y. 1989. Verb movement, universal grammar, and the structure of IP. *Linguistic Inquiry* 20: 365–424.

Poortvliet, M. 2016. Copy Raising in English, German and Dutch: Synchrony and Diachrony. *Journal of Germanic Linguistics* 28: 370–402.

Portner, P. & Zanuttini, R. 2000. The force of negation in wh exclamatives and interrogatives. In *Studies in Negation and Polarity: Syntactic and semantic perspectives*, L. R. Horn & Y. Kato (eds.) 201–39. Oxford: Oxford University Press.

Portner, P. 2004. The syntax of imperatives within a theory of clause types. In *Proceedings of the 14th Semantics and Linguistic Theory Conference*, K. Watanabe & R. Young (eds.) 235–52. Ithaca, NY: Cornell University.

——2007. Imperatives and modals. *Natural Language Semantics* 15: 351–83.

Portner, P. & Yabushita, K. 1998. The semantics and pragmatics of topic phrases. *Linguistics and Philosophy* 21: 117–57.

Postal, P. M. 1966. On so-called pronouns in English. In *Report on the Seventeenth Annual Round Table Meeting on Linguistics and Language Studies*, F. Dinneen (ed.) 177–206. Washington, DC: Georgetown University Press.

——1971. *Cross-Over Phenomena*. New York: Holt, Rinehart and Winston.

——1972. On some rules that are not successive cyclic. *Linguistic Inquiry* 3: 211–22.

——1974. *On Raising*. Cambridge, MA: MIT Press.

Postal, P. M., & Pullum, G. K. 1988. Expletive noun phrases in subcategorised positions. *Linguistic Inquiry* 19: 425–49.

Potsdam, E. 1998. *Syntactic Issues in the English Imperative*. New York: Garland.

——2018. *Syntactic Issues in the English Imperative*. London: Routledge.

Potsdam, E. & Runner, J. T. 2001. Richard returns: Copy-raising and its implications. *Chicago Linguistic Society Proceedings* 37: 206–22.

Preminger, O. 2012. Agreement as a fallible operation. PhD diss. MIT.

——2014. *Agreement and its Failures*. Cambridge, MA: MIT Press.

Prince, E. 1981a. Topicalization, Focus-Movement, and Yiddish-Movement: A pragmatic differentiation. *Berkeley Linguistic Society Proceedings* 7: 249–64.

——1981b. Toward a taxonomy of given-new information. In *Radical Pragmatics*, P. Cole (ed.) 222–55. New York: Academic Press.

——1984. Topicalization and left dislocation: A functional analysis. *Annals of the New York Academy of Sciences* 433: 213–25.

——1990. Syntax and discourse: A look at resumptive pronouns.

Berkeley Linguistics Society Proceedings 16: 482–97.

——1995. On *kind*-sentences, resumptive pronouns, and relative clauses. In *Towards a Social Science of Language: A Festschrift for William Labov*, G. Guy, J. Baugh & D. Schiffrin (eds.) 223–35. Cambridge: Cambridge University Press.

——1997 On the functions of left-dislocation in English discourse. In *Directions in Functional Linguistics*, A. Kamio (ed.) 117–43. Amsterdam: Benjamins.

Puskás, G. 2000. *Word Order in Hungarian: The Syntax of Ā-positions*. Amsterdam: Benjamins.

——2003. Floating quantifiers: What they can tell us about the syntax and semantics of quantifiers. *Generative Grammar in Geneva* 3: 105–28.

Quirk, R. S. 1957. Relative clauses in educated spoken English. *English Studies* 38: 97–109.

Quirk, R., Greenbaum, S., Leech, G. & Svartik, J. 1985. *A Comprehensive Grammar of the English Language*. London: Longman.

Rackowski, A. & Richards, N. 2005. Phase edge and extraction: A Tagalog case study. *Linguistic Inquiry* 36: 565–99.

Radford, A. 1980. On English exclamatives. Ms. University College of North Wales, Bangor.

——1981. *Transformational Syntax*. Cambridge: Cambridge University Press.

——1982. The syntax of verbal wh-exclamatives in Italian. In *Studies in the Romance Verb*, N. Vincent & M. Harris (eds.) 185–204. London: Croom Helm.

——1988. *Transformational Grammar: A First Course*. Cambridge: Cambridge University Press.

——1989. The Status of exclamative particles in French. In *Essays on Grammatical Theory and Universal Grammar*, D. J. Arnold, M. Atkinson, J. Durand, C. Grover & L. Sadler (eds.) 223–84. Oxford: Oxford University Press.

——1997a. *Syntactic Theory and the Structure of English*. Cambridge: Cambridge University Press.

——1997b. *Syntax: A minimalist introduction*. Cambridge: Cambridge University Press.

——1997c. Verso un'analisi delle frasi esclamative in italiano (= 'Towards an analysis of clausal exclamatives in Italian'). In *La Linguistica Italiana Fuori d'Italia*, L. Renzi & M. Cortelazzo (eds.) 93–123. Rome: Bulzoni, Società Linguistica Italiana.

——2004a. *Minimalist Syntax: Exploring the structure of English*. Cambridge: Cambridge University Press.

——2004b. *English Syntax: An introduction*. Cambridge: Cambridge University Press.

——2008. Feature correlations in nominative case-marking by L1 and L2 learners of English. In *The Role of Formal Features in Second Language Acquisition*, J. M. Liceras, H. Zobl & H. Goodluck (eds.) 81–102. Mahwah, NJ: Laurence Erlbaum Associates.

——2009a. *Analysing English Sentences*. Cambridge: Cambridge University Press.

——2009b. *An Introduction to English Sentence Structure*. Cambridge: Cambridge University Press.

——2013. The complementiser system in spoken English: Evidence from broadcast media. In *Agreement, Information Structure and the CP*, V. Camacho-Taboada, Á Jiménez-Fernández, J. Martín-González, & M. Reyes-Tejedor (eds.) 11–54. Amsterdam: Benjamins.

——2016. *Analysing English Sentences*, 2nd edition. Cambridge: Cambridge University Press.

——2018. *Colloquial English: Structure and variation*. Cambridge: Cambridge University Press.

——2019. *Relative Clauses: Structure and variation in everyday English*. Cambridge: Cambridge University Press.

——2020. *An Introduction to English Sentence Structure*, 2nd edition. Cambridge: Cambridge University Press.

Radford, A. & Iwasaki, E. 2015. On swiping in English. *Natural Language and Linguistic Theory* 33: 703–44.

Radford, A., Felser, C & Boxell, O. 2012. Preposition copying and pruning in present-day English. *English Language and Linguistics* 16: 403–26.

Ramat, P. 2014. Categories, features and values in the definition of a word class. *Italian Linguistic Studies* 52, 2.

Raposo, E. 1986. On the null object in European Portuguese. In *Studies in Romance Linguistics*, O. Jaeggli & C. Silva-Corvalan (eds.) 373–90. Dordrecht: Foris.

——1987. Case theory and Infl-to-Comp: The inflected infinitive in European Portuguese. *Linguistic Inquiry* 18: 85–109.

Rawlins, K. 2008. (Un)conditionals: An investigation in the syntax and semantics of conditional structures. PhD diss. University of California, Santa Cruz.

Reed, A. M. 2010. The discourse function of floated quantifiers. *Journal of Pragmatics* 42: 1737–61.

Reed, L. 2011. *Get*-passives. *The Linguistic Review* 28: 41–78.

Reich, I. 2017. On the omission of articles and copulae in German newspaper headlines. *Linguistic Variation* 17: 186–206.

Reid, J. 1997. Relatives and their relatives: Relative clauses in conversational Australian English. PhD diss. La Trobe University.

Reiman, P. W. 1994. Subjectless sentences in English. *UTA Working Papers in Linguistics* 1: 141–52.

Reinhart, T. 1981. Pragmatics and linguistics: An analysis of sentence topics. *Philosophica* 27: 53–94.

Rett, J. 2012. Exclamatives, degrees and speech acts. *Linguistics and Philosophy* 34: 411–42.

Rezak, M. 2004. Elements of cyclic syntax: Agree and Merge. PhD diss. University of Toronto.

——2006. The interaction of Th/Ex and Locative Inversion. *Linguistic Inquiry* 37: 685–97.

——2010. φ-agree versus φ-feature movement: Evidence from floating quantifiers. *Linguistic Inquiry* 41: 496–508.

——2011. Building and interpreting nonthematic A-positions: A-resumption in English and Breton. In *Resumptive Pronouns at the Interfaces*, A. Rouveret (ed.) 241–86. Amsterdam: Benjamins.

Richards, N. 1999. Dependency formation and directionality of tree construction. *MIT Working Papers in Linguistics* 34: 67–105.

——2003. Why is there an EPP? *Gengo Kenkyu* 123: 221–56.

——2010. *Uttering Trees.* Cambridge, MA: MIT Press.

——2016. *Continuity Theory.* Cambridge, MA: MIT Press.

Riemsdijk, H. van 1985. On pied-piped infinitives in German relative clauses. In *Studies in German Grammar*, J. Toman (ed.) 165–92. Dordrecht: Foris.

——2006. Free relatives: A syntactic case study. In *The Blackwell Companion to Syntax*, M. Everaert & H. van Riemsdijk (eds.) 336–78. Oxford: Blackwell.

Riemsdijk, H. van & F. Zwarts. 1974. Left dislocation in Dutch and the status of copying rules. Ms. MIT and University of Amsterdam. Reprinted as van Riemsdijk & Zwarts (1997).

——1997. Left dislocation in Dutch and the status of copying rules. In *Materials on Left Dislocation*, E. Anagnastopoulou, H. van Riemsdijk & F. Zwarts (eds.) 13–30. Amsterdam: Benjamins.

Ritter, E. & Wiltschko, M. 2014. The composition of INFL: An exploration of tense, tenseless languages and tenseless constructions. *Natural Language & Linguistic Theory* 32: 1331–86.

Rivero, M.-L. 1978. Topicalization and wh-movement in Spanish. *Linguistic Inquiry* 9: 513–7.

——1980. On left-dislocation and topicalization in Spanish. *Linguistic Inquiry* 11: 363–93.

——1989. Barriers and Rumanian. In *Studies in Romance Linguistics.* C. Kirschner & J. A. DeCesaris (eds.) 289–312. Amsterdam: Benjamins.

Rizzi, L. 1982. *Issues in Italian Syntax.* Dordrecht: Foris.

——1986. Null objects in Italian and the theory of *pro. Linguistic Inquiry* 17: 501–57.

——1990. *Relativised Minimality.* Cambridge, MA: MIT Press.

——1994. Early null subjects and root null subjects. In *Language Acquisition Studies in Generative Grammar*, T. Hoekstra & B. Schwartz (eds.) 151–76. Amsterdam: Benjamins.

——1996. Residual verb-second and the *wh*-criterion. In *Parameters and Functional Heads*, A. Belletti & L. Rizzi (eds.) 63–90. Oxford: Oxford University Press.

——1997. The fine structure of the left periphery. In *Elements of Grammar*, L. Haegeman (ed.) 281–337. Dordrecht: Kluwer.

——1998. Remarks on early null subjects. *Proceedings of the Annual Boston University Conference on Language Development* 23: 14–38. Reprinted as Rizzi 2000a.

——2000a. Remarks on early null subjects. In *The Acquisition of Syntax*, M.-A. Freidemann & L. Rizzi (eds.) 269–92. London: Longman.

——2000b. *Comparative Syntax and Language Acquisition*. London: Routledge.

——2001. On the position 'Int(errogative)' in the left periphery of the clause. In *Current Issues in Italian Syntax*, G. Cinque & G. Salvi (eds.) 287–96. Amsterdam: Elsevier.

——2003. Relativised minimality effects. In *The Handbook of Contemporary Syntactic Theory*, M. Baltin & C. Collins (eds.) 89–110. Oxford: Blackwell.

——2004a. Locality and Left Periphery. In *The Cartography of Syntactic Structures, Vol. 3: Structures and beyond*, A. Belletti (ed.) 223–51. Oxford: Oxford University Press.

——2004b (ed). *The Cartography of Syntactic Structures, Vol. 2: The structure of IP and CP*, Oxford: Oxford University Press.

——2005. On some properties of subjects and topics. In *Proceedings of the XXX Incontro di Grammatica Generativa*, L. Brugé, G. Giusti, N. Munaro, W. Schweikert & G. Turano (eds.) 203–24. Venice: Cafoscarina.

——2006a. On the form of chains: Criterial positions and ECP effects. In *Wh-Movement: Moving On*, L. Cheng & N. Corver (eds.) 97–133. Cambridge, MA: MIT Press.

——2006b. On intermediate positions: Intervention and impenetrability. Handout for talk presented to EALing 2006. ENS, Paris.

——2006c. Grammatically-based target-inconsistencies in child language. *University of Connecticut Occasional Papers in Linguistics* 4: 19–49.

——2007. On some properties of criterial freezing. *CISCL Working Papers on Language and Cognition* 1: 145–58.

——2010. On some properties of criterial freezing. In *The Complementizer Phase: Subjects and Operators*, E. P. Panagiotidis (ed.) 17–32. Oxford: Oxford University Press.

——2011. Syntactic cartography and the syntacticisation of scope-discourse semantics. Ms. Universities of Siena and Geneva.

——2012. Delimitation effects and the cartography of the left periphery. In *Discourse and Grammar: From sentence types to lexical categories*, G. Grewendorf & T. E. Zimmermann (eds.) 115–45. Berlin: De Gruyter Mouton.

——2013a. Notes on cartography and further explanation. *Probus* 25: 197–226.

——2013b. A Note on locality and selection. In *Deep Insights, Broad Perspectives: Essays in honor of Mamoru Saito*, Y. Miyamoto, D. Takahashi & H. Maki (eds.) 325–41. Tokyo: Kaitakusha.

——2013c. Topic, focus and the cartography of the left periphery. In *The Bloomsbury Companion to Syntax*, S. Luraghi & C. Parodi (eds.) 436–51. London: Bloomsbury.

——2014a. Some consequences of criterial freezing. In *The Cartography of Syntactic Structures, Vol. 9: Functional structure from top to toe*, P. Svenonius (ed.) 19–45. Oxford: Oxford University Press.

——2014b. The Cartography of syntactic structures: Locality and freezing effects on movement. In *On Peripheries: Exploring clause initial and clause final positions* C. Cardinaletti, G. Cinque, & Y. Endo (eds.) 29–59. Tokyo: Hituzi Syobe Publishing.

——2015a. Cartography, criteria and labelling. In *The Cartography of Syntactic Structures, Vol. 10: Beyond functional sequence*, U. Shlonsky (ed.) 314–38. Oxford: Oxford University Press.

——2015b. Notes on labelling and subject positions. In *Structures, Strategies and Beyond: Studies in honour of Adriana Belletti*, E. Di Domenico, C. Hamann & S. Matterini (eds.) 17–46. Amsterdam: Benjamins.

——2016a. Uniqueness of left peripheral focus: Further explanation and introduction. In *Order and Structure in Syntax*, L. R. Bailey & M. Sheehan (eds.) 333–43. Language Science Press.

——2016b. Labeling, maximality and the head–phrase distinction. *The Linguistic Review* 33: 103–27.

——2017. Types of criterial freezing. *Rivista di Grammatica Generativa* 39: 1–19.

——2018. Subjects, topics and the interpretation of *pro*. In *From Sound to Structures: Beyond the veil of Maya*, R. Petrosino & P. Cerrone (eds.) 510–529. Berlin: Mouton de Gruyter.

——2020. Notes on the map of the left periphery in Danish. In *The Sign of the V: Papers in honour of Sten Vikner*, K. R. Christensen, H. Jørgensen & J. L. Wood (eds.) 489–501. Aarhus: Department of English, School of Communication and Culture, Aarhus University.

Rizzi, L & Bocci, G. 2017. Left periphery of the clause: Primarily illustrated for Italian. In *The Wiley-Blackwell Companion to Syntax*, 2nd edition, M. Everaert & H. van Riemsdijk (eds.) 1–30. Hoboken, NJ: John Wiley & Sons.

Rizzi, L. & Cinque, G. 2016. Functional categories and syntactic theory. *Annual Review of Linguistics* 2: 139–63.

Rizzi, L. & Shlonsky, U. 2006. Satisfying the subject criterion by a non-subject: Locative inversion and heavy NP shift. In *Phases of Interpretation*, M. Frascarelli (ed.) 341–61. Berlin: Mouton de Gruyter.

——2007. Strategies of subject extraction. In *Interfaces+Recursion = Language?* U. Sauerland & H.-M. Gärtner (eds.) 115–60. Berlin: Mouton de Gruyter.

Roberge, Y. 1991. The recoverability of null objects. In *New Analyses in Romance Linguistics: Selected papers from the XVIIIth linguistic symposium on Romance languages*. D. Wanner & D. A. Kibbee (eds.) 299–312. Amsterdam: Benjamins.

Roberts, I. 1987. *The Representation of Implicit and Dethematized Subjects.* Dordrecht: Foris.

——1993a. *Verbs and Diachronic Syntax.* Dordrecht: Kluwer.

——1993b. The nature of subject clitics in Franco-Provençal Valdotain. In *Syntactic Theory and the Dialects of Italy,* A. Belletti (ed.) 319–53. Turin: Rosenberg & Sellier.

——2004. The C-system in Brythionic Celtic languages and the EPP. In *The Cartography of Syntactic Structures, Vol. 2: The structure of IP and CP,* L. Rizzi (ed.) 297–328. Oxford: Oxford University Press.

——2010. *Agreement and Head Movement: Clitics, incorporation and defective goals.* Cambridge, MA: MIT Press.

Roberts, I. & Roussou, A. 2002. The extended projection principle as a condition on the tense dependency. In *Subjects, Expletives and the EPP,* P. Svenonius (ed.) 125–55. Oxford: Oxford University Press.

Rochemont, M. 1986. *Focus in Generative Grammar.* Amsterdam: Benjamins.

Rochman, L. 2010. Why float? Floating quantifiers and focus marking. In *The Sound Patterns of Syntax,* N. Erteschik-Shir & L. Rochman (eds.) 72–92. Oxford: Oxford University Press.

Rodman, R. 1974. On left dislocation. *Papers in Linguistics* 7: 437–66. Reprinted as Rodman 1997.

——1997. On left dislocation. In *Materials on Left Dislocation,* E. Anagnastopoulou, H. van Riemsdijk & F. Zwarts (eds.) 31–55. Amsterdam: Benjamins.

Rodriguez, C. 2004. Impoverished morphology and A-movement out of case domains. PhD diss. University of Maryland.

Roehrs, D. 2008. High floating quantifiers: Syntactic or 'delayed' V2? *Snippets* 17: 7–8.

Rogers, A. D. 1971. Three kinds of physical perception verbs. *Chicago Linguistic Society Proceedings* 7: 206–23.

——1972. Another look at flip perception verbs. *Chicago Linguistic Society Proceedings* 8: 303–15.

——1974. Physical perception verbs in English: A study in lexical relatedness. PhD diss. UCLA.

Rohrbacher, B. 1999. *Morphology-driven syntax: A theory of V-to-I raising and pro-drop.* Amsterdam: Benjamins.

Romero, M. 1997. The correlation between scope reconstruction and connectivity effects. *Proceedings of the West Coast Conference in Formal Linguistics* 16: 351–65.

——1998. Focus and reconstruction effects in wh-phrases. PhD diss. University of Massachusetts, Amherst.

Rooryck, J. 1994. Generalized transformations and the *wh*-cycle: Free relatives as bare *wh*-CPs. In *Minimalism and Kayne's Asymmetry Hypothesis.* C. J.-W. Zwart (ed.) 195–208. Groningen: Groningen University.

——2000. *Configurations of Sentential Complementation: Perspectives from Romance Languages.* London: Routledge.

Rooth, M. 1985. Association with focus. PhD diss. University of Massachusetts, Amherst.

——1992. A theory of focus interpretation. *Natural Language Semantics* 1: 75–116.

——1996. Focus. In *The Handbook of Contemporary Semantic Theory,* S. Lappin (ed.) 272–97. Oxford: Blackwell.

Rosen, S. T. 1990. *Argument Structure and Complex Predicates.* New York: Garland.

Rosengren, I. 2000. Rethinking the adjunct. *ZAS Papers in Linguistics* 17: 217–40.

——2002. A syntactic device in the service of semantics. *Studia Linguistica* 56: 145–90.

Ross, J. R. 1967. Constraints on Variables in Syntax. PhD diss. MIT. Published as Ross 1986.

——1969. Guess who. *Chicago Linguistic Society Proceedings* 5: 252–86.

——1973. Ross, J. R. The same side filter. *Chicago Linguistic Society Proceedings* 9: 549–67.

——1986 *Infinite Syntax!* Norwood, NJ: Ablex Publishing Corporation.

Rothstein, S. D. 1983. The syntactic form of predication. PhD diss. MIT.

——1995. Pleonastics and the interpretation of pronouns. *Linguistic Inquiry* 26: 499–529.

Roussou, A. 2000. On the left periphery: Modal particles and complementizers. *Journal of Greek Linguistics* 1: 65–94.

Rouveret, A. 2002. How are resumptive pronouns linked to the periphery?

Linguistic Variation Yearbook 2: 123–84.

——2011 (ed.) *Resumptive Pronouns at the Interfaces.* Amsterdam: Benjamins.

Ruda, M. 2014. Missing objects in special registers: The syntax of null objects in English. *Canadian Journal of Linguistics* 59: 339–72.

——2017. *On the syntax of missing objects: A study with special reference to English, Polish and Hungarian.* Amsterdam: Benjamins.

Rudolph, R. E. 2019. A closer look at the perceptual source in copy raising constructions. *Proceedings of Sinn Und Bedeutung* 23: 287–304.

Rühlemann, C. 2012. Conversational Grammar. *Wiley Online Encyclopedia of Applied Linguistics.* https://doi .org/10.1002/9781405198431 .wbeal0220 .

Rupp, L. 1999. Aspects of the syntax of English imperatives. PhD diss. University of Essex.

——2003. *The Syntax of Imperatives in English and Germanic: Word order variation in the minimalist framework.* New York: Palgrave Macmillan.

——2005. Grammatical constraints on nonstandard *-s* in expletive *there* sentences. *English Language and Linguistics* 9: 225–88.

Ruppenhofer, J. & Michaelis, L. A. 2010. A constructional account of genre-based argument omissions. *Constructions and Frames* 2: 158–84.

Sabel, J. 1996. *Restrukturierung und Lokalität: Universelle*

Beschränkungen für Wortstellungsvarianten. Berlin: Akademie Verlag.

——2000. Expletives as features. *Proceedings of the West Coast Conference on Formal Linguistics* 19: 411–24.

——2002. A minimalist analysis of syntactic islands. *The Linguistic Review* 19: 271–315.

Sadock, J. M. 1974. Read at your own risk: Syntactic and semantic horrors you can find in your own medicine chest. *Chicago Linguistic Society Proceedings* 10: 599–607.

Sæbø, K. 2006. Explaining clausal exclamatives. *3ième Journée de Sémantique et Modélisation.* Paris: ENS.

——2010. On the semantics of 'embedded exclamatives'. *Studia Linguistica* 64: 116–40.

Safir, K. 1986a. *Syntactic Chains.* Cambridge: Cambridge University Press.

——1986b. Relative clauses in a theory of binding and levels. *Linguistic Inquiry* 17: 663–90.

——1999. Vehicle change and reconstruction in A-bar chains. *Linguistic Inquiry* 30: 587–620.

Sag, I. 1978. Floating quantifiers, adverbs and extraction sites. *Linguistic Inquiry* 9: 146–50.

——1980. *Deletion and Logical Form.* New York: Garland.

——1997. English relative clause constructions. *Journal of Linguistics* 33: 431–83.

Saito, M. 2012. Sentence types and the Japanese right periphery. In *Discourse and Grammar:*

From sentence types to lexical categories, G. Grewendorf & T. E. Zimmermann (eds.) 147–76. Berlin: de Gruyter.

Sakamoto, A. & Ikarashi, K. 2017. Subjectless sentences in conversation and the defectiveness of their syntactic structures. In *Studies on Syntactic Cartography*, Fuzhen Si (ed.) 336–51. Beijing: China Social Sciences Press.

Salvi, G. 2005. Some firm points on Latin word order: The left periphery. In *Universal Grammar and the Reconstruction of Ancient Languages*, K. É. Kiss (ed.) 429–56. Berlin: Mouton de Gruyter.

Salzmann, M. 2006. Resumptive pronouns and matching effects in Zurich German relative clauses as distributed deletion. *Leiden Papers in Linguistics* 3: 17–50.

——2011. *Reconstruction and Resumption in Indirect A'-dependencies: On the syntax of prolepsis and relativization in (Swiss) German and beyond.* Berlin: Mouton de Gruyter.

Samek-Lodovici, V. 2006.When right dislocation meets the left-periphery: A unified analysis of Italian non-final focus. *Lingua* 116: 836–73.

——2009. Topic, focus and background in Italian clauses. In *Focus and Background in Romance Languages*, A. Dufter & D. Jacob (eds.) 333–57. Amsterdam: Benjamins.

Sato, Y. & Dobashi, Y. 2013. Functional categories and prosodic phrasing in English: Evidence from *that*-trace effects and pronominal object shift. Ms. National University of Singapore and Niigata University.

Sato, Y. & Kim, C. 2012. Radical pro drop and the role of syntactic agreement in Colloquial Singapore English. *Lingua* 122: 858–73.

Sauerland, U. 1998. The meaning of chains. PhD diss. MIT.

——1999. Two structures for English restrictive relative clauses. In *Proceedings of the Nanzan GLOW*, M. Saito (ed.) 351–66. Nagoya: Nanzan University.

——2003. Unpronounced heads in relative clauses. In *The Interfaces: Deriving and interpreting omitted structures*, K. Schwabe & S. Winkler (eds.) 205–26. Amsterdam: Benjamins.

Sauerland, U. & Elbourne, P. 2002. Total reconstruction, PF movement and derivational order. *Linguistic Inquiry* 33: 283–319.

Sawada, H. 1995. *Studies in English and Japanese Auxiliaries: A multistratal approach*. Tokyo: Hituzi Syobo.

Schachter, P. 1973. Focus and relativization. *Language* 49: 19–46.

Schaeffer, J. 1994. The split INFL hypothesis: Evidence from impaired language. *First Language* 14: 334–35.

Schirer, K. C. 2008. Have you heard the new theory? A syntactic analysis of null subjects and null auxiliaries in English. MA thesis. University of Kansas.

Schmerling, S. 1973. Subjectless sentences and the notion of surface structure. *Chicago Linguistic Society Proceedings* 9: 577–86.

Schneider-Zioga, P. 2007. Anti-agreement, anti-locality, and minimality: The syntax of dislocated subjects. *Natural Language and Linguistic Theory* 25: 403–46.

Schönenberger, M. 2010. Optional doubly-filled COMPs (DFCs) in wh-complements in child and adult Swiss German. In *Variation in the Input*, M. Anderssen, K. Bentzen & M. Westergaard (eds.) 33–64. Dordrecht: Springer.

Schütze, C. 1996 *The Empirical Basis of Linguistics: Grammaticality judgments and linguistic methodology*. Chicago: University of Chicago Press.

——1999. English expletive constructions are not infected. *Linguistic Inquiry* 30: 467–84.

——2001. On the nature of default case. *Syntax* 4: 205–38.

——2009. Web searches should supplement judgements, not supplant them. *Zeitschrift für Sprachwissenschaft* 28: 151–56.

Schütze, C. & Sprouse, J. 2014. Judgment data. In *Research Methods in Linguistics*, R. J. Podesva & D. Sharma (eds.) 27–50. Cambridge: Cambridge University Press.

Schwarz, B. 1999. On the syntax of either ... or. *Natural Language and Linguistic Theory* 17: 339–70.

——2000. *Topics in Ellipsis* Amherst, MA: GLSA Publications.

Schwarz, F. 2012. Situation pronouns in determiner phrases. *Natural Language Semantics* 20: 431–75.

Schwenter, S. A. 2006. Null objects across South America. In *Selected Proceedings of the 8th Hispanic*

Linguistics Symposium, T. L. Face & C. A. Klee (eds.) 23–36. Somerville, MA: Cascadilla Proceedings Project.

Schwenter, S.A. & Silva, G. 2002. Overt vs. null direct objects in spoken Brazilian Portuguese: A semantic/pragmatic account. *Hispania* 85: 577–86.

Scott, K. J. 2004. Diary drop in English: A syntactic and pragmatic analysis. MA thesis. University College London.

——2010. The relevance of referring expressions: The case of diary drop in English. PhD diss. University College London.

Sells, P. 1984. Syntax and semantics of resumptive pronouns. PhD diss. University of Massachusetts, Amherst.

——1987. Binding resumptive pronouns. *Linguistics and Philosophy* 10: 261–98.

Seppänen, A. 1997: Relative *that* and prepositional complementation. *English Language and Linguistics* 1: 111–33.

Seppänen, A. & Kjellmer, G. 1995. The dog that's leg was broken: On the genitive of the relative pronoun. *English Studies* 76: 389–400.

Seppänen, A. & Trotta, J. 2000. The *wh+that* pattern in present-day English. In *Corpora Galore: Analyses and Techniques in Describing English*, J. M. Kirk (ed.) 161–75. Amsterdam: Rodopi.

Shaer, B. & Frey, W. 2004. Integrated and non-integrated left-peripheral elements in German and English. *ZAS Papers in Linguistics* 35: 465–502.

Shan, C.-C. & Barker, C. 2006. Explaining crossover and superiority as left-to-right evaluation. *Linguistics and Philosophy* 29: 91–134.

Sharvit, Y. 1999. Resumptive pronouns in relative clauses. *Natural Language and Linguistic Theory* 17: 587–612.

Sheehan, M. 2006. The EPP and null subjects in Romance. PhD diss. University of Newcastle-upon-Tyne.

——2013a. The resuscitation of CED. *Proceedings of the North East Linguistic Society* 40: 135–50.

——2013b. Some implications of a copy theory of labelling. *Syntax* 16: 362–96.

Shibata, K. 2017. Subject ellipsis in English: The perception verbs *feel*, *look*, *sound*, *smell*, and *taste*. PhD diss. Kyoto Prefectural University.

Shlonsky, U. 1991. Quantifiers as functional heads: A study of quantifier float in Hebrew. *Lingua* 84: 159–80.

——1992. Resumptive pronouns as a last resort. *Linguistic Inquiry* 23: 443–68.

——1993. Agreement in COMP. *The Linguistic Review* 11: 351–75.

——1997. *Clause Structure and Word Order in Hebrew and Arabic: An essay in comparative Semitic syntax*. Oxford: Oxford University Press.

——2010. The Cartographic enterprise in syntax. *Language and Linguistics Compass* 4: 417–39.

——2014. Subject positions, subject extraction, EPP, and the Subject

Criterion. In *Locality*, E. Aboh, M. T. Guasti & I. Roberts (eds.) 58–85. Oxford: Oxford University Press.

Shlonsky, U. & Soare, G. 2011. Where's 'why'? *Linguistic Inquiry* 42: 651–69.

Shlonsky, U. & Bocci, G. 2019. Syntactic cartography. *Oxford Research Encyclopedia of Linguistics*. https://doi.org/10.1093/acrefore/9780199384655.013.310

Shnukal, A. 1981. There's a lot mightn't believe this ... Variable subject relative pronoun absence in Australian English. In *Variation Omnibus*, D. Sankoff & H. Cedergren (eds.) 321–8. Carbondale, IL: Linguistic Research.

Shormani, M. 2021. Imperatives in Arabic: Syntax, discourse and interface. *International Journal of Arabic Linguistics* 7: 19–50.

Shorrocks, G. 1982. Relative pronouns and relative clauses in the dialect of Farnworth and district (Greater Manchester County, formerly Lancashire). *Zeltschrift für Dialektologie und Linguistik* 49: 334–43.

Sichel, I. 2014. Resumptive pronouns and competition. *Linguistic Inquiry* 45: 655–93.

Siemund, P. 2015. Exclamative clauses in English and their relevance for theories of clause types. *Studies in Language* 39: 698–728.

Sifaki, E. & Sitaridou, I. 2007. EPP revisited: Evidence from null subject languages. In *Selected Papers in Theoretical and Applied Linguistics: 17th International Symposium, English Department,* *Aristotle University*, vol 1, 188–98. Thessaloniki: Monochromia.

Sigley, R. 1997. The influence of formality and channel on relative pronoun choice in New Zealand English. *English Language and Linguistics* 1: 207–32.

Sigurðsson, H. Á. 2010. On EPP effects. *Studia Linguistica* 64: 159–89.

Sigurðsson, H. Á. & Maling, J. 2007. On null arguments. In *Proceedings of the XXXII Incontro di Grammatica Generativa*, M. C. Picci & A. Pona (eds.) 167–80. Alessandria: Edizioni dell'Orso.

——2010. The Empty Left Edge Condition. In *Exploring Crash-Proof Grammars*, M. Putnam (ed.) 57–84. Amsterdam: Benjamins.

Simonin, O. 2012. Adverbial and relative *to*-infinitives. *Journal of English Linguistics* 41: 4–32.

Simpson, A. 2011. Floating Quantifiers in Burmese and Thai. *Journal of the Southeast Asian Linguistics Society*, 4: 115–46.

Simon-Vandenbergen, A. M. 1981. *The Grammar of Headlines in The Times 1870-1970*. Brussels: Paleis der Academiën.

Šímová, P. 2005. The transition between restrictive and nonrestrictive adnominal relative clauses. PhD diss. Charles University, Prague.

Sistrunk, W. 2012. The syntax of zero in African American relative clauses. PhD diss. Michigan State University.

Smit, J. 2014. An investigation into the adequacy of Cinque's functional theory as a framework for the analysis of adverbs in Afrikaans. MA thesis. Stellenbosch University.

Smith, P. W. 2015. Feature mismatches: Consequences for syntax, morphology and semantics. PhD diss. University of Connecticut.

——2017. The syntax of semantic agreement in English. *Journal of Linguistics* 53: 823–63.

——2020. Object agreement and grammatical functions: A re-evaluation. In *Agree to Agree: Agreement in the minimalist program*, P. W. Smith, J. Mursell & K. Hartmann (eds.) 117–47. Berlin: Language Science Press.

Smith, P. W., Mursell, J. & Hartmann, K. (2020). Some remarks on agreement within the minimalist program. In *Agree to Agree: Agreement in the minimalist program*, P. W. Smith, J. Mursell & K. Hartmann (eds.) 1–29. Berlin: Language Science Press.

Sobin, N. 1987. The variable status of Comp-trace phenomena. *Natural Language and Linguistic Theory* 5: 33–60.

——1997. Agreement, default rules and grammatical viruses. *Linguistic Inquiry* 28: 318–43.

——2002. The Comp-trace effect, the adverb effect and minimal CP. *Journal of Linguistics* 38: 527–60.

——2003. Negative Inversion as non-movement. *Syntax* 6: 183–212.

——2004. Expletive constructions are not 'lower right corner' movement constructions. *Linguistic Inquiry* 35: 503–08.

——2009. Prestige case forms and the Comp-trace effect. *Syntax* 12: 32–59.

——2016. The halting problem. *Proceedings of the Linguistic Society of America* 1.3: 1–10.

Sorace, A. 2000. Gradients in auxiliary selection with intransitive verbs. *Language* 76: 859–90.

Speas, M. 1986. Adjunction and projections in syntax. PhD diss. MIT.

——1994. Null arguments in a theory of economy of projection. *University of Massachusetts Occasional Papers in Linguistics* 17: 179–208.

Speas, P. & Tenny, C. 2003. Configurational properties of point of view roles. In *Asymmetry in Grammar*, A. M. di Sciullo (ed.) 315–45. Amsterdam: Benjamins.

Spector, I. 2008. Hebrew floating quantifiers: A non-derivational approach. MA thesis. Hebrew University of Jerusalem.

——2009. Hebrew floating quantifiers. In *Proceedings of the LFG09 Conference*, M. Butt & T. H. King (eds.) 520–40. Stanford, CA: CSLI Publications.

Spencer, A. 1991. *Morphological Theory*. Oxford: Blackwell.

Spinillo, M. G. 2004. Reconceptualising the English determiner class. PhD diss. University College London.

Sportiche, D. 1986. A theory of floating quantifiers. *Proceedings of the North East Linguistics Society* 17: 581–94.

——1988. A theory of floating quantifiers and its corollaries for constituent structure. *Linguistic Inquiry* 19: 425–49.

——2008. Inward bound: Splitting the wh-paradigm and French

Relative *qui*. https://ling.auf.net/lingbuzz/000623

——2015. Relative clauses: Head raising only. http://www.ciscl.unisi.it/ad60/doc/sportiche_abs.pdf

——2017. Relative clauses. Ms. UCLA. https://ling.auf.net/lingbuzz/003444

Sprouse, J. 2011. A test of the cognitive assumptions of magnitude estimation: Commutativity does not hold for acceptability judgments. *Language* 87: 274–88.

Sprouse, J. & Almeida, D. 2011a. Power in acceptability judgment experiments and the reliability of data in syntax. Ms. University of California, Irvine and Michigan State University.

——2011b. A formal experimental investigation of the empirical foundation of generative syntactic theory. Ms. University of California, Irvine and Michigan State University.

——2012. Assessing the reliability of textbook data in syntax: Adger's *Core Syntax*. *Journal of Linguistics* 48: 609–52.

——2013. The empirical status of data in syntax: A reply to Gibson and Fedorenko. *Language and Cognitive Processes*. 28: 229–40.

Sprouse, J., Caponigro, I., Greco, C. & Cecchetto, C. 2013. Experimental syntax and the crosslinguistic variation of island effects in English and Italian. Ms. Universities of California, Irvine and San Diego, and Milan-Bicocca.

Sprouse, J. Schütze, C. & Almeida, D. 2013. A comparison of informal and formal acceptability judgments

using a random sample from *Linguistic Inquiry* 2001–2010. *Lingua* 134: 219–48.

Starke, M. 2001. Move dissolves into Merge: A theory of locality. PhD diss. University of Geneva.

Stassen, L. 2013. Zero copula for predicate nominals. In *The World Atlas of Language Structures Online*, M. Dryer & M. Haspelmath (eds.) feature 120A. Leipzig: Max Plank Institute for Evolutionary Anthropology.

Stepanov, A. 2001. Late adjunction and minimalist phrase structure. *Syntax* 4: 94–125.

——2007. The end of CED? Minimalism and extraction domains. *Linguistic Inquiry* 10: 80–126.

Stockwell, R., Schachter, P. & Partee, B. 1973. *The Major Syntactic Structures of English*. New York: Holt Rinehart and Winston.

Stowell, T. 1981. Origins of phrase structure. PhD diss. MIT.

——1990. C-command effects found in newspaper headlines. Ms. UCLA.

——1991. Abbreviated English. *Glow Newsletter*, March.

——1996. Empty heads in abbreviated English. Ms. UCLA.

——1999. Words lost and syntax found in Headlinese: The hidden structure of abbreviated English in headlines, instructions and diaries. Paper presented at York University, Toronto.

Stradmann, M. 2013. Reviewing the Binary Branching Hypothesis. BA thesis. Utrecht University.

Straumann, H. 1935. *Newspaper Headlines: A study in linguistic*

method. London: George Allen &
Unwin Ltd.

Suárez-Gómez, C. 2014. Relative
clauses in Southeast Asian
Englishes. *Journal of English
Linguistics* 42: 245–68.

Suñer, M. 1998. Resumptive
restrictive relatives: A
crosslinguistic perspective.
Language 74: 335–64.

Suñer, M. & Yépez, M. 1988. Null
definite objects in Quiteño.
Linguistic Inquiry 19: 511–19.

Svenonius, P. 2002a (ed.) *Subjects,
Expletives and the EPP*. Oxford:
Oxford University Press.

——2002b. Subject positions and
the placement of adverbials. In
Subjects, Expletives and the EPP,
P. Svenonius (ed.) 199–40. Oxford:
Oxford University Press.

——2017. Syntactic features. Ms.
CASTL, University of Tromsø.

Szczegielniak, A. 1999. *That*-trace
effects cross-linguistically and
successive-cyclic movement. *MIT
Working Papers in Linguistics* 33:
1–26.

——2005. Two types of resumptive
pronouns in Polish relative clauses.
Linguistic Variation Yearbook 5:
165–85.

Szendrői, K. 2001. Focus and the
syntax-phonology interface. PhD
diss. University College London.

Tagg, C. 2009. A corpus linguistics
study of SMS text messaging. PhD
diss., University of Birmingham.

Tagliamonte, S. 2002. Variation and
change in the British relative
marker system. In *Dialect Contact
and History on the North Sea*

Littoral, P. Poussa (ed.) 147–65.
Munich: Lincom Europa.

Taglicht, J. 1984. *Message and
Emphasis: On focus and scope in
English*. London: Longman.

Takahashi, H. 2004. The English
imperative: A cognitive and
functional analysis. PhD diss.
Hokkaido University.

Takano, Y. 2013. Movement of
antecedents and minimality.
Nanzan Linguistics 9: 193–214.

Tanaka, T. 2008. Aspectual restriction
for floating quantifiers. *Nanzan
Linguistics* 3: 199–228.

Tateishi, K. 1995. *The Syntax of
'Subjects'*. Cambridge: Cambridge
University Press.

Teddiman, L & Newman, J. 2010.
Subject ellipsis in English:
Construction of and findings from
a diary corpus. In *Handbook of
Research on Discourse Behaviour
and Digital Communications:
Language structures and social
interaction*, R. Taiwo (ed.) 281–95.
Hershey, PA: IGI Global.

Tel, A. 2020. Article omission in
headlines: A comparison between
the physical and digital version
of a newspaper. BA thesis. Leiden
University.

Terada, H. 2000. Multiple expletive
construction. *English Linguistics*
17: 1–25.

——2003. Floating quantifiers as
probes. *English Linguistics* 20:
467–92.

Thornton, R. 1995. Referentiality and
Wh-Movement in Child English:
Juvenile *D-Link*uency. *Language
Acquisition* 4: 139–75.

Thrasher, R. 1973 A conspiracy on the far left. *University of Michigan Papers in Linguistics* 1: 169–79.

——1974. Shouldn't ignore these strings: A study of conversational deletion. PhD diss. University of Michigan.

——1977 *One Way to Say More by Saying Less: A study of so-called subjectless sentences.* Kwansei Gakuin University Monograph Series Vol. 11. Tokyo: Eihosha Ltd.

Ticio, M. E. 2003. On the structure of DPs. PhD diss. University of Connecticut.

——2005. Locality and anti-locality in Spanish DPs. *Syntax* 8: 229–86.

Tonoike, S. 1996. A note on floating quantifiers. *Metropolitan Linguistics* 16: 1–9.

Torrego, E. 1996. On quantifier float in control clauses. *Linguistic Inquiry* 27: 111–26.

Torrence, H. 2013. *The Clause Structure of Wolof: Insights into the left periphery.* Amsterdam: Benjamins.

Torres Cacoullos, R. & Travis, C. E. 2014. Prosody, priming and particular constructions: The patterning of English first-person singular subject expression in conversation. *Journal of Pragmatics* 63: 19–34.

Totsuka, M. 2015. On phasehood of the functional categories in the left periphery. PhD diss. Tohoku University, Sendai.

——2017. On ellipsis in the left periphery: A view from transfer. *English Literary Society of Japan Regional Proceedings* 9:

45–52. https://doi.org/10.20759/elsjregional.9.0_45

Tottie, G. 1997a. Relatively speaking: Relative marker usage in the British National Corpus. In *To Explain the Present: Studies in the changing English language in honour of Matti Rissanen*, T. Nevalainen & L. Kahlas-Tarkka (eds.) 465–81. Helsinki: Société Néophilologique.

——1997b. Overseas relatives: British-American differences in relative marker usage. In *Studies in English Language Research and Teaching*, J. Aarts & H. Wekker (eds.) 153–65. Amsterdam: Rodopi.

Trotzke, A. & Giannakidou, A. 2019. Exclamatives as emotive assertions of intensity. https://ling.auf.net/lingbuzz/004838

Trudgill, P., Nevalainen, T. & Wischer, I. 2002. Dynamic *have* in North American and British Isles English. *English Language and Linguistics* 6: 1–15.

Truswell, R. 2007. Extraction from adjuncts and the structure of events. *Lingua* 117: 1355–77.

——2009. Preposition stranding, passivisation, and extraction from adjuncts in Germanic. *Linguistic Variation Yearbook* 8: 131–77.

——2011. *Events, Phrases, and Questions.* Oxford: Oxford University Press.

Tsai, W.-T. D. 2008. Left periphery and *why-how* alternations. *Journal of East Asian Linguistics* 17: 83–115.

Tsoulas, G. 2003. Floating quantifiers as overt scope markers. *Korean Journal of English Language and Linguistics* 3: 157–80.

Uchibori, A. 2000. The syntax of subjunctive complements: Evidence from Japanese. PhD diss. University of Connecticut.

Ura, H. 1994. Varieties of Raising and the feature-based phrase structure theory. *MIT Occasional Papers in Linguistics*, no. 7.

——1995. Multiple feature checking. PhD diss. MIT.

Ussery, C. 2009. Optionality and variability: Syntactic licensing meets morphological spellout. PhD diss. University of Massachusetts, Amherst, MA.

——2012. Case and phi-features as probes. *Proceedings of the West Coast Conference on Formal Linguistics* 29: 127–35.

Valmara, V. 2008. Topic, focus and quantifier float. In *Gramatika Jaietan*, X. Artigoitia & J. A. Lakarra (eds.) 837–57. Bilbao: EHU.

Varlokosta, S. 1994. Issues on Modern Greek sentential complementation. PhD diss. University of Maryland.

Vat, J. 1981. Left dislocation, connectedness and reconstruction. *Groninger Arbeiten zur Germanistischen Linguistik* 20: 80–103.

Vater, H. 1980. Quantifier float in German. In *The Semantics of Determiners*, J. van der Auwera (ed.) 232–49. London: Croom Helm.

Vergnaud, J. R. 1974. French relative clauses. PhD diss. MIT.

Vikner, S. 1995. *Verb Movement and Expletive Subjects in Germanic Languages*. Oxford: Oxford University Press.

Villa-García, J. 2010. Recomplementation and locality of movement in Spanish. Second general examination paper, University of Connecticut, Storrs. Published as Villa-García 2012c.

——2011a. On COMP-t effects in Spanish: A new argument for rescue by PF deletion. Paper presented to GLOW 34, University of Vienna.

——2011b. On the Spanish clausal leftedge: In defence of a TopicP account of recomplementation. Paper presented to 41st Linguistic Symposium on Romance Languages, University of Ottawa.

——2012a Characterizing medial and low complementizers in Spanish: Recomplementation *que* and jussive/optative *que*. In *Current Formal Aspects of Spanish Syntax and Semantics*, M. González-Rivera & S. Sessarego (eds.) 198–228. Newcastle upon Tyne: Cambridge Scholars.

——2012b The Spanish complementizer system: Consequences for the syntax of dislocations and subjects, locality of movement, and clausal structure. PhD diss. University of Connecticut, Storrs.

——2012c Recomplementation and locality of movement in Spanish. *Probus* 24: 257–314.

——2015 *The Syntax of Multiple-que Sentences in Spanish: Along the left periphery*. Amsterdam: Benjamins.

Villalba, X. 2000. *The Syntax of Sentence Periphery*. Barcelona: Servei de Publicacions.

——2001. The right edge of exclamative sentences in Catalan. *Catalan Working Papers in Linguistics* 9: 119–35.

——2003. An exceptional exclamative sentence type in Romance. *Lingua* 113: 713–45.

——2008. Exclamatives: A thematic guide with many questions and few answers. *Catalan Journal of Linguistics* 7: 9–40.

Vishenkova, A., & Zevakhina, N. 2019. Wh-exclamatives with and without predicates in Russian. *Russian Linguistics* 43: 107–25.

Visser, J. 1996. Object Drop in Dutch imperatives. In *Linguistics in the Netherlands 1996*, C. Cremers & M. den Dikken (eds.) 257–68. Amsterdam: Benjamins.

Wagner, M. 2012. Focus and givenness: A unified approach. In *Contrasts and Positions in Information Structure*, I. Kučerová & A. Neeleman (eds.) 102–47. Cambridge: Cambridge University Press.

Wagner, S. 2012. Null subjects in English: Variable rules, variable language? Post-doctoral diss. Chemnitz University of Technology:

——2016. Never saw one: First-person null subjects in spoken English. *English Language and Linguistics* 22: 1–34.

Wal, J. van der 2016. Diagnosing focus. *Studies in Language* 40: 259–301.

Ward, G. & E. Prince. 1991. On the topicalization of indefinite NPs. *Journal of Pragmatics* 15: 167–77.

Watanabe, A. 1993. Agr-based case theory and its interaction with the A-bar system. PhD diss. MIT.

——1994. The role of triggers in the extended split INFL hypothesis: Unlearnable parameter settings. *Studia Linguistica* 48: 156–78.

Weir, A. 2008. Subject pronoun drop in informal English. MA thesis. University of Edinburgh.

——2009a. Subject pronoun drop in informal English. Ms. University College London.

——2009b. Article drop in English headlinese. MA thesis. University College London.

——2012. Left-edge deletion in English and subject omission in diaries. *English Language and Linguistics* 16: 105–09.

——2013. Article drop in headlines and truncation of CP. Text of paper presented to LSA Annual Meeting, Boston, 3–6 January.

——2014. Fragments and clausal ellipsis. PhD diss. University of Massachusetts, Amherst.

——2016. The prosodic licensing of left-edge ellipsis and implications for clausal ellipsis. Presentation to the Ellipsis and Prosody Workshop, Leiden University.

——2017. Object drop and article drop in reduced written register. *Linguistic Variation* 17: 157–85.

——2018. Left-edge ellipsis and clausal ellipsis: The division of labor between syntax, semantics and prosody. Talk at workshop on The Timing of Ellipsis, at the annual meeting of the Societas Linguistica Europaea, Tallinn University.

——2022. Fragments and left-edge ellipsis: The division of labour between syntax, semantics, and prosody. In *The Derivational Timing of Ellipsis*, G. Güneş & A. Lipták (eds.) 253–90. Oxford: Oxford University Press.

Weisler, S. 1980. The syntax of *that*-less relatives. *Linguistic Inquiry* 11: 624–31.

Weiß, H. 2005. Inflected complementisers in Continental West Germanic dialects. *Zeitschrift für Dialektologie und Linguistik* 72: 148–66.

Wen, H. 2020. Relative clauses in Mandarin Chinese. PhD diss. Queen Mary, University of London.

Weskott, T. & Fanselow, G. 2011. On the informativity of different measures of linguistic acceptability. *Language* 87: 249–73.

Wexler, K. & Culicover, P.W. 1980. *Formal Principles of Language Acquisition*. Cambridge, MA: MIT Press.

Wharton, T. 2010. Recipes: Beyond the words. *Gastrononomica* 10: 67–73.

Wierzba, M. 2014. What is special about fronted focused objects in German: A study on the relation between syntax, intonation and emphasis. MA thesis. University of Potsdam.

——2019. Focus projection: Extending the empirical data base. Talk presented to the Phonology Colloquium, Goethe Universität Frankfurt, 6 November.

Wilder, C. 1989. The syntax of German infinitives. PhD diss. University College London.

——1994a. Coordination, ATB, and ellipsis. *Groningen Arbeiten zur Germanistischen Linguistik* 37: 291–329.

——1994b. Some properties of ellipsis in coordination. *Geneva Generative Papers* 2: 23–61.

Wiljergård, E. 2011. The use of articles in newspaper headlines: Omission and retention in a British quality paper and tabloid. BA thesis. Linnaeus University.

Williams, E. 1984. *There*-insertion. *Linguistic Inquiry* 15: 131–53.

——2002. Adjunct modification. *Italian Journal of Linguistics* 12: 129–54.

——2006. The subject-predicate theory of *there*. *Linguistic Inquiry* 37: 648–51.

Williams, P. 2013. 8 grammar rules for writing newspaper headlines. englishlessonsbrighton.co.uk

Willim, E. 2012. On the feature valuation/interpretability biconditional in minimalist theory. https://www.researchgate.net/publication/298215508

Wiltschko, M. 1998. On the syntax and semantics of (relative) pronouns and determiners. *Journal of Comparative Germanic Linguistics* 2: 143–81.

——2001. The syntax of pronouns: Evidence from Halkomelem Salish. *Natural Language and Linguistic Theory* 20: 157–95.

Woolford, E. 1991. VP-internal subjects in VSO and nonconfigurational languages. *Linguistic Inquiry* 22: 503–40.

——2006. Case-agreement mismatches. In *Agreement Systems*, C. Boeckx (ed.) 317–39. Amsterdam: Benjamins.

Wurff, W. van der 2007 (ed.) *Imperative Clauses in Generative*

Grammar: Studies in honour of Frits Beukema. Amsterdam: Benjamins.

Wurmbrandt, S. 2006. Licensing case. *Journal of Germanic Linguistics* 18: 175–236.

——2019. Cross-clausal A-dependencies. *Chicago Linguistic Society Proceedings* 54: 585–604.

Xu, L. 2003. Choice between the overt and the covert. *Transactions of the Philological Society* 101: 81–107.

Yamakoshi, K. 2002. Wh-drop in child languages and adult ASL. In *Proceedings of the GALA 2001 Conference on Language Acquisition*, M. J. Freitas (ed.) 217–31. University of Groningen.

Yamato, N. 2010. The left periphery of Japanese exclamatives. *Studia Linguistica*: 64: 55–80.

Yang, Y. 2009. Infinitival relative clauses in English. *English Language and Linguistics* 28: 137–55.

Yatabe, S. 1990. Quantifier floating in Japanese and the θ-hierarchy. *Chicago Linguistics Society Proceedings* 26: 437–51.

Yoo, E.-J. 2001. English floating quantifiers and lexical specification of quantifier retrieval. *Language and Information* 1: 1–15.

——2002. A lexical approach to English floating quantifiers. *Berkeley Linguistic Society Proceedings* 28: 351–62.

Yuan, M. 2016. Subordinate clause types and the left periphery in Kikuyu. Handout of paper presented to LSA meeting in Washington, DC.

Zaenen, A. 1997. Contrastive dislocation in Dutch and Icelandic. In *Materials on Left Dislocation*, E. Anagnastopoulou, H. van Riemsdijk & F. Zwarts (eds.) 119–48. Amsterdam: Benjamins.

Zagona, K. 1987. *Verb Phrase Syntax.* Dordrecht: Kluwer.

Zamparelli, R. 2000. *Layers in the Determiner Phrase.* New York: Garland.

Zanuttini, R. 2008. Encoding the addressee in the syntax: Evidence from English imperative subjects. *Natural Language and Linguistic Theory* 26: 185–218.

Zanuttini, R. & Portner, P. 2000. The characterization of exclamative clauses in Paduan. *Language* 76: 123–32.

——2003. Exclamative clauses: At the syntax-semantics interface. *Language* 79: 39–81.

Zeijlstra, H. 2004. Sentential negation and negative concord. PhD diss. University of Amsterdam.

——2012. There is only one way to agree. *The Linguistic Review* 29: 491–539.

Zeller, J. 2006. Raising out of finite CP in Nguni: The case of fanele. *South African Linguistics and Applied Language Studies* 24: 255–75.

Zevakhina, N. 2013. Syntactic strategies of exclamatives. *The Journal of Estonian and Finno-Ugric Linguistics* 4: 157–78.

Zhang, S. 1990. The status of imperatives in theories of grammar. PhD diss. University of Arizona.

Ziegler, J. 2014. Copy raising and phase theory: Finite complementisers look like they're defective too. Poster presented at the Linguistic Society of America's 88th Annual Meeting, Minneapolis.

Ziv, Y. 1994. Left and right dislocations: Discourse functions and anaphora. *Journal of Pragmatics* 22: 629–45.

Zribi-Hertz, A. 1984. Prépositions orphélines et pronoms nuls. *Recherches Linguistiques* 12: 46–91.

Zubiaguirre Sebastián, Z. 2017. The syntax of English and Basque wh-exclamatives. BA diss. University of the Basque Country.

Zubizaretta, M.-L. 1998. *Prosody, Focus and Word Order*. Cambridge, MA: MIT Press.

——2009. The syntax and prosody of focus: The Bantu-Italian connection. *Iberia* 2: 1–39.

Zwart, J.-W. 1993. Dutch Syntax: A minimalist approach. PhD diss. University of Groningen.

——1997. *A Minimalist Approach to the Syntax of Dutch*. Dordrecht: Kluwer.

——2000. A head raising analysis of relative clauses in Dutch. In *The Syntax of Relative Clauses*, A. Alexiadou, P. Law, A. Meinunger & C. Wilder (eds.) 349–86. Amsterdam: Benjamins.

——2006. Complementiser agreement and dependency marking typology. *Leiden Working Papers in Linguistics* 3: 53–72.

Zwicky, A. M. 1988. On the subject of bare imperatives in English. In *On Language: Rhetorica, phonologica, syntactica: A festschrift for Robert P. Stockwell*, C. Duncan Rose and T. Vennemann (eds.) 437–50. London: Routledge.

——2002. I wonder what kind of construction that this example illustrates. In *The Construction of Meaning*, D. Beaver, L. D. Casillas Martínez, B. Z. Clark & S. Kaufmann (eds.) 219–48. Stanford, CA: CSLI Publications.

——2005. Saying more with less. Language Log post, 19 March. http://itre.cis.upenn.edu/~myl/languagelog/archives/001995.html

Zwicky, A. & Pullum, G. K. 1983. Deleting named morphemes. *Lingua*, 59: 155–75.

Zwicky, A. M. & Zwicky, A. D. 1971. How come and what for. *Ohio State University Working Papers in Linguistics* 8: 173–85.

——1981. Telegraphic registers in written English. In *Variation Omnibus*, D. Sankoff & H. J. Cedergren (eds.) 535–44. Edmonton: Linguistic Research Inc.

——1982. Register as a dimension of linguistic variation. In *Sublanguage: Studies of language in restricted semantic domains*, J. Lehrberger & R. Kittredge (eds.) 213–18. Berlin: De Gruyter.

Zyman, E. 2018a. On the driving force for syntactic movement. PhD diss. University of California at Santa Cruz.

——2018b. Quantifier float as stranding: Evidence from Janitzio P'urhepecha. *Natural Language and Linguistic Theory* 36: 991–1034.

——2022. On the definition of Merge. Ms. University of Chicago.

Index

9 781009 322935